# APPLIED ORGANIZATIONAL COMMUNICATION

## Perspectives, Principles, and Pragmatics

# COMMUNICATION
# TEXTBOOK SERIES
Jennings Bryant—Editor

---

# Applied Communication
Teresa Thompson—Advisor

---

# APPLIED ORGANIZATIONAL COMMUNICATION
## Perspectives, Principles, and Pragmatics

**Thomas E. Harris**
*The University of Alabama*

**LEA** LAWRENCE ERLBAUM ASSOCIATES, PUBLISHERS
1993   Hillsdale, New Jersey                    Hove and London

Lawrence Erlbaum Associates, Inc., Publishers
365 Broadway
Hillsdale, New Jersey 07642

**Library of Congress Cataloging-in-Publication Data**

Harris, Thomas E., Ph.D.
    Applied organizational communication : perspectives, principles,
and pragmatics / by Thomas E. Harris.
        p.     cm. — (Communication textbook series. Applied
communication)
    Includes bibliographical references.
    ISBN 0-8058-0050-6. — ISBN 0-8058-1212-1
    1. Communication in organizations.  I. Title  II. Series:
Communication textbook series. Applied communications.
    HD30.3.H372   1993
    658.4'5—dc20                                      92-31201
                                                         CIP

Books published by Lawrence Erlbaum Associates are printed on acid-free
paper, and their bindings are chosen for strength and durability.

Printed in the United States of America
10  9  8  7  6  5  4  3  2

This book is dedicated to Barbara, my wife and very best friend. She gives me love, laughter, encouragement, and support, and has remained my best friend throughout this effort.

I wish to include Edward and Jean Harris, my parents, who gave me guidance and direction in my early years; Beatrice Stephens, my grandma, who has always provided me with unconditional love; and Anissa, my daughter, who is a very special person to me.

# Contents

# Preface

After 20 years as a university teacher and an organizational consultant, I am convinced that an understanding of organizational communication is a prerequisite for being a successful organizational member and for assuming productive leadership positions. This text reflects my own experience as a consultant to a wide variety of organizations where I introduced, developed, and expanded their abilities to utilize applied organizational communication concepts. In order to become more effective in the communication process, individuals must understand the basic perspectives, the underlying principles, and the pragmatic aspects of organizational life. As the reader will discover, each chapter presents an extensive analysis of the selected topics, coupled with a broad base of research to develop and support the conclusions. Hopefully, my own enthusiasm for a communication approach to understanding organizations shows in each chapter.

Organizations are facing constant change – or permanent white water, as one observer noted. The next 10 years will witness major changes in organizations ranging from significant demographic shifts to changes in work group design, downsizing of some organizations to transnational competition for others, and new leadership techniques to accommodate technological linkages of individuals, units, and organizations. Regardless of the investigator's background, effective communication practices are seen as the key to surviving and flourishing during this period. An applied approach to studying organizational communication allows the reader to understand why certain actions stand a greater likelihood for success, and they set a cutting edge view for innovative alternatives.

We must have a solid strong theoretical understanding of organizational communication. To this end, the text covers three broad issues: perspective, principles, and pragmatics.

The first three chapters are concerned with the perspectives necessary to understanding the interrelationship between communication and organizations. Chapter 1 develops a transactional communication approach and provides the link between communication and a systems approach to understanding organizations. In chapter 2, the critical role of perception in organizations is outlined. Because we must understand why organizations do what they do, chapter 3 provides an extensive discussion of the major organizational and management theories that have set the stage for the modern organization. In each chapter, current examples are used to explain the concepts.

Organizational communication is a complex topic. Using traditional labels, chapters 4–8 provide in-depth analysis of significant communication issues in organizations. Each chapter utilizes communication theory and organizational examples to exemplify the issues. Chapter 4, on verbal communication, presents an organization's eye view of how language functions and malfunctions. Chapter 5, on nonverbal communication, draws from the broad research available and applies the relevant information to organizations. Because organizations must depend on the interdependence of individuals, chapter 6 explains listening and feedback. At a different level, but with the same importance, chapter 7 examines the important concepts of networks and channels. At this point, the reader is armed with the basic theoretical and practical communication tools. Chapter 8, on symbolic behavior, returns to the providence most comfortably controlled by communication. Although acknowledged as important by numerous authors, this chapter provides a specific discussion of the role of symbolic behavior in organizational success.

Anyone dealing with organizations recognizes specific areas in special need of consideration. Chapters 9–14 isolate interpersonal and small group communication, leadership, conflict management, motivation, and new communication technologies for an exhaustive analysis. As with the earlier chapters, although the titles are traditional, the analysis is filled with up-to-date examples and insights placed in perspective with communication theory.

The text is intended to be comprehensive, clear, interesting, current, and accessible. The most exciting aspect of my own career has been the application of academic theories to actual organizational communication situations. Throughout this text, I have tried to offer the same opportunity for the reader.

## ACKNOWLEDGMENTS

I would like to express my appreciation to the numerous organizations and individuals that have provided insights into the organizational communication processes as I have functioned as a facilitator, consultant, and trainer. These experiences, ranging from change management to leadership and motivation, provide a vital bridge between organizational communication and behavior theories and specific applications of these theories.

In addition, Jennings Bryant (University of Alabama) has provided editorial assistance and he deserves a special thank you.

*Thomas E. Harris*

# Adopting a Perspective

For anyone planning a career, there are two realities. First, a fuller understanding of organizations is a vital ingredient at every forward step of the career process, and, second, communication is a primary element for understanding how organizations function and how we should, even must, behave in organizations if we are to advance our careers. The first part of this statement—that organizations permeate all parts of our postbaccalaureate careers—only underscores the social complexity of our modern age. There are practically no activities a college graduate can engage in that do not require membership in some type of organization. For each of us, understanding how organizations function is synonymous with the pursuit of rewarding employment. Except for the unusual, and most likely unemployable individual, the need to operate effectively within organizations is as real a skill and an occupational necessity as knowing how to find a job or learn a vocation.

The goal of this book is to provide an understanding of organizational communication that will be useful to you throughout your involvement with organizations. Although we could focus on managerial communication or leader-centered behavior, this unnecessarily limits your options as you choose and develop your career or careers. Different positions require different skills and understanding, and during your progression through any organization you will be alternatively both in charge and a relative newcomer. Therefore, your repertoire of knowledge and skills is more important than any one procedure. As you read the various chapters of this text, you will understand, of course, a great deal about managerial behavior, which will lead you to be a better supervisor or manager. You also will understand how to use communication as a neophyte in a particular organization, during your transitions from one position to another, and throughout the various organizational activities you will engage in.

## COMMUNICATION IN ORGANIZATIONS

Because organizations are an intricate part of practically any activity we undertake, the second part of our observation becomes even more important. Simply put, communication is one of the most dominant activities occurring in any work setting (Daniels & Spiker, 1991, pp. 4–8). The need to study, understand, and effectively use organizational communication has been, for many individuals, an after-the-fact enlightenment. As such, individuals in various occupations refer to the inability of others to communicate well, the lack of listening skills displayed by their colleagues, or the unwillingness of subordinates to follow instructions. Individuals will suggest that people fail to communicate and they are almost mystified that other people do not hear them in the manner they intended. As a result, "experts in management theory and human relations training have been preaching the need for improved communication for nearly four decades" (Hill, 1982, p. 117). Unfortunately, being aware of the need for improved communication does not always translate into better understanding or use. Drucker, in 1971, concluded: ". . . the results to date have been meager. Communications are, by and large, just as poor today as they were twenty or thirty years ago when we first became aware of the need for, and lack of adequate communication in modern organizations" (p. 65). His conclusion is updated and reinforced by a recent survey in the *Wall Street Journal*, which shows a declining trend in the quality of at least some aspects of organizational communication (see Table 1.1). A closer examination of the importance of communication in organizations indicates its significance to the organization as a whole and to executives, managers, supervisors, and employees.

### Importance of Communication to the Organization

Kennedy (1984), coauthor of *Corporate Cultures*, concluded: "Maintaining a . . . healthy, organizational culture depends in part on high quality communication, internal and external" (p. 30). General Electric ("Survey: GE," 1984), in their study of 10,000 employees, found a direct link between good communication with the employee's immediate supervisor and job satisfaction in the specific categories of general problems, feedback, salary discussions, career counseling, and performance appraisal. Studies of other organizations have concluded "that communication between employees and immediate supervisors remains a key influence on employee happiness and productivity" (Pincus, 1984, p. 28). The Business–Higher Education Forum (1985) report titled *America's Business Schools: Priorities for Change* argued: "Because effective communications are indispensable ingredients for successful management activities in all areas—from problem solving to negotiations—skill training in these disciplines should be incorporated throughout the entire [MBA] curriculum" (pp. 3, 16). One summary of observations about the importance of organizational communication produced the following list of metaphors: Communication is the lifeblood of the organization, the glue that binds the organization, the oil that

TABLE 1.1
Lack of Communication—Surveyed Employees Say Their Companies
Are Doing a Poorer Job of Talking to Them

|  | Agreeing | |
| --- | --- | --- |
|  | *1984* | *1980* |
| Company tries to keep employees well-informed | 68.5% | 74.1% |
| Official communication doesn't tell the full story | 68.2% | 64.6% |
| Communication is a two-way street within the company | 52.3% | 55.2% |
| Communication is candid and accurate within this company | 48.9% | 54.4% |

*Note.* From *The Wall Street Journal*, July 2, 1985, p. 1. Reprinted by permission.

smooths the organization's functions, the thread that ties the system together, the force that pervades the organizations, and the binding agent that cements all relationships (Goldhaber, 1986, p. 5).

During my own consulting work with various companies, one of the tools used to determine the direction for training and development is a needs analysis given to members of the organization. The analysis involves 40 question areas, which are translated into 10 specific categories in need of additional training. In the last 5 years, the analysis has been given to a major banking corporation, two plastic manufacturing companies, the headquarters of an international moving company, a steel manufacturing company, a large regional medical center, and several specialized companies. In every case, communication is ranked as first, or sometimes second, as the area in need of improvement within the organization. Invariably, the other top item is motivation, which also will be discussed later in this text. These two items rank above many traditional organization issues such as delegating, teamwork, time management, leadership, or job structure and planning. When people actually working are asked to decide where improvement needs to be made in an organization, they focus on communication.

## Importance of Communication to Leaders

In addition to being important to the organization, communication is critical to the leader, manager, or supervisor. A survey of vice presidents, presidents, and CEOs concluded that business communication courses were more important to their success than any other business courses, including finance and accounting (Hildebrandt, 1982, p. 8; see also Table 1.2).

A 20-year longitudinal study of Stanford MBA graduates showed communication to be an important part of their success in business and organizations and "a

TABLE 1.2
How Important Are These Courses in Preparing for a General Management Career?

| Course | Mean | Very Important | | | Very Unimportant | |
|---|---|---|---|---|---|---|
| | | 1 | 2 | 3 | 4 | 5 |
| Business communication | 1.357 | 72.2 | 21.5 | 5.1 | 1.1 | 0.2 |
| Finance | 1.428 | 63.1 | 31.9 | 4.3 | 0.6 | 0.2 |
| Accounting | 1.578 | 55.9 | 33.7 | 7.7 | 2.2 | 0.6 |
| Business policy/planning | 1.695 | 47.2 | 39.1 | 11.3 | 2.0 | 0.5 |
| Computer information systems | 1.848 | 34.1 | 50.0 | 13.1 | 2.5 | 0.2 |
| Marketing | 1.862 | 37.7 | 42.8 | 15.7 | 3.3 | 0.6 |
| Business economics & public policy | 1.908 | 35.5 | 43.1 | 16.8 | 4.2 | 0.3 |
| Business law | 2.246 | 19.5 | 46.0 | 25.8 | 7.5 | 1.1 |
| Personnel/industrial relations | 2.311 | 17.5 | 44.2 | 29.1 | 8.2 | 1.0 |
| Production/operations | 2.352 | 15.9 | 43.7 | 30.7 | 8.7 | 1.0 |
| International business | 2.506 | 11.2 | 40.5 | 36.9 | 9.5 | 2.0 |
| Statistics | 2.627 | 10.2 | 37.4 | 34.8 | 14.3 | 3.1 |
| Advertising/sales promotion | 2.722 | 8.1 | 34.5 | 38.0 | 15.6 | 3.7 |

From Hildebrandt (1984). Copyright © 1984 by The International Association of Business Communicators. Reprinted by permission.

clear dominance in the importance of oral communication over written communication" (Harrell & Harrell, 1984). The Stanford study also indicated that a large number of the MBA students had chosen to become entrepreneurs or work with small businesses and found their communication abilities to be a significant asset in their success. Both of these studies provide further credence for the Business–Higher Education Forum's (1985) conclusions mentioned earlier.

Top executives, and those aspiring to become top executives, provide an equally important barometer of the need for better organizational communication. Any review of the top 10 best-selling, nonfiction books would include 2 or 3 dealing with the ingredients needed to be successful in business. These books almost universally draw the conclusion that behavior, which is manifested through communication with other members of an organization, is the key to executive success. For example, in *Theory Z: How American Business Can Meet the Japanese Challenge*, Ouchi (1981) concluded, among other suggestions, that managers should practice MBWA or "management by wandering around" (p. 176). This same bias toward action is discussed repeatedly in Peters and Waterman's (1982) *In Search of Excellence: Lessons From America's Best-Run Companies*, where organizational members go to great lengths to reinforce the communication processes (pp. 13–16). Peters and Austin (1985) followed this analysis with their own, titled *Passion for Excellence*, where they identified MBWA as one of the four elements practiced by outstanding organizational leaders, which is supported by careful attention by the leaders to effective listening. Each of these books noted that the type of communication activity used by the excellent organizations and by successful leaders is markedly different from the traditional types of managerial behavior.

## Importance of Communication to the Individual

Not only is the ability to communicate effectively an important factor for organizations and leaders, it also is a vital skill for the individual (Conrad, 1990, pp. 4–5). In a recent paper, Di Salvo, Dunning, and Homan (1982) reviewed the findings of 45 studies of communication in organizations ranging from hospitals to research and development companies and concluded: "It is quite clear that communication is one of, if not the most important, aspects of organizational activity. Proficiency in various communication skills is essential, required and expected, is often valued above technical expertise or skills, and is likely to play an important role in promotions" (p. 26).

Finally, the amount of time actually spent in communication activities in an organization underscores the importance of understanding communication. A survey of industrial research personnel indicated that first-level supervisors spend 75% of their time communicating, second-level managers spent 81% and third-level managers spent 87% (Hinrochs, 1964, p. 199). Another survey of over 3,000 research and development individuals indicated that they spent 69% of their time communicating (Klemmer & Snyder, 1972). When asked to identify the source of trouble in their job, over 80% of the managers picked communication (Cox, 1968, p. 7).

## UNDERSTANDING ORGANIZATIONAL COMMUNICATION

In spite of the importance of communication in and to an organization, studying the subject seems to present a paradox for many individuals. On the surface, communication, especially in the nonprint areas, would seem to be too simple to really need to be carefully analyzed. After all, once we tell people that communication is important, and that "breakdowns" should be avoided, what else is there really to be studied? If employees should be listened to more often, then some type of general directive or meeting should make all the supervisors and managers aware of the problem so there would seem to be little reason to try and examine something so obvious. A perusal of current management magazines will yield a variety of articles on communication ranging from effective language use to listening, and generally, the articles will be two to five pages in length. The suggestions for improvement are usually to the point, but the manager often learns that implementing the suggestions is not as surefire as the article makes them appear.

As we become more and more aware of the ineffective uses of communication in organizations, the more the concept seems to be all-inclusive and difficult to study. For example, the well-meaning manager, using an ongoing program of MBWA, could create a strong sense of identification between management and employees.

At the same time, the manager might be seen by employees as too intrusive or over-bearing, merely using a gimmick, or simply increasing an unwanted "policing" tendency. The more we learn about communication, the more we understand that all behavior is potentially communicative. In the communication process, each individual is both an actor and a reactor to the communication events. We introduce our own interpretation of events. So, in addition to achieving the intended goal, different behaviors can become contradictory, allow us to direct and respond to other behaviors, provide us with a means to rationalize why specific behaviors do not necessarily create the desired goals, or be misunderstood. Because we simultaneously produce and respond to behaviors, the possible implications are truly astonishing. Each time we choose a particular behavior, the communication impact is highly dependent on a host of circumstances.

This seeming paradox can be resolved through a systematic study of organizational communication. Individuals tend to rely on intuitive responses to situations that may or may not be appropriate. For recent college graduates, for example, the merits of their job-related skills are often overshadowed by a lack of awareness of how to use communication in an organization, thereby slowing career development (Blotnick, 1984). Tavemier (1981), an associate editor of *Management Review*, concluded: "managers need to be able to communicate with a high degree of skill to be effective. But I believe these skills are not natural to people. A manager must be taught to communicate" (p. 14). One national management consulting organization called this the paradox of experience, because we become accustomed to doing particular activities that seem to work and we therefore are not likely to question their actual effectiveness ("Model-Netics," 1980). This would apply to recent college graduates who do not adapt their communication to the organizational setting or to managers, departments, or organizations who simply are continuing communication practices that may, or may not, be the most effective.

Providing you with the knowledge necessary to be successful in your communication is the goal of this textbook and you will find this information useful to you throughout your entire career in any organization. This will be true in at least three circumstances. First, even when we are effective in our communication processes, we may lack the theoretical underpinnings to be able to explain why. When this happens, we cannot be certain of replicating our successes. Second, if we do not succeed, it is equally important to be able to examine the situation to identify and correct, if possible, those factors that caused the failure. Finally, when we face new or different situations, we need to be able to predict, with some degree of success, what communication behaviors will be likely to produce the results we would like to have. Because effective communication is fundamental to an individual's success, the systematic study of communication provided by this book will give you a significant advantage in your own career.

## PERSPECTIVES

Two perspectives must be understood to develop our organizational communication skills: (a) Communication is a process, and (b) organizations can be viewed most usefully as systems of behavior.

### Communication as a Process

Identifying communication as a process is one of the most important additions to communication theory in the last 20 years. Humans usually try to predict or control the results of their behaviors. One means available for understanding communication is to attempt to provide a model of the important factors in order to understand and quantify or qualify the impact of various communication behaviors in order to predict outcomes.

The first models of communication were *linear* in nature and involved tracing a one-way flow of messages with the speaker or sender developing or encoding a message that would be sent over a channel or channels to be received by a listener or receiver. These models were very simple in form and were effective in drawing attention to certain aspects of the communication process. They work well in situations where there is no need for feedback. For example, the specific procedures for operating a cash register or some computer programs normally are set and should be followed in a step-by-step manner. Someone speaking in a situation where no feedback is expected, needed, or possible also could be an example of the use of this type of model. As you probably can predict, this model is not very reliable or valuable in an organizational setting. If you cannot receive feedback regarding your communication, then you have no means for finding out if the message has been received correctly. In human communication, the idea that we can put something into a clear message that will be understood by other people is an ideal rather than an everyday reality.

The limitations of the linear model for depicting the communication process lead to the *interactional* models of communication. These models took into account the critical importance of feedback and focused on the reciprocal message exchanges that occur between senders and receivers. From this perspective, feedback was any kind of signal or message that tells the sender what is happening at the receiving end of the process (Rothman, 1972). By accepting the importance of both participants in the eventual success or failure of the communication process, the interactional approaches were better able to explain the dynamic nature of human communication. No longer was it necessary to focus on senders alone, because each participant was both a sender and receiver. An early Sperry Univac advertisement for better listening in business depicted communication as a ping-pong game, and this analogy fits the interactional model well. Both players take turns sending and receiving and both must be active participants to make the process work. But, this model still assumed an interactive nature for the communication process.

### Can Communication Breakdowns Occur?

A fundamental problem with these conceptualizations is that they lead to misnomers, and therefore misunderstandings, regarding the actual event called communication. Both of the models present an incomplete explanation of the communication process. The simplest means of demonstrating the problem is to use a popular notion, "the communication breakdown" (Harris, 1980). When individuals are unable to achieve their goals in an operation, procedure, or relationship, they frequently say that they have a "communication breakdown" or a "failure to communicate." The assumption is based on either a linear or a step-by-step depiction of communication. Somewhere in the process there is a breakdown. Naturally, if we could find the breakdown, we could correct the communication problem. The linear model would examine the sender's techniques or approaches. The interaction model would trace the sequence of events. Although both of these explanations have an appeal because of their simplicity, the dynamics of the communication process are not this easy to explain.

In the communication process, senders and receivers are simultaneously sending and receiving messages and neither person nor element in the communication activity can fail to communicate. This view of communication means "one cannot not communicate" once a transaction has occurred between individuals (Watzlawick, Beavin, & Jackson, 1967).

Communication is a process where there is a mutual assignment of meaning, simultaneous responses by all persons in the transaction, ongoing giving and receiving of multiple messages, circularity, and numerous channels of communication (Berlo, 1960, pp. 106–131). Any form of human communication is an attempt to create meaning as long as it is purposeful (Miller & Steinberg, 1975). Anytime someone makes an effort to give a message, some signal or meaning is received as long as there is mutual perception.

This view of communication as a transaction leads to several conclusions:

1. The process is complex and dynamic.
2. Transactions are contextual and therefore irreversible, unique, and unrepeatable.
3. As a process, communication has no necessary beginning or end, so labeling participants as senders and receivers is an arbitrary, although sometimes useful, decision.
4. Each participant is simultaneously affected and affects every other member of the transaction.
5. Encoding and decoding are occurring simultaneously by each participant in the transaction (Wilmot & Wenburg, 1973).

Two important premises underlie these conclusions. First, human beings behave toward each other and, as living organisms, cannot not behave (Bateson, 1972, p. 9). As apparent as this conclusion might seem, it explains the axiom that one cannot not communicate. You might be concerned that this perspective leaves everything we do within the realm of communication.

However, the second premise is that the behavior, as we already have mentioned, also must be meaningful because it tries to elicit some response. So, the behavior must have some meaning for the person or persons to which it is aimed, sent, or directed. When we add this element, we free ourselves from including all behavior and we also free ourselves from the expectation that the intended message will be the one received.

Cherry (1978), in *On Human Communication*, provided a useful cognitive perspective: "Communication is the use of words, letters, symbols, or similar means to achieve common or shared information about an object or occurrence" (p. 216). We are interested in the various behaviors because each one can be a potential problem in the organizational communication process, and with a clear understanding, can be a great asset for enhancing the quality of our communication.

Difficulties arise in the communication process when there are incongruences in the meanings in a transaction (Rath & Stoyanoff, 1982). You are probably familiar with the problem you have in responding to someone who gives different messages during a transaction. A classic example of this problem in an organization is the request by management for suggestions from employees regarding the procedures being followed in the organization. All too often, the suggestions are not responded to or implemented. Employees are left with conflicting messages because there is a contradiction between management's stated desires and actions. Ironically, management often means a little, or a lot, of both messages and therefore continues to present the confusing behaviors.

Many organizations have started calling their employees "associates," which is a wise symbolic move. However, this new "title" does not always carry with it the full power of being anything more than an employee who must follow the same orders or directives in the same manner. Once again, the problem arises out of the confusion or incongruence within the transaction because the language and the actions contradict each other. Our earlier example of the manager who attempts to use management by walking around but finds the interpretation by employees is quite different from his or her intended meaning provides another illustration of this communication characteristic. It also could be that he or she lacks the savoir faire or knowledge of how to effectively use the technique and it comes across as a stratagem or trick rather than a sincere attempt at better management. Communication is based on the meaning attached to behavior by the participants. So, even when good intentions are behind certain activities ranging from soliciting suggestions to MBWA, we can only respond to the behaviors we can observe. To extend our example, the manager might react to employee cynicism by eliminating the practice of MBWA. However, the communication transaction already has begun, so the manager now will experience an important corollary to one cannot not communicate. Once a transaction has begun, although you can stop giving expression, you cannot stop giving off expression because meaning can be attached to any change in behavior. So, employees might be able to justify their initial distrust by observing the cessation of MBWA. The manager is not necessarily between the proverbial rock and a hard place in this example. With experience in using communication effectively, new behaviors should not come across as insincere.

In summary, communication is transactional. As an ongoing process, communication is the study of behaviors that elicit or produce meaning between individuals, groups, or organizations.

## Organizations as Systems

Organizations are systems of behavior that are interrelated and interacting rather than a "chartable" or static structure. Organizations are entities that have been put together to accomplish some type of purpose. The organization provides many of the rules, roles, and behaviors that individuals will and should follow to maintain the organizations, and, to a large extent, individuals and groups determine the development of an organization. An organization's structure, and tasks and methods, evolve out of the history of the organization's transactions with its changing members and environment. How the components work in relationship to each other is the vital question.

The systems perspective is potentially seductive for looking at organizations, because a "systemized pattern of behavior" is practically a synonym for the concept of organization. More properly, an organization should be viewed as a system because it is the sum total of the various parts and those parts determine the output and growth of the process (Downs, 1964; Thayer, 1968; Weick, 1979). Several terms are important to this concept.

First, the organization as a system is a perspective or framework toward organizations and not necessarily a theory (Katz & Kahn, 1978, p. 752). Our consideration is with the *integrated whole* of the organization you are examining, which is made up of *interacting and interrelated parts*. Thus, the whole can range in size from a partnership to IBM. Our goal is to understand the interacting parts of this system. The benefit of this view is it relieves us from looking at certain subgroups, such as managers, supervisors, marketing, operations, sales, or any other group, for understanding because this can create a myopic view of what actually occurs in the organization. To focus on a relationship with one colleague, for example, tends to neglect the critical influence of other parts of the organization. The systems view of organizations provides a framework for looking at the organization as a whole in terms of process-related subsystems (Katz & Kahn, 1978). Each subsystem in an organization, whether it be departments, job categorizations, or promotions, is separate and definable, but it is also interrelated and interdependent. All organizations are conglomerations of many subsystems, ranging from the annual company picnic organizing committee to the board of directors or trustees (Miller, 1972; Seiler, 1967). If we are looking at an organization as part of an entire industry, we could have the system (the organization), the subsystems (components of the organization), and suprasystem or the industry as a whole (Farace, Monge, & Russell, 1977, pp. 48–49). For example, the local Holiday Inn could comprise the system, the people working for the Inn would make up some of the subsystems, and the Holiday Inn chain would operate as the suprasystem. Systems are arranged hierarchically, so every system is a suprasystem for systems contained within it and a subsystem for systems containing it. In this case, the Holiday Inn chain is a system to the hotel industry suprasystem.

Second, all organizations exist within an *environment* and are both created and controlled by the environment. Organizations involve a pattern of recurrent activities in which resources, or *inputs* (energy, matter, money, materials, personnel, or information) are imported from their environment. These are *transformed* through various *processes* (means, methods, procedures, how-to-do-its, or techniques) in some fashion or another, and the resulting *outputs* (products or services) are exported back into the environment. All human organizations function in varying states of openness or responsiveness to their environment, because their boundaries are permeable and they constantly are engaged in interactions. When the organization tends toward isolation from its environment, it moves toward a *closed* status (Bertlanffy, 1968; Hall & Fagan, 1956). Actually, organizations cannot remain isolated for long because they are highly dependent on the consumer, supplier, and often government for their growth, stability, or survival. Inputs or resources such as money, materials, and information are provided by the environment, which in turn receives outputs from the organizations, which can be products, services, and revised information. Because this is an ongoing process, to the degree that the outputs respond well to the inputs, the system will remain open and growth will occur. No living system is ever totally open or totally closed, but successful organizations do not ignore input from their environments. In contrast with closed systems, which are best demonstrated by classical Newtonian physics, *open* systems maintain themselves with a constant interchange with the host environments, so there is a continual exchange of energy between the system and its environment.

Thus, an open system can be represented as a recurring cycle of input, transformation, and output. Both the input and output characteristics of the open system keep the system in constant commerce with the environment, whereas the transformation process is contained within the system. An effective open system requires a balance among the three stages of the cycle, with the input taking into account both environmental demands and the capacity of the transformation cycle, and the transformation process absorbing the flow from the input and moving to the output stage. This system is a vital model for organizational life because it is concerned with the elements of the system, the structure of the system, the interdependency of the elements of the system, and the way the system is embedded in the environment.

At all levels of an organization from individuals within the organization to the environment surrounding the organization, communication is the process used to connect and coordinate the system and its subsystems (Rothman, 1972). As you already may have concluded, there is an excellent fit between the two perspectives presented in this chapter. Both communication and organizations can be understood best as open, living systems that are dynamic in nature. This is true for communication between individuals, within teams, departments or groups, or throughout the organization.

### Feedback

In order to maintain a steady state, an open system needs adaptive processes to receive information about its activities, which is called *feedback* (Bennett, 1987). Feedback represents the ability of the system to generate and utilize evaluative information. Without such information, the system is blind to itself and the consequences of its actions. Although Ford Motor Company's attempt to sell the Edsel automobile is an obvious example of a lack of feedback and a tendency toward being a closed system, the failure rate for new businesses often is traced to the unwillingness of the entrepreneur to obtain information or follow advice, which is feedback, regarding how to operate (Hisrich, 1990; Rothman, 1972).

Two types of feedback are possible. When the feedback reinforces, accentuates, or adds to the direction being taken by the system it is positive. The feedback is negative when it corrects a deviation. Communication is how the feedback process works (Jacker, 1964, p. 5). When the process of feedback is confined to the system itself, it would be considered closed (Parsegian, 1973, p. 48), which we already have indicated would be a destructive factor in an organization. So, when there is an interchange between the system and its environment through feedback, it is considered open (Young, 1969, p. 47).

Negative feedback decreases the difference between the desired results (goal) and the actual results of the interaction (Rothman, 1972). Positive feedback increases the differences (Beck, 1982). To illustrate these two types of feedback, remember our manager who is trying to follow the advice of organizational consultants by practicing MBWA. Managers can employ MBWA as a system-maintaining mechanism to receive information (input) in order to increase their understanding (transformation) of their interrelated subsystems or, in this case, the employees, in order to be more effective managers (output). Hopefully, employees will feel free to reinforce current managerial actions (negative feedback), explain why some procedures are not working well in helping the department meet its goals (negative feedback), or call for fewer work rules and greater freedom in individual actions (positive feedback). Although the call for less control is not necessarily system maintaining, the insightful manager still can use this information to make some decisions regarding current practices toward employees and, if a change in work rules appears to be helpful to the organization, the information could become negative feedback.

The manager also has the opportunity during the wandering to use both types of feedback. If some behavior that is out of line with the expectations of a work unit is occurring, the manager might correct the subordinates about the actual work they are doing. This most likely would be considered negative feedback because it would be system correcting. If the manager wanted greater innovation by a group of individuals, then positive feedback could be used to reinforce the changes.

Obviously, both types of feedback have an important role to play in an organization. Too much negative feedback creates a loss of initiative because employees soon learn that doing it "by the book" will create the least amount of difficulty. Organizations must maintain a steady state, however, so the manager must impose some system-maintaining behavior. Too much positive feedback could result in each person "doing their own thing" with no coordination or direction. Eventually, the department would be unable to "organize" its actions and slowly work toward entropy.

## *Entropy*

Systems tend toward disorganization or *entropy*. Human organizations are capable of negative entropy because they can maintain and increase their supply of energy and their level of organization. An organization must provide tangible and intangible outputs to its environment that enable it to receive the inputs necessary to its survival. Systems cannot survive in the absence of negative feedback or information that enables them to detect deviations from course. All information inputs undergo a coding process, which filters some information and transforms other into information to which the system is attuned. An organization maintains a dynamic equilibrium (steady state), which includes the basic "character" of the organization (manifested in recurring cycles of events). This steady state is highly stable even though the organization evolves over time in response to internal and environmental chances. Maintaining an organized structure is achieved through information processing. The processing is dependent on the interpretation (coding process) and how the information is filtered and passed on.

An examination of Allegis, a short-lived conglomerate, should make these concepts clear. On April 30, 1987, United Airlines changed its name to Allegis to reflect plans to develop a full-service travel giant, which already included Hertz Rental Cars Corporation, and the Westin and Hilton hotel chains, in addition to United Airlines. This change was championed by Chairman Richard Ferris and it represented the combination of two words, *allegiant* (loyal) and *aegis* (protection), to appeal to travelers. The change involved a year of planning, included a $7 million advertising campaign, and lasted 6 weeks. The board of directors accepted the information as provided by Ferris. On June 9, 1987, Ferris resigned and the name of Allegis was moved toward oblivion. The initial change was based on the desires of Ferris to have a new concept in travel. However, several external environmental influences provided feedback to the board of directors about these plans. The Coniston Partners mounted an effort to oust members of the board of directors by buying 13%

of the Allegis stock. They were prepared to force a leveraged buyout, which would have left the board of directors with no organization to direct. The United Airlines Pilot Association also fought the diversification efforts and expressed an interest in an employee-owned organization. Finally, the board of directors accepted the feedback from these external sources that their current direction was not the best possible one.

Initially, the board was allowing its own internal positive feedback (deviation enhancing) from Ferris to encourage the diversification of United Airlines. The external information, which included a great deal of financial leverage, functioned as negative feedback (system maintaining) and forced the board to reject the changes. The judgment of the external sources of information was that Allegis was becoming entropic, or locked into a strategy that would not succeed, and the board was able to accept the energy and respond with organization (return to the original structure). The board interpreted the threat of a leveraged buyout as real and accepted the information. In addition to forcing the resignation of Ferris, the original name of United Airlines was reinstated and Hertz, Westin, and Hilton were sold. Regardless of the type of organization, the systems perspective can be applied to the subsystems or internal structure.

### Organizational Subsystems

In all organizations, two internal subsystems continually operate. One consists of the groups within the organization and the other consists of the dyadic or individual relationships (Bertlanffy, 1968). The elements of these two subsystems are discussed in detail when we examine the principles and pragmatics of organizational communication in the last two thirds of this text.

The system called the organization also has a *formal structure* with definite lines of responsibility and authority. These often have been the basis for organizational charts, which define the formal lines of authority and responsibility within an organization. All organizations also have a much less easily defined *informal structure*, which includes emerging leaders, power politics, assumed authority, and so on (Luciano, 1979). The formal structure outlines the authority whereas the informal structure outlines the influence. At all times, these can be the same, different, or an interesting combination of both of these characteristics. The third-shift foreman or supervisor, for example, may have the authority to require the crew to skip their break time, but several recalcitrant members have the potential influence of voicing a grievance concerning the decision. If the recalcitrants are listened to, then temporary power or influence is shifted.

**Rational Objectives.**     Whenever people are gathered together in an organization, it is for some specific purpose. These objective goals, or "things to do," are established by the mandate behind the organization's existence and usually are divided into attainable subtasks or short-range targets. Within these subtasks are the specific tasks for each individual within the organization to accomplish. Frequently, the reasons why someone was hired and gets paid are the objectives.

***Methodology.*** Organizations also are structured around some ways of doing the tasks through training, tools, background, expertise, and procedures. This is, for all practical purposes, the definition of technology. In its narrowest sense, technology is the machinery, the physical things used—the banker uses various equipment to process money, the moving company uses vans, and so on for all occupations and organizations. But in its truest sense, the technological subsystem in an organization includes the way the tools are employed and how things get accomplished. The banker uses the machinery in a certain way and the moving company calculates costs, with various distance and load specifications, to obtain specific and attainable ends. These techniques are procedures developed from knowledge about and experience with the best ways to do a job at any particular point. The standard operating procedure establishes how a job is to be done and is part of the technological subsystem.

***Management.*** All organizations have a subsystem that organizes and controls the other subsystems, causing them to interact and resulting in increased effectiveness of the total organization. Although the term most often applied to this concept is boss or supervisor, in a real sense, managers are those individuals who integrate the system and subsystems for the goals of the organization. They are the ones that control the output. In the most basic terms, power, authority, decision making, and coordination all represent this ability to manage. Whenever power and authority are being exercised, resources are affected, or someone is directing people in their efforts toward a common goal, that process represents the managerial structure.

All of these factors tell us that to make a change in one subsystem requires that some consideration be made regarding the implications for the other subsystems. By examining the level of interdependence, or asking what effect the change will have on other subsystems (environment, people, structure, objectives, technology, and management), it is possible to be aware of the values, or lack of value of the particular change.

Two additional concepts complete this initial examination of organizations as systems. The first is that the interactions between the systems in an organization are *nonsummative*, which means the whole is greater than the sum of its parts. The interactions between the various components of the organization create a *synergy*, or increased energy, to the system. When the various parts of the system work together, the end product is greater than what each of the departments, individuals, or groups originally contributed to the process.

In addition, a systems approach also points to the principle of *equifinality*, which means the same end product or outcome can be reached through a variety of conditions. In other words, there are numerous ways to accomplish the same goal or reach the same conclusion. This aspect of a systems approach explains why different organizations and departments can achieve comparable successes without necessarily following the same route or process. One of the best examples of this concept lies in the development of general systems theory. The basic principles and elements of systems thinking were agreed upon even though the scholars' backgrounds ranged from biology (Bertlanffy, 1968) to economics (Boulding, 1977).

At the beginning of the chapter we presented some of the metaphors used to describe communication in organizations and they included the glue that binds, the thread that ties the parts together, and the organization's lifeblood. Both synergy and equifinality depend on communication between individuals and subsystems and are examples of the interlocking nature of communication and organizational systems. The perspectives of communication as a process and organizations as systems stem from the same philosophical base regarding living systems. As open systems, people and organizations are not static entities, but are dynamic, ongoing, and ever changing.

## APPLYING OPEN SYSTEMS CONCEPTS

In addition to the organizations as systems concepts already discussed, we examine three attempts to be more specific about the relationship between systems theory and organizations. Each of these approaches highlights important aspects of systems thinking that we already have discussed, but they provide a useful focus.

In the first, Thompson (1967) characterized organizations as open systems continually trying to become less so. Uncertainty, caused by the continual interaction with the environment, requires some means to minimize its impact. Organizations respond by developing some norms of rationality. The organization's power comes from its ability to manage its niche or its area of dominance. The organization takes a rational approach to attempting to control the impact of the environment on its activities. A technical core, which can range from expertise to a product to a procedure, exists in the organization that needs to be protected from the environmental turbulence so control is exercised on the inputs and outputs of the organization. For example, an organization might purchase a large supply of raw materials to prepare for an expected increase in demand. Or, an organization might adopt the "Just-In-Time" process popularized by the Japanese where parts for production are literally purchased on the same day or in the same week in which they are needed. In this case, the organization is reducing the possible cost of oversupplying itself when demand changes. Thompson's approach explains the push by organizations for a rational perspective in order to reduce uncertainty, but it does not fully account for the various living subsystems in an organization and their tendency to act irrationally in spite of a need for rationality.

A second attempt is provided by Weick (1969) with his theory of organizing. Weick's definition of organizing is: "the resolving of equivocality in an enacted environment by means of interlocked behaviors embedded in conditionally related processes" (p. 91). Each of the concepts in his definition deserves discussion. First, a system's behavior continually influences the environment it experiences. So, we only experience being in a particular place because our own behavior led us there. Our past and present behaviors influence the nature of the place that we experience. Because of the mutual influence, there is a circularity between the interaction of systems. The system's behavior continually influences the environment that it experiences.

Second, there is always equivocality, or uncertainty, in the enacted environment, because the outside world is complex and changing. When relationships form (patterns of interlocking behaviors), organizing occurs that begins to reduce the uncertainty in the environment. Weick (1969) made an important point when he suggested that the term organization is static whereas living systems are continually in the ongoing process of organizing. If these processes of organizing stop, entropy takes over and the organization begins to disintegrate.

So, organization, Weick (1969) argued, is information that has been produced by processes that reduce equivocality. Living systems continually are trying to increase their certainty about the world in which they reside. Although Weick provided a very sophisticated systems/cybernetic view of "organizing," his theory is unnecessarily abstract. Suggestions for applying the theory have been provided (Kreps, 1990, pp. 115–118), but information still remains a subset of the overall functioning of organizations and what happens to the information as it is perceived by the various components of the organizations still remains the determining variable. Attempts to reduce uncertainty, a major premise behind Thompson's (1967) and Weick's (1969) theories, are important variables when looking at organizational systems and explain even further how organizations operate.

Finally, the sociotechnical systems view applies concepts from systems theory. A classic study of the relationship between technological and social systems was provided by Trist and Bamforth (1951) on changes in British coal mining. Essentially, they demonstrated that when changes in the methods by which coal was mined (technological) caused problems in the social relationships between miners (social), the miners resisted the changes.

Rice (1963) expanded this concept into a general perspective of organizations as open, sociotechnical systems. He saw a basic drive in individuals to work if the work is meaningful (p. 252). He focused on the impact of leadership whose primary task, he argued, is to manage the system's relationship with its environment. The leader is responsible for ensuring that the system will acquire the needed inputs from and provide the suitable outputs to the environment.

In each of these three uses of systems theory, we have specific verifications of particular aspects of the systems concepts presented in this chapter. The organization and environment interdependence and the role of information as a critical variables for all organizations are themes held in common by all of these three different applications of systems thinking.

## SYSTEMS AS CULTURES

One of the most useful approaches for understanding the particular organizational system in operation is to examine organizational cultures. Every organization has a culture, which is based on the various interactions that occur or "the way we do things around here" (Deal & Kennedy, 1982, p. 125). The type of culture operating is dependent on the organization's environment and the interactions of the subsystems within the organization. The various communication activities are what keep the organization operating and provide the cultural foundation. These communication processes provide the behaviors which lead to ". . . a pattern of basic assumptions — invented, discovered, or developed, by a given group (or organization) as it learns to cope with its problems of external adaptation and internal integration — that has worked well enough to be considered valid and, therefore, to be taught to new members as the correct way to perceive, think, and feel in response to those problems" (Schein, 1985, p. 9). The assumptions include the values, style, written and unwritten rules of conduct, plus the history, structure, past and present leaders, mission, goals and objectives, and finances (Senn, 1986, p. 16). The way individuals, groups, and subsystems communicate provides the "primary vehicle(s) for the active creation and maintenance of cultures" (Sypher, Applegate, & Sypher, 1985, p. 17).

The cultural perspective is developed fully in chapter 3 as we examine the various approaches currently being used to understand organizations. At this point, you already have seen the clear connection between a systems approach and the cultural perspective. An organizational cultural approach, as defined by this text, incorporates the various disparate views of how and why organizations do what they do. When we combine the study of communication as an analysis of the process of behaviors — the way we do things around here — with an understanding of the living systems nature of organizations — cultures — we have an excellent basis for understanding how to develop our own organizational communication abilities. Rather than focus on isolated, although important factors, such as information or leadership, the cultural approach explains why behaviors become meaningful. Not only is there an interest in information, but we also can understand what happens to the information as it is processed by the various living systems in the organization ranging from individuals through departments to the organization as a whole.

Organizational communication is the study of meaningful behaviors within the system and subsystems of the organizational culture. These meaningful behaviors constitute the specific areas of study that we examine in this text.

## CONCLUSION

We started this chapter by observing how important effective communication is to any organization. We then demonstrated the general impact of communication on the organization and to leaders and members of the organization.

By understanding the two perspectives introduced in this chapter—communication as a process and organizations as systems—we can begin a systematic analysis of how to be effective. Communication is an ongoing, coactive process, between individuals, groups, and systems. Organizations are interrelated systems of behavior that are interdependent. Both of these perspectives require further amplification through a specific discussion of the various communication processes in an organization, which is the focus of the remainder of this text. The organizational culture perspective is our means for unifying the two perspectives within the context of organizational behavior.

In chapter 2 we explain the impact perception has on all the behavioral activities we engage in while we function in our job. Chapter 3 traces the development of management and organizational theories as a means of explaining current approaches to understanding organizations.

Chapters 4–8 outline the principles that underlie communication in an organization—verbal, nonverbal, networks and channels, listening and feedback, and symbolic behavior. The titles of the chapters have been chosen arbitrarily to fit familiar categories in both the fields of communication and business and management. Each chapter, however, develops various approaches and insights to the general concept drawing from current research. Chapters 9–14 provide pragmatic application of these principles to those areas most likely to require additional understanding. These include interpersonal communication, group communication, leadership, conflict management, motivation, and new communication technologies. In the end, you will have a proactive capacity to both understand and effectively use organizational communication. Because you will have established a broad-based perspective regarding perception, communication, and organizational behavior, and you will have developed a basic understanding of the underlying principles of organizational communication, you should be able to deal with new or different issues as they arise.

## REFERENCES

Bateson, G. (1972). *Steps to an ecology of the mind*. New York: Ballantine.

Beck, D. E. (1982). Beyond the grid and situationalism: A living systems view. *Training and Development Journal, 36*, 76–83.

Bennett, T. E., Jr. (1987, June). What do bankers want? *INC.*, pp. 149–150.

Berlo, D. K. (1960). *The process of communication*. New York: Holt, Rinehart & Winston.

Bertlanffy, L. V. (1968). *General systems theory*. New York: Braziller.

Blotnick, S. (1984, May). The corporate steeple chase: Predictable crisis in a business career. *Psychology Today*, p. 72.

Boulding, K. E. (1977). The universe as a general system. *Behavioral Science, 22*, 299–306.

Business–Higher Education Forum. (1985, May). *American business schools: Priorities for change*. Washington, DC: Business–Higher Education Forum.

Cherry, C. (1978). *On human communication: A review, a survey, and a criticism*. Cambridge, MA: MIT Press.

Conrad, C. (1990). *Strategic organizational communication* (2nd ed.). Orlando, FL: Holt, Rinehart & Winston.

Cox, H. L. (1968). Opinions of selected business managers about some aspects of communication on the job. *Journal of Business Communication, 5,* 7.

Daniels, T. D., & Spiker, B. K. (1991). *Perspectives on organizational communication* (2nd ed.). Dubuque, IA: Brown.

Deal, T. E., & Kennedy, A. A. (1982). *Corporate cultures: The rites and rituals of corporate life.* Reading, MA: Addison-Wesley.

DiSalvo, V. S., Dunning, D., & Homan, B. (1982, April). *An identification of communication skills, problems, and issues for the business and professional communication course.* Paper presented at the annual meeting of the Central States Speech Association, Milwaukee, WI. (ERIC Document Reproduction Service No. EDRS 216 398)

Downs, A. (1964). *Inside bureaucracy.* Santa Monica, CA: Rand Corporation.

Drucker, P. F. (1971). *The effective executive.* New York: Harper & Row.

Farace, R. V., Monge, P. R., & Russell, H. M. (1977). *Communicating and organizing.* Reading, MA: Addison-Wesley.

Goldhaber, G. M. (1986). *Organizational communication* (4th ed.). Dubuque, IA: Brown.

Hall, A. D., & Fagan, R. E. (1956). Definition of system. *General Systems Yearbook, 1,* 18–28.

Harrell, T. W., & Harrell, M. S. (1984). *Stanford MBA careers: A 20 year longitudinal study* (Research Paper No. 723). Stanford, CA: Stanford University, Graduate School of Business.

Harris, T. E. (1980). Dispelling the myth of the communication breakdown. *Management World, 10,* 31–32.

Hildebrandt, H. W. (1982). Executive choice: Business communication. *Journal of Communication Management, 11,* 8–10.

Hill, A. W. (1982, June). The supervisor as manager: Contributions and conflicts. *Personnel Administrator,* pp. 114–117.

Hinrochs, J. R. (1964). Communication activity of industrial personnel. *Personnel Psychology, 17,* 198–199.

Hisrich, R. D. (1990). Entrepreneurship/intrapreneurship. *American Psychologist, 45*(2), 209–222.

Jacker, C. (1964). *Man, memory, and machines: An introduction to cybernetics.* New York: Macmillan.

Katz, D., & Kahn, R. (1978). *The social psychology of organizations* (2nd ed.). New York: Wiley.

Kennedy, A. (1984, November). Back-fence conversations: New tools for quality conversations. *Communication World,* p. 30.

Klemmer, E. T., & Snyder, F. W. (1972). Measurement of time spent communicating. *The Journal of Communication, 11,* 142–158.

Kreps, G. L. (1990). Organizational communication (2nd ed.). New York: Longman.

Luciano, P. R. (1979). The systems view of organizations: Dynamics of organizational change. In J. E. Jones & J. W. Pfeiffer (Eds.), *The 1979 annual handbook for group facilitators* (pp. 140–144). La Jolla, CA: University Associates.

Miller, G. R., & Steinberg, M. (1975). *Between people: A new analysis of interpersonal communication.* Chicago: Science Research Associates.

Miller, J. G. (1972). Living systems: The organization. *Behavioral Science, 17,* 1–182.

*Model-Netics.* (1980). Sacramento, CA: Main Event Management Corporation.

Ouchi, W. (1981). *Theory Z: How American business can meet the Japanese challenge.* New York: Addison-Wesley.

Parsegian, V. L. (1973). *The cybernetic world of men, machines, and earth systems.* Garden City, NY: Doubleday.

Peters, T., & Austin, N. (1985). *Passion for excellence: The leadership difference.* New York: Random House.

Peters, T. J., & Waterman, R. H., Jr. (1982). *In search of excellence: Lessons from America's best-run companies.* New York: Harper & Row.

Pincus, D. (1984, November). Study links communication and job performance. *Communication World,* pp. 28–29.

Rath, G. J., & Stoyanoff, K. S. (1982). Understanding and improving communication effectiveness. In J. W. Pfeiffer & L. D. Goodstein (Eds.), *The 1992 annual for facilitators, trainers, and consultants* (pp. 166–173). San Diego: University Associates.

Rice, A. K. (1963). *The enterprise and its environment*. London: Tavistock.

Rothman, M. A. (1972). *The cybernetic revolution*. New York: Franklin Watts.

Schein, E. H. (1985). *Organizational culture and leadership*. San Francisco: Jossey-Bass.

Seiler, J. A. (1967). *Systems analysis in organizational behavior*. Homewood, IL: Irwin.

Senn, L. (1986). Corporate cultures: Does your corporate culture stimulate innovation or foster apathy? *Management World, 15*, 16–17.

Survey: GE campaigns to boost execs' job satisfaction. (1984, March). *World of Work Report*, p. 1.

Sypher, B. D., Applegate, J. L., & Sypher, H. E. (1985). Culture and communication in organizational contexts. In W. Gudykunst, L. Stewart, & S. Ting-Toomey (Eds.), *Communication, culture and organizational processes* (pp. 13–29). Beverly Hills, CA: Sage.

Tavemier, G. (1981, February). Improving managerial productivity: The key ingredient is one-to-one communication. *Management Review*, p. 14.

Thayer, L. (1968). *Communication and communication systems*. Homewood, IL: Irwin.

Thompson, J. D. (1967). *Organizations in action*. New York: McGraw-Hill.

Trist, E. L., & Bamforth, K. L. (1951). Some social and psychological consequences of the long-wall method of goal-setting. *Human Relations, 5*, 3–38.

Watzlawick, P., Beavin, J. H., & Jackson, D. D. (1967). *Pragmatics of human communication: A study of interactional patterns, pathologies, and paradoxes*. New York: Norton.

Weick, K. E. (1969). *The social psychology of organizing*. Reading, MA: Addison-Wesley.

Weick, K. E. (1979). *The social psychology of organizing* (2nd ed.). New York: Addison-Wesley.

Wilmot, W. W., & Wenburg, J. R. (1973, May). *Communication as transaction*. Paper presented at the International Communication Association Convention, Montreal.

Young, J. F. (1969). *Cybernetics*. London: Lliffe.

# Perception

Perception is the overriding influence surrounding our understanding of organizational communication (Laing, Phillipson, & Lee, 1972, p. 5). Focusing on perception is one of the advantages of a communication perspective for the study of organizations. Because the living system of an organization, by definition, can include a large number of variables, the behaviors we choose to "pay attention to" or select from the available data become the determining factors in our own behavior within the organization. Our view of reality, both in an organization and during our entire lives, is based on our perceptions (Altman, Valenzi, & Hodgetts, 1985).

Gaining an insight into the perception process may be the most important factor in helping us become effective organizational communicators. According to Cohen (1969), "Perception is defined as the meaningful interpretation of sensations as representatives of external objects; perception is *apparent* [italics added] knowledge of what is out there" (p. 86). As the word *apparent* [italics added] indicates, perception is our interpretation of reality. Although we do not always have the option of determining what it is that we will perceive, our efforts to make sense out of the information and multiple inputs we receive is a prerequisite to knowing how to respond. As Galvin and Book (1973) put it, "Perception is the process by which you filter and interpret what your senses tell you so you can create a meaningful picture of the world" (p. 22). This is an immensely complex procedure, which is often synonymous with growing up, learning to make decisions, understanding how to act correctly and appropriately, plus a host of other behaviors we undertake in an organization.

We obtain two benefits by understanding the role of perception in an organization. First, we can adjust our own perceptual capacities to enhance our performances, and second, we can learn to better understand other people's actions and responses. Because we only can respond to behaviors, the facts and knowledge we have about a situation are based on the process of obtaining the information, imposing sequence and arbitrary order to the vast amount of potential data, and making choices regarding our willingness even to pay additional attention to particular information. People perceive the world with information that is filtered through their sensory systems—both conscious and unconscious—which gives them the data to know how to respond to the outer world (Bandler & Grinder, 1975). We depend on sensations from seeing, hearing, tasting, smelling, or touching something to provide us with an interpretation of its meaning.

The process of perception is defined as the selecting, organizing, and interpreting of sensory stimulations into a meaningful and coherent picture of the world (Myers & Myers, 1976, p. 19). This process of discrimination has the inherent by-product of never being "able to see it as it is," but only as we interpret it to be. Reality, both within organizations and throughout our lives, is a function of the interpretation we assign to our own perceptions. Perception is never more than what is apparently correct about reality. However, it is very real to each individual. Peters and Austin (1985), in *A Passion for Excellence*, concluded that "there is only perceived reality, the way each of us chooses to perceive a communication, the value of a service, the value of a particular product feature, the quality of a product. The real is what we perceive" (p. 71).

Hence, our reality in an organizational system is derived from the perceptual base we bring to the system and the development of that base as we operate within the system. For example, why are you more concerned with organizational communication than acid rain? The answer, assuming that this is a correct assumption, lies in your response to a large number of stimuli. You have selected specific data to pay attention to and excluded other information.

In many ways, perception is both the instrument with which we succeed by making sense out of the world and the limitation on our ability to see greater or different issues that might be critical to our effective functioning in an organization. For instance, the most obvious characteristic of "experts" is their ability to perceive certain things that other people do not necessarily notice. An art expert is someone who can tell the good from the bad or the authentic from the fake. And, as is always the case, this does not mean that other people cannot see the differences between the two. The art expert is more likely to see particular characteristics as important. As anyone specializes in an activity, they develop this ability to perceptually "hone" their view to the exclusion of unnecessary information. The tendency of the expert to see things simultaneously that other people might not see and to do this at the necessary expense of other information is a working definition of perception.

Some companies hire efficiency experts who concentrate on how employees use their time. After studying the organization, one finding could be that the methods used for job assignments must be revamped in order to decrease wasted time and increase productivity. Other variables, such as worker satisfaction, would be excluded because they do not deal directly with the issue of efficient use of time. This example focuses on the concept that one person's trash is another person's treasure,

or one manager's unnecessary coffee breaks are another's social gratification periods. In a tongue-in-cheek indictment of some investigations, cynics have observed
that organizational research experts begin to know more and more about less and
less until they know everything about nothing. Perception always involves leaving
out some details in favor of others. In fact, making selective decisions about which
stimuli we will attend to is, by definition, creating the potential for exclusion of
significant information.

As the pressure for change and product development continues in organizations,
seminars frequently are offered in an effort to increase creativity. Being creative,
however, does not just happen and many of our limitations are a result of how we
perceive. Figure 2.1 shows a popular exercise for outlining perceptual blocks to
creativity. Can you connect the nine dots by (a) using four straight lines and (b)
not lifting your pencil or pen off of the page? We return to this example later in
the chapter.

## UNDERSTANDING OUR PERCEPTUAL BASE

There are three primary sources for our perceptual base. These include our past
experiences which provide us with a personal "reference file," our present organizational experiences or our "updating" of the file, and the actual physical limitations
while obtaining the information (Hostort, Schneider, & Polefka, 1970, pp. 5–6).

### Past Experiences

McLuhan and Fiore, (1967) communication commentators and philosophers, drew
attention to our tendency to engage in "rearview mirrorism" in our attempts to explain
current events and changes. In this process, "we march backwards into the future,"
because we tend to refer to the past to explain the present and the future (p. 26).

Given the barrage of sensory material available to use, our attention necessarily
is based selectively on those stimuli that have been significant to us in the past. The
response people have to an event is not so much the reality of what is occurring,
but which part of the event they are responding to. What we perceive is a combination of the event and our own perceptual system. When managers try to choose certain issues to increase their staff's teamwork they face a difficult task (Orsburn, Moran,
Musselwhite, & Zenger, 1990, pp. 9–13). This is because, for some people in an
organization, their department or team is the most important factor. For others, personal success tends to be the key motivating factor. Obviously, for others a combination of the two operates or perhaps the quality of the organization's product or
external competitiveness is the real issue. Some members might have had good or
bad experiences with teams and this influences their responses. Finally, in certain
cases, individuals simply do not care about their jobs.

FIG. 2.1.  A popular exercise for outlining perceptual blocks to creativity.

In a similar manner, organizations face a difficult task with customer service because "[t]he individual [customer] perceives service in his or her own unique, idiosyncratic, human, emotional, end-of-the-day, irrational, erratic terms" (Peters &
Austin, 1985, p. 71). Some customers want a great deal of attention, some want
to be left alone, and some need to complain about prices. As the sales representative
approaches these different individuals, understanding the uniqueness of individual
perception is often a prerequisite to success.

As we discuss the psychological factors in perception later in this chapter, the
impact of these sets will become much clearer. At this point, we should emphasize
that one of the major reasons for learning about organizational communication is
to expand this personal reference file through cross-checking and updating. This
expanded knowledge will allow you to operate more effectively in an organization.
In fact, the application of this expanded perceptual base will be useful in all communication activities from interpersonal experiences to absorbing mass media. Understanding that perception is selective and limited by our own background is an excellent
beginning to being a more effective organizational communicator.

If you have connected the nine dots in Fig. 2.1 and followed the instructions,
then you are the exception to the rule for most individuals trying this exercise. The
most common explanation for our inability to connect the dots, as shown in Fig. 2.2,
is an unwillingness to go outside the artificial "square" created by the dots. Our perception of the problem limits our ability to expand our creative problem-solving ability.

## Present Organizational Experiences

When we enter the culture labeled "gainful employment," most of us recognize that
our behavior must be adaptive in order to fit in and maintain our job. In most cases,
we accept additional inputs into our own personal perceptual system in the form

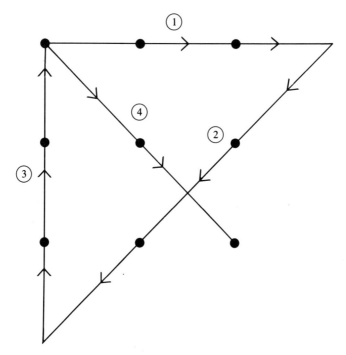

FIG. 2.2.    An example of the most common explanation for an inability to connect the dots.

of instructions regarding the job requirements and performance, the rules and regulations regarding the culture, and the apparent interpersonal patterns. We slowly make "sense" of this new sensory data and, as we remain on the job, certain perceptions become permanently associated with the organization. These all become part of our orientation toward organizational behavior and our attitudes toward lunch hours, office location, or weekly staff meetings are all formed in the ongoing process of being part of the organizational system.

In a more general sense, our present experiences provide the information we have regarding the specific organizational culture. Banks offer significantly different experiences than do computer development companies or the armed services. Financial institutions are not limited to banks and can range from credit unions to savings and loan associations, to local, regional, or national banks, to small loan companies, to a loan shark, and they all provide very different types of perceptual information.

Each subsystem within the culture provides unique inputs. Marketing focuses on very different behaviors than does the shipping department although both subsystems are concerned with the environment outside of the immediate office. Our interpersonal activities also provide substantial inputs regarding our impressions and this formulation begins during the interview process and our early transactions with the culture. Individuals differ regarding their feelings toward the first day on the job or their interview, but no one ever seems to forget the process itself and each of us can relate very specific lessons learned by our perceptions of this event.

## Actual Situational Limitations

We soon become aware that no one can know or, for that matter, should know, everything about everything in an organization. In fact, we are hired to do very specific tasks, and even those with extensive oversight responsibilities carry with their position specific physical limitations including what type of access they have to data, which part of it they will detect as being important, and how they will use that information as they interpret the meaning. Each of these three factors can work to prevent us from fully understanding a particular issue within an organization. Our position, including the circumstances and staff surrounding it, combined with all the other constraints—available information, resources, time, and so on—always work to control perception (Dearborn & Simon, 1958; Myers, 1991, pp. 2–8).

Later in this text, we examine the networks and channels that enhance and prevent information from reaching the people who should receive it. In every organization, there is filtering of messages as they proceed through the organization (Goldhaber, 1990, pp. 136–137). Because we cannot be all places at all times, we operate with less than complete information.

Past and present experiences, combined with situational limitations, operate in almost all of our decision-making activities. In an organization, for example, we look to past successes and failures with particular ideas and behaviors before making certain choices. Then we look to our present knowledge of the organization's structure to determine the best or most appropriate persons to approach regarding the issue. Finally, we incorporate the present information for acting on the choices.

In a recent article on obtaining bank loans, Bennett (1987) concluded, "New businesses tend to fail for one of two reasons: poor management or inadequate financing" (p. 112). To prevent the lack of financing, Bennett outlined the perceptual issues in obtaining a loan: (a) "We bankers are not all alike," (b) "most loan officers are doing what their bosses want done so they can get a raise and a promotion," (c) "your proposals (for a loan) will be viewed in light of where a loan officer is sitting on a particular day," and (d) "loan officers get burned on particular types of loans and don't forget" (p. 108). If you were seeking a business loan, the advice states: Do not depend on past experiences with bankers (a), understand situational constraints (b), be aware of the impact of particular events (c), and be cognizant of the banker's perceptions based on past experiences (d).

Perceptual limitations have an impact on numerous issues in all organizations. One of the most important, and recurring, problems any organization faces is how to effectively motivate employees. Individual perceptions figure prominently in the misdirecting of some of the motivation efforts used by management to motivate workers. We discuss the actual motivational process extensively later in this text, but the issue itself provides us with an important example regarding perception.

In an effort to test the correctness of certain motivational efforts, employees and managers were asked to rank from 1 to 10 a list of items in order of their importance to the employee. The goal of the test was to determine if there was any difference between those items employees thought were important versus those that management thought were important for the employee. As Table 2.1 indicates, employees ranked their preferences quite differently from the ranking by the employers.

The explanation for the differences lies, to a large extent, in the managers' attempts to apply their own experiences and backgrounds to the employees and thereby attributing to the employees' motives that simply do not apply. With little difficulty, we can see that the source of this misapplication lies in the three factors we discussed. The rankings reported in Table 2.1 are based on in-house training seminars conducted in 1982–1984. The actual test has been repeated numerous times in the last 10 years, with a large number of organizations, and the important point is the perceptual differences between management and employees occur every time regardless of the type of organization.

## SENSORY AND SYMBOLIC BASIS
## FOR PERCEPTION

No matter how acute our own perceptual abilities might be, the reality we carry with us is essentially less than the actual event. A story about three baseball umpires comparing notes on how they do their job indicates the function of reality in perception. The first umpire stated: "I call them either balls or strikes!" The second umpire, in an attempt to sound like a better umpire, asserted: "I call them as I see them!" The third umpire, with what is probably the strongest statement about labeling and reality, declared: "They ain't nothing until I calls them!" For each of the umpires, their reality was based on their perception of their own role and their environment. In terms of perception, each of the umpires was correct.

In the umpire story, no one disagreed that there was such a thing as a ball or a strike or that there was a need, for the benefit of the culture called baseball, to have someone call them. The issue was who would construct the reality.

In all cases, we are aided by a group construct concerning reality and this is especially important in an organizational culture. On the job, for example, we have a group definition of a "good" or "bad" worker. What constitutes a good or bad worker is essentially a group decision based on the combined past experiences each person brings to the job and the present environment. In some places, "beating the time clock" by punching in other workers who are late is applauded behavior, whereas at other locations being late is considered a violation of group norms. The famous, and now partially abandoned, IBM white-shirt-and-suit uniform is an example of group requirements. Dress codes, by and large, rarely have to be enforced due to

TABLE 2.1
Summary of Rankings by Employees and Management of 10 Items
Which are Important to Employees at Work

| *What employees say they want from their jobs* | *What managers think employees want* |
|---|---|
| 1. Interesting work | 1. Good pay |
| 2. Full appreciation of work done | 2. Job security |
| 3. Feeling "in" on future developments | 3. Promotion and career growth |
| 4. Job security | 4. Good working conditions |
| 5. Good pay | 5. Interesting work |
| 6. Promotion and career growth | 6. Tactful disciplining |
| 7. Good working conditions | 7. Management loyalty to workers |
| 8. Management loyalty to workers | 8. Help with personal problems |
| 9. Help with personal problems | 9. Full appreciation of work done |
| 10. Tactful disciplining | 10. Feeling "in" on future developments |

group expectations. We explain the impact of nonverbal issues, such as dress and the IBM dress standard, in our nonverbal chapter.

We also must realize that, as with the umpires, reality is always based on incomplete data. We cannot observe all the accompanying information to an event. This does not free us from having to form some type of perception because we must put the observed data in some context so that it makes sense to us. To do this, we abstract from reality and develop a symbolic construct. To us, this reality is no less valid than the one that would be based on all possible information. From a practical standpoint, meticulously gathering and evaluating all reports, advice, and communiques would prove impossible and probably unnecessary.

A very good example of the problems encountered with perception at the workplace occurs in the attempts by organizations to obtain increased input from workers. Abernathy (1980), a professor at the Harvard University Graduate School of Business Administration, explained: "Management frequently complains that workers don't make suggestions that fit into company plans. This shouldn't be surprising. Workers, after all, usually aren't part of the planning process. And in many companies, they're made to feel that they're not, which further discourages them from suggesting improvements" (p. C1). Abernathy summarized nicely the impact of our own perceptions of our place within the organization and its subsystems.

The final consequence of perception is the tendency of our perceived realities to "lock-in outcomes" (LaBrecque, 1980, p. 36). Essentially, we tend to persevere in our judgments even when the evidence is overwhelming that they are wrong. If we have a particular image in a work situation, we often opt for *perceptual constancy* rather than accept contradictory information. Hence, once the perceptual image has been formed, we interpret subsequent events in light of the original perception and not the new information. Our preconceived notion of reality becomes reality itself.

Our perceptions are also a function of the availability of reinforcement. Events are judged as likely or unlikely depending on the readiness to which they come to our mind. A communication professor observes to a friend: "Did you ever notice how many communication professors are chosen as the outstanding teacher at their universities? I'll bet it has to do with the way their background and education guide them in approaching their jobs." In spite of the apparent desirability of this claim, the basis for this observation probably has more to do with the likelihood of hearing about and noticing this particular phenomenon more than the activities of other professors in other disciplines. Many of the concepts held by individuals of where minorities, women, and older people fit into the workplace are based on built-in biases, which are reinforced by selective perception (Morrison & Von Glinow, 1990). We make behavioral observations based on selecting information and cues that we have learned to pay attention to and use.

Reality is based, then, on our perceptions combined with the group and environmental data that we use to modify our original concepts. By definition, we use incomplete data in the process of forming an abstraction. This symbolic representation tends to lock us into particular views of the world (Nisbett & Ross, 1980).

## PSYCHOLOGICAL FACTORS IN PERCEPTION

There are at least six psychological determinants of our perceptual abilities. In many cases, these categories cross over because we are not a mental computer that can freely catalogue all incoming data into a precise set of files containing discrete files of past inputs. In fact, most people cannot attend to more than five to seven separate pieces of information at one time (Miller, 1956).

### Attitude Set

An attitude is a predisposition to respond favorably or unfavorably to some person, object, idea, or event (Simons, 1976, p. 80). This reaction tends to create a bias, which can be carried to the extreme and result in *tunnel vision*. Individuals who cannot see the forest for the trees are often accused of having tunnel vision. In an organization, each of us has our own specialty that is more important to us than the others. Most individuals in sales, for example, argue that organizations cannot exist without sales because the cash flow generated by sales is the lifeblood of the company. Increasingly, computer specialists make the same type of claim, only they refer to the mind or memory of the system.

The impact of attitude set can be observed in organizations doing business as usual even when there are multiple signs that this is an inadequate response to a changing environment (Bolman & Deal, 1991). The call for the "tried and true" processes is not incorrect, but taken to the extreme it eliminates system adaptation and innovation. We return to the importance of effectively adapting to change several times in this text.

Performance appraisals provide another excellent example. Most organizations now use these reviews or appraisals annually, semiannually, or quarterly. During the session, the superior will indicate to the subordinate the areas of strength and weakness that have emerged during the period being appraised. The actual performance appraisal can be an important factor in improving performance and employee satisfaction. From the organization's view, it is also an important permanent document regarding future decisions concerning the employee.

In one organization where I consulted, reviews were ranked by employees as the major source of dissatisfaction. They felt they were frequently "sandbagged" or set up during the semiannual process, and that the meeting served no real benefit for the employees. Employees viewed it as a forum for the supervisor to comment on the employee's areas of weakness with some cursory comments regarding some progress by the employee. In this organization, employees were called in for a 20-min semiannual meeting where their performance files were reviewed. Up to that point, no employee was aware of exactly what was contained in the performance file. The meeting was used to inform the employee of the contents.

In searching for a means to overcome this problem, we encountered resistance to change by the managers and supervisors. The most frequent defense of the current system was in the form of tradition or "that's the way it's always been done." Some of the supervisors and managers also pointed to other organizational experiences where similar procedures had been employed. After several meetings regarding the options available for overcoming this major employee complaint, we decided that the appraisal form, which constituted a summary of the employee's file, would be made available to the employee a week before the performance appraisal so that sandbagging would not be a complaint. Because all the managers already had indicated that setting up the employee was not the intent of the sessions, no one openly voiced any objection to this modification. In fact, the only issue throughout the discussion was the attitude set regarding the accepted procedure. After a year of using the new system, which included two sessions for each employee, this major area of dissatisfaction for the employees was significantly reduced. By altering procedures and behaviors, we were able to modify the attitude set and, hopefully, enhance the success of the performance appraisal sessions.

Our own attitude set is an excellent paradigm for the discussion of perception because attitude set is neither good nor bad. However, when this set becomes carved in stone, tunnel vision can occur. Of course, a complete lack of attitude set would lead to indecision and potential chaos. Because humans prefer certainty over uncertainty the propensity is toward an attitude set that becomes closed and can create needless errors as we operate in an organization. Imagine the surprise on the part of the employee whose attitude had lead him or her to expect the semiannual sandbagging when he or she received the completed initial document a week before the actual meeting with the ascribed goal and expectation that it would enhance discussion in the actual meeting!

The expectancies we have regarding a particular event tend to determine how we will respond to that event. We often hear what we expect to hear and see what we expect to see. With this particular organization we were attempting to enhance the positive expectancies held by both the managers and the employees regarding the performance appraisal process (Hartman, Harris, Crino, & Griffeth, 1986).

The higher education culture has numerous examples of holding onto procedures and practices simply because they always have been done a certain way. A ready example of this type of attitude set is the current offering by many universities of the traditional Master's of Business Administration (MBA) degree. The rigorous MBA program requires each student to become an active leader and decision maker. One of the learning tools used is to require the future manager to explain effectively a large number of case problems to the satisfaction of the faculty along certain guidelines of decision making.

This format, created when business schools first offered the MBA, increasingly has been criticized for being removed from the reality of the business world. In the last few years, articles have appeared with titles such as "If All the Business Schools in the Country Were Eliminated . . . Would Anyone Notice?" In this article, Muse (1983), Vice Chancellor for Academic Programs for Texas A & M University, lamented "the continuing lack of willingness or ability on our part [business schools] to focus our energies on developing the skill most lacking, yet most desired by our graduates—the ability to communicate" (p. 4). Muse then indicated that the reason for the lack of focus on communication abilities lies in the apparent desire of business schools to be academically justifiable. In an effort to do this, they have made research and publication the major criteria for determining the quality of the business school. In the process, business faculties have downplayed, he argued, practical business experience in favor of the conceptual and analytical models where there are theoretically correct answers. The attitude set toward academic credibility has created a tendency to draw a dichotomy between research and the practical management skills used on a daily basis. Because the professor is rewarded for academic rigor rather than teaching ongoing management skills, critics argue that "The M.B.A.: Losing Some of Its Luster" (Hechinger, 1981).

As we indicated in chapter 1, business schools are now becoming fully aware of this limitation and are attempting to change. To the degree the schools are operating as open systems, they can adapt and change. These articles indicate a strong attempt within the schools themselves to alter the educational offerings to be more beneficial to the students and the employers.

Opening our perceptual systems is not always easy and this process is often the focus of training and development sessions. In Fig. 2.3, how many squares can you count? In training sessions, the responses range from 17 to 30 or more. You may have a different answer. In any case, our perceptual abilities are tested by this exercise because different individuals have a wide variety of answers. Normally, I put individuals into small groups to work out the correct answer in order to lead into a discussion of synergy and the importance of expanding perspectives. After lengthy discussion, each group usually will arrive at 30 squares as the correct answer.

## Count The Squares

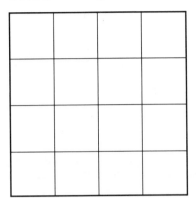

FIG. 2.3.   An exercise to test perceptual systems.

**I see _____ squares**

However, a few years ago, one group correctly pointed out that there were 32 squares in the illustration. Why? The word *squares* appears twice on the paper in addition to the actual squares. So, both answers of 30 and 32 are correct and underscore the importance of opening our perceptual systems.

## Stereotypes and Self-Fulfilling Prophecies

Once we have an established attitude set, the application of that set can lead to *stereotyping*. In an organization, it can be applied through *allness*, *indiscrimination*, and *time binding*. When this occurs, the final outcome can be a self-fulfilling prophecy. In organizations, stereotyping is the tendency to lump all of a particular group of subsystems or systems into a particular characterization. Hence, for a long time we believed all Japanese products were cheaply made, or all German cars were well designed. But, we leave off the word *all* and simply assume the generalization to be true. So, some people assume women cannot be effective managers or would rather be at home and that retirement should or should not occur at 65 years of age. Although we may be aware of the necessary caution that should be applied when speaking of minorities, such as all Latin men are passionate, all Yuppies are materialistic, or all blondes are dumb, consider the manner in which we proceed to discuss other classifications such as supervisors, management, unions, MBAs, high school dropouts, CEOs, today's youth, and many other job-related categories, and never pause to add the term *some*.

Unfortunately, this allness can lead to a self-fulfilling prophecy (Livingston, 1969). This phenomenon is the powerful influence our expectations can have on the outcome of a particular event. Currently, many organizations are grappling with the impact of automation, and not the least of the problems is the built-in bias that the "new-fangled" devices simply cannot work. When we set unnecessarily low expectations, our perception tends to preordain the failure of the event. One of the most difficult elements to successfully introduce in any organization—change—suffers from the conviction that it will not work.

In a moment, we return to the self-fulfilling prophecy. Our second general category is indiscriminate application of our limited perception. Within a short period of time on the job, many individuals create concrete reactions to concepts such as unions (good or bad), time clocks (very helpful or an insult to integrity), and many others depending on the particular occupation. Because all categories are collections of subsystems, any attempt to apply an across-the-board statement always will be less than accurate.

Finally, we time bind events and individuals and fail to recognize that people, objects, events, and organizations change over time. Tom Wolfe coined the phrase "You can never go home again," His point was that home cannot be time bound because it always will evolve in some direction. As a living system, which home must be because it includes people, whoever or whatever it was that made up the concept of home will change and this same evolution will occur to any individual who is away from home.

One certainty in any organization is that the system will respond to the environment in some manner. To maintain growth, the organization must respond in an open system manner, and any organization that refuses to respond to the environment tends toward being a closed system and eventually will deteriorate (Naisbitt & Aburdene, 1985; Waterman, 1987). As with individuals, organizations cannot not communicate, and they almost always will reflect some adaptation to circumstances. As a result, our specific tasks rarely remain the same, and interacting with the surroundings is never time bound. To the degree that we try to apply this type of limited perspective on our environment, we will perceive incorrectly the factors that we should be aware of in order to effectively do our job.

In varying ways, these three perceptual limitations bring about self-fulfilling prophecies. In applying this concept to the manager–subordinate relationship, Single (1980) concluded:

> The self-fulfilling prophecy, documented in a number of case studies prepared during the last decade for major industrial concerns, has revealed the following:
> * What a manager expects of his subordinates and the way he or she treats them largely determines their work performance and career progress.
> * A unique characteristic of superior managers is their ability to create high performance expectations that subordinates fulfill.
> * Less effective managers fail to develop similar expectations, and, as a consequence, the productivity of their subordinates suffers.
> * Subordinates, more often than not, do what they believe they are expected to do. (p. 19)

For each of us, the application is much broader because our expectations, based on our stereotyping, will tend to forecast the outcome for any number of our organizational experiences. These will range from learning a new skill to performance reviews to interacting with individuals within the organization. If we are convinced, for example, that a particular job will be too difficult, our perception will tend to create a greater likelihood for failure. Cyberphobia, meaning fear, distrust, or hatred of computers, is seen as a major impediment for many middle managers in their attempts to learn to use the computer (Rice, 1983).

When viewing people, this process has been appropriately labeled the *self-fulfilling stereotype* (Snyder, 1982). Through the preconceived image of the other individual, people tend to focus on particular characteristics of these individuals and therefore receive behavioral confirmation of their beliefs. The stereotype influences our work relationships in such a manner as to create the illusion of reality.

In one study regarding this phenomenon, a welding instructor at a vocational training center was told that five of his trainees had an unusually high aptitude for being excellent welders, when in fact the five were selected at random by the researchers. All five showed substantial changes in performance during the training period including fewer absences than other workers, better knowledge of the basics in half the usual training time, and scored a full 10 points higher than the other trainees on the welding test. The other trainees also noticed the improvement and chose the five as their preferred co-workers. When informed of the study, the instructor was unaware that he had treated the five in any different manner. The only actual difference between these five and the rest of the group was the self-fulfilling prophecy.

In reviewing this study, and many others, Snyder (1982) concluded:

> Might not other expectations influence the relationships between supervisors and workers? For example, supervisors who believe that men are better suited for some jobs and women to others may treat their workers (wittingly or unwittingly) in ways that encourage them to perform their jobs in accordance with the stereotypes about differences between men and women. These same stereotypes may determine who gets the job in the first place. Perhaps some personnel managers allow stereotypes to influence, subtly and not so subtly, the way in which they interview candidates, making it more likely that candidates who fit the stereotypes show up better than job-seekers who do not fit them. (p. 68)

Stereotyping and the self-fulfilling prophecy are important perceptual issues for us in the organizational setting because of their potential negative impact.

## Closure

Not knowing all the information regarding a situation often leads to *closure*. In this process, we fill in the gaps because the human mind has the need for apparent completeness in a given situation. In many organizational settings, it is impractical to gather all the facts about a situation. Depending on the structure of the system, it very well may be unnecessary. So, we fill in the vacuums with our versions of the appropriate information so that the event will make sense. In addition, if there is a gap in the story, individuals will provide the information in order to make the recollection of the event follow more coherently. Eyewitness accounts regarding accidents or crimes frequently incorporate this tendency toward closure in order to fill in the missing information.

## Selectivity

In our presentation of perceptual biases, we indicated the impact our own attitudes and beliefs have on our perception. Selectivity is the tendency to interpret communication messages using those biases. As an unconscious filtering process, selectivity tends to exclude certain aspects, groups, or behaviors as we operate in an organization (Hostort et al., 1970, pp. 19–25). What we are doing is accepting into our perceptual system certain facts or happenings that are consistent with our past experiences and beliefs. This occurs in three ways: *exposure bias, selective retention, and similarity and liking.*

**Exposure Bias.**   We are more likely to attend to messages that are consistent with our existing beliefs and attitudes. If we buy a new car, we are suddenly surprised to see many of that particular model on the road. What we have done is change our perception because we are now interested in a particular event. This is an ongoing activity in which we attend to the same types of behaviors, and therefore meanings, with the result being a continual exposure to the same data. Each prevailing interest we have tends to be accentuated by the selective exposure we have toward all of the possible events we could pay attention to. The manner in which we choose to read the different sections of a newspaper is an example of this bias. Even choosing to read the *Wall Street Journal* indicates a particular set regarding the information we are seeking.

In organizations, we tend to read memos for information that applies directly to our own area of interest. If your particular area is marketing, there is little likelihood that you will be concerned with the decisions regarding the typing pool in the payroll department.

**Selective Retention.**   This tendency is highlighted by the process of *selective retention*. Not only do we notice particular messages, but we also tend to remember those that are consistent with our needs, beliefs, and attitudes.

In spite of the need to recognize the interrelatedness of each part of an organization, Dearborn and Simon (1958) found executives unlikely to go beyond selective retention. They concluded: "Each executive will perceive those aspects of the situation that relate to the activities and goals of his department" (p. 144). The executives are using *habituation*, which is "blocking out of consciousness extraneous or unimportant messages in any situation" (Kreps, 1990, p. 30). In an organization, we must pay attention to those elements that have a direct bearing on our particular role. But, we do so at the expense of other information.

*Similarity and Likings.* The final aspects, *similarity and liking*, are our tendencies to see positive attributes in those individuals we like and negative ones in those we do not like. This can be carried to an extreme in an organization and result in what is now popularly known as *The Peter Principle* (Peter & Hull, 1969, p. 26). This principle argues that within an organization, those individuals who perform well at one level or in one position will be promoted to the next level under the assumption that they will perform well there also. The classic example is when an organization likes the individual who is a successful salesperson and promotes that person to manage all of the salespeople. Based on this principle, the use of liking as a means for making the decision is potentially disastrous, because the person who is a competent salesperson might not want to be a manager, or might lack the necessary skills to be an effective manager. Even more fundamentally, doing one task well hardly indicates that the individual can do other tasks with the same proficiency. The issue is one of using selective traits the person provides to the job they are presently doing for the organization and generalizing to all possible organizational activities.

## Self-Concept

These three aspects of selectivity often are accentuated by each individual's need to maintain his or her own self-concept. We need to have a sense of cognitive consistency in which our own personal conceptual integrity is somehow held in tact. We have certain beliefs which lead to a self-image that is an integral part of each of our makeups. In many ways, this self-concept requires that the incoming information be consistent with the preconceived premise under which we operate (Thompson & Van Houton, 1970, p. 55). We carry an evaluative frame of reference that predisposes us to respond to particular information in a manner that maintains our own internal equilibrium between new information and the already accepted premises. In the process, we have the tendency to maintain our own self-concept. Some authors have argued that for most individuals, the overriding concern is this maintenance of personal mental integrity (Heider, 1958).

Our need to defend our self-concept has been most appropriately described by Gibb (1961) in his analysis of defensive communication. The specific principles are discussed later in this book, but in general Gibb observed that communication that is essentially evaluative will cause the receiver to become defensive and will prevent effective interactions because the individual will feel the need to defend his or her self-concept.

On the other side of the coin, if we are given supportive messages that are consistent with our self-image, there is a greater likelihood we will act on them in a manner befitting the situation. Simply put, we do not correctly perceive things we do not like or that threaten our self-concept as well as ones that fit neatly into our perceptual set.

## ORGANIZATIONAL ROLE CONSTRAINTS

Within all positions are certain limitations on exactly what we can perceive. These are real in the sense that we cannot be everywhere and certainly cannot observe all activities. In addition, there are those limitations imposed because we simply do not wish to wander out of the limitations that make good sense to us. We may choose to say genuinely "not my job, man" due to the reality that it is indeed not our job or because we do not want any additional responsibility. Even if we are free from all other perceptual limitations, the particular system we operate within still would put specific constraints on our ability to perceive all information. For example, in studies of the perceptual differences within organizations, Maier, Hoffman, and Reed (1961) found a significant difference between the way superiors and supervisors saw their subordinates' jobs and the way the subordinates saw their jobs. Interviews with 58 superior–subordinate pairs from upper management levels in five different corporations showed that 85% of the dyads agreed on half or more of the subordinate's job duties, 64% agreed on half or more of the subordinate's job requirements, 68% agreed on less than half of the obstacles to the subordinates performing their jobs, and 50% agreed on less than half of the future changes that would affect the subordinates' jobs. We already have indicated the difference in perceptions regarding employee motivation by managers earlier in this chapter.

This limited perception because of role constraints is indicated in a large number of studies (Fachrenbach & Rosenberg, 1983), with the conclusion being that the person's position in the organization and the necessary constraints placed as a result of the position occupied magnifies the tendency to see things differently. At this point, you might be thinking that the entire discussion of perception and its impact on organizational communication is interesting and obviously important, but the problem should be easy to overcome simply by making this information available to active members of organizations.

Unfortunately, the issue is too complex for a simple solution. Recall that we all operate within the organizational system as a whole while we also are operating within specific subsystems. Faced with the complexity of the entire system, we tend to concentrate on our own presentations of what we perceive to be effective roles. As we act out our roles within the system, we consciously and unconsciously neglect other factors within the organization. As guidelines, we have an overriding sense of what the culture will accept as proper, and we have the immediate influence of the subsystem, whether it be a department, a specialty, or a group goal, on our ongoing behavior. The stimuli we choose to respond to will determine how we perceive a particular situation.

An extended program I used with one corporation's personnel directors regarding their own perceptual limitations in their hiring practices demonstrates the issue. Personnel directors are under a large number of constraints when they choose to interview a candidate for possible employment. For example, most personnel directors have a list of questions they may not ask a candidate. The goal of the program was to demonstrate some of the significant perceptual constraints that come into play in spite of the general belief that hiring practices must be fair.

The group of about 30 was divided into six task forces to determine whether to hire a specific individual. The picture in Fig. 2.4 was distributed with three of the task forces receiving a description of an older woman, at least 55 years of age, who had been a secretary for many years and was certain of how to do her job. Her attributes included confidence and the ability to follow through on work assignments. The other three received a description of a young woman, around age 25 years, who had been to secretarial school and was very confident in her approach to her job. Although she had a flair for overdressing, she was a serious worker. Both candidates had excellent references. The rest of the description for both candidates was identical except for adjustments for the age of each person. The position to be filled required secretarial skills and the ability to manage 10 other members of the same office staff.

If you already have seen two individuals in the picture, congratulations. The members of the seminar did not fare as well. Being under tremendous constraints created

FIG. 2.4. The picture used to test perceptual constraints that may come into play in hiring practices.

by their own organizational roles, their apparent perception of potential peer pressure, and the immediate context of having to act out their abilities as personnel directors, each group went about the task as it was described. Those persons who initially advocated the existence of two faces, and there were surprisingly few, quickly dropped their observation in order to facilitate the group problem-solving process. The immediate task became the overriding issue.

Each group's deliberations regarding whether to hire the individual or not were recorded. At one point or another in the discussion, practically all of the perceptual limitations that we have predicted might occur in an organizational setting did occur in these groups. For example, in all six groups age was an important issue with comments ranging from "older people make the best workers" or "experience is the best teacher" to "youthful enthusiasm is best for the changing workplace" or "schooling is the secret to present knowledge." Many of the individuals argued from their own experiences regarding past employees.

Because reality is also a group construct, there developed a consensus complete with attitude sets, stereotyping, closure, and selectivity. Each person also was concerned with maintaining their own self-concept within the group, which was evident in relation to their own positions as personnel directors. In reviewing the exercise for the participants, we were able to identify the perceptual issues we have discussed in this chapter as the major impediment to effective hiring practices.

The final step in this exercise was to ask each group to discuss their decision and the rationale for it. Each group was asked to choose a representative who then presented the findings. At this point, it should have been obvious that there were two faces in the picture. However, the perceptual set was so great that most of the groups refused to accept the other possibility. The group leaders became more concerned with their presentations and the maintaining of their own self-image. The leaders were also in a position of publicly forwarding the group's decision. These elements combined to create a highly defensive reaction to the challenges from the other perspectives.

This type of study has been conducted for various other purposes with the same general result (Mulford, 1978). For this group, the hoped-for result was a greater understanding of the perceptual limitations with which we all work.

The personnel managers also brought to my attention an important saying, which summarizes the apparent paradox regarding perception: "Always remember that you are absolutely unique—just like everyone else." This is the type of dilemma we face with perception. In order to adequately understand information as we receive it, we need to see it in groupings in order to make sense of the data. At the same time, this tendency to see things as being the same because they carry the general characteristics means that we miss the absolutely unique nature of each event. This chapter highlights the areas where we must work to resolve the apparent paradox. An awareness of the perceptual influence on our ability to communicate in an organization is the critical step. Often, we are limited in our ability to understand perception because "we are too close to be able to see it clearly" (Platt, 1970, p. 25).

## CONCLUSION

Before we can effectively understand the various issues in organizational communication, we must appreciate the significant impact perception has on all parts of an organization. Once we understand the impact of perception, we can begin to overcome our own tendencies to be perceptually limited. In addition, we can understand the impact of perception on all the individuals we work with and on the cultures of every organization. As we learn to more effectively select, organize, and interpret the various sensory stimulations in our organizational cultures, we will be more successful as organizational communicators.

Each of the remaining chapters in this textbook provides new information that will assist you in expanding your personal reference file toward organizational communication. With increased sensitivity toward our perceptual blinders and sets, we become better able to correctly respond to the various behaviors occurring in an organization. Rather than depend on past experiences to explain current activities, we can interpret more accurately exactly what is occurring and respond in a more effective manner. Equally as important, we can become more effective in understanding other people. As you continue your organizational communication studies, carefully examine your assumptions in light of the new information being provided.

## REFERENCES

Abernathy, W. J. (1980, November 2) In J. Miller. Better ideas need more watts. *The New York Times*, p. C1.

Altman, S., Valenzi, E. R., & Hodgetts, R. M. (1985). *Organizational behavior: Theory and process*. New York: Academic.

Bandler, R., & Grinder, J. (1975). *Structure of magic*. Palo Alto, CA: Science & Behavior Books.

Bennett, T. E., Jr. (1987, February). How to choose a bank. *Inc.*, pp. 108–112.

Bolman, L. G., & Deal, T. E. (1991). *Reframing organizations: Artistry, choice, and leadership*. San Francisco: Jossey-Bass.

Cohen, J. (1969). *Sensation and perception: Vol. 1. Vision*. Chicago: Rand McNally.

Dearborn, D. C., & Simon, H. A. (1958). Selective perception: A note on the departmental identifications of executives. *Sociometry, 21*, 140–144.

Fachrenbach, J., & Rosenberg, K. (1983). Employee communication index: How are we doing? *IABC Journal, 7*, 3–9.

Galvin, K., & Book, C. (1973). *Person-to-person: An introduction to speech communication*. Skokie, IL: National Textbook.

Gibb, J. R. (1961). Defensive communication. *Journal of Communication, 11*, 141–148.

Goldhaber, G. M. (1990). *Organizational communication* (5th ed.). Dubuque, IA: Brown.

Hartman, S. J., Harris, O. J., Crino, M., & Griffeth, R. (1986, August). *The effects of rater and candidate sex, candidate personal characteristics, and job type on assessment center evaluations*. Paper presented at the annual meeting of the National Academy of Management, Miami, FL.

Hechinger, F. M. (1981, January 4). The M.B.A.: Losing some of its luster. *The New York Times*, p. E1.

Heider, F. (1958). *The psychology of interpersonal relations*. New York: Wiley.

Hostort, A. H., Schneider, D. J., & Polefka, J. (1970). *Person perception*. Reading, MA: Addison-Wesley.

Kreps, G. L. (1990). *Organizational communication: Theory and practice* (2nd ed.). New York: Longman.

LaBrecque, M. (1980, June). On making sounder judgments: Strategies and snares. *Psychology Today*, pp. 32–42.

Laing, R. D., Phillipson, H., & Lee, A. R. (1972). *Interpersonal perceptions: A theory and a model of research*. New York: Harper & Row.

Livingston, J. S. (1969, July-August). Pygmalion in management. *Harvard Business Review*, pp. 81–89.

Maier, N. R. F., Hoffman, L. R., & Reed, W. H. (1961). *Superior–subordinate communication in management*. New York: American Management Association.

McLuhan, M., & Fiore, Q. (1967). *The medium is the massage*. New York: Bantam.

Miller, J. A. (1956). The magical number seven, plus or minus two: Some limits on our capacity for processing information. *Psychological Review, 63*, 81–96.

Morrison, A. M., & Von Glinow, M. A. (1990). Women and minorities in management. *American Psychologist, 45*(2), 200–208.

Mulford, W. R. (1978). Young/old woman: A perception experiment. In J. W. Pfeiffer & J. J. Jones (Eds.), *The 1978 annual handbook for group facilitators* (pp. 40–45). La Jolla, CA: University Associates.

Muse, W. V. (1983, Spring). If all the business schools in the country were eliminated . . . would anyone notice? *Collegiate News & Views*, pp. 1–5.

Myers, G. E., & Myers, M. T. (1976). *The dynamics of human communication* (2nd ed.). New York: McGraw-Hill.

Myers, M. S. (1991). *Every employee a manager*. San Diego: University Associates.

Naisbitt, J., & Aburdene, P. (1985). *Re-inventing the corporation*. New York: Warner.

Nisbett, R., & Ross, L. (1980). *Human inference: Strategies and shortcomings of social judgment*. Englewood Cliffs, NJ: Prentice-Hall.

Orsburn, J. D., Moran, L., Musselwhite, E., & Zenger, J. H. (1990). *Self-directed work teams: The new American challenge*. Homewood, IL: Business One Irwin.

Peter, L. J., & Hull, R. (1969). *The Peter principle: Why things always go wrong*. New York: Morrow.

Peters, T., & Austin, N. (1985). *Passion for excellence: The leadership difference*. New York: Random House.

Platt, J. (1970). *Perception and change*. Ann Arbor: University of Michigan Press.

Rice, B. (1983, August). Curing cyberphobia. *Psychology Today*, p. 79.

Simons, H. W. (1976). *Persuasion: Understanding, practice, and analysis*. Reading, MA: Addison-Wesley.

Single, J. L. (1980, November). The power of expectations: Productivity and the self-fulfilling prophecy. *Management World*, pp. 18–20.

Snyder, M. (1982, July). Self-fulfilling stereotypes. *Psychology Today*, pp. 60–68.

Thompson, J. D., & Van Houton, D. R. (1970). *The behavioral sciences: An interpretation*. Reading, MA: Addison-Wesley.

Waterman, R. H., Jr. (1987). *The renewal factor*. New York: Bantam.

# Management and Organizational Theories: An Overview

In order to understand how organizational communication functions, you need to be familiar with the various theories that have shaped the development of present companies, businesses, and corporations. These theories provide information regarding the underlying premises that guide the behaviors in organizations. Knowing more about these theories will help you increase your ability to adapt and develop. Because each of these views represents some important conclusions regarding the proper structure for management, employee, and systems relationships, an insight into the premises supporting them will be very beneficial.

This chapter outlines and discusses four major perspectives. Because this chapter is a general introduction and overview, this division is somewhat arbitrary, and not every approach to organizational design and behavior is examined. For our purposes, looking at the development of organizational and management theories from four views is useful because each one does represent a fundamentally different outlook and position on how the *behaviors* of the members and the organization should occur (Albanese, 1988). At the end of this chapter, you will be able to understand the basic differences between scientific management, humanistic management, human resource management and contingency theory, and the cultural perspective. These theories are explained further by examining them from a structural, human resources, political, and symbolic frame of reference (Bolman & Deal, 1991). Each of these frames carries fundamentally different perspectives regarding organizations.

## THE INDUSTRIAL REVOLUTION

As the modern organization emerged, the need to be able to effectively *manage* large groups of people engaged in a coordinated activity became a reality. Each organization has specific purposes for its operation, which may include making a profit, providing a service, solving a problem through research and development, and any number of other activities. For the organization to achieve its goals, whatever they may be, some type of structure and coordination is required.

Prior to the industrial revolution, most goods and services were generated within the family unit and most needs were met by the family itself or with the help of neighbors. Within larger families, management was mostly a matter of tradition. The state and the church represented organized authority and their dictates usually were followed because of compliance by decree or perhaps because of fear of retribution. In many cases, a certain sense of duty and devotion added to the ability of these large organizations to manage and govern.

In the earliest stages of organizational development, the problem was how to coordinate most effectively the work of several employees who had gathered for a common purpose. Before this occurred, most "overseers" of large organizations — plantations and estates — simply assigned specific tasks to certain individuals and the need to work jointly for a particular final product was not really an issue. The farm or estate either was well managed because the specific jobs were accomplished, or it was not, and having people work well together was more of a convenience than an absolute necessity.

The industrial revolution changed all of this as machine power became the major source of production. With the movement by the population to the cities, services and needs had to be provided effectively to those individuals who no longer could depend on the family unit. Individuals operating the factories and assembly lines had to concern themselves with scheduling, coordinating, and rewards in terms of wages. Although the industrial revolution continued to provide better technology, the skills needed for coordinating and managing workers were still in an infant stage. Instead of being able to rely on the innate abilities of workers gathered for a common purpose, organized attempts at production needed some clear management direction. The beginning of the 20th century witnessed the development of various theories of management.

## SCIENTIFIC MANAGEMENT

Three theorists stand out for their contributions to early management theory and practice. Taylor (1911) is the best known advocate of scientific management. We examine his approach to organizational design and then explain the important contributions of two other theorists, Fayol (1949) and Weber (1947).

Early in the 20th century, Taylor (1911) looked at the typical production line and noticed there could be any number of workers performing the same job and each one would be using a different method. He concluded that management would benefit greatly from studying these jobs, determining the best means for performing them, and then teaching all the employees with the same job the preferred method. This assumption of *managerial responsibility* for the worker's job underlies the concept of *scientific management*. In most cases, managers were responsible to owners for the profitable operation of the assembly line. So, managers were expected to educate the workers and provide the proper tools for getting the job done. For the employees at the time, who were uneducated and relatively unskilled, the system worked well. The phrase "hired hand" developed during this period because the "hands" were being hired to do a job. Taylor called for a clear *job design* by management for these unskilled workers.

Scientific management is based on the classical theory of organizations where the *structuring* of the system is of primary importance. As the term scientific management implies, *predictability* and *control through careful design* are the basic elements of scientific management. Productivity could be maximized, scientific management advocates assumed, "by reducing workers' jobs to minute, specialized, even mindless tasks" (Hickman & Silva, 1987, p. 23).

Taylor (1911) demonstrated the application of his concepts in his study of shoveling at Bethlehem Steel Company. Recall the impact on management of hiring a large number of workers for a particular organized task mentioned earlier. On a small farm, workers would come to work with whatever tools they already had available. At the Bethlehem Steel Company, the same procedure was used. Taylor studied, through time-and-motion analysis, scaling the top performer's ability to shovel more coal than other individuals. Through a "science of shoveling" he was able to find the optimum shovel size for the job that would allow the most productivity with the least worker fatigue. He then used an incentive payment, based on the top worker's production, for paying all individuals. The results were excellent. With fewer workers, efficiency went up.

The exact details of Taylor's (1911) study provide interesting reading. They also helped establish the legitimacy of scientific management. By using standards of good performance, tight scientific means could be used for managing people. Taylor assumed all individuals could be top performers if scientifically assigned to the correct task. He believed performance was directly related to pay and the only real incentive needed for good work was good and fair pay. The use of clear-cut goals would enhance the potential for workers to perform well.

The nicely mechanistic nature of this approach made his concepts quite popular. Many of his followers, such as Frank and Lillian Gilbreth (Pugh, 1971, pp. 126–127), and numerous organizations, operated on the premises of control, predictability, efficiency, and task orientation. The Gilbreths extended their use of scientific management principles to "the challenge of raising their twelve children efficiently, and their lives and experiences are the subject of the book and film *Cheaper by the Dozen*" (Albanese, 1988, p. 41). From the factory to large families, scientific management did seem to fit the needs of organizations at the time it was introduced.

Although scientific management frequently is associated with Taylor, Fayol and Weber deserve major credit for developing the premises of the classical theory of management. Fayol, a French coal-mining manager, wrote extensively about the nature of effective management based on his experience as a manager (Fayol, 1949).

He became widely known for his concepts regarding the proper design of work based on certain principles of management.

Essentially, Fayol (1949) wanted a classical, hierarchical pyramid of command for each organization. At the top would be a chief executive, or at least a single executive authority, and at the bottom would be the on-line worker. Within this structure, there would be strict specialization and accountability. Levels of command and the sources for control would be clear at all times. With no exaggeration, the modern analogy would be a military operation during a time of strife. Management would be concerned with the planning, organizing, commanding, coordinating, and controlling of all aspects of the operation. Maximum efficiency would be accomplished through the most rational approach to management. The goal of an organization, after all, was to develop material rewards for those in charge, and Fayol's concept would guarantee that result. Extensive organization charts used by many companies are examples of this desire. Establishing the proper channels for determining who is in charge is an important, and often essential, characteristic of any organization. Fayol indicated how to make the entire operation as predictable as possible.

Fayol (1949) also recognized the need to go beyond the traditional structure in order to enhance coordination. Managers at the same level should be able to contact each other directly and discuss and coordinate their activities without going through a common boss and at a higher level. This "gangplank" approach is known as *Fayol's Bridge*. At the time, the bridge was quite innovative as an approach to organizational structure, and it has had a useful impact on organizational theory. However, Fayol saw this moving between the direct chain of command as something that would be done in exceptional cases and not as a general rule. His principles were based on his own practical experience, which supported his concepts: specialized jobs, single chain of command, one person ultimately in charge, scaler direction from the top down and back up, and some potential for decentralization when needed. Although Taylor (1911) is known as the "Father of Scientific Management," Fayol's theories best clarify the concepts behind the classical approach to organizing.

Weber (1947), a great German sociologist, postulated the view that bureaucracy, or order through clear rules, was the best form of human organization. People, Weber argued, respond to clear authority. The best and most effective means for using authority is for it to be free from tradition. Depending on family structure, or the church's and king's traditional authority, or the charisma of great leaders, are unreliable means for obtaining results. Instead of these preindustrial forms of authority, organizations should have impersonal leadership which would be established through rules and regulations. In many ways, this is a logical extension of Smith's (1776/1937) concept of division of labor forwarded in *The Wealth of Nations*. Strict adherence to rules based on competence of individuals provides the ideal means of managing. Instead of making decisions based on favoritism, administrators would make all decisions according to specific rules, policies, regulations, and behaviors spelled out in a uniform manner.

Bureaucracy often is associated with negative attributes. A popular joke in

Washington, DC concerns a new missile, recently introduced by the Navy, which was causing problems: "It's called the civil service. It won't work and you can't fire it." The very rigidity of the system tends to lead to excesses in impersonal behavior and lack of personal accountability.

However, a structure that chooses individuals based on their ability to do a specific job is certainly an improvement over the pre-1900 method of dispensing positions based on family ties or simply availability. Weber's (1947) bureaucracy eliminated special privileges in hiring, promoting, or firing and therefore would be concerned with the individual's technical competence. As long as the individuals did their job to the specifications of the guidelines, they would be rewarded appropriately.

Taken together, Taylor (1911), Fayol (1949), and Weber (1947) represent the basic tenets of scientific management. There are numerous other individuals who have contributed to the theory and implementation of the basic concepts of a clearly functional approach to management where purpose, and its corresponding form, personnel policy and procedures, are clearly defined through specific tasks, direct lines of authority, task training for personnel, and accountability. This bureaucracy should function effectively because competence is rewarded. Their combined approach was straightforward and not laden with any ambiguities or paradoxes. Given the choice, practically any manager at the beginning of the 20th century would choose the approach that provided clarity over ambiguity and scientific management quickly became the predominant mode of managing. Henry Ford, one of the early users of these concepts for increased productivity through standardization, work simplification, motion studies, and clear controls, expressed the essence of the implementation of the scientific management philosophy: "All we ask of the men is that they do the work that is set before them" (Hall, 1965, p. 2). The method worked. After Ford introduced his new touring car for a record low price of $290.00 complete, half of the automobiles in the world were Model T Fords. So, scientific management was successful and accomplished its particular ends. In a recent reevaluation of Taylor's (1911) theory, Locke (1982) pointed out that many modern organizations still use Taylor's basic premises.

## HUMAN RELATIONS MANAGEMENT

One of the potential problems with any successful managerial approach is its overuse. We return to the continued use of scientific management several times during this chapter because the rationale behind scientific management is that predictability, control, and clear expectations are important parts of any effective managerial approach. Because organizations always are striving to be as successful as possible, events that show a better way to achieve productivity always will gain a great deal of attention.

The human relations movement resulted from some dramatic findings in the mid-1920s in what are now known as the *Hawthorne Studies*. Because these studies

challenged some of the basic conclusions of the scientific management practitioners, we discuss them before outlining the major premises behind the human relations movement.

## Hawthorne Studies

Between 1927 and 1932, a series of studies were conducted at the Western Electric
Company's Hawthorne Works (Roethisberger & Dickson, 1939). The original design of the research was to discover the relationship between production and the
level of lighting at the plant. The goal of the studies was to determine the best possible working conditions that would be needed to maximize worker productivity—a
classic scientific management approach. Manipulating the level of illumination at
the plant in order to make the employees more efficient and harder working is probably the most famous of the various and extensive Hawthorne experiments. One
group of workers was subjected to increased and decreased lighting to see if there
was a correlation between lighting levels and the amount of work produced. The
other group, functioning as a control group, received the same level of lighting at
all times. To the surprise of the researchers, output went up regardless of the level
of lighting. So, increases and decreases both brought about increases in output. In
addition, the control group began to respond to the new environment—they saw that
they were picked for some reason—and their output also increased.

   Researchers, at first baffled by these results, were forced to conclude that increased attention, a nonmaterialistic reward, was causing the changes. The apparent capacity of workers to increase productivity, regardless of the better or worse
working conditions imposed by management, indicated the possibly ironic impact
of management controls, which had been to restrict productivity to preestablished
goals.

   The impact of increased attention could be explained when the changes imposed
were viewed as surrogate management. The workers saw the changes as an indication that the organization was paying attention to them. In fact, the experimenters
were de facto managers because they used extensive contacts, structured the work
day, and helped the group maintain contact with the organization. Prior to the experiment, workers had predictable and impersonal jobs with a great deal of structure and numerous controls.

   The Harvard University researchers, headed by Mayo, interpreted the results as
indicating the need for greater emphasis on the human relations aspects of the work
setting. By improving the social aspects of work, employees presumably would be
more content with their jobs and therefore would be more productive. This interpretation of the Hawthorne Studies called into question many of the major premises
behind the scientific management view regarding a "day's pay for a day's work was
all that was needed," and had a major impact on management practices (Roethisberger & Dickson, 1939). A large number of innovations were developed, which
ranged from better break times and rooms to broader conveniences, such as air con-

ditioning, which represented factors not directly related to the strict scientific management approach.

The Hawthorne Studies are important because they experimentally questioned the prevailing assumptions about organizational management and design, and brought an awareness of the need for greater attention to human needs, motives, and relationships at work. Various scholars have offered alternative interpretations to explain the unexpected results of the studies. For example, in the original study, the supervisor assigned to the experimental group was one of the best in the plant, the workers were encouraged to develop a team effort, and there was a high degree of individual control in the workplace (Carey, 1967; Franke & Karl, 1978). Taken together, the studies and the various interpretations all point to the impact of social conditions on productivity.

## Goals in Conflict

Mayo and his associates provided the groundwork for the humanistic movement. The philosophical issue behind the problems of scientific management was outlined by Argyris (1957), who postulated that there were goals in conflict between the organization's needs and the worker's needs. He noted that the goals of an organization can be met most effectively through a posture on the part of individuals of submissiveness, passivity, and dependency. The use of specific job requirements, met through particular job skills, and rewarded through material benefits would create these conditions in workers. Individuals, he argued, need to be able to grow and have some sense of self-control. These two needs are bound to be in conflict.

Argyris (1957) saw individuals as needing growth in a large number of areas beyond the payment for services rendered. Material benefits will meet the basic needs of individuals, but once these have been met, greater needs also must be addressed. People also need to develop personal maturation and interpersonal comptency, which often are thwarted by the organization's need for control and rationality. In fact, the "rational/legal bureaucratic" organization creates an atmosphere that is short-sighted and centered only on the organization.

The system, through its tendency to try to evaluate and control individuals, creates a defensive attitude on the part of the individual. The outcome is that the organization produces in the individual an infantile perspective because it uses fear, control, and dependence, which carry with them behaviors characterized by indifference, irresponsibility, and passivity. Argyris (1957) argued that these difficulties will occur because the organization does control the workaday world, requires a single-job perspective, and encourages the perfection of a few skills for the good of the product.

Argyris (1957) saw in these issues a vicious spiral because management will react to the employees' behavior with greater controls, as long as the scientific perspective is maintained. Workers, of course, will escalate their own behavior and will retaliate with greater deviations and indifference. Employee thefts, for example, often are blamed on management's excessive concern for control ("Boss' Pockets," 1983). Industrial sabotge, especially when it is clearly directed as a statement of frustration, probably grows out of this conflict.

Following the Hawthorne Studies and the various criticisms regarding the impact of scientific management, numerous attempts were made to develop greater people-oriented management behavior. Rather than placing production as the most important issue, supervisors and managers were told to try to make the individual worker feel more important in relation to the goals of the organization and the specific tasks required. As Bendix (1956) put it, "The failure to treat workers as human beings came to be regarded as the cause of low morale, poor craftsmanship, unresponsiveness, and confusion" (p. 287).

Because the managers did not want poor productivity, they adopted the apparent means for implementing the humanistic approach. In an effort to decrease alienation by the workers, management tried to increase participation in various decisions and to treat the workers in a more friendly manner. Supervisors frequently were given "charm school" seminars to overcome the prevailing production orientation. Unfortunately, many managerial personnel saw this increased sensitivity as an opportunity to manipulate their employees into acceptance of management decisions (Rush, 1972). At its best, the human relations school created higher morale and undoubtedly made workers feel more appreciated while doing their jobs. However, just as the emphasis on productivity by scientific management had been excessive, depending on high morale to cause high production was also an error. Happy people are not necessarily the best and most productive workers (Albanese, 1988, p. 53). Some amazingly harsh criticism was directed at the human relations approach (Hertzberg, 1968, p. 55). In reality, "The overwhelming failure of the human relations movement was precisely its failure to be seen as a balance to the excesses of the rational model, a failure ordained by its own equally silly excesses" (Peters & Waterman, 1982, p. 95). In an effort to counteract the possible negative influence of managerial control, organizations became too likely to move in the direction of allowing petty issues to prevail. Comfort won out over consistency, personal indulgence over organizational perseverance, and so on to the point that the humanistic approach allowed individual needs to supersede the needs of the organization.

Top-down control used by the scientific management school was replaced by bottom-up control, and the results were a lack of productivity for organizations. As a consequence, the humanistic side of management became discredited and a large number of organizations reverted to scientific management techniques. A short visit to most assembly lines in the major industries, such as steel or automobile, in the 1960s would have provided ample evidence of the predominant use of managerial control.

In smaller ways, time clocks, piecework, bonus systems, and accountability with commensurate rewards and punishments still exist in many organizations. For example, with the increased use of computer terminals for many workers, some organizations also are using the terminals for computer monitoring, which is used to establish standards and evaluate performance. In 1986, at least one third of the 4 million to 6 million individuals using video terminals were being electronically monitored by their companies with the information being used to evaluate performances (Memmott, 1987). In some ways, this binary measurement is replacing Taylor's (1911) shovel size for determining the amount of work completed. The impact of the new communication technologies, including computers, is examined in chapter 14.

In a thorough and fascinating analysis of the PATCO Air Controllers' Strike, "What would make 11,500 people quite their jobs?," Bowers (1983) effectively documented the impact of a stringent scientific management aproach on the work force. The strike, he argued, was almost a classic (scientific management) outcome: the destruction, or near destruction of a system. In his lengthy examination of the evidence surrounding the strike, he concluded that the outcome was "perhaps the greatest labor relations disaster in the history of modern public administration" (p. 19). The management team refused to alter their own view of how to run an organization and therefore prevented any conciliatory moves on the part of the work force. Excessive reliance on scientific management created a crisis which, according to Bowers, could have been alleviated by greater utilization of human relations. The PATCO strike acted out Argyris' (1957) concept of goals in conflict. Excessive control, leading to stress and burnout, forced air controllers to take action. In 1987, arguing that little had changed since the PATCO strike, the air controllers again responded to what they perceived as excessive use of managerial control and insensitivity, and formed another air traffic controllers union ("Air Controllers," 1987, p. B1). Stress is a common concern. One study indicated that one in three Americans seriously thought about quitting their jobs because of stress burnout caused by a lack of personal control ("One in Three," 1991, p. A6). The efficiency and control generated by scientific management techniques can dehumanize the workplace and create serious problems.

## Summary: Scientific and Humanistic Management

Scientific management provided essential processes for the efficient and productive use of manpower after the industrial revolution. However, the perspective was limited to enhancing productivity through clear and precise controls. This concern for production remains one of the key variables in any managerial theory.

Mayo and the Harvard researchers discovered an equally important issue when they applied scientific management techniques to the Hawthorne Electric Works. After various interpretations, the basic finding from those studies seems to indicate that how people are treated is an equally important variable. This concern for people provides the other variable in almost any approach for understanding how organizations operate effectively.

Humanistic management correctly noted the debilitating impact of a production orientation. Argyris (1957) articulated the basic dilemma between the concerns of the organization and the needs of the individual, and the dangers of a headlong pursuit of production goals on the individual's ability to work. Unfortunately, many of the attempts to apply the concepts of humanistic management became equally manipulative and quite dishonest because they were really disguised attempts to pursue production goals at all costs. But the underlying premise behind the school of thought that workers must be treated as an important part of the organization, and must be dealt with as people, remains an important tenet of organizational theory.

## HUMAN RESOURCE MANAGEMENT

The extreme use of either scientific management or human relations management does not seem to provide an adequate approach to effectively managing people. Both of these approaches have provided necessary information in the development of human resource management techniques. This approach recognizes the need for structured development combined with an awareness of human needs. In addition, it argues for a *contingency approach* to managing organizations by observing that there rarely are simple answers. Finally, people are seen as resources that work with other factors in an organization for solutions to important managerial issues.

As with the first two views of management, human resource management comes from a large number of theorists and practitioners. We discuss McGregor's (1960) Theory X–Theory Y and Likert's (1967) System 4 as important insights into the development of human resource management. Then we examine the premise behind the contingency theory—there is no one best way—and some specific applications of the contingency theory approach.

McGregor (1960) approached the general issues raised by Argyris (1957) with a different perspective. He saw the incongruences between management and labor as being based more on how the manager views the workers than a statement of conflicting goals. To McGregor, the conventional manner used by management in dealing with workers is based on *Theory X*. Management harbors erroneous assumptions regarding the kinds of employee motivations that operate on the job. Argyris' dilemmas are seen by McGregor as being misinterpretations by management in their interactions with the various subsystems of an organization, including superiors, subordinates, peers, and the formal and informal structure of the organization. Theory X assumes an inherent laziness on the part of individuals, a lack of ambition, an indifference to organizational needs, a built-in resistance to change, and a need for careful supervision. As such, Theory X organizations and managers rely on coercion, control, and possibly overt and covert threats.

McGregor (1960) also postulated a *Theory Y* for management, which creates opportunities for growth, expects the best from individuals who are treated fairly, and assumes human beings will welcome the chance to work given the proper conditions. People, in other words, want meaningful work and will provide the input needed to make that work meaningful if they are given the chance.

McGregor (1960) reaffirmed the perceptual nature of organizational behavior and the communication conditions surrounding it. After noting that McGregor's theory "is one of the most frequently cited theories in the management literature" (p. 1), Jacoby and Terborg (1976) further summarized his perspective:

> Briefly, McGregor believes that human behavior is seldom a direct response to objective reality, but is rather a response reflecting the individual's perception of that reality. A manager's personal beliefs about the nature of man and about cause–effect relationships in human behavior exert considerable influence over the actual behavior exhibited by that manager when directing the activities of others. (p. 1)

Theory X managers believe their fellow workers tend to be indifferent or lazy, are motivated only by extrinsic gratification, and would prefer to work as little as possible while still receiving strong rewards. Based on this type of distrust, these managers tend to be authoritarian and manipulative when working with others because coercion would seem to be the only means for obtaining the organizational output needs.

Theory Y managers view organizational members as potentially self-actuated and desiring responsibility. People are not innately lazy or irresponsible. In fact, with the proper opportunities for growth and development, people will produce extremely well. Unnecessary conflicts can be avoided because the only motivation needed for the work force is acceptable treatment with emotions and social development always being considered. The manager determines the conditions likely to help the individual succeed, and then provides them. At no time did McGregor (1960) argue that all workers are responsive and productive. By using the Theory Y approach, with its emphasis on individual respect, managers would be encouraged to accept Argyris' (1957) goals in conflict stance and alleviate it by shifting the issue to enhancing individual growth within the framework of work.

McGregor's (1960) Theory Y is one of the backbones of human resource management. The other major contributor is Likert (1967), who developed a more complex process for determining the characteristics of the two contrasting management styles. In *New Patterns of Management* (Likert, 1961), he certainly agreed with McGregor that there have been two contrasting styles of management.

These trends were characterized by the scientific or production-oriented perspective and the humanistic or employee-oriented perspective. Rather than seeing the two styles as contrasting or inherently in conflict, Likert (1967) argued that an employee-centered management with a clear task orientation will develop the most effective production *team*. This is his System 4 or participative process where group methods are used for decision making and supervision. His *linking pins*, who are managers and supervisors, uphold the principle of supportive relationships as opposed to the traditional "we–they" process between management and employees. Supervisors serve as linking pins from one level in the organization to the next, all the way up and down the hierarchy. Each supervisor and subordinates form a team or family group. At the same time, the supervisor is a member of another team consisting of his or her peers and a superior. Because the supervisors act as linking pins between these levels, the organization continually builds a sense of personal worth for the employee because the potential for communication at all levels is maximized.

System 4 would demonstrate complete trust in subordinates. Based on this trust, decisions would be decentralized and all employees would exert considerable self-control over their activities. Supervisors and their teams would be expected to set high performance goals. Communication is between groups and individuals rather than top to bottom. Likert's (1967) principle of supportive relationships concluded:

> The leadership and other processes of the organization must be such as to ensure a maximum probability that in all interactions and all relationships with the organization each member will, in light of his background, values, desires, and expectations, view the experience as supportive and one which builds and maintains his sense of personal worth and importance. (p. 103)

Likert (1967) also characterized three other systems, with System 1 being exploitative-authoritative (scientific), conforming to McGregor's (1960) Theory X, System 2 being benevolent-authoritative run by a paternalistic despot, and System 3 being consultative at the lower levels with decision-making authority remaining concentrated at the upper levels. In studies of the four systems, which are outlined in Table 3.1, Likert found the use of System 4 was most likely to lead to greater productivity. System 1, as the scientific management approach, tended to be the least effective.

McGregor (1960) and Likert (1967) offered an excellent transition from the human relations to the human resources approach. The underlying premise for the human resources model is the *impact of participation* by members of the organization in decision making. Although the human relations approach pays careful attention to individual needs and tries to make conditions in the work environment as positive as possible, the human resources model actively seeks greater input from members of the organization in decisions.

In an analysis of these two approaches, Miles (1965) found middle managers expecting more willingness on the part of "their superiors to recognize and make full use of [the middle managers'] own currently wasted talents" (p. 148). In so doing, the superiors would be imlementing a human resources model where it is the manager's "obligation to encourage ideas and suggestions from his subordinates" (p. 152). At the same time, these middle managers tended to use human relations toward their own subordinates "by showing interest in the employees' personal success and welfare" (p. 152). Participation, from the human relations viewpoint, is designed to make individuals "*feel* a useful and important part of the overall effort" (p. 149).

This is a useful distinction. Although human relations overcame the depersonalized approach of scientific management, it did not necessarily provide for individual fulfillment at work. As McGregor (1960) and Likert (1967) indicated, people have

TABLE 3.1
LIKERT'S SYSTEM IV
Explanation of the Four Systems

---

SYSTEM 1 – EXPLOITATIVE-AUTHORITATIVE
1. Top-to-bottom chain of command – one-way communication.
2. Employees not trusted by management.
3. Fear is the major motivator for employees.
4. Mistrust permeates communication atmosphere.
5. At lower levels of the organization, an informal organization develops with different goals from
   leadership.

SYSTEM 2 – BENEVOLENT-AUTHORITATIVE
1. Majority of decisions made at the top.
2. Some decisions made at lower levels.
3. Motivation based on rewards and punishment.
4. Management gives off signals of trusting employees.
5. An informal organization develops that might work with the overall goals of the organization.

SYSTEM 3 – CONSULTATIVE
1. Lower level management actually implements policies set by upper management.
2. Two-way communication between different levels of the organization.
3. A strong, informal organization operates that may resist or support the organization.
4. Workers have considerably more control and responsibility.
5. Management exhibits some significant trust in employees.

SYSTEM 4 – PARTICIPATIVE
1. A team effort is used for decisions.
2. Trust exists throughout the organization.
3. Extensive communication at all levels and between all levels.
4. Formal and informal structures have common goals and might be the same.
5. Motivation arises from participation by employees.

---

great potential for adding to the success of an organization and using people as
resources will enhance motivation and productivity.

## No One Best Way

The scientific and humanistic schools shared one characteristic invaluable for anyone studying organizations. Both theories were universal, straightforward, and took
a definite stand regarding which variables should be emphasized. Classical theorists
wanted central control and management by a few whereas humanistic theorists wanted
individual needs emphasized. In many ways, McGregor (1960) and Likert (1967)
seemed to be pointing to one best way – Theory Y or System 4.

As a final development of the human resources approach, an additional approach
has been offered, which assumes that the best organizational structure and management style should vary from situation to situation. Four important examples of *contingency theory* are provided by Burns and Stalker (1961), Lawrence and Lorsch

(1967a, 1967b) Chandler (1962), and Woodward (1965). We examine *contingency leadership* after establishing the basic concepts behind contingency thinking.

Contingency theory does not deny many of the premises of all approaches offered in this chapter. It merely tells us that all the variables must be considered before making a decision, designing an organization, and so on. This *situational approach* to management suggests that the tasks required and the environment surrounding the organization are critical variables.

Burns and Stalker (1961), in their study of several industrial firms in England, concluded that the structure of the organization should be determined by the task to be accomplished (pp. 80–83). So, a *mechanistic* approach, basically a classical structure, was appropriate when the task was routine and unchanging because of a stable environment. All of the attributes of efficiency through procedural control did work well in those types of organizations where the jobs remained the same. In mechanistic organizations, managers rely on a command style "in which managers' instructions and decision govern work operations. Communication tends to be one-way, or top-down, since managerial instructions dictate what subordinates do" (Courtright, Fairhurst, & Rogers, 1989, p. 774).

Many modern organizations must respond to changes in the environment. For this type of organization, an *organic* approach, or a human resources model, is the most appropriate. The organic approach responds to a rapidly changing environment and tends to decrease rules and regulations in favor of innovation and development. Individuals become increasingly important to the organization rather than a dependence on the chain of command. Burns and Stalker (1961) provided us with important information regarding the need to vary the structure as well as the treatment of individuals in order to respond to the environment. They also reaffirmed the potential usefulness of some of the tenets of scientific management for organizations operating in a stable environment. The organic type of organization emphasizes communication, group decision making, self-control, and motivation. Team self-management, an issue we discuss at length in our chapter on small groups, is an example of an organic approach being embraced by many U.S. companies (Courtright et al., 1989, p. 775).

Lawrence and Lorsch (1967b) expanded this concept of structural diversity by demonstrating the diversity within an organization of departmental structure depending on the functions or tasks. They examined three types of departmental structures within various organizations: marketing, economic-technical, and scientific. Their hypothesis was that certainty is related to the structure of the subsystem (Lawrence & Lorsch, 1967a). According to Lawrence and Lorsch, and Burns and Stalker (1961), the more predictable the environment, the greater the likelihood that there would be a scientific approach to structure.

There are three key concepts to Lawrence and Lorsch's (1967a, 1967b) theory. When the subsystems (e.g., departments, units, sections) are *differentiated*, each having its own tasks and environment, the structures will vary appropriately. Differentiation is a more sophisticated term for division of labor. The process that ties these differentiated subsystems together is *integration* or coordination. Finally, the rate of change in technological development and product demand, and the amount of turnover in employees, create the *environmental uncertainty* surrounding the organization. These three factors interact to determine the best structure of the organization. Obviously, this theory can become quite complex in application, but it clearly underscores the concept, along with Burns and Stalker (1961), that there is no one best way to organize.

Chandler (1962) pulled these two studies together with his basic thesis that "structure follows strategy." He examined the histories of almost 100 of America's largest industrial organizations. He concluded that there is a strong relationship between the establishment of an organization's *strategy*, such as greater sales or increased productivity; the organization's environment, such as larger sales force or more automation; and *structure*, or what type of organizational system best supports the desired goals. This is the exact opposite of classical theory or one best way of organizing.

Woodward (1965) conducted an extensive investigation of over 100 firms trying to determine which type of structure operated in particular settings. She hoped to link the type of management used with the success of the organization. Although she found no universal link between management type and success, she did discover that a company's production technology also affects how the company should be organized. The managerial practices were important, of course, but the particular technology, or how the product was made, was a more important variable in the type of organization needed for success. Woodward did not provide a clear explanation for the apparent lack of relationship between structure and success. However, she did demonstrate that there is no one best way for a given type of production process to be managed. A more recent study did find a possible explanation in the degree of employee professionalism as the most important variable (Blau, Fable, McHinley, & Tracy, 1976). The more employees are required to deal with unforeseen problems, the more likely they are to operate well in an organic, as opposed to mechanistic, environment. If the work is routine, then a mechanistic structure works well.

Contingency theories offer the important conclusion that different organizational structures should be used for different tasks. There are no simple, surefire answers for how to run an organization. Because each set of circumstances has different contingencies, the methods of communication, decision-making processes, types of structure, and styles of leadership must be situational. The complexity of contingency theories has kept them from being as popular as some other methods of organizing and managing. However, their very complexity tends to bring them closer to organizational realities.

## Situational Leadership

One important area of research for applying contingency theory has been in relationship to the particular style of leadership that would be the most successful for a manager. A useful example to investigate for understanding how contingency theories have been developed was provided by Fiedler (1967). His approach is instructive for it sets the tone for many of the later developments (Fiedler, Chemers, & Mahar, 1978).

Fiedler (1967) hypothesized that the relationship between managerial style and a variety of organizational outcomes was mediated by an elaborate array of contingencies. In theory, the manager can articulate the relevant contingency in a given situation and therefore can determine the effects of a particular leadership behavior on the situation's outcome. His emphasis is on the work group, and Fiedler predicted that the group's effectiveness will be dependent on the leader's ability to match her or his style with the contingencies of the situation.

Fielder (1967) saw two styles of leadership. One style provides the leaders with satisfaction from performing the task. This style, he argued, is more effective in group situations that are either very favorable or very unfavorable to the leader. The leader will be more effective with a relationship-oriented style when there is an intermediate degree of favorableness, which Fiedler defined as "the degree to which the situation enables the leader to exert control over his group" (p. 13).

Fiedler's (1967) contingency theory stresses the difference between leadership behavior and leadership style. Behaviors are the acts the leader performs while directing and coordinating the activities of group members. Fiedler postulated that "the effectiveness of a group is contingent upon the relationship between leadership style and the degree to which the group situation enables the leader to exert influence" (p. 15). The premise underlying this approach is important. Leaders must realize the impact of their particular style on group success. Although there have been conflicting research results regarding his model, the situational nature of leadership has become an important tenet for additional research and management training (Kotter, 1990).

House, for example, saw the leader's basic role as one that complements the subordinate's work setting (House & Mitchell, 1974). The Vroom–Yetton model requires the leader to choose a style on a continuum from autocratic to democratic depending on the problem and its contingencies (Vroom & Yetton, 1973). The most important application of these three theories has been in training managers to make more realistic decisions regarding the leadership style they choose. Put in terms we are already familiar with, there is no one best way for a manager to manage or lead. There have been numerous extensions of contingency thinking (Schermerhorn, Hunt, & Osborn, 1982), which are discussed in our chapter on leadership.

Contingency thinking has been translated pragmatically into two approaches. The first, as we already have mentioned, observes that there is no single management style that is right for all organizations at all times. In fact, there are always a variety of possible approaches whose rightness is contingent on a particular situation. The second concludes that the results and performances wanted can be obtained with a careful linking of stimulus and response to behavior and reward, in a chain of contingencies. Because individuals, organizations, and the multiple subsystems are constantly changing in response to the environment, each situation requires specific analysis. Tosi and Hammer (1982), in *Organizational Behavior and Management: A Contingency Approach*, provided a large number of possible tools and techniques to be used in the workplace.

For many individuals in managerial positions, accepting uncertainty as a perspective is very uncomfortable. Ideally, most persons in charge want some specific means for improving managerial performance even if they accept the general premise of the contingency approach. One of the attractions, after all, of the scientific approach is the certain prescriptions given to the leader. One of the better answers to this issue is provided by Dyer (1982) in *Contemporary Issues in Management and Organization Development* with his core-contingency model of management. Briefly, this model states that although every organization needs its own style, based on its particular contingency factors, there are also certain core behaviors that are consistently related to high productivity and morale. These include, he suggested, personal concern, allowing employees to have influence over their work life, keeping them informed, fairness, and appropriate job structure. These core behaviors are combined by the successful manager with applications to their own organizational structures.

Human resources management combines the strengths of both the scientific and humanistic approach to management. It accomplishes this by recognizing the need for structured approaches to the development of individuals and groups within an organization. Using the premise that there are no simple, easy answers, various contingency approaches have developed that call for an awareness of the situation and the environment before making any decisions. Human resources management sees individuals as untapped resources that can be developed with the proper atmosphere. The conditions, or contingencies, surrounding an individual will determine how well that person will develop. The same issue demands attention for the organization as a whole and significant core contingency approaches have been developed for both managers and organizations.

## ORGANIZATIONAL CULTURES

At this point, you should have a basic understanding of how various organizational and managerial theories have developed. In spite of the chronological development of this chapter, you should keep in mind that all three approaches we have outlined still are being used. Because we are most interested in how these theories affect behavior, we now discuss what is one of the most promising approaches to understanding how and why organizations function as they do.

The organizational culture perspective is an extremely useful means for understanding why events actually occur in an organization and for studying of organizational communication. The culturual orientation demonstrates how the behavior in organizations is determined by the processes used by management and employees (Schein, 1990). As you will recall from chapter 1, communication is based on the behaviors that occur between interacting systems.

We first examine the rationale for this view of organizational behavior. Then we discuss the 7-*S* model and Theory Z. Third, two different schemes for explaining behavior in organizational cultures is provided. Fourth, specific applications of this cultural view to small enterprises are examined. Finally, we compare and contrast the means of operating in the excellent company cultures with the traditional operating procedures used in American corporations. Throughout this section, you should notice the reappearance of many of the organizational traits already discussed in this chapter. The difference will be the successful placing of particular behaviors in the context of the overall culture of the organization.

## Revising Managerial Perspectives

Just as success breeds imitation by other organizations, as in the case of the scientific and humanistic methods of management, waning prosperity brings a search for new alternatives. The late 1970s witnessed a relative decline in U.S. productivity and invited comparisons with other, more productive economies. The most predominant example is the Japanese. Ouchi (1981), in *Theory Z: How American Business Can Meet the Japanese Challenge*, summarized the reason for the growing interest in Japanese management techniques: "We know productivity in Japan increased at 400 percent the rate in the United States over the postwar years. More seriously, we know that productivity in the United States is now improving more slowly than in any European nation, including the much-maligned United Kingdom" (pp. 3–4). We discuss Ouchi's Theory Z later in this section where it is compared to traditional American managerial techniques.

The rationale for examining the Japanese model for insights into a new perspective is clearly summarized by Pascale and Anthos (1981) in *The Art of Japanese Management*:

> Our managerial set is being challenged persistently on three fronts. First, we are challenged on the frontier of managerial *practice*, where even bigger doses of what we already do will yield diminishing returns. Sometimes more is needed to get our organizations to run effectively. Second, we are challenged by shifting values within our society which lead people to expect different things from organizations and to seek different meaning from work itself. And, third, the competition is killing us. (p. 25)

However, as correctly as this statement summarizes the call for new management, and in spite of the willingness of some American management to consider change, Pascale and Anthos also summarized the reason why many organizations have been slow to adopt this particular perspective:

> While technological advances have been tremendous and our formation of capital enormous, Western organizations run themselves in 1981 in much the same way as in 1940. There is still troublesome tension between boss and subordinate, and between the firm

and the public good, broadly defined. There are still negative attitudes toward necessary collective efforts, notably toward meetings and activities outside groups. We still esteem the tough, individualistic, and dominating U.S. leadership that prevailed in the past centuries. (p. 32)

The reliance on a leader-oriented managerial style simply is not working as well as other alternative approaches.

## The 7-S Model

Pascale and Anthos (1981) felt that Western organizations have placed a great deal of faith and effort into the *three hard S's: strategy, structure, and systems*. These lead to a fixation on individual glory and the joys of winning through intimidation. The example they use of the prototypical corporate leader is former International Telephone and Telegraph chairman, Genee, who ran a management-by-inquisition operation and once said that he would do everything himself, "if I had enough arms and legs and time."

In contrast, the *four soft S's: staff, skills, style, and superordinate goals* have received a relative lack of emphasis. These four skills, however, provide the backbone of the successful Japanese corporation. As we point out later in this chapter, adopting an entirely new managerial perspective is normally impossible because of the organizational structure. In the case of American organizations, management has tended to set the culture based on the three hard *S*'s (Waterman, Peters, & Phillips, 1980).

The title of Pascale and Anthos' (1981) book, *The Art of Japanese Management*, nicely highlights the issues they discussed throughout their analysis. For a moment, consider the use of the word *art* at one end and the word *management* at the other. With little doubt, one of the greatest difficulties Western management seems to have in adopting new tools such as soft management is that they do not consider management an art. They perceive management as a quantifiable science and art as a leisure activity. Hence, the number of organizations who have been able to incorporate the 7-*S* model in the United States is not great. Pascale and Anthos acknowledged that Westerners often find the concept "at best, remote, at worst, elusive" (p. 35), and that few American business leaders will mimic the Japanese style.

## Theory Z

However, the desire for more successful and productive organizations remains, and to satisfy this interest, many organizations and managers have turned to Ouchi's (1981) *Theory Z*. Table 3.2 contrasts the basic differences between the traditional American organization and Theory Z. You should examine the contrasts carefully for they

TABLE 3.2
Contrast Between Traditional and Theory Z Management and Cultural Manifestations

| *Traditional* | *Theory Z* |
|---|---|
| 1. Impersonal | 1. Personal |
| 2. Direct from authority | 2. Work with personnel |
| 3. Suspicion of workers | 3. Trust of workers |
| 4. Individual oriented | 4. Group oriented |
| 5. Mobility from job to job; employer to employer | 5. Long-term employment |
| 6. Inflexibility in structure & response | 6. Flexibility in structure & response |
| 7. Rapid evaluation of job performance | 7. Slow evaluation of job performance |
| 8. Specialized career for individuals | 8. Nonspecialized career for individuals |
| 9. Individual decision making | 9. Collective decision making |
| 10. Segmented concern | 10. Collective concern |
| 11. Internally competitive | 11. Internally noncompetitive |
| 12. Formal relationships | 12. Informal relationships |
| 13. Resistant to change; slow to alter methods & procedures | 13. Adaptive |

highlight the traditional approaches taken by American management and compare them to the developments needed in order to use Theory Z.

Most Western firms, Ouchi (1981) argued, are characterized by mutual distrust between employees and management, formal relationships, decision making only at the executive level, specialized training and narrow career paths, quick employee evaluation, and short-term employment. The Theory Z style is characterized by mutual trust between employees and management, informal relationships, employee involvement in decision making, nonspecialized careers, slow evaluation process for employees, long-term employment, and flexibility and adaptation.

This ability to distinguish between the hard and soft *S*'s and to implement a strategy that successfully uses both had been used in a variety of organizations. For example, York Russell developed a new management style starting in 1979 in response to the merger of a previously successful Canadian steel company, Hugh Russell, Inc., with a failing steel fabricator, York Steel Construction, Ltd. (Hurst, 1984). Prior to the merger, Hugh Russell used the approach of the structure-follows-strategy school where all elements are clearly defined and relationships are clearly measurable. In order to meet the new challenge created by this change, the managerial team developed a new approach. As they observed:

> The hard rational model isn't wrong; it just isn't enough. There is something more. As it turns out, there is a great deal more. At York Russell we have had to develop a "soft", intuitive framework that offers a counterpart to every element in the hard rational framework. . . . [I]n the soft model, roles are the counterparts of tasks, groups replace structure, networks operate instead of information systems, the rewards are soft as opposed to hard, and people are viewed as social animals rather than rational beings. (Hurst, 1984, p. 79)

In other organizations, this change toward a Theory Z type of organization is seen with increases in activities, such as *quality circles*, which are now used in a wide range of organizations. The quality circle is "a relatively autonomous unit composed of a small group of workers (ideally about ten) usually led by a foreman or senior worker and organized in each work unit" (Cole, 1980, p. 24). The unit works with most of the attributes of Theory Z within the organization itself. Numerous American firms have now adopted some version of the quality circles concept. These firms represent a broad spectrum ranging from American Airlines and Hughes Aircraft to General Motors and Honeywell Corporation. With the emphasis on worker participation in the decision-making process, the quality circle concept is a major shift from the traditional organizational structure. When we discuss small group behavior and processes later in this book, we return to the concept of quality circles. They serve to indicate the willingness of American organizations to attempt to adapt in order to experience potential increases in quality and productivity.

Ouchi (1981) did not suggest a full adaptation of Japanese management style for U.S. companies. In fact, there are excellent reasons why the Japanese means of operating organizations cannot, and perhaps should not, be applied to American companies (Briggs, 1982; Whitsell & Yorks, 1983). Theory Z offers the potential for expanding managerial perspectives in order to increase adaptations and change.

Improvements such as hands-on management already are used in many organizations and have been very successful (Peters & Austin, 1985, p. 33). Effective managers, Ouchi (1981) felt, spend less time behind their desks and more time with subordinates and colleagues. This leads in turn to increased communication between supervisor and staff, better understanding by managers of employees and their job requirements, a fuller appreciation for work-related problems, and improved relations between supervisor and employees. This movement toward a concept "we are in this together" is having a substantial impact on American organizations, as we see later in this chapter.

Specific tools for using the Theory Z approach stand out as being important in making organizations work. When surveyed regarding which courses should be taken for anyone planning careers in general management, "just over 96 percent of Asian executives . . . ranked business communication first" ("Asian Executives," 1983). Communication, as outlined in discussing the various processes involved in a Theory Z approach, constantly is referred to by Japanese executives as a critical variable. In an article entitled "Communication Spurred Japanese Growth," Tamotsu Marabe (1983), secretary general of the Japanese Federation of Employers Associations, concluded: "Organizational communication will become even more important. . . . The role of communication is in solving problems related to labor-management relations and other human relations inside an organization, and preventing conflicts with the public at large" (p. 5). Because the Soft *S*'s and Theory Z require effective interpersonal, small-group, and organizational behavior, productive communication remains a vital link.

## Defining Organizational Cultures

An extremely important tool for examining organizations is an understanding of the impact of organizational cultures. The culture is an organization's shared beliefs and values—its distinct identity (Harris, 1990). Culture often is referred to as the "social glue holding the company together" (Baker, 1980, p. 8).

Deal and Kennedy (1982), in *Corporate Cultures: The Rites and Rituals of Corporate Life*, correctly declared: "Every business—in fact, every organization—has a culture" (p. 4). As groups and organizations learn to survive, adapt, and solve problems over a period of time, a culture emerges (Schein, 1990, p. 111). The factors that constitute the culture include "the various rituals which members regularly or occasionally perform" (Pacanowsky & O'Donnell-Trujillo, 1983, p. 136). Deal and Kennedy continued:

> Culture, as Webster's New Collegiate Dictionary defines it, is "the integrated pattern of human behavior that includes thought, speech, action, and artifacts and depends on man's capacity for learning and transmitting knowledge to succeeding generations." Marvin Bower, for years managing director of McKinsey & Company and author of *The Will to Manage*, offered a more informal definition—he described the informal cultural elements of a business as "the way we do things around here." (p. 4)

## Perspectives on Studying Cultures

In recent years, organizational cultures have gained a great deal of attention both within the business community and by scholars (Smircich & Calas, 1987). What appears to be a simple enough definition, "the way we do things around here," can be clarified by highlighting two different orientations toward the study of organizational cultures (Smircich, 1983). The *functionalist* perspective is concerned with what an organization has that constitutes the culture. The current artifacts in the organization that can be observed and possibly altered, reinforced, eliminated, or added to are the focus of concern. The information produced by functionalistic research is used to create and sustain a system of beliefs for knowing and managing organizational experience. For many organizational leaders, these are the factors that must be worked with to enhance the ultimate success of the organization (Baker, 1980). The *interpretionist* perspective focuses on the interactions that lead to a *shared meaning*. This perspective is more interested in understanding the process by which the culture is created and maintained (Bormann, 1983). The functionalist perspective is oriented toward making the cultural aspects of the organization as effective as possible in helping the organization obtain its goals, whereas the interpretionist perspective is interested in explaining the various processes that lead to shared meanings.

This division of the organizational culture concept is useful, and both views reaffirm our need to attend to the behavioral aspects of organizational life. In fact, organizational events include situations "where individuals assign symbolic meanings [through] stories, myths, rituals, ceremonies, and nonverbal objects of the organizational cultural inventory" (Putnam, 1982, p. 199). Once individuals assign the meaning, they are more likely to act as if it is reality. Clearly a manager with a functionalist view would be wise to consider how he or she can have an impact on this shared reality.

For you to be fully competent in understanding organizational cultures, you will need to be aware of the artifacts and the shared meanings because both are critical to the organization. Put another way, you will need to be an active learner of the expected behaviors so you eventually can use the culture, and you also must be excellent at gathering information so you continually can understand the general impact of culturally shared meanings.

Using a different approach, Schein (1985) made the distinction between the *ethnographic* and a *clinical* perspective: "The ethnographer obtains concrete data in order to understand the culture he is interested in, presumably for intellectual and scientific reasons" (p. 13). The ethnographic perspective brings to the situation a set of presumptions that motivated the research in the first place. So, examining the impact of a particular type of culture on member satisfaction, for example, presumes that member satisfaction is important and should be tested. As we learned in chapter 2 on perception, as soon as we focus on a particular orientation, we run the risk of excluding other important information.

On the surface, the clinician is similar to the functionalist and is more interested in the ongoing factors in an organization that must be changed to enhance growth and development. The majority of organizational consultants take this perspective. However, they do not always establish a dichotomy between the functionalist and interpretive views of organizations. Instead, they discuss the level of cultural analysis.

For example, Schein (1985) saw three levels of culture that can be examined (pp. 13–21). Level 1, artifacts and creations, is the most visible level of the organizational culture. These elements constitute the physical and social environment, including the overt behaviors. The central values that provide the day-to-day operating procedures by which the members guide their behaviors are in this category.

Level 2, the values, provides normative or moral functions in guiding the organizational or group members in dealing with certain key situations. These are the "ought to be" concepts as opposed to Level 1's description of what actually is occurring. When these espoused values become congruent with the behavior of the organization, as with IBM and its belief in people, or 3M's "never be responsible for killing an idea," then these values can become part of the philosophy of operating. Slogans and creeds, such as Merrill Lynch's "a breed apart," Delta Airlines' "The Delta family feelings," or General Electric's "progress is our most important product," can become actual operating values. But, these values might not explain fully the functioning of the organization's culture.

Level 3, the assumptions, are essentially the same as Argyris' (1976) theories in use, which are the implicit assumptions that actually guide behavior, and that tell group members how to perceive, think about, and feel about things (Argyris

& Schon, 1974). These assumptions tend to be nonconfrontable and nondebatable. As you work to understand an organizational culture, each of these levels will be very useful to you. In looking at organizational cultures, the divisions offered between functionalist and interpretive and ethnographic versus clinician are helpful in focusing our attention.

Perhaps the most important point is that the culture of each organization, and its subunits, is generally distinct, even though certain types of organizations tend to have a large number of similarities due to the environments they operate in and with. However, just as there are cultural variations from the North and South, so do the attributes of various cultures vary from organization to organization and between the subsystems such as the grounds crew and payroll, or planning and service.

## Contexts of Organizational Cultures

The current interest in organizational cultures is explained in Peters and Waterman's (1982) study, *In Search of Excellence*: "Without exception, the dominance and coherence of culture proved to be an essential quality of the excellent companies" (p. 75). Exactly what comprises cultures is important, but the overriding quality of all strong cultures resides in the communication patterns. Kennedy (1983), coauthor of *Corporate Cultures*, was asked what ingredient is needed to build strong corporate cultures and responded as follows:

> The answer, pure and simple, is through effective communication—to employees, customers, shareholders, public officials, and the public at large. Companies and organizations that do the best job thinking through what they are all about, deciding how and to whom these central messages should be communicated and executing the communication plan in a quality way invariably build a strong sense of esprit within their own organization and among the many constituents they serve. (p. 26)

The cultural perspective's value is its ability to explain the behaviors of organizations instead of simply isolating types of leadershp. In a predominant number of cases, leaders come and go, but organizations remain. Excellent leaders help shape the excellent cultures, and many of the shortcomings in some organizational cultures lie in their leadership activities (Kilmann, 1982; Zaleznik, 1989, pp. 11–35), but the organizational cultures will shape the behaviors of specific individuals (Kotter, 1988, pp. 98–102). No matter how well equipped a manager might be with an excellent background in human resources development and contingency leadership, if the culture is not prepared to accept the individual's activities, his or her initiatives will not succeed (Skinner, 1981). So, we need to understand the cultural view of organizations in order to understand how organizations work.

## Categorizing Cultures

There are at least three specific ways to categorize cultures. The first is to divide them into three distinct types which reflect, to some extent, the previous discussion in this chapter of organizational and management theories. These three types are authoritarian, compromise, and performance. Table 3.3 outlines the differences.

The authoritarian culture reflects many of the features of scientific management, especially as they apply to the behavioral characteristics. As we indicated earlier in this chapter, autocratic organizations still exist and flourish, ranging from law firms (Cook, Glaberson, & Moskowitz, 1985) to investment firms (Miller, 1985).

Both the compromise and the performance cultures reflect some of the elements of the human relations model and most aspects of the human resources model. All three cultures are more concerned with the way things occur in an organization than the particular managerial style being used, although organizational and managerial performance are always interdependent.

The compromise culture is the nearest to the human resources model because it considers the group the fundamental strength for any actions. This approach requires a supportive atmosphere with a great deal of cultural backing. Attempts to introduce team-oriented innovations, such as quality circles, which can be a powerful technique for allowing employees to analyze work-related problems and propose solutions, will face serious obstacles unless they are supported by a compromise culture (Marks, 1986, p. 38). In our chapter on small groups, we discuss quality

TABLE 3.3
Types of Organizational Cultures

| | *Behavioral Characteristics* | | |
|---|---|---|---|
| | *1*<br>*Authoritarian/*<br>*Bureaucratic* | *2*<br>*Compromise/*<br>*Supportive* | *3*<br>*Performance/*<br>*Innovative* |
| Basis for Decisions | Direct from Authority | Discussion, Agreement | Directions from Within |
| Forms of Control | Rules, Laws, Rewards, & Punishments | Interpersonal/Group Commitments | Actions Aligned With Self-Concept |
| Sources of Power | Superior | What "We" Think & Feel | What I Think & Feel |
| Desired End | Compliance | Consensus | Self-Actualization |
| To Be Avoided | Deviation from Authoritative Direction | Failure to Reach Consensus | Not Being "True to Oneself" |
| Time Perspective | Future | Near Future | Now |
| Position Relative to Others | Hierarchical | Peer | Individual |
| Human Relationships | Structured | Group Oriented | Individually Oriented |
| Basis for Growth | Following the Established Order | Peer Group | Acting on Awareness of Self |

circles and team development in depth. The compromise culture has many of the attributes of Likert's (1967) System 4 discussed earlier. McGregor's (1960) Theory Y manager would be required for this type of culture to be successful, but the dependence on group control is the prevailing feature of the compromise culture. Clearly, the new managerial perspectives would be most likely to work within this type of culture.

The performance culture is highly dependent on self-motivation and personal growth (Hopkins, 1982). Sales-oriented organizations often strive for developing this type of culture (Deal & Kennedy, 1982, p. 113). Once well established, this type of culture probably would use the human relations approach.

These categorizations of cultures explain how things are done. Simply realizing that managerial style is only a part of the overall culture would be of great help to you in understanding organizations. Any attempt, by a manager or anyone else, to impose an unacceptable behavior pattern into one of these cultures probably will lead to a rejection by the culture itself. This traditional, generic three-part division of organizational cultures provides us with a better understanding regarding how to use leadership, communication, groups, and numerous other activities.

A second means for dividing cultures is to reintroduce the systems perspective discussed in chapter 1. Within the organization, there are five operating subsystems (Kast & Rosenzweig, 1984, p. 7). These include:

1. A goals and values subsystem—people with a purpose.
2. A technical subsystem—people using knowledge, techniques, equipment, and facilities to accomplish goals.
3. A structural subsystem—people whose activities are differentiated and integrated (e.g., tasks, work groups, information, procedures, authority, and work flow).
4. A psychological subsystem—people engaged in social interactions because of their common activities (e.g., human resources, attitudes, perceptions, and leadership).
5. A managerial subsystem—people who coordinate the subsystems by planning and controlling the overall endeavor (e.g., goal setting and organizing).

These five factors encompass the various interacting variables in an organization.

The overriding influence on all of these subsystems is the environmental suprasystem. Kast and Rosenzweig (1984) provided two polar characteristics of organizational cultures—closed/stable/mechanistic and open/adaptive/organic—and tied the impact of these two types of cultures to each of the five subsystems. We discuss the subcategories as we progress through this book. Table 3.4 shows the dramatic differences between the two types of cultures in terms of "how we do things around here."

TABLE 3.4
Descriptions of Organizational Cultures

| | Polar Characteristics | |
|---|---|---|
| *Systems* | *Closed/stable/mechanistic* | *Open/adaptive/organic* |
| Environmental Suprasystem -general nature- | placid, certain, fixed, few participants, well-defined boundaries | turbulent, uncertain, many participants, varied & not well-defined boundaries |
| Goals and Values | single-goal, efficient performance, managerial hierarchy | adapting, problem solving & innovation, extensive participation |
| Technical System | repetitive tasks, homogenous input, fixed output, programmed methods | varied tasks, varied input & output, nonprogrammed methods |
| Structural System | formalized organization, many rules & procedures, concentrated authority | few written rules, informal enforcement, networks |
| Psychosocial System | clearly defined status, based on hierarchy, use of extrinsic rewards, Theory X view, autocratic leadership, concentrated power | status based on expertise, roles change with tasks, intrinsic rewards Theory Y view, collaborative leadership |
| Managerial System | hierarchical, autocratic decision making, fixed planning process, conflicts resolved by superiors | network of control, participative decision making, reciprocal power, group conflict resolution |

*Note.* Adapted from Kast, F. E., & Rosenweig, J. E. (1984).

## Corporate Cultures

The environment in which the organization operates provides the framework for the entire culture. Within this environment, the degree of risk and the relative speed of feedback from the environment tend to determine how the organization operates. Deal and Kennedy (1982) applied these principles to American corporations. Although this focus on major corporations limits the general applicability somewhat, the impact of organizational culture is clearly outlined by the groupings. Table 3.5 summarizes the attributes of the Macho/Tough Guy, Work Hard/Play Hard, Bet Your Company, and Process cultures.

The degree of risk associated with the companies' activities, and the speed with which the companies—and their employees—get feedback on whether decisions or strategies are successful, determine the culture. With these two criteria, the four types can be defined further.

The tough guy/macho culture is characterized by high risks and quick feedback on whether actions were right or wrong. Examples include construction, entertainment, and others identified in Table 3.5. The obvious uncertainty of the entertainment field, with the extremely costly outlays for a movie or television program, and the speed with which the critics, box office, or Neilson ratings define success, provides a good example of this category.

**TABLE 3.5**
Four Types of Corporate Cultures

| | Macho/Tough Guy-Gal | Work Hard/Play Hard | Bet Your Company | Process |
|---|---|---|---|---|
| Business Environment | | | | |
| Degree of Risk | High risk, expensive outlays for risks | Small risks | High risk, research and development | Low risk |
| Feedback on decision's success | Quick | Quick—by volume of sales | Slow—future of the company | Virtually none or reactive & negative |
| Represented by shared values of: | Youth, intense pressure, fast pace, early rewards, "all or nothing" | Fun & action, high level of activity which is everything | Deliberateness, long-term, careful decision making | Technical perfection how things because what cannot be managed |
| Use of rites and rituals Types of behavior expected | Extensive, often superstitious, bonding meetings | Contests, morale boosting conventions, language for sales | Titles & formalities business meetings | Drawn-out meetings, memos & reports that disappear |
| Attitude of employees | Individualistic | Center on customer—fill needs well | Be right & be careful | Conservative & trivial |
| Paradigms of corporate types | Construction Cosmetics Management consulting Venture Capital Movies Publishing Advertising Television Sports Entertainment | Sales Real estate Computer companies Automotive distributors Door-to-door sales Mass consumer companies Retail stores | Capital goods Mining Large-system business Oil companies Architectural firms Investment banks Computer design co's. Actuarial end of insurance companies | Banks Insurance Financial services Utilities Large chunks of government Heavily regulated industries— e.g., pharmaceuticals |

*Note.* From Deal, T.E., & Kennedy, A. A. (1982).

The work hard/play hard culture is typified by sales organizations, where employees take few major or costly risks, with quick feedback on their activities. Employees know of their successes immediately, but lose little with any one failure. For example, in a retail store, the actual success of a particular new style of Levi jeans, or a specific toy, is not that important because the sales-oriented organization is concerned with moving products rather than creating them. The initial decision to produce a product, a research and development issue, is much riskier than simply deciding to offer it for sale.

The bet-your-company culture exists in a high-risk, slow feedback environment. Organizations who fall into this category are large business systems such as investment banks. Where research and development costs are high and the feedback is slow, this type of culture is likely to be operating. Deciding to fund the building of a shopping mall, an investment issue, centers on very different types of decisions than does deciding to offer a product for sale.

The process culture concentrates on how things are done, so it is hard for employees to measure what they do. There is virtually no risk and practically no feedback. If there is feedback, it becomes directed at the procedure, not the product. Examples include insurance companies and utilities. When the focus of the organization is on an extremely long-range planning cycle, organizational members do not feel that they have much to do with the actual operation. Any organization operating with substantial external control or regulation, such as a utility company, tends to become process oriented because there is little of consequence that organizational members can do to alter the organizations' course.

Deal and Kennedy's (1982) analysis is valuable because it indicates the impact of the suprasystem on the specific subsystems in an organization. A careful reading of their analysis also shows how difficult it is to separate the functional and interpretive views of cultures. Although Deal and Kennedy have been labeled functionalist by some observers (Daniels & Spiker, 1987, pp. 108–109), their framework and extensive discussion of cultural variables provide an excellent background for an understanding of the shared, subjective meanings in various cultures. Because these cultures define the philosophy of the system which in turn defines the behavior, understanding each of them can be of great benefit to you.

You might be tempted to combine Tables 3.3, 3.4, and 3.5, and the discussion, in an attempt to predict some of the requirements for a given industry, corporation, or organization. In a sense, this would be a wise strategy for it would make you more likely to understand the culture instead of simply approaching it in an "Alice in Wonderland" fashion. However, Deal and Kennedy (1982) warned us that: "No one company fits perfectly into any of these molds, and different parts of the same organization will exhibit each of the four types of cultures. Still, most companies have overall tendencies toward one of the cultures because they are responding to the needs of their marketplace" (p. 125). They pointed to three specific companies to underscore the point. Procter & Gamble, Pepsi Cola, and Bloomingdale's department store are companies that logically would be work hard/play hard cultures, but that are actually macho/tough guy organizations who actively pursue competition, both within the company and with competitors.

Each company culture also has a cast of characters, which includes storytellers, priests, whisperers, gossipers, secretarial sources, spies, and cabals, a "group of two or more people who secretly join together to plot a common purpose – usually to advance themselves in the organization" (Deal & Kennedy, 1982, p. 94). Inevitably, meetings serve as the symbolic reaffirmation of status with the setting, the table's shape, who sits where, number and composition of attendees, conduct, and number held acting as statements regarding the culture. These examples are used to indicate the importance of observing the behavior of the participants in an organization in order to fully understand why things are done. According to Deal and Kennedy, "It is important for all managers – or employees for that matter – to have a good and precise sense of the culture of their companies. Once you know more exactly the type of culture you're dealing with, you will have a better idea of how to get things done in an effective way" (p. 127). As Table 3.5 indicates, there are a large number of variables that you will want to consider as you examine the various cultures. The impact of cultures also can be seen in smaller organizations. The most obvious example would be in the use of quality circles, or the emphasis on analysis of the work process by all the employees, which reflects a company's culture. However, the basic cultural aspects outlined in Theory Z must be transferred in two important cultural areas – heightened interpersonal skills and analytical techniques.

A corporate culture grid also can be constructed based on the amount of participation and the tendency toward reactive or proactive behaviors (Ernest, 1985). This provides four cultures as shown in Fig. 3.1. The interactive culture is high with individual participation, but slow to react, and McDonald's and Sears fall into this quadrant. Apple Computer is an integrated culture where there is high participation and very proactive behavior. A systematized culture is reactive and uses little individual participation, which used to be the case with Ford Motor Company. An entrepreneurial culture is proactive but not highly participative in its decision making. A company like Merrill Lynch, for example, may be bullish on America, but bearish on seeking out individuals for their input. This grid is intended to be used by management before they try to introduce innovations or change to see if the culture will accept the alterations.

Creating a new culture can be accomplished through practices emphasizing the values of communication and participation. Cillinge (1983), Vice President and General Manager of Owen-Illinois' Closure Division, in reflecting on the successful implementation of a new culture in the Berlin, Ohio plant, reaffirmed two basic elements in any organizational culture: "A positive work culture is not automatically self-sustaining, but requires constant attention and updating" through various participatory and MBWA procedures based on communciation, and "a positive work culture is not a specific set of rules and procedures, but an environment from which innovative management can evolve" (p. 2). For example, the workers chose to eliminate time clocks, special status for managers, and rigid hours.

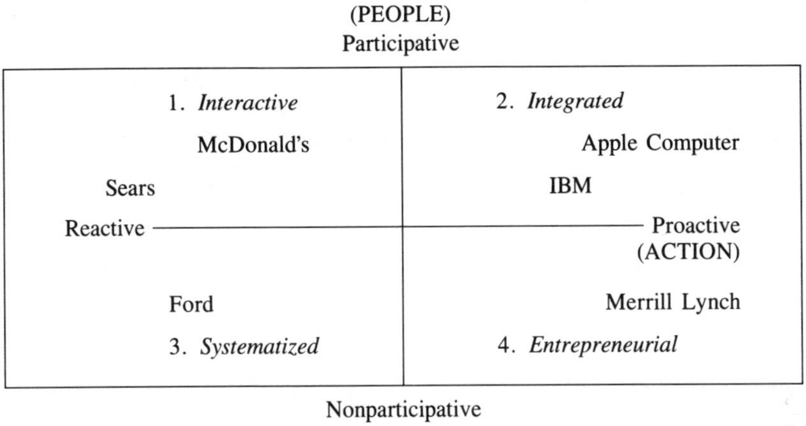

(PEOPLE)
Participative

| 1. *Interactive* | 2. *Integrated* |
|---|---|
| McDonald's | Apple Computer |
| Sears | IBM |

Reactive ———————————————————— Proactive
(ACTION)

| Ford | Merrill Lynch |
|---|---|
| 3. *Systematized* | 4. *Entrepreneurial* |

Nonparticipative

FIG. 3.1.   Corporate Culture Grid (from Ernest, 1985). Copyright © 1985 by *Personnel Administrator*. Adapted by permission.

Understanding the cultures of all types of organization is important. Although larger organizations often are cited as examples of effective and ineffective cultures, 99% of the companies in the United States qualify as small businesses. The big corporations have great impact because they generate about half of all revenues, but there is a greater likelihood that you will be employed by one of the 14 million smaller businesses (Austin, 1986; Peters, 1987, pp. 23–29; "Tomorrow's Jobs," 1986).

In addition, since the recession in 1980, most of the new jobs have been created by fast-growing small and medium-size companies. For example, in 1983, the 100 most rapidly expanding U.S. firms employed an average of 506 workers each. For these firms, this represented a rise of 835% since 1979. By contrast, Fortune 500 companies have lost 2.2 million jobs, or 10% of their workers, in the same time period (Bureau of Labor Statistics, 1984). This trend has been increased by mergers and acquisitions, failures and downsizing, the expanding service sector, and the international challenge confronting American organizations (Offermann & Gowing, 1990, pp. 98–99).

Changing an organization's culture is difficult precisely because it is the underlying factor in the functioning of an organization. Throughout this textbook we indicate how the cultural variables influence leadership, teams, decisions, and every other part of the organization. The culture is not the only factor; it simply is the prevailing one. Some authors have questioned the ability to alter cultures (Uttal, 1983), but there are a substantial number of examples of successful cultural shifts that act to deny this perception ("Changing a Corporate Culture," 1984; Feuer, 1985; Solberg, 1985; Ulrich, Clack, & Dillon, 1985; "A Winning Trio," 1985).

A second, and equally important lesson, is that strategic planning is not likely to be a tool that you will be using in most organizations (Bradford & Cohen, 1984; Hayes & Abernathy, 1980; Kiechel, 1982). Conceived as a means for developing corporate portfolios, financial controls, management by the numbers, and adherence to particular guidelines, the concept has been replaced by a stronger orientation to getting the work done by management involvement. Effective planning is a vital tool (Smircich, 1983; Tregoe & Zimmerman, 1980). Strategic planning, as a means for some grand design, simply will not have immediate application for the vast majority of individuals entering the job market. A balance between understanding how an organization functions in order to enhance its culture, and what must be done based on a competitive analysis in order to choose a strategic position, is required for organizations to be effective (Mintzberg, 1991). As in the case of the overuse of scientific management, or human relations, the overuse of strategic planning fails to account for the impact of the organization's culture.

## Excellent Companies

Excellent companies should have the best attributes and characteristics we have been moving toward with this discussion of cultures. In fact, the best companies do reflect the concepts of an excellent culture. In a study which was to become a huge bestseller, Peters and Waterman (1982) selected 62 companies that had been top performers for the last 20 years, of which they actually analyzed 43, to decide what managerial techniques were being successfully employed. *In Search of Excellence* describes those characteristics that distinguish the excellent performers.

The companies and industries surveyed by Peters and Waterman (1982) represent a broad range of organizations including high-technology companies such as Digital Equipment, consumer goods companies such as Procter & Gamble, general industrial goods companies such as Minnesota Mining and Manufacturing (3M), service companies such as Delta Airlines, project management companies such as Bechtel, and resource-based companies such as Atlantic-Richfield (ARCO). The book identifies and discusses the qualities shared by these diverse organizations. In picking their sample of 43 companies, they chose ones who had excellent financial performance to support their "halo of esteem" in the business world. The organizations covered were measured by six long-term measures of superiority, which included growth and wealth creation over a 20-year period. They excluded banks because they traditionally have been too heavily regulated, preventing Peters and Waterman from applying their 20-year standard. Overall, their "major concern was and is how big companies stay alive, well, and innovative" (p. 4).

On eight different characteristics, there are fundamental distinctions between traditional procedures and the excellent companies. A careful analysis of Table 3.6 shows the difference between the two. In general, organizations have allowed structure to become an end in and of itself and control to be the management technique most likely to be used. The excellent companies contrast sharply.

Throughout their analysis, Peters and Waterman (1982) referred to the intensity of interactions between the various members of the successful companies. Using the term *fluidity,* they saw excellent companies responding well because they shun

TABLE 3.6

Characteristics of the Excellent Companies: Comparison of America's
Best-Run Companies with Traditional Practices

| *Best-Run Companies* | *Traditional View* |
|---|---|
| 1. *A bias for action* — being oriented toward getting things done. | 1. *Paralysis by analysis* — complicate it, debate it, wait. |
| 2. *Staying close to the customer* — catering to the needs of the customer. | 2. *Close to the organization* — use of frills, "statue of liberty plays," specials. |
| 3. *Productivity through people* — making all people feel part of the process. | 3. *Cost control by controlling people* — "forced labor must be made to work." |
| 4. *Autonomy and Entrepreneurship* — breaking the organization into working, independent units. | 4. *Top-down control* — produce well, it's your job. |
| 5. *Hands-on, value driven* — executives must keep in touch (MBWA). | 5. *Driven by remote control* — policy manuals, executives in the background. |
| 6. *Stick to the knitting* — staying with primary business. | 6. *Diversify* — Apples & Oranges = Synergy |
| 7. *Simple form, lean staff* — few administrative levels, small upper level. | 7. *Layering, Matrices* — complex structure, large upper level. |
| 8. *Simultaneous loose–tight properties* — dedication to central values combined with a tolerance for all employees who accept the values. | 8. *Totalitarianism or anarchy* — unbending controls OR unbridled "actualizing." |

*Note.* Adapted from Peters & Waterman (1982). Copyright © 1982 by Harper & Row. Reprinted by permission.

the traditional organizational structure. This "rich, informal communication" is the name of the game for these organizations:

> The nature and uses of communication in the excellent companies are remarkably different from those of their nonexcellent peers. The excellent companies are a vast network of informal, open communications. The patterns and intensity cultivate the right people's getting into contact with each other, regularly, and the chaotic/anarchic properties of the system are kept well under control simply because of the regularity of contact and its nature (e.g., peer versus peer in quasi-competitive situations). (pp. 121–122)

Critical to the success of this communication is the use of the small group. As Peters and Waterman put it, "Small groups are, quite simply, the basic organizational building blocks of excellent companies" (p. 126). Rather than the strict organizational building blocks made of the accepted structure, these small groups are based on flexibility and often take the form of task forces that have single purposes, and when finished, are disbanded. Rather than formal reports, actions are taken to resolve whatever difficulties were the reason for the group being formed in the first place. Coupled with this overall belief in small groups is the previously discussed policy of MBWA. In the excellent companies, all of the management team believes in being involved with the activities of the members of the organization. Peters and Waterman concluded: "The free-wheeling environments in which ad hoc behavior flourishes are only superficially unstructured and chaotic. Underlying the absence of formality lie shared purposes, as well as an internal tension and a competitiveness that make these cultures tough as nails" (p. 134).

*In Search of Excellence* provides an important set of information for individuals interested in organizational communication. Perhaps as instructive has been the mixed fate of the excellent companies since Peters and Waterman (1982) did their analysis. Fourteen of the companies changed their means of operating, varied on at least one of the eight operating principles, and ran into difficulties within two years of the book's publication ("Who's Excellent," 1984). The eight interacting principles indicate the interdependence of a large number of behaviors in the making of an organizational culture. By 1990 only fourteen of the original companies still carried the excellence label (Pascale, 1990). The others had stopped using one of the eight principles or failed to respond to a changing environment.

Taken together, the books and authors discussed in this section on culture combine to emphasize the importance of people over strategy in an organization. From a variety of perspectives ranging from Theory Z and 7-*S* to cultures and *In Search of Excellence,* the key to making an organization work effectively is summarized by Ouchi (1981): "Involved workers are the key to productivity" (p. 4). The concepts of trust, shared values, closeness to customers, and hands-on use of technology permeate all these new approaches to management.

## Organizational Climate

An important concept for describing the behaviors that determine the type of culture is organizational climate. Climates tend to be nurturing or stultifying in their willingness to support the types of cultures described in the best companies discussed by Peters and Waterman (1982). In their examination of *The 100 Best Companies to Work for in America,* Levering, Moskowitz, and Katz (1985) outlined numerous efforts taken by these companies to help employees identify and feel good about the organization. As they put it, "People are proud to work for companies that treat them well. They become linked to these companies in more than an employer/employee relationship. It is the presence of this feeling more than any other, perhaps, that sets these 100 companies apart from the great mass of companies in America" (p. xii). In their study, they did not include all of the companies discussed by Peters and Waterman. They did point to the fact that "small companies are better than big companies—as places to work" (p. xiii).

Organizational climate is a reflection of how employees feel they are being treated by the organization—the employees' perception (Campbell, Dunnette, Lawler, & Weick, 1970; Poole & McPhee, 1983). Because perception often determines reality in an organization, as we discussed in chapter 2, feelings by employees of supervisory and managerial fairness or friendliness, for example, become critical to the effective operation of the organization and function as affirmations of the existing culture.

Numerous studies have been done in an attempt to measure climates. The categories have ranged from structure, responsibility, rewards, warmth, and risk (Litwin & Stringer, 1968; Muchinsky, 1976; Sims & LaFollette, 1975) to attempts to determine which climate best matches which type of organizational goal (Drexler, 1977). Jones and James (1979) analyzing 35 factors that seemed to be important to climates and reduced these to five basic dimensions, including professional and organizational esprit, perceived work-group cooperation, friendliness and warmth, perceived leader facilitation and support, perceived job challenge, importance, and variety, and perceived conflict and ambiguity.

You probably have noticed some analogies between the groupings for climates and the concept of organizational cultures. In fact, cultures are the overriding influence on how the climate is set up, supported, and developed. Organizations with a bureaucratic orientation will make employees feel confined and closed in (Frederiksen, 1966), but more often the leader's behavior is the most important variable for determining the climate (Kouzes & Posner, 1990, pp. 189–216; Litwin & Stringer, 1968). Redding (1972) listed five elements that should be fostered in the organization's climate to facilitate effective communication: participative decision making, high performance goals, trust/credibility, openness, and supportiveness (pp. 139–142). These couple well with the 7-S framework and the concept of MBWA to indicate the necessity to work on positive communication behaviors.

Although we do not limit our view of organizational communication to these five factors, they are of great importance in bridging the theory of MBWA, for example, and the actual practices of openness, trust, and supportiveness (Amsbary & Staples, 1991). Allowing culture to be the overriding construct then allows us to utilize correctly the various factors that mold the organizational climate.

Organizational climate is an important term because many of the approaches to improving communication behavior in an organization are based on improving the climate. If the culture will support the behaviors, then working to maintain and improve the climate is an important task for all individuals in the organization. For the leader, it is the most important communication task for developing the company.

If you review the comparison charts presented earlier in the discussions of Theory Z and *In Search of Excellence,* you will see many of the supportive and positive behaviors of an excellent climate being emphasized over the traditional approaches to management. The soft S's are highly dependent on successful uses of leadership behavior that foster an excellent climate.

Each of the factors that are important for an effective climate is discussed later in this book. At this point you need to understand the impact of employees' perceptions of the behaviors manifested by the organization, its leaders, and its members because climate reinforces the reaction individuals have to their environment. Without a positive climate, there is little likelihood for an organization to effectively move toward excellence.

## INTERPRETATIONS OF ORGANIZATIONAL PROCESSES

At this point, you probably have found some of the theories and approaches closer to what you actually believe than others. We all organize our experiences, as we examined in chapter 2, and make sense of the information that is being provided to us. In other words, we all have a selective, and subjective, reality based on our own interpretation of how organizations work. Based on these perceptions, we then implement or act out what we think are the best approaches for obtaining the goals we perceive as being important. If we are not careful, we act as if our perception of organizational reality is the correct one.

One useful means for examining how these different interpretations operate in an organization is to consider these perspectives under four different frames of reference (Bolman & Deal, 1991). When it comes to perception, a frame is a window on the world through which we see, and fail to see, things. These frames help us to make order in our world and decide what action to take. As Bolman and Deal (1984) explained, "Every manager uses a personal frame, or image, of organizations to gather information, make judgments, and get things done" (p. 25). But, just as theories can explain ongoing events, they also can exclude important insights into how and why things actually are occurring.

Bolman and Deal (1984, 1991) provided an excellent division of the four primary approaches individuals take when they analyze their organizations. As with the discussion on specific cultures, you will want to remember that there are very few "pure" perspectives. Most individuals combine parts of several managerial perspectives. But, it is useful to try and divide the multiple perspectives on organizational behavior into some manageable structure. Although their division might appear somewhat arbitrary—remember, most people have some of each perspective—organizations tend to be managed based primarily on one of these four views. Or, at least, the people in the organization follow these perspectives or beliefs.

The four frames are structural, human resources, political, and symbolic. Each of these has its own vision of reality. Although many successful individuals intuitively have merged parts of each of these frames, they still hold significant, and quite different, views regarding the maintenance and development of an organization.

The *structural frame* is concerned with the goals, rules, and technology of the organization. So, this frame concentrates on the goal direction, structural clarity, and task accomplishment in an organization. It assumes that organizations exist to accomplish established goals, that a structure can be developed that is appropriate to these goals, the environment, technology, and the participants. From this perspective:

1. A rational approach is the best.
2. Specialization leads to better individual expertise and performance.

3. Coordination and control are accomplished best through the exercise of authority and impersonal rules.
4. Structures can be systematically designed and implemented.

The underlying belief is that organizational problems usually reflect inappropriate structure and can be resolved through redesign and reorganization. How to structure itself is one of the central issues facing any organization and this frame concentrates on it. You may recognize the influence of Taylor (1911) and scientific management with his interest in breaking tasks into minute detail and retraining workers to get the greatest output. The work by Fayol (1949) falls into this frame because of his interest in a set of principles for managers regarding specialization, span of control, authority, and delegation of responsibility.

Weber (1947) also fits in this frame and, after World War II, his model of bureaucracy was extended by other researchers with an examination of the impact of structure on morale, productivity, and effectiveness (Blau & Scott, 1962; Perrow, 1970).

In summary, this organizational framework has two axes: (a) differentiation (allocation of tasks and responsibilities across individuals and unites), which creates a structure of roles, each with specified responsibilities and expectations; and (b) linkages (relationships between roles that create interdependence). Roles and interdependencies are coordinated vertically by authority and rules, and laterally through meetings, task forces, teams, and coordinates.

The structural frame helps create the more stable and formal aspects of human behavior in organizations. Activities and relationships are influenced by goals, roles, rules, and procedures. Any attempt to make people work well together requires some type of coordination. But, much of organizational life falls outside the jurisdiction of organization charts, policy, and formal authority.

This gives credence to the *human resources frame* used by many individuals as they try to understand how organizations work. As we discussed earlier in this chapter, the human resources frame focuses on individual needs, feelings and prejudices with a strong underlying belief in the potential for development of each person. It looks for an effective response to human needs in order to effectively use human resources. The human resources perspective believes there exists a strong interdependence between the individual and the organization and that the search for collective purposes should be behind attempts to manage organizations. Whereas the structural frame is concerned with the way structure develops in response to an organization's task and environment, the human resource perspective adds the issue of the interplay between organization and people. From this perspective, people are the most critical resource in an organization and through their ideas, energy, skills, insights, and commitment the organization can be made or broken. Organizations can make a choice between being dehumanizing, alienating, and frustrating or energizing, exciting, and productive. The fit between the individual and the organization is of critical importance.

This frame focuses on the human needs, an issue we deal with extensively in our chapter on motivation, and draws on Maslow's (1970) hierarchy of needs, which range from the physiological to the final level of self-actualization. We discussed McGregor's (1960) input regarding managerial behavior and Argyris' (1957) analysis of goal in conflict. Likert's (1967) System 4 also fits within the human resources frame. When the importance of culture and organizational values are added to the human resource frame, parts of Ouchi's (1981) Theory Z and Pascale and Anthos' (1981) 7-*S* approach fit in as well.

However, human resource theorists have had little to say about power and the allocation of scarce resources. As Bolman and Deal (1984) observed, "The works of Argyris, McGregor, and Likert devote much attention to concepts like communication, feedback, and leadership but rarely mention power" (p. 105). Human resource theorists believe that it is possible to make improvements that will benefit employer and employee at the same time, therefore avoiding the problem of power.

The human resource frame arises from the prediction that organizations will concentrate on structure and fail to pay attention to the needs of individuals and this will cause strife. In fact, many of these predictions have come to pass.

From the structural frame, organizations are designed to be rational systems where the central question is how to design the most effective system. The human resource frame also sees the organization as rational but finds mismatches between individual and organizational needs.

The *political frame* focuses on interest groups concerned with dividing scarce resources. Coalitions are formed, often based on very different views of reality, with organizational goals emerging from ongoing processes of bargaining, negotiation, and jockeying for position between individuals and groups. Because of the inherently scarce resources, conflict and power are central fixtures in organizational life. Although the human resources theorists see conflicts as open to a possible win/win resolution with enough time and effort by all parties, the political theorist is more likely to view divergent interests and conflicts over scarce resources as an enduring fact of life.

Gamson's (1968) analysis of political processes focuses on two major players in a social system: authorities and partisans. The authorities must exercise social control and the partisans may choose to challenge it and even overthrow it. So, the people seeking power use a variety of rewards to control the individuals including authority, expertise, control of rewards, coercive power, and personal power (French & Raven, 1959; Kanter, 1977). Authorities have the exclusive access to power of position, but they are only one of many contenders for power. All contenders have access to power ranging from sheer numbers to specialty forms. You will recall that we made this observation in chapter 1 when we outlined the various parts of the system's perspective and discussed formal and informal power.

The existence of conflict is downplayed by both the structural and human relations schools. The political perspective does not worry about resolving conflict, but instead looks at the strategies and tactics of conflict. If you want to understand how organizations work, this frame argues, look at the natural pursuit of self-interest and how power is used to achieve personal interests.

Although carrying a certain amount of organizational reality (Gibson, Ivancevich, & Donnelly, 1991, pp. 347–353), this perspective is likely to become a self-fulfilling prophecy. In addition to being overly cynical and pessimistic, it underplays the importance of rational and collaborative processes. An example of this overly skeptical perspective is seen in Ritti and Funkhouser's (1979) *The Ropes to Skip and the Ropes to Know,* which makes the issue of correct decisions unimportant, and the knowledge of skills and technical expertise of little importance. Instead, political savvy and skills in using symbols are of greater importance. Doing a good job is not the issue, but appearing to do a good job is critical. The political frame says some very important things about the way organizations function. But, its cynical view tends to diminish what people actually do. Argyris and Schon (1974) suggested that people, in fact, often fail to learn from their own areas of ineffectiveness and persist in self-destructive, self-defeating cycles of behavior. Each new win produces more losses. These individuals create a major problem for organizations because they see their own self-interest as being at odds with others, thereby creating a win/lose attitude toward other people. The political frame does say some very important things about organizations more clearly than the structural or human resource frame, but it depicts the ongoing battles as too pervasive. Block's (1987) *The Empowered Manager: Positive Political Skills at Work,* for example, recognized the inherent conflict between the entrepreneurial approach needed by companies and the entrenched bureaucratic thinking of many organizations. He therefore called for a specific approach for managers that is highly political in an effort to cut through all the "red tape" and obtain political empowerment. Some political savvy is critical, but an overreliance on this perspective makes organizational life an ongoing game rather than a goal-oriented activity. We discuss the issue of power extensively in our chapter on conflict and power.

In sum, these three frames illuminate different aspects of organizations. The structural frame focuses on roles, relationships, and more formal ways of coordinating diverse efforts toward common directions. In the human resource frame, individual needs are central and the basic issue is how to design settings in which individual and organizational needs can be integrated. From the political perspective, organizations are networks of special interests: Coalitions, conflicts, and bargaining translate power into action. Groups that win the political battles are able to steer the organization in the directions they choose.

These frames are different, but they share some characteristics. They assume a world that is relatively certain—goals provide direction, effectiveness can be seen, needs can be identified, power can be understood, developed, and used. So, the world is substantially rational. Decisions are made by choosing the best alternative. People act rationally, as least judged by their own needs and beliefs. Groups behave rationally in attempting to further their own self-interests. Finally, the world is relatively linear. Goals are established to guide action, people determine what they want and take action to get it. Policies are developed through a sequential process of bargaining and conflict. The frames vary, of course, with the structural being strongest in believing in certainty, rationality, and linearity, and the political the least. These three frames, along with the symbolic frame, are summarized in Table 3.7.

The *symbolic frame* says that what is most important about any event is not what happened, but the meaning of what happened. The meaning of an event is determined not only by the event itself, but by the ways humans interpret, or perceive the event.

Many of the significant events and processes in organizations are substantially ambiguous or uncertain. As we work, it is often difficult or impossible to know what happened, why it happened, or what will happen next. Unpredictability undermines rational approaches to analysis, problem solving, and decision making. To make sense out of this uncertainty, humans create symbols to reduce the ambiguity, resolve confusion, increase predictability, and provide direction. Events may remain illogical, random, fluid, and meaningless, but human symbols make them seem otherwise. As we discussed in chapter 1, the reduction of equivocality is a major driving force behind much of our organizational behavior (Weick, 1969).

Symbols and symbolic phenomena have been studied for a long time from a variety of disciplines (Bolman & Deal, 1984, p. 151). The symbolic frame concentrates on the concepts of meaning, belief, and faith. Various methods are available for making organizational life more understandable. For example, myths provide explanations, reconcile contradictions, and resolve dilemmas (Cohen, 1969). Metaphors make confusion comprehensible. Scenarios provide direction for action in areas where the correct actions are not clear (Ortner, 1973). We discuss each of the concepts in depths in chapter 8, Symbolic Behavior. Examples of each of these symbolic behaviors were presented earlier in this chapter when we outlined the four culture types discussed in *Corporate Cultures* (Deal & Kennedy, 1982).

The symbolic frame assumes that organizations are full of questions that cannot be answered, problems that cannot be solved, and events that cannot be understood or managed. Although traditional views see organizations as rational and objectively real, the symbolic frame counterpoises a set of concepts that emphasizes the complexity and ambiguity of organizational phenomena and the extent to which symbols mediate the meanings of organizational events and activities. Myths and stories provide drama, cohesiveness, clarity, and direction to events that are confusing and mysterious. Rituals and ceremonies provide ways of taking actions in the face of confusion, unpredictability, and threats.

In the end, we need some order, predictability, and meaning in organizations, which often seem to be filled with ambiguity and uncertainty. Rather than admit that we cannot solve these problems, we create symbolic solutions. Organizational structure and processes then serve as myths, rituals, and ceremonies that promote cohesion inside organizations and bond organizations to their environment.

Bolman and Deal (1984, 1991) provided us with an excellent means for understanding each of the major perspectives that people use as they operate in an organi-

TABLE 3.7

Four Interpretations of Organizational Processes

| Process | Structural | Human Resource | Political | Symbolic |
|---|---|---|---|---|
| Planning | strategies to set objectives | gatherings to promote participation | arenas to air conflict & alter power | ritual to signal responsibility, negotiate meaning |
| Decision making | rational | open-to produce commitment | power opportunity | ritual for support |
| Reorganizing | realign roles & responsibility | balance human & formal roles | redistribute power & form new coalitions | negotiate new social order; maintain image |
| Evaluating | used to distribute rewards and penalties | helps individual to grow and improve | opportunity to exercise power | opportunity to play roles in a ritual |
| Approaching conflict | authorities resolve | have individuals learn to confront | bargaining, forcing, power opportunity | develop shared values & use conflict for meaning |
| Goal setting | used to direct organization | keep involvement & open communication | allows interests to be known | develop shared values & symbols |
| Communication | transmit facts & information | exchange information, feelings, needs | vehicle to influence or manipulate | telling stories |
| Meeting | formalized place to make decisions | informal place to be involved | competitive place to win points | sacred place to celebrate & transform culture |
| Motivating | monetary rewards | growth, self-actualization | coercion | symbols |

*Note.* Adapted from Bolman and Deal (1984). Copyright © 1984 by Jossey-Bass. Reprinted by permission.

zation. As Table 3.7 indicates, each of the four frames emphasizes particular views of organizational reality. The creation of meaning, the underlying premise behind communication, seems to fit in the symbolic frame. However, each of the four frames provides a guide to action, which is then interpreted by organizational members to have meaning. So, all four perspectives function to provide communication and are seen as evidence of communication. If you behave in a political manner, for example, or you believe it is the most appropriate behavior to adopt, what you do will be *communication*, which is the focus of this text. So, our actions take on symbolic meaning even though our motives for acting can come from any of the four frames.

*In Search of Excellence* often is cited as a study of organizational cultures (Goldhaber, 1990, pp. 71–72; Kreps, 1990, pp. 128–132). These four frames can be applied effectively to the eight characteristics outlined earlier as demonstrated in Table 3.8. So, although the general analysis contained in *In Search of Excellence* is cultural, the tools used to obtain those ends range across three of the four frames. The absence of the political frame does not mean these behaviors do not occur in the excellent organizations. But, the values perpetuated by these organizations diminish the potential for extensive political behavior that is rewarded by the culture.

## Putting It Into Perspective

We also can put these four approaches to organization and management theory into perspective by examining two interacting variables—the type of actor and the type of system. Each of the four theories makes certain assumptions regarding the role of the action—either rational or social—and the type of system—either closed or open—in which the organization member will be operating (Bolman & Deal, 1984, pp. 225–226). These interactions are based on the theories used by management sultants who see themselves as physicians are likely to be different from consultants who see themselves as salesmen or rain dancers" (Bolman & Deal, 1984, p. 164). If an organization is perceived as a fighting unit (military metaphor), a well-oiled machine set all the rules and regulations. This would be done through careful analysis of the job requirements and a strict adherence to certain standards of performance by workers. The primary reason for interactions between individuals was to get the job done as quickly and cheaply as possible while maintaining performance standards.

Humanistic management approached workers and the managers or supervisors as social actors and the primary job of the managerial staff was to initiate openness and a feeling of appreciation for the workers to establish a good work setting. Being cognizant of the workers' needs was of great importance and the work force used communication interactions to express those needs. The system remained closed, however, because the manager was still "in charge" and made all the production decisions without consulting the workers.

With the awareness that workers have a great deal of information that could be useful to the operation of an organization, human resources management moved back

TABLE 3.8
Applying the Four Frames to the Eight Characteristics of the Excellent Companies

| Characteristics | Applicable Frames |
|---|---|
| 1. Bias for action | Structural—eliminates the impact of a confining structure.<br>Symbolic—shows a culture supportive of risk taking. |
| 2. Close to the customer | Human resource—customers are a human resource to the company. |
| 3. Productivity through People | Human resource—people are most important-actual belief.<br>Symbolic—extended family. |
| 4. Autonomy and entrepreneurship | Human resource—encourage risk, extensive communication.<br>Structural—decentralized. |
| 5. Hands-on, value-driven | Symbolic—story telling, values continually transmitted. |
| 6. Stick to the knitting | Human resource—managers avoid trying to manage "new" things.<br>Symbolic—do not try to transfer cultural values to different types of businesses. |
| 7. Simple form, lean staff | Structural—remain free from large central staff, decentralize. |
| 8. Simultaneous loose–tight | Human resource—people are committed to each other.<br>Structural—decentralized.<br>Symbolic—the characteristic that makes the organizations work—the culture that holds the excellent companies together. |

The *political* frame does not occur because of the cultural values of these excellent companies. In other companies, political behavior does occur and carries cultural messages to the rest of the organization.

*Note.* Adapted from Bolman and Deal (1984). Copyright © 1984 by Jossey Bass. Reprinted by permission.

to a rational actor status but opened the system to worker input. Decisions about how the operation should be carried out were opened up to the work force in general.

The final stage of theoretical development is represented by the newer approaches to the managerial process. The work force is seen as a vital part of the open system and the manager is a social actor who works with the employees in an effort to forward the organization's goals (Myers, 1991). Using a cultural perspective, all factors are considered intertwined and the manager's job is to be part of the process. The open system, social actor view allows for a fuller understanding of the cultural perspective.

## Merging Perspectives

Because organizations are a major factor in everyone's life, it is not suprising to find a large number of explanations for why they do what they do and numerous prescriptions made for how to manage them more effectively. Rather than assume that a particular approach is the most useful, organizational theories increasingly are becoming combinations of the various approaches we have discussed in this chapter.

As we pointed out earlier in this chapter, this duality of perspective is summarized nicely by the conclusion that the hard rational model is not wrong, it just is not enough. We must be careful not to assume that differences mean other perspectives are incorrect. For example, when attempts are made to divide cultural investigations into two approaches, a great deal of information is missed when one approach is assumed to be better than the other. The old saying, "there are only two kinds of people, those that divide people into two kinds and those that don't," demonstrates the problem with trying to establish any clear dichotomies.

There are very few absolute divisions when we consider organizational communication. The Eastern perspective, which suggests that human behavior is both/and rather than either/or, is an appropriate perspective to take regarding organizational communication. The excellent companies surveyed by Peters and Waterman (1982) are simultaneously loose and tight, competitive and compassionate, the 7-S model incorporates both hard and soft management factors, and situational theory requires this same multiperspective approach. Rather than looking for quantifiable results as the only justified source of information, as is often the case with behaviorists, or qualifiable results, as the humanists tend to seek, we gain much greater insights into organizational behavior by understanding that both views are substantially correct.

## CONCLUSION

We have examined the four major developments in organizational and managerial theory since the industrial revolution. Scientific management emphasized the importance of job design and efficiency. Management's key function was to effectively structure the work setting so that the organization's production goals were met. This structured, well-designed approach allowed top-down control of all the factors in the work setting.

With the Hawthorne Studies' conclusions challenging many of the premises behind scientific management, human relations management moved toward an emphasis on the work setting as a social force. Adding the importance of social interaction as a motivational tool is the major contribution of this perspective.

In an attempt to balance the excesses of the humanistic approach without returning to the strict control features of scientific management, human resources management approaches workers as human beings capable of self-direction if provided the proper work setting and goals. People are a potential resource, which can be used effectively to enhance the organization's growth and productivity. Leadership is a critical variable in this approach and has led to a vast number of studies on contingency design and leadership style.

The final approach to organization and managerial theory takes an overview of the various approaches and looks at organizations as cultures. Based on serious criticisms of the present approaches to organizational development, the cultural approach offers us an excellent perspective for understanding the behavioral aspects of organizations. This view provides us with an important starting point for the full understanding of the power of organizational communication. The principles and pragmatic sections develop a further understanding of these concepts. As we demonstrated, the new managerial perspectives give a great deal of credibility to cultural studies, but include the other theories as part of the process of organizing.

This chapter is basic to your understanding of why organizations do what they do. Because each of the perspectives offered tells us about successful processes in management, you should understand the major contributions of scientific management, humanistic management, and human resources management. The important result of numerous studies indicating that there is "no one best way" tells us that the contingencies involved in organizational communication must be understood fully if we are going to be successful as members of organizations. Membership requires us to view organizations as cultures that have a large number of contingencies based on the factors making up the structure.

You probably are asking the logical question: If the new managerial perspectives are basically correct, then why worry about the other three views? There are at least two reasons. First, when we discussed cultures, we carefully included all four views. For example, the 7-S Model and Theory Z explain to us what ought to be important in the running of an organization. But when you first join an organization, adapting to it effectively will be more important than worrying about the validity of the type of managerial style. By adding cultures as a concept, you are also aware that the external environment greatly influences the type of culture operating.

Second, each of the views discussed works. In many cases, the manner in which the management perspective is employed is not as successful as it could be. However, you will see a large number of businesses, companies, and organizations successfully operating in spite of the type of management, or, in some cases, because of it.

What we have provided you are excellent maps of the territories you will be joining. With the information provided in the remainder of this book, you will have the tools needed for settling in effectively and productively. Few things can be more rewarding than learning to be successful at your chosen profession, and organizational communication is an important link in that success.

## REFERENCES

Air controllers form union. (1987, June 23). *Wall Street Journal*, p. B1.

Albanese, R. (1988). *Management*. Cincinnati: South-Western.

Amsbary, J. H., & Staples, P. J. (1991). Improving administrator/nurse communication: A case study of "management by wandering around." *Journal of Business Communication, 28*(2), 101–111.

Argyris, C. (1957). *Personality and organization*. New York: Harper & Row.

Argyris, C. (1976). *Increasing leadership effectiveness*. New York: Wiley-Interscience.

Argyris, C., & Schon, D. A. (1974). *Theory in practice: Increasing professional effectiveness*. San Francisco: Jossey-Bass.

Asian executives give communication top priority. (1983, October). *Communication World*, p. 8.

Austin, W. M. (1986). *The job outlook in brief*. Washington, DC: U.S. Department of Labor.

Baker, E. L. (1980, July). Managing organizational culture. *Management Review*, pp. 8–13.

Bendix, R. (1956). *Work and authority in industry*. New York: Wiley.

Blau, P., Fable, C. M., McHinley, W., & Tracy, P. (1976, March). Technology and organizing in manufacturing. *Administrative Science Quarterly, 21,* 20–40.

Blau, P. M., & Scott, W. R. (1962). *Formal organizations: A comparative approach.* San Francisco: Chandler.

Block, P. (1987). *The empowered manager: Positive political skills at work.* San Francisco: Jossey-Bass.

Bolman, L. G., & Deal, T. E. (1984). *Modern approaches to understanding and managing organizations.* San Francisco: Jossey-Bass.

Bolman, L. G., & Deal, T. E. (1991). *Reframing organizations: Artistry, choice, and leadership.* San Francisco: Jossey-Bass.

Bormann, E. G. (1983). Symbolic convergence: Organizational communication and culture. In L. L. Putnam & M. E. Pacanowsky (Eds.), *Communication and organizations: An interpretive approach* (pp. 99–122). Beverly Hills, CA: Sage.

Boss' pockets being picked of huge sums. (1983, June 11). *The Evansville Courier,* p. 1.

Bowers, D. G. (1983, Winter). What would make 11,500 people quit their jobs? *Organizational Dynamics,* pp. 5–19.

Bradford, D. L., & Cohen, A. R. (1984). *Managing for excellence.* New York: Wiley.

Briggs, B. (1982, May 17). The dangerous folly called Theory Z. *Fortune,* pp. 41–53.

Bureau of Labor Statistics. (1984). *Occupational outlook handbook.* Washington, DC: U.S. Department of Labor.

Burns, T., & Stalker, G. M. (1961). *The management of innovation.* London: Tavistock.

Campbell, J. P., Dunnette, M., Lawler, E. E., III, & Weick, K. E., Jr. (1970). *Managerial behavior, performance and effectiveness.* New York: McGraw-Hill.

Carey, A. (1967). The Hawthorne studies: A radical criticism. *American Sociological Review, 32,* 403–416.

Chandler, A. D., Jr. (1962). *Strategy and structure.* Cambridge, MA: MIT Press.

Changing a corporate culture. (1984, May 14). *Business Week,* pp. 130–133, 137–138.

Cillinge, R. B. (1983, June). *ASTD national report,* p. 2.

Cohen, P. S. (1969, April). Theories of myth. *Man,* p. 4.

Cole, R. E. (1980, September). Learning from the Japanese: Prospects and pitfalls. *Management Review,* pp. 23–35.

Cook, D., Glaberson, W. B., & Moskowitz, D. B. (1985, March 4). Is this any way to run a bigtime law firm? *Business Week,* p. 98.

Courtright, J. A., Fairhurst, G. T., & Rogers, L. E. (1989). Interaction patterns in organic and mechanistic systems. *Academy of Management Journal, 32,* 773–802.

Daniels, T. D., & Spiker, B. K. (1987). *Perspectives on organizational communication.* Dubuque, IA: Brown.

Deal, T. E., & Kennedy, A. A. (1982). *Corporate cultures: The rites and rituals of corporate life.* Reading, MA: Addison-Wesley.

Drexler, J., Jr. (1977). Organizational climate: Its homogeneity within organizations. *Journal of Applied Psychology, 62,* 38–42.

Dyer, W. G. (1982). *Contemporary issues in management and organizational development.* Reading, MA: Addison-Wesley.

Ernest, R. C. (1985). Corporate cultures and effective planning. *Personnel Administrator, 30,* 49–50, 52–56.

Fayol, H. (1949). *General and industrial management.* New York: Pittman.

Feuer, D. (1985, November). Florida power corporation: Focus on performance. *Training,* pp. 57–60.

Fiedler, F. E. (1967). *A theory of leadership effectiveness.* New York: McGraw-Hill.

Fiedler, F. E., Chemers, M. N., & Mahar, L. (1978). *Improving leadership effectiveness.* New York: Wiley.

Franke, R., & Karl, J. (1978). The Hawthorne experiments: First statistical interpretations. *American Sociological Review, 43,* 623–643.

Frederiksen, N. (1966). *Some effects of organizational climates on administrative performance* (Research Memorandum No. RM 66-21). Princeton, NJ: Educational Testing Service.

French, J. R. P., & Raven, B. H. (1959). The bases of social power. In D. Cartwright (Ed.), *Studies in social power* (pp. 150–167). Ann Arbor: University of Michigan Press.

Gamson, W. A. (1968). *Power and discontent.* Homewood, IL: Dorsey.

Gibson, J. L., Ivancevich, J. M., & Donnelly, J. H., Jr. (1991). *Organizations* (7th ed.). Homewood, IL: Irwin.

Goldhaber, G. M. (1990). *Organizational communication* (5th ed.). Dubuque, IA: Brown.

Hall, J. (1965). *Management's changing theory.* Conroe, TX: Telemetrics, International.

Harris, T. E. (1990). Organizational culture: An examination of the role of communication. In S. Thomas & W. A. Evans (Eds.), *Communication and culture: Language, performance, technology, and media* (pp. 143–155). Norwood, NJ: Ablex.

Hayes, R. H., & Abernathy, W. J. (1980). Managing our way to economic decline. *Harvard Business Review, 58*(4), 67–77.

Hertzberg, F. (1968). One more time, how do you motivate employees? *Harvard Business Review, 46*(1), 53–62.

Hickman, C. G., & Silva, M. A. (1987). *The future 500: Creating tomorrow's organizations today.* New York: New American Library.

Hopkins, T. (1982). *How to master the art of selling.* New York: Warner.

House, R. J., & Mitchell, T. R. (1974). Path-goal theory of leadership. *Journal of Contemporary Business, 5,* 81–97.

Hurst, D. K. (1984). Of boxes, bubbles and effective management. *Harvard Business Review, 62*(3), 78–97.

Jacoby, J., & Terborg, J. R. (1976). *Development and validation of theory x and theory y scales for assessing McGregor's managerial philosophies.* Conroe, TX: Teleometrics International.

Jones, A., & James, L. (1979). Psychological climate: Dimensions and relationships of individual and aggregated work environment perceptions. *Organizational Behavior and Human Performance, 23,* 201–250.

Kanter, R. (1977). *Men and women of the corporations.* New York: Basic.

Kast, F., & Rosenzweig, J. (1984). *The nature of management.* Chicago: Science Research Associates.

Kennedy, A. (1983, November). Back-fence conversations, new tools for quality conversations. *Communication World,* p. 26.

Kiechel, W., III. (1982, December 27). Corporate strategists under fire. *Fortune,* pp. 32–39.

Kilmann, R. H. (1982). Getting control of the corporate culture. *Managing, 3,* 11–17.

Kotter, J. P. (1988). *The leadership factor.* New York: Free Press.

Kotter, J. P. (1990). *A force for change: How leadership differs from management.* New York: Free Press.

Kouzes, J. M., & Posner, B. Z. (1990). *The leadership challenge.* San Francisco: Jossey-Bass.

Kreps, G. L. (1990). *Organizational Communication: Theory and practice* (2nd ed.). New York: Longman.

Lawrence, P. R., & Lorsch, J. W. (1967a, June). Differentiations and integration in complex organizations. *Administrative Science Quarterly, 12,* 1–47.

Lawrence, P. R., & Lorsch, J. W. (1967b). *Organization and environment.* Boston: Harvard University, Graduate School of Business Administration, Division of Research.

Levering, R., Moskowitz, M., & Katz, M. (1985). *The 100 best companies to work for in America.* New York: New American Library.

Likert, R. (1961). *New patterns of management.* New York: McGraw-Hill.

Likert, R. (1967). *The human organization.* New York: McGraw-Hill.

Litwin, G., & Stringer, R., Jr. (1968). *Motivation and organizational climate.* Boston: Harvard University, Graduate School of Business Administration.

Locke, E. A. (1982). The ideas of Frederick Taylor: An evaluation. *Academy of Management Review, 7,* 14–25.

Marabe, T. (1983, June). Communication spurred Japanese growth. *Communication World,* p. 5.

Marks, M. L. (1986, March). The question of quality circles. *Psychology Today,* pp. 36–42.

Maslow, A. H. (1970). *Motivation and personality* (2nd ed.). New York: Harper & Row.

McGregor, D. M. (1960). *The human side of enterprise.* New York: McGraw-Hill.

Memmott, M. (1987, June 8). Big brother taps into computers at work. *USA Today*, p. 8E.

Miles, R. E. (1965). Keeping informed – Human relations or human resources? *Harvard Business Review, 43*(4), 148–163.

Miller, G. (1985, April). Bob Forman: Is being rough still enough? *Institutional Investor*, pp. 58–64.

Mintzberg, H. (1991, Winter). The effective organization: Forces and forms. *Sloan Management Review*, pp. 54–67.

Muchinsky, P. (1976). An assessment of the Litwin and Stringer organizational climate questionnaire: An empirical and theoretical extension of the Sims and LaFollette study. *Personnel Psychology, 29*, 371–392.

Myers, M. S. (1991). *Every employee a manager.* San Diego: University Associates.

Offermann, L. R., & Gowing, M. K. (1990). Organizations of the future: Changes and challenges. *American Psychologist, 45*(2), 95–108.

One in three thought about quitting their jobs last year. (1991, May 8). *The Evansville Courier*, p. A6.

Ortner, S. (1973). On key symbols. *American Anthropologist, 75*, 138–1346.

Ouchi, W. G. (1981). *Theory z: How American business can meet the Japanese challenge.* New York: Avon.

Pacanowsky, M. E., & O'Donnell-Trujillo, N. (1983). Organizational communication as cultural performance. *Communication Monographs, 50*, 126–147.

Pascale, R. T., & Anthos, A. G. (1981). *The art of Japanese management.* New York: Warner.

Pascale, R. T. (1990). *Managing on the edge: Companies that use conflict to stay ahead.* New York: Simon & Schuster.

Perrow, C. (1970). *Organizational analysis: A structural view.* Monterey, CA: Brooks/Cole.

Peters, T. (1987). *Thriving on chaos: Handbook for a management revolution.* New York: Knopf.

Peters, T., & Austin, N. (1985). *A passion for excellence: The leadership difference.* New York: Random House.

Peters, T. J., & Waterman, R. H., Jr. (1982). *In search of excellence: Lessons from America's best-run companies.* New York: Harper & Row.

Poole, M. S., & McPhee, R. D. (1982). A structural analysis of organizational climate. In L. L. Putnam & M. E. Pacanowsky (Eds.), *Communication and organizations: An interpretive approach* (pp. 195–219). Beverly Hills, CA: Sage.

Pugh, D. S. (1971). *Organization theory.* Baltimore: Penguin.

Putnam, L. L. (1982). Paradigms for organizational communication research: An overview and synthesis. *Western Journal of Speech Communication, 46*, 192–206.

Redding, W. C. (1972). *Communication within the organization.* New York: International Communication Council.

Ritti, R. R., & Funkhouser, G. R. (1979). *The ropes to skip and the ropes to know.* Columbus, OH: Grid.

Roethisberger, F. L., & Dickson, W. (1939). *Management and the worker.* Cambridge, MA: Harvard University Press.

Rush, H. M. F. (1972). The world of work and the behavioral sciences: A perspective and overview. In F. Luthers (Ed.), *Contemporary readings in organizational behavior* (pp. 11–28). New York: McGraw-Hill.

Schein, E. H. (1985). *Organizational culture and leadership.* San Francisco: Jossey-Bass.

Schein, E. H. (1990). Organizational culture. *American Psychologist, 45*, 109–119.

Schermerhorn, J. R., Jr., Hunt, J. G., & Osborn, R. N. (1982). *Managing organizational behavior.* New York: Wiley.

Sims, H., Jr., & LaFollette, W. (1975). An assessment of the Litwin and Stringer organizational climate questionnaire. *Personnel Psychology, 28*, 421–433.

Skinner, W. (1981). Big hat, no cattle: Managing human resources. *Harvard Business Review, 59*(5), 102–114.

Smircich, L. (1983). Implications for management theory. In L. L. Putnam & M. E. Pacanowsky (Eds.), *Communication and organizations: An interpretive approach* (pp. 221–242). Beverly Hills, CA: Sage.

Smircich, L., & Calas, M. B. (1987). Organizational culture: A critical assessment. In F. M. Jablin, L. L. Putnam, K. H. Roberts, & L. W. Porter (Eds.), *Handbook of organizational communication* (pp. 228–263). Newbury Park, CA: Sage.

Smith, A. (1937). *The wealth of nations.* New York: Modern Library. (Original work published 1776)

Solberg, S. L. (1985, Fall). Human resource management in action—Changing culture through ceremony. *Human Resource Management, 24,* 329–340.

Taylor, F. W. (1911). *The principles of scientific management.* New York: Harper & Bros.

*Tomorrow's jobs: Overview.* (1986). Washington, DC: U.S. Department of Labor.

Tosi, H. L., & Hammer W. C. (1982). *Organizational behavior and management: A contingency approach* (3rd ed.). New York: Wiley.

Tregoe, B. B., & Zimmerman, J. W. (1980). *Top management strategy.* New York: Simon & Schuster.

Ulrich, D. O., Clack, B. A., & Dillon, L. (1985). Blue Cross of California: Human resources in a changing world. *Human Resource Management, 24,* 69–80.

Uttal, B. (1983, October 17). The corporate culture vultures. *Fortune,* pp. 66–70, 72.

Vroom, V. H., & Yetton, P. W. (1973). *Leadership and decision making.* Pittsburgh: University of Pittsburgh Press.

Waterman, R. T., Peters, T., & Phillips, J. R. (1980, June). Structure is not organization. *Business Horizons,* pp. 14–26.

Weber, M. (1947). *The theory of social and economic organizations* (A. M. Henderson & T. Parsons, Trans.). New York: Free Press.

Weick, K. E. (1969). *The social psychology of organizing.* Reading, MA: Addison-Wesley.

Whitsell, D., & Yorks, L. (1983, Summer). Looking back at Topeka: General Foods and the quality-of-work-life experiment. *California Management Review,* pp. 93–110.

Who's excellent now? (1984, November 4). *Business Week,* p. 21.

A winning trio: Quality in, quality out. (1985, November). *Training,* pp. 46–47.

Woodward, J. (1965). *Industrial organization: Theory and practice.* London: Oxford University Press.

Zaleznik, A. (1989). *The managerial mystique: Restoring leadership in business.* New York: Harper & Row.

# Verbal Communication

Verbal communication is a primary vehicle organizations use to maintain contact with their internal and external environments. Through the use of oral and written language, organizations—and all of their subsystems—coordinate, control, and manage individual and group behavior. According to one estimate, two thirds of the United States' work force is involved in the processing of information (Naisbett, 1984, p. 4), which is dependent on verbal communication.

Organizations are affected by verbal communication in at least three ways. First, the environment provides extensive information to an organization through verbal communication. Second, individuals use verbal communication to direct, manage, comprehend, and respond. Finally, verbal communication is a principal means for creating and developing organizational intelligence. Organizational intelligence is the memory of the system, which is maintained through its cultural communication processes (Kreps, 1986, pp. 153–154). Language is used to create and define meaning (Huber & Daft, 1987, p. 151).

Verbal communication also allows us to understand the complex nature of communication in an organization, because we are brought directly in touch with an apparent contradiction. On the one hand, clarity and directness are required to be effective in giving instructions, making assessments, and dealing with colleagues (Bittle, 1980; Murphy & Hildebrandt, 1984, pp. 38–47). On the other hand, language is powerful precisely because it is highly symbolic of much broader meanings (Lee, 1941, p. 264). In a sense, language becomes almost magical when it reinforces and motivates, creates an esprit de corps, or enhances a company image (Kotter, 1990, pp. 55–59). This second category includes stories, myths, heroes, metaphors, and humor (Huber & Daft, 1987, pp. 151–154).

In a very real sense, verbal communication requires both clarity and ambiguity.

This duality of perspective is an essential tool for understanding the complexity of verbal communication (Stohl & Redding, 1987). Symbols, stories, and myths, for example, can be understood only in the context of the underlying values and assumptions of the organization's culture (Schein, 1990, p. 112).

We are making an arbitrary division between verbal and nonverbal communication in order to facilitate our analysis. However, these two factors are, for all practical purposes, not separable. By and large, organizational members, because of their organizational roles or personal preferences, learn to depend on particular means of communication for specific needs and outcomes, but the verbal and nonverbal aspects are always in play. Before discussing the functions of verbal communication, we examine its importance to organizations.

## VERBAL COMMUNICATION IN ORGANIZATIONS

Language, the underpinning of verbal communication, allows us to assign meaning to things (Condon, 1975, pp. 36–38). As we assimilate into the organization, we create individual realities based on language, so we can predict and control our own behavior. We are forced to decipher from a variety of clues what messages mean and which messages are important. As such, verbal communication provides the written and unwritten, spoken and unspoken rules and procedures. These lead to a common purpose, or a set of ground rules, which constitute the process of organizing the various subsystems. Understanding the nature of verbal communication can be difficult because "language is both commonplace and enigmatic, both superficially simple and infinitely complex" (Bowman & Targowski, 1987, p. 22). How language functions in an organization has a major impact on all individuals and shapes their organizational reality. Verbal communication is written and oral.

### Written Communication

Written messages have numerous organizational functions (Gilsdorf, 1987, pp. 36–37). A partial list includes corporate goals and values, short- and long-range plans, job descriptions, work orders, announcements, bulletins, informal notes, house magazines and organs, annual reports, handbooks, procedures, official guidelines, regulations, codes, contracts, performance appraisals, and meeting agenda and minutes. Written job descriptions can help employees understand the goals of an organization (Boyd, 1984, pp. 53–54).

The organization's public statements, such as annual reports or press releases, provide a great deal of information about the type of culture an organization would like to project (Deal & Kennedy, 1982, p. 131). No less important are the ongoing memos, letters to an organization's customers and other interacting systems in the organization's environment, and the written credos, sayings, and general culture-forming messages surrounding the workplace.

Managers consider written communication important, and they spend a significant amount of their working day engaging in this activity (Flatley, 1982, pp. 46, 49). But, "most executives [75%] said they either 'hate' or merely 'tolerate' business writing (John Rost Associates, 1984, p. 14). Managers are not pleased with the written communication they receive and "nearly 60 percent described it as 'fair or poor,' and they had several other words for it: unclear, wordy, disorganized, impersonal" (John Rost Associates, 1984, p. 14).

Each year, the prestigious "Percy" award is given to the worst business letters and memos. The award is named after the pompous legalistic phrase "pursuant to your request." The award-giver's goal is to reduce poor business writing. An insurance company won top honors for the Percy award for the following letter it sent to its independent contractors: "Please note that IRS regulations promulgate that our company must submit Form 1099 for their use of 'Unincorporated Independent Contractors' with respect to services received when the aggregate amount paid exceeds $600.00. The Form W-9 must be completed and returned so payments may be issued without further delay. Thank you" ("Miserable Memos," 1988, p. 11). Managers, it would appear, are justified in being critical of some business writing. The U.S. Department of Commerce (1984) concluded: "When a company simplifies its language, it builds business and saves time and money. It streamlines procedures, eliminates unnecessary forms, and reduces customer complaints. Its employees, as well as its customers, get a better grasp on how the company does business. This increases productivity and customer satisfaction" (p. v). The Southern California Gas Company simplified its billing statement and estimates it will now save $252,000 a year because of fewer customer inquiries ("Simply Stated," 1987). Organizations demonstrate their belief in the importance of effective written communication through in-house training programs (Leonard, 1982; Rothwell, 1983).

The memorandum is the most frequently used means of written communication (Flatley, 1982, p. 41). One memo cited in the Percy award search demonstrates some of the potential problems in written communication: "You should to the greatest extent possible strive for symmetry in your involvement with the business and professional staffs as this relates to the level of person you meet with on a regular, formal basis." (A Washington, DC magazine publisher; "Miserable Memos," 1988, p. 11).

At Procter & Gamble, the fabled one-page memorandum is their statement of "a language of action—the language of the systems" (Peters & Waterman, 1982, p. 150). The one-page memorandum has become an embodiment of the organization's managerial philosophy. In one survey, "recent college graduates indicated that the memorandum (81.3%), computer networks (68.8%), and the informational report (65.6%) are the most used forms of communication in their position in today's organization" (Bednar & Olney, 1987, p. 22). Letters (43.8%), analytical reports (40.6%), oral presentations (37%), video teleconferencing (10%), and audio teleconferencing (6.3%) complete the types of internal and external business communication formats surveyed (Bednar & Olney, 1987, p. 22).

For the neophyte in a large corporation, writing is especially significant. As

Mitchell and Burdick (1983) put it, "In terms of the beginning executive's career, writing is even more important than speaking. Upper management generally will see your written work before they ever meet you. And to many of your business contacts, you are what you write" (p. 131).

Most managers anticipate an increased reliance on modern technology such as computers (Rader & Kurth, 1988, pp. 476–493), word processors, and dictating machines (Flatley, 1982, p. 47). Electronic bulletin boards and fax machines have added an almost instantaneous transmission of written messages. Computerized electronic communication systems are used extensively (Olcott, 1984, p. 7). These interactive, computerized systems expedite document preparation and transmission, allow immediate information access, and provide almost unlimited information storage possibilities (Mitchell, Crawford, & Madden, 1985, p. 9). Because these new communication technologies are so pervasive, we provide an extensive analysis in chapter 14.

Organizations carefully consider the impact of their written communication when it concerns policy and personnel actions. Written communication is critical to contracts (Scott & Bain, 1987, pp. 10–14), job descriptions, business plans (Bangs & Osgood, 1988), work rules, recommendations, resumes, reports, and many other activities (Brusaw, Alred, & Oliu, 1987).

Written messages provide a substantial amount of information regarding the organizational culture, ranging from themes — "IBM means service" — to employee handbooks. Members of an organization also assign meanings. For many IBM employees, IBM stands for "I've Been Moved," because the company is famous for moving its management to different locations. As you can see, written communication is vitally important to organizations.

## Oral Communication

In chapter 1, we indicated the strong bias toward oral communication in organizations. Managers (Mintzberg, 1975, p. 52) and supervisors (Bittel, 1980, pp. 175–190) prefer speaking to writing.

Oral communication is used in practically any activity requiring coordination. For example, interviewing, delegating, meetings, performance appraisals, giving and receiving orders, public statements, and instructing are primarily verbal. The telephone, and the telecommunications industry, are extending oral communication to virtually every aspect of organizational behavior (Weitzen, 1987; Williams, 1987, pp. 73–82).

The less formal oral communication behaviors are just as important and include "howdy," "attagirl," and "attaboy" comments, break time, and the ritualizing of particular informal, but expected behaviors. Organizations have rich oral traditions surrounding events that have happened in the past, which are passed from work group to work group and form a substantial body of the known and commonly accepted data. As Albert (1987) put it, "Organizational stories are presented as metaphors or as descriptions of actual events" (p. 71), which are used to maintain and promote the underlying cultural values.

Written and oral communication are important to every organization. The functions of verbal communication need to be considered before we develop a further understanding of how it operates in an organization.

## Functions of Verbal Communication

Verbal communication is used in three ways: first, to enhance task accomplishments; second, to make sense out of content; and third, to supply the bridge between myth and reality (Morris, 1971; Watzlawick, Beavin, & Jackson, 1967, pp. 51–54).

The first level, *task ordering,* involves cognitive meaning, which focuses on either/or choices. At this level, when given instructions, we either follow them, or we do not; understand them or not; or comprehend them or not. In many ways, contracts involve this level of meaning. This is a task orientation.

Two examples are company rules and organizational charts. First, certain company rules are absolute. Prohibitions against the use of alcohol and drugs in most factories are, for example, clear-cut statements regarding employee behavior that almost always lead to dismissal if ignored. Certain safety violations simply will not be tolerated. On a broader scale, organizational charts, which outline job functions and responsibilities, are efforts at task ordering.

In chapter 3, we observed that some individuals use this task-ordering level when they contend one particular theory or frame is the only valid explanation for understanding organizational behavior. We concluded that rather than accepting one theory or explanation as correct, we needed to adopt a multidimensional approach that accepted "both/and" as correct.

When we think about content, we are in the process of sense making. At this point, we are adding meaning to the hard reality of the language initially used, and developing a more complex understanding of what is actually occurring. This is level two, *affective,* which accepts the concepts of both/and, and isolates issues in terms of degrees of difference rather than absolute choices. At this level, someone can be both a good worker and often late to work. This same worker can violate an important safety rule and still be worth retaining.

Level two is a process orientation. So, returning to chapter 3, effective management requires both hard and soft techniques, or management is both an art and a science.

Two terms should make this second level clear. When we talk about *leadership,* many of us feel we have a relatively clear, recognizable, cognitive definition. A leader is someone who leads, commands, or is in charge of others. When we are using the first level, task ordering, we say someone is or is not a good leader. In fact, excellent leaders quickly learn that simply being in command or in charge does not make for successful leadership (Kotter, 1990). Instead, a leader is someone who plans, organizes, sways, conjures, persuades, reprimands, and carries out many other functions (Roethlisberger, 1985; Schutz, 1985). They are leading rather than just being the leader. The emphasis moves from simply being a good or bad leader to the process of leading.

Excellent leadership can require almost paradoxical views of the job requirements. For example, managers are expected to produce harmony through healthy conflict, facilitate change by providing stability, draw strength from being vulnerable, and have fun while working (Bissell, 1988).

In the same vein, the word *organization* may be more appropriately labeled *organizing*: "Organizing is used to denote the processual, sequential, time-varying nature of the behaviors of members in an organization" (Farace, Monge, & Russell, 1977, p. 19). Because organizations are both static and dynamic, predictable and chaotic, and understandable and mystical, they are not fixed or set simply because there is a particular label attached such as IBM or Atlas Van Lines. IBM is, of course, International Business Machines (or "I've Been Moved"). It is also a complex set of subsystems that are constantly changing, even though there is an international system called IBM. Atlas Van Lines is a moving company, but is also a set of independent agents who operate under the national banner. Both organizations are constantly organizing their subsystems. Although their organizational charts outline the structure, the process of behavior more correctly explains what actually occurs.

In the article, "Of Boxes, Bubbles, and Effective Management," Hurst (1984) articulated the need to accept both the rational (hard) and the symbolic (soft) views of management. He provided an outline of the two aspects they label *boxes* and *bubbles* as shown in Table 4.1. In order to develop as an organization, the author found that a soft, intuitive framework was needed along with the hard, rational model. Value judgments emerge from both cognitive and affective processes.

This leads to the third level, *narrative,* which involves the combination of myth with reality. The things we say, for example, become both very real, in that we accept them as valid, yet they are based on a narrative form of proof. This level most accurately reflects how we actually think.

Great leaders or outstanding organizations are often such because individuals pass on stories about them. Once these narrations are assigned credibility, we believe in the characterizations.

At this point, we use metaphors, irony, humor, paradoxes, and the vast array of stories that fuel all organizational cultures. Organizational decisions often are "lucked into" through rational appearing processes (Baron, 1983, pp. 356–357). This becomes a backward decision-making process, where organizational members look back on a decision and see why it was rational. This process is used to make sense of complex, ever-changing situations, so that they can be managed (Conrad, 1985, p. 154).

Concepts, at this third level, are transformable, reversible, and simultaneously reality and myth. These stories provide individuals with the understandable, shared reasons for why things occur. In every organization, stories exist to explain what leadership actually is supposed to be. IBM becomes bigger than life because of its

TABLE 4.1
Boxes and Bubbles

| | |
|---|---|
| Tasks. . . .&. . . . | Roles |
| static, clarity, content, fact, science | fluid, ambiguity, process, perception, art |
| Structure. . . .&. . . . | Groups |
| cool, formal, closed, obedience, independence | warm, informal, open, trust, autonomy |
| Information Systems. . . .&. . . . | Networks |
| hard, written, know, control, decision | soft, oral, feel, influence, implementation |
| People. . . .&. . . . | People |
| rational, produce, think, tell, work | social, create, imagine, inspire, play |
| Strategy. . . .&. . . . | Mission |
| objectives, policies, forecast, clockworks, right, target, precise, necessary | values, norms, vision, frameworks, useful, direction, vague, sufficient |
| Compensation System. . . .&. . . . | Rewards |
| direct, objective, profit, failure, hygiene, managing | indirect, subjective, fun, mistake, motivator, caring |
| Boxes. . . .&. . . . | Bubbles |
| solve, sequential, left brain, serious, explain, rational, conscious, learn, knowledge, lens, full, words, objects, description | dissolve, lateral, right brain, humorous, explore, intuitive, unconscious, remember, wisdom, mirror, empty, pictures, symbols, parable |

*Note.* From Hurst (1984). Copyright © 1984 by The President and Fellows of Harvard College. Reprinted by permission.

halo of esteem. Atlas Van Lines has an international reputation that is based on stories passed on from customer to customer and agent to agent.

The transformable nature of meaning can be demonstrated by seeing how consultants suggest organizations handle customer complaints. Virtually every customer service consultant suggests that the complaint can be viewed as an opportunity (Albrecht, 1988, pp. 219–221; "Capitalizing," 1987). By shifting the emphasis, the employee's reality concerning the complaining customer is altered. This same shifting of perspectives is used to encourage organizations, and managers and supervisors, to solicit employee suggestions and complaints. When we discussed the self-fulfilling prophecy earlier in this text, we indicated the dramatic shift that can occur when people use a different perspective to view a problem or issue.

This third level of language use is vital to an organization. In the extreme, plans are offered to make an organization appear to be on course and carefully structured. As Weick (1987) explained: "Thus language trappings of organizations such as strategic plans are important components of the process of creating order. They hold events together long enough and tightly enough in people's heads so that they act in the belief that their actions will be influential and make sense" (p. 98).

At first glance, delineating these three levels might appear unnecessarily complex. However, we need to understand the three ways we establish meaning through the use of language. The cognitive level involves the explicit choices we make. We either take a job, for example, or we do not. But the word *job* does not describe what we actually do. Chances are the affective level, where the job is both interesting and boring, or easy and hard, comes closer to describing our daily activities. The very nature of organizations leads us to the third level of narrative. Organizations often jerk, lurch, and slide into decisions and directions, and we are able to follow the organization because of the rich body of myths and stories that provide a guiding force for us.

## UNDERSTANDING VERBAL COMMUNICATION

Two aspects of verbal communication are important: (a) the relationship between language and perception, and (b) the symbolic nature of language.

### Language and Perception

Language, the basis for verbal communication, is the most logical place to being our discussion. Language both facilitates and hinders our effectiveness in communication. However, because we do place a strong belief in the written word, as manifested in contracts, policy statements, and possible legal challenges, the impact of language in an organization can be one of the first issues we encounter. Our business and legal ethics mandate a dependence on language. To "get it in writing" or have the statement "signed" or "initialed" provides written proof of commitment. We also are guided in how to do our jobs by written and oral language. As Irvine (1970) observed, "A good deal of operational information flow in industry and commerce is in the form of instructions — verbal, written, or best of all, written in an instruction book and explained verbally" (p. 196).

In many ways, language is the best paradigm of the influence of perception on our understanding of reality. There is "the inescapable relation of language to the user's and the receiver's schemes of perception. To say things in a particular way is to advance a particular way of seeing — a way based on values" (Rentz & Debs, 1987, p. 38). Managers are counseled: "When planning an important communication, the focus should be on language, because it's language that governs thought, persuasion, and the perception of character, attitudes and values" (Blake, 1987, p. 43). Both of these statements reflect the capacity of language to do more than just relay facts. In organizations, there is a strong belief in the potential for persuading and changing attitudes in order to motivate people. This involves both the cognitive and affective aspects of verbal communication.

The language used can determine how a decision is made. In one study, managers who were told that a hypothetical business maneuver has an 80% chance of succeeding usually opted for the decision (McCormick, 1987). In a similar group, when told the decision had a 20% chance of failure, the overwhelming majority of managers decided not to accept the maneuver. As McCormick put it, "Decision makers often allow a decision to be 'framed' by the language or context it's presented in" (p. 2).

Killer statements, as shown in Table 4.2, often stop creative thinking because of the statements' ability to reframe an idea in a negative fashion.

Organizations frequently resist change because of the framing of the alternatives (Kehrer, 1989). In the United States, organizations held onto the concept that products made in Japan were inferior and therefore provided no real competition in the marketplace (Nora, Rogers, & Stramy, 1986, pp. 2–7). With the spectacular successes by Japanese corporations in numerous arenas, American corporations are recognizing the incorrect framing of the decision-making process (Nora et al., 1986). Public opinion researchers refer to *response bias* to explain how the wording and context of a question can "trigger connotations or interpretations in the respondent's mind that can have a major effect on how a question is answered" (Jaroslovsky, 1988, p. 56). Language, or how the problem is described, can influence our perception. In order to understand how language influences perception we also need to examine the process of identification or naming.

## Naming

A fundamental characteristic of language is its capacity to name things. During the naming process, language necessarily provides signification to the item and excludes everything else from that particular category. Language provides both division and unity because it excludes certain factors and allows a common understanding of previously disparate ones (Burke, 1969, p. 22). If someone is called a student, union leader, or IBMer, this label provides a category that explains what the person is not as well as including what the person is. Perception, you will recall from chapter 2, is the selecting, organizing, and interpreting of sensory stimulations into a meaningful and coherent picture of the world. Language is a primary mechanism used to accomplish this end. Imagine for a moment waiting to be introduced to your new manager and having one of your colleagues label the manager a "real stickler for detail." If you accept a job with the organization, you probably will be influenced by the initial description of the manager's biases. Although your job might entail a large variety of tasks, it will be difficult to not focus on paying attention to detail as a major priority in everything you do.

## Language and Understanding

Assigning a name or label to an event allows us to actually use the process in our thinking. The label or name makes the item more understandable. For example, a substantial amount of American factory jobs are now located in Mexico in *maquiladoras,* a Spanish colloquialism meaning assembly plants. In 1987, there were over 1,000 maquiladoras in operation employing over 300,000 people (Jacobson, 1988; Poppa, 1986). Although you may have little need for this term at this point, if you work for any of the major auto manufacturers, this term will be part of your everyday vocabulary (DuBay, 1987).

TABLE 4.2
Examples of Killer Statements.

1. We tried that before.
2. Our place is different.
3. It costs too much.
4. That's beyond our responsibility.
5. That's not my job.
6. We're all too busy to do that.
7. It's too radical a change.
8. We don't have the time.
9. Not enough help.
10. That will make other equipment obsolete.
11. Let's make a market research test of it first.
12. Our office is too small for that.
13. Not practical for operating people.
14. The staff will never buy it.
15. Bring it up in 6 months.
16. We've never done it before.
17. It's against company policy.
18. Runs up our overhead.
19. We don't have the authority.
20. That's too ivory tower.
21. Let's get back to reality.
22. That's not our problem.
23. Why change it, it's still working OK.
24. I don't like the idea.
25. You're right, but . . .
26. You're 2 years ahead of your time.
27. We're not ready for that.
28. We don't have the money, equipment, room, personnel.
29. It isn't in the budget.
30. Can't teach an old dog new tricks.
31. Good thought, but impractical.
32. Let's hold it in abeyance.
33. Let's give it more thought.
34. Top Management would never go for it.
35. Let's put it in writing.
36. We'll be the laughing stock.
37. Not that again.
38. We'd lose money in the long run.
39. Where'd you dig that one up?
40. We did all right without it.
41. That's what we can expect from the staff.
42. It's never been tried before.
43. Let's shelve it for the time being.
44. Let's form a committee.
45. Has anyone else ever tried it?
46. Customers won't like it.
47. I don't see the connection.
48. It won't work in our company.
49. What you are really saying is . . .

*(Continued)*

**101**

TABLE 4.2
*(Continued)*

---

50. Maybe that will work in your department, but not in mine.
51. The Executive Committee will never go for it.
52. Don't you think we should look into it further before we act?
53. What do they do in our competitor's company?
54. Let's all sleep on it.
55. It can't be done.
56. It's too much trouble to change.
57. It won't pay for itself.
58. I know a fellow who tried it.
59. It's impossible.
60. We've always done it this way.

---

The number of terms that have been added to business since the advent of the computer is remarkable. A PC now has universal meaning, whereas in 1970 there were only 23 video display terminals in use in industry (Evans & Clarke, 1984, p. 2). A new field of study, *cyberphobes,* has been developed to understand the 20% of adults who have a fear of computers, or *computerphobia* (Byrne, 1984).

However, naming also limits the application of the word because we now have specific reference for our symbol. Although we are certainly dependent on nonverbal, and sensual messages, verbal communication provides the basic underpinning for how we will interpret our world. In the case of organizational communication, it tells us how we will order and understand the events in the particular culture.

Navistar, Unisys, Contel, Trinova, and USX are all examples of words invented to establish a very specific meaning. In 1986, a record 1,382 corporations adopted new names, and the pace for 1987 was even greater ("Corporate Name," 1987). Sony Corporation's leaders chose the name Sony for its ease of pronunciation in a variety of countries. An organization coins a particular name because it "gives the company the connotations it wants for the corporate image and flexibility for the future" ("Corporate Name," 1987, p. 4B). The name is designed to provide a cognitive meaning for the organization so we know we are dealing with Unisys and not IBM. Unisys, the result of the merger of Burroughs and Sperry in 1986, cost up to $15 million in advertising, printing, signs, and other costs (Johnson, 1987, p. 6B). At the same time, the name means a variety of things to people at the affective level, and these two levels quickly become transformable and myth and reality are combined. This process was demonstrated with the Allegis discussion in chapter 1. The millions of dollars spent on finding "Allegis is thought to be one of the most expensive logo projects in history" (Winburne, 1989, p. F1). The word *Xerox* is now in the dictionary and operates on many levels of meaning.

## Denotative and Connotative Meaning

One useful way to understand the impact of language is to distinguish between *denotative* and *connotative* meanings. Both verbal and nonverbal communication have these two levels of meaning. With language, the denotative meaning is what the word literally represents. There is no disagreement about what is meant because the reference is explicitly clear to everyone. On the surface, people should have little difficulty in clearly understanding each other. We use about 2,000 words in our daily conversations, which should facilitate shared meaning. But, the 500 most used words have over 14,000 dictionary definitions (Griffin & Patton, 1976, p. 161). Many words, such as "F.Y.I.," "T.G.I.F.," or "time clock," do have denotative meanings, but people have a variety of interpretations of the meanings based on their individual experiences (Haney, 1967, pp. 63–73).

Connotative meanings depend on our own subjective reality much more than do denotative meanings (Ogden & Richards, 1953). We have a fuller meaning for each word than its specific denotative intent (Locker, 1992, pp. 142–145). The emotional and affective responses that a word evokes from us are the connotative meanings. This is a powerful perceptual issue for organizations because it involves the impression or aura surrounding the word, based on experience instead of the prescribed meaning. So, words such as *strike, union,* or *management* will be reacted to quite differently depending on who responds to the word (Schwartz, Stark, & Schiffman, 1970). Walkins (1987) offered the following advice to managers and supervisors: "Consider using the word 'quality' instead of 'productivity.' Many workers interpret productivity as meaning insecurity, loss of jobs, working harder, making profit for the company and getting nothing back" (p. 1).

When you put ASAP on a request, you probably mean you want it as soon as possible and you are expressing a sense of urgency. In recent consulting activities, I have been intrigued to find that the shipping departments in five different organizations interpret ASAP as meaning whenever possible, so take your time. The reason is that the phrase had been so overused by managers and salespeople that there is no credibility assigned to ASAP. In addition to indicating serious internal combat, the shipping people provide us with an excellent example of the connotative meaning of a phrase.

Connotative meaning also extends to a collective interpretation of a phrase, word, or concept that does not have to be explained (Hall & Nordby, 1973, pp. 38–53; Thass-Thienemann, 1968). When an organization is described as being on the "cutting edge," people seem to understand the characterization even though it is unlikely that everyone knows what the phrase really means. The organizations studied in *In Search of Excellence* initially were chosen because of a halo of esteem (Peters & Waterman, 1982). IBM frequently is named as the most admired company in *Fortune* magazine's annual survey of companies. Yet few individuals would be able to explain the specific reasons why they feel it is an excellent company.

## Jargon

Although increasingly part of everyone's communication, concepts such as perks, quality circles, "just-in-time" suppliers, VAM (value-added manufacturing), TQC (total quality control), robotics, and MBWA originated in certain organizations. Each of these terms began as jargon, which is the specialized or technical language used in an organization. It functions as a shorthand code comprehensible to co-workers. As Kunerth (1983) explained, "A single word of jargon can identify an object, concept or task that would require an elaborate explanation for someone outside the field. The special language of an occupation speeds communication within a closed fraternity of workers, while effectively excluding others" (p. 1). Each organizational culture develops specific terms for describing events.

Jargon serves to both include members of the profession and exclude outsiders. Jargon can be wielded as an instrument of power, intimidation, and evasion. A physician might refer to "axilla bromidromsis" instead of an armpit's foul-smelling odor and make the patient fearful of a problem that might simply be a long shower away from being cured (Kunerth, 1983, p. 17). Legal terminology is beyond the grasp of the uninitiated. Some college professors appear to be guilty of judging the competence of an article partially by its reading difficulty with increased difficulty being positively related to increased competence (Armstrong, 1980). Tracy and Lee's (1984) article, "Acculturation of Graduate Business Students to Academic Values: Abstruseness as a Criterion of Competence," discusses the impact of higher education jargon on the MBA student who eventually learns to like using it because the faculty assigns it greater credibility.

The government frequently uses terms such as *revenue enhancement* for tax increases and organizations use *selective cutbacks* to mean firings. The Department of Defense seems to be especially adept at using jargon to alter meaning. A hammer is called "a manually powered fastener-driving impact device," a steel nut is a "hexiform rotatable surface compression unit," and a tent is a "frame-supported tension structure" (Marklein, 1987, p. D1).

When discussing the Challenger tragedy, NASA called it an "anomaly," the astronauts' bodies "recovered components," and their coffins "crew transfer containers." An Air Force Cruise missile "terminated 5 minutes earlier than planned" because it "impacted with the ground prematurely." Finally, one set of high school football players was just "deficient at a grading period" rather than failing their classes (Marklein, 1987, p. D1). Chrysler received the 1989 English teachers' doublespeak award "for telling AMC [American Motors Corporation] workers their new 'career alternative enhancement program' meant they were fired" ("The Envelope," 1989, p. D1).

Although these euphemisms were used to obscure meaning, careful wording also can help prevent offending people. Officials at Expo 86 in Vancouver, British Columbia expected "the occasional protein spill" from people on park rides, police were "security hosts," and rest rooms were "guest relations facilities."

Gummidge's Law was formulated because jargon can be abused. The law states: The amount of expertise varies in inverse proportion to the number of statements understood by the general public (Dickson, 1978, p. 109). If we can make something difficult to decipher, people are more likely to believe us. The law originated from the following story:

> The scene opens at Instant College, where a student is being briefed by key faculty members on the importance of learning jargon on the way to becoming an Expert. Dr. Gummidge, professor of sociology, tells the student, "Remember Gummidge's Law and you will never be *Found Out*." Gummidge illustrates by telling the student how he would tell a student's mother that he was a lazy, good-for-nothing: "The student in question is performing minimally for his peer group and is an emerging under-achiever." (Dickson, 1978, p. 109)

As you can see, irony is one means of dealing with language abuses.

Letters of reference and written performance reviews can use carefully selected terms to provide an insider's knowledge of the true meaning as shown in Table 4.3. Being obscure is a tactic that is not limited to the use of jargon.

TABLE 4.3
Decoding Device for Letters of Reference and Performance Review

| CODE WORDS-THIS | TRANSLATION-MAY REALLY MEAN |
|---|---|
| "careful thinker" | won't make a decision |
| "strong principles" | stubborn |
| "spends extra hours on the job" | miserable home life |
| "average employee" | not too bright |
| "active socially" | drinks too much |
| "zealous attitude" | opinionated |
| "takes pride in work" | conceited |
| "uses logic on hard problems" | finds another to do the job |
| "forceful" | argumentative |
| "conscientious" | scared |
| "meticulous attention to detail" | nitpicker |
| "of great value to the organization" | gets to work on time or turns in work on time |
| "has leadership qualities" | is tall or has a loud voice |
| "average" | not too bright |
| "exceptionally well qualified" | has committed no major blunders |
| "unlimited potential" | will stick until retirement |
| "quick thinking" | offers plausible excuses for error |
| "indifferent to instruction" | knows more than his or her superiors |
| "tactful in dealing with superiors" | knows when to keep mouth shut |
| "takes every opportunity to progress" | drinks with the boss |
| "gets along well with superiors & subordinates" | is a crowd |
| "unusually loyal" | nobody else wants him or her |
| "alert to company developments" | is a gossip |

*Note.* Adapted from Fritz (1985). Copyright © 1985 Prentice-Hall. Reprinted by permission.

*Buzzwords,* or business slang, are a special category of jargon. In a recent survey of the Fortune 1,000 vice presidents, buzzwords were seen as being inappropriate for formal reports, but useful for a variety of other business related activities. As Gilsdorf (1983) related, "Most respondents feel that business slang can sometimes improve communication, make talking easier, make talking more comfortable, be amusing, or be the most precise and exact way to say a thing. Many also felt, however, that business slang expressions are boring, almost four-fifths said they sometimes do not understand a given business slang expression" (p. 41). Table 4.4 shows the buzzwords included in the survey.

A good example of a universal buzzword is "here's my card." The business card has become the organizational coin of the realm and provides an excellent paradigm for seeing the impact of written communication, and understanding how representation (the card) becomes presentation (the perceived impact). Most large corporations have a specific type of card format for everyone from the beginning salespeople to the president. At the other end of the scale, entrepreneurs make their cards memorable by using metal, leather, wood, plastic, backed adherence for easy placing in Rolodex files, and a large number of color symbols and metallic lettering alternatives. The business card's importance can be gauged partially by the $50 million a year spent in printing the cards ("Business Cards," 1983). The card's design can be used to project a specific image. Jargon is a specialized form of verbal communication that occurs in all organizations and professions.

## SEMANTIC/SYMBOLIC ANALYSIS

Semantics offers an explanation for why organizations simply can develop new names, or why words are so open to multiple interpretations. Three principles of semantics help us understand how verbal communication operates.

First, meaning is in people, not words. Words do not mean, people mean. These two sentences are popular summations of the important principle that everyone has his or her own interpretation of reality (Keltner, 1970, p. 69).

Second, language is *representational.* As we already have seen, the word is not the thing. The word is merely a symbolic representation of an idea or object (Condon, 1975, p. 13). We are free to create whatever words we choose, and our only limitation is what other people interpret the words to mean. We can take a term and make it represent a reality, but the shared meaning is *transactional.*

In 1987, Ford Motor Company surpassed General Motors in profit for the first time since the Model T, and many individuals attributed the success to the types of behaviors fostered by the slogan "Quality is Job 1" (Eaton, 1987, pp. E1–E2). Suppliers to Ford must obtain a "Q101" rating from Ford. For every company involved, Q101 has become part of their language, used on an everyday basis throughout the organization, even though it has no actual meaning. However, based on my consulting experience with some Ford suppliers, and their production departments,

TABLE 4.4
Examples of Buzzwords

| | |
|---|---|
| gopher | blind side |
| sweating bullets | parameters |
| K (for thousand) | GIGO |
| entropy | liaison function |
| eyeball-to-eyeball | logistics |
| reinventing the wheel | modality |
| back to square one | mentoring |
| hands-on | viable |
| conventional wisdom | case in point |
| glitch | vis-a-vis |
| mid-course correction | watershed |
| reworking | RIF-list |
| accountability | ball park figure |
| counterproductive | mindset |
| hardball | bottom line |

*Note.* From Gilsdorf (1983). Reprinted by permission.

reactions to Q101 vary dramatically depending on what type of threat is involved in being required to meet the Q101 standards. Not meeting Q101 standards means not getting the contract. Some suppliers might see the concept as an open demand that they alter their means of production just to please Ford, which could lead to resentment and possible resistance. Words then are arbitrary because there is no one-to-one relationship between words and things. Words are assigned to things by agreement or by social and cultural convention (Hayakawa, 1972, pp. 150–154; Korbinski, 1933, chapter 25).

Third, both *observations* and *inferences* occur when we use verbal communication. This semantic distortion needs to identified, although there is little likelihood you would want to eliminate it. A statement of observation is factual, can be observed and verified, and is about the past or the present. Inferences can be made by anyone about anything in any time frame (Haney, 1967, pp. 63–73). In other words, inferences are much less reliable if we are interested only in the facts. However, inferences comprise a substantial portion of organizational communication.

Organizations spend a great deal of time trying to prevent overly abstract instructions. In one organization, there is a large sign saying "never ASS-U-ME" anything is clear, unless both individuals can agree on the exact meaning. Too many errors occur because people assume they have been understood and end up making the sign come true.

In conclusion, we have focused on three principles: Meaning is in people not words, language is representational, and there is an important distinction between observations and inferences.

Part of the confusion regarding verbal communication comes from its multiple uses. In an organization, language has at least four functions (Fisher, 1981, pp. 98–99). The *expressive function* is where language is used to provide information about ourselves. The *social structuring function* is where talk maintains and enhances relationships. When we are telling others what to do, we are using the *directive function*. Finally, there is a *ritual function* where certain ceremonies are used to convey on others special honors or distinctions. Obviously, success in each of these four functions requires a different communication emphasis.

## VERBAL COMMUNICATION—ORGANIZATIONAL USES

Our second area of interest is the use of symbolic verbal communication. First, every organization uses specific means for obtaining organizational goals, and language is one of the most important. A sense of identification between the individual and an organization is vital. In essence, organization members must buy into an "organizational personality . . . accepting the values and goals of the organization as relevant to on-the-job decisions" (Thompkins & Cheney, 1983, p. 125). Even more fundamentally, "language is the primary vehicle in this process of identification, and the ways in which it is shaped and used by the individual often reveals his or her organizational personality—the extent to which the person has adopted the values of the organization" (Rentz & Debs, 1987, p. 44). Very little of this type of information is obtained through the cognitive level. In fact, organizations operate at the affective level and myths become reality.

### Stories and Myths

A tremendous amount of information is passed on to members of an organization through the telling of stories and myths (Peters, 1987, pp. 418–419). These tell "about how the organization dealt with key competitors in the past, how it developed a new and exciting product, how it dealt with a valued employee, and so on, not only to spell out the basic mission and specific goals (and thereby reaffirming them) but also to reaffirm the organization's picture of itself, its own theory of how to get things done and how to handle internal relationships" (Schein, 1985, p. 81). Although an organization's formal documents spell out the official statements of ideology, these informal means are what actually guide the organization. Sony cofounder Akio Morito tells this story to all of his salespeople: "Two shoe sales representatives find themselves in a rustic backwater of Africa. The first writes back to the head office, 'No prospect of sales. Natives do not wear shoes.' The second writes, 'No one wears shoes here. We can dominate the market. Send all possible stock.' "

This story could become simply another of the "great salesperson" stories that dominate all sales cultures. But, it takes on a mythical nature because it clearly spells out the need for optimism and opportunity hunting by Sony salespeople. Because it is delivered by the cofounder to all sales recruits, the story has an added dimension and significance. It becomes perceived reality for how a Sony salesperson must think and act.

In chapter 3, we outlined the characteristics of a sales-oriented organizational culture which can be labeled as work-hard, play-hard. As Deal and Kennedy (1982) explained, "Language plays a big part in the business rituals of the work-hard culture. The perfect sales pitch enjoys a special position in the folklore" (p. 115).

All organizations have stories about past events. Of particular value to many organizations are the "stories recounting the histories of these visionary heroes [which] pass from generation to generation of managers" (Deal & Kennedy, 1982, p. 44). Tom Watson (IBM), William Kellogg, and Charles Steinmetz (GE) all have extensive stories told about them that reinforce the importance of the individual with a vision to the success of a corporation. During each generation, new heroes emerge who "are known to virtually every employee with more than a few months tenure in the company. And they show every employee 'here's what you have to do to succeed around here' " (Deal & Kennedy, 1982, p. 14). In a nutshell: "Through stories, parables, and other forms of oral and written history, an organization can communicate its ideology and basic assumptions—especially to newcomers, who need to know what is important not only in abstract terms but by means of concrete examples that can be emulated" (Schein, 1985, p. 82).

In organizations where the culture does not foster positive employee responses to management, heroes still emerge among the individuals who are working for the company. Stories about these "counterculture heroes" also provide employees with rules, only these explain how to beat the system rather than support it.

## Transmitting Values

The values ". . . are the basic concepts of an organization; as such they form the heart of the corporate culture. Values define 'success' in concrete terms for employees—'if you do this, you too will be a success'—and establish standards of achievement within the organization" (Deal & Kennedy, 1982, pp. 13–14). An organization that carries the message "never be responsible for making a mistake" (or at least getting caught) passes on a very different sense of values from the 3M Company which states: "Never be responsible for killing an idea" (Deal & Kennedy, 1982, p. 151). The use of *slogans and creeds* allows companies to emphasize their organizational culture's particular emphasis, as shown in Table 4.5.

Heroes personify the values of the culture and act as role models for other employees to follow. All of this information is transmitted through the cultural network. As the primary (and informal) means of communication within an organization, the cultural network is the primary "carrier" of the corporate values and the heroic mythology. Storytellers, spies, priests, cabals, and whisperers form a hidden hierarchy of power within the company. Working the network effectively is the only way to get things done or to understand what is really going on (Deal & Kennedy, 1982, p. 15). Chapter 6, Networks and Channels, outlines in detail the roles each of these individuals play in an organization. The means they use is verbal communication.

TABLE 4.5
Slogans, Creeds, and Shared Values

| | |
|---|---|
| Continental Bank: | *"We'll find a way"* |
|   Expresses a concern for meeting customer needs. | |
| Merrill Lynch: | *"A breed apart"* |
|   Statement about belief in stock market investments and policies. | |
| American Telephone & Telegraph: | *"Universal service"* |
|   Commitment to reliable service. | |
| Delta Airlines: | *"The Delta family feeling"* |
|   Development of team orientation. | |
| Toshiba: | *"In touch with tomorrow"* |
|   Product development. | |
| Honeywell: | *"Together, we can find the answers"* |
|   Teamwork and research. | |
| General Electric: | *"Progress is our most important product"* |
|   Product development. | |
| DuPont: | *"Better things for better living through chemistry"* |
|   Product development, with an emphasis on chemicals. | |
| Sears, Roebuck: | *"Quality at a good price"* |
|   Orientation to middle America. | |
| Rouse Company: | *"Create the best environment for people"* |
|   Orientation toward distinctive housing developments. | |
| Leo Burnett Advertising Agency: | *"Make great ads"* |
|   Restatement of business philosophy. | |
| Dana Corporation: | *"Productivity through people"* |
|   Commitment to and from employees. | |
| Chubb Insurance Company: | *"Underwriting excellence"* |
|   Summation of goals. | |
| Price, Waterhouse & Company: | *"Strive for technical perfection"* |
|   Accounting firm's clear statement. | |

## Metaphors

Metaphors operate as verbal statements about the organizational culture and the individual member's perception. They function to symbolize something as if it were something else. When we say the world's a stage, we are stating a great deal about our view of reality. Metaphors, like stories and myths, compress complicated issues into understandable images and allow members to make sense out of the organization (Pettigrew, 1985). Metaphors "affect our attitudes, evaluations, and actions. A college president who sees the university as a factory will probably be different from a president who sees the university as a craft guild or a shopping center. Consultants who see themselves as physicians are likely to be different from consultants who see themselves as salesmen or rain dancers" (Bolman & Deal, 1984, p. 164). If an organization is perceived as a fighting unit (military metaphor), a well-oiled machine (structural and mechanistic metaphor), or a winning team (a sports metaphor), three entirely different assumptions of reality are being presented. Table 4.6 presents some

TABLE 4.6
Metaphors

---

*Metaphors Applied to Organizations*

---

These metaphors have been used to compare an organization or a department to another type of activity. By speaking about one thing as if it were another, greater clarity can be gained in understanding the underlying feelings and operation.

| | | |
|---|---|---|
| Big happy family | Police department | Cornucopia |
| Athletic team | Santa Claus | Volcano |
| Zoo | Military unit | Battlefield |
| Well-oiled machine | Disneyland | Insane asylum |
| Play pen | Circus | Garbage can |
| Penitentiary | Garden | Snake pit |
| Pyramid | Boiling cauldron | Steamroller |
| Circle | Dragon | Swamp |
| Windmill | Quick sand | Stage |
| First class | Explorers | Warriors |

*Metaphors Applied to Four Frames*

---

The four-frame approach can be further understood by applying metaphors to each frame.

| Frame | Metaphor |
|---|---|
| Structural | Well-oiled machine |
| Human Relations | Big, happy family or team |
| Political | Chain of command, troops, flank attack |
| Symbolic | Productivity through people (Dana Corp.) |
| | The Delta Family Feeling |

commonly used metaphors and show how the four frames presented in chapter 3 can be applied. According to Redding (1984), "One of the best ways, for instance, to identify a manager's style of managing is to listen carefully for the metaphors he or she uses when referring to the company, the job, or to employees" (p. 105). In *The Corporate Warriors,* Ramsey (1986) discussed business in terms of battles involving the strategies of maneuvering, unity of command, and security with the ultimate goal for the leader to be a successful general leading troops to victory. If there is a preponderance of military metaphors, then there will be "war." Anyone following Ramsey's advice would lean toward a military approach.

## Language and Management

Managers and supervisors are encouraged to use language that makes people feel good about themselves and the job they are doing. This demand for the use of positive reinforcement through language shows a strong belief in the power of the spoken word (Redding, 1984, pp. 107–123). In addition, numerous suggestions have been made for managers to learn to use the right word at the right time to enhance employee motivation. One article advises: "But you can motivate through a compliment and helping to motivate subordinates is part of your job. Just give some thought to the why, when and how of delivering the 'good word' " ("The Right," 1982). The trick, or needed insight, for the manager is to choose the correct wording for the situation by accurately perceiving the needed symbolic message. For example, managers must be adept at giving less than positive feedback in order to correct problems without damaging the relationship.

Not only is verbal communication used to motivated, it also is used to predict, control, manage, coordinate, and perpetuate organizations. Managers must define for other employees exactly what is expected of them in a given situation and the various means of verbal communication provide an excellent avenue. Moving from connotative to denotative language is encouraged as a means to avoid emotionally charged words (Denton, 1987, p. 10). Sometimes, managers are required to turn down various requests by subordinates. According to Izraeli and Jick (1986), "The art of saying 'no' then is a process of redefining the situation and of managing meaning. The situated activity in which this is done we call a 'refusal ceremony' " (p. 285). How effectively the manager succeeds in saying no while maintaining a sense of commitment probably will turn up in the stories told to other members of the group about the encounter by the subordinate.

## Inconsistencies

When faced with difficult verbal communication situations, organizational members may choose to present inconsistent statements to maintain the strategic advantage of being able to claim deniability. Negotiators of contracts may "deliberately use ambiguous or unclear language to avoid squabbles that might slow down or prevent a settlement" (Scott & Bain, 1987, p. 10). This same pressure often influences the manager who may say one thing and mean quite another. As Table 4.7 shows, the stated message actually has a much deeper meaning. The difference between these messages and euphemisms is that managers are monitored directly by subordinates who must implement the vague statements. Eisenberg (1984) made a strong case for the importance of some strategic ambiguities in organizations as a means for maintaining interpersonal relationships and supporting status distinctions. There are times when the only way to deal with apparently impossible situations is to be unclear. We all have been faced with a situation where a compliment was required for something we did not think was well done. So, we issued an ambiguous comment like: "that's certainly different," or "you don't see many done that way anymore," or "only you would think to put those items together."

Likewise, public relations specialists, or spokespersons and wordsmiths, often are placed in the position of having to make statements that are ambiguous or unclear. Presenting a positive organizational image to the public is one of the goals of a good spokesperson. However, in a moment of crisis, or in responses to difficult

TABLE 4.7
Management Inconsistencies

| We say: | We mean: |
| --- | --- |
| I plan. | Objectives are vague and contradictory. |
| I make decisions based on facts. | Emotions, opinions, and personalities come first. |
| I manage by objectives. | They may be *my* objectives, but the people who will do the work have not been involved. |
| I believe in job enrichment. | Pay is all I care about. |
| I use control systems to measure progress. | The things that we're measuring aren't important. |
| I do my job. | Much of my time is wasted on organizational politics and power plays. |

*Note.* Adapted from Fritz (1985). Copyright © 1985 by Prentice-Hall. Reprinted by permission.

questions, the wordsmith often tries to forward the best possible company image (Daniels & Spiker, 1987, pp. 219–220). Protecting this image, or working toward the greatest possible profits for the organization, has led to cover-ups, changes in the facts presented, or simple denial. Because of abuses, which often have included lying or strongly altering the truth, public relations has a negative image in the minds of many individuals (Grunig & Hunt, 1984, pp. 63–64). Most recent texts on public relations have counseled the spokesperson to try to avoid the behaviors that often backfire (e.g., Grunig & Hunt, 1984; Pinsdorf, 1987). However, the spokesperson is put in the incongruent position of protecting the organization while seeming to disclose fully to the public. So, the wordsmiths, who are paid to present a good public image, and not put the organization in a bad public light, are forced to resolve an incongruency between truth and job security.

Paradoxes also can occur in the nature of commands, such as the manager who tells you "don't regard everything I say as an order, and that's an order," or the parent who tells the child "I've told you a million times, don't exaggerate!" To be told that all generalizations about organizations are incorrect also would appear to be paradoxical, although perhaps true (another paradox). The need for more employee creativity has become apparent to many organizations. In response, they have ordered employees to "be creative" which, as you probably already have noticed, is a *paradoxical injunction.* It often can be turned into a *double bind* when there is a time limit placed on when the solution must be ready. So, if the employee takes the time to be creative, the answer will be late. If the answer is on time, it might not be very creative.

The oxymoron provides a nice example of the paradoxical phrase. According to Blumenfeld (1986), "An oxymoron is two concepts that do not go together but are used together. It is the bringing together of two contradictory terms" (p. 36). For example, near miss, even odds, justifiably paranoid, almost candid, intense apathy, postal service, deliberate speed, qualified success, almost perfect, eloquent silence, negative benefit, original copy, routine emergency, same difference, minimum competency, functional illiterate, pure filth, a firm maybe, extensive briefing, awfully good, objective rating, second deadline, constant variable, pretty ugly, perfect misfit, and pure nonsense are oxymorons that appear in a variety of organizations and conversations (Blumenfeld, 1986, 1989). Although many of these are humorous, a large number of these terms are actually the strategic use of ambiguity. By saying something is a qualified success, the originator of the comment still can criticize the outcome because the praise is carefully hedged.

## Humor

Humor is an excellent example of the importance of incongruences. Most humor is based on paradoxes and incongruences (Smith & Williamson, 1985, pp. 262–263). Although managing and work are supposed to be "serious business," humor provides organizational members with a means for coping with the various paradoxes and incongruences that are inherent in any organized activity (Lippitt, 1982). Sometimes laughter is the best medicine for tough organizational situations that are steeped in tension (Gibson, Ivancevich, & Donnelly, 1991, p. 253). In fact, "it is less important to ask why people are humorous in organizations than to ask why they are so serious" (Bolman & Deal, 1991, p. 266).

Humor can be used to "share messages, relieve stress, motivate employees" (Sleeter, 1981, p. 25), make a point in a strategic manner, relay interest, enhance group behavior (Duncan, 1982), facilitate team building (Kiechel, 1986), and allow the discussion of delicate issues without requiring a full commitment (Smith & Williamson, 1985, p. 279). Humor can be an excellent means of conveying messages and meanings to people, which also can increase the listener's acceptance (Frost, Mitchell, & Nord, 1986, pp. 361–362). According to Bolman and Deal (1984), in organizations:

> Humor integrates, expresses skepticism, contributes to flexibility and adaptiveness, and indicates status. Humor is a classic device for distancing, but it can also be used to socialize, include, and convey membership. Humor can establish solidarity and promote face saving. Most importantly, humor is a way of illuminating and breaking frames to indicate that any single definition of the situation is arbitrary. (p. 164)

In one organization, in response to the demand that supervisors improve the work climate, a plaque began appearing that stated: "firings will continue until morale improves." Because the supervisors could not openly question the order, paradox and humor were used to partially alleviate the stress. Humor often involves nonverbal as well as verbal communication (Boland & Hoffman, 1986). The various rites and rituals of a work group often are tied to the humor used by the members (Roy, 1960).

When I first started teaching, one of my colleagues remarked that teaching would be a great job if it was not for the students. Although his comment was funny, the paradox he raises actually exists when it comes to customer service. The Confederation of British Industry (Berstein, 1983) started its book *Working for Customers* with this story: "A local authority, told that its bus drivers were 'speeding past queues of people with a smile and a wave of the hand' replied that it's impossible for drivers to keep their timetables if they have to stop for passengers" (p. 3). In these two examples, the communicator is able to express an idea without fully indicating the source of the humor. The professor simply was overworked because of pressures to publish and serve on committees. Members of organizations often are told to treat customers with respect, but always meet production deadlines and reduce expenditures. Table 4.8 is used to highlight the errors managers may make when they evaluate subordinates. Because it overstates the potential biases, managers can simultaneously smile at the examples and identify their own tendencies to make incorrect judgments.

Organizations can be characterized in a humorous fashion. Weick argued that instead of viewing organizations as smooth running machines, we instead should see them as garrulous, clumsy, haphazard, hypothetical, monstrous, octopoid, wondering, grouchy, and galumphing (Bolman & Deal, 1984, p. 165). March and Olsen (1976) went one step further with their garbage can metaphor. Organizations are portrayed as organized anarchies where problems, solutions, participants, and choice opportunities interact almost in a random fashion as the organization moves toward the future. After enough people sift through the contents, some type of decision emerges out of a process of interpretation (Robey, 1991, pp. 39–41). Both of these depictions of organizations debunk the concept of a rational model of organization and decision making.

These characterizations strike a cord of reality for organizational researchers,

TABLE 4.8
How to Distinguish Between a Subordinate You Like and One You Do Not Like

| *The one you like:* | *The one you do not like:* |
| --- | --- |
| IS AGGRESSIVE | IS PUSHY |
| IS GOOD ON DETAIL | IS PICKY |
| GETS DEPRESSED FROM WORK PRESSURES | CAN'T STAND THE HEAT |
| IS CONFIDENT | IS CONCEITED |
| DRINKS BECAUSE OF EXCESSIVE WORK PRESSURES | IS A LUSH |
| IS A STERN TASKMASTER | IS IMPOSSIBLE TO WORK FOR |
| IS ENTHUSIASTIC | IS EMOTIONAL |
| FOLLOWS THROUGH | DOESN'T KNOW WHEN TO QUIT |
| STANDS FIRM | IS BULLHEADED |
| HAS SOUND JUDGMENT | HAS STRONG PREJUDICES |
| ISN'T AFRAID TO SAY WHAT HE/SHE THINKS | IS MOUTHY |
| IS CLOSE-MOUTHED | IS SECRETIVE |
| CLIMBED THE LADDER OF SUCCESS | MARRIED INTO THE BOSS'S FAMILY |

or practicing managers, who are trying to make sense out of certain organizational behaviors. Organizations are not always "tightly run ships" that concern themselves with rational decision making. At the same time, Weick and March and Olsen have been challenged for their tendencies to overgeneralize (Pettigrew, 1985). One obvious limitation relates to the size of an organization. A small family business will operate with a much smaller "trash can," and probably will be a little less monstrous and octopoid, simply because the store or business must be opened on a daily basis. In addition, the chaotic description carries more validity with upper level management, who are in charge of the planning functions, than with front-line supervisors or managers. However, in both of these examples, the individuals involved still must deal with the external environment replete with whatever octopoid tendencies it may possess (e.g., government regulations, incompetent bosses, late delivery of supplies).

This short discussion underlines the requirement made in the beginning of this chapter, and at the end of chapter 3, that a both/and perspective is most likely to assist you in understanding organizations. Organizations are chaotic and predictable. Decisions are justified after the fact and also carefully planned. Both are true and the popularity of Murphy's Laws may be attributable to the unpredictable nature of organizations, as shown in Table 4.9.

We have discussed the impact of stories, myths, metaphors, inconsistencies, and humor in organizations. The particular type of culture operating also has an effect on the verbal communication. In turn, the verbal communication perpetuates the predominant culture.

## VERBAL COMMUNICATION AND CULTURES

One means for you to understand the types of verbal communication used by the various cultures would be to reexamine the discussion of cultures in chapter 3. Our working definition of culture, the way we do things around here, provides an insight into the type of verbal communication being used. In Table 3.8, four interpretations of organizational processes, the communication process was outlined for the structural, human resources, political, and symbolic frames. In the structural view, communication is used to transmit facts and information. This coincides with our opening discussion of the uses of verbal communication. The goal of the communication is to direct the organization. In this type of organization, stories, myths, and humor do not disappear, they become part of a subculture that is not necessarily approved of by management.

The human resource frame uses verbal communication to exchange information, feelings, and needs. Involvement and open communication are the primary goals of this managerial approach. In addition to the handing out of information, there would be a much greater use of the stories, myths, and metaphors to create a participatory organization. Although management would not actively seek to create

TABLE 4.9

Murphy's Laws

1. If anything can go wrong, it will.
2. Nothing is ever as simple as it seems.
3. Everything takes longer than you expect.
4. If there is a possibility of several things going wrong, the one that will go wrong first will be the one that will do the most damage.
5. If you play with something long enough, you surely will break it.
6. Left to themselves, things go from bad to worse.
7. If everything seems to be going well, you have obviously overlooked something.
8. If you see that there are four possible ways in which a procedure can go wrong, and circumvent these, then a fifth way, unprepared for, will probably develop.
9. Nature always sides with the hidden flaw.
10. It is impossible to make anything foolproof, because fools are so ingenious.
11. If a great deal of time has been expended seeking the answer to a problem with the only result being failure, the answer will be immediately obvious to the first unqualified person.
12. Murphy applied to the collegiate experience:
    a. During an exam, the pocket calculator battery will fail.
    b. Exams will always contain questions not discussed in class.
    c. All students who obtain a B will feel cheated out of an A.
    d. Campus sidewalks never exist as the straightest line between two points.
    e. At five minutes before the hour, a student will ask a question requiring a ten minute answer.
    f. When a student finally does a homework assignment, the instructor will not ask for it.
    g. If an instructor says "it's obvious," it isn't.
    h. If a student has to study, he will claim the course is unfair.
    i. Students who obtain an A for a course will claim that the instructor is a great teacher.
13. and so on . . .

myths, they certainly would support any verbal communication behavior that enhances individual and group development.

When conflict becomes the predominate view of organization leaders, the verbal communication is seen as a means to influence or manipulate. The dominance of power leads to careful selection of verbal communication techniques. Stories about "wins and losses" predominate and language is carefully selected to make certain no one can "score."

Symbolic approaches opt for the telling of stories to enhance shared values. Ritual is a vital part of these cultures and verbal communication is basic to all rituals.

As we indicated in chapter 3, these are not definitive categories. In any organization or office, there are likely to be some of each of these orientations. How communication is used varies depending on the perception of the organization's members.

In general, the means with which people "make common" their understanding of the organization's written and unwritten rules provides specific information about verbal communication. All organizations have cultures and innumerable stories, myths, heroes, and villains. When management fails to nurture proactive cultural attributes, various subcultures or "undergrounds" still will provide stories of the heroes or guerilla leaders, and the various battles, successes, and failures. These counterculture heroes also epitomize important symbolic messages to other organizational members about how to respond to the organization.

## CONCLUSION

Verbal communication is a critical part of every organization's behavior system. It acts as the link between the various groups, subsystems, and individuals in the organization. Both written and oral communication are important, although practicing managers and supervisors prefer oral communication.

Language has a direct impact on our perception of our organizational reality. That reality is cognitive, affective, and narrative and we continually move between these three perspectives. As Crow (1988) put it, "The language of the workplace . . . thrives at the workplace itself, in the thoughts and values—not just the words— of those who use it" (p. 94). Language allows us to label parts of our working environment and, in so doing, provide signification. By naming someone blue collar, white collar, pink collar, gray collar, or gold collar, we both include and exclude individuals. Gold collar is a term being applied by personnel directors to recent college graduates who expect to receive excellent jobs immediately upon graduation. Denotative and connotative meaning occur every time we use verbal communication. Calling someone a "suit" has a connotative meaning that is much more important than the denotative description of a person's working attire.

Two approaches provide important information regarding verbal communication. The first, based on semantics, explains the tendency of language to move from the specific to the general. When instructions are considered, for example, it is in the best interest of all concerned to make the information clear. Jargon is an excellent example of the impact of naming on organizational reality. However, "no two people can ever have exactly the same meaning for the same word" (Millar & Millar, 1976, pp. 38–39).

The second approach deals with an organization's need to function in spite of ambiguity. Common cultural appeals provide a direction. In addition, the lack of clarity allows appeals to much loftier and more abstract concepts. In the use of metaphors, myths, stories, and humor lies the impact of cultures and the capacity to motivate. For you to be successful in understanding a particular organization, you must understand both levels of language use in verbal communication.

## REFERENCES

Albert, M. (1987). Transmitting corporate culture through case stories. *Personnel Journal, 64,* 69–73.
Albrecht, K. (1988). *At America's service.* Homewood, IL: Dow Jones-Irwin.
Armstrong, J. R. (1980). Unintelligible research and academic prestige. *Interfaces, 10,* 80–86.
Bangs, D. H., Jr., & Osgood, W. R. (1988). *Business planning guide.* Portsmouth, NH: Upstart.
Baron, R. A. (1983). *Behavior in organizations.* Boston: Allyn & Bacon.

Bednar, A. S., & Olney, R. J. (1987). Communication needs of recent graduates. *The Bulletin, 50,* 20–22.

Berstein, D. (1983). *Working for customers.* London: Confederation of Business Industry.

Bissell, D. (1988). The manager's balancing act. *Management World, 17,* 39–40.

Bittel, L. R. (1980). *What every supervisor should know* (4th ed.). New York: McGraw-Hill.

Blake, L. (1987). Communicate with clarity: Manage meaning. *Personnel Journal, 66,* 43–45.

Blumenfeld, W. S. (1986). Business communication versus the ubiquitous, but insidious, oxymoron: A semantic gotcha. *The Bulletin, 44,* 33–36.

Blumenfeld, W. S. (1989). *Pretty ugly: More oxymorons & other illogical expressions that make absolute sense.* New York: Perigee.

Boland, R. J., Jr., & Hoffman, R. (1986). Humor in a machine stop: An interpretation of symbolic action. In P. J. Frost, V. F. Mitchell, & W. R. Nord (Eds.), *Organizational reality* (3rd ed., pp. 371–376). Glenview, IL: Scott, Foresman.

Bolman, L. G., & Deal, T. E. (1984). *Modern approaches to understanding and managing organizations.* San Francisco: Jossey-Bass.

Bolman, L. G., & Deal, T. E. (1991). *Reframing organizations: Artistry, choice, and leadership.* San Francisco: Jossey-Bass.

Bowman, J. P., & Targowski, A. S. (1987). Modeling the communication process: The map is not the territory. *The Journal of Business Communication, 24,* 21–34.

Boyd, L. E. (1984, November). Why "talking it out" almost never works out. *Nation's Business,* pp. 53–54.

Brusaw, C. T., Alred, G. J., & Oliu, W. E. (1987). *The business writer's handbook* (3rd ed.). New York: St. Martin's Press.

Burke, K. (1969). *A grammar of motives.* Berkeley: University of California Press.

Business cards. (1983, October 25). *Chicago Tribune,* Sec. 3, p. 3.

Byrne, R. B. (1984). Overcoming computerphobia. In S. H. Evans & P. Clarke (Eds.), *The computer culture* (pp. 76–101). Indianapolis: White River Press.

Capitalizing on complaints. (1987, September). *INC,* p. 112.

Condon, J. C., Jr. (1975). *Semantics and communication* (2nd ed.). New York: Macmillan.

Conrad, C. (1985). *Strategic organizational communication.* New York: Holt, Rinehart & Winston.

Corporate name changes. (1987, July 8). *USA Today,* p. 4B.

Crow, P. (1988). Plain English: What counts besides readibility? *The Journal of Business Communication, 25,* 87–95.

Daniels, T. D., & Spiker, B. K. (1987). *Perspectives on organizational communication.* Dubuque, IA: Brown.

Deal, T. E., & Kennedy, A. A. (1982). *Corporate cultures: The rites and rituals of corporate life.* Reading, MA: Addison-Wesley.

Denton, D. K. (1987). If you want your ideas approved. In *Problem solving* (pp. 10–14). New York: American Management Association.

Dickson, P. (1978). *The official rules.* New York: Dell.

DuBay, K. (1987, August 25). Auto plants payrolls are mushrooming south of the border. *The Evansville Courier,* p. 7.

Duncan, J. W. (1982, January). Humor in management: Prospects for administrative practice and research. *Academy of Management Review, 7,* 136–142.

Eaton, J. (1987, February 18). Ford's better idea: Quality, workers no. 1. *The Denver Post,* pp. E1–E2.

Eisenberg, E. M. (1984). Ambiguity as a strategy in organizational communication. *Communication Monographs, 51,* 227–242.

The envelope, please. (1989, January 1). *The Sunday Courier,* p. D1.

Evans, S. H., & Clarke, P. (1984). Introduction. In S. H. Evans & P. Clarke (Eds.), *The computer culture* (pp. 1–8). Indianapolis: White River Press.

Farace, R. V., Monge, P. R., & Russell, H. M. (1977). *Communicating and organizing.* Reading, MA: Addison-Wesley.

Fisher, D. (1981). *Communication in organizations.* St. Paul, MN: West.

Flatley, M. E. (1982). A comparative analysis of the written communication of managers at various organizational levels in the private business sectors. *The Journal of Business Communication, 19,* 35–49.

Fritz, R. (1985). *Rate yourself as a manager.* Englewood Cliffs, NJ: Prentice-Hall.

Frost, P. J., Mitchell, V. F., & Nord, W. R. (1986). Humor. In P. J. Frost, V. F. Mitchell, & W. R. Nord (Eds.), *Organizational reality* (3rd ed., pp. 361–362). Glenview, IL: Scott, Foresman.

Gibson, J. L., Ivancevich, J. M., & Donnelly, J. H., Jr. (1991). *Organizations.* Homewood, IL: Irwin.

Gilsdorf, J. W. (1983). Executive and managerial attitudes toward business slang: A fortune-list survey. *The Journal of Business Communication, 20,* 27–42.

Gilsdorf, J. W. (1987). Written corporate communication policy: Extent, coverage, costs, benefits. *The Journal of Business Communication, 24,* 36–37.

Griffin, K., & Patton, B. R. (1976). *Fundamentals of interpersonal communication* (2nd ed.). New York: Harper & Row.

Grunig, J. G., & Hunt, T. (1984). *Managing public relations.* New York: Holt, Rinehart & Winston.

Hall, C. S., & Nordby, V. J. (1973). *A primer on Jungian psychology.* New York: New American Library.

Haney, W. V. (1967). *Communication and organizational behavior: Text and cases* (rev. ed.). Homewood, IL: Irwin.

Hayakawa, S. I. (1972). *Language in thought and action* (3rd ed.). New York: Harcourt Brace Jovanovich.

Huber, G. P., & Daft, R. L. (1987). The information environments of organizations. In F. M. Jablin, L. L. Putnam, K. H. Roberts, & L. W. Porter (Eds.), *Handbook of organizational communication* (pp. 130–164). Newbury Park, CA: Sage.

Hurst, D. K. (1984). Of boxes, bubbles, and effective management. *Harvard Business Review, 62*(3), 78–87.

Irvine, A. (1970). *Improving industrial communication.* London: Gown.

Izraeli, D., & Jick, T. J. (1986). The art of saying no: On the management of refusals in organizations. In P. J. Frost, V. F. Mitchell, & W. R. Nord (Eds.), *Organizational reality* (3rd ed., pp. 283–296). Glenview, IL: Scott, Foresman.

Jacobson, G. (1988, July). The boom on the Mexican border. *Management Review,* pp. 20–24.

Jaroslovsky, R. (1988, July/August). What's on your mind, America? *Psychology Today,* p. 56.

John Rost Associates. (1984). U.S. execs rate business writing. *Training and Development Journal, 38,* 14.

Johnson, H. C. (1987, May 4). *USA Today,* p. 6B.

Kehrer, D. (1989). *Doing business boldly.* New York: Simon & Schuster.

Keltner, J. W. (1970). *Interpersonal speech communication: Elements and structure.* Belmont, CA: Wadsworth.

Kiechel, W., III. (1986). Executives ought to funnier. In P. J. Frost, V. F. Mitchell, & W. R. Nord (Eds.), *Organizational reality* (3rd ed., pp. 363–366). Glenview, IL: Scott, Foresman.

Korbinski, A. (1933). *Science and sanity: An introduction to non-Aristotelian systems and general semantics.* Lancaster, PA: Science Press.

Kotter, J. P. (1990). *A force for change: How leadership differs from management.* New York: Free Press.

Kreps, G. (1986). *Organizational communication.* New York: Longman.

Kunerth, J. (1983, September 13). Behind the jargon: How the language of our work works. *Chicago Tribune,* p. 1.

Lee, I. J. (1941). *Language habits in human affairs.* New York: Harper & Bros.

Leonard, A. (1982). An annotated bibliography of recent articles in company communications training. *The Bulletin, 45,* 48–52.

Lippitt, G. (1982). Humor: A laugh a day keeps the incongruities at bay. *Training and Development Journal, 36,* 98–100.

Locker, K. O. (1992). *Business and administrative communication* (7th ed.). Homewood, IL: Irwin.

March, J. G., & Olsen, J. P. (1976). *Ambiguity and choice in organizations.* Bergen, Norway: Universitetsforlaget.

Marklein, M. B. (1987, November 24). Wayward ways with words. *USA Today,* p. D1.

McCormick, J. (1987, August 17). Decisions. *Newsweek,* p. 62.

Millar, D. P., & Millar, F. E. (1976). *Messages and myths.* New York: Alfred.

Mintzberg, H. (1975). The manager's job: Folklore and fact. *Harvard Business Review, 53*(2), 49–61.

Miserable memos get the "Percy" award. (1988). *Management Review, 77,* 11.

Mitchell, C., & Burdick, T. (1983). *The extra edge: Success strategies for women.* Washington, DC: Acropolis.

Mitchell, R. B., Crawford, M. C., & Madden, R. B. (1985). An investigation of the impact of electronic communication systems on organizational communication patterns. *The Journal of Business Communication, 22,* 9–16.

Morris, C. (1971). *Writing on the general theory of signs.* The Hague, Netherlands: Mouton.

Murphy, H. A., & Hildebrandt, H. W. (1984). *Effective business communication* (4th ed.). New York: McGraw-Hill.

Naisbett, J. (1984). *Megatrends.* New York: Warner.

Nora, J. J., Rogers, C. R., & Stramy, R. J. (1986). *Transforming the workplace.* Princeton, NJ: Princeton Research Press.

Ogden, C. K., & Richards, I. A. (1953). *The meaning of meaning.* New York: Harcourt Brace Jovanovich.

Olcott, W. A. (1984, May). Office automation: Is the message getting through to American business? *Office Administration and Automation,* pp. 7–9.

Peters, T. (1987). *Thriving on chaos.* New York: Knopf.

Peters, T. J., & Waterman, R. H., Jr. (1982). *In search of excellence: Lessons from America's best-run companies.* New York: Harper & Row.

Pettigrew, A. M. (1985). Examining change in the long-term context of culture and politics. In J. M. Pennings (Ed.), *Organizational strategy and change* (pp. 283–284). San Francisco: Jossey-Bass.

Pinsdorf, M. K. (1987). *Communicating when your company is under siege.* Lexington, MA: Heath.

Poppa, T. (1986, December 21). Assembly plant is king in Juarez. *The Sunday Courier,* pp. F1, F5.

Rader, M. H., & Kurth, L. A. (1988). *Business communication for the computer age.* Cincinnati: South-Western.

Ramsey, D. K. (1986). *The corporate warriors: Six classic cases in American business.* New York: Houghton Mifflin.

Redding, W. C. (1984). *The corporate manager's guide to better communication.* Glenview, IL: Scott, Foresman.

Rentz, K. C., & Debs, M. B. (1987). Language and corporate values: Teaching ethics in business writing courses. *The Journal of Business Communication, 24,* 27–48.

The right word at the right time. (1982, November). *Manager's Magazine,* p. 18.

Robey, D. (1991). *Designing organizations* (3rd ed.). Homewood, IL: Irwin.

Roethlisberger, F. J. (1985). The administrator's skill: Communication. In E. G. C. Collins (Ed.), *The executive dilemma* (pp. 543–556). New York: Wiley.

Rothwell, W. J. (1983). Developing an in-house training curriculum in written communication. *The Journal of Business Communication, 20,* 31–45.

Roy, D. F. (1960). Banana time: Job satisfaction and informal interaction. *Human Organization, 18,* 156–168.

Schein, E. H. (1985). *Organizational culture and leadership.* San Francisco: Jossey-Bass.

Schein, E. H. (1990). Organizational culture. *American Psychologist, 2,* 109–119.

Schutz, W. C. (1985). The interpersonal underworld. In E. G. C. Collins (Ed.), *The executive dilemma* (pp. 521–542). New York: Wiley.

Schwartz, M. M., Stark, H. F., & Schiffman, H. R. (1970). Responses of union and management leaders to emotionally-toned industrial relations terms. *Personnel Psychology, 23,* 361–367.

Scott, C., & Bain, T. (1987). How arbitrators interpret ambiguous contract language. *Personnel Journal, 64,* 10–14.

*Simply stated* (1987). Washington, DC: American Institute for Research.

Sleeter, M. (1981). Are you "humoring" your employees? *Management World, 10,* 25–27.

Smith, D. R., & Williamson, L. K. (1985). *Interpersonal communication: Roles, rules, strategies, and games* (3rd ed.). Dubuque, IA: Brown.

Stohl, C., & Redding, W. C. (1987). Message and message exchange processes. In F. M. Jablin, L. L. Putnam, K. H. Roberts, & L. W. Porter (Eds.), *Handbook of organizational communication* (pp. 451–502). Newbury Park, CA: Sage.

Thass-Thienemann, T. (1968). *Symbolic behavior.* New York: Washington Square Press.

Thompkins, P., & Cheney, G. (1983). Account analysis of organizations: Decision making and identification. In L. L. Putnam & M. E. Pacanowsky (Eds.), *Communication and organizations: An interpretive approach* (pp. 123–146). Beverly Hills, CA: Sage.

Tracy, L. N., & Lee, J. A. (1984, Fall-Winter). Acculturation of graduate business students to academic values: Abstruseness as a criterion of competence. *Collegiate News and View,* pp. 37–41.

U.S. Department of Commerce. (1984). *How plain English works for business: Twelve case studies.* Washington, DC: U.S. Government Printing Office.

Walkins, O. (1987, January). Words that motivate. *Communication Briefings,* p. 1.

Watzlawick, P. W., Beavin, J. H., & Jackson, D. D. (1967). *Pragmatics of human communication: A study of interactional patterns, pathologies, and paradoxes.* New York: Norton.

Weick, K. E. (1987). Theorizing about organizational communication. In F. M. Jablin, L. L. Putnam, K. H. Roberts, & L. W. Porter (Eds.), *Handbook of organizational communication* (pp. 97–122). Newbury Park, CA: Sage.

Weitzen, H. S. (1987). *Telephone magic.* New York: McGraw-Hill.

Williams, F. (1987). *Technology and communication behavior.* Belmont, CA: Wadsworth.

Winburne, P. R. (1989, June 18). Logos help in picturing business. *The Evansville Courier,* p. F1.

# CHAPTER 5

# Nonverbal Communication

Although estimates of the impact of the nonverbal communication on a specific message's meaning vary from 93% (Mehabian, 1981, p. 77) to 65% (Birdwhistell, 1970, p. 158), the importance of nonverbal communication cannot be doubted. One summary concluded that nonverbal messages "can convey affiliation, positive regard, interest, dominance, credibility, or status; can reinforce or punish; [and can] affect what others learn, what attitudes develop, what approaches will be modeled, and what is expected" (Tresch, Pearson, Hunter, Wyld, & Waltman, 1986, p. 78).

Nonverbal communication principles have wide organizational application. Topics range from detecting deception in interview situations (Harrison, Hwalek, Raney, & Frits, 1978), to helping managers and supervisors understand their employees (Beegle, 1971; Ehat & Schappner, 1974), to making managers aware of the nonverbal messages they are sending to employees (McCroskey, 1979). National sales training programs outline the various assumptions that can be made depending on the client's office set-up and what signals a successful salesperson should watch for in order to close the sale. Clearly, nonverbal communication is considered an essential factor in understanding organizations.

In addition to the interpersonal impact, organizations are also keenly aware of the importance of certain nonverbal behaviors, and many corporations go to great lengths to create the desired impression on visitors, clients, and employees through office and building design (Seiler, 1982). Individuals often use their offices as extensions of their own territory.

Because understanding nonverbal communication carries a implicit sense of power, some consultants are tempted to provide advice that goes well beyond the scope of nonverbal studies. For example, in reviewing recent audio tapes for the business person, Case (1987) concluded:

**123**

It would be nice if these were the worst of a bad lot (of business tapes). But surely that honor has to go to *The Power of Subliminal Selling* by Ken Delmar. Delmar has so much advice for salespeople! Like, always look at the prospect so he can see both your ears. With certain kinds of prospects, sit close—but watch their blinks, and if they blink too much, move back. Keep your hands in a "log cabin," fingers interlaced, and "lay your log cabin on your lap or hold it just above your lap." Now psychologically, "you are safe inside your log cabin." And Delmar is *serious* about this. (p. 22)

This chapter outlines the aspects of nonverbal communication that are generally predictable, gives you specific advice about certain behaviors, and stays away from unsupported "log cabin" generalizations.

## VERBAL VERSUS NONVERBAL COMMUNICATION

The first step in understanding nonverbal communication is to define the concept and delineate the differences between verbal and nonverbal communication. Nonverbal communication is "a process whereby people, through intentional or unintentional manipulation of normative actions and expectations express experiences, feelings, and attitudes in order to relate to and control themselves, others, and their environments" (Hickson & Stacks, 1985, p. 15). The four major differences between verbal and nonverbal communication will make this definition even clearer.

First, the vast majority of nonverbal behaviors are intuitive and are based on normative rules. Except for behaviors such as good manners or etiquette, little formal training is provided for nonverbal communication. Verbal communication is highly structured and is reinforced through an extensive formal and informal learning process. There is no clear-cut linguistic structure for nonverbal communication even though researchers have found some consistencies in how people interpret nonverbal behaviors (Malandro & Barker, 1983, pp. 6–10). Although nonverbal communication has little or no formal structure, it does have a natural set of rules which are recognized through cultural norms.

Second, verbal communication is confined to the use of language. Nonverbal communication, then, is any part of communication that does not use words (Hickson & Stacks, 1985, p. 9). For the sake of analysis, this is a useful division. However, "nonverbal communication is so inextricably bound up with verbal aspects of the communication process that we can only separate them artificially. In actual practice, such separation does not occur" (Knapp, 1972, p. v). There are nonverbal behaviors that stand by themselves, such as a hitchhiker's thumb, but most nonverbal communication occurs in conjunction with some verbal act. For example, silence becomes a significant nonverbal act because it represents a break in the verbal aspects of a transaction.

Nonverbal communication operates in the present and is highly dependent on the context, which provides a third distinction, and an important defining characteristic. In chapter 1, we introduced the concept one cannot not communicate along with nothing never happens. Both of these phrases apply very specifically to nonverbal communication. Goffman (1959) concluded that we can stop giving expression, but we cannot stop giving off expression during interactions with other individuals (p. 2). Returning to the definition, all intentional and unintentional behavior is potentially meaningful and your communication is rich with nonverbal behaviors. Any nonverbal behavior one or both parties chooses to assign meaning to becomes communication. This third distinction also means that we cannot stop nonverbal communication without actually removing ourselves from the context.

These three lead to the fourth distinction. The communicative capability of nonverbal behavior is also dependent on the potential for a behavioral response or feedback (Burgoon & Saine, 1978, p. 9). A great writer, or an ineffective memo, always can be read at a different time or place and have meaning. Some type of response must occur to nonverbal behavior when it happens for the behavior to carry meaning and have an impact on the transaction.

Based on these four distinctions, you probably have concluded that nonverbal communication is less rule-bound than verbal communication and is judged more by the situational variables than the absolute correctness of the behavior. This is a valid conclusion.

The remainder of this chapter provides two means for further understanding nonverbal communication. First, based on the research used in this chapter, 14 principles can be generalized that apply to nonverbal communication. These include 8 guiding principles for all nonverbal communication and 6 principles governing nonverbal communication in an organizational setting.

Second, specific nonverbal behaviors relevant to organizations are presented. These allow you to understand the manner in which nonverbal communication operates in an organization and, with some caution, to generalize to other behaviors.

## PRINCIPLES OF NONVERBAL COMMUNICATION

The eight guiding principles for all nonverbal communication are:

1. The quality of relationships is judged through nonverbal cues (Hickson & Stacks, 1985, p. 228). When people try and determine if they have a good, bad, or mediocre relationship, nonverbal cues provide the supporting information that indicates the strength of the bond. For example, although handshakes are standard fare in business transactions, how the handshake is given, including other concurrent nonverbal behaviors, gives the participants information about the relationship.

2. Nonverbal communication is more likely to be believed than is verbal communication when there is an inconsistency or incongruence between the two message systems (Knapp, 1972, pp. 22–23; Malandro & Barker, 1983, p. 12; Mehrabian,

1981, pp. 74–88). What someone says can be overridden by what is done. The expression "actions speak louder than words" is fundamentally correct. Members of organizations are sometimes criticized because they "talk the talk but don't walk the walk." Waterman (1987), in his analysis of the renewal factors required for companies, concluded, "*Visible* management attention, rather than management exhortations, gets things done. Action may start with words, but it has to be backed by symbolic behavior that makes those words come alive" (emphasis added; p. 11).

3. Nonverbal communication can be assigned meaning if only one of the parties chooses to do so (Hickson & Stacks, 1985, p. 228; Smith & Williamson, 1985, p. 192). Perception is the key term, as we discussed in chapter 2. Inadvertent actions on the part of one person still can be very meaningful to the other person. With the complexity of most organizations, there is vast potential for nonverbal behaviors to become meaningful, even when there is no intent on the part of an individual. Fortunately, the overriding parameters for our behaviors, provided by the cultural norms, prevent a large number of miscues.

4. Because perception is the key variable, forward leans, relaxed posture, decreased distance, increased touching, and enhanced attention all seem to provide positive messages in a transaction (Hackman & Johnson, 1991, p. 163; Johns, 1988, p. 366). By doing the opposite, negative messages are perceived.

5. The rules for nonverbal behavior vary depending on the age, sex, and the various cultures involved (Berko, Wolvin, & Wolvin, 1985, pp. 82–83, 100; Knapp, 1972, pp. 125, 244–246, 336–367). These cultures can include group, regional, organizational, national, and international and all the possible combinations of these five cultures. Therefore, the nonverbal rules in a group or organization are likely to be idiosyncratic.

6. The context, social situation, and power relationships help determine the rules and roles for nonverbal communication (Hickson & Stacks, 1985, p. 228; Knapp, 1972, pp. 75, 127, 339–340; Mehrabian, 1981, pp. 2–7; Richmond, McCroskey, & Payne, 1987, pp. 262–277). Where the behavior occurs and with whom it occurs are vital to interpreting the nonverbal communication.

7. Women are generally more sensitive to nonverbal cues and more accurate in sending nonverbal messages (Hickson & Stacks, 1985, p. 228; Knapp, 1972, p. 22).

8. Although people can learn to interpret others' nonverbal cues more accurately, greater success will be achieved by concentrating on our own nonverbal behavior to make it consistent with our desired message(s) (Hackman & Johnson, 1991, pp. 96–97, 162–163; Hickson & Stacks, 1985, p. 228).

These eight principles apply to all nonverbal communication. For the purposes of understanding organizational communication, we provide six additional principles that apply more specifically to organizations:

9. Applying the eight guiding principles is contingent on the specific cultural expectations of the organization (Gordon, Tengler, & Infante, 1982, p. 434; Hickson & Stacks, 1985, pp. 193–213). So, in addition to the general concept in the aforementioned Principle 5, occupational role(s), group affiliation(s), and any sub-culture(s) (e.g., management vs. union, faculty vs. administration, engineers vs. production, computer designers vs. computer users, nurses vs. doctors, etc.), all further clarify and define the specific, acceptable behaviors.

10. By and large, organizational cultures will reward individuals who adapt nonverbal behaviors to cultural expectations, and punish those who do not (Goldhaber, 1986, pp. 204–218; Lareau, 1985; Richmond, McCroskey, & Payne, 1987, pp. 223–239). Both the rewards and punishments tend to be subtle and reflected in actions such as promotions, type of office space, or inclusion in meetings.

11. Organizational members learn and adapt their own nonverbal cues intuitively as they become part of the culture (Adler, 1983, pp. 39–48; Wilson, Goodall, & Waager, 1986, pp. 107–109). Individuals tend to reflect more and more of the occupational or group behaviors exhibited by other members of the organization.

12. Business settings provide individuals with an opportunity to prove their abilities at culture adaptation and thereby increase acceptance (e.g., dress, mannerisms, addressing behavior, punctuality) (Korda, 1975; Lareau, 1985, pp. 4–5; Molloy, 1988, pp. 38–39).

13. In organizations, nonverbal communication is more important than verbal communication in informal settings (Conrad, 1985, p. 91; Mehrabian, 1981, pp. 15–16; Richmond, McCroskey, & Payne, 1987, pp. 80–81). Power and affiliation are indicated by the type of nonverbal behavior used. As with all nonverbal communication, credibility, assertiveness, and awareness of others are transmitted nonverbally.

14. Because most nonverbal communication can be interpreted in a variety of ways, conservative, "safe" behavior is a norm in most organizational cultures (Lareau, 1985, p. 5; Molloy, 1988, pp. 1–3). Organizations that support deviations from traditional dress standards communicate their acceptance through the culture (Johns, 1988, p. 245).

These 14 guiding principles are presented at the beginning of this chapter because most nonverbal experts agree on their importance in understanding and using nonverbal communication. As we discussed in chapter 2, Perception, all generalizations are subject to question and these principles are no exception.

Finally, nonverbal communication serves six specific organizational communication functions. Table 5.1. outlines these for you.

In conclusion, there are 14 specific principles that can be applied to the general understanding of nonverbal communication. We now discuss facial display, eye contact, paralanguage, body language, appearance, and proxemics.

TABLE 5.1
Functions of Nonverbal Communication

| Function | Explanation |
|---|---|
| Repetition | Reinforcing verbal messages with nonverbal behaviors. *Examples:* A supervisor moving his or her arms while giving instructions. Telling *and* showing someone how to do a job. Giving an O.K. signal, or a pat on the back, *along with* verbal praise. |
| Substitution | Using a nonverbal behavior in place of a verbal one. *Examples:* A head nod to indicate yes, a "pat on the back," a "knowing glance," or a "thumbs up" for success. When the action is symbolic, it is called an emblem. |
| Accentuation | Nonverbal communication can provide emphasis. *Examples:* The loudness of a person's voice often conveys the true strength of the message. A secret *can* be forecast by a whisper. A wink or a furrowed brow *can* add to the impact of the verbal message. Distance *can* indicate seriousness. |
| Contradiction | The nonverbal and verbal messages are incongruent. *Examples:* A colleague's facial expression, or vocal inflection, gives a message opposite to the verbal one. Sarcasm is one of the best examples since the tone of voice provides a meaning that is quite different from the stated one. Making someone wait and then telling them they are important can be an example. Someone asks you what is wrong because of your appearance and you say, defensively, "nothing," is another example. |
| Regulation | Using nonverbal behaviors to initiate, continue, interrupt, or terminate interactions. *Examples:* Eye contact, gestures, nods, head motions, and numerous other behaviors indicate how the interaction should progress. |
| Complementing | Using nonverbal messages to supplement, expand, modify, or provide details to a verbal message. *Examples:* Looking confident while conducting a briefing enhances the quality of the presentation. Speaking softly while discussing delicate information. |

## FACIAL DISPLAY

Your face provides vital information regarding your own internal views about how things are going. One estimate is that 55% of feeling is communicated through facial expression (Frank, 1982, p. 118). With no formal training, observers of facial expressions can distinguish a variety of emotions including interest/excitement, enjoyment/joy, suprise/startle, distress/anguish, shame/humiliation, anger/rage, contempt/disgust, and fear/terror (Tomkins, 1962). In organizations, we tend to work toward less facial expression so that we can control the setting. Showing too much excitement, joy, rage, or humiliation is not professional. One consultant advises: "Your object should be to showcase your positive feelings and to disguise your negative feelings, unless letting them show will help you get something accomplished" (Gray, 1983, p. 28).

We are quite adept at hiding our emotions, which is an expected behavior in most organizational cultures. Apparently, we are more able to distort factual information than emotional information (Comadena, 1982). Three specific areas of facial display deserving further discussion are smiles, hair, and makeup.

## Smiles

The smile is a useful example of how the face is used. Although a smile can be indicative of a wide range of feelings ranging from happiness to nervousness, in the business world smiles generally are considered positive communication behaviors. In sales, smiles not only create rapport, they also have been linked to success (Lau, 1982; Moore, 1982). Smiling people are perceived as more intelligent than those who do not smile (Grazian, 1987). People who smile are judged to have an honest face (Hickson & Stacks, 1985, p. 202). However, as with any nonverbal behavior, there are exceptions. For example, some research has concluded that female managers would be wise to consider when they use a smile. Although not calling for the elimination of smiling, the study does point to the potential double bind facing individuals as far as knowing when to smile and when to have a serious business face (Williams, 1984).

Finally, Ekman and Friesen (1987) concluded that a smile's message—along with feelings of anger, disgust, fear, happiness, sadness, and surprise, when expressed through facial changes—is internationally recognizable from simple photographs. In the cultures they studied worldwide, these same facial expressions provided the same messages.

Smiling is a worthwhile nonverbal facial gesture. How the smile and face are framed add to the nonverbal message. Hair is one important method.

## Hair

As a general rule, organizations seek individuals who fit into their particular cultural expectations. These expectations are created by the environment that surrounds the culture. For example, although length of hair does not determine a man's ability to do a job, "to most people, long hair connotes an artistic, aesthetic, romantic, and casual mode of life. Discipline, seriousness, and business ethics are not suggested by long hair. Very short hair represents the energetic, precise, athletic, and youthful type, while the moderate length suggests pragmatic, executive, business-like, serious, and decisive qualities of an individual" (Hickson & Stacks, 1985, p. 82). Any organization wishing to forward either a professional or an energetic image, or both, would be likely to hire and promote someone who fits that image.

Changing our hair style, length, or amount are all examples of *body adaptors*. Body adaptors are different from the general term adaptors, which refers to movements that are mostly reflexive, such as scratching our head or drumming our fingers, and are learned early in life. You will recall that the fifth general principle indicated that nonverbal rules vary depending on the age, sex, and cultures involved. This principle certainly applies to facial display for men and women in organizations. To demonstrate this point, we consider a gender-specific issue for men and women that underscores the overall importance of understanding how nonverbal communication operates in organizations.

Being aware of the importance of hair style and a youthful appearance, some businessmen have tried to restrict the balding process through hair transplants. It would appear that these men believed the ads that promise rejuvenated job opportunities if they would adapt their bodies by changing their hair. Although we can predict the problems with long hair for a man, investing in a hair transplant in an effort to look younger is not worthwhile (Fenton, 1986, p. 193). In a survey of personnel managers from the 1,000 largest corporations in the United States, only 2% thought a hair replacement would be useful. Thirty-six percent disagreed strongly and 28% disagreed somewhat about the value of such a move (Ward, 1987).

The survey results reaffirm that it is risky to make predictions regarding nonverbal communication. However, as we discuss later under Dress, if the hair transplant makes the man feel more confident, there is every reason to believe that the investment might be worthwhile.

The same conclusions can be drawn regarding men's facial hair. Of 1,000 chairmen of the largest U.S. service and industrial firms, 94% were clean shaven. Of the rest, 4% had mustaches and 2% had beards (Sloan, cited in Cervera 1987). As a general piece of advice, beards are not recommended. If mustaches are worn, they should be carefully trimmed and not eccentric (Hickson & Stacks, 1985, p. 82). Facial hair also underscores the situational nature of nonverbal signals. In 1973, two studies concluded that men with increased facial hair were judged as more positive than a nonbearded counterpart (Kenny & Fletcher, 1973; Pellegrini, 1973). Apparently, the times have changed and facial hair may not be a positive nonverbal signal when one initially enters an organization. In addition, the two studies used college classes as evaluators. Although a college audience can make reliable predictions regarding some organizational behaviors, accepting the conclusions of the people who actually work in organizations probably is safer. Obviously, once the prevailing norms of the culture are known, you can make your own decisions regarding appropriateness.

## Makeup

The use of makeup by women provides an additional example of the complexity of facial manipulation. The explanations are not entirely clear, but when combined with other artifacts such as glasses or clothing style, makeup cues do make a difference (Hamid, 1952; Knapp, 1972, p. 174). Molloy (1977), who studied the management of nonverbal signals in an organizational setting, concluded that any flashy additions, ranging from bright nail polish to extravagant lipstick, provide the wrong cues to the receiver and should be avoided as unprofessional image presentations (pp. 85–86). Other sources have granted greater freedom for many of the body adaptors Molloy cautioned against, but the advice is still to look conservative, including not displaying long hair (Mitchell & Burdick, 1983, pp. 103–122, 152–153).

At this point, we have examined two gender-specific nonverbal examples. For men, the type of facial hair is important. For women, the use of makeup seems to make a difference.

All of these examples and advice, whether they are directed at men or women, center on the concept of a particular organization's cultural expectations. Most businesses are interested in projecting a conservative image (Molloy, 1988, pp. 1–6, 38–39). We are somewhat uncomfortable in making a sweeping generalization regarding conservative facial adaptation. We can make the observation that you will be most successful if you examine the particular culture and then adapt. You will find it is easier to start out somewhat conservative, smile, keep your hair within acceptable norms, and judiciously use makeup. Once you have obtained status and position, you can consider altering your facial adaptors.

We have provided a discussion of several facial factors in the work setting. One additional example should underscore the importance of understanding the cultural expectations.

The showing of emotions through overt actions, such as crying, stands as a clear violation of most organizational cultures: "The impact of tears depends on the field you're in, the company's culture and what's tolerated in a particular setting. In highly creative fields such as TV, public relations, and advertising, people aren't expected to be as much under control as in banking, law, accounting, and corporate business" (Edelson, 1987, p. D4). Studies conclude that there is a double standard regarding crying at work (Butler, 1987; Edelson, 1987; O'Connell, 1991). Because men traditionally do not display overt emotions, such as crying, they are more likely to get mad than shed tears. Women are more likely to cry to express anger or frustration (Plas & Hoover-Dempsey, 1989). Most organizational cultures are not the highly creative types and overly emotional displays, such as crying, simply are rejected as being inappropriate. Women therefore must alter their responses to particular situations more drastically than men. This is not a new insight for the vast majority of women. In a survey of 8,033 *Working Women* readers, 78% said "crying in the office quashes professionalism" (Hellmich, 1988, p. D1). The point is, of course, that the behavior is examined in light of the expectations established by the cultural norms and not the legitimacy of the behavior itself.

The impact of facial display, through smiles, hair adaptations, and makeup, underscores the general principles provided at the beginning of this chapter. In addition to the examples discussed, there are numerous types of temporary adornments, including various extensions of clothing, wigs, perfume, and so on, that can be used to alter someone's appearance (Morris, 1977, p. 222). Again, the success in using these adornments will depend on the fit between the addition and the organization's expectations.

## EYE CONTACT

Eye contact may indicate a liking for the other person. It also serves as simultaneous communication because eye contact allows people to send and receive messages at the same time.

Direct eye contact is seen as an indication of honesty and credibility (Burgoon & Saine, 1978, p. 181). In seminars we have conducted with professional interviewers, they are convinced that direct eye contact, which should be distinguished from staring, is an indication of self-confidence and forthrightness. Eye contact ranks second only to dress as an important nonverbal factor in an interview (Burgoon, Buller, & Woodall, 1989, p. 452).

Status and power are shown by eye contact. In meetings, organizational members with the most power will be looked at more often (Duncan, 1975). Leaders can gaze more directly and with greater frequency than subordinates (Richmond, McCroskey, & Payne, 1987, p. 230). Showing deference to power often is accomplished through diminished eye contact by subordinates.

Interestingly, speakers attribute more control and power to receivers who do not look at them (Burgoon & Saine, 1978, p. 181). This may be due to the lack of simultaneous feedback. A total elimination of eye contact with reflective sunglasses creates a "Darth Vadar" effect, which causes fear and resentment in the receiver (Boyanowsky & Griffiths, 1982). Because all possibility for feedback is eliminated, receivers feel as if they have lost control of the transaction.

You are seen as being more confident if, as the sender, you maintain eye contact (Frank, 1982, p. 118). However, once you achieve high status and power, you can choose not to use eye contact and this decision will have little impact, because the power differential is already known (Hickson & Stacks, 1985, p. 202).

Eye contact also is used to control interactions. This regulating of the flow of the transactions can be simply failing to acknowledge someone's presence. Clearly, the potential for a response from someone is decreased if the amount of eye contact is minimal. Studies indicate eye contact is diminished during the telling of bad news or the providing of critical feedback (Frank, 1982, p. 118). Eye contact is used to monitor feedback. Listeners and speakers tend to look away when a difficult subject is being discussed (Knapp, 1978, p. 299).

The type of eyeglasses you wear also sends a message. In the business world, your eyeglasses should make you look older, traditional, and authoritarian. Molloy (1975) suggested that men and women wear heavy plastic glasses (p. 123), and counseled women to consider contacts for social occasions (Molloy, 1977, p. 89).

In general, eye contact is a powerful means for establishing relationships and indicating an open, honest approach. Once you become more familiar with the specific cultural requirements, you can better judge how to use eye gestures. Certainly, it is a must in an interview situation. Any presentation will be assigned greater credibility if you use eye contact. However, staring is not an acceptable norm in most organizations.

## PARALANGUAGE

The manner in which something is said is paralanguage. It includes "accents, emphases, vocal qualities, pitch, rate, pauses, to include silences, (a form of vocalic behavior), anything that adds to the meaning we associate with the verbal" (Hickson & Stacks, 1985, p. 107). Because all behavior is potentially meaningful, each of these paralinguistic factors can alter a message.

A person's dialect, whether it be foreign, southern, general American speech, or any other, does have an impact on the initial impression, although the effect is short-term (Burgoon & Saine, 1978, pp. 182–183). A pleasing voice logically would make people more likely to listen to us. A conversational voice is seen as more attractive and as indicating a better education and a higher socioeconomic position than is a dynamic voice (Pearce & Brommel, 1972; Pearce & Conklin, 1971).

The rate of speech also effects credibility. Within reason, listeners judge a speaker as being more competent as the rate of speech increases (Street & Brady, 1982). According to the same study, people are seen as more attractive by listeners if the sender speaks at a more rapid rate. Finally, the slowest rate of speaking is the least attractive.

Salespeople have enhanced their sales presentations by manipulating paralanguage. According to Moore (1982), "By changing their speech, volume, and tone, the best sales agents are able to give certain phrases the effect of commands" (p. 51).

Paralanguage also is used to regulate the transaction. Interesting research has been conducted on the concept of turn taking, or deciding who should be the sender and who should be the receiver. Middle-class speakers, for example, use turn-taking processes differently from lower class speakers (Robbins, Devoe, & Wiener, 1978). In organizations, there are unstated rules regarding who is allowed to begin, regulate, and end conversations.

Silence has several important uses. First, it is used to create interpersonal distance (Marlando & Barker, 1983, p. 299). In response to a variety of emotions, individuals simply may choose to remain silent. These emotions can range from fear to a desire to hurt someone. In a conflict situation, for example, remaining silent can be the wisest response available.

Second, silence is used in response to authority. Most individuals will allow the more powerful organizational member to speak and will remain silent until the authority figure indicates they can respond. At the same time, defying authority by remaining silent also can send a strong message (Bruneau, 1973; Newman, 1982). In all cases, silence sends a message and knowing when to use silence is an important communication skill.

Paralanguage includes a large group of behaviors including pitch, tone, rate, silence, and other vocal behaviors that add to the words. Sometimes referred to as *vocalics,* these behaviors provide information about emotions, reinforce meanings, and demonstrate understanding of the specific organizational communication skills expected.

## BODY LANGUAGE

*Kinesics,* or the study of body language, provides important information regarding behavior in an organization. Without even using body movement, a person's height and physique send messages.

### Height and Physique

For example, a male executive's height can be correlated to his job prospects and salary. In a study of 1,433 alumni of the University of Pittsburgh's Graduate School of Business, the average 6-ft 2-in. tall man earns $6,000 a year more than does one who is 5 ft 4 in. tall (Olson & Frieze, 1987). Frieze, one of the study's authors, concluded that we subconsciously view taller men as being dominant and assertive. The same survey found men judged to be 20% or more overweight earned $4,000 less than those of average weight.

These same biases were observed in a study of the hiring practices used for picking prospective high school principals (Bonuso, 1979). Roughly identical resumes were sent to New York State school superintendents with pictures that varied in body type from short/overweight to tall/ideal weight. The superintendents judged the tall, lean applicants as most qualified, and their ratings fell consistently with shorter, heavier applicants. Finally, a person's beginning salary is correlated to their height (Knapp, 1978, p. 167). From a business perspective, "a lack of height has always been considered a sign of inferiority. We can 'fall short' of a goal, 'think small,' be 'shortsighted,' or be 'looked down on.' Being lower is a sign of servility. . . . We constantly favor people with a height advantage" (Cooper, 1979b, pp. 21–22).

In the same book, Cooper (1979b) advised businesspeople to maintain a trim weight so you will "fit the mold" because "there is a definite relationship between a sound body and business success" (pp. 55–56). As with obtaining a hair transplant, being more physically fit probably does allow an individual to project greater self-confidence, which would work to a person's advantage in an organization (Cash, Winstead, & Janda, 1986).

The Pittsburgh survey (Olson & Frieze, 1987) also revealed a gender difference. Of the 349 women surveyed, tall women were not significantly better paid than shorter ones and weight did not seem to be an important variable. Freize (1974) concluded from the survey results that being slim is not considered a plus, and "if you're a woman and you're too attractive, you're perceived as being incompetent" (p. 16). Another study found that attractiveness aided women seeking only nonmanagerial positions, whereas it was an asset for men at all times (Heilman & Sarugatari, 1979).

In the most subtle of ways, there are significant differences between how men and women are treated professionally. In a study of salesclerks' responses to customers, men received better service regardless of the type of products being purchased. The study includes salesclerks in 300 departments in large stores in five cities. The products included men's goods, women's products, and goods appealing to both sexes. The study's authors concluded that salespeople are discriminating against some of their better customers (Stead & Zinkhan, 1987).

Although we cannot increase our height or change our sex, we can pay attention to weight. More fundamentally, we can be aware of our own tendency to discriminate on non-performance-based criteria.

## Body Movement and Gestures

How individuals use their bodies provides messages to other organizational members. Specific characteristics include synchrony, gestures, etiquette, and smoking behavior. The last two issues offer useful insights into how organizations evaluate body movement and gestures.

*Synchrony.* First, establishing *synchrony* in interpersonal body movements is a basic characteristic of successful communication between equals: "Rhythm seems to the fundamental glue by which cohesive discourse is maintained" (Erickson, 1987). This rhythmic synchrony may be critical to how well individuals work with other people and it varies from culture to culture and job to job. Salespeople are encouraged to mirror the movements of their clients to help make a sale. As Moore (1982) explained it, "The best sales people first establish a mood of trust and rapport by means of *hynotic pacing*—statements and gestures that play back a customer's observations, experience, or behavior. Pacing is a kind of mirror-like matching, a way of suggesting: 'I am like you. We are in sync. You can trust me' " (p. 52).

However, as with any generalization about nonverbal behavior, the context determines the actual effectiveness of a specific action. According to Hickson and Stacks (1985), "Research indicates that mirroring the behaviors of others is a sign of conceding or according status or power to them" (p. 202). Numerous studies indicate that the higher status individuals in an organization have a more relaxed posture and greater movement (Burgoon & Saine, 1978, p. 182).

*Gestures.* Gestures in an organization tend to be evaluated based on how well the movements reinforce or challenge the existing relationships. Subordinates are expected to display appropriate attention to superiors through correct facing behaviors, apt attention, and tightness of stance (Cooper, 1979a, pp. 18–21). Superiors can manipulate their body movements and gestures in order to enhance the quality of the interaction whereas subordinates are more likely to be expected to fit the cultural norm.

Earlier in this chapter, we indicated that an open posture tends to enhance communication. Specifically, folding arms across the chest indicates an unwillingness to communicate, whereas opening the arms shows an interest in the other person's ideas.

Hand gestures can indicate a wide array of meanings. *Illustrators,* movements that enhance the message by literally adding nonverbal reinforcement, are positive, are expected with dynamic individuals, and increase the likelihood of message acceptance (McGinley, LeFevre, & McGinley, 1965). *Adaptors,* which include various self-touching behaviors, are taken as indications of nervousness or quasi-courtship. Because nervousness and quasi-courtship behaviors challenge organizational norms, they provoke negative meanings. As we indicated earlier in this chapter, these adaptors are different from body adaptors, which are changes we make to our body's appearance.

The palm of the hand seems to indicate openness whereas the back of the hand has the opposite connotation. Being given the back of the hand means we are striking others and clenched fists or slicing movements carry very strong meanings. Most of us have been schooled not to point and this advice probably applies to organizational behavior as well. Pointing is something school teachers do and it is a clear dominance behavior. So, you would be safe to conclude that movements indicating withdrawal or aggression should be avoided unless the circumstances clearly dictate them.

**Etiquette.** Etiquette provides a good example of the impact of gestures. Although etiquette clearly includes verbal behaviors, such as correct introductions, titles, and addressing, good manners also demand close adherence to specific nonverbal expectations. Because a great deal of executive business occurs in social settings, a gaffe or faux pas may signal that the individual lacks the acumen to be granted credibility in other business dealings. During the job-interviewing process, for example, candidates must accept that they are on stage and are being judged. As Forbes (1990) put it, "Employers want people who know how to live in a social world and interact in a business environment" (p. C10). The judging process can be quite specific. J. C. Penney and Henry Ford based their management hiring decisions on whether or not candidates salted their food before tasting it (Sabath, 1990). Their reasoning, valid or not, was that someone who salts their food before tasting it implies they decide before checking all the facts. Although Penney and Ford may have been rash and their actions indicative of a perceptual bias (e.g., chapter 2), their preconceived notion of correct etiquette demonstrates how important actions can be in the organizational environment.

Organizations pay up to $2,500 a day for 20-person seminars on etiquette (White, 1987). For this fee, individuals learn to give clients the preferred seat in a restaurant—a power and deference move; to keep jackets buttoned when standing, unbuttoned when seated—a willingness to accept cultural norms; to place handbags and briefcases out of sight during meals—a statement that business will not be discussed before meals; and, to not drink alcohol or smoke unless the client does. These same general guidelines apply to an individual on a job interview, except interviewees should not drink hard liquor or smoke, even if invited to or raise business matters before the host does (Mitchell, 1991). Company parties often act as opportunities for managers to prove they can demonstrate the correct behaviors and not drink too much or draw too much negative attention (Raudsepp, 1983, p. 30).

To a significant degree, properly performed etiquette goes unnoticed. Errors, as violations of expectations, can create unwanted attention to an individual's lack of cultural knowledge.

**Smoking.**    Smoking provides another interesting paradigm. Studies indicate that the smoker's credibility is effected depending on the type of artifact used (Hickson, Powell, Hill, Holt, & Flick, 1979). Pipe smokers have been found to be more credible than cigarette or cigar smokers.

Increasingly, organizations are restricting smoking on the job. The reasons vary, ranging from health costs, to work or co-worker safety, to the response of customers to a salesperson who smokes. In 1987, over 35% of American organizations had some type of no-smoking policy (Derk, 1987). One fourth of the 283 companies surveyed in 1989 by the Administrative Management Society were smoke-free, up 14% from 1987 (Lawlor, 1990). One nonverbal means used by companies to find out if an applicant is a smoker is to put out an ashtray and ask if he or she wants to smoke. In justifying this procedure, one manager remarked: "Nobody ever gets turned off by a non-smoker. You don't hear, 'Gee, if only that person smoked, then I'd like him' " (Banzhaf, 1987). Many companies simply ask if an applicant smokes. This nonverbal behavior, not smoking, has become a desired attribute by many organizations.

Both etiquette and accepted smoking behavior provide us with examples of the importance of nonverbal communication in an organization. On a broader scale, being socially awkward provides the wrong nonverbal impression for many organizations.

## APPEARANCE

Physical appearance and clothing provide important nonverbal messages. In addition to obvious examples such as uniforms or priest's collars, every organization has written and/or unwritten codes regarding dress. Manufacturing plants have specific dress requirements ranging from the amount of clothing that must be worn to certain safety equipment, such as reinforced toes in shoes or safety glasses. Some manufacturing organizations use the Labor Day to Memorial Day tie and white shirt requirement for all managers and supervisors. During summer months, they do not need to wear ties.

In the gray- to white-collar professions, the codes might not be as tightly stated, but clothing is still a vital nonverbal consideration. In the service sector, the major rental car agencies dress their agents in distinctive uniforms. Some real estate organizations have their representatives wear the same color sports jackets. Most fast-food chains, such as McDonald's, require a certain uniform. Many delivery people wear easily identifiable uniforms.

Clothing is highly symbolic, which is why many organizations are so concerned with it. Waterman (1987) discussed one of the most famous examples, the IBM White Shirt:

> [It] stems from Tom Watson Sr.'s conviction that being a salesman was a respectable, desirable calling, far from the reputation for double-dealing and phoniness that sales-men carried in the first half of the century . . . Allen J. Krowe, a senior executive at IBM, told us the legend (which may be somewhat apocryphal) of how the White Shirt got started. "You've heard it a hundred times," he protested, but we assured we hadn't. "Tom Watson, Jr., is visiting a bank president and they get on an elevator. Another guy gets on who is dressed like he is heading out to the racetrack—big, loud tie, garish suit. Tom says to the bank president: 'I'm surprised one of your employees is allowed to dress like that.' And the bank president says, 'Tom, he works for you.' That's all that Tom needed. He decided we were going to have a dress code. He didn't want his people looking like they were heading out to the racetrack." (IBM never had a written dress code, as Krowe later points out, but Thomas Watson, Jr., did continu-ously urge all his people to dress conservatively, and once he did so in a memo. It had the power of a written dress code.) (p. 266)

Krowe continued to say that he wears the classic IBM white shirt and dark suit be-cause it gives him an edge in business.

## Uniforms

Uniforms, worn by over 23 million Americans, serve at least two functions (Solo-mon, 1987, p. 31). First, they differentiate one class or group from another. A waiter or waitress, a priest, or an officer of the law can be singled out because of their uniform and they are treated differently. For the service industries, uniforms act as confidence boosters because they indicate a "uniform" standard of performance. The service company's selling points, ranging from professionalism to simple good taste, can be signaled by the type of uniform used. So, the law-and-order police officer, the efficient and professional rug cleaner, or the clean nurse all present a message to the outside about the activity the group is engaged in.

Second, uniforms provide a common sense of identification for the group wear-ing them. Members of the police force feel a certain kinship with other members when they are all in uniform. The same concept applies to putting uniforms on fac-tory workers. Rather than divide between the blue, gray, and white collars, one uni-fied outfit can provide common ground for the group. As Solomon (1987) said, "Many organizations believe uniforms contribute to productivity and morale and ensure the workers are loyal to the organization's goals" (p. 30). A uniform enhances the abili-ty of an employee to identify with the company because they are living representa-tions of the organization.

In many Japanese corporations, uniforms are issued to each employee with only minor differences in style depending on the employee's position. The uniforms, of course, do not lead to a better organization. They do allow for a concentration on the task and not on the obvious status differences pointed out by dress ("Egalitarian Rules," 1987; Ouchi, 1981, p. 109). Toyota, Honda, and other Japanese-owned corporations have implemented dress codes in their American plants. Several organizations I work with have adopted a standard, uniform dress procedure. Although I was somewhat skeptical concerning the willingness of an American-based work force to accept these types of changes, the results have indicated the value of decreasing status distinctions in light manufacturing plants. The dress code is not less rigid for other professions, as I indicate later in this chapter.

On the other side of the coin, the leveling process brought about by a common uniform also can diminish an individual's sense of importance and achievement. Individual recognition for outstanding performance can be more difficult to observe because everyone looks alike. To the degree receiving personal acknowledgement is important, being dressed like everyone else can act as a demotivator.

## Clothing and Messages

For a variety of reasons, clothing is very important to organizations. Regardless of the type of business, some dress requirements exist and the rationale is clear. As Morris (1977) explained, "It is difficult to wear clothes without transmitting some type of message. Every costume tells a story, often a very subtle one, about its wearer. Even those people who insist they despise attention to clothing, and dress as casually as possible, are making specific comments on their social roles and their attitudes towards the culture in which they live and work" (p. 213). Morris put it another way:

> People are social animals, and clothing is very much a social invention. It is laden with symbolism that provides information about social and occupational standing, sex-role identification, political orientation, ethnicity and esthetic priorities. Clothing is a potent — and highly visible — medium of communication that carries a flood of information about who a person is, who a person is not, and who a person would like to be. It is an important mediator of social life. (p. 216).

## Functions of Clothing

Clothing has three functions: comfort and safety, modesty, and cultural display. Comfort, and especially safety, are both subject to clearly defined rules in most organizations. Modesty is an expectation in most organizations and the unwritten dress codes set the standards.

Cultural display includes statements regarding our willingness to accept the restrictions and requirements of an organization. For example, many stores and restaurants have signs saying "no shoes, no shirt, no service." According to Solomon (1986):

Dress requirements exist for many events and "tie required" is displayed in some eating establishments. Ties are clearly cultural displays. The tie, like so many other details of costume, is unimportant either as a comfort device or as a modesty covering. Instead, it operates as a cultural badge, slotting the wearer neatly into a particular social category. This is the most ancient use of clothing, preceding even its protective and modesty roles, and it remains today of supreme importance. (p. 20)

In a survey of personnel managers, 69% responded that it was never acceptable for a male executive to come to work not wearing a tie and 26% said it was generally not acceptable (McLean-Ibrahim, 1988). Only 5% thought it could be acceptable. Clothing demonstrates an understanding of the cultural requirements of the social situation. A recent Gallup survey found that two-thirds of working people want a dress code at work because the code clarifies the cultural expectations (Peterson, 1991).

## Clothing and Perception

People make many decisions based on someone's clothing. Among the information inferred from dress are economic level and background, educational level and background, social position and social background, level of success, degree of sophistication, trustworthiness, and moral character (Thourlby, 1978, p. 1). This is vital information because "research has proven that people form impressions and make judgments about others based on what they see within the first few moments of interaction" (Brothers, 1986, cited in Berry, 1986). Tom Wolfe, a well-known author, made the following comment regarding blue suede shoes, which is very much on target: "I love them and I wear them, even though you can't get a bank loan when you do" ("People," 1987).

In an initial job interview situation, the type of clothing is an important factor (Watson & Smeltzer, 1982). During the interview, how the applicant looks ranks as the most important nonverbal cue. Other nonverbal factors include eye contact, facial expression, and gestures. But the willingness to mirror the dress of the interviewer shows an understanding of the cultural demands of the organization and increases acceptance by the interviewer.

As dressing correctly for an interview is important, formal uniforms facilitate certain activities. Bickman (1974a) conducted a study to see the impact on individuals of uniforms. He had four men stop adults asking them to do one of the following: (a) pick up a bag, (b) put a dime in a parking meter for someone else, or (c) stand on the opposite side of a bus stop sign. The men's apparel included civilian, milkman, and guard. He found that regardless of individual characteristics, more people (83%) obeyed the uniformed authority figure than the other two (46%).

In another study, Bickman (1974b) varied the type of dress for individuals from high status—the men wore suits and the women dresses—to low status—the men wore working clothes and the women wore inexpensive skirts and blouses and looked unkempt. He was interested in finding out if people would be more honest with the high- or low-status individual. In the study, Bickman's participant approached the individual, told him or her that he may have left a dime in the phone booth earlier, and asked the caller if he or she had found it. Regardless of the sex, race, age, and status of the subject, more people (77%) returned the dime to the person with high-status attire compared to 38% for the low-status dress. As Cope (1987) reported, "A survey of 292 patients regarding doctors' clothing concluded: Appearance is an important aspect of the way doctors communicate with patients and doctors should pay attention to it. If doctors look good, they are taken seriously by their patients, and the patients believe they will be well taken care of" (p. 7). The study linked dress to the willingness of the patient to follow the doctor's advice (credibility), and to a sense of well-being instead of worry. The study, which was first reported in the *Archives of Internal Medicine*, found patients wanted their doctors to look like doctors. Carrying a stethoscope was a prime appearance factor expected by patients. Finally, patients do not like their physicians—male or female—to be overweight or have hair that is too long. So, the dress and perception are intertwined and the style of dress influences interactions in a variety of circumstances.

Molloy (1975, 1977) authored two books that have had a remarkable effect on the perception of correct business dress. In *Dress for Success*, Molloy (1975) recommended darker attire because it demonstrates greater authority. Gray and dark blue enhance credibility. Pinstripes are also useful for the executive. Ties should be solid or diagonal. In *The Woman's Dress for Success Book* (Molloy, 1977), he called for women to wear medium grays and blues, with whites and pinks being acceptable for blouses. Women should not try to look like men, but they should be very professional and predominately conservative. Molloy has been a clothing consultant for over 400 companies, and his only substantial revision since the books came out is that businesspeople must learn to wear different clothing in different cities. If a Chicago executive moves to New York, he "should shed his 'Chicago Browns' which are seen as executive in Chicago but 'peon' in New York" (Swanson, 1983). *John T. Molloy's New Dress for Success* (Molloy, 1988) reaffirms the impact of correct attire for men in the business world. Women are counseled to wear "the intimidation suit"—a dark, elegantly cut suit—by *Working Woman* magazine (Hellmich, 1988). Sixty-four percent of the 8,033 professional and managerial women responding to a survey by *Working Women* said a professional image was more important for women than men and 48% said they abide by the adage "dress for the position you aspire to" (Hellmich, 1988).

Regardless of the occupation, clothing does make a difference in how people are perceived. From the initial job interview to professional activities, correct attire is necessary to maintain the proper image with other people.

## Clothing and Self-Perception

On the flip side of the dress for success formula is the impact dressing has on each of us. As Molloy (1988) put it, "The meanings transmitted by clothing profoundly affect the perception and thinking not only of the viewer, but of the wearer as well" (pp. 38–39). You are already aware that when you feel well dressed, you are also likely to be more self-confident. There is a self-fulfilling prophecy operating because individuals perceive that they are dressed in an acceptable manner and act accordingly. People's self-perception is enhanced by the realization that they are fitting into the culturally expected behaviors. Remember the IBM vice president's feeling of having a competitive edge because of his dress.

In one study, students on job interviews, who were dressed appropriately for the role, thought they had made a better impression on the interviewer than those not well dressed (Berry, 1987). According to the study, proper dress increased the self-confidence of a person being interviewed for a job including a willingness to ask for a starting salary $4,000 higher than those individuals not well dressed.

People depend on clothing to ease their transformation from a familiar role to one that is less familiar. According to Solomon (1986), "Many people believe that the business suit, for example, can function as a magic amulet that protects the wearer during the rite of passage to a new role as an 'executive' " (p. 30).

The importance of dress ultimately may be reduced to a "which came first, the chicken or the egg" type of analysis. People who are well dressed tend to project an image that is more likely to be accepted in the business world. The business world represents specific cultural interests that will be preserved by choosing individuals who do not threaten the organization. A major cue for the organization is an indication by the individual that he or she understands the "dress code." An inability to show an understanding of the underlying codes of conduct probably will lead to being rejected. Finally, there is every reason to believe that each individual behaves in a more confident manner when dressed for effect.

One very interesting study found that employees were more likely to be friendly toward customers if they were dressed in company smocks and wearing name tags, than if the employees were simply well dressed. The researcher believed this "reflects the process of employees 'putting on' an organizational face when they put on their smock and name tag" (Fischman, 1988, p. 17). The uniforms seemed to act as cues for employees to follow company policy and smile, use eye contact, and thank customers. Given the importance of customer relations for service industries, the apparent relationship between uniforms and effective employee behavior is significant.

The transactional nature of communication leads to a synergistic effect because the acceptance by others will make individuals behave more successfully. So, wearing the wrong clothing probably will subject individuals to messages that they are inappropriately uniformed or costumed for the event. In chapter 1, the interdependence of living systems was emphasized. Nonverbal communication provides excellent proof of this interdependence.

## Clothing and Power

Once information is available that can be used to differentiate some groups from others, it can be used to establish power. Traditionally, people who were the "suits" were management and had some additional control because of their dress. Dress-down Fridays, otherwise known as "jeans day," or "grub day," are used by many organizations to build morale and show a willingness to change (Gottschalk, 1989). Ministers, professors, lawyers, and many other professions can use appropriate dress to indicate a superior position. The medical profession, police, and trainers are three examples of where dress is used to create a specific impression.

Members of the medical profession often use dress to communicate power and status. Burgoon and Saine (1978) observed, "One of the ways doctors, nurses, and medical students reinforce their power position is through the conspicuous display of the badges of their profession. They were never without their white lab coats, stethoscopes, name tags, insignia, and beepers. Doctors wore their lab coats everywhere – to the cafeteria, the bookstore, to meetings, and even to their cars" (pp. 186–187). The importance of dress to the patient already has been established. We like our doctors to look like doctors and the medical profession likes being treated with all the respect due their profession. Clothing and appearance are primary means for achieving both these goals.

Uniformed police officers usually are treated as if they have power, so they do have power and can use it if they wish. Organizations hire official-looking security guards because of the deterrent effect. The popular notion of *power dressing* (e.g., the intimidation suit) is invoked to justify changes from solid ties to striped ties (and back) and for prescriptions regarding the type of shirts, shoes, and jacket.

In an analysis of the use of dress for a training and development person, the advice, according to Lean (1984), is:

> The trainer should choose colors according to the audience and the relationship he or she wants to establish with them. . . . In most cases, the trainer should balance a serious, professional color image with one of likability and trustworthiness. The dark blue or black solid or pinstripe suit that comes so highly recommended nowadays carries too heavy a power message for the trainer, unless he or she is working with a power group, of top managers, for instance. (p. 49)

So, the use of any generalization regarding proper dress must be balanced by the audience and purpose of the transaction.

Intuitively, you probably are aware of the importance of dress and appearance. Pragmatically, how you appear effects all your transactions. In an organization, knowing the appropriate costume for the role is a fundamental requirement for gaining credibility. Individuals must present the appropriate front because the organizational culture is the ultimate determinant for acceptable appearance. As Davidson (1987) put it, "If your image is not helping you to advance in your career, identify your problems and do something about them" (p. 7).

Returning to our original observations about cultures, the Navy provides a useful concluding example. In 1987, the Navy decided it was permissible for Navy men to carry umbrellas (Black, 1987). This decision came after an 18-year debate over the issue. At the same time, the umbrellas must be plain, solid black, without ornamentation, and must be carried in the left hand to permit saluting. Because it took almost two decades to decide this issue, it is not surprising that it is still an "optional uniform item" not allowed in formal ceremonies or parades. The military culture, requiring a sign of readiness to serve and defend the country, did not like the concept of men carrying umbrellas. To allow umbrellas threatened the desired image. The compromise was to require a particular, uniform umbrella that must be used in an exactly correct manner. Organizations, such as ALCOA, Southwest Airlines, Citicorp, and Mellon Bank, allow casual attire to reward participation in fund-raising (e.g., United Way) activities, to encourage creativity, and to motivate employees (Agins, 1992). However, ALCOA employees still keep a suit or other appropriate wear for business lunches and other public settings. Clothing speaks.

At this point, we have discussed facial display, eye contact, paralanguage, body language, and appearance as shown in Fig. 5.1. Each of these nonverbal characteristics focuses primarily on the individual. The remainder of this chapter discusses *proxemics* and *chronemics* as specific issues.

## PROXEMICS

At the beginning of this chapter, we noted that organizations are aware of the importance of territoriality for presenting a corporate image. Individuals also are able to manipulate space, environment, and territorality. *Proxemics* "pertains to how we structure, use and are affected by space in our interactions with others" (Harper, Wiens, & Matarazzo, 1978, p. xii). Hall (1963), the originator of the concept of proxemics, originally placed his emphasis on the unconscious structuring of space. Increasingly, individuals and organizations are aware of many of proxemics' ramifications and intentionally manipulate space.

✔**FACIAL DISPLAY**   **EYE CONTACT**✔
Smiles                Recognition
Hair                  Control
Make-up               Manipulation
Emotions              Power

✔**PARALANGUAGE**   **APPEARANCE**✔
Tone, Rate            Uniforms
Quality               Clothing
Silence               Messages
                      Self-Perception

✔**BODY LANGUAGE**
Height & Physique
Body Movement & Gestures
Synchrony
Self-Perception

FIG. 5.1.   Individual nonverbal communication behaviors.

## Access and Control of Space

A subtle example of the relationship between territorality and a person's place in the hierarchy is their freedom to use the space. First, if you have relatively free access to your territory, you are probably more powerful than many others in an organization. For example, high-level executives can arrive and leave with greater freedom, vary their lunch hours, use their telephone at their own leisure, lock their door, and so on.

Organizations let every individual know just what their capacity is in determining how much of their territory is really their own. If some individuals wish to display pictures on their office walls, for example, they can. This discretion is not universally available. In organizations I have consulted with, ranging from an international moving company to a major bankcorp, the cubicles assigned to each member have strict "dress requirements," including the number and size of personal photographs that can be displayed. How much control individuals actually have over their use of space is a statement of status and power.

Second, if you have the ability to limit other people's access you probably have a certain degree of status. In most organizations, the person with higher rank can enter freely a lower ranking person's territory whereas the lower ranking person must make special arrangements, such as an appointment, to enter the "boss's" territory.

Psychologist Robert Sommer called attention to the roles of keys to a person's position in an organization by developing a formula:

$S = D/K$. S is the status of the person in the organization. D is the number of doors he must open to perform his job and K is the number of keys he carries. A higher number denotes a higher status. Examples: The janitor needs to open 20 doors and has 20 keys ($S = 1$), a secretary has to open two doors with one key ($S = 2$), but the president never has to carry any keys since there is always someone around to open doors for him (with a $K = 0$ and a high D, his S reaches infinity). (Dickson, 1978, p. 137)

To make this discussion of territorality clear, we divide the analysis into two aspects: personal space and touch; and semifixed and fixed space including offices, meeting arrangements, and buildings.

## Personal Space

Hall (1959, 1966) identified four distances between individuals that help define the relationship. Within these four distances are a close phase and a far phase which, when combined with the four distances, provide eight different spatial dimensions. The four identified distances are intimate, personal, social, and public.

*Intimate distance* ranges from 0 to 18 in. with the close phase being actual touch and the far phase of 6 in. to 18 in. where we are fully aware of the other's presence. Physical contact and involvement are easy and activities, such as lovemaking and comforting, occur. In the far phase, individuals still can touch hands and tend to not use a great deal of verbalizations. Because of the closeness, this distance is not considered acceptable in organizations. We discuss touch more extensively once the four distances have been presented.

*Personal distance* ranges from 18 in. to 4 ft. Everyone has a *personal bubble* or protective space around them, which is an invisible boundary between themselves and others. This bubble travels with each individual and expands and contracts under varying circumstances dictated by the elements of each transaction. At the close phase, which is 18 in. to 2½ ft, we are comfortable in accepting our loved ones. In the far phase, we still can touch someone and can detect details about the other person. If an individual has sweat on their upper lip, dandruff on their shoulder, or severe halitosis, it could be detected at this distance, which is between 2½ ft and 4 ft. DeVito (1986) elaborated:

> This distance is particularly interesting from the point of view of body odors and the colognes designed to hide it. At this distance, we cannot perceive normal cologne or perfume. Thus it has been proposed that cologne has two functions: First, it serves to distinguish the body odor or hide it; and, second, it serves to make clear the limits of the protective bubble around the individual. The bubble, defined by the perfume, signals that you may not enter beyond the point where you can smell me. (p. 242)

In an organization, this far phase is used for personal business between very close colleagues. Individuals still can touch or reach someone else, but only with conscious effort. Therefore, each individual has a certain amount of control over the interaction.

The vast majority of business transactions occur in the *social distance.* When two managers discuss company policy, they are likely to do so within social distance's close phase, which would be from 4 ft to 7 ft. In the close phase of social distance, individuals are able to conduct business and are fully aware of the other person's presence. An informal meeting at the water fountain, or conversing about information on a computer screen, could be conducted at this distance. In the far phase, which is 7 ft to 12 ft, the business discussion becomes more formal. People become more dependent on the other nonverbal behaviors, such as eye contact and volume, to maintain the transaction. Social distance, then, is 4 ft to 12 ft. The somewhat dramatic difference between 4 and 12 is reflected in the type of business transacted. Often the far phase of social distance is used to maintain contact without the need for constant interactions.

Once individuals are out of the arena of direct involvement with another individual, they are at a *public distance.* Any distance beyond 12 ft is considered public. The close phase is 12 ft to 15 ft. It allows people to understand the nature of someone else's actions, and they easily can defend themselves or take the appropriate actions toward someone.

However, when people are in the far phase, which is over 25 ft, there is no necessary recognition of individuals. People become part of the setting. A good example would be the president of a major corporation addressing all of the employees at a Christmas party. In an almost automatic fashion, a distance of 25 ft would set up around the president. In addition, the president would be under no obligation to deal with any single individual. Often, briefings to large groups of employees occur at this distance.

There is substantial research suggesting the importance of distance to the attitudes held by the participants. People who are located in close proximity are seen as warmer, friendlier, and more understanding than are people located further away (Patterson, 1968). As our example of the president would suggest, research also indicates that status differences are emphasized by physical distance and minimized by greater closeness. According to Mehrabian (1969), "The findings of a large number of studies collaborate one another and indicate that communicator-addressee distance is correlated with the degree of negative attitude communicated to and inferred by the addressee" (p. 363). Unless the situation calls for reinforcing differences in status through public distance, it would be wise to work toward reducing the distance between individuals to a level that is clearly consistent with the goals of the transaction.

Interpersonal distances include intimate, personal, social, and public. Within each of these categories are the close and far phases. Congruency between the distance used and the content of the transaction is vital.

## Touch

Sometimes called *zero proxemics* (Hickson & Stacks, 1985, p. 47), the use of touch in a business setting is culturally regulated. Handshakes are a well-known mechanism for greetings, agreements, and farewells. A handshake that is too hard, long, "feminine," or flaccid can result in an impression not actually intended (Hickson & Stacks, 1985, p. 200). In a survey of personnel managers at 30 companies, 90% indicated that a firm handshake by the applicant is important (Forbes, 1990).

Touch has a variety of other uses in an organizational setting. Depending on the relationship between individuals, touch can be used for consolation, support, and congratulations.

Power and dominance also are expressed through touching behavior. Henley (1977), in *Body Politics,* pointed to specific examples of when certain individuals can put their arm on another's shoulder or put their hand on another's back (pp. 104–109). In the following dyads, you should have no difficulty in deciding who could put their hand on the other person with the greatest of ease, and with the least violation of cultural rules. The examples are manager and worker, teacher and student, doctor and patient, businessperson and secretary, and minister and parishioner. Because the first person in each dyad also has higher status, they could touch with greater ease. This freedom to touch acts, according to Henley, as a power and dominance behavior for men. When women use touch, she argued, it is interpreted in a sexual, rather than political or power-oriented, way.

Mehrabian (1981) explained touch in a different manner. Using the *immediacy principle,* he concluded that people are drawn toward persons and things they like, evaluate highly, and prefer, and they avoid or move away from things they dislike, evaluate negatively, or do not prefer (pp. 22–23). In this context, touching is a statement of liking rather than power. Research on interpersonal attraction seems to support the concept that we touch people we like and avoid ones we do not like (Berscheid & Walster, 1969; Huston, 1974).

Somewhere between Henley's (1977) political orientation and the interpersonal attraction studies would be the concept forwarded in some managerial literature that calls for a "pat on the back" of an employee after they have been disciplined (Blanchard & Johnson, 1982). This pat can be either actual or symbolic, but the impact is to reestablish trust and caring between the superior and the subordinate.

The organizational world uses the concept of touch in many symbolic ways, including "out-of-touch," "touching," "bruising," "touch base," "keep in contact," "stroking," "rubbing the wrong way," and someone's a "soft touch." In chapter 3, we mentioned the concept of a hired hand. We hand someone power; use hands-on or hands-off approaches; hire a handy man or woman; get a handle on a crisis; an agreement is at hand; organizations are handcuffed by rules; managers are heavy-handed; some people do not want to get their hands dirty; people are on hand; and numerous other terms using touch or hands to explain organizational processes. These lists are indicative of the many ways that the importance of touch is expressed.

Increasingly, actual touch is regulated in organizations. Part of the impetus stems from recent court cases regarding sexual harassment, which also have established new limits on a superior's right to touch a subordinate (Machlowitz & Machlowitz, 1987). In a sense, these cases step between Henley's (1977) and Mehrabian's (1981) positions and point to the possible abuses by superiors of touching.

### Stigmas

Goffman (1963) observed that we maintain greater distances from individuals who have stigmas. He was referring to individuals who are "possessing an attribute that makes him different from others in the category of persons available for him to be, and of a less desirable kind—in the extreme, a person who is thoroughly bad, or dangerous, or weak" (p. 3). In a very real sense, stigmas exist throughout the specialized cultures of various organizations. The discredited manager, the loud and complaining employee, the outlandish dresser, or the failed salesperson, for example, would seem to elicit greater distancing than people who accept or reflect the organizational norms. When you decide to leave one organization to work for another, do not be suprised if suddenly you are treated as an outsider who no longer is invited to parties or involved in decisions.

When stigmatized individuals invade our personal space, they often are treated as nonpersons. A crowded elevator provokes most people simply to ignore the other person's presence by directing eye contact to the ceiling or the floor. Intrusions into our intimate space by an obnoxious or extremely outgoing person cause most individuals to treat the intruder as a nonperson or a "dummy" (Burgoon & Saine, 1978, p. 97). This reaction allows people to deny that the invasion actually is occurring.

In summary, the area around each individual that is used to regulate transactions with other individuals is the first category of proxemics. Everyone has an invisible, flexible bubble that surrounds them or a "body buffer zone" (Horowitz, Duff, & Stratten, 1964, p. 651) so potential invasions have communication impact. Both distances and touch have specific rules of conduct which frequently are not stated, but are very real.

## Territoriality

There is a biological tendency for individuals to own the space around them (Smith & Williamson, 1985, p. 220). Individuals literally extend out into the surrounding space and set up boundaries. The various territories surrounding each person, ranging from their car to their home to their parking spot, become part of who they are and they establish ownership.

While working with several major hospitals and a regional medical center, I continually come across the concept of "GOMERS." For many individuals, hospitals are foreign territories that provoke some misgivings. In discussing why patients and visitors might have this negative reaction, someone would talk about GOMERS. The rest of the group of managers and doctors would nod understandingly. Naturally, I asked what a GOMER was. The term stands for *Get Out Of My Emergency Room.* Emergency room doctors have a strong territorial perspective and resent anyone not truly ill invading the space. So common are their complaints about hypochondriacs and nuisance cases, that the phrase GOMER has been coined and in use for a long period of time.

Regardless of the organization, individuals will take over space around them. Supervisors or line managers will individualize their stations. Secretaries apply personal touches to their desks.

Understanding this natural tendency also explains why there is a biological advantage to the possessor of the space, and why there is a relationship between space and social hierarchies. In organizations, a person's office often is set up in such a manner as to provide comfort, and therefore an advantage, in any transaction. Consultants frequently suggest that important issues be discussed away from anyone's own personal office. Labor union leaders and management representatives always seek neutral territory to discuss contracts.

Hall (1972) provided three dimensions for understanding how territoriality can be divided: *dynamic, semifixed,* and *fixed-feature.* A discussion of each of these follows.

### Dynamic

Dynamic involves the use of space as people communicate. Each of Hall's (1959, 1966) four categories we outlined at the beginning of the discussion of proximity operate in the dynamic use of space. Cooper (1979) noted:

> There is a wealth of information to be gained from observing how attendees mill around before a meeting or "shoot the breeze" around the cooler. It is easy to determine which person is the leader of a group. When a superior is talking with a number of subordinates, the configuration often takes on a "choir effect." The leader, at the top of the diagram, is given more space; the others are facing the leader in a semicircle. The "choir" will usually stand attentively, rarely turning to leave unless someone else arrives to fill the gap. (p. 18)

When people arrange furniture or other objects in the environment to control their transactions with other people, they are using the semifixed process. This can include where someone chooses to sit at a meeting, or how they arrange their office.

### Semifixed

The possibilities for arranging furniture and seating patterns is practically endless. We discuss three aspects of the semifixed concept to demonstrate what the issues are. The three are dyadic sitting positions, meeting arrangements, and office setup.

**Dyadic Seating Positions.**   Several studies have been conducted that indicate that people will choose to sit in different positions depending on what they perceive are the goals of the transaction. Sommer (1969) reported four specific differences in where people will position themselves depending on the desired outcomes (pp. 28–29, 39–57). Figure 5.2 shows the four positions. Other studies have collaborated Sommer's findings (Cook, 1970; Lang, Calhoun, & Selby, 1977).

In *competitive* situations, individuals will sit across from one another. By facing an opponent, individuals can react to all of the possible moves or threats that might occur. People also feel safer because of the table. Finally, most competitive games are based on a "face-off" or "taking sides," so it makes sense that people would choose this positioning.

In my consulting experience, I have observed that this seating operates as a self-fulfilling prophecy because people became competitive even when there was no apparent reason. This positioning maximizes the potential for sending and receiving conflicting messages. It has the greatest interpersonal distance, which also helps explain the tendency toward combat rather than collaboration.

Sitting with a corner between the participants is called *cooperative* by some authors and *conversation* by others. The presence of the corner allows some protection of our personal bubble and still guarantees a concentration of the transaction because there is little personal distance. Information-gathering interviews often use this arrangement.

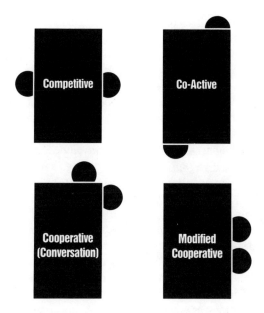

FIG. 5.2.   Four possible seating arrangements. Illustration provided by W. G. Griffin with permission.

Sommer (1969) labeled sitting next to another person as *modified cooperative.* The side-by-side position allows the participants to concentrate on the task at hand. In organizations, individuals who are trying to work through the same task will adopt such a seating pattern. Because there is little interpersonal distance, or opportunities for conflicting nonverbal messages, individuals tend to concentrate on the job rather than on each other.

When distance is a desired element in the interaction, the coactive arrangement is used. In this situation, individuals can discuss specific issues without continually being in active verbal discourse. As Fig. 5.2 shows, each of the these positions provides different communication opportunities.

***Meeting Arrangements.***   In meetings, sitting at the end of a rectangular table is a statement of leadership (Reiss & Rosenfeld, 1980). Participants wanting to be considered part of the group frequently will choose the middle chairs. Cooper (1979b) concluded: "You should be familiar with the dominant and subordinate positions around a rectangular business meeting table. The dominant positions are the ends. The middle of the table is a secondary dominant position and is usually used for active defense or disagreement with the leader on the end. The weakest positions are in between the powers, in the 'dead zone' of status" (p. 33).

Sometimes meetings provoke a King Authur arrangement. As the myth is told, King Authur used a round table to make certain no knight was given greater status over any other. As it turns out, the person sitting closest to the king was considered the "right-hand" man and still accorded the greatest status. In modern organizations, the king is ambidextrous because the positions to the left and the right on a rectangular table are considered power positions (Cooper, 1979b, p. 34).

Korda (1986), whose major concern is with power in an organization, described *power spots* around a table. At a rectangular table, the corner spots are the best for asserting power. When a circular table is used, the most powerful position at 12 o'clock high, and the power decreases clockwise around the table from this spot (pp. 145–146).

At this point you might be concerned that the advice varies depending on the expert's personal perspective. Sitting at a meeting begins to look more like a game of musical chairs than an opportunity to engage in serious discussion. As you will recall from chapter 3, political perspectives regarding organizational behavior do lead to game playing.

So, where should you sit? A good question and a valid concern. The answer lies in returning to some of the earlier information regarding nonverbal communication. Because eye contact is one of the most powerful means of communication, placing yourself in a position where you can be in direct contact with those individuals you wish to focus on would seem to be the key. The King Authur arrangement requires the lesser "knights" to look at you and the king. A power spot view focuses on the danger of being away from the *activity centers* at a table. A place at the table that is across from the leader provides an opportunity to directly challenge the king, but it could also leave the challenger out of the discussion if the leader demanded attention. Without invoking the political concepts, we still can predict that being outside the points of convergence of the discussion will isolate an individual. So, realistically, if you wish to be paid attention to, pick a high-profile spot.

As trite as some of this maneuvering may seem, power is a major concern in many organizations. Even if a political perspective, with its power orientation, is not the issue, we should worry about the seating arrangement. Where people sit, and who they sit next to, does regulate individual participation.

Much of the expert advice centers on an individual's desire to lead or dominate a meeting. Although the advice by authorities differs, leadership clearly is established by sitting where an individual can control the transaction. As opposed to a dyadic meeting, where sitting across from someone can create conflict, having all eyes centered on a leadership position in a larger meeting obviously is desirable. Both ends of a rectangular table tend to be leadership positions. Various configurations are used to reduce power positioning, and one means that is gaining increased popularity is the oval-shaped table.

**Office Setup.**   The last aspect to examine is the office setup. Because territoriality always gives the advantage to the possessor, office setup can be used by the office holder to send messages and control transactions.

Assuming you can change your office layout, Korda (1986) provided three specific furniture arrangements for three different types of control (pp. 145–146). The first setup allows the visitor to sit next to the desk, which provides the greatest comfort for the visitor. In this arrangement, dominance is minimized and interpersonal contact maximized.

The second arrangement creates more power for the occupant. The chairs are arranged so the desk is a barrier between the individuals. In addition to creating the competitive arrangement, the office possessor has all the implements of power provided by the desk at his or her disposal. Files, telephone, and so on, are part of the desk's instruments of power.

In the third arrangement, the visitor's chair is placed so it is in a corner, away from the door, with little space. The occupant can move around with some freedom, whereas the visitor must remain "cornered."

Depending on how much power an individual feels like imposing, additional actions can include placing the visitor in a soft chair or one with shorter legs. This would maximize the *angle of inclination* between the power holder and the chair's occupant. Being forced to look up to someone replicates power situations such as a teacher-student, parent-child, or speaker-audience. We discussed the natural tendency to assign credibility to height and this type of manipulation creates a taller image or impression. An important caveat is that once people recognize the ploys and strategies, the competitive advantage is neutralized.

For many individuals, creating the best possible climate, by minimizing power differentials, is the goal. In my work as a consultant, I have found most managers eager to rearrange their offices to enhance the quality of interactions. One obvious change is to use the first office-seating arrangement. In addition, creating a neutral territory within the office, such as a sofa and chair or a small round table with two or three chairs, removes the desk as a barrier. An additional alternative is to seek a neutral meeting spot, such as a conference or break room.

The selection, display, and arrangement of objects also provide strong nonverbal messages. Diplomas, awards, and other artifacts emphasize expertise and background, whereas plants and other decorations might focus on comfort. Once again, Korda (1986) argued for a careful selection of symbols and emphasized simplicity as the ultimate power symbol (p. 149). The image that someone is too important to be dealing with a variety of trivial matters does seem powerful. Korda also listed many dated power symbols including framed diplomas (p. 149). The number of keys formula mentioned earlier in this chapter relates to this concept.

Individuals expect some indications of expertise when they visit a doctor's or lawyer's office. Although most lawyers do not constantly refer to the law books in their offices, it is highly reassuring to know the lawyer would be able to locate the necessary information, because of the displayed reading material.

Arranging an office and applying certain decorations are both examples of semifixed features. Returning to the definitions at the beginning of this chapter, any behavior to which someone assigns meaning can be nonverbal communication. Even the option of closing an office door for a meeting, as opposed to being in a shared office, can be an important nonverbal message.

A major *perk* in most organizations is a premium parking space. Parking privileges frequently are based on an individual's status in the organization. Even when the size of the organization would not seem to warrant parking privileges, the owner or manager inevitably will be provided a special spot.

In some organizations, the best parking place is now given to outstanding employees, rather than the president or CEO, as a reward. As a clear statement of status, the parking space draws attention to special contributions by individual employees. The best salesperson, the most valuable suggestion giver, the person who acts as the best customer service representative, or the holder of the best attendance record are all possible candidates. Whatever behavior the organization wishes to reinforce can be the basis for assigning the space.

### Fixed-Feature

The fixed-feature arrangement includes "internal, culturally specific configuration, and external environmental arrangements such as architecture and space layout" (Hall, 1972, p. 210). The elements that go into the office, such as furniture, are fixed. These visible appurtenances do vary greatly depending on status, with larger offices, bigger desks, and no file cabinets indicative of the highest level of achievement (Fabun, 1968, pp. 25–26). Fixtures that cannot be moved easily make the strongest statement. Decisions regarding office design and type, and who receives the best offices, fall into this last category.

The modern office building evolved through three major phases (Stone & Luchetti, 1985). The first phase was a *row or militarylike arrangement.* In the early 1900s, office managers used the factory management procedures discussed in chapter 3 and put clerks into rows. According to Stone and Luchetti (1985), "As organizations grew, many companies in which management preferred private, walled offices came to have depressingly long hallways lined with closed doors. Needless to say, in these places, informal communication was discouraged" (p. 104). This setup still exists in numerous organizations. For example, the U.S. Postal Service mail distribution centers have clerks sitting in rows tapping out zip codes from letters. The major feature of this type of setting is a full concentration on individual work and little interaction with colleagues. This is a *structural* approach to organizational design.

The second phase came from the Quickborner team in Germany, who called for eliminating both the factorylike setting and the private cells. Instead, an *open* setting was used to encourage interaction.

However, many Americans are not fully comfortable with this totally open design. As a bridge between the closed doors and the open space, a *landscaped partitioning* process became popular and lead to *cubicleland.* For many organizations, this design allows individuals to feel as if they have privacy without erecting walls. People have their own territory within the open, but structured, design of the organization.

Open spaces do leave people vulnerable to numerous distractions because of competing stimuli. Individuals need visual and acoustic space, as well as their own physical autonomy. For example, the capacity to conduct important, and often confidential, business is more difficult in an open setting. So, the use of *workstations* presents a viable alternative to rows or closed doors.

Organizations also have surrounded offices in glass, thereby providing privacy in conversations, while retaining a sense of common purpose. The managers at one major plastics corporation dubbed the glass offices "fishbowls," but they appreciated the added privacy of the enclosed space over the cubicles. In other words, they were afforded the acoustic, but not the visual privacy.

*Activity centers* are the third phase of office design and are being used with increased efficiency by various organizations. The goal is to provide the privacy needed for certain activities and still utilize open communication whenever possible. The terms are fully descriptive of the change in moving from workstations to activity centers. Different parts of an organization are set up for particular needs. So, specialized equipment can be scheduled for different groups at various times. Rather than expecting all activities to be conducted in a particular space, the individuals or groups move around from conference rooms to computer centers to other settings conducive to particular activities. The human expertise is movable, providing the most efficient use of space.

The major stumbling block to this third phase is the traditional equation of office size and location with status (Stone & Luchetti, 1985, p. 106). Although it is logical to share equipment and facilities, there is a desire for individualized offices. The counterbalancing force is the need for flexibility and the immense cost of giving everybody their own fully outfitted workstation.

Seiler (1984) discussed this from a broad perspective: "Buildings influence behavior by structuring relationships among members of the organization. They encourage some communication patterns and discourage others. They assign positions of importance to units of the organization. They do these things according to a plan that fits the company's strategic design, or to a nonplan that doesn't. They have effects on behavior, planned or not" (p. 120). The use of rows, individualized offices, cubicleland's workstations, or activity centers all help form certain behaviors by the employees.

Designing a building requires some insightful considerations. One example of design intended to control behavior is the seating arrangement and chair comfort (or lack of) in modern airports (Knapp, 1978, p. 101). As fixed features in the waiting areas, the rows of chairs make speaking to more than a couple of people at a time practically impossible. In addition, the chairs are intentionally hard. Both of these factors force patrons to move into more comfortable settings, such as the restaurant, cocktail lounge, or shops. The airport therefore discourages crowding by family and friends at the exit areas and encourages everyone to spend money at the various concessions.

Design also includes aesthetics and lighting. Several studies have demonstrated that people in beautiful settings perform more effectively than do people in ugly settings (Knapp, 1978, p. 96). When the surroundings send a message of quality, there is an increased likelihood of quality outcomes.

The Hawthorne Studies discussed in chapter 3 demonstrated a correlation between changes in lighting and performance. The performance changes have been attributed to the increased attention. However, "generally speaking, researchers have found that the brighter the room, the better the performance" (Meer, 1985, p. 60). Meer developed a set of premises for what type of lighting is most likely to produce which results. Based on current research, lighting changes affect the type of conversation, sense of satisfaction, and the amount of interaction. Direct, overhead lighting is not as effective as indirect lighting, and uniformed lighting made people feel that the room was larger. As with other types of fixed-feature issues, lighting does make a difference.

*Ergonomics* is the field of study that concentrates on making a workplace as compatible as possible with the physical and psychological needs of the people who do the job (Gaines, 1987). The term is derived from the Greek, *ergo,* meaning work, and *nomics,* meaning management or law. With the increase in specialization, such as computers or robotics, semifixed equipment's design must be considered carefully for its impact on workers' comfort and productivity ("VDTs [Video Display Terminals]: Fitting," 1991). The external environmental control placed on organizations by the Occupational Health and Safety Administration, for example, has forced companies to install specific equipment for specialized tasks ranging from computer workstations to hazardous occupations.

**Size and Location.** Larger desks and offices and ones located higher up in buildings are normally indicative of highest status (Fabun, 1968, pp. 25–26). The number of barriers between an individual and a visitor also can be an indication of status. If a secretary answers someone's phone, or an appointment is necessary to meet with the person, this usually is taken as a power or status cue. In spite of the pressure to manage by wandering around, and to afford open access to high-ranking corporate officers, the majority of organizational leaders still limit access to a select few (Bennis, 1990, pp. 140–141).

For individuals who want to increase their influence, Korda (1975) argued that office placement is the most significant factor. He found that corner offices were most often the power spots (pp. 63–105, 232). A 1983 American Society of Interior Designers survey of 143 chief executives showed that 75% of the CEOs had corner offices with big or wide views. Sixty-one percent had offices on the top floor and 59% had the building's largest office (Ward, 1986). In addition, 67% had original artwork, 62% had private washrooms, 51% had custom rugs, 36% had custom furniture, 25% had antiques, 13% had a dining room, and 12% had a wet bar. Although the luxuries are impressive, the most important message about these offices is the occupant's ability to alter the fixed features.

Modern technology is also changing the impact of territoriality. The automobile, for example, provides a traveling office for numerous salespersons.

For some individuals, their vehicle is of primary importance. For example, the Steelcase furniture company does not allow a new driver to take a vehicle on the road for 6 months (Waterman, 1987, pp. 269–270). During this initiation period, new drivers wash the trucks and wait for their opportunity to earn the right to drive the trucks. From that point on, each driver takes immense pride in the cleanliness of the truck. The same type of story can be told about UPS trucks and drivers. Territoriality extends well beyond office buildings.

About 10 million Americans use their home as their office (Verrengia, 1987). The type of profession ranges from doctors and lawyers to home repair businesses. Technology has created a specialized type of home office for an estimated 600,000 workers who are *telecommuters* (Verrengia, 1987). These people work at home with electronic equipment supplied by their company. Organizations report improvements in productivity of up to 50%. Three explanations for this remarkable increase are (a) individual control over goals and work design, (b) freedom from distractions such as walk-ins and phone calls, and (c) individual control over the environment. Because computer hookups make the actual location of the equipment a moot point, territoriality can be anywhere an individual telecommuter desires (Shirley, 1986). Changes in territoriality can lead to significant gains or losses in productivity.

Everyone is affected by the use of space and territoriality. Ranging from zero proxemics through various configurations of an organizational setting, how a transaction is arranged influences the communication.

### Territoriality and Symbolic Behavior

Office size and location, parking spaces, and surroundings are all examples of territoriality that has symbolic impact. In addition, the design of meeting rooms and office buildings makes statements about the intended message for employees and visitors.

An interesting example of the tendency to own space is the *NIH* factor. *Not Invented Here* is "a fairly well-known phenomena in the management of technology. [It] refers to the fact that engineers are not predisposed to like things that other engineers have invented" (Waterman, 1987, p. 81). At several major computer companies, and at Ford Motor Company, the concept is called "tossing it over the wall." One division creates the design, then it is "tossed over" to another division which engineers the design, and then the design plans are "tossed over" to the manufacturing and production divisions who make the final product. Each division proceeds to redefine the concept as a means of resisting the foreign input into their part of the process. Therefore, teamwork and cooperation are sacrificed in favor of territorial defense. Whether it is someone's office, truck, or pet project, ownership is part of how people approach territoriality.

In summary, territoriality is a major nonverbal factor in organizations. The tendency to own space, the biological advantage afforded to the owner, and the status attributed to space all make territoriality a critical issue. Territoriality is manifested through the variations in the dynamic or interpersonal, semifixed or office and meeting arrangements, and fixed-feature factors.

Organizations have approached the allocation of space in three ways. The first, a military-like setting, is based on factory design, and a structural view of organizations. Offices in rows, structure, and everything in its proper place have characterized this type of space allocation. This purpose of allocating individual offices increases the tendency toward political concerns because battles of office location and size tend to surface.

The second form of space allocation is the most predominant in the United States. Rather than the military rows, space use ranges from open spaces to the extensive use of partitions and cubicles. Pressure from the human relations approach, discussed in chapter 3, led to the reduction of barriers.

How the barriers are manipulated to alter the organization's communication patterns becomes very important symbolically. In an effort to bridge the gap between private offices for rank and cubicles for efficiency, many organizations provide offices for the higher status members and divided space for lower management and staff.

Activity centers are the final type of space design being forwarded in the modern organization. This use of design is work oriented. The acceptance of this space design will be slow because of the political and symbolic views of personal space. As with clothing, space allocation in buildings speaks and the messages help control communication.

For a large number of workers, their office is mobile or at home. In both cases, the impact of territoriality is shifted, but the importance is not diminished.

## CHRONEMICS

Chronemics is the study of the use of time. Western cultures are very oriented to time as an important part of the workday (Hall, 1959; Hobbs, 1987; Lakein, 1973). Factory workers are "on the clock," people receive "hourly wages," managers receive and give "annual" performance reviews, appointments are "on time," and so on. Time is how we measure and quantify work by using seconds, minutes, hours, days, weeks, months, seasons, and years. We are paid for our time and are congratulated for getting tasks completed ahead of schedule or on time. Time is money in our culture.

Punctuality is an important message. Being late for a job interview, for example, is tantamount to saying you are not interested in the position (Burgoon & Saine, 1978, pp. 102–103). People in high power positions have the luxury of setting the meeting time for appointments and being late (Burgoon & Saine, 1978, p. 185).

Waiting, the consequence of how time is used, has two functions (Levine, 1987). First, individuals measure someone's importance by how long they are willing to wait for them. The greater the person's prestige, the longer people will wait patiently. How much prestige would you assign, for example, to a medical doctor that you did not have to wait to see? An empty waiting room, an assembly line approach, or easy access might make you somewhat suspicious about the doctor's reputation or credentials. In many cases, people value what they wait for and devalue what comes quickly (Levine, 1987, p. 30). Levine further stated, "The rules and principles that govern waiting—who waits up front, who waits in the back and who waits not at all—are part of the silent language of culture, seldom expressed but carrying a message that speaks louder than words" (p. 26).

Two especially important rules are: Status dictates who waits, and the privileged do not wait. Both of these rules mean "time is the ultimate symbol of domination. Those who control others' time have power, and those who have power control others' time" (Levine, 1987, p. 30).

Second, individuals tend to equate the amount of time someone will spend with them as a message regarding how important they are to the time spender. The reverse is also true, because individuals tend to spend more time with individuals who are most important to them. On a job interview, for example, a 5-min audience would leave the impression that the individual was not being considered seriously for the job.

From a structural or scientific view, time is how organizations measure an individual's worth. Seventy percent of American factories use time clocks to monitor employee promptness and attendance ("Business and Legal," 1987). *Just-in-time* (JIT) inventory management has become a popular structural management tool for reducing the buildup of supplies by the manufacturer before they are needed and eliminating waste in the organization (Peters, 1987, pp. 117–118). In a true implementation of the adage that time is money, JIT shifts the control of the quality process from top management to the factory floor thereby eliminating delays (Myers, 1991, pp. 47–68). Saving time leads to a competitive advantage and an important involvement of employees. So, when correctly implemented, JIT moves from a structural approach to a human resources strategy that leads to important symbolic and cultural changes (Myers, 1991).

The human resources approach tries to make time for every employee and create informal opportunities to spend time. Responding to these pressures, managers frequently point to a lack of time as their major impediment to being effective. In response, "a great deal of management training comes right under the heading: Learn How To Manage Your Time" (Kast & Rosenzweig, 1984, p. 44). Human resource approaches try to enhance the use of time by helping individuals do the right things rather than just doing things right.

There is also an increased awareness of the circadian rhythms that reflect our natural body clocks. Individuals working split shifts, for example, have greater difficulties at work because the rotating shifts leave an impact similar to jet lag (Painter, 1986; Van, 1983). So, efforts are made in many organizations to bridge the gap between our body clocks and the needs of the workplace.

A political or power-oriented approach makes people wait or manipulates time. A favorite political ploy is to schedule a meeting for less time than necessary so the leader has tremendous control over the agenda.

Increasingly, organizations are approaching time from a symbolic view. Time clocks, for example, are being eliminated in some organizations to indicate management's trust of employees (Peters, 1987, p. 291). In managing, the amount of time the leader spends with a work group, a project, or an individual is often more important than what occurs during the time (Peters, 1987, p. 414). Both of the symbolic actions have created significant results.

With the expanding interest in international business, most business leaders who have met with their Latin American counterparts will relate an anecdote about being punctual and then having to wait for the other party (Burgoon & Saine, 1978, p. 103; Hall, 1985). Pursuing Japanese manufacturing plants and Chinese business in order to get them to locate in a particular part of the United States has become a preoccupation by American political and business leaders (Bowman, 1986; Buckley, 1988). Americans are suprised by the slow, time-consuming pace of oriental business decisions (Hall & Hall, 1987; Ohmae, 1987). Any change of cultural boundaries will bring to light differences in how time is perceived and used.

Chronemics, then, is an important nonverbal communication mechanism. In a variety of ways, the manipulation of time sends messages.

## FORM AND CONTENT

What we say and what we do are often interrelated. As we pointed out at the beginning of this chapter, form—how things are done and said—and content—what is verbally communicated—are both important. One of the experiences shared by anyone who has submitted a research paper or analysis is to be criticized about the style of the paper. Although we justifiably can call for a focus on our content, the form often "speaks" louder than the content. Two examples should underscore this point.

In studies of effective resumes, keeping the format brief is critical and avoiding common mistakes, such as spelling errors and sloppiness, are most important to recruiters according to the National Association for Corporate and Professional Recruiters (Laird, 1987). Next to telling the truth and being qualified for the job, how the resume looks makes a vital difference.

The second example is the Dillion Hypothesis of Titular Colonicity (Perry, 1985). J. T. Dillion (1982) and others have found a correlation between the placement of a colon in a scholarly paper's title and its likelihood to be accepted as important scholarship. A form issue, the colon, seems to be linked to the scholarly outcome. Although the resume example is vital to obtaining a job, the colon issue simply points to the importance of "proper dress" even in some scholarly activities.

## CONCLUSION

Nonverbal communication is a vital aspect of organizational behavior. Nonverbal communication is different from verbal communication because: It is based on normative rules; it includes all behavior not verbal; it operates in the present, all behavior can be meaningful, and it cannot be stopped; and it is dependent on context.

Any attempts to understand organizational behavior without also focusing on non-verbal communication will be less than comprehensive.

Because nonverbal communication is so broad, 14 guiding principles should be applied. Eight of these principles apply to all nonverbal communication and 6 are applied specifically to organizations. As with all rules of human behavior, exceptions are clearly possible.

Specific nonverbal communication issues provide paradigms for understanding how organizations use and respond to behaviors. Facial display, eye contact, paralanguage, body language, and appearance are the five individual subjects. Proxemics and chronemics are concepts more dependent on external factors.

Facial display includes smiles, use of hair and makeup, and the display of emotions. The face is a major method for transmitting meaning. Eye contact is a powerful mechanism for controlling transactions and numerous messages are created through eye behavior. Paralanguage is the manipulation of various aspects of the voice that provides explanation for the verbal messages.

Body language is concerned with how the body is used to communicate. Height and physique give messages in organizations. The use of body movement and gestures explains how synchrony works. Specific gestures allow illustration and adaptation and etiquette and smoking are examples of how expectations exist in organizations regarding body language.

All organizations have specific appearance expectations or dress standards. Uniforms are the most obvious form of dress requirements and are used widely to enhance the quality of organizations. Clothing sends messages to other people and has specific functions for each individual. In addition, clothing affects other people's perception of our abilities and changes our self-perception. Dress influences a person's power. How an individual dresses makes a significant difference.

Proxemics is a broad concept explaining how people use space. Access and control of space are general issues underscoring an individual's position in an organization. Personal space, touch, stigmas, and territoriality are four additional issues in proxemics. Intimate, personal, social, and public are the four types of personal space. Touch is zero proxemics. Power, dominance, interpersonal liking, and effective management are all displayed through the use of touch. A stigmatized, or discredited, individual makes us withdraw touch.

Territoriality can be explained by examining dynamic, semifixed, and fixed features. The dynamic concepts include the various uses of personal space. Semifixed features of territoriality include dyadic seating, meeting arrangements, and office setup.

In two-person positions in seating, where people sit can indicate a competitive, cooperative, modified cooperative, or coactive psychological set. When people gather for meetings, specific seating arrangements tend to create activity spots or power centers. Regardless of the perspective taken, where someone sits does make a difference in terms of how much they will actively participate and possibly lead.

Offices offer opportunities for changing the seating arrangement to affect the type of transactions occurring. Angle of inclination and the display of artifacts also influence the transaction. Where an individual is assigned parking is symbolically important in many organizations.

Fixed-feature aspects of territoriality divide into organizational layout and design and the symbolic uses of space. A military or factory setting, open spaces, partitions and cubicles, and activity centers are the three general fixed-feature layouts. The use of lighting and aesthetics does influence individuals.

In addition, the size and location of an office are important nonverbal messages. For many Americans, their car and home have become their offices reinforcing the systems nature of all organizations discussed in chapter 1. Because territoriality is significant to all living systems, its symbolic uses should be understood.

Chronemics is the use of time. How time is used is determined culturally. Because of the control aspects of organizational life, punctuality and waiting are clear nonverbal messages.

As indicated at the beginning of the chapter, all communication behavior is interrelated. So, although content, or the verbal aspects, is important, the form, or nonverbal conditions, also must be considered. We have risked belaboring our analysis of nonverbal communication because it is very important to our understanding of organizational communication. Too often, log cabin advice is given, and believed, instead of developing in-depth knowledge of the critical issues. Any attempt to explain organizational communication without fully examining nonverbal communication simply would be incomplete.

## REFERENCES

Adler, R. B. (1983). *Communicating at work.* New York: Random House.

Agins, T. (1992, March 23). Breaking out of the grey flannel suit. *The Wall Street Journal,* pp. B1, B8.

Banzhaf, J. F. (1987, August 2). Bans on smoking at work may lead some to kick habit. *St. Louis Post Dispatch,* p. 5C.

Beegle, B. B. (1971, February). The message that is sent without words. *Supervisory Management,* pp. 12–14.

Bennis, W. (1990). *Why leaders can't lead: The unconscious conspiracy continues.* San Francisco: Jossey-Bass.

Berko, R. M., Wolvin, A. D., & Wolvin, D. R. (1985). *Communicating: A social and career focus* (3rd ed.). Boston: Houghton Mifflin.

Berry, M. (1986, August 10). Do looks make the woman: You bet they do. *The Evansville Sunday Courier and Press,* p. D1.

Berry, M. (1987, October 26). How mini is too mini? At work you still can't cut it too short. *The Evansville Courier,* p. 6.

Berscheid, E., & Walster, E. H. (1969). *Interpersonal attraction.* Reading, MA: Addison-Wesley.

Bickman, L. (1974a). The social power of a uniform. *Journal of Applied Social Psychology, 4,* 47–61.

Bickman, L. (1974b). Social roles and uniforms: Clothes make the person. *Psychology Today, 7,* 48–51.

Bickman, L. (1987). The effect of social status on the honesty of others. *Journal of Applied Social Psychology, 4,* 87–92.

Birdwhistell, R. L. (1970). *Kinesics and context: Essays on body motion communication.* Philadelphia: University of Pennsylvania Press.

Black, N. (1987, November 11). Navy decides umbrellas OK in left hand. *The Evansville Courier*, p. 2.

Blanchard, K., & Johnson, S. (1982). *The one minute manager*. New York: Morrow.

Bonuso, C. (1979). *Phi Delta Kappan, 64*. Cited in *Psychology Today, 17*, 17.

Bowman, J. S. (1986, September). The rising sun in America. *Personnel Administrator, 31*, 63–67, 114–117.

Boyanowsky, E. O., & Griffiths, C. T. (1982). Weapons and eye contact as instigators or inhibitors of aggressive arousal in police–citizen interaction. *Journal of Applied Social Psychology, 12*, 398–407.

Bruneau, T. J. (1973). Communicative silences: Forms and functions. *Journal of Communication, 23*, 17–46.

Buckley, J. (1988, May 9). We learned that they may be us. *U.S. News & World Report*, pp. 48–57.

Burgoon, J. K., Buller, D. B., & Woodall, W. G. (1989). *Nonverbal communication: The unspoken dialogue*. New York: Harper & Row.

Burgoon, J. K., & Saine, T. (1978). *The unspoken dialogue*. Dallas: Houghton Mifflin.

Business and legal reports. (1987, June 5). Cited in *USA Today*, p. B4.

Butler, A. (1987, December 29). It's a crying shame if it is at office. *The Sunday Courier*, p. F9.

Case, J. (1987). The sounds of silence: Why aren't there any good business tapes? *INC, 9*(10), p. 22.

Cash, T. F., Winstead, B. A., & Janda, L. H. (1986). The great American shape-up. *Psychology Today, 20*, 30–37.

Cervera, L. (1987, May 8). Facial hair. *USA Today*, p. B4.

Comadena, M. E. (1982). *Nonverbal correlates of deception: A contextual analysis*. Paper presented at the Speech Communication Association Convention, Louisville, KY.

Conrad, C. (1985). *Strategic organizational communication*. New York: Holt, Rinehart & Winston.

Cook, M. (1970). Experiments in orientation and proxemics. *Human Relations, 23*, 61–67.

Cooper, K. (1979a). *Bodybusiness: The sender's and receiver's guide to nonverbal communication*. New York: AMACOM.

Cooper, K. (1979b). *Nonverbal communication for business success*. New York: AMACOM.

Cope, L. (1987, August 3). Study shows patients like doctors to look traditional. *The Evansville Courier*, p. 7.

Davidson, J. P. (1987). *Blow your own horn*. New York: AMACOM.

Derk, J. (1987, August 16). The smoker: Facing extinction? *The Sunday Courier*, p. B1.

DeVito, J. A. (1986). *The communication handbook: A dictionary*. New York: Harper & Row.

Dickson, P. (1978). *The official rules*. New York: Dell.

Dillion, J. T. (1982). In pursuit of the colon: A century of scholarly progress: 1880–1980. *Journal of Higher Education, 53*, 93–99.

Duncan, S., Jr. (1975). Interaction units during speaking turns in dyadic, face-to-face conversations. In A. Kendon, R. Harris, & M. Key (Eds.), *Organization of behavior in face-to-face interaction* (pp. 199–213). The Hague: Mouton.

Edleson, H. (1987, August 25). Too many tears can dampen your career. *USA Today*, p. D4.

Egalitarianism rules in Japanese plants. (1987, December 28). *The Evansville Courier*, p. 5.

Ehat, D. M., & Schappner, M. (1974, August). What your employee's nonverbal cues are telling you. *Administrative Management*, 64–66.

Ekman, P., & Friesen, W. V. (1987, October 28). Universal facial expressions. *USA Today*, p. D8.

Ekman, P., & Friesen, W. (1969). The repertoire of nonverbal behavior: categories, origins, usage, and coding. *Semiotica, 1*, 49–98.

Erickson, F. (1987). The beat goes on. *Psychology Today, 21*, 38.

Fabun, D. (1968). *Communications: The transfer of meaning*. San Francisco: The International Society of General Semantics.

Fenton, L. (1986). *Dress for excellence*. New York: Rawson Associates.

Fischman, J. (1988). Service with a smile. *Psychology Today, 22*, p. 17.

Forbes, C. (1990, April 12). Firm handshake more important than buttering a role, etiquette expert says. *Birmingham Post-Herald*, p. C10.

Frank, A. D. (1982). *Communicating on the job.* Glenview, IL: Scott, Foresman.

Frieze, I. H. (1974). *Nonverbal aspects of femininity and masculinity which perpetuate sex-role stereotypes.* Paper presented at Eastern Psychological Association, Boston, MA.

Gaines, S. (1987, October 11). Employers wake up to worker well-being. *Chicago Tribune,* Sec. 7, p. 1.

Goffman, E. (1963). *Stigma: Notes on the management of spoiled identity.* Englewood Cliffs, NJ: Prentice-Hall.

Goffman, E. (1959). *The presentation of self in everyday life.* Garden City, NY: Anchor.

Goldhaber, G. M. (1986). *Organizational communication* (4th ed.). Dubuque, IA: Wm. C. Brown.

Gordon, W. I., Tengler, C. D., & Infante, D. A. (1982). Women's clothing predispositions as predictors of dress at work, job satisfaction, and career advancement. *The Southern Speech Communication Journal, 47*(4), 422–434.

Gottschalk, M. (1989, July 23). Dress-down Fridays help boost morale in Silicon Valley. *The Birmingham News,* p. 12E.

Gray, J. G., Jr. (1983). *Image impact: The business and professional man's personal packaging program.* Bethesda, MD: Media Impact.

Grazian, F. (1987, September). Smiling equals trust. *Communication Briefings, 6,* p. 6.

Hackman, M. Z., & Johnson, C. E. (1991). *Leadership: A communication perspective.* Prospective Heights, IL: Waveland.

Hall, E. T. (1959). *The silent language.* Garden City, NY: Doubleday.

Hall, E. T. (1963). A system for the notation of proxemic behavior. *American Anthropologist, 65,* 1003–1026.

Hall, E. T. (1966). *The hidden dimension.* Garden City, NY: Doubleday.

Hall, E. T. (1972). Proxemics: The study of man's spatial relations. In L. A. Samovar & R. E. Porter, (Eds.), *Intercultural communication: A reader* (pp. 210–217). Belmont, CA: Wadsworth.

Hall, E. T. (1985). Social time: The heartbeat of culture. *Psychology Today, 19,* 33.

Hall, E. T., & Hall, M. R. (1987). *Hidden differences.* New York: Anchor.

Hamid, P. N. (1952). Some effects of dress cues on observational accuracy: A perceptual estimate, and impression formation. *Journal of Social Psychology, 36,* 241–244.

Harper, R. G., Wiens, A. N., & Matarazzo, J. D. (1978). *Nonverbal communication: The state of the art.* New York: Wiley.

Harrison, A. A., Hwalek, M., Raney, D. F., & Frits, J. G. (1978). Cues to deception in an interview situation. *Social Psychology, 41,* 156–161.

Heilman, M. E., & Sarugatari, L. R. (1979). When beauty is beastly: The effect of appearance and sex on evaluations of job applicants for managerial and non-managerial jobs. *Organizational Behavior and Human Performance, 23,* 360–372.

Hellmich, N. (1988, September 23). Career women's code of conduct for the office. *USA Today,* p. D1.

Henley, N. M. (1977). *Body politics: Power, sex, and nonverbal communication.* Englewood Cliffs, NJ: Prentice-Hall.

Hickson, M. L., Powell, L., Hill, S. R., Holt, G. B., & Flick, H. (1979). Smoking artifacts as indicators of homophily, attraction, and credibility. *Southern Speech Communication Journal, 44,* 191–200.

Hickson, M. L., & Stacks, D. W. (1985). *NVC nonverbal communication studies and applications.* Dubuque, IA: Wm. C. Brown.

Hobbs, C. R. (1987). *Time power.* New York: Harper & Row.

Horowitz, M. J., Duff, D. F., & Stratten, L. O. (1964). Body buffer zones. *Archives of General Psychology, 11,* 651–656.

Huston, T. L. (Ed.). (1974). *Foundations of interpersonal attraction.* New York: Academic Press.

Johns, G. (1988). *Organizational behavior: Understanding life at work* (2nd ed.). Glenview, IL: Scott, Foresman.

Kast, F. E., & Rosenzweig, J. E. (1984). *The nature of management.* Chicago: Science Research Associates.

Kenny, C. T., & Fletcher, D. (1973). Effects of beardedness on person perception. *Perceptual and Motor Skills, 37,* 413–414.

Knapp, M. L. (1972). *Nonverbal communication in human interaction.* New York: Holt, Rinehart and Winston.

Knapp, M. L. (1978). Nonverbal communication in human interaction (2nd ed.). New York: Holt, Rinehart and Winston.

Korda, M. (1975). *Power! How to get it, how to use it.* New York: Ballantine.

Korda, M. (1986). Symbols of power. In P. J. Frost, W. F. Mitchell & W. R. Nord, (Eds.), *Organizational reality: Reports from the firing line* (3rd ed.). (pp. 145–156). Glenview, IL: Scott, Foresman.

Laird, B. (1987, October 2). Resume report: Keep it simple. *USA Today,* p. 4B.

Lakein, A. (1973). *How to get control of your time and your life.* New York: Signet.

Lang, G. T., Calhoun, L. G., & Selby, J. W. (1977). Personality characteristics related to cross-situational consistency of interpersonal distance. *Journal of Personality Assessment, 41,* 274–278.

Lareau, W. (1985). *Conduct expected: The unwritten rules for a successful business career.* Piscataway, NJ: New Century.

Lau, L. (1982). The effect of smiling on person perception. *Journal of Social Psychology, 117,* 63–67.

Lawlor, J. (1990, November 15). Smokers are put out as firms crack down. *USA Today,* p. B1.

Lean, E. (1984). Color me training. *Training and Development Journal, 38,* 43–50.

Levine, R. (1987). Waiting is a power game. *Psychology Today, 21,* 26.

Machlowitz, M., & Machlowitz, D. (1987, July 1). Hug by the boss could lead to a slap from the judge. *Wall Street Journal,* p. 41.

Malandro, L. A., & Barker, L. (1983). *Nonverbal communication.* Reading, MA: Addison-Wesley.

McCroskey, M. B. (1979). The hidden messages managers send. *Harvard Business Review, 57*(2), 135–148.

McGinley, H., LeFevre, R., & McGinley, P. (1965). The influence of a communicator's body position on opinion change in others. *Journal of Personality and Social Psychology, 31,* 686–690.

McLean-Ibrahim, E. (1988, August 17). Strong ties to business. *USA Today,* p. B1.

Meer, J. (1985). The light touch. *Psychology Today, 19,* p. 60.

Mehrabian, A. (1969). Significance of posture and position in the communication of attitude and status relationships. *Psychological Bulletin, 71,* 359–372.

Mehrabian, A. (1981). *Silent messages: Implicit communication of emotions and attitudes* (2nd ed.). Belmont, CA: Wadsworth.

Mitchell, C., & Burdick, T. (1983). *The extra edge.* Washington, DC: Acropolis.

Mitchell, W. (1991, January 13). Do not forget why you were invited. *Parade Magazine,* p. 23.

Molloy, J. T. (1975). *Dress for success.* New York: Warner.

Molloy, J. T. (1977). *The woman's dress for success book.* Chicago: Follett.

Molloy, J. T. (1988). *John T. Molloy's new dress for success.* New York: Warner.

Moore, D. J. (1982). To trust, perchance, to buy. *Psychology Today, 16,* 50–54.

Morris, D. (1977). *Manwatching: A field guide to human behavior.* New York: Harry N. Abrams.

Myers, M. S. (1991). *Every employee a manager.* San Diego: University Associates.

Newman, H. M. (1982). The sounds of silence in communicative encounters. *Communication Quarterly, 30,* 142–149.

O'Connell, L. (1991, June 30). Experts wary of expressing emotions at work. *The Birmingham News,* p. 9E.

Olson, T. E., & Frieze, I. H. (1987, February 4). Survey: Tall men get big raises. *USA Today,* p. 6B.

Ohmae, K. (1987). *Beyond national borders.* Homewood, IL: Dow Jones-Irwin.

Ouchi, W. C. (1981). *Theory z: How American business can meet the Japanese challenge.* New York: Avon.

Painter, K. (1986, November 24). Your inner clock may need a hand. *USA Today,* p. D4.

Patterson, M. (1968). Spatial factors in social interaction. *Human Factors, 2,* 351–361.

Pearce, W. B., & Brommel, B. J. (1972). Vocalic communication in persuasion. *Quarterly Journal of Speech, 58,* 298–306.

Pearce, W. B., & Conklin, F. (1971). Nonverbal vocalic communication and perception of speaker. *Speech Monographs, 38,* 235–241.

Pellegrini, R. J. (1973). Impressions of male personality as a function of beardedness. *Psychology, 10,* 29–33.

People. (1987, August 11). *USA Today*, p. 4D.

Perry, J. A. (1985). The Dillion hypothesis of titular colonicity: An empirical test from the ecological sciences. *Journal of the American Society of Information Science, 36,* 251–258.

Peters, T. (1987). *Thriving on chaos: Handbook for a management revolution.* New York: Alfred Knopf.

Peterson, T. (1991, December 30). O.K. button up—and button down. *Business Week*, p. 48.

Plas, J. M., & Hoover-Dempsey, K. V. (1989). *Working up a storm.* New York: W. W. Norton.

Raudsepp, E. (1983). The politics of promotion. *Office Administration, 44,* 28–32.

Reiss, M., & Rosenfeld, P. (1980). Seating preference as nonverbal communication: A self-presentational analysis. *Journal of Applied Communications Research, 8,* 22–28.

Richmond, V. P., McCroskey, J. C., & Payne, S. K. (1987). *Nonverbal behavior in interpersonal relations.* Englewood Cliffs, NJ: Prentice-Hall.

Robbins, O., Devoe, S., & Wiener, M. (1978). Social patterns of turn-taking: Nonverbal regulators. *Journal of Communication, 28,* 38–46.

Sabath, A. M. (1990, September). A quiz on business meals. *Communication Briefings, 9,* 4.

Seiler, J. A. (1982). Architecture at work. *Harvard Business Review, 62*(1), 111–120.

Shirley, S. (1986). A company without offices. *Harvard Business Review, 64*(1), 127–137.

Smith, D. R., & Williamson, L. K. (1985). *Interpersonal communication: Roles, rules, strategies, and games* (3rd ed.). Dubuque, IA: Wm. C. Brown.

Solomon, M. R. (1986). Dress for effect. *Psychology Today, 20,* 20.

Solomon, M. (1987). Standard issue. *Psychology Today, 21,* 31.

Sommer, R. (1969). *Personal space: The behavioral basis of design.* Englewood Cliffs, NJ: Prentice-Hall.

Stead, B. A., & Zinkhan, G. M. (1987). *Sex Roles, 15,* 601–611, cited in *Psychology Today, 21,* 11.

Stone, P. J., & Luchetti, R. (1985). Your office is where you are. *Harvard Business Review, 63,* 103–106.

Street, R. L., & Brady, R. M. (1982). Speech rate acceptance ranges as a function of evaluative domain, listener speech rate, and communication context. *Communication Monographs, 49,* 290–308.

Swanson, S. (1983, September 14). Dress for success, revisited. *Chicago Tribune,* Sec. 1, p. 15.

Thourlby, W. W. (1978). *You are what you wear.* New York: New American Library.

Tomkins, S. S. (1962). *Affect, imagery, consciousness.* New York: Springer.

Tresch, R., Sr., Pearson, P., Munter, M., Wyld, L. D., & Waltman, J. L. (1986). Nonverbal communication. In S. P. Golen (Ed.). *Methods of teaching selected topics in business communication* (pp. 75–80). Urbana, IL: The Association for Business Communication.

Van, J. (1983, May 1). The night syndrome. *Chicago Tribune,* Sec. 4, pp. 1–2.

VDTs [Video Display Terminals]: Fitting the job to the person. (1991, January/February). *Labor Relations Today, 6.* Washington, DC: U.S. Department of Labor.

Verrengia, J. B. (1987, November 29). Many say computing via home terminal beats commuting. *The Sunday Courier,* p. F12.

Ward, S. (1986, April 14). Corporate offices. *USA Today,* p. E2.

Ward, S. (1987, September 9). Promotion by a hair. *USA Today,* p. B2.

Waterman, R. H., Jr. (1987). *The renewal factor: How the best get and keep the competitive edge.* New York: Bantam.

Watson, K. W., & Smeltzer, L. R. (1982, June). Perceptions of nonverbal communication during the selection interview. *The ABCA Bulletin,* pp. 30–34.

White, L. (1987, August 5). Firm minds business manners. *USA Today,* p. 5B.

Williams, M. (1984, February 16). Something as simple as a smile may make or break a female manager. *Wall Street Journal,* p. 35.

Wilson, G. L., Goodall, H. L., Jr., & Waagen, C. L. (1986). *Organizational communication.* New York: Harper & Row.

# CHAPTER 6

# Networks and Channels

*Networks* and *channels* are the methods used for exchanging messages and information in organizations. As the patterns of communication interactions become regularized, they are labeled networks (Burgess, 1969; Monge & Eisenberg, 1987; Tichy & Formbrum, 1979). This chapter allows us to connect the verbal and nonverbal techniques for message transmission with a systems view of organizations. Communication acts as the lifeblood of an organization and networks and channels function as the veins that connect and carry the various messages. This analogy to the human body is particularly appropriate because the configurations and directions for the flow of communication can be as complex as in any living system. This chapter examines networks and channels of communication.

Organizations are communication networks dependent on interlocking behaviors (Tichy, 1981; Weick, 1979, pp. 3, 19–20). When we study the networks individuals form with the internal subsystems of an organization, and the external environment, we are analyzing these connecting activities. Networks transmit information, influence, affect, and goods and services.

Channels sanctioned by the organization are labeled *formal* and are related to the functional aspects of communication, such as giving and receiving information. These channels are either downward, upward, or horizontal. *Grapevines* are the informal channels of communication. Because getting the job done is the primary goal of an organization, formal restrictions are used to control and channel these patterns of communication (Gibson, Ivancevich, & Donnelly, 1991, pp. 538–539; Katz & Kahn, 1966). As Greenberg (1983) put it, "The link between organizational structure and communication is a very basic and important one. Simply put, an organization's structure dictates who can or must communicate with whom. An organization's lines of authority shows the pathways through which messages have to flow within organizations" (p. 319). Within all organizations there are formal restrictions regarding the communication process. Making certain you go through the proper channels, or following the chain of command, are two expressions that reflect this demand for control and structure.

If organizational charts were truly reflective of how message flow in an organization, then these distinctions would be very useful. In fact, because of the systems nature of organizations, communication tends to be both upward and downward, combined with a large number of lateral transactions. People meet at the copy machine, over coffee, and at social events, for example, and share a great deal of information. Understanding the impact of upward, downward, and horizontal communication patterns is important.

The grapevine operates in all organizations as the carrier of informal communication. Many of the attributes of networks and grapevines are the same. However, in many organizations, the term grapevine carries special meaning so we analyze it when we discuss channels.

Networks and channels have an interacting effect on each other. For the purposes of clarity, this chapter examines networks, or patterns of interaction first, then the channels of communication.

## NETWORKS

Numerous networks of colleagues, co-workers, or other individuals exist in every organization. In fact, according to Roberts (1984), "In the last few years, most organizational communication research has looked at organizations as giant networks" (p. 27).

The importance of networks lies in their transactional nature (Bossevain, 1974, p. 25). Everything that occurs in the linking process can be a message. According to Tichy (1981), "All organizations consist of multiple networks through which flow goods and services, information, influence or affect. These networks may overlap considerably or be quite separate" (p. 227). Past attempts to understand networks often have concentrated on the information properties rather than the transactional process of networks.

### Defining Networks

Networks are the systems of interactions, both formalized and informalized, that are used in an organization and between organizations. Or, as Lipnack and Stamps (1982) put it, "Networks are the lines of communications, the alternative express highways that people use to get things done. In crisis and in opportunity, the word spreads quickly though these people-power lines" (p. 1).

In general, a network is a web of free-standing participants linked or connected

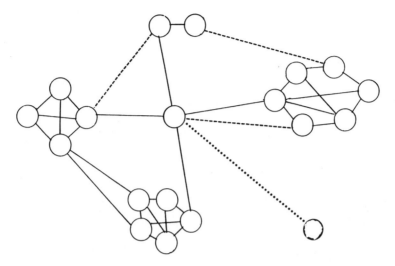

FIG. 6.1. Typical network structure.

by one or more shared values. These values may have a task or social orientation, or both. Figure 6.1 indicates a typical network structure.

At first glance, a network might appear to be a communication analogue to the sociological concept of a group. However, a network is distinct from a group in that it refers to a number of individuals (or other units) who persistently interact with one another in accordance with established patterns. Although all groups are networks, not all networks are groups (Beebe & Masterson, 1986, pp. 3–5). According to Goldhaber (1986), "A communication network may consist of only two people or an entire organization" (p. 160).

Finally, and perhaps most important, a network's operational definition is often a function of the investigator's specific area of interest. Table 6.1 indicates some of the network functions discussed by researchers. Network types can range from electronic media (e.g., telemediated, computer-based, video screens, telephones) to a friendship network meeting over lunch. Network goals can include responding to specific occupational needs, meeting certain group needs, or providing information regarding job functions.

People belong to a variety of networks, which can operate independently or in conjunction with numerous other networks (Tichy, 1981). In addition to task-related behaviors, investigations into the structure of networks reveal "behavior in a human system at a macro level of communication links. It focuses on the communication-social structure and process within which people live" (Mueller, 1986, p. 49). Networks are microcosms of the patterns of communication in all organizations. Therefore, networks are complex and broad-based.

Networks perform a variety of important tasks because they connect people. In order to fully understand networks, we need to examine network properties.

TABLE 6.1
Types of Networks

| Function | Activities |
|---|---|
| Structure | Reflects the formal chart of the organization. This involves the passing of messages through the correct channels from the top to the bottom and back. |
| Information | Who actually controls the data that makes decisions. |
| Task-expertise | The "how-to-do" information about processing a decision. |
| Status | Cliques of individuals who occupy the same type of organizational role. |
| Friendship | Based on interpersonal attraction and affiliation. |
| Social | Concerned primarily with the relationships with the ultimate goal being friendship or companionship. |
| Expertise | Concerned with obtaining necessary professional information and assistance in planning and organizing tasks. |
| Authority | Concerned with connecting the right power or authority individuals through various channels. |

Each of these network functions will overlap, depending on the situation, individuals involved, and organizational culture.

## Network Properties

There is a difference between classic organizational charts and networks. An *organigram* is used to provide a graphic representation of an organization's structure through charts (Greenberg, 1983, p. 316). A hierarchy is arranged by indicating to whom each person is responsible and which persons the individual is responsible for. This static view of organizations emphasizes that although individuals do fill jobs, the structure of the organization does not change just because someone leaves. Individuals occupy certain positions, but the position will exist regardless of the presence of any particular person. An organizational chart does indicate the *prescribed network*. This is also the basis for formal channels of communication, which will be discussed later in this chapter.

The ongoing patterns of influence are more dynamic. A great deal of communication is not formalized, does not travel in required directions, and may not be concerned with authority.

At the same time, messages do not flow randomly through organizations. They tend to go in predictable directions and follow patterns, which can be traced using a *sociogram* (Tichy, 1981, p. 227). A sociogram is developed after the fact, and explains how the flow of messages occurs. It provides a graphic representation of emerging relationships among individuals. This working model represents a set of elements related to one another through multiple interconnections—a network (Moreno & Jennings, 1960).

Both prescribed and *emergent* networks are important. The prescribed network indicates the direction for reporting and of influence. The emergent network explains the flow of information, affective exchange, or actual influence. There can be considerable overlap between all of these networks (Schon, 1971, p. 108).

The sociogram also identifies the roles performed in networks. Before outlining the various roles, we examine the concepts of coupling and connectedness and the importance of weak ties.

**Coupling.** A useful label for explaining the relationship process is *coupling* (Glassman, 1973; Weick, 1976). *Loosely coupled subsystems* are related but not highly interdependent. When subsystems are highly interdependent, they are *tightly coupled*. In a tightly coupled situation, a change in one of the subsystems immediately will effect or influence the other.

The first, loosely coupled relationships, exist in a variety of organizations. Departments at a university, for example, tend to be loosely coupled. Although each department's activities and personnel need to be coordinated with the general university plan, there is little reason for constant interactions. Autonomous units set up by organizations to research and develop new products often are loosely coupled with the other organizational activities. Peters and Austin (1985) referred to the "*skunkworks*, those small off-line bands of mavericks that are the hallmark of innovative organizations" (p. 116). Within the skunkworks, there is tight coupling.

Many universities and innovative organizations are organic cultures, as explained in chapter 3, which have more loose coupling. Their subsystems are allowed to pursue their own means for reaching the general organizational goals. Loose coupling leads to a larger number of independent networks operating to solve specific problems. Kidder's (1981) fascinating account of Data General's development of a new computer, through the use of an independent research team of engineers, is a good example of the power of loosely coupled groups within an organization. Organic cultures use lateral relations and open access to information to keep the organization coordinated, which allows for groups and individuals to pursue their own directions within the generally accepted cultural norms. Local adaptation is encouraged because the subsystems and individuals can concentrate on their particular needs without necessarily involving the rest of the organization.

On the other hand, when having a variety of subsystems pursuing their own agendas is not appropriate, tight coupling is necessary. As you will recall from chapter 3, some types of organizations require an authoritarian form of control to maintain uniformity of standards.

For example, McDonald's is known for requiring strict adherence to national standards that cannot be altered by local franchises. If a local McDonald's does veer from the established policies, the national McDonald's office can arbitrarily withdraw the franchise. Peters and Austin (1985) reported the following:

Ray Kroc (McDonald's Chairman) once visited a Winnepeg franchise. It's reported that he found a single fly. The franchisee lost his McDonald's franchise two weeks later. . . . Even one fly doesn't fit with QSC&V (Quality Service, Cleanliness and Value). You'd better believe that after this story made the round a whole lot of McDonald's people found nearly mystical ways to eliminate flies—every fly—from their shops. Is the story apocryphal? It doesn't really matter. Mr. Kroc did do things like that. (p. 99)

The focus McDonald's has on customer satisfaction, and its almost dictatorial set of rules for a franchise's operation, are cornerstones of the organization. In theory, every Big Mac served in any McDonald's in the world should taste the same. This is tightly coupled!

Coupling, then, is related to the amount of interdependence between subsystems. On the surface, this would seem to be a restatement of the dichotomy between scientific management, which is very formal, versus humanistic management, which is more likely to promote local, team, or departmental decisions. In fact, "coupling does not depend so much on the degree of formalization in organizational structure as it does on the level of interdependence that actually exists among subsystems" (Daniels & Spiker, 1987, pp. 94–95).

The impact of coupling is very evident in studies of the change process. Organizations who become overcommitted to projects that cannot succeed reveal an overreliance on procedures and rules, or tight coupling, leading to an administrative lethargy regarding change (Shaw & Ross, 1988). The organization becomes so involved with the original plan or goal that it loses perspective regarding the chances for success. Although high interdependence works well for McDonald's national standards, it can be counterproductive when change clearly is required (Weick, 1976). Coupling provides an important basis for understanding organizational communication. Daniels and Spiker (1991) elaborated, "[T]he study of organizational communication should be less concerned with traditional distinctions between formal and informal communication and more concerned with identifying and understanding the coupling characteristics of organizational communication networks" (p. 104).

In all organizations, there will be examples of loose and tight coupling within the general organizational structure. Some organizations encourage more loose coupling whereas others demand strict adherence to specific rules or guidelines.

***Connectedness.*** A term used in network studies that further clarifies coupling is *connectedness*. Connectedness describes the extent to which network members identify with the goals of other members of their network. When connectedness is related to a specific network, it is a measure of group cohesiveness (Pearce & David, 1983). Both coupling and connectedness refer to the degree of interdependence between the subsystems or systems. Coupling is concerned with the structural interdependence whereas connectedness is concerned more with the psychological interdependence.

At one extreme are *highly connected networks*. Family networks, based on common blood and a great deal of integration of perspectives, would be an example of a very highly connected network. Rural area farmers or coal miners' families are obvious examples. Family businesses, which pass from parents to children, are often highly connected networks.

In England, there is the Massingberg 500. These are the 500 key network families in Great Britain who have consistently produced "men and women" of prominence over the last three generations (Heald, 1983, p. 106). Less positive examples might be the Hatfields and McCoys' feud, or the infamous crime families such as the Mafia. Somewhere shy of these very highly connected examples are the large number of networks composed of union members, classmates, long-time friends, professional acquaintances, and family members, who work together or who trade professional favors.

There are three advantages to a high degree of connectedness. First, for the organization, increased connectedness among units appears to lead to improved performance. Studies of successful organizations show a high degree of employee identification with the basic goals of the organization (Peters & Waterman, 1982). A survey of 500 insurance company executives indicated that greater employee participation and involvement, or high connectedness, lead to a 20% increase in productivity (St. John, 1986).

You are already familiar with the Hawthorne Effect which explains increases in productivity as a consequence of greater attention by management to employees. Increasing connectedness goes one step further and provides employees with a purpose or rationale for doing better work (Myers, 1991, pp. 57–58). When asked what topics they would like to see in their company publications, employees chose information about their company plans over all other topics including feature stories about other employees, news about employee social events, or personal information such as marriages or births (St. John, 1986). Employees are interested in knowing more about their organizations, and networks facilitate this connectedness. When employees use the network as a means of understanding why they do what they do, a greater sense of identification occurs.

Second, intergroup connectedness provides greater power to a group within an organization. If one unit is highly involved with another unit, the members of each unit have more power (Blau & Alba, 1982). By being connected, members of units have a greater opportunity for influencing other networks and increasing the cluster's resources.

Third, a highly connected network has increased information because the network's members receive multiple inputs from a variety of sources. Sometimes, organizations unexpectedly realize the power of networks. For example, as Peters (1987) reported:

Pieter Martin, manufacturing manager of Buckman Labs in Ghent, Belgium wanted to improve communication between departments. . . . [He] invested $5,000 in walkie-talkies for eighteen employees that would allow the warehouse workers to contact the shipping department, for instance, or the lab supervisor to call the production line without bothering the maintenance crew. But the walkie-talkies of two of the workers didn't work right—they picked up all the interdepartmental chatter. Martin says, "They didn't tell us. And eventually I noticed that at meetings these two were so involved, asking lots of questions and offering solutions to problems in other departments." When he discovered the reason was the "flawed" walkie-talkies, he didn't try to get them fixed. Instead, he traded them in for a downgraded system to allow everyone to listen to everyone else. (p. 287)

The mechanical error created an increased connectedness for the entire organization. This synergistic process is one of the major values of high connectedness. With the increased dependence on technology in organizations, networks offer the means for making certain that people get the right information, at the right time, and in the right form (Penzias, 1989, p. 206).

**The Strength of Weak Ties.**   The happenstance of the introduction of new information and perspectives demonstrated by the walkie-talkie episode, and its impact, can be explained further by examining the *strength of weak ties.* As the walkie-talkie example demonstrates, organizations must be *permeable,* or open to information that ordinarily would not find its way into specific networks.

The concept of weak ties becomes clearer through an examination of strong ties and the commensurate dangers. Once we have examined strong ties, we look at individual uses of weak ties, organizational weak ties, and the small-world phenomenon.

When individuals are close to their colleagues, and the network is highly integrated, they have strong ties. As Roberts (1984) explained, "The strength of a tie between two individuals in a network is defined by the amount of time, emotional intensity, intimacy, and reciprocal services that characterize the tie" (p. 30). When these ties become intense, they tend to create a likeness of mind which can lead to a closing of the system. Precisely because networks can become closed, they are susceptible to rehashing the same information and perspectives, rather than infusing new data and viewpoints.

The strength of weak ties theory argues that people must form weak ties with other networks in order to increase resources, information, and innovation (Granovetter, 1973; Liu & Duff, 1972). So, although an esprit de corps is a desirable attribute for departments, teams, or organizations, being linked to information from outside sources is also vital to prevent errors and add new inputs. Groupthink and freezethink are two good examples of the potential problems with strong ties.

**Groupthink and Freezethink.**   Janis (1972) labeled the closed decision-making process *groupthink.* When individuals become insulated from outside information, they are likely to perceive external inputs as a threat rather than as important information (pp. 9, 13, 212–214). The group develops a likeness of thinking, or purpose, which blinds them to additional information. The examples Janis used to support his theory are not limited to friendships. In fact, they are more linked to the closed nature of the network to outside information during the decision-making process. Janis counseled the establishment of weak ties to prevent the group from being closed.

As a careful analysis of the 1986 Challenger spacecraft disaster demonstrates, the pressure to launch the spacecraft apparently allowed individuals to reject outside information and proceed with a deeply flawed decision (Gouran, Hirokawa, & Martz, 1986). The result was a tragic loss of lives and a decrease in credibility for NASA. One author has labeled the process *freezethink,* because the commitment to launch was so great that the decision makers failed to examine crucial evidence (Kruglanski, 1986). Studies of the Challenger disaster indicate that the information was available to justify aborting the flight, but it was ignored, discredited, downplayed, or reframed to appear less ominous.

***Using Weak Ties.*** The tendency toward being closed to information and messages can be countered with the effective use of weak ties. Four examples further explain weak ties.

First, the Johnson and Johnson (J & J) handling of the 1983 Tylenol crisis demonstrates how incorporating weak ties can assist in making effective decisions and handling a crisis. At the end of September 1983, seven deaths related to the ingestion of extrastrength Tylenol were reported in 2 days and J & J had to decide how to respond to the crisis, which included a major drop in sales (Trujillo & Toth, 1987, p. 221). J & J immediately established a seven-member strategy team, cooperated fully with the press, and integrated key organizational structures and functions (Trujillo & Toth, 1987, pp. 222–223). The deaths were the result of cyanide poisoning and J & J correctly assumed that maintaining the public's trust was the most important task. J & J's proactive approach to handling the crisis by seeking increased relations with the public and the press, and increased information regarding the best strategy, allowed the company actually to increase their stock value and regain much of the market within 5 months (Trujillo & Toth, 1987, p. 221). Although this represents a public relations coup, it is even more dramatic as an example of the effective use of weak ties. J & J effectively opened up their organizational network, incorporated diverse opinions, and resolved the problem.

Second, most individuals use weak ties to enhance their own decision-making process. Choosing a college or university, for example, usually involves incorporating the opinions of close friends and family, or strong ties, and some outside reading and the advice of counselors and other sources, or weak ties. Perhaps your first contact with the school of your choice was through a mass mailing by the university.

People outside your group of strong ties are a fertile source of information about employment opportunities (Fowler, 1987, pp. 32–33, 61–66). One study of professionals who had changed their jobs indicated the majority learned about the new position through sources to whom they were weakly tied: "The thesis was that those to whom we are weakly tied move in different circles than we do and have different information than we do. The findings bore this out in that the vast majority of people who found new jobs through personal contacts were in touch with those contacts occasionally (more than once a year but less than twice a week) or rarely (once a year or less)" (Roberts, 1984, p. 30). A U.S. Department of Labor report "indicates that at least 48% of job leads come from personal contacts and the higher up the executive ladder, the more jobs are filled by word of mouth" (DeWine, 1983, p. 90).

Expanding our immediate network makes intuitive sense. In fact, weak ties often provide information and perspectives not available otherwise. The problem, of course, is we are most comfortable dealing with individuals and information that are familiar to us. Consultants, project teams, workshops, training programs, and many other inputs are used by organizations to introduce some weak ties by offering a different view of a situation.

A third use of weak ties are regular, informal contacts, which function as de facto networks. As Mueller (1986) explained, "All large organizations have their interpersonal networks for exchanging favors on which much business depends. The very life of social systems has been dependent on the operation of informal networks" (p. 65). When information is sought, most professionals have a select group they call on for consulting, advice, or insight. One analysis of networks calls these people *GWRKs,* which stands for "gals and guys who really know" (Jordan, 1976, p. 673). Regardless of the label, every professional has a list of individuals who are contacted for specific information about certain issues. For some, they are the "good ol' girl," "good ol' boy," or "old school tie" networks.

Interorganizationally, there are *occupational communities* made up of individuals from particular professions who develop their own networks (Van Maanen & Barley, 1984). These occupational communities often help set standards, develop operating procedures, and monitor certain activities. So, in addition to the personal contacts each individual is likely to maintain, this professional networking process is used to advance people's careers and provide support and help. These networks often are formed by individuals with similar backgrounds, such as gender, education, or expertise, to formalize the weak ties. Table 6.2 shows how such a network can be created and used by an individual. According to Peters (1987), "Word-of-mouth communication can take on many different forms. Industry participants form 'old boy networks' to keep each other informed about new developments. One recent market-research report showed that such a network plays a key role in the telecommunications industry. Gaining access to the network is critical to success" (pp. 239–240).

The vast majority of my current organizational consulting is the result of individuals asking a colleague from another organization to recommend someone who can deal with organizational communication issues. It seems that it pays to know the people who are thought to really know!

Often, this *cross-organizational communication* is more influential than internal network behavior. Interlocking directorates, for example, are powerful influences on organizations. These directorates are made up of leaders of various organizations serving on each other's board of directors. So, although a board of directors

TABLE 6.2
Steps For Developing a Network

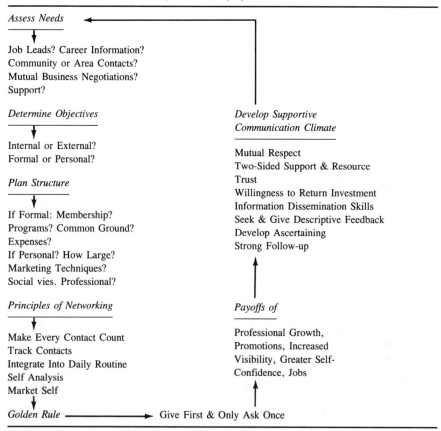

*Assess Needs*

Job Leads? Career Information?
Community or Area Contacts?
Mutual Business Negotiations?
Support?

*Determine Objectives*

Internal or External?
Formal or Personal?

*Plan Structure*

If Formal: Membership?
Programs? Common Ground?
Expenses?
If Personal? How Large?
Marketing Techniques?
Social vies. Professional?

*Principles of Networking*

Make Every Contact Count
Track Contacts
Integrate Into Daily Routine
Self Analysis
Market Self

*Golden Rule* ⟶ Give First & Only Ask Once

*Develop Supportive*
*Communication Climate*

Mutual Respect
Two-Sided Support & Resource
Trust
Willingness to Return Investment
Information Dissemination Skills
Seek & Give Descriptive Feedback
Develop Ascertaining
Strong Follow-up

*Payoffs of*

Professional Growth,
Promotions, Increased
Visibility, Greater Self-
Confidence, Jobs

*Note.* From DeWine (1983). Reprinted by permission.

is supposed to oversee an organization's management, these close, informal ties between the leaders of each organization can pervert the process.

Some individuals characterize entire industry clusters as networks. Rogers and Larsen (1984) dub Silicon Valley, California as not just a geographical area, but as a network of the key computer companies. The telecommunications industry, interlocking directorates, and Silicon Valley are all examples of message flows that are not necessarily constant, nor part of the formal communication structure, but are highly influential.

A fourth example of the power of weak ties is the *small-world phenomenon.* Sociologist Stanley Milgram (1965) wanted to see just how powerful informal networks can be. He selected a volunteer person in Omaha, Nebraska and a target person in Boston. The volunteer was sent the target's name and some information about the target and then asked to send a packet. The volunteers did not know the target personally. The original source, or volunteer, was asked to find someone else who was also likely to know someone who could pass it on to the final target. Milgram repeated the study several times. The number of successful completions of this intercontinental task ranged from 12% to 33% with the number of links averaging from five to eight.

Responding that "It's a small world, isn't it!" is not an unusual occurrence. You may have been shocked in a conversation to find out that both participants knew the same person. What is not as surprising is to find out that you have an acquaintance who might know a particular person or work in the same organization as that person. If you were bent on getting a message to the target in the organization, you probably would be able to employ weak ties to deliver it.

The strength of weak ties points to the importance of establishing a broad, loosely constructed network to enhance our effective functioning in an organization. In addition to the importance of weak ties, the serious problems associated with a closed network must be considered. Although your personal experiences might not be as dramatic as groupthink, freezethink, or unemployment, examining how we establish and maintain our perspectives and information sources is obviously very important. All organizations depend on weak ties to accomplish their goals. The small-world phenomenon provides one final example of the strength of weak ties.

*Clusters.*  Connectedness has been classified further by looking at *clusters,* which are more richly connected, coupled, or tied than the general network. In addition to the prescribed clusters, such as committees and work groups, there are coalitions and cliques.

A *coalition* is a perceived linkage among several individuals who believe that their ability to dominate organizational relationships is greater as a group than as individuals. So, coalitions tend to be temporary alliances with the goal being to control some type of activity. In addition to domination, "coalitions often form when there are unusual or nonroutine demands, perhaps when firms develop new products or when the environment appears threatening" (Roberts, 1984, pp. 29–30). The entire process of building a project management team requires a clear understanding of how to set up a temporary network structure (Dinsmore, 1984). Once the project is completed, the rationale for the coalition disappears and it probably will be disbanded.

A *clique* is a set of actors in a network who are connected to one another by strong relations; or, as Pace (1983) put it, "A clique is a group of individuals who have at least half of their contacts with each other" (p. 158). Friendship networks are cliques. The more cohesive the group, and the more friendship ties that exist, the more active the process of communication. This, in turn, will lead to a greater uniformity of attitudes, opinions, and behaviors (Burt, 1982, pp. 31–32). Cliques have frequent communication and share information as a single unit (Rogers & Agarwala-Rogers, 1976, pp. 142–143). In a clique, all the members are linked and their communication can be about issues other than their friendship ties. Cliques are tightly coupled and connected. When a few members dominate the clique, there is likely to be less connectedness (Rogers & Agarwala-Rogers, 1976, p. 143).

As Table 6.3 indicates, there are significant differences between behaviors in coalitions and cliques. Network research has identified specific roles that members may play.

## Roles

Each individual in a network is important. Research has identified liaisons, gatekeepers, stars, bridges or linking pins, cosmopolites, and isolates as specific roles. Individuals who have neither minimum nor maximum contact with others are referred to as members (Roberts, 1984, p. 31). One study indicates that the group member role has more variety in task assignments as determined by the number of activities performed and pieces of equipment used in accomplishing the job (Dallinger, 1985). Group members often perform different roles at different times. Although some research has tended to neglect this category, a systems approach makes clear that merely being a member of the network creates the potential for messages. One of the specific roles that has received a great deal of attention is the liaison.

*Liaisons.*   *Liaisons* are individuals who serve as intermediaries among various emergent work groups within a department or an organization. They provide the ties between the clusters and networks. Liaisons are not members of a cluster but function as the link between two or more clusters. Liaisons are critical to the effective functioning of an organization (Pace, 1983, pp. 159–160). Liaisons receive more feedback and have more opportunities to deal with others in their jobs. Some organizations use the label *road warriors,* because these liaisons travel between different groups and factions passing on information and solving problems.

Liaisons also are known as *network bridges,* when the bridge belongs to one of the networks. These are group members who are connected with members of other groups. *Fayol's Bridge,* discussed in chapter 3, is a good example.

Another example would be a supervisor or manager who acts as a liaison between various groups of subordinates, or between a group of employees and the upper level management. Likert's *linking pin* approach, also discussed in chapter 3, is representative of this concept. The individual who is a linking pin is a superior in one group acting as the supervisor or manager, and a subordinate in another group composed of supervisors and their superior. This person carries information upward and downward, and acts as a coordinator between the two levels in the organization. A linking pin belongs to multiple clusters, and bridges whatever gaps there may be in an effort to enhance cooperation.

Organizational liaisons include specialists assigned either temporarily or permanently to work in units other than their own. Computer specialists, or health, safety,

TABLE 6.3
Networks, Coalitions, & Cliques

| Network Properties | Explanations | Characteristics of: Coalition | Cluster |
|---|---|---|---|
| Transactional content | The four media of exchange are: (a) expressions of affect, (b) influence, (c) information, (d) goods and services. | Influence Information | Affect Information |
| Characteristics of Links | | | |
| Reciprocity | To what degree are relationships symmetrical rather than asymmetrical or nonsymmetrical? | High | High |
| Clarity of norms | How clear are the ways participants should behave in relationships? | Very | Moderately |
| Intensity | To what degree will one participant disregard personal costs in order to fulfill obligations? | Low | Moderate |
| Multiplexity | In how many ways are one pair of participants related? | Few | Many |
| Structural Characteristics | | | |
| Organizational Density | What portion of the organizational members participate in this network? | Moderate | Small to Moderate |
| Clustering | How many dense regions, such as coalitions or cliques does this network contain? | Moderate | One |
| Size | How many people participate in this network? | Moderate | Few |
| Visibility | Can uninvolved observers tell who participates in this network, and can participants themselves map their network? | Easily | Moderately Well |
| Membership Criteria | How clear are the criteria for recruitment or membership? | Very | Very |
| Openness | How many relationships does this network have with other networks? Are the participants cosmopolitans or locals? | Moderate Both | Few Locals |
| Stability | How long is this network expected to survive? | Short | Long |
| Connectedness | Of all possible relationships among participants, what portion actually exist? | Moderate | Most |
| Reachability | What is the average number of links separating two participants? | Moderate | Few |
| Occupational Density | What portion of all the occupations in the organization are included in this network? | Large | Moderate |
| Vertical Density | What portion of all hierarchical levels does this network encompass? | Moderate | Small |
| Centrality | Does this network include many sociometric stars or only a few? | Centralized | Moderately decentralized |

*Note.* From Tichy (1981). Copyright © 1981 by Oxford University Press. Reprinted by permission.

and personnel monitors, or anyone else with a particular expertise, contribute valuable and identifiable links in the organization's overall communication network.

Because of the importance of the linking process, a great deal of research has been conducted regarding liaisons. Among other findings, Goldhaber (1986) reported that liaisons are more satisfied, hold higher official positions, and exercise greater influence because of their integrative role (p. 163). The liaison is a critical part of any organization. Tichy (1981) observed, "Most network studies find that five to twenty percent of an organization's members act as liaisons" (p. 237). However, research has not yet measured the stability of liaisons, so it is conceivable that the role passes between various network members.

Each of the three terms used, liaison, bridge, and linking pin, points to slightly different connecting roles. The liaison does not belong to the different clusters, a bridge belongs to at least one, and the linking pin is involved in both.

**Gatekeeper.**   A *gatekeeper* regulates the flow of information. This individual has the strategic capacity to decide what information will be forwarded to the other members of the clique (Katz & Lazarfeld, 1965, p. 119). Gatekeeping has positive and negative effects in an organization.

One valuable attribute is the person can prevent information overload by filtering and screening messages (Rogers & Agarwala-Rogers, 1976, p. 108). There is a classic cartoon that shows one executive secretary saying to another executive secretary: "I will *not* put my boss on the phone until you put your boss on the phone!" Both secretaries are functioning as gatekeepers.

The importance of the gatekeeping role should not be mistaken. The "your boss must come to the phone first" cartoon is a reflection of a genuine problem for managers. One estimate is that the average business executive wastes 5–7 hr each week playing telephone tag, talking with callers who should have been screened, and wishing that long-winded talkers would get to the point (Walther, 1986, p. 7).

Obviously, the negative aspects of the gatekeeping role lie in the potential for screening out important messages. When we discuss serial communication (which is communication that proceeds through a chain of individuals) later in this chapter, we further analyze this gatekeeping problem.

Two important factors to keep in mind at this point are: (a) The messages the gatekeeper receives may or may not be forwarded, and (b) the messages may be filtered. The gatekeeper can make the decision to reduce, change, hold back, or push ahead one message over any other messages. This position's power lies in the control of access to messages and information.

For example, when you apply for a job, several gatekeepers may make important decisions regarding your qualifications before you ever have the opportunity to interview for the position. The actual decision maker in the hiring process may not even see your resume if it does conform to the gatekeeper's notion of what the job entails. The opposite outcome also could occur if the gatekeeper decides to place your name first on the list of potential candidates.

**Stars.**   *Stars* are the focus of most communication within the group and they have many relationships with the other members. In an organization, stars tend to have a great deal of "on the job" influence with most group members.

Sometimes, this role is labeled the *opinion leader,* because the person is the center of network communication activity. Opinion leaders tend to be powerful, respected, and followed, without having any formal leadership role (Pace, 1983, p. 162). These individuals are listened to by other network members (Peterson, 1973).

**Cosmopolite.**   A *cosmopolite* is an individual who has a relatively high degree of communication with the system's environment (Tichy, Tushman, & Fombrun, 1979). When they take on the role of providing information to the environment and bringing information back to the organization from the environment, they are called *boundary spanners.* These individuals often link one organization with another.

Both boundary spanners and cosmopolites function as an interlocking element between the organization and its surroundings (Tichy et al., 1979). By reporting external information to the network, they help keep it alive and operating. Through contacts external to the system, the cosmopolite provides vital information to the network regarding the activities of the rest of the world. These connecting behaviors are, as we discussed earlier in this chapter, critical.

**Isolates.**   Some individuals have practically no contact with the network. These *isolates* are decoupled from the network, removed from the regular flow of communication, and tend to be out of touch with the rest of the network.

Determining how to apply the term isolate is relative (Pace, 1983, p. 159). First, someone can be an isolate with some decisions and deeply involved with others. Realistically, some group members tend to be isolated from certain decisions because they have nothing to add.

Second, being removed from network activity can be by choice. For example, people doing field work (e.g., linesman, sales, or deliveries), or a professor on sabbatical leave, are intentionally decoupled to enhance the individual's ability to work. Isolates report that their jobs are characterized by more autonomy and more identity than other role incumbents (Dallinger, 1985).

In any case, being out of touch with the activities and decisions of the network has two important consequences. First, the information flow is restricted, either by a function of the individual's personality, or by choice. This lack of information can make it difficult for the network to maintain the isolate's commitment or to coordinate the group's activities.

Second, by being on the fringe of the network, isolates develop some delimiting characteristics. For example, one author has concluded that isolates tend to be less self-assured, motivated by achievement, or willing to interact with others (Goldhaber, 1986, p. 163). Isolates can be less powerful, they may withhold information, they often perceive the system as closed to them, and therefore they would tend to be dissatisfied. In the end, the isolate cannot be an active part of the esprit de corps because few expressions of affect will take place.

These characteristics would suggest that being an isolate is not a particularly desirable role. At the same time, there are excellent reasons for individuals to be temporary isolates at different times in their organizational careers.

Although it is tempting to see the liaison as a highly valuable role, and the isolate as a problem role, rapid changes in the environment may require that each role be used at various times depending on the demands of the situation. More than anything, the specific task function of the isolate tends to determine if being apart from the network is a positive or negative attribute.

Specific network roles include liaisons, gatekeepers, stars, cosmopolites, and isolates. Figure 6.2 shows the various network roles. How these roles operate is even more apparent when we analyze the network types.

In conclusion, networks accomplish three very important goals for their members. First, by their relational influence, they increase an individual's, group's, or department's power. A team's, cluster's, or clique's involvement with other groups enhances its power (Blau & Alba, 1982). Second, they allow for the influx of information that might not occur if there were fewer external contacts. Finally, they offer affect or friendship-oriented bonds. These relational bonds can create a more effective individual or group climate.

Specialty networks, such as skunkworks or project management teams, can be created for the very purpose of isolating the members from interactions with the rest of the organization. The goal is to enhance the quality of the single network away from the influence of the rest of the organization. These types of networks also overcome the apparent paradox between the need for teamwork and togetherness, as evident in successful organizations, and the dangers of groupthink.

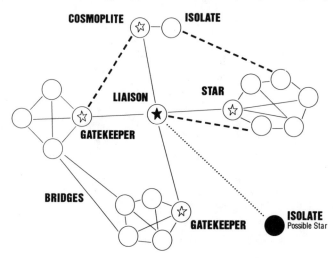

FIG. 6.2.   Various network roles.

## TYPES OF NETWORKS

Two different approaches can be used to identify networks. The first represents studies of micronetwork configurations and information flow and the second shows the various working models for network design.

### Micronetwork Analysis

Beginning in the 1950s, a host of experiments were conducted on the impact of centralized versus decentralized micronetworks. Focusing on small groups of three, four, or five members, these studies have investigated the numerous configurations for communication flows (Farace, Monge, & Russell, 1980). Figure 6.3 shows six examples of the group structures with five members.

Several conclusions can be drawn regarding the effect of network design on information flow. These appear on Table 6.4. Over time, these differences in performance disappear and one of the most important findings is that the artificial nature of the experiments tended to limit the generalizability of the conclusions. Apparently, as living systems, adaptation occurs as the network structure becomes part of the working world.

In small-group meetings, being aware of the importance of information flow on member satisfaction is quite important, and the findings from micronetwork analysis can be applied easily. Individuals out of the mainstream of communication in a small group will experience less satisfaction and the group will have less creative solutions to difficult problems. If efficiency is the goal, then controlling the

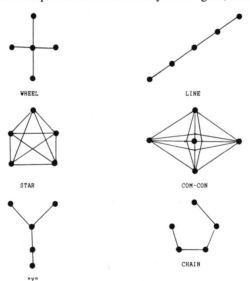

FIG. 6.3.   Six examples of five-member group network structures.

TABLE 6.4
Characteristics of Networks

| | Wheel or Star | Line or Chain | Circle* | All Channel or Com-Con* |
|---|---|---|---|---|
| *Example* | *Formal work group* | *Chain of Command* | *Committee or task force; Autonomous work group; Team* | *Informal Communication; Grapevine* |
| Centralization of Power & Authority | Moderately High | High | Low | Very low |
| Speed of Communication | Simple tasks: Fast / Complex tasks: Slow | Moderate | Members together: fast / Members isolated: slow | Fast |
| Accuracy of Communication | Simple tasks: High / Complex tasks: Low | Written: High / Verbal: Low | Members together: high / Members isolated: low | Moderate |
| Level of Group Satisfaction | Low | Low | High | High |
| Speed of Decisions | Moderate | Fast | Slow | |
| Group Commitment to Decisions | Moderate | Low | High | |

*Note.* From Steers (1988). Adapted by permission.
*The emphasis on teams, interdepartmental co-operation, and the crossing over of numerous boundaries means these two types often interplay and cross-over.

**185**

communication flow is important. In chapter 5 we discussed the impact of meeting arrangement.

In spite of the extensive research on configurations, few organizations reflect the simplified version of communication analyzed by the studies. Communication patterns tend to vary depending on the specific task. Networks, however, are very important and we now examine some examples.

## Specific Applications of Networks

The terminology, roles, and importance of networks can be understood further by examining network analysis, leadership use of networks, specialized networks, teamwork, and innovation. Each of these processes provides specific examples of how networks are used.

From a broad perspective, network analysis can include communication studies, power and political processes, career advancement, socialization, and relationships between organizations. According to Tichy (1981), "Network analysis is capable of linking the micro and macro approaches to organizational behavior, and network concepts account for phenomena heretofore described only anecdotally or implicitly" (p. 227). Tichy asserted that "all organizational relations [can be categorized] in terms of networks" (p. 227). Because organizations involve more than the networking process, it is safer to say that networks provide an excellent manner for understanding the role of communication in organizations.

Technical, political, or cultural systems can be explained using a network approach, as shown in Table 6.5. In addition to this broad, organizational application, networks exist in much more specialized forms.

### Systematic Management Networks

Managers use *systematic networks.* Kotter's (1982) study of what successful general managers actually do provides a useful insight regarding networks. He observed 15 successful general managers over a 5-year period. As Fig. 6.4 indicates, general managers establish broad networks with a variety of groups and individuals. Table 6.6 shows how those networks are used in terms of content and process.

Kotter (1982) concluded, "The GM job places the incumbent in a position of dependence on a lot of people over whom he has little direct control. Under those circumstances, developing, maintaining, and shaping an informal network of relationships is probably essential. Without such a network, getting things done (implementing the agenda) may well be impossible. One is not in a powerful enough position; the network gives one power" (p. 78). Being a general manager is a demanding job in any organization. Kotter's general conclusion is insightful:

In other words, these effective executives did not approach their jobs by planning, organizing, motivating, and controlling in a very formal sense. Instead they relied more

TABLE 6.5
Network Analysis—by Systems Type

| Foci of Attention | Technical Systems | Political Systems | Cultural Systems |
|---|---|---|---|
| Interorganizational Networks | How do organizations acquire information: forecasting, marketing research, intelligence gathering? | What forms of co-optation, cooperation, and competition link organizations? What makes interorganizational conflicts constructive? | How do societal values and traditions affect organizational cultures? What norms do new members carry into organizations? |
| Organizations | How does an organization's structure relate to its missions, strategies, and environments? How hierarchical is influence? | What coalitions, if any, dominate? How hierarchical is control of resources? What coalitions occur? | How are members indoctrinated? How homogeneous are values? What subcultures occur? |
| Clusters | What communication patterns occur in a work group? How does a clique buffer itself against external influence? | How much autonomy does a work group possess? Where do conflicts occur within a coalition? | How do norms and beliefs relate to tasks and technologies? |
| Roles | Who bridges boundaries? Who are the stars in communication networks? | Who are the power brokers? Who resolves conflicts? | What conflicts occur between role expectations and the values of the role incumbents? |

*Note.* From Tichy (1981). Copyright © 1981 by Oxford University Press. Reprinted by permission.

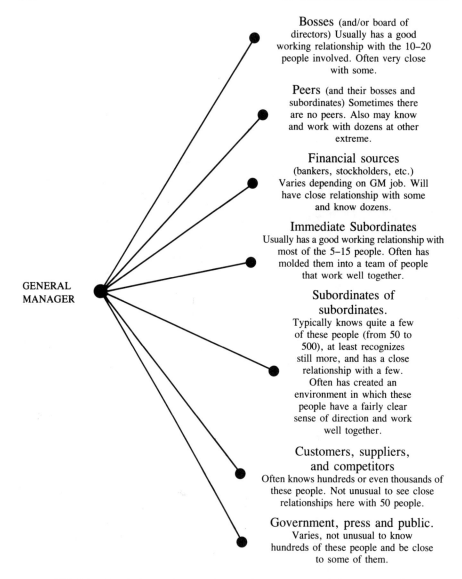

**Bosses** (and/or board of directors) Usually has a good working relationship with the 10–20 people involved. Often very close with some.

**Peers** (and their bosses and subordinates) Sometimes there are no peers. Also may know and work with dozens at other extreme.

**Financial sources** (bankers, stockholders, etc.) Varies depending on GM job. Will have close relationship with some and know dozens.

**Immediate Subordinates** Usually has a good working relationship with most of the 5–15 people. Often has molded them into a team of people that work well together.

**Subordinates of subordinates.** Typically knows quite a few of these people (from 50 to 500), at least recognizes still more, and has a close relationship with a few. Often has created an environment in which these people have a fairly clear sense of direction and work well together.

**Customers, suppliers, and competitors** Often knows hundreds or even thousands of these people. Not unusual to see close relationships here with 50 people.

**Government, press and public.** Varies, not unusual to know hundreds of these people and be close to some of them.

GENERAL
MANAGER

FIG. 6.4.   A typical general manager's network. From Kotter (1982). Copyright © 1982 by Free Press. Reprinted by permission.

on continuous, more informal, and more subtle methods to cope with their large and complex job demands. The most important products of their approach were agendas and networks, not formal plans or organizational charts. . . . [T]heir networks were not necessarily inconsistent with the "formal structure," but they were different. (p. 127)

As Fig. 6.4 and Table 6.6 indicate, general managers establish and maintain a variety of networks in order to effectively complete their work.

TABLE 6.6
General Managers' Use of Networks

---

I. CONTENT: the general managers created networks of cooperative relations that
 \*included hundreds or thousands of people;
 \*included subordinates, subordinates of subordinates, bosses, peers, and outsiders such as customers, suppliers, the press and bankers;
 \*were different from formal structure;
 \*included a variety of types and intensities of relationships to and among people;
 \*often included very strong ties to and among subordinates.

II. PROCESS: the general managers created networks by
 \*focusing on people they felt dependent on, or people they felt were needed to implement their emerging agendas;
 \*making others feel obligated to them;
 \*encouraging others to identify with them;
 \*establishing their reputation in the eyes of others;
 \*making others feel dependent on them;
 \*replacing or removing incompetent subordinates;
 \*changing suppliers or bankers or other outsiders;
 \*shaping the "environment" especially among their subordinates, to foster teamwork, minimize politics, etc., by using both formal management tools (e.g., planning, processes, organization structure, control systems) and more informal methods.

---

*Note.* From Kotter (1982). Copyright © 1982 by Free Press. Reprinted by permission.

Regardless of your area of specialization, you will develop a variety of informal and systematic networks. If you are in the personnel department, for example, you probably will join some version of the local or regional personnel managers association and learn to rely on several other personnel directors for information. In addition, within your organization, you will learn who is most likely to be able to give good advice and who you must contact to accomplish specific activities. Within a short period of time, the informal and systematic networks probably will cross over each other. You will use networks to collect information from different hierarchical levels within the company, to dispense information throughout the organization, and to exchange information, knowledge, and persuasion concerning whatever is being communicated within the organization at any time (Wilson, Goodall, & Waagen, 1986, p. 98).

As a neophyte, you might find it useful to find a *mentor* who will provide linking information to aid your entry and development in the organization. The mentor is wise to the workings of the organization and can facilitate your entry into important networks. Many organizations encourage and sponsor the mentoring process because it does link individuals (Hurley, 1988). The actual value of the mentoring process in aiding career development is not quite as clear (Merriam, 1983). However, being tied to someone who is linked to important information regarding an organization is helpful, and the mentoring concept is an additional example of how networks operate.

Networks are a vital part of an effective manager's repertoire. Effective managers are highly connected with various individuals and groups inside and outside the organization. All organizational members can learn from this analysis of effective managers and develop their own networks. The same conclusion can be stated regarding the excellent companies as we demonstrate next.

### Networks and Organizations

Three approaches show how networks aid organizations. The first is using specialized structures, the second is enhancing teamwork, and the third is including employees in the ownership of the organization. In the companies considered to be among the best, "working the network effectively is the only way to get things done or to understand what is really going on" (Deal & Kennedy, 1982, pp. 14–15).

**Specialized Networks.**   Specialized networks are intended to make certain innovations occur by encouraging effective interactions. As Mueller (1986) explained:

> It is not happenstance that in a 1984 study we found a common positive attribute of ten innovative companies: an organizational style with easy communication and human networking. The art of innovation depends on a changing series of champions. The champions network directly with different elements of the organization and environment in which they exist. The bureaucratic and hierarchical power flow are short-circuited by collaboration with those who really know. (p. 58)

We already have examined the effective use of networking. Examples such as skunkworks and the J & J Tylenol case demonstrate this process of making certain the right people get in touch with each other. The result of this cooperative ethic is summarized in *Re-inventing the Corporation* by Naisbitt and Aburdene (1985): "The top-down authoritarian management style is yielding to a networking style of management, where people learn from one another horizontally, where everyone is a resource for everyone else, and where each person gets support and assistance from many different directions" (p. 72).

Creating specialty groups to solve particular problems is a successful approach used in many organizations. Peters (1987) offered this example: "Ford and IBM both say that they wasted years before realizing that most quality improvements opportunities lie outside the natural work group. Tennant and Milliken launched multifunction teams from the start. In fact, Tennant's first team was a multi-function group working on an automatic floor scrubber; it reduced defects per machine from 1.3 to 0.4 in its first year of existence" (p. 76).

Three examples of "effectively working the network" are project management, research and development groups, and *intrapreneurship*. First, these multifunctional groups are present in project management, which we discussed earlier in this chapter. To reiterate, project management is a mixture of people, systems, and techniques used to complete a project successfully (Dinsmore, 1984). This type of project manipulates the organizational structure and functions as a tool to help people work together to reach challenging goals. In many cases, project management types of teams are tightly coupled coalitions more than cliques, because their major goals are short-term, pragmatic, and result oriented.

Successful research and development projects, where supervisors act as boundary spanners, and provide the key links to the rest of the organization, provide a second example. These individuals link the project teams to outside sources and guarantee greater project success (Katz & Tushman, 1983). Other project members, labeled internal liaisons, link project colleagues to information both inside and outside the organization. As Katz & Tushman put it, "Research has consistently demonstrated that interpersonal communications are the primary means by which engineering professionals acquire and disseminate important ideas and information" (p. 256). In the end, the quality of the boundary-spanning supervisors, who both integrate their group with outside sources and act as gatekeepers limiting some outside access, were the key variables in the effectiveness of a laboratory's communication and information processing. In organizations, these groups are closer to cliques because they are long-term and develop numerous close ties. The supervisor or manager relies on interpersonal influence and knowledge to guide the project team (Robey, 1991, pp. 221–224).

A final example of allowing subunits of an organization to make important decisions is intrapreneurship. This is the process of creating entrepreneurial ventures within large organizations (DuBrin, Ireland, & Williams, 1989, p. 542). The classic example of a separative, or isolate, would be an entrepreneur. In an effort to capture the entrepreneurial spirit, and still keep separatives within an organizational structure, a large number of companies have encouraged intraprenuers. As the term implies, these are people with entrepreneurial skills employed in organizations. As a consequence, some companies are reinventing themselves as confederations of entrepreneurs, operating under the main tent of the corporation (Gregore, 1983). This confederation represents a tightly connected network, which is loosely coupled with the organization's structure. A key purpose of intrapreneurial ventures is to make big organizations more flexible and responsive by establishing small, project-oriented networks. Organizations can cultivate the creativity and risk-taking characteristics of entrepreneurs through the intrapreneurial process (DuBrin et al., 1989, pp. 542–544).

These are three examples of effectively using networks within the organizational structure. Actually, there are unlimited possibilities for the manipulations and configurations that can be used on the basic concepts presented by these three examples. A more generic concept, based on effective networks, is teamwork.

**Teamwork.**    Creating speciality networks is not always practical or applicable to a particular task or organization. In these cases, teamwork is used to maximize interactions. Teamwork is virtually synonymous with organized activities. The secret is to effectively network as a team (Blake, Mouton, & Allen, 1987, pp. 4–12). Table 6.7

TABLE 6.7
Seven Keys to Effective Team Building

1. Leadership. Team building cannot occur without a formal team leader. The leader has to be involved and committed—not indifferent or tongue-in-cheek.
2. Leader's role. Team leaders must be willing to examine their roles in relation to the team.
3. Member commitment. All team members must be committed and willing to take responsibility for making the effort work.
4. Examining process. All team members must continually study the team process and critique their own performance.
5. Regular meetings. Team building requires group meetings. One-on-one meetings by the leader will not succeed because members cannot relate face to face. Manager/member meetings allow the manager to control the flow, content, and direction of information.
6. Daily process. Team building cannot be done in special sessions or off-site meetings. Team members should be committed to use materials gained in the daily meetings.
7. Ongoing process. Team building has to be understood as a process of continued diagnosis, action planning, implementation, and evaluation—not a one-shot process.

*Note.* From Hanson and Lubin (1986). Copyright © 1986 by *Organization Development Journal*. Adapted by permission.

shows the seven steps needed for team building. Although many networks are less formally composed, teams are ongoing, coordinated groups of individuals working together even when they are not in constant contact. You will recall that networks are not small groups. Teams provide a specific justification for that conclusion. A team shares common boundaries, interdependent tasks, articulated purposes, and understood, "owned," goals (Egan, 1988a, pp. 145–156). As such, teams may start as coalitions, but in a short period of time they operate as a clique form of a network.

*Quality circles* (QCs) and *employee stock ownership plans* (ESOPs) are two specific examples that illustrate the methods used to incorporate team concepts. A quality circle is a group of 3 to 10 people from the same work area that voluntarily meets on a regular basis—usually 1 hr, once a week—to identify, analyze, and solve problems in that work area. These individuals focus on a specific issue to resolve a quality problem (Bain, 1982, p. 202). QCs are good examples of increasing network potential by making certain the right people are placed in a decision-making position. The QC allows for better creative problem-solving processes and improved management practices. When QCs have failed, it is most frequently the result of poor training in process, excessive control, or a lack of support by the organization (Karp, 1983). A QC, or a team, needs different players for different tasks. They represent a network of relationships rather than a group of people. So, in a given QC, there might be a producer who knows how to get the job done, an administrator whose strength is planning, an entrepreneur who has vision and creative problem-solving abilities, and an integrator who transforms individual goals into group goals (Blanchard, 1987).

Although QCs generally are designed to be used by production personnel, there are few limits to the potential for such a networking approach. The power of involvement, created by QCs, applies to white-collar situations as well as production personnel (U.S. Department of Labor, 1987a). For example, Herman Miller, a furniture manufacturer, expects teams and networks: "Everyone from the CEO on down is organized into a network of work teams, caucuses, and councils. The aim is to enlist every employee in the drive to increase productivity, reduce costs, and improve customer services, and to make sure that employee complaints are resolved" ("Teams at Herman," 1986, p. 1). We return to QCs, and a much more complete discussion of employee involvement, later in this textbook when we discuss specific applications of small-group communications. At this point, we can conclude that the networking process is the underpinning of successful QCs.

***Employee Ownership.*** A growing number of companies are giving employees a real stake in the business through programs such as employee stock ownership plans *(ESOPs)*, pension and savings plans, and retiree medical plans. If all the worker-owned stock in the United States is counted, employees have more than $150 billion worth, and "employee ownership shows no sign of slowing" (Bernstein, 1991, p. 110). By creating ownership, organizations increase employee motivation.

At Seymour Speciality Wire Company, a "Workers Solving Problems" (WSP) was set up to make the employees part of the decision-making process (U.S. Department of Labor, 1987b). The WSP provided for each working group on each shift to meet for 20 min every 2 weeks on company time to discuss productivity issues and other matters. A shop-floor representative was elected from each group to serve as its chairperson for a year. The representative worked closely with the foreman or section manager. The 21 WSPs took up 165 problems in the first quarter. Sixty-eight were solved at the point of production, 44 still were being discussed, and 53 were referred to higher management levels. Of those 53, 25 were resolved. Evaluators spotted potential problems including lack of action on items, use of WSP as a stalling versus solving mechanism, unskilled or uninterested foremen, fear of reprisals, and some ineffective procedural mechanisms.

The Seymour Speciality Wire Company provides a useful working example of how networks intertwine with the formal channels of communication. Although the linking pin, the shop-floor representative, forwards the important information regarding problems, there is still a vertical power structure that dictates who actually can solve approximately one third of the issues. At the same time, the program meets the employees' desire for more say and control in the workplace. Finally, it meets the central issues of asking the people who actually do the work how to make the process more productive.

So, networks are a means for making certain the right people get in touch with each other at the right time. QCs and ESOPs are two examples of this process. At this point, we should return to networks. The examples provided so far represent relatively stable, ongoing networks.

## Loosely Coupled Systems Revisited

With increasing regularity, groups are put together with specific problems to resolve. These groups represent the use of loosely coupling procedures, which is one means of dealing with a rigid, centralized bureaucratic structure (Metcalfe, 1981, p. 509). The intent is to have nearly decomposable subsystems that allow for innovation and creativity without challenging the overall design of an organization. The organization is able to adapt to specific demands by the combination of subsystems' existing programs rather than the construction of entirely new programs. The Tylenol case discussed earlier provides a good example. The groups are tightly connected internally, and with the issue at hand. Perhaps the most challenging task for organizations is change. The effective use of networks is an underpinning to successfully implementing change.

## Networks and Change

The change process places the analysis of networks in perspective. All organizations must change by adapting to the environment, evolving to remain competitive, or altering procedures and products simply to survive (Schein, 1985, pp. 314–372). Every organization will grow, diminish, gain and lose personnel, alter product lines, have new and different customers, and be influenced by a number of other environmental factors. To adapt to these changes, organizations engage in various processes of change. Successfully managing change is very difficult. Simply because a new procedure makes sense does not mean it will be accepted by members of the organization.

Information about new or different products and procedures spreads through a process called *diffusion of innovation*. In numerous studies, Rogers (1983) examined how new ideas and new products are disseminated. Of particular interest to Rogers is why excellent product ideas, or operating procedures, take so long to be accepted. In many cases there have been 30-year and 40-year delays in the widespread dissemination of innovations, even when products and services demonstrate a crystal-clear, decisive advantage from the start. His dozens of studies have analyzed new commercial products, the adoption of birth control techniques, and agricultural technology.

Rogers' (1983) studies demonstrate the overriding power of networks. Most individuals do not evaluate an innovation on the basis of any "scientific," objective study of its consequences. Instead, they depend mainly on the subjective evaluation of an innovation that is conveyed to them from other individuals like themselves who previously have adopted the innovation. This dependence on the communicated experience of near-peers suggests that the heart of the diffusion process is the imitations by potential adopters of their network partners who have adopted previously. According to Peters (1987), "Study after study Rogers reviews reveals that: (1) an innovation takes off only after interpersonal networks have become activated in spreading subjective evaluations and (2) success is related to the extent that the change agent or marketer worked through opinion leaders" (p. 241).

Rogers (1983) isolated five adopter categories. These are the innovators, who are the first people to try an innovation; the early adopters, who are well respected in the organization; the early majority, who compose the critical mass of acceptance; the late majority, or skeptics; and the laggards, who are the last group to accept any change. Strategically, these five categories operate to explain how to use the networking process. By isolating the innovators and early adopters, who are the people most likely to try a change, the enormous time lag in acceptance of change can be circumvented (Pinchot, 1983; Rogers, 1983).

This *linking role* has been found to be crucial to the innovation adoption process. *Linkers* are the individuals who disseminate and utilize scientific knowledge. The originator of knowledge communicates to an intermediary, who carries the information to the user, or the liaison.

Organizational development efforts often involve an inside change agent, who links the knowledge of an outside change agent with the organizational user of the knowledge (Egan, 1988b; Havelock, Guskin, Frohman, Hill, & Huber, 1969). This use of an insider–outsider change agent team is a primary means now used to enhance organizational development and shows the power of networks. You will remember when we discussed the various types of roles, we indicated the various ways that liaisons operate in an organization. From a change perspective, the isolate would correspond to the late majority or laggard. However, in the actual change process, the isolate also might be the innovator or, sometimes, the star.

For many years, managers have been cautioned to be aware of the *two-step flow of information* (Gannon, 1979, p. 162). In most work groups, there is an informal leader who influences the other group members. If a manager wants to introduce a new product or procedure, the advice is to convert these informal leaders first. Then the rest of the work group will be likely to follow. Essentially, this is a pragmatic use of the linking pins, opinion leaders, and boundary spanners in the organization.

Our discussion of networks clearly does not incorporate all the specialized networks. As you become part of an organization, you probably will be engaged in computer-conferencing networks, networking for specific goals, and various other links using personal computers, communication technology, and conference software. We examine these activities in chapter 14. You will recall that a network can be almost any set of relationships an investigator chooses to isolate.

## Conclusion

Before moving to a discussion of channels, consider what we now know about networks. First, networks are regularized patterns of interaction in an organization. Individuals belong to a variety of networks. Although organigrams describe the prescribed directions for communication, the sociogram shows the predictable patterns that actually occur.

Second, networks have properties including coupling, connectedness, and roles. Coupling is a reflection of the amount of interdependence between subsystems. The amount of identification by network members with the goals of the network is called connectedness. The strength of weak ties phenomenon is a good example of how networks function.

Groupthink and freezethink show the problem with overconnectedness. Organizations, as well as individuals, can use weak ties to overcome some of these problems.

Third, clusters can be divided into coalitions and cliques with specific roles. Coalitions are linkages for political or pragmatic purposes. A clique is created because of high connectedness.

There are numerous network roles. Research has identified liaisons, gatekeepers, stars, bridges or linking pins, cosmopolites, and isolates. Each role has a function in the network. In general, liaisons seem the most active and isolates are outside the network. However, different people play different roles at different times in a network.

Specific applications of networks include systematic management networks, specialized structures, teamwork, and employee ownership. Networks also provide a useful means for understanding the change process.

At this point, you might be tempted to conclude that an understanding of networks would be sufficient as a perspective on communication flow in an organization. However, because channels are the sanctioned means of organizational communication, they must be examined carefully.

## CHANNELS

In all organizations, there is an intertwining of networks and channels. Although networks often operate in a de facto manner in the decision-making process, most organizations assign a great deal of de jure, or sanctioned importance, to channels.

Communication is channeled through an organization. This flow is downward, upward, and horizontal. When individuals and groups follow these *prescribed channels,* they are using the *formal communication mechanisms.* Individuals frequently communicate without using the formal channels, and this *informal process* is called the *grapevine.* Many of the properties and behaviors in the grapevine are analogous to networks. For the purposes of making the concepts clear, however, we discuss grapevines as a specific type of communication channel. Because the term grapevine is widely used in organizations, you need to be able to differentiate grapevines from the other channels of communication.

## Channel Characteristics

Vertical channels have five characteristics. These include one-way or two-way communication, channels as organizational memories, channels as a managerial prerogative and responsibility, channel properties as intervening variables, and the different perspectives of the channel users.

*One-Way, Two-Way Communication.* First, communication patterns can be analyzed as being one-way or two-way, although this only applies to a very strict definition of information flow. When no opportunity is provided for feedback, the communication is one-way. In situations where orders are given, memos are posted, or directives are passed down from upper levels, the flow tends to be one-way downward. An example of one-way upward flow would be when employees make suggestions and the employees never receive a response.

One-way communication can be useful for managers in situations where there really is no need for discussion. Certain safety regulations, for example, are not open to question. Many organizations post rules. Employee responses to some types of questions are essentially one-way. If the sender and receiver have a good working relationship, it might be a waste of time to engage in two-way communication.

Many communication training sessions begin with an analysis of the problems with one-way communication. In chapter 1, we discussed the impossibility of not communicating. This impact of the communication process can lead to an *arc of distortion* between the intended and the perceived message (Albanese, 1988, p. 492).

All communication activity, including silence, or the absence of an intentional message, can be meaningful! Unintended messages, or interpretations of messages, result from nonverbal factors such as word choice, physical posture, or setting (McCaskey, 1979, p. 27). The potential discrepancies between the intended message, and the multiple messages actually received, lead to the possible distortion. Most managers and supervisors are counseled to avoid one-way communication. However, in an effort to facilitate work activities, many managers and supervisors employ one-way techniques to save time, or in the mistaken belief that more control over the message is occurring (Zaleznik, 1989, pp. 93–95, 104). Hence, the rather sarcastic sign in many offices and factories observing: "There's never time to do a job right, but there's always time to do it over."

To avoid this distortion between individuals, two-way communication is considered the most useful. In any organization, channels operate both in a one-way and a two-way manner.

*Channels as Organizational Memories.* Second, these message-processing systems are the source of data for the *memory systems* of an organization. The how, why, and what comprising the channel's content tells a great deal about the type of organization operating (Roberts, 1984, p. 35). The content can be information and/or affect messages.

Each management perspective uses channels for different purposes (Daniels & Spiker, 1987, p. 84). In chapter 3, the various frames used to organize and manage were explained. The organization's view of what is required to effectively manage will determine how channels are used (Bolman & Deal, 1984, 1991).

From the pragmatic position taken by the structural or scientific management school, channels transmit the information required for coordination. In this mode of operation, managers set objectives and direct employees with the information necessary to understand and complete the work. Employees let management know if there are any major impediments to accomplishing the work.

The human relations school directs communication efforts toward providing rationale to employees in order to enhance compliance, in other words, treating employees as competent and deserving of sufficient information to make their tasks acceptable. An important benefit would be the generation of positive reactions. This attention and inclusion should enhance motivation. Because of the supportive operating climate, employees will express their feelings and attitudes to managers.

Effective utilization of each individual's potential input is the goal of managers following the human resource perspective. Rather than telling, selling, or counseling employees, the human resources approach tries to bring employees into the communication process. Because employees are a resource, extensive uses of communication channels prevail. Communication channels are used to exchange information, feelings, and needs.

The political perspective sees channels as power opportunities. So, channels are used as vehicles to influence or manipulate. In a very real sense, information can be power. When competition and conflict are the primary aims of an organizational system, then the outcome is likely to be coercive.

From the symbolic or cultural perspective, communication literally is the glue that provides sense-making data for everyone and provides a unifying concept for the organization. In other words, the memory of the system is influenced by the type of information and messages, which ultimately are determined by the goal of the managing process or philosophy. So, although disseminating information is the ascribed goal of communication channels, perpetuation of the organization's cultural values are an inherent by-product. In our discussion of organizational cultures, you will recall that this by-product is often the cornerstone of effective organizations because there are shared beliefs and attitudes.

The information and messages organizations facilitate through the communication channels provide insights into the type of organizational culture operating. The scientific, human relations, human resources, political, and cultural perspectives all utilize channels in different fashions. In any organization, there is likely to be a mixture of how individuals and groups use channels.

***Channels as a Managerial Prerogative and Responsibility.***   Third, channels of communication are controlled primarily by management. Initiating communication is usually a managerial decision as are the form, location, and time (Harriman, 1974). DeVito (1986) put it as follows:

> In both upward and downward communication, management is in control of the com-
> munication system. The managers are the ones who have the time, the expertise, and
> the facilities to improve the communication that takes place in an organization. . . .
> This is not to say that the workers or lower levels are absolved of their responsibility;
> effective communication is a two-way process. Nevertheless, management bears the
> larger responsibility for establishing an effective and efficient internal communication
> system. (p. 102)

Ironically, this sense of responsibility tends to lead to overcontrol by managers who
are attempting to do a good job of opening channels (Bradford & Cohen, 1984, pp.
25–55). Managers might give off the message: "I talk, you listen," rather than creating a two-way communication process. Without the necessary training and skill in
communication, changing the operating environment is extremely difficult.

**Channel Properties as Intervening Variables.** The various properties of
channels themselves provide the fourth characteristic. The communication channel
process is controlled by four intervening variables (Smeltzer & Golen, 1984). *Channeling, timing, editing,* and *abstracting* all occur as messages are passed through
an organization. Table 6.8 explains each of these factors. Channeling explains why
messages are sent to particular individuals; timing outlines what happens, in terms
of possible delays; editing involves the process of modification the message under-
goes; and abstracting shows what different sources do as a message is passed on.

*Serial transmission,* which is the sending of messages along a chain of people
or links, is the label often applied to many of these processes. The popular child's
game, telephone, where one person whispers a message to another, who proceeds
to pass it on to another, until the final person states the message they received, illustrates this problem. For children, this experience is funny because the final message
form is always very different from the original. When this same process is illustrat-
ed to managers, they are suprised. However, in any large, complex organization,
there are numerous links through which messages must travel.

Messages will become distorted. Table 6.9 shows a humorous, and widely used,
example of the possible distortions in downward communication. One researcher
found another version of the same story, printed 20 years later in the same magazine, which is shown in Table 6.10. Various aspects of serial transmission operated
to change the message substantially from the first version to the second.

Three characteristics of serial transmission create the principal problems. They
are *condensation, closure,* and *expectations* (Bedeian, 1986). Condensation is caused
when individuals use fewer words or details as they pass the message along. Someone might assume the information is irrelevant and simplify the message. In the
process, vital information might be lost. Closure occurs because people tend to have
a low tolerance for ambiguity. Relayers of messages fill in the missing information
so that it makes more sense. When the relayers add meaning to a message based

TABLE 6.8
Information Transmission

---

## CHANNELING

---

1. The probability that information will be accepted by an organizational member through any channel is related to the perceived quality of the source.
    Quality is dependent on accuracy, timely, and reliable.
    Quality is dependent on perception.
2. The probability that information will be transmitted to an organizational member is related to the costs of communicating with that member.
    Efficiency increases the use of a communication channel.
    Physical and structural accessibility determines frequency.
    Location of information helps determine its use.
3. The probability of an organizational member transmitting information is related to the perceived work load of the member.
    Low priority items are destroyed with high work loads.
    Perceived work load is the critical variable.
4. The possibility that a message will be routed to an organizational member is related to the perceived relevance of the contents for that member.
    The greater the task interdependence, the more frequent the communication.

---

## TIMING

---

5. Senders delay the message until they perceive the receiver is ready to attend to the message.
6. Senders delay sending messages if they are busy with other tasks considered more important.
7. The delay of the message is directly related to the number of links in the communication chain.

---

## EDITING

---

8. Message editing/modification is related to the extent that the sender believes that the modification will result in greater goal attainment.
    People distort upward communication by exaggerating favorable data and minimizing the unfavorable information.
    Senders alter messages more if they do not trust the motives of the receivers.
9. The extent of information editing is related to the ability to choose the message format.
10. The tendency to edit a message is directly related to the perceived ambiguity of the data on which the information is based.
    People perceive what they are ready to perceive (perceptual readiness).
    Objective and tangible subject matter makes people feel they are communicating accurately.
    Conversely, the more subjective the material, the greater doubt.
    Decisions makers rely on credible or trustworthy sources, and ignore others.
11. The extent of editing is related to the number of sequential links in the communication chain between sender and receiver.

---

## ABSTRACTING

---

12. The extent of abstracting the information is related to the cost of storing and sending the information.
13. The extent of message abstracting is related to the perceived work load of the receiver.
    People on the top demand abstracting.
14. The extent of message abstraction is related to the links in the communication chain connecting the sender and the receiver.

---

*Note.* From Smeltzer and Golen (1984). Adapted by permission.

TABLE 6.9

Serial Transmission – 1

---

*Eclipse of the Sun: The Operation of the Chain of Command*

---

### THE COLONEL TO THE EXECUTIVE

At nine o'clock tomorrow there will be an eclipse of the sun, something which does not occur every day. Get the men to fall out in the company street in their fatigues so that they will see this rare phenomena, and I will explain it to them. In case of rain, we will not be able to see anything so take the men to the gym.

### THE EXECUTIVE TO THE CAPTAIN

By order of the Colonel, tomorrow at nine o'clock there will be an eclipse of the sun; if it rains you will not be able to see it from the company street so then, in fatigues, the eclipse of the sun will take place in the gym, something that does not occur every day.

### THE CAPTAIN TO THE LIEUTENANT

By order of the Colonel in fatigues tomorrow at nine o'clock in the morning the inauguration of the eclipse of the sun will take place in the gym. The Colonel will give the order if it should rain, something which occurs every day.

### THE LIEUTENANT TO THE SERGEANT

Tomorrow at nine the Colonel in fatigues will eclipse the sun in the gym, as it occurs every day if it is a nice day; if it rains, then in the company street.

### THE SERGEANT TO THE CORPORAL

Tomorrow at nine the eclipse of the Colonel in fatigues will take place by cause of the sun. If it rains in the gym, something which does not take place every day, you will fall out in the company street.

### COMMENTS AMONG THE PRIVATES

Tomorrow, if it rains, it looks as if the sun will eclipse the Colonel in the gym. It is a shame that this does not occur every day.

---

*Note.* From Bedeian (1986). Reprinted by permission.

on their own expectations, we have the third type of serial transmission problem. All three of these serial transmission problems are important because the changes are not a result of willful distortion, but are, instead, attempts to make sense of a message as it is passed along.

Changes in messages would appear to be inherent in the use of channels. Figure 6.5 indicates how the message, by the time it gets to the employee, contains only 20% of the original message. Whether the changes in a message are intentional or merely convenient, making the decisions to alter a message also can change the message's usefulness.

**Different Perspectives.** Finally, superiors and subordinates have different information needs. One of the reasons managers or employees do not necessarily

TABLE 6.10
Serial Transmission—2

---

*That's No Eclipse—It's A Blackout.*
*Chain of Command, J5 Directorate, to All Officers, From J5*

---

Director: Gentlemen, tomorrow at 1315 hours there will be a total eclipse of the sun. This is a rare phenomena and I would like the officers of J5 to internalize this experience in order to broaden their cognitive awareness. All personnel will fall out on the parking area and I will explain the circumstances which cause eclipses of the sun and the moon. Should there be inclement weather, we will not be able to see the eclipse, but I will speak to all personnel in the J6 conference room.

Deputy Director: Gentlemen, by order of the director, there will be an eclipse of the sun. If it rains, you won't be able to see it from the parking lot, so the eclipse will take place in the J5 conference room. This is a rare phenomenon which does much to enhance the individual officer's internalization of broad awareness.

Ch. M. Sgt.: Tomorrow, the director and the deputy director will eclipse the sun. If it rains or snows, this'll take place in the conference room. If not, it'll happen outside.

Ch. P&S: My officers don't need an eclipse of the sun.

Ch. Plans: Let's include this in our insurgency prevention plan.

Ch. Weapons: Can you eat an eclipse?

Action Officer: It looks as though the J5 Directorate will be eclipsed tomorrow. It is a shame that this doesn't occur every day.

---

*Note.* From Anonymous (1983, cited in Bedeian, 1986).

| MESSAGE | | AMOUNT RECEIVED |
|---|---|---|
| Written by the board of directors | | 100% |
| Received by the vice-president | | 63% |
| Received by the general supervisor | | 56% |
| Received by the plant manager | | 40% |
| Received by the general foreman | | 30% |
| Received by the worker | | 20% |

FIG. 6.5. Serial transmission—Downward (From Killan, 1968). Copyright © 1968 by American Management Association. Reprinted by permission.

appreciate or understand information passed on to them is they are operating with very different perspectives.

Someone who runs machinery, makes sales calls, types all day, makes deliveries, or does any other job that is somewhat routine will have little interest in certain information that might seem very important to the supervisor. Subordinates probably have little appreciation for a manager's time allocation problems, for example, because the subordinate's time is prescribed throughout the day. Superiors, who have more control of their days, are likely to see some employee's complaints, or observations, as trivial. The problem is, as Katz and Kahn (1966) explained, "The information requirements of superior and subordinates are not symmetrical. What the superior wants to know is often not what the subordinate wants to tell him; what the subordinate wants to know is not necessarily the message the superior wants to send" (p. 239). So, even when the other channel characteristics are working to enhance effective communication, different perspectives always exist.

In summary, the five characteristics of channels are: (a) They can be one-way or two-way, (b) they provide important information about the organization's memory, (c) they are primarily a managerial prerogative, (d) they are subject to numerous intervening variables, and (e) they are affected by different perspectives.

To fully understand channels, each of the directions for communication—vertical, as demonstrated by downward and upward messages, and horizontal—needs further analysis.

## Downward Communication

Downward communication is the messages sent from superiors to subordinates. The majority of these messages are reaffirmations of the hierarchical structure and tend to reinforce control. Downward communication is used in a variety of fashions. We discuss five of the most prevalent types and messages.

### Functions of Downward Communication

The five functions are (a) giving job instructions, (b) providing job rationale, (c) explaining procedures, policies, and practices, (d) furnishing performance feedback, and (e) transmitting information regarding the organization's mission and goals (Katz & Kahn, 1966, pp. 239–243).

*Job Instructions.* The tasks expected from employees, as explained in directives, contracts, operating manuals, union contracts, and job descriptions, are all part of the job instructions. The goal is to let employees know what they are supposed to do and how they are supposed to do it. This type of communication can be oral and/or written and is an ongoing job function of any supervisory or management position.

For example, one of the skills taught to beginning supervisors is how to train others by using the tell-show-and-do method for routine tasks such as sorting mail or cleaning up. The supervisor tells workers what they are supposed to do, shows them how to do it, and then watches them do it. For more complex tasks, supervisors are advised to break down the work into specific subtasks (Shout, 1977, pp. 56–57). A suprising number of supervisors are unaware of how to get the message across. So, insightful organizations provide training, or job instructions, to beginning supervisors on what they must know about their role as instruction givers (Bittel, 1980, p. 271).

*Job Rationale.*   Letting employees know how their job and tasks relate to other individuals, positions, tasks, and overall objectives is an important function of downward communication. Increasingly, companies are spending more time on explaining this aspect of each individual's job so employees will know how their particular task fits into the overall success of the organization (Koehler, Anatol, & Applbaum, 1981, p. 81). Letting the employee see the "big picture" is the goal behind many orientation, or perhaps indoctrination, programs.

*Procedures, Policies, and Practices.*   The various policies, benefits, customs, processes, and rules are explained, and often reaffirmed later, with downward communication. Bulletin boards, memos, and meetings are often forums and employee handbooks tend to spell out the expected behaviors. Training manuals are employed to explain procedures and can be good examples of one-way communication.

*Performance Feedback.*   In the most pragmatic sense, continued employment operates in all organizations as feedback (if you are not fired, you must be doing a satisfactory job). In large factory-type settings, feedback usually is directed to a specific task not being accomplished well or a specific job requirement, such as being on time, not being fulfilled.

As individuals move up in an organization, they are more likely to receive performance appraisals where specific discussions occur between superior and subordinate over various aspects of the subordinate's performance. Unfortunately, many managers practice *management by exception* where the only feedback, or management recognition, is when something is wrong or needs to be corrected.

Knowing when to provide feedback can be tricky. Many employees do not need or want constant supervision. In these instances, managers often are cautioned to use management by exception for very positive reasons. When employees need to be left alone, the phrase management by wandering around is changed to management by wandering away. We return to feedback in the next chapter.

*Information Regarding the Organization's Missions and Goals.*   Becoming familiar with the organization's ideological perspective is important. Employees need to know why an organization does what it does and the excellent companies go to great lengths to make certain every employee can identify the specific goals of the organization (Koehler et al., 1981, p. 10). The goal in many organizations is to effect the integration of employees into the total picture. In a sense, the acculturation process can be started with the information provided about the company in the first training sessions. Peters (1987) explained:

> Disney, IBM, Federal Express, Stew Leonard, and Nissan provide models: their training "overemphasizes" the skills that define their uniqueness. Leonard focuses on courtesy and communication skills; the shoddy training of most retail clerks focuses on how to run the cash register—and what a message that sends! Disney teaches Walt's vision directly, as well as acting and atmospherics; it sends another clear message through its extensive training—in customer service skills—for sweepers, parking-lot attendants, and ticket sellers. Federal Express has made a science of training its Memphis-based customer service force in how to deal with antsy customers. (pp. 326–327)

As Peters indicated, the issue is what type of message will be provided rather than if a message regarding the company's missions and goals is sent.

All five of these downward communication processes are important to employees. In one survey, employees said the most important information to them at work concerns employee benefit programs (82%), pay policies and procedures (78%), company's plans for the future (73%), how to improve work performance (65%), and how my work fits into the total picture (61%) (The Hay Group Research for Management Database, 1985, p. 21).

Consultants continuously hammer home the importance of having a well-informed work force and urge managers to spend their time trying "to catch people doing something right" rather than using management by exception. Uniformly, textbooks argue for keeping employees well informed to make certain they will be more productive.

### Analysis of the Process

Unfortunately, the downward communication process is not always successful. One study of 30,000 employees found that only 40% of the respondents felt their organizations did a good or very good job of communicating downward (Morgan & Schiemann, 1983, p. 16). The International Association of Business Communicators surveyed 32,000 employees in 26 U.S. and Canadian organizations (Foehrenbach & Rosenberg, 1982). The participants responded as follows: 70.9% felt that their organizations tried to keep employees well informed, 65.3% thought they were given enough information to perform their jobs, and 51.1% thought their organization's downward communication was candid and accurate. Although 70% would appear to be a major improvement over the 40% figure from the first study, the results indicate that one third (29.1%) of the employees felt their organization was not trying to keep them informed.

Of equal interest is the ranking employees place on sources of information. As Table 6.11 indicates, the current ranking and the preferred ranking for sources of

TABLE 6.11
Sources of Organizational Information

| Preferred Rank | Source | Major Source For | Current Rank |
|---|---|---|---|
| 1 | Immediate supervisor | 92.3% | 1 |
| 2 | Small group meetings | 63.0% | 3 |
| 3 | Top executives | 55.5% | 10 |
| 4 | Annual employee business report | 45.8% | 8 |
| 5 | Employee booklets | 41.2% | 5 |
| 6 | Orientation program | 41.1% | 11 |
| 7 | Local employee publication | 40.4% | 7 |
| 8 | General employee publication | 38.5% | 6 |
| 9 | Bulletin board(s) | 37.1% | 4 |
| 10 | Upward communication programs | 33.8% | 15 |
| 11 | Mass meetings | 30.3% | 9 |
| 12 | Audio-visual programs | 23.2% | 14 |
| 13 | Union | 20.4% | 12 |
| 14 | Grapevine | 10.5% | 2 |
| 15 | Mass media | 8.8% | 13 |

*Note.* From Goddard (1985). Copyright © 1985 by American Management Association. Reprinted by permission.

information are quite dissimilar. The exception is the immediate supervisor who is both the most used source for information and the preferred source.

Based on this particular listing, employees do not seem overly impressed with media approaches or written materials. As a general rule, when giving instructions, managers and supervisors should limit written messages to situations where the information is critical  omplex, or will need to be referred to in the future (Braid, 1985). Oral messages seem to be preferable both because employees seem to want this method of transmission, and because it provides for greater flexibility in explanation.

On the surface, then, downward communication is important and needs to be more effective. This conclusion, however, is not a new one. So, what prevents superiors from more effectively communicating information downward? In addition to the problems with serial transmission discussed earlier, certain specific issues for downward communication deserve further elaboration.

**Barriers to Downward Communication.** First, there is a problem deciding the type (e.g., financial data, management concerns, employee issues) or content (e.g., amount of detail, specifics) of downward communication. At the risk of sounding like a heretic, one national consulting firm argues that management should tell employees everything! Their point, of course, is that current management practices are to carefully filter information and decide what employees need to know (Davis, 1968; Redding, 1972, p. 391).

As we already have discussed, control of the channels and the content is primarily in the hands of management. So, managers can determine how the information is passed on. A recent management textbook listed the most effective upward and downward communication channels as shown in Table 6.12. To the degree that managers follow this textbook's prescription, they may be limiting their effectiveness, because employees are most interested in face-to-face communication.

A second barrier to the effectiveness of written forms of downward communication is the surprising rate of functional illiteracy in the work force. In 1988, the *Personnel Journal* reported "rates of functional illiteracy of 29% among semiskilled workers, 30% among unskilled, and 11% among managers" (p. 3). The how part of the downward communication process has a potentially significant weak link of 11% to 30% of the message recipients. In some settings, 1 out of 10 managers might not be able to utilize a written message and around one third of the work force probably will not be able to act on many of the messages being sent.

Much of the difficulty in message transmission can be alleviated through face-to-face, or dyadic, communication between superior and subordinates. Because this is a specialized form of communication, we deal with it in much greater depth later in this text.

In conclusion, there is little likelihood that employees and management will share the same goals (what) or channel preference (how), so the information passed on to employees often can lack relevance (DeVito, 1986, p. 102). Some filtering may be important because not all information is valuable to employees.

The third downward communication problem, then, is the *relevancy* of the information. Simply providing more information does not mean that people will be better informed. The information must be useful to employees and this is where there is likely to be a problem. When information has little application, any efforts in communicating it are largely wasted and may discredit the source (Koehler et al., 1981, pp. 86–87). To the degree there is an unlimited, or perhaps unending, amount of downward communication, there will be *overload*. This occurs when the capacity of the communication channel, or the individual, to process the information is

TABLE 6.12
Effectiveness of Specific Upward and Downward Communication Techniques

| Rank | Upward Communication Techniques | Rank | Downward Communication Techniques |
|---|---|---|---|
| 1 | Informal Discussion | 1 | Small Group Meeting |
| 2 | Meeting with Supervisors | 2 | Direct Organizational Publications |
| 3 | Attitude Surveys | 3 | Supervisory Meetings |
| 4 | Grievance Procedures | 4 | Mass Meetings |
| 5 | Counseling | 5 | Letters to Employees' Homes |
| 6 | Exit Interviews | 6 | Bulletin Boards |
| 7 | Union Representatives | 7 | Pay Envelope Inserts |
| 8 | Formal Meetings | 8 | Public Address Systems |
| 9 | Suggestion Boxes | 9 | Posters |
| 10 | Employee Newsletter | 10 | Annual Reports, Manuals, Media Advertising |

*Note.* From Azilagyi (1981). Reprinted by permission.

exceeded. Faced with message overload, employees simply will behave in a manner that reduces the problem.

Put another way, the employee filters the messages and decides which ones are the most important (Albanese, 1988, pp. 497–498). This filtering can range from employees incorrectly using the information, to disregarding it, to removing themselves from the information flow. Obviously, none of these is a desirable outcome for the manager or supervisor.

This information adequacy versus information overload creates an apparent paradox (Daniels & Spiker, 1987, p. 85), and shows that our national consultant might be a heretic indeed! Just providing information is not sufficient to satisfy the needs of employees. The issue is how to effectively choose what information to provide to employees, rather than the volume. Enlightened management can bypass the dilemma by using genuine team development techniques where subordinates are an integral part of the information system (Bradford & Cohen, 1984, pp. 283–289; Rees, 1991, pp. 11–27). The advantages of a strong organizational culture also minimize the information dissemination problem.

Our consultant is incorrect to suggest "dumping of information." However, in many organizations any additional information would seem to create some benefit, even if only to reaffirm the Hawthorne Effect (see chapter 3).

In conclusion, "there appears to be no absolute relationship between information adequacy and employee satisfaction within the organization" (Koehler et al., 1981, p. 86). Simply providing more information does not guarantee greater productivity or satisfaction. However, numerous examples exist of the importance of a well-informed and involved work force (Osburn, Moran, Musselwhite, & Zenger, 1990, pp. 3–17). Although it is difficult to prove a direct causal link between information adequacy and performance, there clearly is a correlation. As Table 6.13 indicates, in the higher performing organizations, both professional and hourly employees were significantly more satisfied with the amount and the quality of the information received. So, quality of information would seem to be the intervening variable. One of the characteristics of the high-performing companies is extensive sharing of information.

Finally, in organizations where there is excellent downward communication, combined with a positive communication climate and personal feedback, there is a correlation to job satisfaction. The critical link in the downward communication process is the supervisor–subordinate relationship. As Pincus (1986) put it, "There is a significant, positive relationship between employee job satisfaction and job performance, and employee's feeling of satisfaction with supervisory communication" (p. 417). As long as the downward communication is put into the context of the impact of the organizational culture, it would be correct to conclude that effective downward communication is a vital part of any organization.

Downward communication, to be effective, must deal with what is communicated, how it is communicated, and if it should be communicated at all. In addition, excellent downward communication will be assigned the greatest credibility if upward communication works well.

TABLE 6.13
Sharing Information—Comparison

| *Higher Performing Organizations* | *Lower Performing Organizations* |
|---|---|
| satisfaction with information received | |
| professional employees | |
| 64% | 34% |
| hourly employees | |
| 59% | 30% |
| favorable attitudes toward information received | |
| professional employees | |
| 79% | 69% |
| hourly employees | |
| 72% | 36% |

*Critical Findings*

More Timely, More Open, More Consistent
Communication Leads to
Improved Company Performance.

*Note.* From Hays (1987). Reprinted by permission.

## Upward Communication

Communication from the lower levels of the hierarchy to the upper levels is upward communication. As we already have established, the very process of passing information through channels creates some problems and these apply to upward as well as downward communication.

### Functions of Upward Communication

Upward communication provides four types of messages: (a) what subordinates are doing, (b) unsolved work problems, (c) suggestions for improvement, and (d) how subordinates feel about each other and the job (Katz & Kahn, 1966, p. 245).

**Subordinates' Activities.** Superiors must be made aware of the success or failures of their subordinates. Upward communication provides information about the progress on a particular job, including the subordinates' achievements and problems. At the least, upward communication is a means of giving "feedback on how accurately downward messages have been received" (Adler, 1986, p. 31). Regardless of the management system being used, some type of upward communication of information about the subordinates' activities is necessary. Supervisors must check the effectiveness of instructions, progress, and ongoing activities (Planty & Machaver, 1952).

***Unsolved Work Problems.***   Supervisors need to know if there are problems in completing the work. Nationally, 29% of the employees ranked equipment breakdown as a critical source of frustration ("Frustration Survey," 1982). Only a lack of recognition, a downward communication factor, was ranked ahead, with 30% of the employees seeing this as their major source of frustration. In some cases, procedures such as filling out unnecessary forms, or participating in worthless activities, cause frustration. If management can be made aware of these types of problems, employee morale and efficiency will be enhanced (Hawkings & Preston, 1981, p. 203).

Some individuals decide to reveal unethical or illegal organizational activities because upward channels of communication are not open. These *whistleblowers* normally feel thwarted in their attempts to change blatant examples of waste, fraud, or corruption, so they go public to gain satisfaction (Glazer & Glazer, 1986). Although their motivations differ depending on the specific example, their activities demonstrate a failure in the upward communication process (Donnelly, 1991). For example, the whistleblower who reported his company for selling faulty helicopter engines to the U.S. Coast Guard did so because he felt something had to be done ("Whistle Blower," 1990). At the time he was not aware that he would also end up receiving $2.7 million under the False Claims Act, an 1863 Civil War era law that gives private citizens a direct financial stake in exposing government fraud (Smart & Schine, 1991). In spite of the potential financial bonanza from reporting fraud in government contracts, the driving force behind whistleblowing remains frustration with the upward communication process and becoming a whistleblower requires courage and knowledge of the facts (Hamilton, 1991; Roberts, 1991).

***Suggestions for Improvement.***   The person actually doing the job is an important resource for organizations ("An Old Idea," 1991, C6). This front-line individual can make suggestions regarding the process and be of great help to management. Procter & Gamble attributes $900 million in annualized cost savings to employees' ideas. IBM says its suggestion plan has yielded ideas for $125 million in savings from some 5,000 of their people. IBM paid these employees $18 million in cash rewards for their suggestions (Waterman, 1987, pp. 73–74). The National Association of Suggestions Systems says its 700 members saved $800 million in 1 year as a result of employee suggestions (Beissert, 1984).

Practically every organization has some type of suggestion box. Too often, the box symbolizes empty offers by management for open channels of upward communication. In the companies that are serious about nurturing this upward communication process, suggestion systems are implemented using idea forms, complete with numbers to track the source of the suggestion, and professional managers to encourage and collect suggestions.

Examples of successful suggestions systems appear in every successful organization. Team Taurus at Ford came up with a want list of over 1,400 ideas from Ford employees for the Taurus (Waterman, 1987, pp. 82–83). Ford incorporated over 50% of the suggestions. At Toyota, a remarkable 5,000 new suggestions are implemented a day, with an average number of suggestions of 32.7 per worker per year. Ninety-five percent of the suggestions are implemented (Peters, 1987, pp. 72, 80). Overall, "American companies are less likely to solicit and use suggestions from their employees than their Japanese counterparts" ("Wanted: More," 1991). At the Mitsubishi Corporation, for example, employees offer an average of 100 suggestions per employee a year. In the United States, the average firm receives approximately one suggestion per year from every seven employees ("Wanted: More," 1991). Conventional wisdom has held that suggestion systems would seem to reap the greatest savings in manufacturing operations where long production runs allow for large returns for changes in the process. Increasingly, effective customer service operations depend on suggestions from employees as an effective means for keeping ahead of the competition (Albrecht, 1988, pp. 167–171). In addition, most organizations can benefit from some type of *gain sharing,* which rewards the suggester with part of the savings obtained from implementing the change.

Sometimes, the opportunity to offer ideas is sufficient to obtain changes. The Scottsdale, Arizona city government asked their people to complete, in writing, the sentence "this seems dumb to me. . . ." (Waterman, 1987, p. 301). Although some of the answers were less than complimentary, the upward communication process was enhanced. The activity, which on the surface appears rather minor, involved employees and made them believe in the process. Asking employees "What do you think?," and using the answer, is the impetus behind many of the Marriott Corporation's successful innovations ("Suggestions at Marriott," 1986).

Obtaining suggestions from employees has two obvious benefits. First, suggestions provide valuable information regarding the organization's procedures and practices. Second, a well-functioning suggestion system can enhance employees' belief in the communication process and the organization.

### How Subordinates Feel About Each Other and Their Job.
Obtaining information from employees regarding how they feel covers many issues such as inequities, real and imagined grievances, harassment, and safety problems. Employees can be tired of always receiving the same assignments or working with difficult people. Being afforded the opportunity to express frustrations or to point to injustices can be vital to an organization's health ("How to Keep," 1987).

Do employees speak up? In a survey of 5,200 high performers in the health-care field, 75% of the individuals leaving their organizations were doing so because they felt it was unsafe to say how they felt ("Managers, Listen," 1987). How they felt included issues such as a lack of advancement chances (67%), unfair pay compared to others (59%), lack of praise and unfair promotion by supervisors (57%), and unfair treatment by supervisors (50%).

Being able to deal with employee problems before they become no longer manageable is in the best interest of any organization. Too often, however, there are psychological and physical barriers to airing complaints.

Upward communication helps the organization in four ways. The existence of upward access for employees seems to be valuable regardless of the other benefits of upward communication. At the same time, effective upward communication is even less likely than effective downward communication.

***Analysis of the Process.*** Universally, organizational communication experts see the upward communication process as less effective than downward communication (Koelher et al., 1981, pp. 96–97). There are at least two reasons.

First, procedures for encouraging upward communication are inadequate. As Rowe and Baker (1984) explained, "The majority of U.S. companies and institutions have no broad, explicit structures for dealing with employee concerns and nonunion appeal channels other than the traditional chain of command" (p. 128). Even if employees are willing to go over the supervisor's or manager's head, they might find themselves in an Alice in Wonderland situation with few rules and less direction.

Many organizations also lack any means for involving employees or junior executives in corporate policy making. According to Miller (1980), "Most corporations, management experts agree, remain largely inflexible, autocratically run entities resistant to change and the 'better idea' " (p. F2). Even if the organizational structure was responsive, management style tends to diminish upward communication.

Second, control by management over workers is a presumption of many organizational systems (Walton, 1985). Although there is a great deal of discussion regarding the importance of open communication, many employees learn early on that comments, complaints, and suggestions are viewed as "rocking the boat."

Traditionally, managers have been correct, so input is not seen as particularly welcomed. Processes that include employee involvement, for example, also challenge the traditional managerial position. We examine this issue when we return to employee involvement in our chapter on small groups.

In many organizations, both of these factors are changing. Through the various processes of downsizing, flattening the structure so there are fewer layers, and the implementation of team work processes, organizations are lessening the debilitating effect of organizational structure on upward communication. However, there are four specific barriers.

***Barriers to Upward Communication.*** There are many reasons why employees do not utilize the upward communication process. Four prominent ones are risk, distortion, manager's use of information, and personal restrictions.

The first issue is risk. There are three types of risk involved in the upward communication. First, when employees admit they are having trouble with a particular task, they also are exposing themselves to being seen as incompetent (Dansereau & Markham, 1987, p. 346). They become vulnerable. One important intervening variable is the amount of trust between the employee and the supervisor (Roberts & O'Reilly, 1974). Obviously, if employees are not happy with their work, speaking to the boss would be a wise decision. However, if the message is taken as one by a malcontent, firing could be the next step. Unless there is a great deal of trust, employees will not risk making personal statements to superiors.

A second risk issue is the fear of reprisal. Especially if the individual plans to take the issue up the ranks past the immediate supervisor (e.g., fails to follow the designated chain of command), there is the fear that in the immediate future, or in the long run, the bypassed individual will be able to even the score.

Supervisors have been encouraged to develop a *middle-management macho ethic* where they are told to handle problems on their own (Rowe & Baker, 1984, p. 129). Employees' complaints seriously undercut this expertise. Supervisors might even be embarrassed, or fear punishment, for not handling the complaint or problem. Even the most secure managers will not be pleased to see a continual stream of subordinates "going over their heads" with issues, problems, or suggestions.

A very subtle example of reprisal and risk is the "you raised it, you solve it" tendency in organizations. Often, when individuals bring problems to the attention of their superiors, they are assigned the task of finding the solution. In addition to being a form of reprisal, subordinates quickly learn that opening a "can of worms" that could lead to unexpected outcomes may not be a wise strategy. Hence, silence becomes golden—or at least very secure. In some cases, delegation of a problem can be the manager's ultimate revenge. A more severe form of reprisal is to eliminate the source of the message.

"Kill the messenger" is the phrase that explains the third risk. In many cases, organizations have learned to kill the carrier of bad news rather than deal with a problem. For some organizations, getting rid of the information might seem to be the same as eliminating the problem. Sadly, this expression has become part of the nomenclature in many organizations. Ryder Truck executives have a solution for "shooting the messenger—Shoot the guy who shoots the messenger" (Waterman, 1987, p. 107).

These three risk factors prevent a great deal of upward communication. When it does occur, it frequently is distorted.

Distortion is the second issue. We already have established the problem with serial transmission. In upward communication, extensive evidence exists that each person distorts information passed upward in the hierarchy. In the extreme, a gatekeeper may simply reroute, or refuse to pass on, some messages.

A more prevalent distortion takes the form of exaggerating favorable and minimizing unfavorable information as it pertains to the person sending the message (Huber & Daft, 1987, pp. 148–149). Trust between the superior and subordinate seems to determine the degree of distortion. Not surprisingly, higher trust encourages more accurate upward messages (Strohl & Redding, 1987, pp. 481–482).

When the person controls the subordinate's fate, the distortion toward positive information becomes even stronger (Bradley, 1978). Employees even will withhold important information that is vital to the decision-making process rather than pass on bad information about themselves (O'Reilly, 1978).

The manager's use of information imposes a third limitation to upward communication. Managers are more likely to use messages that are positive, timely, supportive of current policy, and have intuitive appeal (Koehler et al., 1981, pp. 95–96). In other words, if the perception by the manager is that the message is worthwhile, it probably will be accepted.

In addition, information can be power (Harris & Bryant, 1986, p. 29). In large, bureaucratic organizations, knowing something that no one else knows can give an individual control over a situation. Even when the information from the subordinate needs to be forwarded, a supervisor might choose to withhold the information for political purposes. Strategically timing the release of information is a common ploy in many situations. When the culture does not encourage collaboration, this use of power can be very tempting.

Finally, the employee might use a self-imposed gag for three reasons. First, because of loyalty to the company, the employee might simply let the issue slide. Rather than risk filing a grievance over a safety issue, for example, an employee might choose to remain silent (Rowe & Baker, 1984, p. 130). This self-discipline could be especially strong when exposure of an issue could lead to lay-offs, head chopping, or legal hassles.

Second, employees simply might believe it is pointless to utilize the channels: "Employees at all levels often think that it's useless to complain about certain kinds of problems" (Rowe & Baker, 1984, p. 130). In some cases, such as highly technical issues, an employee might feel inadequate to raise the issue. In other cases, such as with co-workers, the issue might seem too trivial or bizarre.

A closely related issue is the Pelz Effect. Employees prefer to communicate with a supervisor who has the ability to satisfy an individual's needs by being connected with those higher in the organization's hierarchy (Dansereau & Markham, 1987, p. 346). If the subordinate perceives the supervisor as lacking upward influence, the problem probably does not get aired because the communication would not be productive.

Finally, employees might find the adversarial relationship in many organizations easier to understand. Workers are often suspicious of any changes because they might lead to a worsening of the working environment (Roth, 1984). The known, even when it is less than perfect, can appear more comfortable than the unknown.

Employees might not communicate upward because of an overriding sense of loyalty, a lack of belief in the system, or a fear of the possible changes a message might create. These barriers are important because they would supersede efforts by management or the organization to encourage upward communication.

Organizations need effective upward communication. It provides vital information about numerous important issues and it may be the most important type of organizational communication (DeVito, 1986, p. 331).

In conclusion, there is a synergistic effect between effective downward communication and the willingness of employees to communicate upward. When subordinates are convinced their supervisors are withholding information, they will follow suit (Danseareau & Markham, 1987, p. 346). This reciprocal relationship between the two forms of communication underscores the importance of formulating an overall communication policy rather than just a few, isolated efforts (Rosenblatt, Cheatham, & Watt, 1982, p. 42).

Often, communication takes place laterally between different parts of the organization. The process of selling a product, for example, requires some connection between manufacturing, shipping, and the sales force. All organizations have horizontal communication.

## Horizontal Communication

Horizontal communication processes were discussed at length at the beginning of this chapter when we analyzed networks. Horizontal communication consists of messages between employees at the same hierarchical level (Koehler et al., 1981, p. 101). The flow of messages across functional areas at a specific level in an organization is horizontal communication. So, the term is used in discussing communication within departments by people of equal rank, or between units in an organization. We confine ourselves to those aspects of horizontal communication that were not covered already when we analyzed networks.

***Functions of Horizontal Communication.*** Horizontal communication accomplishes five functions. These are task coordination, problem solving, sharing information, conflict resolution, and building rapport (Koehler et al., 1981, pp. 101–102; Mann, 1961).

When General Motors (GM) introduced automation at the Lordstown, Ohio plant, employees started using *doubling* (Waterman, 1987, p. 77). Under this system, four workers might agree among themselves to become an informal team. For a set period of time, usually 15–30 min, two members of the team would work like crazy while the other two chatted and rested. The workers claimed this enhanced the quality of their work because the frantic pace meant they had to concentrate on an otherwise boring and routine task. The workers had great job satisfaction because they could talk with each other during their time off. The efficiency experts at GM could not deal with all the workers not being busy at the same time, so they disciplined the individuals who doubled. In response, workers became angry, grievances were filed, and the quality of work went down.

There are two messages from this story. First, horizontal communication is a valuable asset in many cases for getting the work done effectively. It can reduce potential conflicts, add to employee satisfaction, and increase efficiency. Employees can short-circuit the process and get to the problem without going through the vertical channels of communication.

Second, many organizations are uncertain how to deal with horizontal communication because it does not fit into the concept of a hierarchy. By not following the chain of command, horizontal communication may be viewed by some supervisors as deviance from the system.

***Analysis of the Process.***   It is imperative that units coordinate their activities for a variety of reasons. Three of the most apparent reasons why there is not more horizontal communication are *rivalry, specialization,* and *lack of motivation* (Goldhaber, 1986, pp. 174–175).

Rivalry can occur between individuals and units if they perceive scarce resources. Often, these resources can be attention from superiors, promotions, or friendships. With the pressure toward downsizing, which usually means elimination of a large number of middle-management personnel, there will be some pressure to work against other individuals or units on the same level.

During the 1987 Grenada invasion by American troops, an Army unit found itself pinned down by enemy fire. The soldiers wanted to call in a fire mission from the Navy ship offshore. However, the soldiers could not communicate with the ship because the Army and Navy did not share codes. So, an Army "officer crawled to a pay phone, made a credit-card call to the operations officer in his home base in Georgia; he in turn called the Navy at the Pentagon, which in turn radioed the ship to order the fire mission" (Wagman, 1991). During Operation Desert Storm in Kuwait and Iraq in 1991, Air Force commanders could not communicate directly with the Navy computers on board ship to send daily targeting information for the Navy aircraft, so they "resorted to hand-delivering floppy disks to each carrier every night" (Wagman, 1991). Although not as dramatic as combat, many organizations find their subunits engaged in turf battles, information hoarding, and needless duplication.

Specialization is part of the modern organization. You are already familiar with the "over-the-wall" problem between units. Figure 6.6 shows what happens when there is a lack of horizontal coordination. Increasingly, people are brought into an organization because of their expertise. Other employees might not want to ask foolish questions or are simply not interested. When the time comes for coordination, the units are divided by their separate expertise.

There may be little reason for employees to work together, especially across units. This lack of motivation can occur because management does not reward cooperation. At times there are physical barriers between units that preclude interactions (Filley, 1975, p. 10). People might just be too busy with their own problems and projects to want to interact. There may be no compelling reason to communicate horizontally. Faced with a need to increase productivity or develop new products, upper management may issue a call for increased cooperation. Without some additional incentive, this appeal could fall on deaf ears.

You will recall from the beginning of this chapter that a remarkable amount of communication occurs horizontally. Managers, employees, and organizations work with other units at the same level to achieve important results. Pressure to decrease organizational complexity and increase employee participation will create even greater demands for effective horizontal communication (Adler, 1986, p. 34). Fayol's Bridge, introduced in chapter 3, is an example of an early attempt to formalize this connection between units. Liaisons serve the same type of function.

In conclusion, horizontal communication is very important to an organization.

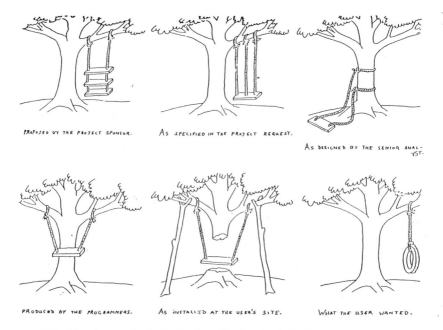

FIG. 6.6.   An example of what happens when there is a lack of horizontal communication.

Because it is not fully sanctioned within an organizational structure, many of the potential benefits are not fully realized. Network analysis explains many of the uses of systems that reduce the dependency on the chain of command (Hickman & Silva, 1987, pp. 240–241). Focusing on horizontal communication issues such as unresolved conflicts, duplication of efforts, and mismatched procedures and priorities is seen as one excellent means for increasing organizational productivity (Bylinsky, 1984; Hale, 1985). When organizations move to formalize the network process, through team building, for example, they are encouraging the horizontal communication process.

## Grapevines

Messages will travel through an organization regardless of management's willingness to send them. When the formal channels of communication lack information, the informal channels take over. The process used for this transmission is the grapevine. When the grapevine's information is generally inaccurate, it is labeled *rumor* (Rosnow, 1980). Because of the informal nature of the grapevine process, much of the information that applies to networks also applies to grapevines.

The term grapevine originated during the Civil War (Davis, 1953). The telegraph wires used to pass intelligence were strung loosely from tree to tree, resembling a grapevine. This stringing procedure tended to cause the messages to be garbled. Grapevine is now applied to messages that travel through an organization with no apparent structure (Davis, 1953; Gibson et al., 1991, p. 548). Grapevine is an excellent metaphor for describing this networking process. Rather than moving in predictable directions, it travels where the ground is most fertile, bears fruit in bunches (clusters), and heads in a variety of directions depending on the climate. Because of the grapevine's inherent presence in any organization, we need to understand both the functions and the process.

*Functions of the Grapevine.*    The three functions of the grapevine are reflecting the quality of the activities within the organization, filling an information void, and providing meaning to activities within the organization.

First, the grapevine serves as a barometer regarding the organization (Gibson et al., 1991, p. 538). It provides vital feedback to management regarding the organization and its employees. Although some managers try to stomp out the grapevine, most theorists feel the grapevine indicates the deep psychological need people have to talk about their company and their jobs (Davis, 1973). The existence of an active grapevine is indicative of the company's health and spirit, and executives can learn a great deal by listening to it (Davis, 1973; Waterman, 1987, p. 269).

Second, the grapevine functions as an important message source. Davis (1953) indicated that the grapevine is most active when (a) there is great upheaval or change within the organization, (b) the information is new, (c) face-to-face communication is relatively easy, and (d) workers cluster along the vine.

Finally, the grapevine provides sense-making information to members of the organization. As messages travel through the grapevine, management's messages get translated into terminology that makes sense to workers. The grapevine helps interpret management for the employee, which makes it a vital aspect of organizational communication (Koehler et al., 1981, p. 119).

So, the grapevine is an important source of messages and information for employees and for management. Does the grapevine perform these functions well?

*Analysis of the Process.*    Yes. There are three specific attributes of the grapevine that make it important and useful. The grapevine's major disadvantage is rumors. In an extensive review of the research on grapevines, Hellweg (1983) provided 33 generalizations, which are summarized in Table 6.14. The grapevine has three general characteristics: It is fast, it is accurate, and it carries a great deal of information (Adler, 1986, pp. 34–36; Timm, 1986, pp. 110–112).

First, the grapevine is fast. We observed at the beginning of this chapter that networks are the express highways of an organization. This is certainly true of grapevines. In situations involving job security or lay-offs, for example, numerous organizations have learned just how quickly the news spreads through the grapevine (Johns, 1988, p. 361).

Second, the grapevine is suprisingly accurate. Rather than being a source of un-

TABLE 6.14

Generalizations About Grapevines

1. The grapevine emerges out of the social and personal interests of employees, rather than formal requirements of the organization.

2. While the grapevine is typically associated with workers in a company, it is just as active among members of management.

3. Five out of every six messages in the organization are transmitted through grapevine channels, rather than formal ones.

4. The grapevine is people oriented, rather than issue oriented.

5. While the formal organization provides a "blueprint" as to ways employees are supposed to behave, the informal one describes ways in which they actually do.

6. The grapevine flows in all directions in an organization—horizontally and vertically (upward and downward).

7. Though the grapevine can operate through single stand gossip or probability transmission patterns, it generally operates through a cluster transmission pattern.

8. The grapevine operates largely through oral communication.

9. The grapevine carries more accurate than inaccurate information.

10. The grapevine can start and stop anywhere in a company.

11. Three types of rumors can travel along the grapevine: anxiety rumors, wish-fulfillment rumors, and wedge-driving rumors.

12. Only a small portion of the informal network consists of rumors.

13. The grapevine often carries information which would be inappropriate for formal channels (e.g., social information).

14. The grapevine has a tendency to carry an incomplete story.

15. Grapevine behavior does not differ as a function of employee sex.

16. Rumors become distorted through sharpening, leveling, and assimilation.

17. Secretaries play a key role in organizational grapevine transmission.

18. Rumors are more prevalent in organizations that foster secrecy.

19. Rumors spread as a function of the importance and ambiguity of the information involved.

20. As the number of individuals in an organization relationship increases, so does grapevine activity.

21. Rumors move more quickly among employees who are close in time and space.

22. The grapevine operates mainly at the work site.

23. Liaisons play a key role in grapevine transmission.

24. The grapevine is fast in transmitting information.

25. The grapevine diminishes as a source of particular information with time.

26. The grapevine is highly selective and discriminating in the information it carries.

27. Formal and informal networks tend to be jointly active or inactive.

28. Of those who receive grapevine information, relatively few transmit it to others.

29. Only a small percentage of employees act as liaisons in grapevine transmission.

30. Rumors may be easily carried over the grapevine, since it offers no reliable source from which individuals can confirm facts.

31. Individuals participating in grapevine activity are not held accountable for distortion of information in the same way that they would be over formal channels, allowing them to treat grapevine information more freely.

32. The grapevine is predictable to the extent that its activity is associated with news events, it may carry information that concerns certain individuals, and it ties to people relationships in the organization.

33. Once a rumor is assigned credibility, other events in the organization are aligned to fit in with it and support it.

Note: From Hellweg (1987). Copyright © 1987 by Ablex Publishing Co. Reprinted by permission.

founded gossip, the grapevine has an accuracy of 75% to 90% for noncontroversial information (Deal & Kennedy, 1982, p. 85; Modic, 1989; Watson, 1982). When errors do occur, they are generally in the area of incorrect emphasis based on incomplete information. The grapevine is not always right, of course, because being 75% to 90% accurate also means that the grapevine is inaccurate 10% to 25% of the time.

Finally, the grapevine contains a significant amount of information. In addition to the messages regarding the organization's health or the employees' sentiments, the grapevine allows organizational members to vent messages that simply do not fit into the formal channels of communication. In the same vein, grapevines can carry socially oriented messages, which develop relationships and enhance a sense of belonging. Often, the formal channels of communication require reinterpretation so that the majority of employees can understand fully the meaning of the messages. All of these functions add to the usefulness of the grapevine (Timm, 1986, p. 111).

The negative features of the grapevine are rumors. These are based on unverified information, which is communicated through the grapevine, that lacks substantial supportive evidence (Rosnow, 1974). The greater the stress, the amount of importance, and the ambiguity in the situation, the greater the likelihood for rumors (Allport & Postman, 1947). Rumors can take on a life of their own and threaten the organization (Light & Landler, 1990).

Two infamous examples of the power of rumors involve McDonald's and Procter & Gamble (Leo, 1987). For McDonald's, there was a persistent rumor in the 1970s in Chicago that they were mixing earthworms into their hamburger meat (Baron, 1983, pp. 332–333). The rumor eventually extinguished itself.

From 1981 to 1991 Procter & Gamble (P & G) fought the rumor that its corporate logo, which had a man in the moon against a field of 13 stars—which stood for the original 13 colonies—was related to Satanism or some other anti-Christ symbol. At one point, P & G had to add employees to handle the 15,000 calls per month they were receiving on a nationwide toll-free consumers' line ("Company Still," 1988). P & G finally redesigned its symbol and eliminated the curly hairs in the man's beard that seemed to look like the number 6 ("P & G Logo," 1991). The number 666 is linked with the devil in the Bible in the Book of Revelations.

A very different type of rumor has cost the Veterans Administration (V.A.) over $1 million (Currie, 1981). For years, a baseless rumor has appeared regarding a new type of G.I. insurance, which would be very useful for any veteran. In spite of official disclaimers, the rumor continues to surface each year. The V.A. spent $309,000 in postage costs in 1 year in an attempt to dispel this pipe-dream rumor. So far, there has been no success. Along the same lines, the aluminum-recycling industry has attempted to squash the rumor that aluminum can pull tabs have a great value or that for every pull tab turned in for recycling, a kidney patient will earn a minute of dialysis (Kipp, 1990). In reality, instead of receiving $40 to $80 for a gallon of aluminum pull tabs, collectors will receive about 60¢ (Robinson, 1991). There is no truth to the dialysis time as a trade for tab tops, but the aluminum industry cannot seem to stop the rumor (Kipp, 1990).

Rumors are powerful forms of grapevine communication because they offer explanations for events or offer hope for certain outcomes. Rumors also can reflect genuine fears held by organizational members. To minimize rumors, managers are counseled to keep employees informed, pay heed to the rumors, act promptly, and enlighten employees (Vickery, 1984). Essentially, feeding the grapevine with a great deal of valid information is the secret to making this important channel of communication productive.

The messages that pass through the grapevine are also vital to the corporate culture. These stories about particular events become the legends of the organization. As Waterman (1987) said, "Procedure manuals might have rules, but stories have morals" (p. 269). Waterman put it another way:

> A CEO can give all the rah-rah speeches and hand out all the T-shirts he wants. But if the legends or the current desk-to-desk whispers are about actions he took that discredit his symbolic behavior, he may as well save his breath. What is the moral in all of this? There are three of them: Listen carefully to the stories that are circulating around your organization; remember that the false stories are just as influential as the true ones; and never underestimate the power of the grapevine.

An entire field of study called Urban Legends relates to the widespread acceptance of stories that have no actual validity (Gillins, 1982). Starting with a phrase like, "It must be true, it happened to . . . ," these examples of modern folklore carry some type of poetic justice or moral about how to deal with certain situations. Organizations have similar legends regarding larger than life heroes who overcame difficult situations. These heroes provide operating information for other members of the organization on what to do. If morale is low, these antiestablishment heroes personify ways to beat the system. In either case, the rumors involve the organization's legends, folk stories, folk heroes, and villains.

Some managers find the grapevine useful when it passes information they like and they call it gossip and rumor when the information is unfavorable. This is a myopic view of communication. Whatever passes through the grapevine provides important information regarding the organization.

Perhaps our heretic's advice earlier in this chapter is once again worth considering. If organizations will feed the grapevine valid, useful, and honest information, it becomes an important channel of communication for the organization's goals.

Studies of dissatisfied customers provide important information regarding informal communication. The average customer who has been burned tells 9 to 10 colleagues. Thirteen percent of the malcontents will spread the news to 20 or more people (Peters, 1987, p. 43). Imagine the same reaction by an employee who is treated unfairly by the organization or the boss. In the absence of information that counters a complaint, the rumor will spread rapidly. When the information is true, but still negative, there is every reason to assume the average person tells 9 or 10 other people.

In conclusion, the grapevine is important, because it reflects the quality of the activities within the organization, fills an information void, and provides meaning to activities within the organization. Contrary to popular assumptions, it is fast, accurate, and oriented toward information rather than gossip. In the absence of information, rumors occur to help explain events. Combating rumors requires a proactive approach to sharing information.

The channels of communication are the sanctioned and recognized means for sending messages. Downward communication is the most used means and upward communication is potentially one of the most effective means. These vertical channels are the most accepted in traditional organizational structures. Many organizations have corporate communication managers who oversee these channels of communication, and control external communication (Harris & Bryant, 1986). These managers perform internal and external public relations activities involving many vertical communication procedures.

Horizontal communication is vital as a means for coordination. Often, subunits at this level need to increase their communication but instead tend to conflict. The grapevine is the least accepted means for communicating in the view of unenlightened management. However, organizations are increasingly aware of the power of the grapevine and are fertilizing it with useful information. In addition to utilizing vertical and horizontal channels, many organizations now are picking the fruit from the grapevine. When organizations neglect the information needs of their employees, rumors begin. Understanding the channels of communication allows us to see how organizations ought to operate.

## CONCLUSION

Networks and channels are the methods used for exchanging messages in organizations. Networks represent the regularized communication interactions. Channels are the sanctioned means of communicating. The grapevine operates in much the same manner as a network.

Networks can be both formal and informal means of communicating. Coupling explains the degree of interdependence between subsystems. Organizations tend to have both loose and tight coupling. Connectedness is the term used to describe the degree of interdependence in a network. Highly connected networks offer advantages to organizations.

The strength of weak ties explains how independent, or loosely connected sources, can influence individuals and groups. Groupthink and freezethink are terms developed to explain the problems with a closed decision-making process. Information can be obtained by using weak ties, which can be used effectively in a variety of decision-making situations.

Connectedness is clarified further by looking at clusters, which are the highly coupled groups within the organizational networks. Coalitions and cliques are the two types of clusters. Coalitions are created to influence organizational relationships. Cliques are connected by strong relations between the members.

Individuals have various roles in a network. In addition to being members, the predominate roles are liaisons, gatekeepers, stars, bridges or linking pins, cosmopolites, and isolates. Each of these roles has specific characteristics that determine the individual's impact on the network. Network members may have different roles at different times.

There are different types of networks. Micronetwork analysis offers specific insights into the impact of configurations on member satisfaction and information flow. Generally, the greater the interaction, the higher the member satisfaction and the better the information flow. Specific applications of networks include network analysis, systematic management networks, specialized networks, teamwork, and innovation. These are examples of the many different applications of networks in organizations. The concept of loose coupling within the larger organizational framework helps explain how the change process operates.

Channels are vertical, horizontal, and the grapevine. Vertical channels have five characteristics. These include one-way or two-way communication, channels as organizational memories, channels as a managerial prerogative and responsibility, channel properties as intervening variables, and the different perspectives of the channel users. Vertical channels include downward and upward communication.

Downward communication has five functions in an organization. As vital as downward communication is to the effective functioning of an organization, the process is ineffective. Information is filtered as it passes downward. In addition, functional illiteracy and lack of relevancy prevent the messages from being used effectively.

Upward communication passes information from the lower levels of the organization through the hierarchy. There are four functions of upward communication. Unfortunately, this process is also ineffective. Little encouragement is offered for upward communication and management is in control of the process. Barriers include risk, distortion, and a self-imposed gag by the employee.

Horizontal communication is the flow of messages between functional areas at a specific level in an organization. Five functions are accomplished through horizontal communication. The process is not as effective as it could be because of rivalry, specialization, and lack of motivation.

The informal channel of communication is the grapevine. This is the system used by employees and management that is not sanctioned by the organization. The grapevine reflects the quality of the activities within the organization, fills an information void, and provides meaning to activities within the organization. The grapevine is fast, accurate, and filled with information. When the information is predominantly groundless, it is called rumor. Enlightened management cultivates the grapevine and listens to the information carried on it.

The study of networks and channels provides us with an insight into how the messages actually flow through the organization. Although it is an overstatement to claim networks, or channels, fully explain how communication works in organizations, the process of message exchange is a vital aspect of organizational communication.

## REFERENCES

Adler, R. B. (1986). *Communicating at work* (2nd ed.). New York: Random House.

Albanese, R. (1988). *Management.* Cincinnati: South-Western.

Albrecht, K. (1988). *At America's service.* Homewood, IL: Dow Jones-Irwin.

Allport, G., & Postman, N. (1947). *The psychology of rumor.* New York: Holt, Rinehart & Winston.

Azilagyi, A. (1981). *Management and performance.* Glenview, IL: Scott, Foresman.

Bain, D. (1982). *The productivity prescription.* New York: McGraw-Hill.

Baron, R. A. (1983). *Behavior in organizations: Understanding and managing the human side of work.* Boston: Allyn and Bacon.

Bedeian, A. G. (1986). The serial transmission effect: Implications for academe. *The Bulletin of the Association for Business Communication, 49,* 35–36.

Beebe, S. A., & Masterson, J. T. (1986). *Communicating in small groups: Principles and practices* (2nd ed.). Glenview, IL: Scott, Foresman.

Beissert, W. (1984, November 26). Suggestion systems pay off. *USA Today,* p. 4B.

Bernstein, A. (1991, July 15). Joe sixpack's grip on corporate America. *Business Week,* pp. 108, 110.

Bittel, L. R. (1980). *What every supervisor should know* (4th ed.). New York: McGraw-Hill.

Blake, R. R., Mouton, J. S., & Allen, R. L. (1987). *Spectacular teamwork.* New York: Wiley.

Blanchard, K. (1987, September). *Quality Circles Journal,* pp. 4–5.

Blau, J. R., & Alba, R. D. (1982). Empowering nets of participation. *Administrative Science Quarterly, 27,* 363–379.

Bolman, L. G., & Deal, T. E. (1984). *Modern approaches to understanding and managing organizations.* San Francisco: Jossey-Bass.

Bolman, L. G., & Deal, T. E. (1991). *Reframing organizations: Artistry, choice, and leadership.* San Francisco: Jossey-Bass.

Bossevain, J. (1974). *Friends of friends.* New York: St. Martin's.

Bradford, D. L., & Cohen, A. R. (1984). *Managing for excellence.* New York: Wiley.

Bradley, P. (1978). Status and upward communication in small decision-making groups. *Communication Monographs, 45,* 33–43.

Braid, R. W. (1985, June). Explaining policies to subordinates. *Supervisory Management, 30,* 19–21.

Burgess, R. L. (1969). Communication networks and behavioral consequences. *Human Relations, 2,* 131–143.

Burt, R. S. (1982). *Toward a structural theory of action.* New York: Academic.

Bylinsky, G. (1984, May 28). America's best managed factories. *Fortune,* pp. 16–24.

Company still fighting Satan rumor. (1988, November 11). *The Evansville Courier,* p. 6.

Currie, W. (1981, January 18). Rumors still flying on GI insurance. *The Chicago Tribune,* p. 22.

Dallinger, J. M. (1985, November). *The influence of task characteristics upon task communication network roles.* Paper presented at the annual meeting of the Speech Communication Association, Denver. (ERIC Document Reproduction Service No. ED 264 625)

Daniels, T. D., & Spiker, B. K. (1987). *Perspectives on organizational communication.* Dubuque, IA: Brown.

Daniels, T. D., & Spiker, B. K. (1991). *Perspectives on organizational communication* (2nd ed.). Dubuque, IA: Brown.

Dansereau, F., & Markham, S. E. (1987). Superior–subordinate communication: Multiple levels of analysis. In F. M. Jablin, L. L. Putnam, K. H. Roberts, & L. W. Porter (Eds.), *Handbook of organizational communication* (pp. 343–388). Newbury Park, CA: Sage.

Davis, K. (1953). Management communication and the grapevine. *Harvard Business Review, 31,* 43–49.

Davis, K. (1968). Success of chain of command oral communication in a manufacturing management group. *Academy of Management Journal, 11,* 379–387.

Davis, K. (1973, July). The care and cultivation of the corporate grapevine. *Dun's Review,* pp. 44–47.

Deal, T. E., & Kennedy, A. A. (1982). *Corporate cultures: The rites and rituals of corporate life.* Reading, MA: Addison-Wesley.

DeVito, J. A. (1986). *The communication handbook: A dictionary.* New York: Harper & Row.

DeWine, S. (1983). Breakthrough: Making it happen with women's networks. In J. J. Pilotta (Ed.), *Women in organizations: Barriers and breakthroughs* (pp. 88–94). Prospect Heights, IL: Waveland.

Dinsmore, P. C. (1984). *Human factors in project management.* New York: AMACOM.

Donnelly, J. H., Jr. (1991). *Organizations.* Homewood, IL: Irwin.

DuBrin, A. J., Ireland, R. D., & Williams, J. C. (1989). *Management & organization.* Cincinnati: South-Western.

Egan, G. (1988a). *Change agent skills A: Assessing & designing excellence.* San Diego: University Associates.

Egan, G. (1988b). *Change agent skills B: Managing innovation & change.* San Diego: University Associates.

Farace, R. V., Monge, P., & Russell, H. M. (1980). Communication in micro-networks. In S. Ferguson & S. D. Ferguson (Eds.), *Intercom: Readings in organizational communication* (pp. – ). Rochelle Park, NJ: Hayden.

Filley, A. C. (1975). *Interpersonal conflict resolution.* Glenview, IL: Scott, Foresman.

Foehrenbach, J., & Rosenberg, K. (1982). How are we doing? *Journal of Communication Management, 12,* 4–7.

Fowler, E. M. (1987). *The New York Times career planner.* New York: Times Books.

Frustration survey. (1982, November 28). *The Sunday Courier & Press,* p. E1.

Gannon, M. J. (1979). *Organizational behavior: A managerial and organizational perspective.* Boston: Little, Brown.

Gibson, J. L., Ivancevich, J. M., & Donnelly, J. H. (1991). *Organizations* (7th ed.). Homewood, IL: Irwin.

Gillins, P. (1982, February 28). Must be true – It happened to. *The Chicago Tribune,* p. 20.

Glassman, R. B. (1973). Persistence and loose coupling in living systems. *Behavioral Science, 18,* 83–98.

Glazer, M. P., & Glazer, P. M. (1986, August). Whistleblowing. *Psychology Today,* pp. 36–43.

Goddard, R. W. (1985, September). Communicate: The power of one-on-one. *Management World,* pp. 8–11.

Goldhaber, G. M. (1986). *Organizational communication* (4th ed.). Dubuque, IA: Brown.

Gouran, D. S., Hirokawa, R. Y., & Martz, A. E. (1986). A critical analysis of factors related to decisional processes involved in the Challenger disaster. *Central States Speech Journal, 37,* 119–135.

Granovetter, M. (1973). The strength of weak ties. *American Journal of Sociology, 68,* 1360–1380.

Greenberg, J. (1983). Communication in organizations. In R. A. Baron (Ed.), *Behavior in organizations* (pp. 87–94). Boston: Allyn & Bacon.

Gregore, T. (1983, January 31). The next step beyond synergy. *Leading Edge Bulletin,* pp. 1–2.

Hale, R. M. (1985). Managing human resources: Challenges for the future. *Enterprise, 9,* 6–9.

Hamilton, J. (1991, June 3). Blowing the whistle without paying the piper. *Business Week,* pp. 138–139.

Hanson, P. G., & Lubin, R. (1986). Team building as group development. *Organization Development Journal, 4,* 27–34.

Harriman, B. (1974). Up and down the communication ladder. *Harvard Business Review, 52,* 143–151.

Harris, T. E., & Bryant, J. (1986). The corporate communication manager. *The Journal of Business Communication, 23,* 19–29.

Havelock, R. G., Guskin, A. E., Frohman, M. A., Hill, M., & Huber, J. (1969). *Planning for change.* Ann Arbor: University of Michigan, Institute for Social Research.

Hawkings, B. L., & Preston, P. (1981). *Managerial communication.* Santa Monica, CA: Goodyear.

Hays Research (1987, February 15). Information sharing. *Behavioral Sciences Newsletter,* p. 2.

The Hay Group Research for Management Database. (1987, September 8). Tell Me More. *The Wall Street Journal,* p. 21.

Heald, T. (1983). *Networks.* London: Hodder & Stoughton.

Hellweg, S. A. (1987). *Organizational grapevines: A state-of-the-art review.* In B. Dervin & M. J. Voigt (Eds.), *Progress in communication sciences* (Vol. 8, pp. 213–230). Norwood, NJ: Ablex.

Hickman, C. R., & Silva, M. A. (1987). *The future 500: Creating tomorrow's organizations today.* New York: New American Library.

How to keep the best people. (1987, October). *Communication Briefings,* p. 3.

Huber, G. P., & Daft, R. L. (1987). The information environments of organizations. In F. M. Jablin, L. L. Putnam, K. H. Roberts, & L. W. Porter (Eds.), *Handbook of organizational communication* (pp. 130–164). Newbury Park, CA: Sage.

Hurley, D. (1988, May). The mentoring mystique. *Psychology Today*, pp. 34–43.

Janis, I. L. (1972). *Victims of groupthink*. Boston: Houghton Mifflin.

Johns, G. (1988). *Organizational behavior: Understanding life at work* (2nd ed.). Glenview, IL: Scott, Foresman.

Jordan, W. A. (1976). On nymphs, GWRK's and other amazing stories. *Chemical Technology, 6,* 672–675.

Karp, H. B. (1983). A look at quality circles. In L. D. Goodstein & J. W. Pfeiffer (Eds.), *The 1983 annual for facilitators, trainers and consultants* (pp. 157–163). San Diego: University Associates.

Katz, D., & Kahn, R. (1966). *The social psychology of organizations*. New York: Wiley.

Katz, D., & Lazarfeld, P. F. (1965). *Personal influence*. New York: Free Press.

Katz, R., & Tushman, M. (1983). The influence of boundary spanning supervision on the turnover and promotion. In K. H. Chung (Ed.), *Academy of management proceedings '83* (pp. 256–260). Dallas: Academy of Management.

Kidder, T. (1981). *The soul of a new machine*. New York: Avon.

Killian, P. (1968). *Managing by design . . . For executive effectiveness*. New York: American Management Association.

Kipp, S. (1990, March 27). Aluminum can pull tabs' high value just rumor. *Birmingham Post-Herald*, p. A9.

Koehler, J. W., Anatol, K. W. E., & Applbaum, R. L. (1981). *Organizational communication behavioral perspectives* (2nd ed.). New York: Holt, Rinehart & Winston.

Kotter, J. P. (1982). *The general managers*. New York: Free Press.

Kruglanski, A. W. (1986, August). Freezethink and the Challenger. *Psychology Today*, pp. 48–49.

Leo, J. (1987, March 16). Psst! Wait till you hear this. *Time*, p. 76.

Light, L., & Landler, M. (1990, December 24). Killing a rumor before it kills a company. *Business Week*, p. 23.

Lipnack, J., & Stamps, J. (1982). *Networking: The first report and directory*. New York: Doubleday.

Liu, W., & Duff, R. (1972). The strength of weak ties. *Public Opinion Quarterly, 36,* 361–366.

Managers, listen or lose best workers. (1987, July 7). *USA Today*, p. 4B.

Mann, J. (1961). Group relations in hierarchies. *Journal of Social Psychology, 54,* 283–314.

McCaskey, M. B. (1979). The hidden messages managers send. *Harvard Business Review, 57,* 21–28.

Merriam, S. (1983). Mentors and proteges: A critical review of the literature. *Adult Education, 33,* 161–173.

Metcalfe, L. (1981). Designing precarious partnerships. In P. C. Nystrom & W. H. Starbuck (Eds.), *Handbook of organizational design* (Vol. 1, pp. 502–540). Oxford, England: Oxford University Press.

Milgram, S. (1965). Some conditions of obedience and disobedience to authority. *Human Relations, 18,* 57–75.

Miller, J. (1980, November 2). Better ideas need more watts. *The New York Times*, p. E2.

Modic, S. J. (1989, May 15). Grapevine rated most believable, management say it's talking more, but. . . . *Industry Week*, pp. 1–12.

Monge, P. R., & Eisenberg, E. M. (1987). Emergent communication networks. In F. M. Jablin, L. L. Putnam, K. H. Roberts, & L. W. Porter (Eds.), *Handbook of organizational communication* (pp. 304–342). Newbury Park, CA: Sage.

Moreno, J. L., & Jennings, H. H. (1960). *The sociometry reader*. New York: Free Press.

Morgan, B. S., & Schiemann, W. A. (1983, March). Why internal communication is failing. *Public Relations Journal*, pp. 13–18.

Mueller, R. K. (1986). *Corporate networking: Building channels for information and influence*. New York: Free Press.

Myers, M. S. (1991). *Every employee a manager*. San Diego: University Associates.

Naisbitt, J., & Aburdene, P. (1985). *Re-inventing the corporation*. New York: Warner.

An old idea returns to the workplace. (1990, September 11). *Birmingham Post-Herald*, pp. C1, C6.

O'Reilly, C. A. (1978). The intentional distortion of information in organizational communication: A laboratory and field approach. *Human Relations, 31,* 173–193.

Osburn, J. D., Moran, L., Musselwhite, E., & Zenger, J. H. (1990). *Self-directed work units: The new American challenge.* Homewood, IL: Business One Irwin.

P & G logo changed. (1991, July 11). *Birmingham Post-Herald,* p. B10.

Pace, R. W. (1983). *Organizational communication: Foundations for human resource development.* Englewood Cliffs, NJ: Prentice Hall.

Pearce, J. W., II, & David, F. R. (1983). A social network approach to organizational design-performance. *Academy of Management Review, 8,* 436–444.

Penzias, A. (1989). *Ideas and information: Managing in a high-tech world.* New York: Norton.

*Personnel Journal.* (1988, April 11). Cited in *Behavioral Sciences Newsletter, 18,* p. 3.

Peters, T. (1987). *Thriving on chaos: Handbook for a management revolution.* New York: Knopf.

Peters, T., & Austin, N. (1985). *A passion for excellence: The leadership difference.* New York: Random House.

Peters, T. J., & Waterman, R. H. (1982). *In search of excellence: Lessons from America's best-run companies.* New York: Harper & Row.

Peterson, B. D. (1973). Differences between managers and subordinates in their perception of opinion leaders. *The Journal of Business Communication, 10,* 27–37.

Pinchot, G., III. (1983, June). Managing for innovation. *Marketing Communications,* pp. 35–38.

Pincus, J. D. (1986). Communication satisfaction, job satisfaction, and job performance. *Human Communication Research, 12,* 411–418.

Planty, E., & Machaver, W. (1952). Upward communication: A project in executive development. *Personnel, 28,* 304–318.

Redding, W. C. (1972). *Communication within the organization.* New York: Industrial Communication Council.

Rees, F. (1991). *How to lead work teams.* San Diego: Pfeiffer.

Roberts, C. (1991, June 30). Blowing the whistle requires courage, command of facts. *The Birmingham News,* pp. 1D, 3D.

Roberts, K. H. (1984). *Communicating in organizations.* Chicago: Science Research Associates.

Roberts, K. H., & O'Reilly, C. A., III. (1974). Failure in upward communication in organizations: Three possible culprits. *Academy of Management Journal, 17,* 205–215.

Robey, D. (1991). *Designing organizations* (3rd ed.). Homewood, IL: Irwin.

Robinson, C. (1991, July 27). Samaritan heeds rumor, 13,000 tops fetch $4.06. *The Birmingham News,* p. 6A.

Rogers, E. M. (1983). *Diffusion of innovations.* New York: Free Press.

Rogers, E. M., & Agarwala-Rogers, R. (1976). *Communication in organizations.* New York: Free Press.

Rogers, E. M., & Larsen, J. K. (1984). *Silicon Valley fever: The growth of high technology culture.* New York: Basic.

Rosenblatt, S. B., Cheatham, T. R., & Watt, J. T. (1982). *Communication in business.* Englewood Cliffs, NJ: Prentice-Hall.

Rosnow, R. L. (1974). On rumor. *Journal of Communication, 24,* 26–38.

Rosnow, R. L. (1980, May). Psychology in rumor reconsidered. *Psychological Bulletin,* pp. 578–591.

Rowe, M. P., & Baker, M. (1984). Are you hearing enough employee concerns? *Harvard Business Review, 62,* 120–128.

St. John, W. (1986). *The best ideas in employee communication.* New York: Communication Briefings. (cited in *Communication Briefings, 6,* 1987).

Schein, E. H. (1985). *Organizational culture and leadership.* San Francisco: Jossey-Bass.

Schon, D. A. (1971). *Beyond the stable state.* New York: Norton.

Shaw, B. M., & Ross, J. (1988, May). Good money after bad. *Psychology Today,* p. 32.

Shout, H. F. (1977). *Start supervising.* Washington, DC: Bureau of National Affairs.

Smart, T., & Schine, E. (1991, January 21). The 1863 law that's haunting business. *Business Week,* p. 68.

Smeltzer, L., & Golen, S. (1984). Transmission and retrieval of information: Statements and hypotheses for research. *The Journal of Business Communication, 21,* 81–91.

Steers, R. M. (1988). *Introduction to organizational behavior* (3rd ed.). Glenview, IL: Scott, Foresman.

Strohl, C., & Redding, W. C. (1987). Messages and message exchange processes. In F. M. Jablin, L. L. Putman, K. H. Roberts, & L. W. Porter (Eds.), *Handbook of organizational communication* (pp. 451–502). Newbury Park, CA: Sage.

Suggestions at Marriott. (1986, October). *Communication Briefings,* p. 2.

Teams at Herman Miller. (1986, August 25). *Behavioral Sciences Newsletter,* p. 1.

Tichy, N. M. (1981). Networks in organizations. In P. C. Nystrom & W. H. Starbuck (Eds.), *Handbook of organizational design* (Vol. 2, pp. 225–249). London: Oxford University Press.

Tichy, N., & Fombrun, C. (1979). Network analysis in organizational settings. *Human Relations, 11,* 923–965.

Tichy, N. M., Tushman, M. L., & Fombrun, C. (1979). Social network analysis for organizations. *Academy of Management Review, 4,* 507–519.

Timm, P. R. (1986). *Managerial communication: A finger on the pulse* (2nd ed.). Englewood Cliffs, NJ: Prentice-Hall.

Trujillo, N., & Toth, E. L. (1987). Organizational perspectives for public relations research and practice. *Management Communication Quarterly, 1,* 218–224.

U.S. Department of Labor. (1987a). *Participative approaches to white-collar productivity* (BLMR Publication No. 116). Washington, DC: U.S. Government Printing Office.

U.S. Department of Labor. (1987b). *Saving jobs and putting democracy to work: Labor-management cooperation at Seymour Specialty Wire* (BLMR Publication No. 11). Washington, DC: U.S. Government Printing Office.

Van Maanen, J. W., & Barley, S. R. (1984). Occupational communities: Culture and control in organizations. In B. M. Shaw & L. L. Cummings (Eds.), *Research in organizational behavior* (Vol. 6, pp. 82–99). Greenwich, CT: JAI.

Vickery, H. B., III. (1984, January). Tapping into the employee grapevine. *Association Management,* pp. 59–62.

Wagman, R. (1991, July 9). Not everything went as planned in Persian Gulf war. *Birmingham Post-Herald,* p. A5.

Walther, G. R. (1986). *Phone power.* New York: Putnam.

Walton, R. E. (1985). From control to commitment in the workplace. *Harvard Business Review, 63,* 77–84.

Wanted: More suggestions. (1991, May 19). *Parade Magazine,* p. 8.

Waterman, R. H., Jr. (1987). *The renewal factor.* New York: Bantam.

Watson, K. M. (1982, June). An analysis of communication patterns: A method for discriminating leader and subordinate roles. *Academy of Management Journal, 25,* 107–122.

Weick, K. E. (1976). Educational organizations as loosely coupled systems. *Administrative Science Quarterly, 21,* 1–16.

Weick, K. E, (1979). *The social psychology of organizing* (2nd ed.). Reading, MA: Addison-Wesley.

Whistle blower due $2.7 million windfall. (1990, July 11). *The Tuscaloosa News,* p. 4.

Wilson, G., Goodall, H. L., Jr., & Waagen, C. L. (1986). *Organizational communication.* New York: Harper & Row.

Zaleznik, A. (1989). *The managerial mystique: Restoring leadership in business.* New York: Harper & Row.

# CHAPTER 7

# Listening and Feedback

Listening is a critical part of the organizational communication process. Communication transactions are dependent on listening. The accurate reception and interpretation of messages is vital for effective organizational communication to take place. The quality of listening is effected by feedback and climate, which we discuss later in this chapter. First, we focus on listening.

Listening is the process of converting sounds into meaning. This includes the four stages of sensing, interpreting, evaluating, and responding (Steil, Barker, & Watson, 1983, p. 22). To better understand the role of listening in organizational communication, this chapter unfolds in the following manner. First, we examine the current status of organizational listening. Then each of the four stages of listening's definition is developed. Third, active, passive, deliberative, and empathetic listening are addressed. Fourth, the special requirements of organizational listening are developed. Finally, feedback, and defensive and supportive climates, are presented.

Two overviews must be understood. First, effective listening is important to individuals and organizations. Second, ineffective listening is costly.

## IMPORTANCE OF LISTENING

Listening's importance can be established in three ways. These are: Effective listening is very beneficial, it is a significant part of the communication process, and it plays a critical role in most occupations, and at every level of the organization. First, effective listening is beneficial.

## Benefits of Effective Listening

The advantages gained through effective listening are almost endless. For example, it leads to satisfied customers, contented employees, managers being trusted by subordinates, and successful salespeople (DiGaetani, 1980, p. 41). As Hackman and Johnson (1991) asserted, "Good leaders are great listeners" (p. 152). In addition, it paves the way toward better personnel relationships, fewer mistakes and errors, more successful meetings, shared viewpoints and perspectives, a stronger culture, and a greater organizational cohesiveness (Wolvin & Coakley, 1985, p. 15). Individuals can achieve greater job success, increase their personal knowledge, improve their interpersonal relations, and protect themselves from unethical persuasion (Floyd, 1985, pp. 3–8). Although these attributes of effective listening might seem remarkable, the second point explains why they occur. Listening creates these benefits because it is an integral part of the communication process.

## Listening and the Communication Process

As the most used channel of communication, listening is a vital link in the communication process. We spend up to 80% of our waking day communicating (Klemmer & Snyder, 1972). Of this 80%, 45% is spent listening, 30% spent speaking, 16% spent reading, and 9% spent writing (Gibbs, Hewing, Hulbert, Ramsey, & Smith, 1985, p. 30).

In organizations, the percentage is frequently greater. The majority of employees in major American organizations spend about 60% of their day listening (Brown, 1982, p. 300). Depending on their job, executives spend between 45% and 93% of their day listening (Keefe, 1971, p. 10). Another study concluded "the busy executive spends 80% of his time listening to people, and still doesn't hear half of what is said" (Nichols & Stevens, 1978, p. 112). Finally, "about three-fifths of the time a manager spends communicating actually involves listening. And the higher up an executive climbs in the corporate hierarchy, the more time he or she must spend listening to others" (Wakin, 1984, p. 46). Although the amount of time spent in listening varies depending on the study, we can conclude that most business personnel spend up to 63% of their day on the job listening (Wolvin & Coakley, 1985, p. 8).

Measured by its ramifications, or by the percentage of communicating time consumed, listening is important. This importance is underscored by examining various occupations and organizational members, which is our third point.

## Listening in Organizations

Listening is a critical part of most occupations and businesses. Numerous trade and professional publications highlight the values of being an effective listener. The readership ranges from administrative managers (DiSalvo, 1980), to salespeople (Steil, 1980), to finance, management, banking, accounting, personnel, and marketing (DiGaetani, 1980, p. 40). The Sperry Corporation has spent over $10 million in its campaign to improve its own listening behaviors and to forward its slogan as the company that listens (Wolvin & Coakley, 1985, p. 4).

Specific research regarding individuals in organizations also justifies our interest in listening. As an overview, organizations require coordination between members, and listening is a vital link in the process. The growth industries (e.g., service, information) and prevailing interests (e.g., quality) have underscored the importance of effective listening. Service industries, which account for more than three fourths of all jobs currently being created in the United States, depend on effective listening. Customer contact is the *sina qua non* of their business (Albrecht, 1988, p. 5).

Information industries, where individuals communicate primarily through machines, have served only to increase the importance of face-to-face communication (Zuboff, 1988, pp. 200–206). As computers focus on specific information-related data, interpersonal contact is decreased. Electronic mail, individual computer workstations, and specific task assignments isolate individuals from interactions. Because the opportunities for human-to-human communication are diminished, each interpersonal listening opportunity takes on even greater importance. Decreased interpersonal contacts create fewer opportunities to double check listening accuracy to make certain an error has not occurred. In addition, as computers allow more individuals to pursue full- or part-time work at home via a computer modem linked to the office system, casual, ongoing work contacts become fewer and fewer. In 1988, nearly 25 million workers, or 23% of the nonfarm work force of 107.1 million, worked out of these electronic cottages (Garties, 1988). In the electronic age, listening must be even more effective because each transaction carries more potential weight. In chapter 14 we examine, in much greater depth, the role of the new communication technologies.

For all organizations, effective listening is of great consequence. For service industries, customer contact is maintained and improved through effective listening. In information-based industries, opportunities to communicate interpersonally are diminished, making each listening event potentially more important. Quality can be achieved only through coordination between individuals and subunits, which requires excellent listening.

Listening's impact is omnipresent regardless of our job or position. For example, a study of 700 middle managers reported listening as the most important skill for subordinates and the fifth most important skill for supervisors (Downs & Conrad, 1982). Other researchers have added: "Listening is essential for the organizational communication effectiveness of both superiors and subordinates" (Hunt & Cusella, 1983, p. 393). We now examine more closely both managers and subordinates and their listening needs.

*Managers.*   You already are aware that managers engage in a great deal of face-to-face communication (Kotter, 1988; Mitzberg, 1973). Managing human resources requires excellent communication skills (Luthans, Hodgetts, & Rosenkrantz, 1988). A supervisor's job is highly dependent on effective transactions (Bittel, 1980, p. 176).

In a survey of the Academy of Certified Administrative Managers, active listening was ranked as the number-one critical skill, as a management ability, from a list of 20 items (Becker & Eldom, 1980, pp. 14, 22). Listening is the number-one problem in accountant-accountant relationships, and for first-line supervisors (Steil et al., 1983, p. 10).

For the manager or supervisor, good listening helps in discovering emerging problems (Niehouse, 1986), dealing with hostile employees (Powell, 1981), enhancing employee morale (Hulbert, 1979), and it adds to the manager's professional image (Morgan & Baker, 1985). Bosses are admonished to "develop formal and informal devices aimed at spurring intense, proactive listening" (Peters, 1987, p. 304) in order to guarantee effective organizational processes.

Listening is important to managers in numerous settings. For example, *downsizing,* a process where large organizations reduce their work force for cost and efficiency purposes (American Management Association, 1988, pp. 13–15), requires managers to effectively listen to a variety of inputs to enhance the potential for successful renewal (Waterman, 1987, pp. 170–171). Because many organizations will be moving toward a flatter structure through downsizing, managers must be able to understand all the ramifications of the change. Effective listening helps in the interviewing process and in meetings (Anastasi, 1982, pp. 65–76, 84–98). Human resource managers must improve their listening skills in order to really understanding their organizations (Tracey, 1988, chapter 1). Listening is a vital key in the process of professional growth and development (Wolff, Marsnik, Tracey, & Nichols, 1983, p. 208). The managerial functions of exchanging job information, receiving and giving directions, seeking and providing information for decisions, coaching and counseling, meetings and conference participation, performance reviews, interviews, and negotiating all require effective listening skills (Tracey, 1988, pp. 4–6). Regardless of the perspective or profession, managers and supervisors need to be good listeners.

*Subordinates.*   For neophytes and subordinates, listening is important. An examination of 24 different studies found effective listening to be the most important skill for entry-level positions (DiSalvo, Larsen, & Seiler, 1976). Once hired, listening is critical to learning, understanding, and participating in communication (Wolff et al., 1983, p. 24). Listening ranks second as the communication problem most identified by subordinates as leading to ineffective communication incidents (Downs & Conrad, 1982). By any measure you may choose, listening is important. Given the impact of effective listening, it is no surprise to find that poor listening is costly, which is our second major point.

## COSTS OF POOR LISTENING

Second, ineffective listening is expensive. For example, a simple $10 mistake, made by each of the over 100 million workers in this country, would cost over a billion dollars (Steil, 1980, p. 65). Unfortunately, most individuals make more than one mistake because of poor listening. Besides the dollar cost, "those little mistakes waste time, cause embarrassment, irritate customers, alienate employees and, ultimately, affect profits" (Wakin, 1984, p. 45). Poor listening can lead to numerous problems, including misunderstanding another person's intentions, confusing an issue, missing valuable information, or antagonizing people (Fritz, 1985, pp. 115–116). Many labor relations problems come down to X-theory managers using poor listening (DiGaetani, 1980, p. 41). In conclusion, "the list of problems caused by ineffective listening is endless, and the exact cost is incalculable" (Gibbs et al., 1985, p. 30).

The evidence is overwhelming that listening, and the concomitant issues of feedback and climate, are important to organizations and must be considered when learning about organizational communication.

## CURRENT STATUS OF ORGANIZATIONAL LISTENING

Based on this universal agreement regarding the importance of listening, you might assume that effective listening is practiced in most organizational settings. Consider several studies and reports that call that conclusion into question.

Fortune 500 vice presidential executives ranked listening as the second most serious problem in the communication in their organization (Bennett & Olney, 1986). Other studies indicate listening is an underdeveloped skill (Hunt & Cusella, 1983; Junge, Daniels, & Karmos, 1984). Listening was identified in a survey of recent college graduates as a needed interpersonal skill (Bednar & Olney, 1987). Listening proficiency is an expected interpersonal skill for subordinates and superiors in organizations (Harris & Thomlison, 1983). Finally, training and development managers feel listening is one of the most important problems leading to ineffective performance or low productivity (Hunt & Cusella, 1983, p. 399).

Many organizations seem immune to evidence and continue to neglect listening as an area for study. According to Wakin (1984), "Most executives still just talk about listening; they do little to actually enhance listening skills" (p. 45). Although listening continually surfaces as the most important communication problem in a survey of 45 companies, only 9 have provided some training (Mundale, 1980, p. 37).

The results are an ineffective listening posture by many individuals. For example, in studies of 10-min presentations, receivers hear, understand, and evaluate correctly only 50% of the message. Within 48 hr, this comprehension is down to 25% (Gibbs et al., 1985, p. 30). Most listening experts accept this estimate (Steil et al., 1983, p. 38; Wolvin & Coakley, 1985, p. 180). We are not good listeners.

Numerous reports point to the importance of listening and the need for additional listening skills. We have risked belaboring the point regarding listening because the case for improved listening would seem to be too great to ignore. If our premise is correct, why is listening not dealt with more effectively by organizations and, in many cases, textbooks on organizational communication?

## DIFFICULTY IN DELINEATION

Three factors make listening a difficult topic to cover. First, listening often falls prey to the same type of reasoning preventing a fuller understanding of organizational communication in general. Either listening is so obvious that we all should be asked simply to be better listeners, or it is too complex to be easily understood (Tracey, 1988, p. 1). If you feel a sense of deja vu regarding this possible dilemma, you would be correct because we confronted the same issue in chapter 1 regarding the study of organizational communication.

Even some organizational communication textbooks pay slight attention to listening. One argument is that listening is too ill-defined to be easily taught or evaluated (Goldhaber, 1986, p. 242). The reasoning may be that listening is so intertwined with communication effectiveness as to make a separate discussion difficult. When listening is not fully explained, it still is recognized as an important factor in supervisory effectiveness (Daniels & Spiker, 1987, p. 158). Often the advice is that individuals learn to listen carefully (Pace, 1983, pp. 33–34). Given the obvious importance of listening, this chapter offers some specific insights into listening effectiveness. These begin with the next two observations.

Second, for all practical purposes, listening cannot be separated from other organizational communication skills (Hunt & Cusella, 1983, p. 399). For example, verbal communication is meaningless unless someone listens aurally (Weaver, 1972, p. 5), and being able to respond to verbal communication is contingent upon effective listening. In addition, listening to the nonverbal aspects of a message is critical to understanding (Wolvin & Coakley, 1985, pp. 120–152). You already are aware that up to 93% of a message's meaning comes from nonverbal communication (Mehrabian, 1981, pp. 43–44). Not only is listening tied to other communication activities, but overt actions by colleagues are an important indication of effective listening.

Third, organizational members conceptualize effective listening by others based on nonverbal and verbal responses during the process (Hunt & Cusella, 1983, p. 399). We are judged to be effective listeners, in other words, by how active we appear to be during the receiving process. In an organizational setting, message sending as well as message receiving determine the effectiveness of listening behavior (Lewis & Reinsch, 1988, p. 53). A listener's overt messages are perceived as an important component of their listening behavior. So, questions, praise, advice, and thanks are positive listening behaviors, along with nonverbal behaviors such as eye contact (Hackman & Johnson, 1991, p. 163).

In conclusion, effective listening is vital to organizational health. Although listening's role seems obvious, organizations often overlook listening precisely because it appears too apparent to require highlighting. When the importance of listening is recognized, the advice often can be superficial.

Three issues must be discussed to understand organizational listening. First, the four listening stages are examined further. Second, the listening behaviors most important to organizations are discussed. Third, the role of listening in the four frames is outlined.

## FOUR LISTENING STAGES

The four listening stages are sensing, interpreting, evaluating, and responding. In most cases, these four stages occur in rapid succession with little awareness on our part. To understand the listening process, we examine each one in greater detail. As we examine each of the stages, we identify many of the reasons people fail to be effective listeners. Simply put, individuals usually have more reasons not to listen carefully than reasons to listen carefully. Because listening is a complex process, understanding each of the stages, and the possible barriers, will enhance our abilities to listen. In most cases, improving our own listening abilities will bring greater rewards than trying to force others to be better listeners. An important exception to this generalization is the power of feedback, which is discussed later in this chapter.

### Sensing

There is a difference between simply hearing and listening with understanding. Hearing involves the biological senses that provide for reception of the message through sensory channels (Cauldill & Donaldson, 1986, p. 22). In addition to the auditory senses, we depend on our visual senses, which sometimes are called our *third ear* (Berko, Wolvin, & Wolvin, 1985, p. 134). A great deal of what we sense actually is obtained because of nonverbal communication cues. Disregarding the nonverbal cues for a moment, the National Institutes of Health estimates that almost 1 in 20 Americans has some hearing impairment ("Hearing Loss," 1982). In addition, there are physical barriers in organizations, such as distance, that prevent listening (Callerman & McCartney, 1985).

Good listening begins with sensing the message. Perception involves screening the message by using the filtering process based on background, experience, and all the other variables that make up the receiver's orientation to the world. In chapter 2, we discussed the numerous perceptual factors that might prevent us from sensing correctly. The possible barriers include external noise, internal noise, organizational distance, selective attention, and our memory systems.

### External Noise

In some organizations, sound levels, distracting stimuli, and competing messages can prevent effective sensing (Tracey, 1988, pp. 5–8). Many manufacturing plants have noise levels, for example, that make listening difficult. Poor acoustics, other ongoing activities, or street sounds can inhibit the listening process. External noise, generated by the environment, can distract someone from sensing the message correctly (Floyd, 1985, pp. 50–52).

### Internal Noise

Internal noise, or interference created by the listener, occurs when we are preoccupied, under pressure, or have other priorities (Anastasi, 1982, p. 10). Sometimes this is referred to as *nonhearing,* because we may be physically present but not processing any messages (Tracey, 1988, p. 3). Some primary candidates for individuals who do not hear could be managers focusing on another issue, employees explaining an unwarranted absence, or leaders overtaken with their own importance. Referred to as an *internal monologue,* the receiver does not give full attention to the task of sensing the message (Howell, 1982, p. 70). Even the time of day can make a difference regarding our listening effectiveness because it influences attentiveness and overall motivation (Wolvin & Coakley, 1985, p. 100). In addition, the amount of time a person has to engage in the listening process also will affect the outcome.

Even when internal noise is not a problem, listeners may *prejudge* the sender. We may decide the individual lacks credibility, is not worth paying attention to, or reminds us of someone we were sorry we listened to at some earlier point. *Stereotyping* can prevent the listener from seeing beyond a sender's outward label of management, union, professor, tall, or any other issue. Sometimes stereotyping leads to distrust between individuals, which can prevent a valid sensing of the message.

If the message is not assigned significance, it is likely to be ignored. Frequently, messages about safety or work rules "go in one ear and out the other," according to people who are in charge of safety. A good example is provided by the story of a worker in a chocolate factory who fell into a vat of chocolate. She began yelling: "Fire! Fire!" Immediately several fellow workers came to the rescue. After they pulled her out, they asked, why did you yell "fire!" She answered, "Would you have come if I had yelled 'chocolate'?" Her fellow workers needed a message they would sense, sort out from competing stimuli, and consider important, in order to prevent her from drowning in a vat of chocolate.

Finally, a listener may be so apathetic or hostile that he or she does not even pick up on the message (Tracey, 1988, pp. 5–8). For example, employees might have a fear of change that prevents them from listening (Wolvin & Coakley, 1985, p. 100). One way to prevent being changed is to refuse to listen, or to alter the message as it is received. A fear of failure created by difficult material or procedures also can create poor listening (Floyd, 1985, pp. 79–80). These three factors of apathy, fear of change, and fear of failure can operate throughout the listening process.

### Organizational Distance

The inherent *organizational distance* between the various job classifications can lead to perceptual differences. Subordinates, after all, are supposed to listen and superiors are supposed to talk (Borman, Howell, Nichols, & Shapiro, 1980, p. 118). Superiors and subordinates have different perceptions of organizational reality. Although a manager might be "fired-up" about a proposed change in procedure, a subordinate might be wondering what additional job responsibilities will be involved. In addition, verbal and nonverbal differences may exist because of cultural backgrounds, or occupational activities, making comprehension difficult.

### Selective Attention

To be effective a listener must fully sense the message. Four explanations are offered to explain why selective attention is given to one particular message over another (Kahneman, 1973). First, there are automatic, unconscious rules, such as focusing on a sender who states our name or mentions a subject important to us. Our chocolate factory story is a good example. Second, we make conscious decisions about which messages we are likely to accept. Choosing to concentrate on the boss's message, rather than a co-worker's simultaneous message, is a normal occurrence in any organization. Third, we may put off by the difficulty of the mental task, because complex tasks require more concentration and energy. Fourth, we have a strong need for consistency. When messages contrast with our preconceived notions, we may dismiss them. Roadblocks exist even as we are receiving the message, which can detour the listening process.

In summary, we have examined how external and internal noise, organizational distance, and selective attention prevent effective sensing of the message. In addition, our memory structure governs how well we remember messages.

### Memory Systems

There are two types of memory systems in operation (Wolvin & Coakley, 1985, p. 59). They are the *short-term memory* (STM) and *long-term memory* (LTM) systems. Although current psychological research has shifted from examining the two systems separately, the perspective provided by understanding that there are two types of memory systems in operation helps explain why listening can be so difficult.

**Short-Term Memory System.** The STM is about 20 sec to 1 min. This *working memory* must decide to preserve incoming messages through the process of rehearsal. Rehearsal involves the silent or vocal repetition of the message, or intentional concentration on the message. If the STM is interrupted, during rehearsal, by "another person's question or request, internal noise, or some other distraction, which results in a shift of attention" (Wolvin & Coakley, 1985, p. 59), the rehearsed message can be lost within 60 sec. The tenuous nature of STM is made even more uncertain by the limited amount of stimuli we can hold simultaneously. Every day experiences confirm the difficulty in concentrating on numerous stimuli at the same time.

One relatively well-accepted principle involves our capacity to remember approximately seven units at one time, or "the magical number of seven, plus or minus two" (Miller, 1956). In other words, we can handle up to seven messages, adding or subtracting two, before we must replace an existing message with an incoming one. The seven-digit phone system is a good example of how this principle is put into operation. The postal zip code, even as it expands beyond the original five digits in many parts of the United States, still remains within the nine-digit range. Public-speaking teachers recommend that presentations contain few main points, which is a good example of the importance of not going over the memory limits (Ross, 1985, pp. 129–130).

Another example is goal setting, which is widely recognized as an important attribute for effective management (Locke & Latham, 1984). To be effective, goals should be few in number and very specific (Quick, 1985, pp. 128–129). Texas Instruments uses the watchwords "More than two objectives is no objectives" (Peters & Waterman, 1982, p. 153). In other words, the effect of memory must be taken into consideration when using goal setting.

The communication purpose also may be an important factor in how the STM is used. Sometimes, the ongoing process of ingratiation, or effective social interaction, is more important than actually retaining many of the messages being transacted (Bostrom & Waldhart, 1980).

Our motivation to listen is perhaps the most important variable in how we apply our STM. If there are compelling reasons for retaining the message, then these will override competing stimuli. For example, when we are introduced to a person who has a great deal of power over us, we are motivated to remember the person's name.

***Long-Term Memory System.*** The LTM's capacity seems to be around 15 min (Berko et al., 1985, p. 135). Whereas the STM has a point where its capacity is "overloaded," the LTM is not so restricted. STM explains how we momentarily retain information. LTM is the storing of messages where we assimilate the data for hours, weeks, months, and years (Wolff et al., 1983, p. 15). The LTM is infinitely expansible, but a message must gain entry to the LTM. Somehow, the LTM must be stimulated to further process and store the message. Persuasion studies, which emphasize that most attitude change is the result of the presentation of several messages over a period of time, rather than a one-shot appeal, provide a good example of this principle (Ross, 1985, p. 4).

For many of us, our only formal listening training occurs if we appear to have a sensing problem. During the first years of formal education, many school systems give auditory tests and hearing problems often are diagnosed. For the remainder of us, hearing is assumed to be okay as long as there are no sensing difficulties. In reality, in organizations, there are numerous reasons why individuals would not sense or hear the message. Even when the message has managed to bypass the numerous barriers and gain entry, effective listening requires interpretation of the message or messages.

## Interpreting

Hearing a message, and then attending to it, are two vital aspects of effective listening. However, the listener must interpret or assign meaning to the message. This is an immensely complex process because we take messages and decide in which category the message belongs (Wolvin & Coakley, 1985, pp. 65–67).

A quick review of some of the issues we have covered so far in this text will underscore the complexity. When we discussed language, for example, we observed that words have numerous meanings and various levels of interpretation. When you started reading this text, some words did not fit into clear categories because the interpretation was unclear. When you read chapter 2, you were introduced to perception as a filter or limiting factor in organizational communication. The nonverbal messages provided to support the linguistic cues also determine the meaning assigned. There are emotional triggers that prevent us from assigning the correct meaning.

Understanding occurs when the listener fully comprehends the other person's frame of reference, point of view, and feelings regarding a subject (Rogers & Roethlisherger, 1952, p. 47). The expression "I know you believe that you understand what you think I said, but I am not sure you realize that what you heard is not what I meant" speaks to the importance of understanding.

A frequently told story regarding the original TAB commercial revolves around the jingle "Let's taste new TAB." A fourth grader wrote to Coca-Cola and explained that it came over the radio as "Less taste, new TAB." Coca-Cola immediately changed the ad.

Finally, consider the following story. A boy is involved in a serious automobile accident. His father was driving the car and was killed instantly. The boy was rushed to the hospital in critical condition. The doctor in the emergency room took one look at the boy and screamed: "Oh my God, it's my son!" What is going in the story? Some individuals are confused because the father was killed in the accident. The answer, of course, is the doctor is the boy's mother. Interpretation, because of preset assumptions, can be inaccurate. This story leads into the third part of the listening process.

## Evaluation

The third stage is evaluation. At this point, we make judgments regarding our acceptance of the messages. These decisions to accept, alter, or reject the messages are based on the receiver's own knowledge or opinions. In theory, this is an important quality control step. The receiver decides if the facts support the point being made, or the individual and the message have credibility. We decide whether or not to agree with the sender (Steil et al., 1983, p. 22). This stage can be used too quickly, resulting in messages being accepted or rejected without any real justification. In many cases, effective listeners are careful to evaluate the message by weighing the evidence, and sorting fact from opinion to make this a useful stage.

*Thought Speed.*   During the interpreting and evaluating stages, listeners can capitalize on *thought speed* to sort through messages. Senders have a normal speaking rate of 125–150 words per min. People think at the rate of 500 words per min (Wolff et al., 1983, p. 15). This differential of 300–400 words can be used to enhance listening.

Television and radio already speed up programs and commercials to save time or to fit within a particular time slot (Wolvin & Coakley, 1985, p. 177). Movies shown on television, for example, that run longer than the allocated time slot can be speeded up. Rather than play two commercials during a certain time slot, three can be used. In both cases, there has been no loss of comprehension by viewers or listeners, which supports the premise that we can use the extra thought speed. Several different studies have indicated that listeners can handle speech at rates of 228–328 words per min (Olsen, 1962; Orr, 1968; Woodcock & Clark, 1968). Individuals have ample mental time for comprehending these compressed messages.

Speeded-up speech, or compressed speech, has been used successfully by mass media, schools, law enforcement, hospitals, and advertising (Wolvin & Coakley, 1985, pp. 89–90). However, it is probably unrealistic to expect senders to rapidly increase their rate of delivery, so listeners must develop additional tools for concentration. You already are aware from the nonverbal chapter that higher credibility is assigned to persuasive speakers who speak quickly. The major impediment, for a speaker, would be the cultural norms of a certain pacing in speaking. The receiver may choose to daydream and wander off and think about other material.

*Role Requirements.*   Role requirements can lead to incorrect evaluations. As Callerman and McCartney (1985) explained, "A supervisor must believe subordinates have experience, ideas, problems, and solutions to contribute to the organization and must demonstrate that belief through active listening so that subordinates will gain greater respect for themselves as individuals and for their supervisors" (p. 39). Subordinates are expected to show interest in their superiors' communication without providing any real feedback (Bormann et al., 1980, p. 118). So, in addition to the organizational distance discussed under sensing, role requirements often impede interpretation and evaluation. Managers can increase their listening effectiveness in the judgment stage by listening for what is not said, considering the other person's emotions and background, and allowing criticisms of a manager's "brilliant" policies (Peters, 1987, pp. 435–442).

The evaluation stage provides us with the opportunity to judge a message's quality.

Thought speed allows for strong analysis. However, role requirements can lead to a lack of credibility by managers to a subordinate's ideas.

## Responding

The final stage is responding. Although some listening experts suggest this step can be covert (Steil et al., 1983, p. 22), in an organization overt responses usually are expected. This final stage is important in most communication settings because it provides data to the sender for judging the success of the communication process (Rhodes, 1987, p. 47). Research indicates that effective listeners provide and use more feedback than do ineffective listeners (Lewis & Reinsche, 1988). Studies of listening in organizations indicate that a listener must make some type of overt response, whether it be verbal or nonverbal, to be judged a good listener (Tracey, 1988, p. 13). Eye contact seems to be closely tied to perceived listening (Rogers, 1970, p. 50). Listeners who strive to understand are highly valued by the people they work with because they confirm the importance of the other person (Wolvin & Coakley, 1985, pp. 75–76). In addition to being able actually to hear what the other individual is saying, receivers must make understanding the other person an important objective (DiGaetani, 1980; Shockley-Zalabak, 1991, p. 158). We further develop this final stage when we discuss feedback.

These four stages explain the listening process. Although we have discussed each one in detail, in the listening process these stages occur rapidly. The examination of each one highlights many of the factors that can limit effective listening. In addition to the listening stages, there are specific types of listening behaviors, which we now explain.

## TYPES OF LISTENING

Listening behaviors can be divided between *passive* and *active* listening, and *deliberative* and *empathetic* listening. We first contrast passive and active listening and then explain the difference between deliberative and empathetic listening.

### Active Listening

When we assume that listening only requires the receiver to be in attendance, we are referring to passive listening. This is listening without directing the speaker verbally or nonverbally. Some individuals are quite adept at pretending to listen, and others simply assume that being present is the same as actually listening (DeVito, 1989, p. 60).

Passive listening may be appropriate in some situations. A lack of overt feedback can allow the sender to fully develop a message (DeVito, 1986, p. 3). However, not providing feedback, in an organizational setting, may not be as productive as being an active listener.

Active listening is a process where the listener sends back to the sender signals indicating what the listener thinks the sender meant (Rogers & Farson, 1969, p. 481). The receiver becomes part of the transaction and takes an active responsibility for understanding the feelings of the other person (DeVito, 1986, p. 3). Understanding the sender's total message, including the verbal and nonverbal information, along with the content and feelings expressed, is the receiver's responsibility. Active listening enables receivers to check on the accuracy of their understanding of what the sender said, express acceptance of the sender's feelings, and stimulate the sender to explore more fully his or her thoughts and feelings (Wilson, Hantz, & Hanna, 1989, p. 96). Receivers provide active verbal and nonverbal cues to senders that they are listening. These cues are intended to provide support and consist of head nods and/or minimum verbal statements such as "uh, huh," "yes," or "tell me more" (DeVito, 1986, pp. 3–4).

Three techniques for developing the active listening process are *paraphrasing, expressed understanding,* and *asking questions* (DeVito, 1986, p. 4). Paraphrasing is stating in your own words what you think the sender meant. This is not an interpretative stage. Instead, you really are providing the sender with your summary of the content of her or his message. This allows you to check the accuracy of your perception of the message. By using objective descriptions, you are responding to the verbal and nonverbal signals given by the sender.

As we already have indicated, fighting the tendency to daydream is especially difficult. In fact, "concentration may be the listener's most difficult task" (Wolvin & Coakley, 1985, p. 169). One means of fighting daydreaming is to paraphrase actively. However, "paraphrasing is both energy-consuming and time-consuming" (Wolvin & Coakley, 1985, p. 238). Paraphrasing can be redundant and annoying if it is simply trading words. The goal is to restate the same meaning presented by the sender, but in a different form. This allows the sender to verify, modify, or reject the listener's interpretation. So, if it seems to be simply parroting the sender, paraphrasing becomes extremely awkward. It is hard to get accustomed to using.

When you echo the feelings of the sender, you are using the second technique. Expressed understanding, or the restatement of the feelings that you hear from the sender as correctly as possible, allows the receiver to check more accurately on how well the sender's feelings have been perceived and understood. Sometimes, this action by a receiver allows the sender to view more objectively her or his own feelings (DeVito, 1986, p. 4). Table 7.1 provides examples of paraphrasing and expressed understanding in greater detail. These five key interactive and supportive behaviors allow the receiver to indicate active listening without sidetracking the sender.

Finally, asking questions designed to stimulate the sender to express the feelings they want to express is important. By allowing the sender to explain fully their thoughts and feelings, we encourage the sender to provide additional information (DeVito, 1986, p. 4). Questions help to clarify areas of uncertainty. Table 7.2

TABLE 7.1
Five Key Interactive and Supportive Behaviors To Use

| Types | Purpose | Examples |
|---|---|---|
| 1. Clarifying | 1. To get additional facts.<br>2. To help explore all sides of a problem. | 1. "Can you clarify this?"<br>2. "Do you mean this. . .?"<br>3. "Is this the problem as you see it now?" |
| 2. Restatement | 1. To check our meaning and interpretation with our partner.<br>2. To show you are listening and you understand.<br>3. To encourage our partner to analyze other aspects of the matter discussed. | 1. "As I understand it, then, your plan is. . ."<br>2. "This is what you have decided to do and the reasons are. . ." |
| 3. Neutral | 1. To convey that you are interested and listening.<br>2. To encourage partner to continue talking. | 1. "I see"<br>2. "Uh-huh"<br>3. "Tell me more about that"<br>4. "That's interesting" |
| 4. Reflective | 1. To show that you understand how your partner feels about what they are saying.<br>2. To help partner to evaluate and temper his/her own feelings as expressed.<br>3. To say you care enough to listen to more than just the surface-level content. | 1. "You feel angry"<br>2. "You're disappointed with yourself because. . ."<br>3. "It must have been a shocking experience for you"<br>4. "You sound hopeful about. . ." |
| 5. Summarizing | 1. To bring all the discussion into focus in terms of a summary or conclusion.<br>2. To serve as a spring board for further discussion on a new aspect of the problem or situation being explored. | 1. "These are the key ideas you seem to be expressing. . ."<br>2. "If I understand you correctly, all we have discussed seems to say you are ready to make a decision on this"<br>3. "So although there have been some problems, you think the future looks positive." |

provides examples of nine types of questions that can help to clarify the sender's message. Not included are questions designed to stymie the sender, such as "Do you still cheat on your travel expense vouchers?"; "Do you still come in late every morning?"; or "You don't still believe that stupid plan will work, do you?"

The concept of *nondirective listening* is analogous to active listening (Nichols & Stevens, 1957, pp. 53–54). By letting the sender know that we accept their problem or opinion as valid, we reaffirm their own self-concept. This provides them with

TABLE 7.2
Effective Questioning

| Type of Question | In-Use Situation | Example |
|---|---|---|
| Open-End | Does not specify what is requested in the way of an answer. It leaves the person asked free to answer as he or she pleases. | "How are things?" |
| Specific | As the term implies, this type of question attempts to elicit detailed, factual information. | "Could you tell me what exactly it is that you are looking for?" |
| Overhead | Such questions are useful for opening a discussion, introducing new phases of a subject, or insuring that those engaged in the conversation have the chance to join in. | "Well . . . that's the situation. Who has some comments to offer right now?" |
| Direct | Used when it is certain the person to whom a question is addressed has the answer, or can get it. | "Junior! Who put that dent on the left side of the car?" |
| Follow-Up | Designed to pursue a discussion further. | "You mentioned at the last meeting the treasury had only $24—isn't that so?" |
| Lead-Off | Helpful in stimulating a discussion. | "Under your present program, what happens when someone quits or retires?" |
| Alternative | Useful for bringing a discussion to a head and forcing a decision. | "Okay! Are we all in agreement that Jim will see the mayor about this?" |
| Justify | Useful in challenging old ideas and developing new ideas as well as securing proof. | "That's an interesting point, but what evidence do you have as proof?" |
| Hypothetical | Helpful when suggesting another approach, even one that's unpopular. Also used to change the course of a discussion. | "Alright . . . let's take Jane's suggestion one step further . . . suppose we did it by . . ." |

*Note.* Reprinted with permission from Dr. Robert K. Burns, founder of Science Research Associates and the Industrial Relations Center, University of Chicago.

greater self-confidence. The guidelines offered for being nondirective include: Take time to listen, be attentive, employ minimal verbal responses, do not probe aggressively for additional data, never evaluate what is said, and never lose faith in the ability of the sender to solve his or her own problems (Koehler, Anatol, & Applbaum, 1981, pp. 114–115). Tables 7.1 and 7.2 provide some examples of nonirective responses. Active or nondirective listening provides credence to the other person's point of view and feelings, and will enhance the ongoing transactions between colleagues, or superiors and subordinates (Gutknecht & Miller, 1986, pp. 138–141). A second means of making distinctions is to examine the differences between deliberative and empathetic listening.

## Deliberative Versus Empathetic

Some authorities divide organizational listening into the two categories of deliberative and empathetic (Koehler et al., 1981, p. 115). Deliberative listening focuses on the listener's capacity to hear, analyze, recall, and draw conclusions from information presented. A large number of training programs and listening tests are concerned with deliberative listening (Papa & Glenn, 1988). Numerous tasks, at all organizational levels, require effective deliberative listening. For example, deliberative listening will help an individual in the use of new technology, such as computers (Anthony & Anthony, 1982, p. 20). Although being accurate in receiving messages is important, there is more to being an effective listener.

Empathy is putting yourself in the other person's "shoes." Many authorities see empathy, or the ability to see an idea or concept from the other's viewpoint, as the key to effective listening (Koehler et al., 1981, p. 115). Empathetic listening concentrates on the feeling part of the sender's message (Rogers & Roethlisherger, 1952). The listener's goal is to relate to what the other person is thinking or feeling, regardless of the content. For this to work, you must be nonevaluative in the listening process (Sorrell, 1975, p. 34). The listener should not interrupt the speaker nor present a threatening environment. In many cases, empathy is required so managers can show they understand and appreciate what the sender is saying (Nichols, 1948).

Empathy is easier to describe than to actually use. How, for example, can a manager really understand what it means to be "on-line" or to deal with numerous angry customers? How can a first-year employee relate to the trials and tribulations of a senior-level executive? The answer lies in truly suspending judgment and accepting, for the moment, that the messages carry validity.

One of the most cited lists of the barriers to effective listening is offered by the Sperry Corporation. Table 7.3 provides a useful, 10-point checklist for examining your own listening habits. Table 7.4 explains the implications of your answers to 10 issues showing the difference between bad and good listeners. To be effective in an organization, understanding and working to overcome these listening barriers are very important. In addition, recent research has provided additional information for effective organizational listening.

## Differentiating Organizational Listening

A significant amount of the early research on listening was conducted in classroom settings. Good listening was tied to mental set, skills and habits, general intelligence, and some specific intelligence traits (Nichols, 1962). A great deal of the subsequent work on listening has been based on this early, pioneering listening research (Nichols, 1957). The focus was on how well the audience could be trained to receive the message (Lewis & Reinsch, 1988, p. 49). The major impediments to listening were identified, and methods were offered to overcome these barriers to listening. Table 7.4 demonstrates this approach.

TABLE 7.3
How to Rate Your Listening Talents

*As a listener, how often do you find yourself engaging in these ten bad habits?*
*Check the appropriate boxes, then tabulate your score, using the key below.*

| How often do you . . . | Almost Always | Usually | Sometimes | Seldom | Almost Never | Score |
|---|---|---|---|---|---|---|
| Call the subject uninteresting? | | | | | | |
| Criticize the speaker's delivery or mannerisms? | | | | | | |
| Get over-stimulated by something the speaker says? | | | | | | |
| Listen primarily for facts? | | | | | | |
| Try to outline everything? | | | | | | |
| Fake attention? | | | | | | |
| Allow distractions? | | | | | | |
| Avoid difficult material? | | | | | | |
| Let emotion-laden words arouse antagonism? | | | | | | |
| Waste the advantage of thought speed? | | | | | | |

Frequency

Total Score

*Key.* Almost Always = 2   Usually = 4   Sometimes = 6   Seldom = 8   Almost Never = 10
*Note.* There is no "correct" score, but the best listeners have the most checks in the "Seldom" and "Almost Never" columns.

Recent research allows us to focus even more directly on organizational listening. The demands on organizational listening are often different from classroom or therapeutic listening (Frank, 1982, pp. 150–154). Classroom listening is oriented primarily toward gaining information. Listening that focuses on the needs of the sender, and concentrates on helping the sender continue their communication efforts, is highly therapeutic and can be extremely helpful to others. These types of listening do have a place in organizations (Lewis & Reinsch, 1988, p. 59), but job-oriented listening behaviors are more likely to be expected by the organization.

Several studies "clearly indicate that [early] conceptions of listening do not correspond to the conception of listening in the work place" (Hunt & Cusella, 1983,

TABLE 7.4
Guide to Listening

| 10 Keys to Effective Listening | The Bad Listener | The Good Listener |
|---|---|---|
| 1. Find area of interest | Tunes out dry subjects | Opportunizes; asks "what's in it for me?" |
| 2. Judge content, not delivery | Tunes out if delivery is poor | Judges content, skips over delivery errors |
| 3. Hold your fire | Tends to enter into argument | Doesn't judge until comprehension is complete |
| 4. Listen for ideas | Listen for facts | Listens for central themes |
| 5. Be flexible | Takes intensive notes using only one system | Takes fewer notes. Uses 4–5 different systems, depending on speaker |
| 6. Work at listening | Shows no energy output. Attention is faked | Works hard, exhibits active body state |
| 7. Resist distractions | Distracted easily | Fights or avoids distractions. Tolerates bad habits, knows how to concentrate |
| 8. Exercise your mind | Resists difficult expository material; seeks light, recreational material | Uses heavier material as exercise for the mind |
| 9. Keep your mind open | Reacts to emotional words | Interprets color words; does not get hung up on them |
| 10. Capitalize on fact that *thought* is *faster* than speech | Tends to daydream with slow speakers | Challenges, anticipates, mentally summarizes, weighs the evidence, listens between the lines to tone of voice |

From Sperry Corporation Listening Program (1979). Copyright © 1979 by Communication Development, Inc. Reprinted by permission.

p. 399). General communication behaviors are more important in an organization than simple recall (deliberative), or concern for someone else's problem (empathetic).

Effective organizational listening is based on the relational aspects of the communication process. Specifically, organizational listening is related to active listening, verbal and nonverbal behavior, relationships, and managerial style.

These relational aspects can be identified further. First, one study of effective organizational listening found the four factors of empathy, receiving skills, receiving instruction-criticism, and giving feedback were most related to organizational success (Hunt & Cusella, 1983). Active listening (empathetic) is more important than recall listening (deliberative) and "listening skills cannot be separated from other communication concerns within the organization" (Lewis & Reinsch, 1988, p. 52). These studies, along with others, "provide clear evidence that classroom listening may differ from work place listening" (Lewis & Reinsch, 1988, p. 49).

Verbal and nonverbal behaviors are tied to perceived listening effectiveness, which is the second element differentiating organizational listening. As Lewis and Reinsch (1988) explained, "In business settings, listening refers to a set of interrelated activities including apparent attentiveness, nonverbal behavior, verbal behavior, perceived attitudes, memory, and behavioral responses" (p. 49). Perceptions of listening effectiveness are affected by both message-sending and message-receiving behaviors. In sum, listening is related to general communication skills.

Third, there are a large number of variables influencing organizational listening including time pressures, ongoing relationships, previous encounters, note-taking activities, and subsequent behaviors after the transaction. These factors are present in all listening settings, of course, but they tend to be more influential in organizational settings. Nonverbal messages are important to perceived listening effectiveness by the receiver (Bradley & Baird, 1977).

Finally, management style and interpersonal communication are closely related to perceived listening effectiveness (Rhodes, 1987, pp. 33–34). Managers opting for a Theory-X approach of "I'm the boss, you're the subordinate" create negative listening habits in subordinates in addition to their own limited listening profile. Because listening is a *relational process* in organizations, feedback is important as an indication of good listening (Barbara, 1971).

An excellent example of the relational impact of management style is the power of *role modeling*. Research indicates that role modeling is the best means for teaching listening behavior (Smeltzer & Watson, 1985, p. 40). So, the advice offered to managers and supervisors to display excellent listening efforts in order to encourage subordinates to also listen is a sound role-modeling approach (Peters, 1987, pp. 305–306). The various processes that encourage managers and executives to be visible through Management by Wandering Around (MBWA) and informal communication give role-modeling information to subordinates. Japanese CEOs and the entire management team depend on this informal listening to establish mutual understanding (Hasegawa, 1986, pp. 27–40).

In organizations, not all messages must be delivered face-to-face and often there is little need for feedback. For example, highly routine messages can be written down and delivered to the receiver without any concern for the specific listening skills. Memos and work orders can be presented without any need for feedback. As the messages become more nonroutine or complex, the requirement for face-to-face communication increases with a commensurate demand for effective listening (Lengel & Daft, 1988). With the increased use of computers for relaying routine messages, interpersonal linkages are diminished (Zuboff, 1988, p. 71). As we discussed earlier, this new communication age requires better interpersonal skills, including listening.

Further clarification regarding listening in an organization can be provided by examining the four frames. No organization operates solely within a single frame, but each frame emphasizes a different goal for listening.

## THE FOUR FRAMES AND LISTENING

The four frames — structural, human resources, political, and symbolic — provide us with a useful perspective regarding how individuals and organizations utilize listening (Bolman & Deal, 1984, 1991). Not only are there differences between organizational and classroom listening, but each frame tends to view listening from a different perspective.

In the structural frame, listening is used to give and receive information. When getting the job done is the focus, we are in the structural frame that places emphasis on effective deliberative listening. Successful listening is determined by fewer mistakes, greater productivity, and orders followed.

The human resources frame focuses on empathy as a means for dealing actively with employee complaints, and relating to colleagues, subordinates, and superiors. The vast majority of sources cited in the beginning of this chapter are concerned with human resources and the role listening plays.

The political frame is represented in some texts on listening and emphasizes the importance of controlling and staying on top through the use of listening (Glatthorn & Adams, 1983). With a political orientation, organizational members use listening as a tool for guarding, gathering, and manipulating. Because most communication is seen as a win/lose proposition, listening is a tool for control.

The symbolic frame is represented by role modeling, MBWA, and other managerial behaviors (Peters & Austin, 1985, pp. 24–25, 390). In addition, symbolic presentations and strong myths provide meaning to individuals, which facilitates the listening process (Peters, 1987, pp. 411–442).

Examining the frames reinforces the varied reasons organizations worry about communication. From reducing mistakes, to keeping customers, to getting ahead, many organizations and individuals are becoming increasingly aware of the importance of listening. Peters and Austin (1985) concluded: "The power of listening: its borders on the bizarre" (p. 25). They are referring to the remarkable successes in any organization that chooses to listen to its people, to its customers, or to its suppliers.

At the same time, one of the difficulties in improving organizational listening may be the different frames being used by the various participants. If a personnel director is using a human resource frame, and the rival department head is operating from a political frame, conflicts will be inevitable, because listening is being used for entirely different purposes.

Now we have outlined values and types of listening. Our final concern is with the use of feedback and the impact of climate in the listening process.

## FEEDBACK

Feedback is the receiver's response to a sender's communication (DeVito, 1986, p. 117). Although feedback can be defined tightly as a message sent in reply to the initial message (Krone, Jablin, & Putnam, 1987, p. 21), in actuality, feedback is an ongoing part of the relational process (Watzlawick, Beavin, & Jackson, 1967). Because one cannot not communicate, feedback occurs at all times, verbally and nonverbally, during a communication transaction. No overt response is still a response. The term feedback has a variety of meanings depending on the source examined and the goal expected from the feedback (Cusella, 1987, pp. 624–630).

In this chapter, we are concerned with the use of feedback as a behavioral aspect of the transaction. To clarify feedback, we should explain *feedforward.*

Feedforward represents predictive messages sent prior to the primary message (Richards, 1968). These messages function as the hypothesis or planning stages for the actual event. Cusella (1987) defined it further: "In organizational terms, feedforward is essentially 'organizational knowledge,' as in the example of the budget planning process" (p. 631). Feedforward also can establish what types of messages are appropriate for a communication event or a particular transaction. In the simplest of terms, a smile can feedforward a metacommunicative message regarding our willingness to receive feedback. Goal setting, a concept that is developed further when we examine motivation later in this text, often functions as a feedforward mechanism, which is then used to provide feedback concerning our success in reaching the goals.

The feedback concept "is central to our understanding of organizational behavior in general and of organizational communication specifically" (Cusella, 1987, p. 624). Feedback helps in maintaining control and developing people in an organization (Basset, 1972). Our focus is on the feedback patterns most useful in enhancing the listening process.

## Positive and Negative Feedback

When originally presented, *positive* and *negative* feedback were used in reference to system-maintaining and system-correcting messages. Positive feedback was an "A-OK" message, and negative feedback called for a change in the manner in which the system was operating.

The more common uses are for the term positive to mean supportive and the term negative to mean modify, change, alter, or correct the source or the source's messages. For example, head nods and smiles might encourage a sender to continue telling a story, whereas frowns might discourage the sender. As we established earlier in this chapter, responses are expected from subordinates. Superiors must use feedback to guarantee successful completion of tasks.

Honest feedback regarding job performance is a requirement for any organization. When it degenerates into harsh criticism, as exemplified by negative feedback, it can have serious effects. In a study of 108 managers and white-collar workers, the poor use of criticism was one of the five most often mentioned causes of conflict at work (Karp, 1987, p. 237). Part of the problem stems from the tendency to manage by exception, or only provide feedback when something is wrong. For most managers, a better strategy would be to spend a great deal of time trying to catch people doing something right and letting them know it (Blanchard & Johnson, 1982). In the extreme, this can mean encouraging subordinates to reveal mistakes in order to open up the communication channels. The chief executive officer of Temps & Co. offers to pay employees $250 for describing an interesting mistake (Levinson, 1987). Although $250 may seem extremely supportive, employees must explain how it happened to their peers in order to prevent repeating the problem. The reward encourages an early detection of potentially serious problems.

You will recall the differences between individual listening patterns and organizational role requirements. Although feedback is vital to a healthy relationship and a successful communication process (Wolvin & Coakley, 1985, p. 97), it takes on an additional role in organizations. In one study, managers and supervisors trained in providing performance-oriented feedback to workers found better communication between themselves and the workers (Tubbs & Widgery, 1978). More important, the factory workers had better job performance and were more satisfied with their work. Effective feedback is seen as vital to an executive trying to be as efficient as possible in communication (Dreyfack, 1983, p. 12). To further understand feedback, we discuss defensive and supportive climates and then effective feedback techniques.

## Supportive and Defensive Climates

One of the most widely used concepts in the teaching of communication is *defensive communication* (Gordon, 1988, p. 53). In his classic article, Gibb (1961) outlined the different consequences from feeling defensive and feeling understood. Gibb's article "is the most requested communication article in the history of the field" (Weick & Browning, 1991, p. 9). The differences between these two types of behaviors appear on Table 7.5. As you can see from the comparison, both verbal and "nonverbal behaviors tend to produce supportive and defensive climates" (Wolvin & Coakley, 1985, p. 217).

The consequences of these two types of feedback responses in organizations are significant (Eadie, 1982). In a longitudinal study at Sears and Roebuck, executives who failed to rise to the highest levels of management had the "fatal flaw" of making

TABLE 7.5
Defensive and Supportive Climates

| *Defensive Climate* | *Supportive Climate* |
|---|---|
| 1. Evaluation: positive or negative judging, blaming | 1. Description: neutral statements of fact— describing without demanding change. |
| 2. Control: attempts to change someone's attitudes, to influence, restrict | 2. Problem orientation: attempts to change problem not person—share concern |
| 3. Strategy: manipulation, use of gimmicks for deceit | 3. Spontaneity: honest, open responses |
| 4. Neutrality: indifference, lack of concern | 4. Empathy: caring, interest, understanding |
| 5. Superiority: expressing power or attitude of being | 5. Equality: willingness to work together, equal partners |
| 6. Certainty: dogmatic, know it all, unchanging, better than others | 6. Provisionalism: tentative conclusions, open to change |

*Note.* From Gibb (1961). Adapted by permission.

the people around them defensive (Horn, 1986, p. 14). Defensive producing feedback affects an individual's self-confidence (Gardiner, 1971). On the other end of the continuum, empathetic understanding promotes greater job satisfaction, lower job turnover among subordinates, and greater mobility within the organization (Gordon, 1988, p. 54).

The tie among listening, feedback, and climate is direct. In fact, "ineffective listening practices are associated with a dysfunctional communication climate" (Hunt & Cusella, 1983, p. 399). In sum, "to the extent you respond genuinely, accurately, positively, without resentment, and in a spirit of mutual equality, you will move toward the establishment of a supportive psychological climate" (Floyd, 1985, p. 125). In addition to Gibb's general suggestions regarding climate, specific information is available regarding effective feedback.

## Effective Feedback Techniques

Judgments should be descriptive in any organizational feedback. The key is to have some objective measure that compares actual behavior with some standard, and a nonevaluative means of providing the feedback (Filley & Pace, 1976). Table 7.6 outlines the basic steps to using effective feedback. Most feedback, in an organizational setting, should deal in specifics, focus on actions, not attitudes, determine the appropriate time and place, and refrain from inappropriately including other issues (Karp, 1987, pp. 238–240).

The underlying power of feedback lies in its capacity to validate the assumptions, constructs, and ideas we have about other people's actions (Harris, 1988). Because making inferences is part of the transactional process, constructive use of feedback, coupled with a supportive climate, allows individuals and groups to move toward clearer interpersonal understanding. In most organizations, people operate toward other individuals based on the behavior that is being observed. So, in addition to listening to an individual, adding the dimension of feedback allows both parties to

TABLE 7.6
Guidelines For Effective Feedback

1. Feedback should be descriptive rather than evaluative.
2. Feedback should be specific rather than general.
3. Feedback should be appropriate, taking into account the needs of the sender, receiver, and situation.
4. Feedback should be directed toward behavior that the receiver can do something about.
5. Feedback should be well timed. Usually, the more immediate the feedback, the more effective.
6. Feedback should be honest rather than manipulative.
7. Feedback should be understood by both parties. Additional input is sought, if needed, to enhance and clarify the feedback process.
8. Feedback should be proactive and coactive. When it requires change in past behaviors, specific directions should be provided for the expected change. Both parties should agree on the need for change and the remedy.
9. Feedback should not be used as an opportunity to "dump" past grievances on an individual. It should be a natural process in the ongoing relationship between superior and subordinate, co-workers, or any subsystem of the organization.

respond to the intended meaning of a message. Although we are presenting feedback as a separate issue, we always are providing feedback. The key is to make certain the feedback is supportive to enhance the quality of the transaction.

## CONCLUSION

Listening is a major communication factor in organizations. Not only is listening important to organizations and individuals, ineffective listening is costly. The current status of organizational listening is not strong. A major reason for this weakness lies in the difficulty in delineating listening factors from the overall communication patterns. In fact, focusing on listening is the most important contribution of this chapter. By being aware of the lack of emphasis, we can be more effective in understanding and using listening.

Examining the four stages of the listening process allows us to focus on the numerous factors that can prevent effective listening. Each stage—sensing, interpreting, evaluating, and responding—is significant in the listening process. Once we examine each stage, we can understand better the complexity of the process.

Active listening is designed to enhance the ability of the sender to successfully complete the message. Sometimes labeled nondirective, active listening is forwarded in most examinations of listening as the best response. Organizations also make different uses of deliberative and empathetic listening. Most important, recent research indicates that active participation by the listener in the communication process is important if the receiver is to be judged an effective listener. As might be expected, each of the four frames uses listening for different purposes.

Feedback and climate are the final areas of concern. Especially in organizations, feedback is vital. However, the transaction can be supported or limited depending on the type of climate. Defensive producing climates limit the willingness of the sender to participate in the transaction. So, feedback must be provided carefully to enhance the listening process.

At the very least, this chapter should provide some important information regarding the relative lack of effective listening in organizations. In spite of overwhelming evidence for the need for better listening, it often is ignored as an important issue. To enhance our own effectiveness, we should concentrate on making our listening behaviors more effective. By and large, good listening encourages others also to listen more effectively.

## REFERENCES

Albrecht, K. (1988). *At America's service.* Homewood, IL: Dow Jones-Irwin.

American Management Association. *Council reports: Insights into issues and trends exclusively for AMA members* (Vol. 2). New York: Author.

Anastasi, T. E. (1982). *Listen! Techniques for improving communication skills.* Boston: CBI.

Anthony, P., & Anthony, W. P. (1982, March). Now hear this: Some techniques of listening. *Supervisory Management, 25,* 18–22.

Barbara, D. A. (1971). *How to make people listen to you.* Springfield, IL: Thomas.

Basset, G. A. (1972). Three I's—Still personal basics, still neglected. *Personnel, 49,* 21–26.

Becker, S. L., & Eldom, L. R. V. (1980). That forgotten basic skill: Oral communication. *Association for Communication Administration, 33,* 14–22.

Bednar, A. S., & Olney, R. J. (1987). Communication needs of recent graduates. *The Bulletin, 50,* 22–23.

Bennett, J. C., & Olney, R. J. (1986). Executive priorities for effective communication in the information society. *The Journal of Business Communication, 23,* 13–22.

Berko, R. M., Wolvin, A. D., & Wolvin, D. R. (1985). *Communicating: A social and career focus* (3rd ed.). Boston: Houghton Mifflin.

Bittel, L. R. (1980). *What every supervisor should know* (4th ed.). New York: McGraw-Hill.

Blanchard, K., & Johnson, S. (1982). *One minute manager.* New York: Morrow.

Bolman, L. G., & Deal, T. E. (1985). *Modern approaches to understanding and managing organizations.* San Francisco: Jossey-Bass.

Bolman, L. G., & Deal, T. E. (1991). *Reframing organizations: Artistry, choice, and leadership.* San Francisco: Jossey-Bass.

Bormann, E. G., Howell, W. S., Nichols, R. G., & Shapiro, G. L. (1980). *Interpersonal communication in the modern organization.* Englewood Cliffs, NJ: Prentice-Hall.

Bostrom, R. N., & Waldhart, E. S. (1980). Components in listening behavior: The role of short-term memory. *Human Communication Research, 6,* 221–227.

Bradley, P. H., & Baird, J. E., Jr. (1977). Management and communicator style: A correlational analysis. *Central States Speech Journal, 28,* 195–203.

Brown, L. (1982). *Communicating facts and ideas in business.* Englewood Cliffs, NJ: Prentice-Hall.

Callerman, W. G., & McCartney, W. W. (1985). Identifying and overcoming listening problems. *Supervisory Management, 28,* 39–40.

Cauldill, D. W., & Donaldson, D. W. (1986). Effective listening tips for managers. *Administrative Management, 47,* 22–23.

Cusella, L. P. (1987). Feedback, motivation, and performance. In F. M. Jablin, L. L. Putnam, K. H. Roberts, & L. W. Porter (Eds.), *Handbook of organizational communication* (pp. 624–678). Newbury Park, CA: Sage.

Daniels, T. D., & Spiker, B. K. (1987). *Perspectives on organizational communication.* Dubuque, IA: Brown.

DeVito, J. A. (1986). *The communication handbook: A dictionary.* New York: Harper & Row.

DeVito, J. A. (1989). *The interpersonal communication book* (5th ed.). New York: Harper & Row.

DiGaetani, J. L. (1980). The business of listening. *Business Horizons, 23,* 39–41.

DiSalvo, V. S. (1980). A summary of current research identifying communication skills in various organizational contexts. *Communication Education, 29,* 283–290.

DiSalvo, V. S., Larsen, D. C., & Seiler, W. J. (1976). Communication skills needed by persons in business organizations. *Communication Education, 25,* 269–275.

Downs, C. W., & Conrad, C. C. (1982). Effective subordinancy. *The Journal of Business Communication, 19,* 27–38.

Dreyfack, R. (1983). *What an executive should know about listening more effectively.* Chicago: Dartnell Corp.

Eadie, W. F. (1982). Defensive communication revisited: A critical examination of Gibb's theory. *Southern Speech Communication Journal, 47,* 163–177.

Filley, A. C., & Pace, L. A. (1976). Making judgments descriptive. In J. W. Pfieffer & J. E. Jones (Eds.), *The 1976 annual handbook for group facilitators* (pp. 128–131). La Jolla, CA: University Associates.

Floyd, J. J. (1985). *Listening: A practical approach.* Glenview, IL: Scott, Foresman.

Frank, A. D. (1982). *Communicating on the job.* Glenview, IL: Scott, Foresman.

Fritz, R. (1985). *Rate yourself as a manager.* Englewood Cliffs, NJ: Prentice-Hall.

Gardiner, J. C. (1971). A synthesis of experimental studies of speech communication feedback. *Journal of Communication, 21,* 17–35.

Garties, G. (1988, November 20). Work at home via computers attracts more baby boomers. *The Sunday Courier,* p. F7.

Gibb, J. R. (1961). Defensive communication. *Journal of Communication, 11,* 141–148.

Gibbs, M., Hewing, P., Hulbert, J. E., Ramsey, D., & Smith, A. (1985, June). How to teach effective listening skills in a basic business communication class. *The Bulletin of the Association for Business Communication, 48,* 29–32.

Glatthorn, A. A., & Adams, H. R. (1983). *Listening your way to management success.* Glenview, IL: Scott, Foresman.

Goldhaber, G. M. (1986). *Organizational communication* (4th ed.). Dubuque, IA: Brown.

Gordon, R. D. (1988). The difference between feeling defensive and feeling understood. *The Journal of Business Communication, 25,* 53–64.

Gutknecht, D. B., & Miller, J. R. (1986). *The organizational and human resources handbook.* Lanham, MD: University Press of America.

Hackman, M. Z., & Johnson, C. E. (1991). *Leadership: A communication perspective.* Prospect Heights, IL: Waveland.

Harris, T. E. (1988). Mastering the art of talking back. *Management World, 17,* 9–11.

Harris, T. E., & Thomlison, T. D. (1983). Career-bound communication education: A needs analysis. *Central States Speech Journal, 34,* 260–279.

Hasegawa, K. (1986). *Japanese-style management.* Tokyo: Kodansha.

Hearing loss: Ways to avoid, new ways to treat. (1982, October 18). *U.S. News and World Report,* pp. 85–86.

Horn, J. C. (1986, April). Executive action. *Psychology Today,* p. 14.

Howell, W. S. (1982). *The empathic communicator.* Belmont, CA: Wadsworth.

Hulbert, J. (1979). They won't hear you if you don't listen. *Administrative Management, 40,* 54–56.

Hunt, G. T., & Cusella, G. T. (1983). A field study of listening needs in organizations. *Communication Education, 32,* 387–395.

Junge, D. A., Daniels, M. H., & Karmos, J. S. (1984). Personnel manager's perceptions of requisite basic skills. *Vocational Guidance Quarterly, 33,* 138–146.

Kahneman, D. (1973). *Attention and effort.* Englewood Cliffs, NJ: Prentice-Hall.

Karp, H. (1987). The lost art of feedback. In J. W. Pfeiffer (Ed.), *The 1987 annual: Developing human resources* (pp. 237–246). San Diego: University Associates.

Keefe, W. F. (1971). *Listen, management!* New York: McGraw-Hill.

Klemmer, E. T., & Snyder, F. W. (1972). Measurement of time spent communicating. *Journal of Communication, 22,* 142–158.

Koehler, J. W., Anatol, K. W. E., & Applbaum, R. L. (1981). *Organizational communication: Behavioral perspectives* (2nd ed.). New York: Holt, Rinehart & Winston.

Kotter, J. P. (1988). *The leadership factor.* New York: Free Press.

Krone, K. J., Jablin, F. M., & Putnam, L. L. (1987). Communication theory and organizational communication: Multiple perspectives. In F. M. Jablin, L. L. Putnam, K. H. Roberts, & L. W. Porter (Eds.), *Handbook of organizational communication* (pp. 18–40). Newbury Park, CA: Sage.

Lengel, R. H., & Daft, R. L. (1988). The selection of communication media as an executive skill. *The Academy of Management Executive, 2,* 228–231.

Levinson, H. (1987, September 28). Congratulations! You made a mistake. *Behavioral Science Newsletter,* p. 3.

Lewis, M. H., & Reinsch, N. L., Jr. (1988). Listening in organizational environments. *The Journal of Business Communication, 25,* 49–67.

Locke, E. A., & Latham, G. P. (1984). *Goal setting: A motivational technique that works.* Englewood Cliffs, NJ: Prentice-Hall.

Luthans, F., Hodgetts, R. M., & Rosenkrantz, S. A. (1988). *Real managers.* Cambridge, MA: Ballinger.

Mehrabian, A. (1981). *Silent messages.* Belmont, CA: Wadsworth.

Miller, G. A. (1956). The magical number seven, plus or minus two: Some limits on our capacity for processing information. *Psychological Review, 63,* 81–97.

Mitzberg, H. (1973). *The nature of managerial work.* New York: Harper & Row.

Morgan, P., & Baker, H. K. (1985). Building a professional image: Improving listening behavior. *Supervisory Management, 28,* 34–38.

Mundale, S. M. (1980). Why more CEOs are mandating listening and writing training. *Training/HRD, 17,* 36–37.

Nichols, R. G. (1948). Factors in listening comprehension. *Speech Monographs, 15,* 154–163.

Nichols, R. G. (1957, July). Listening is a 10-part skill. *Nation's Business,* p. 4.

Nichols, R. G. (1962). Listening is good business. *Management of Personnel Quarterly, 1,* 2–9.

Nichols, R. G., & Stevens, L. A. (1957). *Are you listening?* New York: McGraw-Hill.

Nichols, R. G., & Stevens, L. A. (1978). Listening to people. In *Paths toward personal progress: Leaders are made, not born* (pp. 112–119). Boston: Harvard Business Review.

Niehouse, O. L. (1986, August). Listening: The other half of effective communications. *Management Solutions*, pp. 27–28.

Olsen, L. (1962). Technology humanized: The rate-controlled tape recorder. *Media and Methods, 15,* 134–141.

Orr, D. B. (1968). Time compressed speech—A perspective. *The Journal of Communication, 18,* 279–289.

Pace, R. W. (1983). *Organizational communication: Foundations for human resource development.* Englewood Cliffs, NJ: Prentice-Hall.

Papa, M. J., & Glenn, E. C. (1988). Listening ability and performance with new technology: A case study. *The Journal of Business Communication, 25,* 5–16.

Peters, T. (1987). *Thriving on chaos.* New York: Knopf.

Peters, T., & Austin, N. (1985). *Passion for excellence.* New York: Random House.

Peters, T. J., & Waterman, R. H., Jr. (1982). *In search of excellence.* New York: Harper & Row.

Powell, J. T. (1981). Listening to help the hostile employee. *Supervisory Management, 26,* 2–5.

Quick, T. L. (1985). *The manager's motivation desk book.* New York: Wiley.

Rhodes, S. C. (1987). A study of effective and ineffective dyads using the systems theory principle of entropy. *Journal of the International Listening Association, 1,* 43–49.

Richards, I. A. (1968, February). The secret of feedforward. *Saturday Review,* pp. 14–17.

Rogers, C. (1970). *Carl Rogers on encounter groups.* New York: Harrow.

Rogers, C. R., & Farson, R. E. (1969). Active listening. In R. C. Huseman, C. M. Logue, & D. L. Freshley (Eds.), *Readings in interpersonal and organizational communication* (pp. 477–485). Boston: Holbrook.

Rogers, C. R., & Roethlisherger, F. L. (1952). Barriers and gateways to communication. *Harvard Business Review, 30,* 45–49.

Ross, R. S. (1985). *Understanding persuasion: Foundations and practice.* Englewood Cliffs, NJ: Prentice-Hall.

Shockley-Zalabak, P. (1991). *Fundamentals of organizational communication* (2nd ed.). New York: Longman.

Smeltzer, L. R., & Watson, K. W. (1985). A test of instructional strategies for listening improvement in a simulated business setting. *The Journal of Business Communication, 22,* 33–42.

Sorrell, B. D. (1975). Is anybody listening? *Data Management, 13,* 33–35.

Steil, L. K. (1980, May 26). Secrets of being a better listener. *U.S. News and World Report,* p. 65.

Steil, L. K., Barker, L. L., & Watson, K. W. (1983). *Effective listening: Key to your success.* Reading, MA: Addison-Wesley.

Tracey, W. R. (1988). *Critical skills: The guide to top performance for human resource managers.* New York: AMACOM.

Tubbs, S. L., & Widgery, R. N. (1978). When productivity lags, check at the top: Are key managers really communicating? *Management Review, 67,* 20–25.

Wakin, L. (1984, February). The business of listening. *Today's Office,* p. 46.

Waterman, R. H., Jr. (1987). *The renewal factor.* New York: Bantam.

Watzlawick, P., Beavin, J. H., & Jackson, D. D. (1967). *Pragmatics of human communication.* New York: Norton.

Weaver, C. H. (1972). *Human listening: Processes and behavior.* Indianapolis: Bobbs-Merrill.

Weick, K. E., & Browning, L. D. (1991). Fixing with the voice: A research agenda for applied communication. *Journal of Applied Communication Research, 19,* 1–19.

Wilson, G. L., Hantz, A. M., & Hanna, M. S. (1989). *Interpersonal growth through communication* (2nd ed.). Dubuque, IA: Brown.

Wolff, F. I., Marsnik, N. C., Tracey, W. S., & Nichols, R. G. (1983). *Perceptive listening.* New York: Holt, Rinehart & Winston.

Wolvin, A. D., & Coakley, C. G. (1985). *Listening* (2nd ed.). Dubuque, IA: Brown.

Woodcock, R. W., & Clark, C. R. (1968). Comprehension of a passage by elementary school children as a function of listening rate, retention period, and I.Q. *The Journal of Communication, 18,* 259–271.

Zuboff, S. (1988). *In the age of the smart machine.* New York: Basic.

# CHAPTER 8

# Symbolic Behavior

The power of communication to create and maintain meaning that is shared by members of an organization is a theme that has permeated this text. In the introductory chapter, we established that communication functions as the lifeblood, and sometimes the embalming fluid, for all organizations. As Petrelle, Slaughter, & Jorgensen (1988) put it, "Communication is a requisite to organizational functioning" (p. 294) for the individual, team, or larger group. This is true regardless of the managerial perspective—structural, human resources, political, or symbolic—being used.

This chapter places in context the most human part of organizations—symbolic behavior that results in various degrees of shared meanings and values between organizational members. According to Faules and Alexander (1978), "Symbolic behavior refers to a person's capacity to respond to or use a system of significant symbols" (p. 5). Symbols allow individuals, groups, and organizations to engage in the complex behaviors required to work together. Because the symbols stand for something else, they can be used to explain past behavior, respond based on past experience, use accumulated knowledge, and cope with the present and future.

Symbolic behavior's impact is evident at the organizational, group, and individual levels. This is hardly an insight at this point in our examination of organizational communication, because you are well versed in the importance of symbolic behavior. Throughout the first seven chapters, you have been provided numerous examples of symbolic behavior in organizations, their cultures, and the various subcultures. Our analysis of verbal and nonverbal communication, networks and channels, and listening underscored the importance of symbolic behavior. This chapter takes these pieces of the jigsaw puzzle, which have appeared at the appropriate points in our discussion of other issues, adds the remaining pieces, and provides a comprehensive picture of symbolic behavior. Although the justifications for a symbolic per-

**257**

spective are strong, you already were forewarned in the beginning of this text that selected views of organizations, including symbolic, can be parochial.

With this disclaimer in mind, this chapter begins the analysis by presenting seven propositions underscoring the symbolic perspective. Then, verbal and nonverbal communication, as the delivery mechanisms for symbolic behavior, are examined. Five important limitations to symbolic behavior are provided to make certain our understanding is complete. Finally, we examine the concept of performance as it relates to organizations.

## BASIC PROPOSITIONS — SYMBOLIC BEHAVIOR

### Overview

The symbolic behavior perspective argues that organizational reality is socially constructed through communication (Putnam, 1982). Because of uncertainty, individuals constantly are organizing themselves by creating and responding to a group-based reality. These processes and interactions create, maintain, and transform the organizational structures (Frank & Brownell, 1989, p. 196). This collective sense making means there can be multiple realities produced through the various cycles of human interactions. The following issues are intertwined with symbolic behavior: complexity, uncertainty, cultural creation and maintenance, interpersonal reality, group behavior, leadership, and the management of incongruences. For the sake of clarity, each of these issues is presented as a proposition.

### Complexity

*Proposition 1.   Organizational complexity creates a reliance on symbolic messages.* Most organizations are too vast, unpredictable, and complex for easy understanding. Organizational membership often creates uncertainty regarding the goals, power structure, road to success, or even how to get the work accomplished (Cohen & March, 1974). Communication complexity is compounded by the multitude of ongoing behaviors including transactions between individuals, individuals and groups, groups to groups, groups to organizations, organizations to organizations, and organizations to public behaviors (Faules & Alexander, 1978, p. 11).

Therefore, our world of work is an interpretative experience (Overington, 1977, p. 138). Tompkins (1987) explained, "As for the present, each member of an organization has directly experienced only a 'sliver' of the nonsymbolic; each member's overall picture is but a construct provided by the symbol systems of words, numbers, and nomenclatures. Refusing to see or acknowledge the dominating role of symbolicity in shaping notions of 'reality' is to cling 'to a kind of naive verbal realism' " (p. 85). In other words, organizations are subjective realities rather than objective phenomena (Pacanowsky & O'Donnell-Trujillo, 1983).

Symbolic messages allow members to make sense out of their environment. Our social reality is made up of symbolic systems (Faules & Alexander, 1978, p. 15). For example, few individuals can comprehend an IBM's international realm or a large university's sphere. When we are unable to grasp the entire scope of an organization, we respond to the organization's essence as it is presented symbolically. Faced with uncertainty, we rely on meaning provided through communication. Highly bureaucratic organizations, such as schools, colleges, and universities, business conglomerates, research and development organizations, political campaign organizations, and many government bureaus have been labeled *organized anarchies* (Cameron, 1980, pp. 70–71). Within these organizations, there are ambiguous connections between structure and expected activities.

Even the smallest business must respond to bureaucratic restraints, such as tax and building codes. Although individuals may be their own bosses, they still are subject to the labyrinth of rules, regulations, and conflicting advice (e.g., make a profit and always place the customer first). And, though complexity and incongruity can leave us feeling helpless, we can identify with the symbolic image (Boulding, 1961).

Organizations develop a standardized set of meanings through microcultural verbal and nonverbal symbols. The mechanisms chosen for delivering the messages— verbal and written channels, nonverbal communications, networks, interpersonally, in groups, by leaders, and electronically—carry significant symbolic consequences, which are created and maintained by the organization or subsystem within which we function.

## Uncertainty and Organizing

*Proposition 2. Uncertainty promotes a continual process of organizing.* The symbolic interpretation of organizational reality deals with the process of sense making. In other words, we are constantly organizing our shared experience. According to Weick (1979), "Organizing is defined as a consensually validated grammar for reducing equivocality by means of sensible interlocked behaviors" (p. 3). Because organizing is complex, meaning is provided through symbols. This meaning is negotiated between individuals, within groups, and during an individual's passage through an organization (Eisenberg & Riley, 1988, p. 131). Organizational members make sense out of the everyday events through a set of shared symbols (Brown, 1986, p. 72). In other words, an organization's "reality is socially constructed through the words, symbols, and behaviors of its members" (Putnam, 1983, p. 35). In fact, this common ground is a prerequisite to effective organizational functioning. As Pfeffer (1981) put it, "One of the important defining characteristics of organizations is that within an organization, there are consensually shared perceptions and definitions of the world" (p. 12).

The symbolic-interactionist perspective pays heed to the symbolic reaction people have to their organizations. The work environment presents us with an elaborate code of values, attitudes, roles, and norms of behavior that are appropriate to the organization (Wood, 1982, p. 156).

Organizational cultures prescribe the ways members react symbolically to organizational phenomena by presenting them with culturally approved explanations, shared perceptions, and a mutual sense of social order (Kreps, 1986, pp. 152–154). This collective interpretation of social reality is vital to the effective functioning of an organization.

## Cultural Creation and Maintenance

*Proposition 3. Symbolic behavior creates and maintains organizational cultures.* All organizations have cultures that are learned, shared, and transmitted. The cultural perspective represents a process orientation to organizational reality with reality being formed through communication (Pacanowsky & O'Donnell-Trujillo, 1982). Wilkins and Dyer (1988) explained, "Organizational culture is socially acquired and shared knowledge that is embodied in specific and general organizational frames of reference" (p. 513). For example, the metaphors—ranging from machines (people are merely part of the production process) to brains (information and intelligence processing) to psychic prisons (toe the company line, bound by golden handcuffs) to voyage (adventure requiring teamwork)—used to characterize organizations set the stage for acceptable and unacceptable activities. If you were told you would become entangled in a psychic prison, you certainly would react differently than if you were invited to join one big, happy family (Clancy, 1989).

Culture is the shadow side of the formal organization as reflected by its unique character, style, energy, commitment, and way of doing things. Culture provides the glue for cohesion and the oil for lubrication. As people perform their culturally sanctioned behaviors, their actions assist in creating and maintaining the organization.

In truth, many organizations could not operate if a strict, rational response was required for every behavior. So, cultures provide direction through the shared assumptions, values, and meanings. If nothing else, people have a reason for committing time, personnel, and resources to a particular activity. The culture provides useful, overriding rationale for activities that otherwise might seem meaningless. This point can be explained with two common organizational activities, meetings and goal setting.

Taking part in the ritual of decision making, by attending meetings and making the right comments, can be as important as actually making a decision because the activity reaffirms the importance of the organization. The reasoning can be: The meeting must be important if this many prestigious members are willing to commit their time and energy. Besides, the importance assigned to the meeting, because of status or expertise, is a reaffirmation that the organization carefully deliberates important issues. In the same vein, almost every book on success calls for extensive goal setting and planning. Although little evidence exists that this goal-setting process is the predominant reason people are successful, these activities impose an image of rationality and reaffirm that the organization, group, or individual is in control (Conrad, 1985, pp. 154–163). So, two-day retreats, often isolated from the day-to-day pressures, provide a vital refurbishing of the esprit de corps by setting goals agreed upon during the retreat that may never be acted upon. In fact, having some direction is rational and spending time sorting through conflicting agendas does provide an overriding purpose.

In the more successful organizations, cultures act as reinforcers for productive behaviors. Cultures assist members in coping with environmental uncertainties and in coordinating activities. *Cultural maps*, made up of general and specific frames of reference, allow individuals "to define a situation they encounter and develop an appropriate response" (Wilkins & Dyer, 1988, p. 523). The organizational frame of reference defines "aspects of the culture such as general definitions of roles, relevant groupings of individuals, relationships between groups and the whole, relationships between the organization and outside groups, ideological orientations about the nature of humans, the kind of work that needs doing, repair strategies when things go awry, and so forth" (Wilkins & Dyer, 1988, p. 523). When an organization says "quality is job one," or "the customer is always right," the slogan provides a *master symbol*, which establishes that goal as paramount and easily understood. According to Waterman (1987), "Man is the maker of meanings in the world that sometimes seems without meaning. Few things help us find meaning more than a cause to believe in, better yet, about which to get excited" (p. 11). This overriding ideology allows members "to take their lead from the organization's own vision" (Mitzberg, 1991, pp. 62–64). One organization boasted "the difficult we do immediately, the impossible takes a little longer." Contrast the power of that group image with a popular sign seen in some small businesses that shows several figures bent over in laughter saying "you want it when?"

*Cultural scenes* outline the relevant times, settings, issues, and so forth to justify switching from one organizational frame to another (Wilkins & Dyer, 1988). For example, moving from a management meeting to an interaction with a customer changes the cultural scene.

There are pluses and minuses regarding organizational cultures. The organization's culture provides guidelines regarding the expected practices and communication functions that individuals use when responding to the symbolic reality. Cultures provide meaning, help organizations capture and direct the collective will, create distinctive norms, promote values, and encourage high performance (Gutknecht & Miller, 1986, pp. 76–77). At the same time, cultures can create dysfunctional norms, groupthink, and counterproductive behaviors. A cynic might observe that even the psychic prison provides meaning, albeit unpleasant, in an uncertain setting. As you are already aware from our earlier discussions, cultures provide values, assumptions, informal ideologies, attitudes, myths, symbols, rituals, language, jargon, rumors, prejudices, stereotypes, social etiquette, dress, and appropriate demeanor (Gutknecht & Miller, 1986, p. 73). Tompkins (1987) put it this way: "Symbolism, in short, *creates* organizational realities and environments as well as the motives of those who act" (p. 83).

In choosing *The 100 Best Companies to Work for in America* (1985), Levering, Moshowitz, and Katz concluded that the best companies have gone "beyond technique" (p. xiv). Rather than a manipulative approach where "we" (management) are trying to do something to "them" (employees), the best companies have "achieved a sense of we are all in it together." The investigators concluded: "The 100 best offer an added benefit of such value that it's difficult to place on the same scale: a working life for thousands of people really worth living and worth looking forward to every waking day" (Levering et al., 1985, p. xiv). Symbolic actions assist the organization in achieving its goals. Fundamental to that success is the impact symbolic behavior has on individuals.

## Interpersonal Reality

*Proposition 4.  Symbols constitute the basis for interpersonal reality.* At the microlevel, humans are symbol users whose behavior is directly attributable to symbolic capabilities (Thayer, 1961). As Frank and Brownell (1989) put it, "The concept of symbol is at the heart of human communication" (p. 199). The stimuli to which we assign meaning create and maintain our own reality. The reverse side of the same issue leads to the conclusion that all "communication processes can be seen as ways in which any organization attains personal meaning for its employees. From talk designed to accomplish tasks to talk designed to spread gossip, communication processes are the lifeblood of any company, because they allow the company to do what it does" (Wilson, Goodall, & Waagen, 1986, p. 107). There is a symbiotic process whereby we communicate with symbols and symbols create the meaning we are responding to (Burke, 1969, p. 136).

Roles, symbols, and interaction deserve further attention. Our roles, constructed by our perceptions of organizational situations, are defined socially through communication (Duncan, 1962; Petrelle et al., 1988, p. 295). We respond to our definitions of the workplace by using certain attributes that we present through our role behavior. Role taking, or role performance, does not represent a false persona. Instead, we are attempting to respond to the demands presented by the situation.

Verbal and nonverbal symbols allow us to formulate an understanding of what otherwise might seem unclear (Brown, 1986, p. 71). Regardless of how objective organizations attempt to be, a great deal of organizational reality is created and maintained through symbolic discourse. There is *symbolic interaction* through the communication of significant symbols (Duncan, 1968; Mead, 1934). Working becomes a *negotiated experience* whereby we participate in creating organizational meaning. Understanding the culture's meaning allows us to better appreciate the organization and perform our roles effectively and productively (Wilson et al., 1986, pp. 18–19).

Interaction is a process that involves the negotiation of shared meaning, and the messages imply each individual's vision of the nature of social and physical reality as well as their values, beliefs, and attitudes (Stephen, 1986, p. 192). In a somewhat more to the point manner, Redding (1984) concluded: "In a technical sense, all that is transferred between the two parties are physical manifestations of symbols" (p. 32). Interaction provides the meaning.

Finally, symbols allow us to understand *proscriptive norms* in an organization. Most organizational norms are proscriptive rather than prescriptive because they specify whether a behavior is appropriate, not which behavior is appropriate. Dressing conservatively, listening to employees, or providing excellent customer service are proscriptive expectations rather than specified means for carrying out the activity. Individual activity is bound by group expectations and sanctions, which brings us to the fifth proposition.

## Group Behavior

*Proposition 5. Groups reaffirm the importance of symbolic behavior*. In the end, individuals identify with the subculture, or group, that they belong to. This community, unit, work group, or department allows us to see that culture "can be best understood as a set of solutions devised by a group of people to meet specific problems posed by the situations they face in common" (Ting-Toomey, 1985, p. 74). These solutions, or procedures, occur in every small group. As Bormann, Howell, Nichols, and Shapiro (1982) put it, "Each small group, formal or informal, has a culture that consists of shared norms, reminiscences, stories, rites and rituals. The group's culture provides the members with a unique symbolic common ground" (p. 96).

Group activities represent highly symbolic behaviors. For example, regularly scheduled education, testing, and accreditation set standards that might be in conflict with the organization's operating mode. Salaried professionals, people who decide to practice their profession within an organization, have an expectation of autonomy that can conflict with the overriding cultural expectations (Raelin, 1989). These professions have a code of behavior that is prescribed by their accrediting organizations, not their employer. These codes can be in sync or conflict with the employer's. Depending on the fit, there can be an *enhancing subculture*, which embraces the dominant culture's values, a *counterculture* that challenges the values, or an *orthogonal subculture* that accepts the values of the dominant culture as well as its own (Duncan, 1989, p. 234). Nurses and doctors present excellent examples of the last type. Although professionals provide us with an illustrative discussion, different departments (e.g., shipping, sales, production), locations (e.g., plant, headquarters, region), and subgroup membership (e.g., union, management, exempt, nonexempt, new, fully acculturated) can create the same subcultures. Inevitably, leaders are called on to coordinate interpersonal and group activities and leaders also rely on symbolic behavior.

## Leadership

*Proposition 6. Leadership requires effective symbolic behavior.* A useful distinction can be drawn between management—as the process of planning, organizing, leading, and controlling—and leadership (DuBrin, Ireland, & Williams, 1989, pp. 15–16). In order to provide legitimacy to the practice of management, quantifiable approaches, based on careful planning, often are used. However, "few people doubt that managers traffic in images and more often act as evangelists or psychologists than accountants or engineers" (Duncan, 1989, p. 229). Effective leaders know how to use symbolic behavior and act as facilitators. They help employees and colleagues identify with the organization (Bradford & Cohen, 1984; Kotter, 1988, p. 124). At the highest level, "executive behavior is mostly talk. It is more symbol-intensive than labor-intensive, requiring the creation of meaning for those doing the direct work" (Jonas, Fry, & Srivastva, 1989, p. 205). In order to be an effective member of an organization, you will need to understand the concept of leadership. Therefore, we devoted an entire chapter later in this text to the numerous issues regarding leadership in organizations. For now, we concentrate on symbolic leadership.

There are two aspects to symbolic leadership. First, symbolic leadership is the vital link between organizational needs and employees' understanding. Second, the organizational culture explains to the manager how the role is to be acted.

Accepting that leadership requires excellent management skills, successful leaders have symbolic, as well as rational, political, and human resource impact. Wise leaders utilize symbolic behaviors. As Peters and Austin (1985) explained, "All business is show business. All leadership is show business. All management is show business. That doesn't mean tap dancing; it means shaping values, symbolizing attention—and it is the opposite of 'administration' and especially, 'professional management' " (p. 265). Consistency of messages by leaders is required to maintain the positive affects of symbolic behavior. According to Waterman (1987), "Visible management attention, rather than management exhortation, gets things done. Action may start with the words, but it has to be backed by symbolic behavior that makes those words come alive" (p. 11). An important admonition is that leaders using empty symbolic messages will be discredited quickly.

*Symbolic management* concentrates on manipulating and developing values, beliefs, and commitments in order to change organizational cultures (Daniels & Spiker, 1987, pp. 117–118). It is required to maintain organizational cultures (Kotter, 1988, pp. 89–90). To reiterate, nonverbal, as well as verbal, communication is important. As Waterman (1987) put it, "People are symbol manipulators. Words provide the set of symbols we manipulate most often. We do it so much and so well that most managers rely too heavily on language and not enough on the great wealth of other symbols available to them" (p. 265).

Leaders, then, influence the culture by paying attention to certain behaviors, attributes, and outcomes (Schein, 1985). National consultants hammer away at the premise: What a leader rewards is what the leader gets (Kerr & Slocum, 1987, pp. 99–107; Peters, 1989, p. 7). Managers, vice presidents, or presidents who visit the hot or unpleasant parts of a plant in the middle of summer, drop by training sessions, or spend time inquiring about particularly difficult jobs are operating on the principle that physical presence is more effective than lip service. When leaders, managers, and employees attempt to use the advice provided by cultural messages, they are confronted with the complexities of the world of work.

## Managing Incongruences

*Proposition 7. Incongruences and paradoxes are managed through acculturation.* In chapter 3, we discussed the inherent conflict between joining an organization in order to gain the benefits and the desire for an individual freedom. We face the irony that in order to enjoy our freedom, we must surrender some of it to earn a living. If we want to advance, we must ascribe to the cultural expectations. For most of us, this is a relatively easy dilemma to resolve because rules, roles, and requirements have been placed on us throughout our lives.

Although uncertainty requires continual organizing, and working requires surrendering some freedoms, incongruences and paradoxes require some action. Paradoxes, dilemmas, and contradictions are part of organizational life. You were introduced to the concepts of paradoxes and double binds in chapter 5, Verbal Communication. Symbols can eliminate ambiguity and tension by providing shared values. A closer examination of managers, employees, and ethics underscores the importance of a symbolic lifeboat.

***Managers.*** Managers are faced with conflicting demands regarding how they should act. After examining the current literature on leadership, a manager could conclude that appropriate behavior includes being enthusiastic but calm, very friendly and approachable but always keeping a distance, candid but a very quiet and deep thinker, firm but flexible, tough but compassionate, and very serious while having a great sense of humor. As if these expectations were not difficult enough to reconcile, organizations pursuing a path of renewal and growth expect managers to foster teamwork and entrepreneurship. How can managers fulfill these apparently contradictory behaviors? The answer, for many, is by accepting the symbolic norms of the job, department, and organization. In some cases, the norms call for control over collaboration (e.g., bureaucracies). In others, anarchy over discipline (e.g., highly creative firms). The excellent organizations have discovered that harmony can be produced through healthy conflict, managers can manage best by learning from first-line employees, listening is power, deviance can be a productive norm, strength can be drawn from vulnerability, change is facilitated through stability, and work can be fun (Biddle, 1988, pp. 39–40; Bradford & Cohen, 1984, pp. 283–289). Managers can draw on the myths, stories, and organizational history to form rough guidelines for their behavior. Because leaders can be expected to be evangelists or psychologists, as well as organizers of work, trafficking in images as a means for resolving paradoxes is a viable, and much used, response (Duncan, 1989, p. 229).

*Employees.*   Organizational members provide a second example. The entire organizing process is filled with paradoxes (Poole & Van De Ven, 1989). Organizational cultures direct individuals toward the solution. Most people do not ponder and are not privy to the organization's plan of action. Instead they are guided by the symbolic messages sent by the culture, manager, or work group.

Clearly there are situations where a generalized response would be inappropriate. *Strategic ambiguity* allows for multiple interpretations by individuals in an organization to the overriding culture (Eisenberg, 1984). So, service can be an overriding goal, but the methods for adequately fulfilling this mandate can be determined by the individual. Many hospitals have rigid structures and hierarchies with clear job functions outlined and a top-down control orientation designed to control costs. At the same time, everyone is called on to perform excellent, individualized patient care. Depending on the quality of the symbolic messages, which is critically tied to the ongoing reinforcement, hospital employees may be able to negotiate this difficult dilemma.

Concepts such as "less is more" when it comes to writing a memo or revising a report, or K.I.S.S. (Keep It Simple, Stupid) when giving instructions or training a new associate, seem paradoxical unless the cultural messages consistently are reinforcing the expected behavior. Our earlier discussion of whistleblowing or glorifying the announcing of mistakes demonstrates how organizational members' attempts to resolve conflicting demands can be helped or hindered. Whistleblowing, in particular, brings us to our third area of interest.

*Ethics.*   One of the best paradigms for showing how the culture provides the direction or tools to deal with uncertainty is ethics. Although many organizations and business people are highly ethical, other organizations seem to provide lip service (Toffler, 1987). Because most organizations must make a profit and be careful "not to give away the store" when conducting business, members can be faced with serious ethical dilemmas. Examples abound. Not reporting health and safety violations or hoping a warranty will run out before an identifiable problem becomes too severe are tempting routes for some business people. Companies, such as Union Carbide and USX, have underreported injuries to avoid Occupational Safety and Health Administration (OSHA) inspections. Information-based machinery, such as computer terminals, may be causing serious problems for the operators. In recent years E. F. Hutton Group Inc. received a $7 million fine for check kiting and General Electric was fined $1.04 million for defrauding the Air Force of $800,000 (Dresang, 1986).

Employees face ethical decisions such as whether to accept gifts from vendors, pad expense accounts, or make personal phone calls at work. The E. F. Hutton employees found guilty of 2,000 counts of mail and wire fraud probably thought they were doing the company a favor, or somehow were trying to advance their own standing based on the prevailing culture. Some critics argue that business ethics is an oxymoron because winning is always rewarded and winning is defined as making a profit.

When the employee or manager may have to decide between the ethical and the profitable, a strong symbolic message supported by a rich cultural heritage can provide help (Peters & Austin, 1985, pp. 68–97). For example, rather than be faced with a set of mixed messages including do everything you can to please the customer and keep your costs down, or give attention to each individual but keep moving from customer to customer so no one waits, excellent customer service organizations make it clear that the customer is always most important (Albrecht, 1988, pp. 62–71). Too often, organizations call for excellent customer service for the frontline employees and managers, but people evaluating the performance of a work unit focus on cost-control measures. Unless employees are empowered to answer the call for better customer service, they are likely to question any excessive cost incurred while satisfying a customer (Cone, 1989).

These seven propositions provide a backdrop for understanding symbolic behavior. We now examine the means used to carry out symbolic activities. We are providing a brush-stroke approach because many of the functions of symbolic behavior have been examined repeatedly in our earlier discussions.

## TOOLS OF SYMBOLIC BEHAVIOR

Anything that provides symbolic meaning to people can be considered a tool. Not only is this consistent with our perspective and definition of organizational communication, it also explains why the manipulation of symbols can be difficult. Examples of the use of symbolic tools have been peppered throughout the first seven chapters. Let us return to some of the categories to further explain symbolic behavior.

### Verbal and Nonverbal Communication

Verbal and nonverbal communication provide symbolic meaning (Koehler, Anatol, & Applbaum, 1981, p. 46). As Deetz (1982) put it, "The conceptual distinctions in an organization are inscribed in the system of speaking and writing" (p. 135). The values of the culture are underscored by the vocabulary because what is talked about receives attention. A partial list of verbal behaviors includes stories, myths, rituals, fantasies, ceremonies, titles, and jokes (e.g., chapter 4). Nonverbal behavior and objects create an additional set of symbolic actions through events, activities, and surroundings (e.g., chapter 5). Stories, titles, slogans, attention, dress standards, and priorities should suffice as support for verbal and nonverbal communication's role.

As you read the following discussion of stories, note the highlighted uses and values. Stories allow the organization to coordinate action at a distance. As they are told and retold, people are reminded of key values. Not only is a common thread provided, but during the sharing process general guidelines develop and are reinforced allowing organizational members to customize diagnoses and solutions to local problems. According to Weick (1988), "Stories are important, not just because they coordinate, but also because they register, summarize, and allow *reconstruction of scenarios that are too complex for logical linear summaries to preserve* [italics added]" (p. 31).

Stories provide guidance to individuals in all organizations. In addition to setting the rules, they can serve "as metaphors for the bureaucracy-busting essential to vitalization of a decentralized company. Bill Hewlett, co-founder of Hewlett-Packard, visited a plant on Saturday and discovered a lab stock area locked. He wanted scientists to have access to labs when they wanted. So, he went to maintenance, grabbed a bolt cutter, and cut the padlock off the lab stock door. He left a note asking them never to bolt the door again signed 'Thanks, Bill' " (Waterman, 1987, p. 267). The story, as it is told and retold, provides actions underscoring changes in the culture, supports innovation, and deals with employees in a personal manner.

Numerous organizations pay attention to titles. In moving from a traditional bank to a merchant bank, Bankers Trust changed titles from senior vice president to partners, and loan officers to associates. According to Waterman (1987), "By paying attention to the messages embedded in titles and rewards, they communicated to everyone that there were some significant changes in 'the way we do things around here' " (p. 268). Viewing employees as associates has assisted numerous organizations in shifting both the subordinates' and superiors' views of reality.

Slogans and attention highlight employee interest. Waterman (1987) suggested, "Use symbols to strengthen what you communicate verbally about your priorities. There's nothing like a well-placed slogan or an unexpected bit of adventure to kick off a new priority. It's amazing how much T-shirts and coffee mugs can do to help focus attention that 'something's changed around here' " (p. 275).

Dress standards are another pervasive example. As Waterman (1987) explained, "The most effective symbols are symbolic and functional. What symbol, for instance, could be more powerful and pervasive than the IBM white shirt? It presents a quandary to IBM competitors. Do we wear a white shirt and appear imitative, or do we wear striped and colored shirts and appear to be somehow less professional?" (pp. 265–266).

Finally, the priorities placed on daily activities in an organization carry enormous symbolic impact. The top officers at Federal Express spend a substantial amount of time on minor personnel grievances as symbolic proof of their people orientation. The senior vice president of personnel at Federal Express observed: "The president and chairman are dead serious about making sure employees are treated fairly. So they spend time on it. If they can spend three or four hours a week on grievances, it is a good symbol" (Levering et al., 1985, pp. 110–111). Although many managers would respond "Where can I find the time?" these individuals underscore the point that time ultimately is saved when people identify with the organization.

These examples might lead you to believe that strong organizations and effective leadership should be centered on symbolic behavior. Although there is a significant amount of evidence leading to that conclusion, there are serious drawbacks.

## LIMITATIONS OF SYMBOLIC BEHAVIOR

Just as human relations was overused following the Hawthorne Studies, an overreliance on symbolic activities can lead to significant problems. These include unethical manipulation, empty or meaningless actions, omnipresence, divisions, and unexpected interpretations.

### Unethical Manipulation

First, it can be unethical. As Waterman (1987) put it, "Because symbolism is such a potent source of influence, it can be used to manipulate people. We all know of the ways it has been put to use in the past" (p. 271). False promises, pie-in-the-sky approaches, and dangerous work assignments are good examples. Skipping over the abuses by some evangelists and used-car dealers, employees and managers can be misled. The use of gimmickry, superficial pleasantness to cover up dishonest activities or intentions, or providing untrue explanations for behaviors are means used by unethical organizations, managers, or co-workers in order to obtain some advantage.

### Full of Sound and Fury, Signifying Nothing

Second, symbolic behavior can be used in place of substance. According to Waterman (1987), on the organizational level:

> . . . symbolic behavior can be a substitute for doing what you are supposed to do. It can convincingly give the appearance that you are going along with written or unwritten rules and norms, while all along you are undercutting them. Dick Huber of Citicorp, who spent many years in Brazil, has a neat Portuguese phrase that describes this phenomenon: *paro Inglese ver*. Literally, it means, "for the Englishmen to see." In practice it manifests as the make-work boondoggles, procrastinations and rear guard actions that look like cooperative activity, even though those involved have absolutely no intention of doing what's wanted. (p. 271)

The U.S. Navy, when they began the Polaris submarine project in the 1950s, used a management center, weekly meetings, and the PERT (Performance, Evaluation, and Review Technique) to demonstrate to observers the care being taken in making decisions. In fact, these three factors, although providing an excellent facade, were not very influential in the outcome. PERT, for example, provided an excellent image. As Deal and Kennedy (1982) explained, "PERT's real value was in convincing the outside world that this project was important" (p. 70).

Organizations invest large amounts of time and money to develop teamwork, yet they may not know what the end product should look like and often assume that a lack of "unsportsmanlike conduct" means teamwork is occurring. Therefore the efforts can be misspent. In 210 B.C., Pertonius Arbiter observed: "We trained hard, but it seemed that every time we were beginning to form into teams, we would be reorganized. I was to learn later in life that we tend to meet any new situation by reorganizing, and what a wonderful method it can be for creating the illusion of progress while producing confusion, inefficiency, and demoralization."

Individuals also can be co-opted by symbolism over substance. Leaders can develop a vested interest in preserving the corporate mythologies. As Zaleznik (1989) put it, "Leadership believes in and passes on and acculturates new groups in, generation after generation (these myths, thereby creating a loss of leadership. People at the top become) ill prepared to lead in the direction of change" (p. 14). Although myths are important, leaders must be careful not to be pulled into a fantasy. Zaleznik observed, "They must remain highly objective and have the capacity to look at the world as it is" (p. 14). If leaders are crippled or blinded by an outdated mythology or supported by an incorrect ethnocentrism, they will misunderstand the real nature of the world they live in (Dalziel & Schoonover, 1988, p. 50). Myths are helpful in dealing with paradoxes, but they can be counterproductive when responses to a changing environment are required. People actually may believe the myths and forget the allegorical nature of the stories and heroes.

In addition, symbolic behavior can replace accomplishment. Without meaning to, we can get caught up in the *activity trap* where style gets substituted for substance (Robbins, 1980). In some organizations, the pressure to be productive can be so overbearing that individuals make certain they look busy even when there is nothing to do. Adding to the problem is the tendency toward *chronic externalitis*. This is the term given to the obsession some managers have in creating a successful image of themselves in the minds of others (Strasser & Loebs, 1985). Overdependence on symbolic messages can lead to an overpowering culture.

## Omnipresence

The symbolic messages can prevent effective change or realistic responses to environmental demands. Esprit de corps, for example, also can lead to a *trained incapacity* regarding external information or influence (Folger & Poole, 1984, pp. 65–66). We discussed groupthink, freezethink, and the impact of collective perception. Because cultures create identification and unity (Tompkins & Cheney, 1983), these trained incapacities can occur in three areas where values are strong or the culture's influence is too pervasive. It is not difficult to find examples. American auto manufacturers operated as if Japanese competition was unimportant. Retailing giants disregarded the impact of discount stores such as Walmart or K-Mart.

Specifically, obsolescence, resistance to change, and inconsistency are the three risks posed by strong values (Deal & Kennedy, 1982, pp. 34–36). All three of these issues can occur with organizations that have gone on an expansion and acquisitions binge, where more is better and diversity is a virtue. The value of growth can blind organizational members to the realities of the marketplace.

Sears and Roebuck provides a familiar example encompassing all three problems. For years a leader in selling to middle-American consumers, Sears failed to recognize the changing expectations of its clientele (Deal & Kennedy, 1982, p. 35). Faced with lagging sales, Sears tried to go upscale with its product line. This shift left the original consumers behind. More fundamentally, Sears employees, for years selling highly functional—if not very glamorous—merchandise, were poorly trained to sell Macy's type products. In an attempt to overcome this malady, Sears reversed itself and slashed prices to appeal to the K-Mart and Walmart loyalists (Diamond, 1991). These maneuvers demonstrate the potential problems with strong values. The original Sears organization was stale and riddled with obsolescent values. When the organization was recast, employees were resistant to change and customers were not interested in a new Sears (Kelly, 1990). Finally, Sears presented an inconsistent message to the public and employees by reversing itself and trying to compete with the discount chains.

Customer service is a second example (Albrecht, 1988). In trying to enhance the quality of customer service, the messages to employees are often out of date (e.g., service programs can be measured and controlled through customer feedback forms), recalcitrant (e.g., service is important, but do not really believe customers), and contradictory (e.g., control costs no matter what). The strong cultural values tend to be top-down, control oriented leading to a disbelief on the part of employees in the new messages calling for a customer service-based culture.

Strong cultures dictate roles and performances, which means individuals can be co-opted by the culture and its messages (Conrad, 1985, pp. 204–208). Although strict adherence to cultural expectations can be vital, such as in the military during combat, there are numerous examples where this can create tunnel vision. We already discussed ethics. Police psychologists argue the alienation between many law enforcement officers and the public is the result of a sick police subculture (Meredith, 1984). Although police must react effectively in life and death situations, the officers' subculture demands a we/they, good guys/bad guys perspective that prevents good judgment. Idealistic young officers begin to mimic the posture and activities, buttressed by the cultural messages contained in police policies, procedures, and actions, and soon respond to issues of law and order based on actions sanctioned by the subculture. The strong police subculture, supported by the very real life-threatening situations and pressure from the public, creates a singlemindedness that can be counterproductive. Earlier we pointed to cultures as effective means for directing individuals during paradoxical situations. Clearly, this direction can lead to errors in organizational and individual behavior.

## Fosters Divisions

The schism between police officers and the public leads to the fourth problem with symbols. Symbols also can create great divisions in an organization. Culture provides both division and unity, and the symbols used to reinforce the organization can create a powerful alienation between individuals and groups.

Titles and rank, as indications of advancement and accomplishment, also reinforce differences between individuals and provide a potential for we/they thinking and acting. The impact of parking spaces, time clocks, and numerous other nonverbal artifacts on the organization's members was discussed earlier.

## Unexpected Interpretations

Finally, symbolism can be unpredictable. Because individuals respond to symbolic behavior through their own frame of reference, attempts to use symbolism can have unintended results. As Waterman (1987) observed, "When Ford Motor wanted to emphasize quality back in 1979, it put a bunch of Japanese cars in the plant to show employees what you could do if you really put your mind to quality. The result was that employees went out and bought Japanese cars" (p. 270). Rather than accept quality as a goal, Ford employees accepted Japanese cars as better cars. Fortunately, Ford recognized the misinterpretation and worked harder at making "Quality is Job 1" clear, as we discussed earlier in this text.

In other cases, when there is a powerful management versus employee climate, employees go to great effort to never be labeled a "company man or woman." The bizarre behaviors of true believers, often misguided by their own interpretations of strong symbolic messages, have occurred throughout history. Placed in the context of an organization trying to establish a common theme, our conclusion must be that a judicious use of symbols is necessary or the wrong action based on the right intent can occur. A powerful sense of organizational pride can lead to dysfunctional responses by employees and managers to symbolic messages.

This is not to suggest that unethical manipulation, empty or meaningless actions, omnipresence, divisions, and unexpected interpretations are the only troublesome outcomes from symbolic actions. As a means of highlighting the possible problems, these five issues are instructive. We now consider the logistics of presenting symbolic messages.

## PERFORMANCES

The stage or drama metaphor provides a useful means for understanding how symbolic behavior is carried out through individual role performances and rituals. A dramatistic perspective allows us to view individuals as actors attempting to fulfill roles that are required by the organization's purpose (Burke, 1969, p. 544).

### Role Performance

Learning to act out appropriate roles is a fundamental aspect of human development. Members of organizations find successfully fulfilling role expectations a requirement for success. In a *theatrical* sense, role performance means portraying someone else. The *dramatistic* perspective refers, instead, to an individual's behavior in society. As we learn to recognize and define social situations, we develop appropriate roles for ourselves and others. The enactments occurring provide us with important information regarding the social situation and mold our own performances. In organizations, roles involve doing the work, which can range from specific assigned tasks to practices that are carried out because they fill the needed requirements of the job as expected by the culture (Pacanowsky & O'Donnell-Trujillo, 1982, p. 124). Taken from this perspective, roles are not counterfeit acts, but behaviors that maintain social stability by facilitating predictability in human interaction (Faules & Alexander, 1978, p. 62). Role constitutes those behaviors necessary to be accepted by others as a colleague, boss, manager, leader, or organizational member. The better the presentation, the higher the credibility assigned, leading to the bestowing of status, position, office, or acceptance.

Three elements in a presentation are an *appropriate front, dramatic realization,* and *mystification* (Goffman, 1959, pp. 22, 30, 67). We make choices about how we want to present our role, which constitutes role enactment.

***Appropriate Front.*** Putting on an appropriate front (e.g., choice of clothes, language, facial expressions, gestures, posture) provides messages to support the role. In theory, we decide to present a drama to an audience, which can be a consumer, a manager, or a colleague. As Goffman (1974) put it, "Indeed, it seems that we spend most of our time not engaged in giving information but in giving shows" (p. 508).

Some individuals seem more adept at saying and doing the right thing at the right time, thereby avoiding malapropisms with some regularity. The role abilities of the individual often determine the acceptability of the act (Pacanowsky & O'Donnell-Trujillo, 1982, p. 130). According to Boulding (1961), "If the role is occupied by individuals who do not have the requisite skills, the image of the role is profoundly modified by all those with whom they come in contact" (p. 105).

Role performance has a situational legitimacy that underscores the symbolic nature of organizational experience. Conrad (1985) observed, "The culture of the organization provides the background in which specific situations arise. It establishes broad parameters for acting" (p. 201). We learn to establish credibility through making the appropriate choices. Normative criteria, based on relative, situational data, allow us to understand the role expectations. It must be remembered that role performance is episodic and often improvised. So, acting a role is not always easy.

***Dramatic Realization.***   Using verbal and nonverbal symbols to fulfill the requirements of the role leads to dramatic realization. The term *performance* brings with it several important concepts. Performances are contextual based on immediacy and the cultural fit. As Conrad (1985) put it, "Organizational communication is addressed to an audience, whose beliefs, biases, goals, and perceptions of the communicators impose constraints on their actions" (p. 201). This fit between audience expectations and your presentation should not be taken lightly. Myers and Myers (1982) asserted, "Your behavior is fair game of the other person, who constructs meaning out of it and then behaves accordingly" (p. 82). So, employees being corrected for poor performance should seem contrite and a hospital should not lose medical records.

Partaking in scripts to reaffirm the culture occurs in almost all settings. For example, although most surgeons would agree that germs are destroyed in about thirty sec, they scrub down for about seven min before an operation (Deal & Kennedy, 1982, p. 68). To scrub for less than seven min would be to violate cultural expectations, appear ill prepared for the operation, and risk informal censure for not being conscientious. Appropriateness to the culture's rules or scripts is the measuring rod for the appropriate front and achieving dramatic realization. One study found a group they labeled *water walkers*. These high performers were set aside from others by a high degree of empathy and interpersonal relations skills and political savvy in how to interact with people in power (Goleman, 1981). Put another way, they understood how to fulfill the role requirements to the satisfaction of the audience.

Image presentation and impression management are popular concepts for these efforts. McKendrick and Mason (1984) observed, "Experts agree that a manager's image and its fit into a particular culture is of utmost importance" (p. 9). Pressure to present an effective image has spurred a variety of courses and books on how to play the role correctly (Rice, 1982).

Ingratiation, "an attempt by individuals to increase their attractiveness in the eyes of others" (Liden & Mitchell, 1988, p. 573), is a part of impression management that occurs when the actor feels the audience controls significant rewards. Much of the emphasis on image presentation can be seen as a realization that some roles require skills that might not be developed fully, and using the stage metaphor draws attention to the role of the audience (Fenton, 1986; King, 1987).

***Mystification.***   A certain amount of mystification is required to put distance between the actor and the audience. You can draw on the verbal and nonverbal chapters for examples of mystification ranging from the outfitting of an office to the language used by certain professions. An interesting case in point is provided by the tests frequently administered during preemployment and advancement sessions. Personnel tests represent a desire for scientific rigor and underscore American expectations for rationality in making decisions (Trice & Beyer, 1985, p. 373). Because the evaluation procedures, or what the results mean, are rarely shared with the test taker, there is mystification in the hiring or promotion process. The ceremonial aspects of the roles of personnel managers are a paradigm for many of the activities undertaken to promote legitimacy. In some cases, the testing, and other selection techniques, used to justify personnel decisions lack empirically demonstrated effectiveness, but do function as symbolic devices to confer legitimacy. This is possible because organizational members accept the general value orientation that accepts scientific evidence as sufficient to justify actions (Beyer, 1981, p. 171).

Along the same lines, most organizations have a semiofficial procedure for interviewing new candidates which may, or may not, lead to better selection. It does create, however, an aura of selectivity (Deal & Kennedy, 1982, pp. 61–70). Imagine the difference between being hired immediately because you will do as a "warm body" and having to wait for two weeks to know if you have the job. At Nissan in Tennessee, a Japanese-managed company, employees must go through extensive testing and wait before they are hired (Buckley, 1988). At NUMMI (New United Motor Manufacturing Inc.), the Toyota and General Motors joint venture in California, applicants undergo three days of testing, interviewing, and evaluating ("Japanese Management," 1987). This process can be seen as a *ritual of arrival*, which is discussed later in this section. As you prepare for job interviewing, a great deal of the advice for success will center on appropriate role performance, intended to enhance dramatic realization, and hovering over some information that can demystify the entire process. Guarding the entry process into exclusive colleges makes acceptance seem more attractive for some students.

### Rituals

Once roles become systematized, they are regarded as rituals. Rituals are acted out by the performances and encompass all repeated activities. Acting correctly, scrubbing down, and being professional are examples of individual rituals. Rituals provide for organizational reality. For our purposes, it is helpful to focus on the rituals of arrival, full participation, belonging, and exclusion.

**Rituals of Arrival.**   At some point everyone is a newcomer. The rituals of arrival include those processes that explain what we must learn in order to be a bonafide member of the organization. For starters, neophytes rarely are afforded full privileges to use equipment, park close, leave their station, arrange their lunch time, pick their desks, and so on (Wilson et al., 1986, p. 108). Even gaining entry to parts of the organization can be difficult.

*Socialization* is the process of indoctrinating new employees to a company's policies (Pascale, 1984). As Wiener (1988) put it, "Organizational socialization applies primarily to new members because their needs for cultural adaptation are most salient, but it also serves as a means of support and renewal for an existing value system" (p. 543). Employees must know what is expected of them. Organizations such as AT&T have instructional development internship programs to teach the proper ways to act including an orientation to teamwork (Bialac & Willington, 1985). Many organizations have adopted a clear acculturation process to guarantee successful socialization (Harris, 1990, pp. 150–152). A commitment to a mentoring process is another example of making acculturation a corporate value. Extensive interviewing processes provide an important hazing experience that is intended to demonstrate the exclusive nature of the organization.

**Rituals of Belonging and Exclusion.**   Once you are part of an organization, there are rituals of belonging and exclusion. Belonging rituals are indications that you are accepted within the organization and/or work group. Being invited to certain meetings, out for a meal, or into a project can show belonging. At the same time, some groups make it clear that you are excluded.

For example, in numerous organizations, being promoted to supervisor from the ranks also means losing a large number of contacts. You literally are excluded from the ranks. Knowing how to act in a period of individual advancement can offer a difficult test. In one study of workers being promoted to managers, the individuals were required to alter successfully their body, dress, and social communication to act managerial while not changing to the point of losing credibility with their co-workers (Caudill, Durden, & Lambert, 1985). This is a tricky issue because failing to change creates a credibility problem with other managers, and being a "company person" will hurt in the process of managing friends and colleagues.

*Social dramas* occur in every group and reinforce the belonging rituals. The drama is processional and occurs when there is a breach of the symbolic system or a particular problem. Dramas are likely to follow four phases: breach, crisis, redressive action, and reintegration or recognition of the schism (Turner, 1980). In a miniform, an employee talking back to a manager in front of other employees is a breach of etiquette, roles, and rules. The turbulence can be handled in a variety of ways, but a crisis has occurred. Perhaps the employee is suspended; or the manager chooses to dress the individual down in front of everyone else; or the traditional "in my office now!"; or the employee is asked to explain the point further. If someone must apologize, a redressive action has taken place. The same would be true if management decided that the employee was correct, there was recognition of the schism, and reintegration develops with new guidelines regarding employee feedback. The drama acts as a means for reaffirming, negotiating, and/or transforming the cultural standards (Carbaugh, 1985, pp. 42–43).

This discussion provides the final, essential issue to a dramatic presentation. As the performance unfolds, the audience must remain front stage. *Backstage* is the region reserved for members of the cast and a correctly staged act does not allow the audience to gain access. If they do, they might discredit the performance. As the show is put on, dramatic realization requires that the audience not get behind the scene, discover flaws in the act, and discredit the performance (Harris, 1984, pp. 54–56). As Goffman (1959) observed, "All roles require a certain degree of skill in the performance of the role as well as an image of the role itself" (p. 216). Impressions are formed based on very little information (Einhorn, Bradley, & Baird, 1982, p. 74). Although putting on a facade invites scrutiny, failing to forward the proper image invites loss of credibility. Guarding the backstage is important during the entire presentation process, from interviewing to participating in the rituals of arrival, to the period of belonging.

Letting the role take over your entire persona is equally destructive. While the play is the thing, the trick, it would seem, is never letting the act overcome the person. So, congruency, fulfilling of expectations, and coordination among actors (team members) is required. If the concept of backstage is still unclear, you have just been provided with a backstage view of the role of testing by some personnel managers.

Consider a second example. Being a team player, and effectively creating a successful team, are positive attributes. But, according to Frank and Brownell (1989), "no one knows exactly what it means to coordinate work groups. Therefore, rituals or specific procedures are developed in the hope that coordination will result" (p. 216).

The list is almost endless. When you are asked to act like a leader, you seek symbolic manifestations of the correct actions which will make you appear to be a leader with an image of ability and confidence (Johnson, 1987). We coordinate and plan without a clear notion of exactly what these two activities mean (Deal & Kennedy, 1982, pp. 69–70). Expected behavior can be tautological when it takes the form of "we know we have good teamwork when everyone is working well together" or "good leaders get things done." No one should assume that careful hiring practices, including extensive testing, are incorrect. Nor should teamwork be discounted or leadership underrated. The point is simply that we try to act correctly, based on past and current symbolic reinforcements, for dramatic realization. It may very well be that we also achieve excellent leadership and teamwork and hire the correct people.

Labeled *organizational rites*, these are "organized and planned activities that have both practical and expressive consequences . . . when this definition is applied to corporate life, such diverse activities as personnel testing, organizational development programs, and collective bargaining can be seen as rites that have not only practical consequences but also express important cultural meanings" (Trice & Beyer, 1985, pp. 372–373).

Rather than letting the correct behavior requirements occur through osmosis, some organizations explicitly include the communication skills needed to be a good performer on their employee performance and development review forms (Brennan, 1989, p. 462). Other organizations make certain new employees learn the ropes, through extensive training and internships, before they are asked to carry out specific duties. All rituals, rites, and activities take place within a scene.

The scene includes the physical properties and artifacts of the organization, office, and the setting — the organization's environment. According to Wilson et al. (1986), "The term scene refers to the physical and psychological setting as it is enacted by participants in the drama — it is the *interpretation* of the situation, and interpretation charged with *cultural attitudes*, expressed in a vocabulary that *belongs* to it" (p. 131).

When someone correctly understands the scene, this "refers to verbal, nonverbal, and analogical perceptions of meaning about an individual's knowledge and place in the organization" (Wilson et al., 1986, p. 108). Messages occur designed to indicate whether or not you have earned your place within the organization. Often, decisions are routed past an individual who has not attained "rank" or acceptance. The meetings you are allowed to attend can indicate how important you are. When you are denied a hearing for new or altered ideas, are questioned regarding motives, or are forced to accept dismissal from a discussion for the benefit of someone else, you have not been given participation. In the same vein, being asked for suggestions is a positive — not having them implemented or considered indicates the problem with symbolic actions for symbolic actions' sake.

Finally, although we concentrate on intraorganizational symbolic behavior, the external reaction to organizations is vital. The "halo of esteem" underpinning *In Search of Excellence* (Peters & Waterman, 1982) is a good example of the power of image. Opinion Research Corporation reported that 89% of 1,010 adults polled in 1989 said that the reputation of the company often determines which products they buy ("Consumers Care," 1989). Four out of five saw charitable donations as an indication that the companies were more likely to be concerned with satisfying their customers.

So, presentation, image, consistency, and all the other activities so important to a well-staged performance for individuals and groups, apply to organizations.

Performances are a useful place to end our discussion of symbolic behavior. As much as we might like to believe that individuals and organizations can control performances, we also are aware that one cannot not communicate. Regardless of the staging, some individuals will be able to see behind an invalid act and discover flaws. Just as symbolic behavior has drawbacks, our paradigm of performances only illustrates the power of symbolic behavior.

## CONCLUSION

For many individuals studying organizational communication, symbolic behavior is the obvious focal point. Because we are symbol users, and symbol abusers, this attention is well deserved.

Seven propositions outline the power of symbolic behavior in an organization. The following issues are intertwined with symbolic behavior: complexity, uncertainty, cultural creation and maintenance, interpersonal reality, group behavior, leadership, and the management of incongruences.

Tools of symbolic behavior can be identified through various types of verbal and nonverbal communication. What we say and do provides significant symbolic messages.

But symbolic behavior also can lead to extremely negative outcomes. These include unethical manipulation, empty or meaningless actions, trained incapacities, divisions, and unexpected interpretations.

Finally, performances highlight the ongoing role of symbolic behavior in organizations. This dramatistic perspective also draws attention to the danger of believing that acting is the same as performing a useful, justified role in an organization.

At this point, we have examined the perspectives regarding organizational communication in the first three chapters, and then provided an in-depth analysis of the principles of organizational communication in chapters 4 through 8. The remaining chapters offer specific insights into the pragmatics of organizational communication.

## REFERENCES

Albrecht, K. (1988). *At America's service*. Homewood, IL: Dow Jones-Irwin.

Beyer, J. M. (1981). Ideologies, values, and decision making in organizations. In P.C. Nystrom & W. H. Starbuck (Eds.), *Handbook of organizational design: Vol. 2. Remolding organizations and their environments* (pp. 162–184). London: Oxford University Press.

Bialac, D., & Willington, C. (1985). From backpack to briefcase. *Training and Development Journal, 39*, 66–68.

Biddle, B. (1988). The manager's balancing act. *Management World, 17*, 39–40.

Bormann, E. G., Howell, W. S., Nichol, R. G., & Shapiro, G. L. (1982). *Interpersonal communication in the modern organization* (2nd ed.). Englewood Cliffs, NJ: Prentice-Hall.

Boulding, K. E. (1961). *The image: Knowledge and life in society*. Ann Arbor: University of Michigan Press.

Bradford, D. L., & Cohen, A. R. (1984). *Managing for excellence*. New York: Wiley.

Brennan, E. J. (1989). *Performance management workbook*. Englewood Cliffs, NJ: Prentice-Hall.

Brown, M. H. (1986). Sense-making and narrative forms: Reality construction in organizations. In L. Thayer (Ed.), *Organization-communication: Emerging perspectives I* (pp. 68–78). Norwood, NJ: Ablex.

Buckley, J. (1988, May 9). We learned that them may be us. *U.S. News & World Report*. pp. 48–57.

Burke, K. (1969). *The grammar of motives and the rhetoric of motives*. Berkeley: University of California Press.

Cameron, K. (1980, Autumn). Critical questions in assessing organizational effectiveness. *Organizational Dynamics*, pp. 66–75.

Carbaugh, D. (1985). Cultural communication and organizing. In W. B. Gutknecht, L. P. Stewart, & S. Ting-Toomey (Eds.), *Communication, culture, and organizational processes* (pp. 30–47). Beverly Hills, CA: Sage.

Caudill, D. W., Durden, K. A., & Lambert, R. P. (1985). The image management puzzle. *Supervisory Management, 30*, 22–26.

Clancy, J. J. (1989). *The invisible powers: The language of business*. Lexington, MA: Lexington.

Cohen, M. D., & March, J. G. (1974). *Leadership and ambiguity: The American college president*. New York: McGraw-Hill.

Cone, J. (1989). The empowered employee. *Training and Development Journal, 43*, 96–98.

Conrad, C. (1985). *Strategic organizational communication: Cultures, situations, and adaptation*. New York: Holt, Rinehart & Winston.

Consumers care about corporate image. (1989, September). *Psychology Today*, p. 14.

Dalziel, M. M., & Schoonover, S. C. (1988). *Changing ways: A practical tool for implementing change within organizations*. New York: AMACOM.

Daniels, T. D., & Spiker, B. K. (1987). *Perspectives on organizational communication*. Dubuque, IA: Brown.

Deal, T. E., & Kennedy, A. A. (1982). *Corporate cultures: The rites and rituals of corporate life*. Reading, MA: Addison-Wesley.

Deetz, S. A. (1982). Critical interpretative research in organizational communication. *Western Journal of Speech Communication, 46*, 131–149.

Diamond, S. J. (1991, February 17). Endless changes fail to breath life into ailing Sears. *The Birmingham News*, pp. 1D, 6D.

Dresang, J. (1986, December 9). Companies get serious about ethics. *USA Today*, pp. B1–B2.

Dubrin, A. J., Ireland, R. D., & Williams, J. C. (1989). *Management and organization*. Cincinnati: South-Western.

Duncan, H. D. (1962). *Communication and social order*. London: Oxford University Press.

Duncan, H. D. (1968). *Symbols in society*. New York: Oxford University Press.

Duncan, W. J. (1989). Organizational culture: Getting a fix on an elusive concept. *The Academy of Management Executive, 3*, 229–235.

Einhorn, L. J., Bradley, P. H., & Baird, J. E., Jr. (1982). *Effective employment interviewing*. Glenview, IL: Scott, Foresman.

Eisenberg, E. M. (1984). Ambiguity as strategy in organizational communication. *Communication Monographs, 51*, 227–242.

Eisenberg, E. M., & Riley, P. (1988). Organizational symbols and sense-making. In G. M. Goldhaber & G. A. Barnett (Eds.), *Handbook of organizational communication* (pp. 131–150). Norwood, NJ: Ablex.

Faules, D. F., & Alexander, D. C. (1978). *Communication and social behavior: A symbolic interaction perspective*. Reading, MA: Addison-Wesley.

Fenton, L. (1986). *Dress for excellence*. New York: Macmillan.

Folger, J. P., & Poole, M. S. (1984). *Working through conflict: A communication perspective*. Glenview, IL: Scott, Foresman.

Frank, A. D., & Brownell, J. L. (1989). *Organizational communication and behavior: Communicating to improve performance (2 + 2 = 5)*. New York: Holt, Rinehart & Winston.

Goffman, E. (1959). *The presentation of self in everyday life*. Garden City, NY: Anchor Doubleday.

Goffman, E. (1974). *Frame analysis*. New York: Penguin.

Goleman, D. (1981, January). The new competency tests: Matching the right people to the right jobs. *Psychology Today*, pp. 1–16.

Gutknecht, D. G., & Miller, J. R. (1986). *The organizational and human resources sourcebook*. Lanham, MD: University Press of America.

Harris, T. E. (1984). The "faux pas" in interpersonal communication. In S. Thomas (Ed.), *Communication theory and interpersonal attraction* (Vol. 2, pp. 53–61). Norwood, NJ: Ablex.

Harris, T. E. (1990). Organizational cultures: An examination of the role of communication. In S. Thomas & W. A. Evans (Eds.), *Communication and culture: Vol. 4. Language, performance, technology, and media* (pp. 143–155). Norwood, NJ: Ablex.

Japanese management in America: Can it work here too? (1987, November 7). *Employee Relations and Human Resources Bulletin*, pp. 1–3, 6.

Johnson, C. J. (1987). *The achievers*. New York: Dutton.

Jonas, H. S., III, Fry, R. E., & Srivastva, S. (1989). The person of the CEO: Understanding the executive experience. *The Academy of Management Executive, 3*, pp. 205–215.

Kelly, K. (1990, November 12). At Sears, the more things change . . . *Business Week*, pp. 66–68.

Kerr, J., & Slocum, J. W. (1987). Managing corporate culture through reward systems. *The Academy of Management Executive, 1*(2), pp. 99–107.

King, N. (1987). *The first five minutes*. New York: Prentice-Hall.

Koehler, J. W., Anatol, K. W. E., & Applbaum, R. L. (1981). *Organizational communication: Behavioral perspectives* (2nd ed.). New York: Holt, Rinehart & Winston.

Kotter, J. P. (1988). *The leadership factor*. New York: Free Press.

Kreps, G. L. (1986). *Organizational communication*. New York: Longman.

Levering, R., Moshowitz, M., & Katz, M. (1985). *The 100 best companies to work for in America*. New York: New American Library.

Liden, R. C., & Mitchell, T. R. (1988). Ingratiatory behaviors in organizational settings. *The Academy of Management Review, 13*(4), pp. 572–587.

McKendrick, J., & Mason, J. (1984). Managing your image. *Management World, 13*, pp. 9–11.

Mead, G. H. (1934). *Mind, self, and society*. Chicago: University of Chicago Press.

Meredith, N. (1984, May). Attacking the roots of police violence. *Psychology Today*, pp. 21–26.

Mitzberg, H. (1991, Winter). The effective organization: Forces and forms. *Sloan Management Review*, pp. 54–67.

Myers, M. T., & Myers, G. E. (1982). *Managing by communication: An organizational approach*. New York: McGraw-Hill.

Overington, M. A. (1977). Kenneth Burke as social theorist. *Sociological Inquiry, 47*(2), 128–140.

Pacanowsky, M. E., & O'Donnell-Trujillo, N. (1982). Communication and organizational cultures. *Western Journal of Speech Communication, 46*, 115–130.

Pacanowsky, M. E., & O'Donnell-Trujillo, N. (1983). Organizational communication as cultural performance. *Communication Monographs, 50*, 477–481.

Pascale, R. (1984, May). Fitting new employees into the company culture. *Fortune*, pp. 28–30, ff.

Peters, T. (1989). Making it happen. *Journal of Quality and Participation, 12*, 1–7.

Peters, T., & Austin, N. (1985). *A passion for excellence: The leadership difference*. New York: Random House.

Peters, T. J., & Waterman, R. H., Jr. (1982). *In search of excellence: Lessons from America's best-run companies*. New York: Harper & Row.

Petrelle, J. L., Slaughter, G. Z., & Jorgensen, J. D. (1988). New explorations in organizational relationships: An expectancy model of human symbolic activity. *The Southern Speech Communication Journal, 53*, 279–296.

Pfeffer, J. (1981). Management as symbolic action: The creation and maintenance of organizational paradigms. In L. O. Cummings & B. M. Staw (Eds.), *Research in organizational behavior* (Vol. 3, pp. 1–52). Greenwich, CT: JAI.

Poole, M. C., & Van De Ven, A. H. (1989). Using paradox to build management and organizational theories. *Academy of Management Review, 14*, 562–578.

Putnam, L. L. (1982). Paradigms for organizational communication research: An overview and synthesis. *Western Journal of Speech Communication, 46*, 192–206.

Putnam, L. L. (1983). The interpretive perspective: An alternative to functionalism. In L. L. Putnam & M. E. Pacanowsky (Eds.), *Communication and organizations: An interpretive approach* (pp. 31–54). Beverly Hills, CA: Sage.

Raelin, J. A. (1989). An anatomy of autonomy: Managing professionals. *The Academy of Management Executive, 3*, 216–228.

Redding, W. C. (1984). *The corporate communication manager's guide to better communication*. Glenview, IL: Scott, Foresman.

Rice, B. (1982, September). Adventures in the image trade. *Psychology Today*, pp. 6–11.

Robbins, S. (1980). *The administrative process*. Englewood Cliffs, NJ: Prentice-Hall.

Schein, E. H. (1985). *Organizational culture and leadership*. San Francisco: Jossey-Bass.

Stephen, T. (1986). Communication and interdependence in geographically separated relationships. *Human Communication Research, 13*(2), 192–205.

Strasser, S., & Loebs, S. F. (1985). Viewpoint: Have our shirts become too starched? *Health Care Management Review, 10*, 81–90.

Thayer, L. O. (1961). *Administrative communication*. Homewood, IL: Irwin.

Ting-Toomey, S. (1985). Toward a theory of conflict and culture. In W. B. Gutknecht, L. T. Stewart, & S. Ting-Toomey (Eds.), *Communication, culture, and organizational processes* (pp. 71–86). Beverly Hills, CA: Sage.

Toffler, B. L. (1987). *Tough choices: Managers talk ethics.* Homewood, IL: Wiley.

Tompkins, P. K. (1987). Translating organizational theory: Symbolism over substance. In F. M. Jablin, L. L. Putnam, K. H. Roberts, & L. W. Porter (Eds.), *Handbook of organizational communication* (pp. 70–96). Newbury Park, CA: Sage.

Tompkins, P. K., & Cheney, G. (1983). Account analysis of organizations: decision making and identification. In L. Putnam & M. E. Pacanowsky (Eds.), *Communication in organizations: An interpretative approach* (pp. 123–146). Beverly Hills, CA: Sage.

Trice, H. M., & Beyer, J. M. (1985). Six organizational rites to change culture. In R. H. Killman, M. J. Saxton, R. Serpa, & Associates (Eds.), *Gaining control of the corporate culture* (pp. 368–379). San Francisco: Jossey-Bass.

Turner, V. (1980). Social dramas and stories about them. *Critical Inquiry, 7,* 141–168.

Waterman, R. H., Jr. (1987). *The renewal factor.* New York: Bantam.

Weick, K. E. (1979). *The social psychology of organizing* (2nd ed.). Reading, MA: Addison-Wesley.

Weick, K. E. (1988). Organizational cultures as a source of high reliability. In J. L. Gibson, J. M. Ivancevich, & J. H. Donnelly, Jr. (Eds.), *Organizations close-up: A book of readings* (6th ed., pp. 22–38). Plano, TX: Business Publications.

Wiener, Y. (1988). Forms of value systems: A focus on organizational effectiveness and cultural change and maintenance. *The Academy of Management Review, 13*(4), 534–545.

Wilkins, A. A., & Dyer, W. G., Jr. (1988). Toward culturally sensitive theories of cultural change. *The Academy of Management Review, 13*(4), 522–533.

Wilson, G. L., Goodall, H. L., Jr., & Waagen, C. L. (1986). *Organizational communication.* New York: Harper & Row.

Wood, J. T. (1982). *Human communication: A symbolic interactionist perspective.* New York: Holt, Rinehart & Winston.

Zaleznik, A., (1989, November 26). Freud and organizations. *The New York Times,* Sec. 4, p. 14.

# Effective Interpersonal Communication in Organizations

Communication between individuals is a major component of organizational behavior at every level. Supervisory and managerial workshops call it face-to-face communication, management textbooks label it person-to-person communication, college courses and majors are titled interpersonal communication, studies focus on dyadic communication, and national training organizations concentrate on human interaction.

Interpersonal communication is the process of transacting meaning between individuals. These relationships are the basic social units of an organization and are vital to your success (Kreps, 1990, p. 50). Some scholars consider dyadic organizational communication the most important type, because it is responsible for getting most of the work done, has significant impact on the climate, and is often the source of difficulties (Goldhaber, Dennis, Richetto, & Wilo, 1979, p. 104). A large body of research supports the importance of effective managerial and supervisory communication with subordinates (Daniels & Spiker, 1987, p. 147). This is a two-way street with managers and supervisors expecting subordinates to be effective communicators (DiSalvo, Dunning, & Homan, 1982). A recent survey of personnel administrators in 428 organizations ranked interpersonal skills as the most important requirement for successful job performance (Curtis, Winsor, & Stephens, 1989). This should be a familiar conclusion to you based on our analysis of the importance of effective listening earlier in this text.

Face-to-face communication can consume 70% to 80% of your time in organizations (Klauss & Bass, 1982, p. 3; Klemmer & Snyder, 1972). This is not really a surprising statistic. You will use interpersonal communication when you interview for a job, learn about specific duties, operate on a day-by-day basis, lead and manage others, go to company-sponsored social events, participate in the mentoring process, sell, take part in numerous specialized issues and events (e.g., perform-

**283**

ance appraisals, coaching sessions), and have meals or enjoy social events with your colleagues. In addition, numerous formats are used for interpersonal communication including informal talks, planned appointments, telephone calls, interoffice memos, letters, and reports.

With 10 million American workers switching jobs every year (Lewis, 1990), and the average worker having six employers during their lifetime ("Jobs Still," 1989), you will find it necessary to adapt your interpersonal skills to each workplace, position, and culture. A survey of 2,000 people who have relocated or been promoted, by the management consulting firm of Moran, Stahl, and Boyer, found that it took these individuals around 8 months to adjust and get up to speed ("Relocation Adjustment," 1987). A good deal of the adjustment time was spent in learning particulars about the new position or job by adapting their interpersonal communication skills.

For organizations, "communication is the linking pin between plans and action" (Bittel, 1985, p. 289). For example, at the new Saturn automobile plant, General Motors' innovative answer to Japanese manufacturers, interpersonal skills are considered much more important than technical ones (Treece, 1990). On a broader scale, communication between employees and their immediate supervisors is a key influence on employee happiness and productivity (Pincus, 1985). Interpersonal communication is a vital part of innovation. DrugCorp found that "interpersonal communication provided researchers with their most important channels of access to information and stimulation of new ideas" (Zuboff, 1988, p. 363). One study determined that personal communication was the crucial factor in 80% of the cases of innovation (Zuboff, 1989).

Earlier chapters have focused on important aspects of effective interpersonal communication, including communication and systems (chapter 1), perception (chapter 2), verbal (chapter 4) and nonverbal (chapter 5) communication, networks and channels (chapter 6), listening and feedback (chapter 7), symbolic behavior—a cornerstone of communication (chapter 8), and the impact of managerial and organizational theory and practice (chapter 3). You should incorporate the concepts provided in those chapters as you develop your understanding of interpersonal communication (Sashkin & Morris, 1984, p. 117). To put it in perspective, effective interpersonal communication, as the basic social unit of an organization, is considered a prerequisite to success, consumes a significant portion of the working day, must be adaptable, and covers a broad range of activities.

This chapter outlines the functions of interpersonal communication in organizations, examines the three definitions of interpersonal communication, looks at differences in perspectives regarding transactions, explains how humans process information, discusses interpersonal communication effectiveness from an interactive management and a humanistic perspective, and concludes with an analysis of social styles, transactional analysis, superior–subordinate transactions, interviewing, and coaching. Because the interpersonal communication in organizations can differ significantly from our daily dyadic conversations, these concepts provide important stepping-stones toward a theoretical and a practical understanding of organizational communication.

## FUNCTIONS OF INTERPERSONAL COMMUNICATION IN ORGANIZATIONS

Although interpersonal communication in organizations shares a large number of attributes with our day-to-day friendships, two task-oriented characteristics differentiate it. First, we are hired to accomplish something. Organizations are goal oriented with their chief concern being the output of goods, services, or information (Cushman & Cahn, 1985, p. 101). When we accept a job with an IBM, the Red Cross, or the local grocery chain, we are expected to assist in achieving specific and general goals. Organizations require a *co-orientation* of behavior, which "involves the elicitation of behavioral coordination among communicators for the accomplishment of commonly recognized goals" (Kreps, 1990, p. 149). Organizations are purposeful and the expectations are that employees will work toward common goals.

Second, individuals rely on others to get the work done. Organized behavior is the heart of an organization and organizational membership means more restrictions on our behaviors (Sashkin & Morris, 1984, p. 22). The majority of interpersonal communication is based on prediction making. As Miller (1990) said, "When people communicate with others, they make predictions about the probable outcomes, or consequences, of differing message strategies, or alternative message selections" (p. 97). In organizations, the higher the level of predictability between colleagues, the greater sense of comfort everyone is likely to feel about working together. The corollary to this statement also holds. The more your co-workers can depend on you, the greater the trust and comfort.

Goal orientation and reliance on others are important concepts for clarifying the role of interpersonal communication in organizations. Although getting along with others and making friends are important skills, they are insufficient interpersonal skills to keep a job. Put another way, organizations view communication as primarily work/task oriented and socioemotional/person oriented (Cummings, Long, & Lewis, 1983, pp. 38–39). You should make a mental note regarding this division. Almost every management style test is based on how you respond to the two variables of task and people.

There are three general types of messages sent: task, maintenance, and human (Redding & Danborn, 1964, p. 43). *Task messages*, or getting the job done, concern the organization's services, products, or activities. *Maintenance messages* are policy centered and deal with regulation. *Human messages* concern the morale, attitudes, and accomplishments of people within the organization (Baird, 1978, p. 7). A recent survey asked personnel decision makers at 1,104 U.S. companies of all types and sizes how much time they thought was spent on small talk by employees

("Small Talk," 1987). Sixty-four percent said the average worker spends at least 30 min a day in discussions about things such as football, families, and weekend activities. Twenty-eight percent said it was more than an hour. Most important, the majority of the bosses thought the non-business-oriented talk was excellent for morale and camaraderie.

Being able to get along with people is the human relations perspective discussed in chapter 3. When this is combined with getting the job done, developing subordinates, and experiencing personal growth, we have moved into the human resources perspective. Concepts such as trust, belief in the importance of employees, responsibility, empathy, open climate, self-disclosure, supportive communication, and understanding are all used to explain the important factors in successful dyadic relationships in an organization (Goldhaber, 1986, pp. 220–232). Each of these issues is discussed later in the chapter.

In summary, communication is necessary to get the work done. One means for understanding the different uses of interpersonal communication is to examine its task, person, and socioemotional functions. However, a more complete definition would seem to be in order. Three definitions of interpersonal communication are available—componential, situational, and developmental (DeVito, 1989, p. 3).

## DEFINING INTERPERSONAL COMMUNICATION

The most obvious means of defining interpersonal communication is to identify the components or elements of the process. A second definition focuses on the situation. The last definition suggests that interpersonal relationships are developmental. Each of these definitions deserves further discussion.

### Componential Definition

Before turning to the situational and developmental definitions, we examine the componential definition. In chapter 1, we discounted linear explanations that depict communication as a one-way process from a sender to a receiver. Instead we opted for a dynamic, ongoing process orientation based on the premise one cannot not communicate (Berlo, 1960; Dance, 1967). Most *transactional* models accept that communication is:

1. A process involving
2. both purposive and expressive messages
3. composed of multiunit and
4. multilevel signals that
5. depend on the context for their meanings
6. interpreted by the interactants (Haworth & Savage, 1989, p. 234).

Figure 9.1 shows a communication model with many of the components involved in the process. In all interpersonal communication situations, there are certain *universals* that are present and a model offers us a means for appreciating the complexity of the transaction process, outlining of areas of potential communication difficulties, and isolating variables (DeVito, 1989, pp. 4–11).

There are obvious advantages to the modeling approach to defining interpersonal communication. The graphic display of components allows us to identify factors and understand more fully the issues involved in communication. At the same time, in examining the model, you are probably struck with the feeling that there must be more to interpersonal communication.

Two important factors missing from the model are the ability to coordinate our activities with another and the possibility of developing lasting relationships. These suggest two additional definitions for examining interpersonal communication. The first argues that dyadic communication is different because of the situation. The second suggests that the development of the dyadic relationship is the most important defining characteristic. With the first, the relationship is *interpenetrative* whereas with the second the relationship hinges on *social penetration*.

## Situational Definition

The interdependence created by a dyad is the most obvious characteristic of interpersonal communication (Smith & Williamson, 1985, p. 27). Organizations establish these interlocking relationships to coordinate work. According to Wilmot (1979), "The dyad begins to function when there is the possibility of the actions of each person affecting the other" (p. 9). So, superior–subordinate relationships, colleagues in a department or office, project team members, or any other working combination are, by definition, examples of interpersonal communication. Once meaning is as-

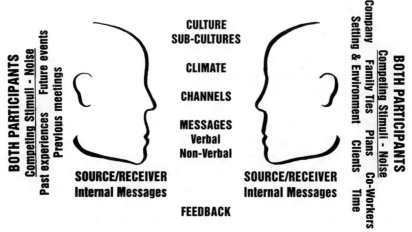

FIG. 9.1.   A transactional communication model.

signed to behavior, communication occurs (Wilmot, 1979, pp. 8–10). Each person affects and is affected by the other person's behavior – their relations are interpenetrative (Wilmot, 1979, p. 13).

This codependence is a critical factor in many working situations. You cannot refuse to work with someone because you do not want to be their friend, and you must cooperate with other people to accomplish many of your assigned tasks. Working effectively with co-workers, bosses, customers, and subordinates is important. These interactions are structured through socially established rules for appropriate and inappropriate behavior, mutual role expectations, and focused attention by each person on the other (DeVito, 1989, p. 15). In fact, the inability to get along with others is the number two reason for employees getting fired ("Personnel Problems," 1990). The others are incompetence (first), dishonesty (third), negative attitude (fourth), and lack of motivation (fifth). On the other side of the coin, the ability to get along with others is the second most important attribute for getting ahead according to *The Wall Street Journal* (Nirenberg, 1989, p. 42). Integrity is the first. Fostering codependence, it would seem, is a prerequisite to keeping a job and advancing. Both the componential and situational definitions of interpersonal communication provide excellent insights, but in many cases there is more to the interpersonal relationship.

## Developmental Definition

Many relationships evolve from work-related interdependence to genuine friendships. This *developmental* perspective focuses on interpersonal communication in organizations as it progresses from first introductions onto the numerous paths any dyad may travel (Miller, 1990, p. 95). This perspective underscores the point that friendships depend on social penetration (Altman & Taylor, 1973), or a willingness to go beyond superficial exchanges regarding the weather, time, or sports. Habitual and routine dyadic experiences (e.g., greetings, leave taking, signing in) do not really demonstrate an interpersonal relationship (Ableson, 1976). Even though the situation is between individuals, the relationship is impersonal.

A relationship is likely to become interpersonal if physical proximity, attitude similarity, and need complementarity occur (Miller, 1990, pp. 104–106). In a nutshell, we are more likely to become friends with someone when (a) we interact with them, (b) we hold somewhat similar attitudes toward social, political, and economic issues, and (c) they somehow meet certain of our psychological needs.

When we first start working with someone, physical proximity is automatic. During the initial stages of the relationship, much of our interpersonal communication is focused on *uncertainty reduction* (Berger, Gardner, Parks, Shulman, & Miller, 1976). In order to understand how to proceed in a relationship, the participants seek information that will help them communicate more effectively. In other words, we want to know what to say after we say hello. Verbal and nonverbal clues, offered during these initial meetings, allow the participants to apply meaning to the relationship. As you are already aware, our judgments are somewhat faulty, but they still provide us with some predictability regarding future interactions. Next time you meet someone, monitor your efforts as you paint a mental picture about the other person so you can interact effectively. In fact, you also are making decisions regarding future interactions. As you work to ingratiate yourself, you also are seeking additional data to see if there is a similarity of attitudes or to discover any capacity by the other person to meet some of your psychological needs. Communicating is the only way to find out whether we are willing to proceed to an interpersonal relationship from the initial impersonal one. The relationship develops its own set of rules rather than depending on socially established ones.

With the communication model in mind, you can use these two additional definitions as you progress through an organization. First, impersonal relationships are important in an organization. Routine behaviors, such as "How are you today?," smiling, or "Howdy" statements, constitute important parts of an organization's rituals. Even more to the point, many routine messages assist in getting the job done but are not intended to lead to social penetration. It would be a remarkable job if everyone you worked with became a friend. Finally, with or without friendship, there always will be some type of interdependence unless you are a true isolate. Even with a working relationship that does not lead to friendship, uncertainty reduction and information are vital to future transactions. You will recall from our earlier discussion that organizations, and individual relationships, constantly are being organized in an effort to make sense of the environment and the interactions (Jablin, 1990, pp. 172–175).

Second, friendships are a vital aspect of organizational life. If you are interested in developing certain dyadic relationships, employing uncertainty-reducing techniques is the key. The key difference that we have outlined at this point between interpersonal communication in organizations and in everyday life is that friendship is a valuable addition, but not a prerequisite, to dyadic behavior in an organization. In truth, all three definitions of interpersonal communication provide significant insights.

## DIFFERENCES IN PERSPECTIVES REGARDING TRANSACTIONS

### Differences That Make Little Difference

Although there is universal agreement concerning the importance of interpersonal communication in organizations, authors differ over which descriptive terms are most appropriate. One school concentrates on messages created by behavior that is assigned meaning by one or both parties (Frank & Brownell, 1989, p. 9), and the other focuses on information that provides the opportunity to reduce uncertainty. This leads to messages that then are transformed into meaning (Kreps, 1990, p.

12). In both cases, communication creates a cognitive awareness of the interpersonal relationship.

Throughout this text, we have opted for the broader perspective offered by the meanings derived from behaviors approach. When someone assigns meaning to a behavior, it is communication. Because of the complexity of organizations, interpersonal transactions tend to be influenced by the seemingly trivial as well as the information-laden behaviors. Our analysis of nonverbal communication and symbolic behavior supports a broad definition that says any behavior can be meaningful if it is perceived and assigned significance.

At the same time, an excellent argument can be made that information is the most important consideration. This perspective posits that information is the outcome of communication that constrains or coordinates the activities of individuals as they establish and maintain organizations (Kreps, 1990, p. 12). For organizations, information is used to reduce uncertainty (Weick, 1969, p. 91). In interpersonal communication, information is something the receiver does not already know (DeVito, 1989, p. 115). The reasoning is that information reduces uncertainty because it is new to the receiver. Armed with this new data, we are better prepared to proceed in the transaction (Ashby, 1964, part 3). For example, there are patterns in interpersonal behaviors, such as routine greetings, that are information free. When there is a deviation from the pattern (e.g., no greeting), information exists (Bateson, 1972, pp. 399–410). Focusing on the reducing of uncertainty through information is a valuable means for studying the communication process.

As you become familiar with the literature on organizations, you will find these terms—communication, information, messages, and meaning—substituted for each other and you need to be aware that many of these differences make little difference. Part of the complexity in terminology comes with the expansion in uses and meanings of the term information.

## Types of Information—Differences That Make a Difference

Everyone agrees that creating meaning is the ultimate goal of communication. To be fully comfortable with the concept of information, it is useful to divide it into information theory, information technology, and human information processing.

*Information Theory.* First, *information theory* rests on the concept of probability and it permits us to quantify and measure certain aspects of communication (Shannon & Weaver, 1949, p. 31). Essentially, we ask "is this new?" or something we did not know before. If we respond yes, we have information. This binary decision is one of the critical attributes of the modern computer (Kidder, 1981, pp. 94–97). For example, a word processor's spelling check only tags words that are "new"— they do not appear in the computer's memory because they are not correct spellings. Computer programs are written in languages that are based simply on endless variations of four human words: "yes," "no," "if," and "what?" Combine them and you have:

"If yes, what?" "If no, what?" These combinations lead to computer reports that can be divided into information-gathering, analysis, and decision-making reports.

The application of information theory to organizations is almost limitless, ranging from inventory control and scheduling to payrolls and buying patterns. When we apply "decision tree" approaches, where we progress through a series of questions about different alternatives, we are applying the information theory approach. Typically, we describe the situation (S) and determine various alternatives $A_1$, $A_2$, $A_3$, and so forth. Then we proceed down the alternatives systematically asking if it is favorable or unfavorable (e.g., binary). If $A_1$ is favorable, we then consider the subissues from a yes/no, accept/reject perspective, which then leads back to the remaining $A_2$, $A_3$ choices. This approach works very well with a purchasing decision, for example, but it also can provide a clear picture for other decisions. When we examine coaching later in this chapter, you will see a simple decision-making map. Whenever there is a binary choice available, this application of information theory can be used.

**Information Technology.** *Information technology* deals with information *transmission*. Although technological innovation is hardly a new phenomenon in the American economy, information and computer-based technology represents a major departure (U.S. Department of Labor, 1989, p. 7). Cheseboro (1990) presented a composite view of the impact of information technology that makes the issue clearer:

> *More than 50% of the U.S. gross national product is attributable to the development of data, exchange of information, manipulation of ideas and the transfer of number.
> *Over 50% of the U.S. labor force is now engaged in some form of transferring, reprocessing, and transmitting information.
> *Some 28% of the labor force is employed in the primary information sector of the economy.
> *Some 24% of the labor force work as information processors in the industrial sector of the economy. (p. 2)

As you examine these statistics, note how much of information's impact is not due primarily to human communication. For example, storing information is more of a mechanical task than an interpersonal one.

Technology increases integration and dependencies across organizational functions. So previously isolated activities, such as the sales and shipping departments, are tied to the rest of the organization. Increased speed occurs, along with greater interdependence. Mistakes and breakdowns become more costly.

Computer-assisted communication (e.g., electronic mail, image transmission devices, computer conferencing, videoconferencing) and decision-making technologies (e.g., expert systems, decision-support systems, on-line management information systems, external information retrieval systems) allow organizations to communicate more easily across time and distance, more rapidly to targeted groups, more reliably in terms of communication events, and more selectively through con-

trol of access (Huber, 1990, p. 50). Just as the telegraph became the primary technology for the railroads, the calculator for brokerage houses, and the radio for ar-
mies, computer technology is having a significant impact on organizations. For
industrial workers, computers transform their jobs from manual tasks to information management (Naisbett & Aburdene, 1985, p. 117). A walk through most modern
factories will provide a complex display of computer technology designed to enhance tasks ranging from inventory control to quality. As Turnage (1990) explained,
"New office automation has transformed organizational communication in many ways
through videoconferencing, teleconferencing, computer conferencing, and electronic
mail" (p. 172).

An important caveat is that "videoconferencing has the most limited utility because videoconferences are not seen as reasonable substitutes for face-to-face meetings" (Long, 1987, p. 21). In an extensive analysis of DrugCorp's use of DIALOG,
a computer conferencing process, Zuboff (1988) concluded that the reality of
managerial life diminishes the potential for the free exchange of messages via computers (pp. 262–284).

Technology's capacity to produce information also has created an information
glut. Consider the following conclusions based on the extensive use of scanner technology (e.g., checkouts at grocery stores). Shagen (1989) said, "Information is the
lifeblood of businesses. But enough, is enough" (p. 41). This conclusion, by the
American Management Association's Sales and Marketing Council, is derived from
the experiences of the users of extensive databases that have gotten so large that
the actual information cannot be utilized. One company hired a chief information
officer as a means for using the 17 million records they have accumulated for their
11 million customers (Marketing Forum, 1989, p. 3). For many executives, wading
through the lists of numbers is like trying to get a drink of water from a fire hydrant
(Rothfeder & Bartimo, 1990, p. 55).

In fact, much of the information derived from modern technology simply is stored.
When articles and books discuss the impact of information, the issue may be the
increased capacity to store and transmit information. The modern computer may
be fast, but more important, it does not forget, tire out, or hesitate to transmit enormous amounts of information in response to a single request.

This draws the critical distinction between the capacity to automate and *informate* (Zuboff, 1989, p. 4). Reducing dependency on human skills, such as keeping
track of inventory, is a type of automation. If you own a phone that can do a dozen
tricks, you are already familiar with how technology can outpace immediate human
usefulness. General Motors already has found a large gap between the technology
it has purchased and the human organization needed to work with the technology
("Technology Outpaces," 1990). Developing strategic advantages is informating.

So, on the positive side information technology offers significant opportunities
to enhance information gathering and use. Communication processes are changed
inherently when information technology is added. The portable phone is an easy
and obvious example of how individuals can be "in the field" or "dealing directly with

customers" and still stay in touch with the home office (Pool, 1983). Increased information processing, transfer, and storage, however, does not necessarily lead to better organizational communication.

The capacity of modern technology to provide solutions to information-processing problems should not be underestimated. Using information theory, organizations like Frito-Lay have developed new programs to interpret the flood of sales data. These software systems allow daily tracking of product performance in supermarkets, for example, by sorting the information into more comprehendible formats (Rothfeder & Bartimo, 1990, p. 55). Just as the newer PC programs are more user friendly, computer programmers are now able to provide more specific and manageable information to decision makers. So the information overload becomes more palatable. The importance of face-to-face communication leads us to the third type of information.

***Human Information Processing.***   *Human information processing* concentrates on information when it becomes meaning. We process the data and through cognition develop some knowledge regarding the information. This is similar to the messages to meaning process we discussed in chapter 1. To examine this process, answer the following question: A hobo can make one whole cigar from every five cigar butts that he finds. How many cigars can be made if he finds 25 cigar butts? The answer is not five (Bartlett, 1979). At first, you might find this story confusing. After all, 25 butts divided by 5 must equal 5. Although a binary reduction might provide the answer, you are more likely to have an "ah, ha" recognition of the correct answer. Regardless of the number of times you apply the criteria of "what's new?," you still will find the answer difficult. As you add reasoning or meaning, you begin to manipulate the information. Each time the hobo smokes a cigar, he is left with a butt. So, the answer is . . . (we confirm your correct answer later in this chapter).

The capacity to analyze, probe, and manipulate messages requires that we go beyond raw data or information. As Naisbett and Aburdene (1985) said, "Information is no substitute for thinking and thinking is no substitute for information" (p. 149). Chess masters consistently outthink the best information-based computer programs. In 1990, Deep Thought, the most sophisticated chess program in the world capable of visualizing 750,000 positions per sec, lost to Anatoly Karpov in less than 2 hr ("Sophisticated Machine," 1990). The reason is that chess masters, or experts in any number of fields, are capable of chunking many small fragments of information into a few, significant issues. By identifying relevant patterns, and being able to dismiss unimportant details, experts (e.g., medical doctors, consultants, technicians) can see patterns that lead to the correct response (Lord & Maher, 1990, p. 14). Couple the ability to shift through information with the fact that information is power (Goldhaber et al., 1979, p. 7), and human information processing frequently is superior to computer processing. The importance of balancing hard data and intuitive skills is increasingly clear to a large number of executives. In one poll, 43%

of the 349 executives surveyed said they relied on intuitive, "gut feelings" when making tough decisions (Pinnacle Group, 1987). Another survey of the senior managers of the 1,200 largest industry and service companies in the United States, 61% of the 300 respondents wanted to be less dependent on numbers and more dependent on intuition (Learning International, 1986). Oh, the answer to the cigar problem is six.

## HOW HUMANS PROCESS INFORMATION

What is clear is we use information as a means for operating in an organization. The chapter on listening examined short-term and long-term memory and the perception discussion explained how we change incoming messages. We now know that there are three different types of information in organizations. You also should be aware that there is some disagreement regarding human information processing. In an extensive analysis of management and psychological literature, Lord and Maher (1990) found four predominant taxonomic systems for information-processing models. The models are rational, limited capacity, expert, and cybernetic.

### Rational Models

*Rational models* assume that people operate in a controlled processing mode using analytic procedures (Lord & Maher, 1990, p. 24). These models are data-based, bottom-up patterns, which assume people can process thoroughly all relevant information to come to a valid outcome. Assigning probability and utility values in an effort to come to a rational solution is how individuals reach decisions, according to this model. But, Lord and Maher cautioned, "The Achilles' heel of such models is that they are not descriptively accurate" (p. 12). People rarely have enough information to behave optimally. To be truly rational, we would have to be omniscient, or, at least, possess extensive knowledge. These models are counterintuitive because they demand some rigor in the information processing. But, few of us actually consider all possible alternatives or have access to all the information. In fact, we often make impressionist decisions based on a sorting process designed to eliminate bad choices.

### Limited Capacity Models

The *limited capacity models*, in contrast to the rational models, show how people simplify information processing. These models accept that we are unlikely to process all possible information before we make a decision. The *satisficing model*, for example, assumes that information processing stops when the first acceptable alternative is identified (Simon, 1955). By using cognitive heuristics and simplified knowledge structures, we work within very limited conceptualization of the problems we are dealing with and consider only a few of all possible alternatives. In many social situations, we are likely to use this model because we cannot wait to accumulate all the information we need. In hunting for a job, we are likely to accept the one that satisfies most of our criteria (i.e., salary, location, working conditions). Note that this sounds like the intuition perspective discussed earlier. However, when a person has been making a judgment for a long period of time, they actually are processing information using the expert model.

## Expert Models

*Expert models* are also dependent on limited capacity, heuristic-driven methods, but we are no longer examining novices dealing with decisions. For example, although anyone can guess at a chess move, the chess master has approximately 50,000 chunks, or familiar chess patterns, in mind (Simon, 1987). These models make the point that people process information very differently when they are experts. Studies consistently show that experts "recognize immediately what novices require great effort to discover. However, it should be stressed that experts are not superior information processors in the general sense; rather, they perform better only within their specific domain of expertise" (Lord & Maher, 1990, p. 14). All three of these models are featured in management literature as means for understanding information processing. Because you already are versed in a systems perspective and a process orientation, you probably are thinking there must be more to how people utilize information. You are correct, although a large number of individuals rely on the rational, limited capacity, or expert models.

## Cybernetic Models

Finally, the *cybernetic* models argue that information is processed over time rather than in a single, static event. So, "behavior, learning, and the nature of the cognitive processes themselves may be altered by feedback" (Lord & Maher, 1990, p. 15). These models consider the future, the present, and the past. Through learning and adaptation, the cybernetic model allows a heuristic answer to be considered and applied over time. When we examined organizations as symbolic, learning, and socially created entities in chapter 8, we were suggesting a cybernetic, information-processing interpretation of organizational reality (Draft & Weick, 1984). These models are also consistent with the *double-loop learning systems* approach, which explains how systems self-correct as they examine their own information processing in light of the surrounding environment. As Frank and Brownell (1989) explained, "Single-loop learning involves detecting and correcting errors in a fixed context: there is no attempt to question, monitor, or change that context" (p. 545). This contrasts with double-loop learning where we examine the underlying premises guiding our actions while we are acting (Argyris & Schon, 1978). This process orientation distinguishes the cybernetic models from the other three.

Each set of models provides a different explanation for information processing in typical work situations. To make certain our point is clear, consider how you decided on which college to attend or which car to buy. Although ample resources are available for making rational choices (e.g., college evaluation books, *Consumer Reports*), you may not have taken the time or made the effort. Maybe you wanted to "get on with the decision" and picked the first college that seemed to fit your needs—the limited capacity model. A second alternative would be to turn to individuals you respect—experts—to provide information regarding your choices. Or, you could take numerous college-level courses over the span of many years and become an expert. Finally, you might have changed college choices and, even more likely, you might have changed your major once you entered college. This cybernetic approach would seem optimal. But, we do not always have the luxury, interest, ability, or time for changing cars or colleges as we proceed through the double-loop learning process. This discussion of information processing highlights that we are not rational decision makers in many organizational situations (Lord & Maher, 1990, p. 24). Table 9.1 outlines the various characteristics of the four information-processing models in greater detail.

To return to our original point, the word information has many meanings. There is no need for you to take a position on the message/information debate. You might want to examine how you process information. Two issues are important. First, you need to be alert to the tendency of management publications to view information workers as primarily clerical and secretarial whereas knowledge workers are seen as professional and managerial (Turnage, 1990, p. 173). In a sense, this is a distinction between the *content* of the communication—information—versus the *process* of communication—meaning (Williams & Huber, 1986, p. 351). Second, you also must be aware that the terms—communication, meaning, messages, and information—are substituted freely depending on the author, theory, and subject. Now that we have a grasp on the concept of interpersonal communication in organizations, we examine how to be successful.

## INTERPERSONAL COMMUNICATION EFFECTIVENESS

Effective interpersonal communication requires a repertoire of skills with which we perform the appropriate acts in response to the situation. These acts must fit the systems' expectations (e.g., culture, department, group, dyad) and they must present the proper image.

First, the actions we take must fall within the expectations of the organization, culture, work unit, and interpersonal relationship. In meeting these criteria, interpersonal actions establish the norm of reciprocity we discussed at the beginning of this chapter (Kreps, 1990, pp. 164–165). Relationships develop over time, so we learn what to expect and how to respond, or reciprocate, to our interpersonal encounters. You may be familiar with the expression "What goes around comes around."

TABLE 9.1

Comparison of Decision-Making and Operating Features for Alternative Information–Processing Models

| Features | Rational | Limited Capacity | Expert | Cybernetic |
|---|---|---|---|---|
| Information requirements | Knowledge of expectancies and utilities for many alternatives | Knowledge of expectancies and utilities for a few salient alternatives | Highly selective use of schema relevant information | Selective use of current information along with recall and evaluation of past actions |
| Choice | Optimization by maximizing expected utility; evaluation of all alternatives | Simplified by heuristic evaluation procedures; and termination when satisfactory alternative is found | Very good alternative recognized by automatic match with information in long-term memory | Feedback guided use of recognition or heuristic processes |
| Perceptual requirements | Accurate perception of environment based on surface features | Accurate perception of limited environment based on surface features | Accurate perception of limited environment based on meaning | Perception of limited environment and ability to shift perspectives over time |
| Short-term memory requirements | Extensive capacity | Moderate capacity | Low capacity | Very low capacity |
| Long-term memory requirements | Extensive information accessed and transferred to short-term memory | Moderate amount of information accessed and transferred to short-term memory | Extensive, highly organized, and accessible long-term memory; minimal information transferred to short-term memory | Varies depending on task familiarity: new task – same as limited capacity; familiar task – same as expert |
| Type of process emphasized | Controlled, serial, analytic | Controlled or automatic use of heuristics; serial | Automatic parallel | Learning; controlled or automatic; serial |
| Timing of processing | Prior to choice or behavior | Prior to choice or behavior | Prior or concurrent with choice or behavior | Intermixed with choice or behavior |

From Lord and Maher (1990). Reprinted by permission.

In organizations, this reflects the impact our interpersonal behaviors have on how others behave. Expectations and reciprocity go hand in hand, because our willingness to complete tasks, for example, creates a cooperative feeling in the relationship. Although it is readily apparent that we are likely to act differently with a company president than with our immediate colleagues, other situations also require the proper adaptation, hence the proper image becomes important.

Second, the performance we present must be consistent with the image desired in the interpersonal encounter. We are striving to be judged as competent. In a job interview, for example, we somehow must put forth a desire to be hired, a sense of confidence in our abilities, and some humility regarding our preparedness at this moment in our careers. In so doing, we are likely to convey a willingness to learn as well as the ability to contribute. The issue, of course, is to know when to show strength and when to show vulnerability, which is the essence of effective interpersonal communication. Learning to understand and adapt to the demands of the situation will make us more effective.

There are a wide variety of explanations for interpersonal effectiveness. DeVito (1989, unit 6) summarized these into two general approaches. They are not mutually exclusive, but they do draw attention to different aspects of dyadic behavior. If success is the desired outcome of your knowledge of interpersonal communication, you probably will be most interested in an *interactive management model*. If you are primarily interested in fostering meaningful and satisfying interactions, the *humanistic model* may be the best direction. Remember, these two approaches can complement each other.

## The Interactive Management Model

The interactive management model is pragmatically based, focusing on interpersonal communication competence (Hunsaker & Alessandra, 1982). Communication competence is clearly situational and, more often than not, dependent on the abilities of both individuals (Haworth & Savage, 1989, p. 234). The most obvious organizational measure is the bottom-line performance. Because there is significant evidence linking communication and productivity (Camden & Witt, 1983; Downs & Hain, 1982; Hellweg & Phillips, 1982), this is not an altogether incorrect measure. Given the complexity of organizational life, however, this is not entirely satisfactory.

A widely used management training approach, which divides individuals into four categories of interpersonal effectiveness, provides an excellent overview. The categories are *conscious competent, conscious incompetent, unconscious incompetent,* and *unconscious competent*. This is an interesting attempt to highlight effective interpersonal communication.

The first group, conscious competent, are just that—individuals who are aware of the reasons for their competence. They can replicate their successes, consciously adapt to changing circumstances, and correct their failures. The conscious incompetent are individuals who are not yet professionals, but they have the advantage of knowing they have to learn. This awareness allows them to experience growth and development. The unconscious incompetent group assumes effective interpersonal communication is easy, comes naturally, and therefore does not take a great deal of work. This group is likely to reach their level of incompetence early in their organizational careers. Finally, the unconscious competent are very good at many of the things they try, but they do not know why. So, when it comes time to replicate particular behaviors, they are not certain what caused the success in the first place. In addition, when these individuals fail, they cannot identify the reasons. Although these four categories are not exclusive, they do draw attention to the pragmatic side of interpersonal communication effectiveness. Being conscious of the needs for development versus "flying by the seat of your pants" is preferable. Being a conscious competent requires a further understanding of the pragmatic approach.

Competent interpersonal communicators utilize five qualities: confidence, immediacy, interaction management, expressiveness, and other-orientation (DeVito, 1989, pp. 104–112). These attributes deserve further analysis.

**Confidence.**  When we are able to handle ourselves with apparent ease, we are judged as being competent. We are perceived by others as being confident. So, organizations encourage managers to take Dale Carnegie Courses, join Toastmasters, and/or attend management development seminars. Although there are many characteristics that can apply to this point, being relaxed in posture communicates a sense of confidence. A degree of flexibility in our voice and body movement, and control over how we appear, make people believe we are in control. When we seem comfortable, at ease, and not shy, we are more likely to be interpersonally successful. For managers, this is the capacity to share power, delegate important work, and involve employees (Bittel, 1985, pp. 82–99, 175–194; Myers, 1990, pp. 138–147). As DuBrin, Ireland, and Williams (1989) put it, "A realistic degree of self-confidence enhances leadership effectiveness" (p. 340).

**Immediacy.**  When an individual seems to be close to us by showing a sense of interest and attention, we are more likely to judge him or her as competent (DeVito, 1986, p. 164). There are various aspects of immediacy. For example, using the other person's name when discussing a job instead of simply saying "I feel . . ." or referring to "our" needs and how "we" will get it done—using joint references instead of you provides a sense of togetherness. In many cases, providing feedback for the other person's remarks and reinforcing the other person draws individuals closer together. Rather than simply working alongside someone else, we show an interest in working with someone else. The level of interaction is extremely high (Brennan, 1989, pp. 13–15). Efforts to encourage leaders to manage by walking around and to listen carefully to feedback are employing the principle of immediacy.

**Interaction Management.**  To be effective, we must control the interaction to the satisfaction of both parties (Watzlawick, Beavin, & Jackson, 1967). During the transaction, both parties should feel as if they are contributing to the interchange.

Managers, for example, must let the subordinates know that they are being listened to. As we are already aware from the listening chapter, verbal and nonverbal acknowledgement are needed. According to DuBrin et al. (1989), "An effective leader has the ability to read people and situations" (p. 338) in order to do the right thing at the right time. The effective interaction manager is able to keep the conversation flowing effectively by being both a sender and listener and by providing appropriate verbal and nonverbal feedback. Questions we can ask regarding interaction management include: "Do you create an atmosphere that encourages people to ask questions, get involved, and trust you?" or "Are you aware of the total impression you are making when you talk to people?" (Matejka, 1989). Effective interaction managers tend to be *proactive* by taking the initiative and responsibility for what occurs, instead of reacting to circumstances or events (Covey, 1989).

Incongruencies need to be minimized. For example, labeling a meeting as important, and then having to cut it short, provides a mixed message that leaves a sense of poor management. Newly appointed managers often find delegating to their previous co-workers difficult because they are uncertain how to keep the past friendship and the current job requirements (i.e., superior/subordinate) congruent. A litmus test for effective interaction management is if people feel comfortable being around you most of the time ("Update," 1985, p. 43).

*Self-monitoring* is a vital part of interaction management (DeVito, 1989, pp. 107–108). Self-monitoring may be viewed as the manipulation of the image we present to others in our interpersonal interactions (DeVito, 1990, p. 45). High self-monitors are able to adjust their interpersonal interactions on the basis of feedback from others (Snyder, 1981). Low self-monitors are more likely to "be themselves" and not alter how they communicate their thoughts or feelings. So, high self-monitors are likely to manipulate their interpersonal actions in order to produce the most desirable effect. This contrasts with low self-monitors who do not seem to be concerned with the image they portray. Research indicates that high self-monitors tend to take charge of situations, are better at detecting deceptive techniques of others, and can see through impression management attempts by other people. In actuality, most people are a little of both. At work, being closer to high self-monitoring would seem to make sense. With friends, less self-monitoring probably is needed. The bottom line on self-monitoring is being able to be a high monitor at work where it probably will be considered an asset. This conclusion was presented when we discussed image presentation in the chapter on symbolic behavior.

**Expressiveness.**    Genuine involvement in the interaction is a sign of expressiveness (DeVito, 1989, pp. 108–110). Providing verbal and nonverbal actions that indicate engagement with the other person, conveying interest in the interaction, and encouraging openness in others are all attributes of expressiveness. The various characteristics of active listening are all indications of expressiveness. In organizations, we are judged by how willing we are to participate in the ongoing transactions. How much we put into indicating an active interest often leads to us being judged as effective or ineffective in managing interactions. Obviously, too much or too little expressiveness is counterproductive to our goal of being judged competent. Overdoing expressiveness can indicate nervousness and withdrawing from an encounter indicates a lack of concern. This leads to the final attribute, other-orientation.

*Other-Orientation.* One of the harshest comments that can be made about people is "they are totally wrapped up in themselves." Constantly talking about ourselves, focusing on our own problems or successes, and doing most of the talking are examples of a "me-orientation." Adopting a political orientation to organizational membership, including employing guerillalike tactics, is an example of a me-orientation and will lead to a "circle the wagons" approach to interpersonal interactions. An expression that summarizes this attribute would be: "they certainly look out for number 1." Clearly, these behaviors do not forward trust or interpersonal effectiveness.

An other-orientation refers to our ability to adapt to the other person (DeVito, 1989, pp. 111–112). We perceive the other person's viewpoint. We display empathy, and interest and attentiveness are communicated through verbal and nonverbal means. Asking for someone's input, confirming the other person's views or perspectives, and asking questions designed to further your own understanding are examples of verbal other-orientation. Confirmation of the other person is a primary skill in interpersonal communication. This "tuning in" to the other person's communication is one of the most effective ways to receive a positive response from your boss, subordinate, or colleague (Wilmot, 1979, p. 230). Nonverbally, smiles, head nods, focused eye contact, and facial expressiveness work well.

These five characteristics—confidence, immediacy, interaction management, expressiveness, and other-orientation—make up the pragmatic model of interpersonal effectiveness. Organizations affect interpersonal communication in at least four ways (Crable, 1981, p. 78). First, organizations create a "backdrop" for interpersonal communication. This context defines a great deal about what can or will occur in the interpersonal relationship. Crying at a movie might be acceptable, but crying at work rarely fits the context. Second, organizations set agendas regarding topics that probably will be discussed. Although few topics are genuinely taboo, many are irrelevant to the job at hand and therefore are excluded from discussion. Third, there are role expectations and membership requirements. How you talk to colleagues might vary greatly from how you converse with the chairman of the board. Nonverbal behaviors, such as dress, are determined by the organization and are expectations that must be met. Finally, there are potential role and membership conflicts stemming from the complexity of life. For one thing, you probably will develop a new self-image that is somewhat different from your general self-concept (Kelly, Lederman, & Phillips, 1989, p. 221). Although you may have been an independent, self-starter before joining a company, the role assigned to you in the organization might require extensive networking, coordinating with others, and dependency on a powerful manager or colleague. Another example could be the demands placed on you by the job. Working overtime rather than being with your family, for example, can place immense pressure on the interpersonal communication patterns. In addition, you are expected to work with people you do not particularly like. Faced with these four issues, the pragmatic model may be the best alternative for succeeding in an organization.

For many of us, opting for a pragmatic perspective might not be completely satisfying. As we already discussed, many business relationships develop into excellent interpersonal friendships. The humanistic approach to interpersonal effectiveness provides those characteristics that are needed to enhance bonding between individuals. At the risk of being overly repetitious, these two approaches are not at opposition to each other. They do represent two different ways of defining and approaching interpersonal communication effectiveness.

## The Humanistic Model

Although managing interactions is a valuable tool in organizations, behaviors that foster meaningful, honest, and satisfying interactions can be vital to long-term effectiveness and our own job satisfaction. In earlier chapters, we discussed the numerous networks managers and leaders use that successfully combine getting the job done with friendships (Kotter, 1990, pp. 89–100). Some applications of interpersonal communication to organizational behavior have focused on the personal relationships within an organization (Bormann, Howell, Nichols, & Shapiro, 1982, p. 21). The impact of supportive climates, listening, and empathy on relationships has been highlighted (Goldhaber, 1986, p. 228). Although status and power differences were acknowledged, the key to using communication for getting and keeping a job seemed to hinge on relational behaviors (Bormann et al., 1982, p. 19).

The humanistic model takes its cue from writers who have sought to define superior human relationships. Five general qualities form this model: openness, empathy, supportiveness, positiveness, and equality (DeVito, 1989, p. 96). Once again, you should recognize some of these terms from our earlier chapters.

*Openness.*   The amount of interaction we are willing to have with other people is called openness. As apparent as this concept might seem, we make conscious and unconscious decisions about just how much information we will share with other people, how reciprocal the openness is, how honestly we react to incoming messages, and how willing we are to "own" our own feelings (DeVito, 1989, pp. 96–97). As Wilmot (1979) put it, "All dyadic participants decide how much information to share with their partner" (p. 236). One of the factors that separates organizational and intimate communication is this willingness to open up to another person.

This somewhat complex process is called *self-disclosure*. Wilmot (1979) asserted that, "No other communication behavior is so closely linked to close relationships as being open—engaging in self-disclosure" (p. 236). Self-disclosure is when we let someone know something about ourselves that they do not already know (Pearce & Sharp, 1973). Self-disclosure creates vulnerability, which indicates trust and helps build a foundation for closeness. Self-disclosure is a requirement for relationship enhancement, but it is not a requirement for many of our professional, productive, and healthy relationships (Wilmot, 1979, p. 237). In fact, in short-term relationships self-disclosure is inappropriate (Gilbert, 1977). In organizations, we would not disclose the same information to our new supervisor that we provide to our close friends.

*Johari's window* is a useful way of envisioning self-disclosure (Luft, 1970). The label *Johari* was derived from the first two names of the two persons who developed the model, Joseph Luft and Harry Ingham. The four selves are open, blind, hidden, and unknown. As Fig. 9.2 indicates, the four quadrants are dependent on the information known to self, not known to self, known to others, and not known to others. As one quadrant gets larger or smaller, it affects the other three. The model underscores that the different aspects of self are not separate pieces but part of the whole person. According to DeVito (1990), "Like the model of interpersonal communication, this model of self is a transactional one in which each part is intimately dependent on each other part" (p. 53).

The *open self* includes all information known to self and to others. In a professional setting, we are likely to withhold information for a variety of reasons ranging from a lack of trust to a need for privacy. If the people we work with know little about us except "rank and serial number," last name, or job function, they have no reason to trust us. With the increase in interdependency in most organizations, successfully getting along with other people requires some disclosure of personal in-

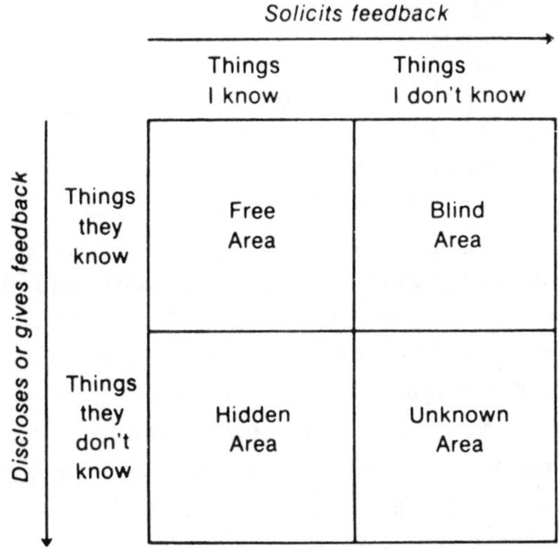

| | Solicits feedback → | |
|---|---|---|
| | Things I know | Things I don't know |
| Things they know | Free Area | Blind Area |
| Things they don't know | Hidden Area | Unknown Area |

*Discloses or gives feedback* ↓

FIG. 9.2. The Johari window.

formation. Often, this includes information such as age, background, interests, family background, and education. As you become more comfortable with the cultural setting in a particular subunit of the organization, you will open up more of this frame of the window. Our willingness to self-disclose is, to a large extent, learned behavior. So, simply being told to provide more personal insights might not help you in the self-disclosing process.

The *blind self* represents those things about yourself that other people know that you do not. Dubbed the "dandruff on the collar" or "bad breath" quadrant, issues in the blind self can range from the trivial to the significant. For example, if every time you are expected to make an important sales call you get sick and snap at people, you are exposing your blind self. Many time management errors (e.g., not returning critical phone calls, being late, setting the wrong priorities or goals) are readily apparent to your co-workers, but not to you.

The *hidden self* includes all the information you know about yourself, but you choose not to disclose. At work, the list of issues that you might not want to make available to other people can be quite extensive. Usually, personal problems are not appropriate for company time. Some fears or recognitions of your own shortcomings may be kept to yourself. An initial feeling that you are "in way over your head" probably will be kept hidden until you are more certain about how well you can work through the problem.

The *unknown self* represents truths that neither you nor others know. To the degree that we open up some of our hidden self, and allow some feedback on our blind self, we can expand the open self and reduce the unknown self.

In theory, appropriate self-disclosure enhances relationships. Obviously, you cannot trust someone you do not know beyond the obvious messages provided by their front. In general, self-disclosure is appropriate when it meets the following six criteria, as outlined by both DeVito (1990, pp. 67–69) and Wilmot (1979, pp. 230–239):

1. It is motivated by a desire to improve the relationship, rather than for selfish purposes. Imposing guilt, for example, is not likely to enhance the relationship. In fact, if the self-disclosure will create undue burdens on the other person, it might not be appropriate. It takes into account the effect disclosure will have on the other person.

2. It fits the communication situation. Disclosing to the wrong person, or at the wrong time, or in the wrong setting only will lead to problems. To be effective, self-disclosure should be a function of an ongoing relationship. The other person should be in a position to provide an open and honest response to the self-disclosure. In addition, it must be well timed so that it fits what is happening.

3. There must be opportunities for the other person to reciprocate.

4. The focus should be on the here and now rather than the past. It should concern what is going on between and within persons in the present.

5. It moves in relatively small increments.

6. It is confirmable by the other person.

From a humanistic perspective, self-disclosure is a must for effective relationships. In organizations, it is important – to be sure – but there must be judicious use for it to be effective. If we are not trusted by our superiors, subordinates, and colleagues, we are in for a very difficult time. In an organization, incremental self-disclosure would seem to be the key.

Actually, every communicative behavior functions as a possible form of self-disclosure. Kreps (1990) observed, "Every time you communicate with another person, you are affecting the relationship you have with that person in some way" (p. 163). Because task competency plays such a critical role in organizations reaching their goals, your ability to perform is a type of self-disclosure. So, consistency and meeting the expectations of others will enhance our effective use of self-disclosure.

***Empathy.*** Empathy is at the core of the human communication process. Regardless of the researcher, empathy is "centrally associated with connectedness, mutuality, relatedness, and the sharing of meaning among people" (Bruneau, 1989, p. 1). By "putting yourself in the other person's shoes," you are better able to understand and communicate. You are already familiar with empathetic listening, which we discussed in chapter 7. Active, empathetic listening behaviors are the key to effective interactions (Frank & Brownell, 1989, p. 347).

Clearly, avoiding evaluating the other person's behaviors is an important part of empathy (DeVito, 1989, p. 98). Indifference, lack of attention, or little feedback cause people to believe that we have no concern or empathy for them. This leads to the third factor, supportiveness.

***Supportiveness.*** Our earlier discussion of the difference between defensive and supportive climates applies here. A supportive climate is fostered when we describe rather than evaluate and are provisional rather than certain. In providing feedback, one of the key goals should be to create a supportive atmosphere where what is being done is discussed rather than the individual doing it. A focus on behavior rather than attitude is fundamental to letting people in an organization know we are discussing the situation, not them (Sashkin & Morris, 1984, pp. 118–119, 142–144).

When we are provisional, we display an open-minded, tentative attitude. By and large, we are willing to listen to opposing points of view and change our own if it is warranted. In other words, we enter the transaction willing to hear and support the other person's perspective. The use of supportive communication as an important organizational behavior is widely prescribed and accepted. It is especially effective when combined with the fourth characteristic, positiveness.

***Positiveness.*** Although it may appear to be a Pollyanna approach at first, presenting a positive perspective regarding other people is an important element in effective humanistic interpersonal communication. Seeing the bright side of things, a question of perception that we discussed in chapter 2, is an appealing characteristic.

In order to do this, we must have a positive self-regard and communicate positively in interpersonal situations. Having a good self-concept allows us to project a strong, positive self. Self-concept is a sum total of numerous social transactions throughout our lives (Wilmot, 1979, pp. 52–55). If you have had a large number of successes, or can change goals when you have faced insurmountable barriers, you are likely to have a good self-concept.

The simplest way to explain positiveness is to examine negative behaviors. When a colleague continually "nay-says" your ideas, or disapproves of your work, or considers your efforts a waste of time, your natural reaction is to shy away from him or her. People who constantly criticize your behavior or find fault with how you handle yourself exhibit negativeness. Because interpersonal relationships develop incrementally over time, the types of messages we send along the way determine the structure and content of the relationship. If we want a productive interpersonal relationship, positive messages seem to be more effective. Clearly, there is a "catch-22" operating here. In order to reciprocate positively, we must feel good about ourselves. In organizations, if the climate is continually negative, the interpersonal communication also will turn sour (Pareek, 1989, pp. 162–163).

Problems can be viewed as challenges or irritants. Mistakes can be seen as something to be tolerated and learned from or as annoyances. Conflicts—natural occurrences in most working situations—can be managed or covered up. All three of these issues provide the difference between positive and negative approaches. In addition, treating other people as our equal tends to enhance interpersonal communication.

**_Equality._**    All relationships have some inequality (Watzlawick, Beavin, & Jackson, 1967, pp. 67–70). A dyad is considered symmetrical when the communicants perceive themselves as equals. A complementary relationship is where there is a hierarchy in which one person is superior to the other in some sense. Both equality and superiority can be slippery concepts. If someone works for you and controls information you need, they will have little difficulty establishing a complementary relationship (and probably you will have little difficulty accepting it) as they brief you. When the office breaks for lunch, you might want the relationships to be more symmetrical. As you are already aware, in almost all organizations there are clear lines of authority and responsibility that override true symmetry. If you announce it is time to return to work, this complementary statement probably will be taken as a command, rather than just a friendly reminder.

So, what is equality? At work, or in any other interpersonal relationship, accepting and approving of someone is the real meaning of equality in interpersonal communication. The issue is atmosphere, not actual equality. When disagreements occur, problem solving is utilized rather than putting the other person down or correcting her or him (Gibb, 1961). In the end, "should" and "ought" statements are eliminated and careful attempts are made to place views in context through phrases such as "I see" or "I understand."

The humanistic model has much to offer for interpersonal effectiveness. If nothing else, many of your colleagues will become friends. Numerous management publications have adopted part of the humanistic approach and many organizations operate as extended families. Depending on the goals of your interpersonal communication, you can concentrate on achieving certain goals or developing a humanistic perspective. Although these are not mutually exclusive, they do come at the process from a different angle.

## SPECIFIC APPLICATIONS
## OF INTERPERSONAL COMMUNICATION BEHAVIOR

Effective interpersonal communication requires choosing the right behavior at the right time. A working definition of communication competence is that your behaviors are appropriate and effective (Infante & Gordon, 1989). But, what is appropriate and effective? Indeed, what guidelines can be established regarding the communication behaviors we should use? Almost all national consulting organizations have their favorite, and often copyrighted, approaches to developing effectiveness. Two directions that have gained widespread application are social styles and transactional analysis.

### Social Styles

One measure of our behavioral preference is our social style. Byrum (1986) wrote, "Social style is defined as patterns of behavior that others can observe and report" (p. 213). It reflects the pervasive communication patterns we have become comfortable with and use habitually. Social style is a method of coping with others that is learned in childhood. This approach to understanding what we do focuses on current, interactive behavior (Merrill & Reid, 1981). Certain styles are perceived as being more favorable than others in certain situations (Snavely, 1981). Because of this attribute, social styles tests, exercises, and seminars are used to train individuals to adapt well to the demands of the situation and the individuals involved (Hunsaker & Alessandra, 1982). LIFO (Life orientation), Wilson Learning Systems, and TRACOM style awareness training are three of the most prominent national programs using some form of social style training. Social style awareness training is based on the values of accepting the differences in others and learning to adapt to them. Because people perform best in positive relationships, and many relationships can be improved, social style approaches argue that knowing yourself, and understanding others, can help (Byrum, 1986, p. 215).

Our interpersonal responsiveness and assertiveness provide the basis for the social style profile. Assertiveness is our willingness to ask or tell and influence or be influenced by others. Responsiveness is the tendency to emote or control our feelings, to display openly or not to express emotion (Byrum, 1986, p. 214). Table 9.2

TABLE 9.2
Social Styles

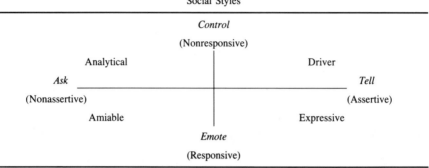

shows how these two behaviors interact to form four styles—driver, expressive, amiable, and analytical. Each of the styles has specific behaviors that lead to increased likelihood of success in certain situations and with particular individuals. By and large, we are most comfortable with people who have the same style, and can experience some tension in dealing with people whose styles have nothing in common with our own (Byrum, 1986, p. 220).

A third criterion is our ability to be adaptable, resourceful, or competent. This is our versatility. If we are inflexible or rigid, we rank low on versatility, and being adaptable and resourceful provides for a higher ranking. The effective interpersonal communicator develops style flexibility in light of the demands of the situation (Goodall, 1990, p. 245). Table 9.3, Characteristics of Four Types, outlines the various behaviors and impact on others. Note the differences in verbal and nonverbal behavior, the habitual actions, and how we are perceived. Using this table, you can make a preliminary analysis of someone's style and other people can do the same for you. Someone's style of communicating gives you the information you need to proceed in a transaction (Norton, 1983). Their actions, as you perceive them, limit your choices as you attempt to effectively adapt. This is not merely hypothetical. National training programs offer in-depth advice regarding how you can respond to other styles and what actions should be taken for effective interpersonal transactions. For example, if you are dealing with a Driver, you should explain what first, proceed rapidly, support the other person's results, talk about immediate action, provide freedom, be businesslike, time conscious, and factual (Byrum, 1986, p. 225). For the Expressive, explain who first, proceed enthusiastically, support the other person's intentions, talk about people and opinions, provide discipline, be stimulating, open, and flexible. The Amiable should be adapted to by explaining why first, proceeding softly, supporting the other person, talking about personal life, providing initiative, being gentle, specific, and harmonious. The Analytical style should be approached by explaining how first, proceeding deliberately, supporting the other person's principles, talking about documented facts, providing deadlines, being patient, organized, and logical.

TABLE 9.3

Social Styles Characteristics of Four Types

*Analytical–Nonresponsive; Nonassertive*
*Thinker–Technical Specialist*

Behaviors: *Verbal*—slower speaking, fewer statements, softer, tends toward monotone, focuses on task, uses facts and data
*Nonverbal*—indirect eye contact, closed hands, rigid posture, controlled facial expression
*Habitual actions*—cautious, maximum effort to organize, slow reaction time, tendency to reject involvement, historical time frame

Perceived by others: *Positive*—industrious, persistent, serious, exacting, orderly
*Negative*—critical, indecisive, stuffy, picky, moralistic

*Driver–Nonresponsive; Assertive*
*Doer–Command Specialist*

Behaviors: *Verbal*—faster speaking, more statements, louder, focuses on task, uses facts and data
*Nonverbal*—direct eye contact, points, leans forward, controlled facial expression
*Habitual actions*—swift reaction time, maximum effort to control, gets involved, rejects inaction, needs for control/results/achievement, present time frame

Perceived by others: *Positive*—strong willed, independent, practical, decisive, efficient
*Negative*—pushy, severe, tough, dominating, harsh

*Expressive–Responsive; Assertive*
*Intuitor–Social Recognition Specialist*

Behaviors: *Verbal*—faster speaking, more statements, louder, more vocal inflection, focuses on people, uses opinions/stories
*Nonverbal*—direct eye contact, points, animated, casual posture
*Habitual actions*—rapid reaction time, maximum effort to involve, minimum concern for routine, future time frame, impulsive, tendency to reject isolation, need for excitement/acceptance

Perceived by others: *Positive*—ambitious, stimulating, enthusiastic, dramatic, friendly
*Negative*—manipulative, excitable, undisciplined, reacting, egotistical

*Amiable–Responsive; Nonassertive*
*Feeler–Relationship Specialist*

Behaviors: *Verbal*—slower speaking, fewer statements, softer, focuses on people, uses opinions/stories
*Nonverbal*—indirect eye contact, casual posture, animated expression
*Habitual actions*—unhurried reaction time, maximum effort to relate, present time frame, supportive time frame, tendency to reject conflict, need for cooperation/acceptance

Perceived by others: *Positive*—supportive, respectful, willing, dependable, agreeable
*Negative*—conforming, unsure, pliable, dependent, awkward

*Note.* From Merrill & Reid (1981). Copyright © 1981 by Chilton Book Company. Adapted by permission.

On the surface, the social styles approach might appear naive or even manipulative. However, most of us have learned to adapt to circumstances and individuals in order to be successful. The definition of interpersonal competence includes the ability to adapt appropriately to situational or environmental variations and to develop interdependence (Bochner & Kelly, 1974, p. 288). The two variables of assertiveness and responsiveness are used in a wide variety of other tests ranging from conflict management to performance appraisal systems to leadership (O'Brien, 1983).

A final application of the styles approach is worth noting. There is a possibility that you have prejudices for or against certain types of behaviors. If this is the case, you "usually attribute your prejudices to the person's personality or character. It is essential that you make a conscious effort to know that you are responding to when you respond to the other's behavior" (Goodall, 1990, p. 243). The styles approach offers us the ability to control our responses and to manage our own behaviors. If you become adept at enhancing your social style, and understanding why you have not been successful with certain people, you are on the road to being a conscious competent communicator.

## Transactional Analysis

How people behave in transactions has been of interest to organizational communication researchers for a long time. In the late 1970s and early 1980s, *transactional analysis* (TA) enjoyed widespread popularity as an approach to help people understand the consequences of certain behaviors in organizations. Its use, and the adoption of many of TA's terms (e.g., stroking, parenting, transactions, adult, child, games), make it worth examining.

TA offers a systematic analysis to understanding why individuals have communication and behavioral difficulties at work. It is an "approach to analyzing and improving transactions between and among people" (DeVito, 1986, p. 325). As an easy-to-understand method to improving organizational practices, TA has enjoyed a strong following and has appeared in various textbooks as a consulting approach (e.g., Goldhaber, 1986, pp. 476–480; Pace, 1983, pp. 111–118). Because of its clear language, specific applications, and easily transferable labels, TA is a useful vehicle for introducing behavioral approaches into organizational learning and practices. The common terminology and references, which are easily understood, provides a good, introductory point for many individuals unschooled in how the behavioral sciences can assist daily transactions.

Although it is difficult to explain TA's demise as a consulting approach, we would be willing to argue that its focus on dyadic behavior, and its apparent simplicity, prevented the transfer of TA's concepts to the political, structural, and cultural aspects of work. TA might enhance the quality of interpersonal transactions, but many of the participants in TA programs we conducted in the late 1970s observed that little was being done to change the realities of organizational life. The popularity of the terminology, the transfer of many of the concepts, and the extent of the training makes a short examination of TA's principles useful in our journey toward understanding how organizations function.

TA focuses on the social intercourse between two or more people (Berne, 1964, p. 13). Berne, the father of TA, argued that each person carries three ego states: parent, adult, and child. These represent relatively consistent patterns of feelings that manifest themselves in certain behaviors. The terms are not related to our chronological state, but to our psychological (e.g., perceptual) orientation at any particular time. So, the *Parent Ego State* is the rule-oriented, controlling, or "mothering" state where we take on the verbal and nonverbal parenting roles. The "should's," "ought-to's," and "don't" statements are part of this state and appear in organizational life in various forms such as "be on time," "I can't change it, it's company policy," and "you should be more conscientious." As a parent would, this state also uses phrases such as "I'll fix it" and "Don't worry." The parent is evaluative and, at work, can be represented by statements such as "You are really doing a fine job" or "If you don't pay more attention, you'll make mistakes." The parent, then, can be supportive, teaching, and helpful or critical, correcting, and defensive producing. The parent is both critical and nurturing and, from the communication model perspective, provides both negative and positive feedback.

These parenting behaviors can be fine, as long as the partner in the transaction is in the *Child Ego State*. The child is the logical receiver of parenting messages. Childlike behavior can be complex. In TA, there are three parts of a child: the Natural Child, the Adapted Child, and the Little Professor. The Natural Child is creative, spontaneous, and rebellious. In this stage, we seek fun, enjoy new things and adventures, and are relatively uncontrollable. The Adapted Child has accepted the rules and roles imposed by the Parent (e.g., society, organization, boss, parent). The Little Professor is, in many senses, a maturing child. This child analyzes information, alternatives, and actions, but is driven by emotion rather than logic. Returning to our earlier example about which car you might buy, when your feelings overtake rationality (e.g., you buy a red Corvette even though it will mean enormous payments, high insurance, and fading paint), you are probably being a Little Professor. During periods of severe lay-offs, keeping "Good Ol' Fred" because he has been a loyal worker comes from the Little Professor or Parent state. The rational or logical choice is represented by the Adult state.

When we are logical, calm, and information seeking, we are acting in the *Adult Ego State*. We are looking for the best decisions based on extensive questioning, accumulating data, and careful analysis. Adults employ tentative behaviors and language, accept the inevitability of change, and understand the inherent complexity of situations, people, and organizations (Goldhaber & Goldhaber, 1976). Clearly, this state appears to be the best one for organizational life. The adult is oriented toward the results and is in touch with the here and now, and is usually most appropriate to business transactions. TA offers a style of human interaction without coercion (Rosenbaum, 1982, pp. 22–23). Managers and employees must be rational and make the best decisions. TA training sessions work at putting the Adult manager in charge most of the time. When innovation or creativity are needed, which are traits many managers subjugate to rules (Parent) or purely rational (Adult) behaviors, discussing the Child Ego State can be useful.

In fact, at times, we will want to tell jokes, "go fishing," or have fun (Child). At other times, we want people to obey the rules and work hard (Critical Parent) or we must teach them how to do a new job (Nurturing Parent). In addition, there will be times that we need someone else to tell us what to do (Parent-Child) and times when we want to discuss rules with someone else who also believes that the rules should be obeyed (Parent-Parent). Note, first of all, how easy it is to use the terminology to describe transactions. In a consulting situation, allowing managers to visualize the transactional process in this elementary fashion can be quite useful. It is especially valuable when discussing the types of transactions.

Transactions may be *complementary*, *crossed*, or *ulterior*. The two examples we used earlier are complementary transactions, which are messages that are sent and received by the appropriate ego state for both members of the transaction. If I want to have a rational (Adult) discussion with you regarding a change in policy, I am trying to address your Adult state. If you respond rationally, we have a complementary transaction. If I say, "These working conditions are disgraceful" (Parent) and you respond, "They are terrible, aren't they" (Parent), then we have a complementary transaction. If you respond to my statement with "I'm sorry," then your Child is in play. Finally, if I say, "Let's figure out a way to improve these working conditions" and you respond "I have some ideas," we are Adult to Adult because we are focusing on problem solving.

A crossed transaction is a message sent to one ego state but responded to by another. Your adult asks my adult, "Given the workload, when would you like to work overtime?" My child responds to your parent with, "Why do you always pick on me?" Our conversation crosses rather than complements. I propose a discussion of a new manufacturing approach (Adult) to you for your input (Adult) and you respond, "You'll never sell that to management" (Parent to Child). The power of discussing crossed transactions to organizational members is to remind managers that employees rarely appreciate the Critical Parent and will become complacent with the Nurturing Parent (Don't worry, I'll figure it out). Suggestion systems are doomed to failure, for example, when ideas are greeted with "It's not in the budget" or "They'll think we're long-haired." Bosses who are authoritarian-paternalistic give off the same parenting messages regardless of the issue. When communication difficulties occur between individuals, the source often can be traced to these crossed messages. Remember the importance of congruency and predictability in the communication process.

Ulterior transactions, the third type, represent hidden or unspoken agendas and are the substance of *game* behavior. Games, of which TA professionals have identified 6,480 types, are attempts to control the transaction covertly (DeVito, 1986, p. 328). Games are an ongoing series of ulterior transactions progressing to a well-defined, predictable outcome, or payoff. Because games are based on ulterior motives, they are considered unhealthy, dishonest, and intimacy reducing. Individuals play games to win, but the winning is based on controlling the transaction. So, genuine, open relationships never can be accomplished through game playing, which involves manipulation in an effort to achieve a desired payoff (Goldhaber, 1986, pp. 248–250). To understand games, we must understand one of the most important contributions of TA, *strokes*.

When we receive recognition, we are receiving strokes. Positive strokes make you feel good about yourself and your work, and negative strokes have the opposite impact. Everyone needs strokes for their psychological and physical health. Stroking directs, controls, and assists organizational members in knowing how and where to establish priorities. Current leadership texts, for example, emphasize "what a leader pays attention to (e.g., puts time, resources) is what gets done" (e.g., Kouzes & Posner, 1990, pp. 9–13, 200–210; Peters, 1987, pp. 411–432). So, if a leader wants better customer service, greater productivity, or cleaner warehouses, then these aspects of organizational life must receive an excessive amount of the leader's attention. TA trainers used to say: "What you stroke is what you get." Clearly, the concepts of feedback and positive reinforcement are based on stroking.

Because we all need strokes, game players seek strokes through the safety of game playing. Games involve covert motives, so the players are protected from the demands of intimacy. The criteria for effective interpersonal communication discussed earlier, requiring self-disclosure, openness, and chances, never can be met. But the game player can receive some attention through games. Why would someone choose pseudointimacy? TA argues that games provide safety because the player always can back out, change players, or change jobs if it looks like they will "lose" the game.

Game titles provide an indication of the widespread application. For example, *Blemish* players find small faults (e.g., two typos in a two-page memo); *If It Weren't for You* players blame others for mistakes thereby discounting the other people (e.g., a manager constantly accusing subordinates of a bad attitude); *Kick Me* players force others into blaming them, which provides for attention, albeit negative (e.g., constantly fouling the new computer system until someone responds that you are, indeed, stupid); *Wooden Leg* players blame some type of physical or psychological malady for their inadequacies (e.g., computers are just too complex for me with my high school education; management never should have promoted me to team leader, because I didn't really want it anyway); and *Happy to Help* players who will volunteer for personal reasons that do not necessarily fit with the goals of the organization or group (e.g., joining a board of directors of an important charity for the recognition). The last group are considered good games, because they benefit the situation, but they are still dishonest. Note that you still have 6,476 games left to consider before you really can analyze game playing. Berne (1964) was careful to include the game *Psychiatry* (e.g., I know what's wrong with you because I have some knowledge of psychiatry). With TA, a little knowledge, when it comes to others, is probably a dangerous thing.

Knowing how our own ego state impacts our colleagues and subordinates can be very valuable. In studies of new workers, it is not unusual to find people leaving jobs because of a supervisor who was unclear, unfair, or tactless (Ramsey, 1987, p. 36). Unfortunately, the search for the mythical ideal supervisor can be never ending, and that person is likely to leave the company soon after we join (e.g., Murphy's Law, paradox). Indignantly moving from one organization to another because supervisors remind us of an unfavorable teacher or relative means we are expecting others to change for us and we are playing "If It Weren't for You" or "Wooden Leg" (e.g., I just can't work for that type of person), among other games.

As you can see, TA provides a clear insight into interpersonal transactions. The decline in TA training can be ascribed to information you are already privy to — there are a variety of perspectives operating in organizations that are complex, unpredictable, and constantly changing. Organizational life is just too uncertain for an approach that focuses on the dyad, or extended dyad, as the source for improving productivity through climate changes. Given the paradoxes, incongruences, and perceptual differences in most aspects of organizational life, TA does not seem sophisticated enough to satisfy managers and supervisors.

In addition, TA makes a case for game-free behavior (e.g., nonpolitical or nonmanipulative). Few individuals seem to be willing to take the plunge until they can be assured that others also will become game-free. Because we cannot force others to change, most participants in TA training report frustration with the "other" people at work. Whether that assessment is correct, or just a defensive reaction (e.g., game playing — If It Weren't for You), TA's transferability became a problem. TA is not wrong; it simply is not enough.

Both social styles and TA offer an opportunity to understand interactions. We do not act alone, and these two approaches are examples of how examining behaviors can help us be more effective interpersonally. Although most people select their interpersonal styles as a reaction to what they anticipate from others, the key to effective relationships lies in proaction (Hall, 1971, p. 12). Being able to fit in, get along with our colleagues, and work well with our superiors and subordinates are vital components for succeeding at work (Walters, 1985). Managing, as represented by the superior–subordinate relationship, provides an ideal paradigm for studying interpersonal communication.

## Superior–Subordinate Relationships

Regardless of our perspective, the most important work-related communication relationships in an organization are between supervisors and subordinates (Eisenberg, Monge, & Farace, 1984, p. 261). As we observed at the beginning of this chapter, interpersonal communication plays an important role from our job interviews to our leaving. In between, there is an entire spectrum of transactions between employees and bosses that span daily work, specific assignments, raises, problems, successes, and social life. Ramsey (1987) asserted, "Supervisors and subordinates alike need a basis for answering questions, solving problems, obtaining feedback, and measuring results" (p. 35). This important observation argues that managers and employees should sharpen their skills in interpersonal communication. Although the manager is, in the end, responsible, employees also can learn to manage up. The Social Styles approach argues that organizational members should make behavioral decisions based on the specific dyadic interaction.

Superiors and subordinates, however, may differ on their perceptions of a wide variety of organizational matters. One summary of current research found differences between superiors and subordinates on the superior's leadership style and the subordinate's, performance and obstacles to good performance, skills and abilities, concern over pay, and authority. In addition, these two groups differed over how much time a job takes to learn and how subordinates should allocate their time (Johns, 1988, pp. 354–355).

## Supervisory Communication Behavior

Based on what we already have outlined earlier in this text, good managers and leaders are skilled at human relations, develop others, make decisions, provide role models, use humor, understand language, use positive nonverbal behavior, develop networks and encourage upward and downward communication, listen effectively, develop strong symbolic messages, and apply power effectively. A prodigious requirement for any manager, and the temptation is to concentrate on task requirements over people issues. Studies indicate that effective managers rely on an understanding of the impact of dyadic relationships, more than the traditional managerial duties of planning, controlling, and decision making (Luthans, Hodgetts, & Rosenkrantz, 1988, chapters 3 & 4). Given the importance of communication skills, we briefly examine how supervisors can enhance their communication.

Supervisors would be well advised to engage in positive, open, and receptive communication (Pace, 1983, pp. 98–100). Various research studies have found that superiors spend from one third to two thirds of their time communicating with subordinates (Jablin, 1985, p. 625). The human relations school established the widely accepted conclusions that successful supervisors employ empathy, communication-mindedness, approachability, openness, sensitivity, information sharing, and an ability to ask rather than tell (Redding, 1972, p. 433). These observations and studies provide a clear direction, but an ideal set of communication characteristics has not been established clearly (Dansereau & Markham, 1987, p. 337). Because superior-subordinate communication does not occur in a vacuum, issues such as climate, culture, task, group size, gender, and occupational type all function as intervening variables.

One example of the difference between a general behavior and a specific activity makes the point. Availability to listen to subordinates—considered an important supervisory trait—and willingness to involve subordinates in the actual decisions are not the same thing. Although being listened to has symbolic importance, some research indicates that job satisfaction for employees in lower level jobs may not be positively affected by being involved in the actual decision-making process (Wheeless, Wheeless, & Howard, 1984). Given the speed with which low-level employees learn of their powerlessness, it is no surprise that being brought into the decision-making process without a commensurate increase in position or salary does little to enhance satisfaction.

The complexity of this relationship makes it difficult to pinpoint exact behaviors that will enhance supervisory effectiveness. Clearly, using supportive, open communication patterns and effective listening are important. One additional finding is that *perceived agreement* was a major contributor in communication satisfaction for both superiors and subordinates (Eisenberg, Monge, & Farace, 1984, pp. 261–271; Lamude, Daniels, & Graham, 1988). When both parties think they are in agreement, regardless of the actual validity of the feelings, they will feel greater satisfaction. Perception plays a significant role for almost all supervisory–subordinate relationships. For example, believing we can approach our supervisor at any time may be much more important than actually walking through that "open door." Unfortunately, managers' claims that they have adopted the ideals of open, supportive trust-based communication behavior may be based more on wishful thinking than fact (Daniels & Spiker, 1987, p. 167).

### Subordinate Communication Behavior

Considering subordinates for a moment, positive listening behaviors increased their ratings by supervisors, as we discussed in chapter 7. This may be a function of perceived agreement because the subordinate is trying to indicate acceptance. Communicating upward to superiors is rarely candid or complete, as you are also aware from the analysis of channels and networks. Subordinates do not communicate openly or honestly with their superiors and distort messages in response to the apparent situational demands. Part of the hesitation arises from differences in power. Although subordinates have power, ranging from information and knowledge to job expertise, they are likely to influence their superiors based on the perceived relationship. In other words, if a hostile environment and climate exists, subordinates resort to covert means of influence.

Subordinates can manage up. This starts with an understanding of your boss's goals and objectives, pressures, strengths, weaknesses, and blind spots, and preferred work style. Then, you should assess your own needs, including strengths and weaknesses, personal style, and predisposition toward dependence on authority figures. Finally, you need to develop and maintain a relationship that fits both parties' needs and styles, has mutual expectations, keeps the boss informed, is based on dependability and honesty, and judiciously uses your boss's time and resources (Gabarro & Kotter, 1986). One example is the *reverse performance appraisal*. According to Dunn (1990), "Among life's stressful encounters, the annual job review ranks high on the scale. Virtually no one enjoys it—and few benefit from it" (p. 134). So, many companies are advising their employees to request a reverse appraisal where the subordinate asks the boss for specific ways to improve his or her performance. Subordinates ask what their strong points are and then the weak points and finally ask for direction and advice on how to improve. Because this appraisal focuses on future improvement, it tends to be coactive and more relaxed. Traditional performance appraisals seem to become perfunctory rituals where grading the past is more important than future improvements.

Willingness to perform a variety of tasks seems to enhance the evaluation by superiors (Harris, 1989). Employees can increase their influence, and therefore their evaluations, by letting the boss perceive them as cooperative and supportive. Although bosses may say they do not want "yes people," in many cases they want at least "yes and no people." Disagreeing with your superiors should only be over significant issues, and subordinates must have the capability of backing off if the issue seems important to the boss. If objections appear to be penny-ante, the subordinate is perceived as an irritant and not a "team player."

### Climate/Context/Situation as Intervening Variables

Finally, it is difficult to separate superior–subordinate relationships from the reality of organizational settings. Although many variables can be controlled in a laboratory, transactions in organizations have high stakes, lack of control by superiors and subordinates, indefiniteness, and ambiguity (Buskirk, 1990, p. 5). In addition, specific transactions have requirements that can change the climate. We examine interviewing, coaching, and use of power.

*Interviewing.* Entire courses and seminars are devoted to learning interviewing skills. For our purposes, we simply touch on the situation as it relates to interpersonal communication. According to Hopper (1984), "The interview is a two-person, goal-centered, planned interaction" (p. 35). In spite of this forceful definition, many interviews are poorly planned, one-sided, and tend to lack goals. For example, the goal of the job (hiring) interview "is to identify the qualified candidates and then select the person who best fits the position and the company" ("The Interview," 1984, p. 61). The employment interviewer is a matchmaker.

Interviews have two specific roles: the interviewer and the interviewee. The interviewer must plan the proposed path of the interview, structure important questions and topics, prepare by reviewing relevant sources of information (e.g., resume, references, detailed job description), find the proper setting, and utilize an objective evaluation system. The effectiveness of the interview depends on the skillful handling by the interviewer of three phases: building rapport to set up the interview and making both parties comfortable, questioning and probing to obtain the needed information, and leaving the respondent by tying together all the loose ends (Sashkin & Morris, 1984, pp. 39–42).

The interviewee must adapt to the demands of the interview and should follow the same general guidelines of being prepared beforehand, utilizing effective interpersonal skills during the interview, and working toward a positive relationship with the interviewer (DeVito, 1986, pp. 167–170). Our discussion regarding both interpersonal effectiveness and social styles would be applicable for the interviewee.

**Coaching.**  This fits within the definition of interviewing, but a separate discussion is worthwhile. As Peters and Austin (1985) explained, "Coaching is the process by which managers help their subordinates to improve performance and develop their full potential" (p. 325). Superiors have the ability to carefully examine the job requirements, the subordinates' needs, skills, and weaknesses, and offer some specific actions for improvement. When done well, coaches lead the subordinates toward the best solution rather than telling them to solve the problem. Effective coaches use problems as opportunities to work with people to build skills, perspectives, and motivation. Taking a positive approach, focusing on solutions, treating the interviewee as an equal, and establishing some measurable goals and milestones will make this important meeting successful. As Table 9.4 indicates, several questions can be asked before making the decision to coach.

Two types of issues are dealt with in a coaching session (Peters & Austin, 1985, pp. 338–340). Job performance problems are the most obvious and are the easiest to change. If the employee lacks the motivation or the skills to do the work, the issue can be dealt with. Unproductive behavior that gets in the way of getting the job done can be corrected by following a coactive, interpersonal coaching session.

The second type are on-the-job interpersonal problems. At first, this may appear to be outside the realm of coaching. However, if a subordinate has difficulties getting along with her or his colleagues, the manager or supervisor must deal with the situation. At the least, the consequences of antisocial behavior must be discussed. In addition, specific human relations training can be suggested (e.g., TA, social styles). When the individual is using dysfunctional behaviors (e.g., excessive drinking, sexual harassment), the issue usually is passed on to a more qualified counselor.

Coaching is a critical managerial skill that is overlooked in many discussions of leadership. We do not make that mistake in our chapter on leadership. At this point, you should recognize that the coach deals openly and honestly with a performance issue using proactive interpersonal techniques. As Kotter (1990) put it, "In a word, it recasts the detached, analytical manager as the dedicated, enthusiastic coach" (p. 10). Coaching offers a one-to-one opportunity to shape values, direct change, encourage innovation, and develop trust. Essentially, coaching involves flexibility so you can adapt your role to the situational demands. According to Peters and Austin (1985, pp. 338–340), there are at least five coaching roles:

1. *Educate*—when goals, roles, or business conditions change; to orient a newcomer; when new skills are needed.
2. *Sponsor*—when an individual can make a special contribution (e.g., skunk works, innovation); to let an outstanding skill speak for itself (e.g., chairs for scholars at universities; sabbatical in a business).

TABLE 9.4
Training/Coaching Analysis:
Decision-making approach to decide what to do involving series
of "binary" choices—proceed based on "yes/no" response

| | | |
|---|---|---|
| Identify need for training or unsatisfactory performance | | |
| Is it worth your time and effort? | NO | Don't waste your time on it. If it is a minor performance problem, let it go. If it is a training issue, let someone else take care of it (e.g., personnel). |
| YES | | |
| Does subordinate know performance is unsatisfactory? | NO | Let subordinate know, give training, feedback, direction. |
| YES | | |
| Does subordinate know what is supposed to be done, how, and when? | NO | Discuss with subordinate, plan work and/or training. |
| YES | | |
| Are the impediments beyond the subordinate's control? | YES | Resolve, remove, alter impediments. |
| NO | | |
| Does the subordinate know how to do it? | NO | Provide practice, training, transfer. |
| YES | | |
| Will subordinate know if the work is poor/incorrect? Will subordinate be informed of errors? Is there negative feedback? | YES | Change feedback to correct problem, transfer, terminate. |
| NO | | |
| Do good things happen regardless of performance? Will pay raises, trips, perks occur because of system? | YES | Change feedback to correct problem, transfer, terminate. Change system. |
| NO | | |
| Could subordinate accomplish task if wanted to? | NO | Change jobs, transfer subordinate, terminate. |
| YES | | |
| Coach, use performance appraisal system, find new/different directions. | | |

3. *Coach*—to make simple, brief corrections; for special encouragement before or after a "first" (e.g., first board meeting, first customer visit).
4. *Counsel*—when problems damage performance; to respond to setbacks.
5. *Confront*—persistent performance problems are not resolved; an individual is failing in his or her current role; an individual seems unable to meet expectations.

Coaching is not adequate in many organizations (Williams & Huber, 1986, p. 386). Managers and supervisors tend to avoid it because it does not deal with the nitty-gritty of a task orientation. But, effectively getting other people to accomplish goals is one of the definitions of good management and leadership. By following the guidelines offered for effective interpersonal communication, and the suggestions made regarding interviews and coaching, you should fare better when you find yourself managing others. Remember, the definition of communication competence is doing the right thing at the right time.

You now have several examples of how interpersonal communication effectiveness is viewed in organizations. Social styles offer an opportunity to examine and understand how our behaviors influence, and are influenced by others. TA provides a clear discussion of the roles we take in trying to adapt socially. The wrong ego state will create difficulties, and the use of the adult approach is seen as the most valuable. Superior–subordinate relationships have received a great deal of attention. Although the superior does hold the power, the subordinate has a variety of tools available for managing the relationship. Interviews and coaching are two specific examples of complementary relationships that occur throughout your organizational career. Clearly, making a conscious effort at developing a proactive, self-correcting interpersonal communication style is important.

Bolman and Deal (1991) put interpersonal communication in perspective when they concluded: "Individual differences and interpersonal dynamics continue to spawn organizational muddles. . . . In organizations, as in the rest of life, many of the greatest joys and most intense sorrows, the highest peaks and deepest valleys, occur in relationships with others" (p. 134). Understanding the dynamics of interpersonal communication, and learning to alter how we behave with others, will allow us to operate more effectively in any organization.

## CONCLUSION

Dyadic relationships are a major influence in most aspects of organizational behavior. This chapter has focused the concept of interpersonal communication so you will be better able to understand, adjust, and adapt.

The functions of interpersonal communication in organizations range from coordinating task and maintenance to developing interpersonal relationships. By understanding the three definitions of interpersonal communication, you will be able to analyze why different groups and people perceive the issue differently. In fact, all three are of value.

The difference in perspectives regarding interpersonal transactions also provides useful insights regarding individual preferences. Information, and information processing, are cutting-edge issues for the 1990s, because the impact of information will continue to grow.

Deciding what is effective interpersonally is difficult. With this in mind, we discussed 10 attributes that lead to being successful. By approaching the issue from an interactive management and humanistic view, we are able to pull together a fuller understanding. More to the point, by concluding with an analysis of various approaches used in organizations to deal with effectiveness, we can pinpoint how dyadic communication is viewed. One of the true insights a communication perspective brings to organizations is the capacity to improve interpersonal communication. This chapter should assist your pursuit of that important goal.

## REFERENCES

Ableson, R. P. (1976). Script processing in attitude formation and decision making. In J. S. Carroll & J. W. Payne (Eds.), *Cognition and social behavior* (pp. 33–45). Hillsdale, NJ: Lawrence Erlbaum Associates.

Altman, I., & Taylor, D. A. (1973). *Social penetration: The development of interpersonal relationships.* New York: Holt, Rinehart & Winston.

Argyris, C., & Schon, D. (1978). *Organizational learning: A theory of action perspective.* Reading, MA: Addison-Wesley.

Ashby, W. R. (1964). *An introduction to cybernetics.* London: University Paperbacks.

Baird, J. W. (1978). *Orientations to organizational communication.* Chicago: Science Research Associates.

Bartlett, S. (1979, May). Two plus two equals four, except. *Psychology Today,* p. 44.

Bateson, G. (1972). *Steps to an ecology of the mind.* New York: Ballantine.

Berger, C. R., Gardner, R. R., Parks, M. R., Shulman, L., & Miller, G. R. (1976). Interpersonal epidemiology and interpersonal communication. In G. R. Miller (Ed.), *Explorations in interpersonal communication* (pp. 149–171). Beverly Hills, CA: Sage.

Berlo, D. K. (1960). *The process of communication.* New York: Holt, Rinehart & Winston.

Berne, E. (1964). *Games people play.* New York: Grove.

Bittel, L. R. (1985). *What every supervisor should know* (5th ed.). New York: McGraw-Hill.

Bochner, A. P., & Kelly, A. P. (1974). Interpersonal competence: Rationale, philosophy, and implementation of a conceptual framework. *The Speech Teacher, 23,* 275–290.

Bolman, L. G., & Deal, T. E. (1991). *Reframing organizations: Artistry, choice, and leadership.* San Francisco: Jossey-Bass.

Bormann, E. G., Howell, W. S., Nichols, R. G., & Shapiro, G. L. (1982). *Interpersonal communication in the modern organization* (2nd ed.). Englewood Cliffs, NJ: Prentice-Hall.

Brennan, E. J. (1989). *Performance management workbook.* Englewood Cliffs, NJ: Prentice-Hall.

Bruneau, T. (1989). Empathy and listening: A conceptual review and theoretical directions. *Journal of the International Listening Association, 3,* 1–12.

Buskirk, W. V. (1990, Winter). Symbolically embedded emotion in organizations: Some implications for culturally based OD interventions (1). *Academy of Management OD Newsletter,* pp. 4–6.

Byrum, B. (1986). A primer on social styles. In J. W. Pfeiffer & L. D. Goodstein (Eds.), *The 1986 annual: Developing human resources* (pp. 213–228). San Diego: University Associates.

Camden, C., & Witt, J. (1983). Manager communicative style and productivity: A study of female and male managers. *International Journal of Women's Studies, 6,* 258–269.

Cheseboro, J. W. (1990). *Pathways to careers in communication.* Annandale, VA: Speech Communication Association.

Covey, S. R. (1989). *The 7 habits of highly effective people.* New York: Simon & Schuster.

Crable, R. E. (1981). *One to another: A guidebook for interpersonal communication.* New York: Harper & Row.

Cummings, H. W., Long, L. W., & Lewis, M. L. (1983). *Managing communication in organizations.* Dubuque, IA: Gorsuch Scarisbrick.

Curtis, D. B., Winsor, J. L., & Stephens, R. D. (1989). National preferences in business and communication education. *Communication Education, 38,* 6–14.

Cushman, D. P., & Cahn, D. D. (1985). *Communication in interpersonal relationships.* Albany: State University of New York Press.

Dance, F. (1967). Toward a theory of human communication. In F. Dance (Ed.), *Human communication theory* (pp. 18–32). New York: Holt, Rinehart & Winston.

Daniels, T. D., & Spiker, B. K. (1987). *Perspectives on organizational communication*. Dubuque, IA: Brown.

Dansereau, F., & Markham, S. E. (1987). Superior–subordinate communication: Multiple levels of analysis. In F. M. Jablin, L. L. Putnam, K. H. Roberts, & L. W. Porter (Eds.), *Handbook of organizational communication* (pp. 343–388). Newbury Park, CA: Sage.

DeVito, J. A. (1986). *The communication handbook: A dictionary*. New York: Harper & Row.

DeVito, J. A. (1989). *The interpersonal communication book* (5th ed.). New York: Harper & Row.

DeVito, J. A. (1990). *Messages: Building interpersonal communication skills*. New York: Harper & Row.

DiSalvo, V. S., Dunning, D., & Homan, B. (1982, April). *An identification of communication skills, problems, and issues for the business and professional communication course*. Paper presented at the annual meeting of the Central States Speech Association, Milwaukee, WI. (ERIC Document Reproduction Service No. EDRS 216 398).

Downs, C. W., & Hain, T. (1982). Productivity and communication. In M. Burgoon (Ed.), *Communication yearbook 5* (pp. 435–453). New Brunswick, NJ: Transaction.

Draft, R. L., & Weick, K. E. (1984). Toward a model of organizations as interpretation systems. *Academy of Management Review, 9*, 284–295.

DuBrin, A. J., Ireland, R. D., & Williams, J. C. (1989). *Management & organization*. Cincinnati: South-Western.

Dunn, D. (1990, March 12). Sitting down with the boss to find out where you stand. *Business Week*, p. 134.

Eisenberg, E. M., Monge, P. R., & Farace, R. V. (1984). Coorientation of communication rules in managerial dyads. *Human Communication Research, 10*, 258–267.

Frank, A., & Brownell, J. (1989). *Organizational communication and behavior*. New York: Holt, Rinehart & Winston.

Gabarro, J. J., & Kotter, J. P. (1986). Managing your boss. In P. J. Frost, V. F. Mitchell, & W. R. Nord (Eds.), *Organizational reality: Reports from the firing line* (3rd ed., pp. 51–62). Glenview, IL: Scott, Foresman.

Gibb, J. (1961). Defensive communication. *Journal of Communication, 11*, 141–148.

Gilbert, S. J. (1977). Effects of unanticipated self-disclosure on recipients of varying levels of self-esteem: A research note. *Human Communication Research, 3*, 368–371.

Goldhaber, G. M. (1986). *Organizational communication* (4th ed.). Dubuque, IA: Brown.

Goldhaber, G. M., Dennis, H. S., Richetto, G. M., & Wiio, O. A. (1979). *Information strategies: New pathways to corporate power*. Englewood Cliffs, NJ: Prentice-Hall.

Goldhaber, G. M., & Goldhaber, G. (1976). *Transactional analysis: Principles and applications*. Boston: Allyn & Bacon.

Goodall, H. L., Jr. (1990). *Small group communication in organizations* (2nd ed.). Dubuque, IA: Brown.

Hall, J. (1971). *Interpersonal style and corporate climate: Communication revisited*. Conroe, TX: Teleometrics.

Harris, G. (1989, September). Flattery can help evaluations. *Communication Briefings*, p. 6.

Haworth, D. A., & Savage, G. T. (1989). A channel-ratio model of intercultural communication: The trains won't sell, fix them please. *The Journal of Business Communication, 26*, 231–254.

Hellweg, S. A., & Phillips, S. L. (1982). Communication and productivity in organizations. *Public Productivity Review, 6*, 276–288.

Hopper, R. (1984). *Between you and me*. Glenview, IL: Scott, Foresman.

Huber, G. P. (1990). A theory of the effects of advanced information technologies on organizational design, intelligence, and decision making. *Academy of Management Review, 15*, 47–71.

Hunsaker, P. J., & Alessandra, P. L. (1982). *The art of managing people*. Englewood Cliffs, NJ: Prentice-Hall.

Infante, D. A., & Gorden, W. I. (1989). Argumentativeness and affirming communicator style as predictors of satisfaction/dissatisfaction with subordinates. *Communication Quarterly, 37*, 83–91.

The interview process: A systematic approach to better hiring. (1984, August). *Small Business Report*, p. 61.

Jablin, F. M. (1985). Task/work relationships: A life-span perspective. In M. L. Knapp & G. R. Miller (Eds.), *Handbook of interpersonal communication* (pp. 615–654). Newbury Park, CA: Sage.

Jablin, F. M. (1990). Organizational communication. In G. L. Dahnke & G. W. Clatterbuck (Eds.), *Human communication theory and research* (pp. 156–182). Belmont, CA: Wadsworth.

Jobs still are being created. (1989, January 13). *The Evansville Courier*, p. 18.

Johns, G. (1988). *Organizational behavior: Understanding life at work* (2nd ed.). Glenview, IL: Scott, Foresman.

Kelly, L., Lederman, L. C., & Phillips, G. M. (1989). *Communicating in the workplace*. New York: Harper & Row.

Kidder, T. (1981). *The soul of a new machine*. New York: Avon.

Klauss, R., & Bass, B. B. (1982). *Interpersonal communication in organizations*. New York: Academic.

Klemmer, E. T., & Snyder, F. W. (1972). Measurement of time spent communicating. *The Journal of Communication, 11*, 142–158.

Kotter, J. P. (1990). *A force for change: How leadership differs from management*. New York: Free Press.

Kouzes, J. M., & Posner, B. Z. (1990). *The leadership challenge*. San Francisco: Jossey-Bass.

Kreps, G. L. (1990). *Organizational communication* (2nd ed.). New York: Longman.

Lamude, K. G., Daniels, T. D., & Graham, E. E. (1988). The paradoxical influence of sex on communication rules coorientation and communication satisfaction in superior–subordinate relationships. *Western Journal of Speech Communication, 52*, 122–134.

Learning International. (1986, November 19). Logic's O.K., gut feeling is better. *USA Today*, p. 5B.

Lewis, R. (1990, April 8). Ten million American workers switch jobs every year. *The Birmingham News*, p. 8D.

Long, R. J. (1987). *New office information technology: Human and managerial implications*. London: Croom Helm.

Lord, R. G., & Maher, K. J. (1990). Alternative information-processing models and their implications for theory, research, and practice. *Academy of Management Review, 15*, 9–28.

Luft, J. (1970). *Group processes: An introduction to group dynamics* (2nd ed.). Palo Alto, CA: Mayfield.

Luthans, F., Hodgetts, R. M., & Rosenkrantz, S. A. (1988). *Real managers*. Cambridge, MA: Ballinger.

*Marketing forum*. (1989, October). New York: American Management Association.

Matejka, K. (1989). *Management solutions*. New York: American Management Association.

Merrill, D. W., & Reid, R. H. (1981). *Personal style and effective performance*. Radnor, PA: Chilton.

Miller, G. R. (1990). Interpersonal communication. In G. L. Dahnke & G. W. Clatterbuck (Eds.), *Human communication theory and research* (pp. 91–122). Belmont, CA: Wadsworth.

Myers, M. S. (1990). *Every employee a manager*. San Diego: University Associates.

Naisbett, J., & Aburdene, P. (1985). *Re-inventing the corporation*. New York: Warner.

Nirenberg, J. (1989). *The American management association executive appointment book*. New York: AMACOM.

Norton, R. (1983). *Communication style*. Beverly Hills, CA: Sage.

O'Brien, R. T. (1983, January). Blood and black bile: Four style behavior models in training. *Training/HRD*, pp. 54–57.

Pace, R. W. (1983). *Organizational communication, foundations for human resource development*. Englewood Cliffs, NJ: Prentice-Hall.

Pareek, U. (1989). Motivational analysis of organizational-climate (MAO-C). In J. W. Pfeiffer (Ed.), *The 1989 annual: Developing human resources* (pp. 161–180). San Diego: University Associates.

Pearce, W. B., & Sharp, S. M. (1973). Self-disclosing communication. *Journal of Communication, 23*, 409–425.

Personnel problems. (1990, March 18). *Parade Magazine*, p. 13.

Peters, T. (1987). *Thriving on chaos: Handbook for a management revolution*. New York: Knopf.

Peters, T., & Austin, T. (1985). *A passion for excellence: The leadership difference*. New York: Random House.

Pincus, J. D. (1985, November). Study links communication and job performance. *IABC Communication World*, pp. 27–30.

Pinnacle Group. (1987, July 21). It takes guts for executives to make the tough decision. *USA Today*, p. 7B.

Pool, I. deS. (1983). *Forecasting the telephone: A retrospective assessment.* Norwood, NJ: Ablex.

Ramsey, R. D. (1987). Now to teach supervisor–subordinate relationships in a basic business communication class. *The Journal of Business Communication, 24,* 35–46.

Redding, W. C. (1972). *Communication within the organization: An interpretative review of theory and research.* New York: Industrial Communication Council.

Redding, W. C., & Danborn, G. A. (1964). *Communication in business and industry.* New York: Harper & Row.

Relocation adjustment time: 8 months. (1987, May 19). *USA Today*, p. 5B.

Rosenbaum, B. L. (1982). *How to motivate today's workers.* New York: McGraw-Hill.

Rothfeder, J., & Bartimo, J. (1990, July 2). How software is making food sales a piece of cake. *Business Week*, p. 55.

Sashkin, M., & Morris, W. C. (1984). *Organizational behavior: Concepts and experiences.* Reston, VA: Reston.

Shagen, A. (1989). Sales and marketing council. *Executive Insights* (2). New York: American Management Association.

Shannon, C. E., & Weaver, W. (1949). *The mathematical theory of communication.* Urbana: University of Illinois Press.

Simon, H. A. (1955). A behavioral model of rational choice. *Quarterly Journal of Economics, 69,* 99–118.

Simon, H. A. (1987). Making management decisions: The role of intuition and emotion. *Academy of Management Executive, 1,* 57–64.

Small talk. (1987, July 28). *USA Today*, p. 4B.

Smith, D. R., & Williamson, L. K. (1985). *Interpersonal communication: Roles, rules, strategies, and games* (3rd ed.). Dubuque, IA: Brown.

Snavely, W. B. (1981). The impact of social style upon person perception in primary relationships. *Communication Quarterly, 29,* 132–142.

Snyder, M. (1981). Impression management. In L. S. Wrightsman & K. Deaux (Eds.), *Social psychology in the eighties* (3rd ed., pp. 35–58). Monterey, CA: Brooks/Cole.

Sophisticated machine no match for man. (1990, February 4). *The Tuscaloosa News*, p. 3A.

Technology outpaces GM staff, adviser says. (1990, January 21). *The Tuscaloosa News*, p. 6E.

Treece, J. B. (1990, April 9). Here comes GM's Saturn. *Business Week*, p. 59.

Turnage, J. J. (1990). The challenge of new workplace technology for psychology. *American Psychologist, 45,* 171–178.

*Update: Today's management know-how.* (1985). Darien, CT: Soundview.

U.S. Department of Labor. (1989). *The challenge of new technology to labor-management relations* (BMLR Publication No. 135-1989). Washington, DC: U.S. Government Printing Office.

Walters, J. (1985, January 2). Getting along can help you get ahead. *USA Today*, p. 3D.

Watzlawick, P., Beavin, J. H., & Jackson, D. D. (1967). *The pragmatics of human communication.* New York: Norton.

Weick, K. E. (1969). *The social psychology of organizing.* Reading, MA: Addison-Wesley.

Wheeless, L. R., Wheeless, V. E., & Howard, R. D. (1984). The relationship of communication with supervisor and decision participation to employee job satisfaction. *Communication Quarterly, 32,* 222–232.

Williams, J. C., & Huber, G. P. (1986). *Human behavior in organizations.* Cincinnati: South-Western.

Wilmot, W. W. (1979). *Dyadic communication* (2nd ed.). Reading, MA: Addison-Wesley.

Zuboff, S. (1988). *In the age of the smart machine.* New York: Basic.

Zuboff, S. (1989). Learning in the age of the smart machine. *Labor Relations Today, 4,* 4.

# Effective Small-Group
# Communication in Organizations

Small groups are the cornerstone of organized behavior, operate at all levels of an organization, and play a major role in informal and formal activities. In the early 1980s, Ford Motor Company wanted to know why their cars were not selling well. As part of the search, Ford researchers formed focus groups to assist in defining the problem areas. When they asked the participants, "Have you driven a Ford lately?," the majority of the focus-group members could not even remember the last time they had ridden in a Ford (Waterman, 1987, pp. 138–140)! These findings, combined with an extensive evaluation of Ford's manufacturing procedures, led to the developments culminating in the successful Ford Taurus and Mercury Sable. At each stage of the production process, Ford implemented teams responsible for quality, customer relations, and numerous other issues (Bolman & Deal, 1991; Osborn, Moran, Musselwhite, & Zenger, 1990). For Ford, the Taurus and Sable became the symbols of renewed quality. More than anything, Ford's turnaround can be traced to the effective use of groups.

The importance of small groups makes sense because the vast majority of tasks accomplished by organizations require more than two people. Once people become a group, there is interdependence to obtain some goal accomplishment. The more the organization tries to achieve, the greater the need to subdivide the work into smaller units.

Any analysis of small-group activities in organizations should consider the scope, the group process, the rationale behind using groups, and the specific methods currently being employed. The first half of this chapter examines small-group behavior in general and the second half explains the use of groups to increase productivity through employee involvement. Before discussing many of the interesting and important uses of groups, we need to lay the groundwork by understanding the scope, definition, types, characteristics, norms, cohesiveness, roles, and meetings.

**325**

## SCOPE OF SMALL GROUPS

Because of their central importance to organizations, groups influence decisions, problem-solving effectiveness, individual self-identity and self-concept, power allocation and application, and symbolic information such as values, justifications, and frames of reference (Daniels & Spiker, 1991, chapter 9). An organization's cultural rules and ongoing procedures are sanctioned by the various groups of individuals forming the immediate work groups. An individual's indoctrination into an organization is carried out by her or his immediate group, team, or unit. Organizational cultures depend on small-group activities to reinforce their rites and rituals (Harris, 1990). You will be a member of a primary work team consisting of your colleagues, supervisors, and assigned activities. In addition, you will be a part of long-standing work teams, project and development teams, and advice units such as committees. One gauge of the prevalence of groups in organizations is the role of meetings.

An estimated 11 million (Watson & Barker, 1990, p. 345) to 20 million meetings (Cole, 1989) take place in organizations in the United States every day! A survey of chief marketing executives of the Fortune 1,000 companies revealed that they work an average of 59 hr a week, spending 21 hr in meetings ("Management Meetings," 1988). In 1987, $7.1 billion was spent on corporate-wide meetings such as conferences, retreats, and strategy sessions ("What Business," 1988). *Industry Week* estimated that organizations commit $37 billion worth of employees' time in meetings each year ("Meetings Unpopular," 1990).

Dependence on groups will expand as organizations attempt to increase productivity and solve problems through team building and specialized task forces (French & Bell, 1984, p. 101; Kouzes & Posner, 1990, pp. 74–75, 140, 170–179; Reich, 1987). This is a wise choice because evidence suggests that "groups produce more and better solutions to problems than do individuals working alone" (Shaw, 1976, p. 78). Even if a solution is not forthcoming, "meetings frequently serve as the focal point for boosting group morale and motivating workers to higher productivity levels" (Cragan & Wright, 1991, p. 239). Groups offer an excellent format for obtaining and reinforcing consensus (Cragan & Wright, 1991, pp. 239–240).

Establishing a small group and successfully using the small-group process are two different things. Your own experiences with small groups at school, work, or socially probably will confirm that observation. Committees, conferences, and meetings have fostered many tongue-in-cheek comments such as: "A meeting brings together a group of the unfit, appointed by the unwilling, to do the unnecessary"; "A camel is a horse designed by a committee"; "A conference is a meeting of people who singly can do nothing, but who collectively agree that nothing can be done"; and "A conference is a meeting to decide when the next meeting will be held." David Ogilvy is credited with the observation: "Search all your parks in all your cities— You'll find no statues to committees." He probably should have excluded those statues erected to war heroes (e.g., Iwo Jima) in his sweeping indictment, but we can suppose that he was remembering his own organizational experiences. In a survey of

2,000 U.S. executives at Fortune 1,000 companies, meetings were picked as the greatest time waster (15.4%) followed by incoming phone calls (11.4%), paperwork (7.3%), travel (6.1%), and gossip (4.2%) (Management Recruiters International, 1986). So, accepting the significance of groups in organizations only provides the first step in being able to use groups effectively. As is the case with most communication behaviors in an organization, directed learning about the activity will enhance our effectiveness. The remainder of this chapter is devoted to providing you with a broad understanding of how groups are utilized in organizations. This chapter progresses in the following fashion: definitions of small groups, types of small groups, characteristics of small groups, group cohesiveness, group norms, roles, group leadership, group development, advantages and disadvantages of groups, tailored group techniques, employee involvement, traditional problem-solving groups, and semiautonomous work units. First, what are small groups?

## DEFINITION OF SMALL GROUPS

In keeping with our definition of interpersonal communication, we can define small-group communication as the process of transacting meaning between three or more individuals. We also could take a cue from the interpersonal communication chapter and define small groups from a componential, situational, and developmental perspective. A more useful approach is to combine the numerous insights provided by small-group communication researchers and create a combined definition.

Nine elements make up our working definition. Small groups include:

1. face-to-face communication (Bales, 1950, p. 33; Campbell, 1958),
2. among a small group of people (3–20 depending on the researcher),
3. who share a common purpose or goal (Beebe & Masterson, 1990, pp. 3–4),
4. perceive a sense of belonging to the group (Cartwright & Zander, 1968),
5. have interdependence (Cragan & Wright, 1991, p. 9; Lewin, 1951, p. 146),
6. create and enforce norms and shared standards (Brilhart & Galanes, 1989, p. 5),
7. exert influence upon one another (Beebe & Masterson, 1990, p. 5),
8. over a period of time,
9. through some structured patterns (Cragan & Wright, 1991, pp. 9–10).

In other words, the fates of the participants are linked together intentionally in the pursuit of some common goal(s) employing some accepted standards and utilizing communication.

In organizations, groups are utilized in a much broader fashion and roam in numerous directions not covered by many traditional definitions (Goodall, 1990, pp. 22–23). As Jablin and Sussman (1983) put it, "An organizational group is a collection of three or more organizational members who interact (more or less regularly) over time, are psychologically cognizant of one another, perceive themselves as a group, and, most important, are embedded within a network of interlocking tasks, roles, and expectations" (p. 12). This expanded perspective allows us to include work teams, quality circles, semiautonomous work units, and skunkworks.

## Differentiating Small Groups

A small group is not just a collection of dyads in one place. With interpersonal communication, "the loss of one is the loss of all" (Wilmot, 1987, p. 19), because the capacity to carry on the relationship has been dissolved. Small groups significantly change the number of interactions possible and alter the interdependence (Bostrom, 1970).

| *Number in the group* | 2 | 3 | 4 | 5 | 6 | 7 | 8 |
|---|---|---|---|---|---|---|---|
| *Interactions possible* | 2 | 9 | 28 | 75 | 186 | 441 | 1,056 |

As we add colleagues to our small group, we radically alter the potential communication between members. We also shift the capacity of some members to contribute, change the potential for creative thinking, and adjust the possible satisfaction obtained by each individual. Small groups increase the number of interactions, and a group can survive (and sometimes flourish) with the departure of any individual or the addition of another.

When we discussed networks in chapter 6, we reached the conclusion that all groups are networks, but not all networks are groups. A network can involve two people or it can extend throughout an entire organization. Our analysis of networks provides you with a great deal of background regarding groups. Of specific interest are the concepts of coupling and connectedness. When subsystems (e.g., members of a department, research and development team) become highly interdependent, they are tightly coupled. Most small groups experience tight coupling when they are concentrating on the task or the social interaction. If your company encourages independent actions by small groups within the corporate structure, your organization is using loose coupling.

Connectedness describes the extent to which network members identify with the goals of other members of their network. We established that increased connectedness enhances employee performance, provides greater power to the group, and offers increased information. As we proceed with our analysis of small groups, you will want to recall the concomitant impact of networks. Effective groups are tightly coupled and highly connected within the group itself. When we examine the use of employee involvement procedures (e.g., suggestions, quality circles, self-managing work teams) later in this chapter, you will see the importance of this concept.

In sum, then, interpersonal communication differs from small groups because of the potential communication opportunities and the interdependence. Network analysis provides a great deal of information regarding effective groups, but not all networks are groups. A further analysis of the types of groups operating in organizations is in order.

## TYPES OF GROUPS

For the purpose of clarification, groups can be viewed as informal and formal. Informal groups do not appear on the organizational chart and are not part of the operating blueprint. Formal groups are sanctioned by the organization and appear on charts, planning documents, or calendars.

### Informal Groups

An informal group emerges naturally from the interaction of members and may or may not have goals related to the organization's goals. These groups structure themselves, develop some type of implicit or explicit membership requirements, and maintain themselves because they have useful social and business purposes. These groups have tremendous power in shaping attitudes and behavior, which ultimately effects production (Gutknecht & Miller, 1986, p. 147).

Informal groups will develop if the elements of physical proximity, attitude similarity, and need complementarity occur, as is the case with interpersonal relationships (Miller, 1990, pp. 104–106). The opportunity for interaction increases the probability of group formation (Johns, 1988, p. 234). For example, groups of middle managers, secretaries, or shipping clerks often have complementary needs and their attitudes can be quite similar because of organizational roles. As with interpersonal communication, doing the same type of work can provide an initial bridge between individuals and group members. Groups also will develop if they can facilitate goal accomplishment for the members. A need complementarity and an attitude similarity are likely if the task simply is too large for any one individual. This is not hypothetical. Developing a new computer or designing a different manufacturing process usually takes more than one person.

A clique, which we discussed in the chapter on networks and channels, is an excellent example (Rogers & Agarwala-Rogers, 1976, p. 113). Group members communicate in an ongoing fashion and set boundaries for belonging (Pace & Faules, 1989, pp. 229–230). Interest and friendship groups formed by employees because of common characteristics (e.g., recreation, age, expertise) are used to obtain a common purpose and can surface in a wide variety of formats. In some cases, the grapevine takes a predictable path creating an ad hoc small group. According to Jablin (1985), "The most influential factors affecting interpersonal communication patterns and relationships among group members are the characteristics of the task on which they are working" (p. 636). How well you function informally depends on your interpersonal communication skills. What the group is trying to achieve effects the group communication process, which brings us to formal groups.

## Formal Groups

Formal groups are sanctioned by the organization. Their primary function is the attainment of organizational goals (e.g., productivity, sales, market strategy). Two broad groupings are functional and task or project. *Functional groups* are specified by the structure of the organization and define the relationship between a supervisor and subordinates. These groups are permanent or quasi-permanent (e.g., advertising department, top management team, the data-processing group, the maintenance crew). The first group you automatically will be part of in an organization is your primary work team.

When employees are brought together for the purpose of accomplishing a specific task (e.g., solve a production problem, create a new credo), they become a *task or project group* (e.g., quality circles, committees, task forces, planning teams). These groups can operate for a short- or long-term period and they are designed to enhance coordination, communication, innovation, interaction, and productivity. Although the functional group will remain until there is a reorganization of the structure, task or project groups are intended to self-destruct after they have accomplished their specific goals.

As you already have realized, we have made several arbitrary divisions for the sake of clarification. In most organizations, groups encompass a wide variety of activities. They can range from informal groups created by a job-related, mutual interdependence (e.g., human resources department and the rest of the organization, shipping and sales departments, loan officers throughout a bank) to those who interact frequently to issue-specific task forces (e.g., reorganization task force, new facilities committee).

Adding to the complexity of understanding groups, organizational scholars are focusing more on *work units* and *work teams* (Sundstrom, De Meuse, & Futrell, 1990). We carefully outline the role of work teams later in this chapter. For now, you should understand that work units are composed of individuals placed in situations with high task interdependence (e.g., traditional assembly line, college faculty), and work teams are individuals involved in mutual goal accomplishment (e.g., self-managing work teams, task forces, quality circles, committees). Now that we have defined and differentiated small groups, it is important to outline the characteristics of small groups.

## CHARACTERISTICS OF SMALL GROUPS

OK, small groups are important. But doesn't the chapter on interpersonal communication suffice to tell you how to work in groups? An excellent question, and the answer is that most of the information does apply, as we indicated when we discussed informal groups. As an overview, groups are more complex, task oriented (e.g., formal) or task related (e.g., informal), and sanctioned by the organization.

Because small groups represent a microcosm of organizations, the four frames or perspectives provide insights into how groups function. In this chapter, we examine the symbolic frame first and then apply the structural, human resources, and political frames.

## Small Groups as Subcultures

Small groups function as subcultures with their own networks, channels, and degrees of effectiveness. From the *symbolic perspective,* "each group develops a history of shared experiences that influences present and future performance" (Frank & Brownell, 1989, p. 224). Small groups provide the rules, roles, and concepts required to understand the organization. This is essentially a provincial, group-based definition of the structural, human resources, and political frames. When an individual joins an organization, the initial influence comes from co-workers who form the immediate group. The informational/sense-making function at the employee's early stages of involvement is substantial, although it diminishes as we are with an organization for a longer period of time (Jablin, 1982, p. 273). During the metamorphosis to a full-fledged member, employees become less dependent on the interpretations of the members of the group and more reliant on their own perceptions and interpretations of reality (Jablin, 1987, p. 710). As newcomers we cannot be fully aware of the group's expectations or standard operating procedures, so we are likely to ask questions or express opinions that are unsettling to older members (Mooreland & Levine, 1982, p. 160).

Groups are living systems, so as new members are being assimilated, the transactional nature of the group requires that the other members also change somewhat by adapting attitudes and behaviors to accommodate the newcomers (Festinger, 1957; Ziller & Behringer, 1960). Living systems also have their own self-sustaining features, so the group also will require or influence the newcomer to fit in to the existing norms. The amount of group cohesiveness, length of time people have worked together, and number of newcomers entering the group all have an impact of the flexibility of the group and the likelihood that rules can be altered by the new member (Jablin, 1987, pp. 711–712).

As you join an organization, you need information regarding "what's going on and how's it done." Nike, who continues to build running shoes that are innovative and appealing to customers, provides a good example (Yang & Buderi, 1990). The 1990 "Air 180" features a large urethane window that affords a 180° view of the heel air bag. This is an extension of the Visible Air line, which was introduced in 1987. These shoes sport a tiny window in the heel and have allowed Nike to overtake Reebok in running shoes sales of $2.2 billion with profits of $243 million. This research effort is carried out behind a cagelike door guarded by a stuffed gorilla. Why? Because the research team is called APEs—advanced-products engineers— who are headed by a "King of the APEs." This team has designed the multisport "crosstrainer" shoe, the "aqua sock" widely used by swimmers, and, for diversity,

Batman's boots and the self-tying sneakers that Michael J. Fox wore in the movie *Back to the Future II*. New product engineers are provided a vast number of cues regarding the team spirit, the sense of uniqueness held by the team, and the sense of humor regarding job titles. All of which underscores the importance of creativity and product development over rules, regulations, and simply getting along. If you join an organized anarchy, which you will recall from chapter 8 involves enormous organizations that are beyond our comprehension, the cues provided by your immediate work group will provide you with the information needed to "make sense of it all." Groups offer rites, rituals, routine, and regime to organizational members.

**Sense-Making Functions of Small Groups.**   You were introduced to the sense-making function of symbolic messages in an earlier chapter. Because the world of work is largely an interpretative experience (Tompkins, 1987, p. 85), small groups provide a primary sense-making service (Bolman & Deal, 1991, p. 143). Groups employ sanctions, develop procedures and processes, and establish shared norms. As the chapter on symbolic behavior explained, you cannot know everything about an organization and what you know is filtered and processed through your organizational experiences.

This *socialization* is the way in which newcomers are transformed from outsiders into effective group members (Gutknecht & Miller, 1986, p. 143). Four influences by groups are worth highlighting (Jablin, 1987, p. 702). First, groups offer explanations regarding the nuances behind the events, rules, procedures, and regulations in every organization. As a newcomer, you will need to know who to turn to for specific advice, what rules are "on the books" but not enforced, and what to avoid at all costs. As you are included in the informal networks, the organization begins to make more sense (Pascale, 1984). What cues, messages, and nuances are presented? Consider the next three points.

Second, joining a new organization is stressful and loaded with uncertainties, and the work group provides a predictable and stable backdrop for comprehending the processes. Upon gaining entrance to the creative advertising department, for example, you quickly become aware of how things are done on a daily basis, who you can approach with questions, and which person or persons are in charge. The computer development organizations in Silicon Valley encourage bureaucracy-busting behavior to foster creativity. This can lead to strange hours, and apparently bizarre group activities (e.g., Nike). Other organizations who are tied to a more rigid set of behaviors (e.g., banks, hospitals) make it clear that specific actions are endorsed and others are prohibited. Once your initial indoctrination with the organization is over, your group ties will increase your understanding of the operating rules and procedures. The group provides a variety of sources for information that facilitates your own capacity to understand the workplace.

Third, the work-related attitudes of the group provide a set of norms for the newcomer. If coffee breaks always extend an extra 5 min, or your department never objects to overtime to complete a project, you are receiving two different messages regarding how the group feels about the company and the job. Finally, the actual job performance of newcomers often is based on modeling the work behaviors and methods of peers. Group members often are aware of their power over the neophyte. Sometimes, "conversations are staged — half consciously — to educate the new employee, and fellow employees volunteer advice about appropriate behavior" (Huber, 1986, p. 159).

In sum, we learn how to do the specific job by modeling ourselves after other members of our work group. Standard operating procedures (SOPs) are almost always different from one organization to another, from the college classroom to a job, and from one group to another. As you can see, small groups create a certain amount of bonding, groupness, or cohesiveness.

## GROUP COHESIVENESS

Groups vary greatly in their effectiveness. Cohesiveness can be defined as unity of purpose and action (Huber, 1986, p. 162). This closeness is a primary component of effective groups and should be pursued (Goodall, 1990, p. 33).

Unity of purpose is achieved by establishing goals (Goodall, 1990, p. 33). The expression "every time you aim nowhere, that's where you get" describes one of the reasons groups flounder. Unity of action, or group cohesion, is based on individuals liking each other, the desirability of group membership, and trust (Gutknecht & Miller, 1986, p. 148). In other words, although we can assign someone to a department, team, or group, unless he or she also values group membership there may not be group cohesion. Groups can make members feel comfortable by reducing member anxiety and attaining sources of satisfaction. Our analysis of group cohesion includes group dynamics, group climate, group talk, group ideology, groupthink revisited, and feedback. Group dynamics are an excellent place to begin.

### Group Dynamics

The forces operating within a group — including methods of organization and supervision, level of participation, team building, and reinforcement for individual members — are all part of group dynamics. The ongoing interpersonal relationships, including all the elements discussed in the interpersonal communication chapter, have a play in effecting the group's relationships.

When a group gets together for the first time, there is a great deal of *primary tension.* This is the uneasiness that group members feel at the beginning of the group's meeting (Bormann, 1975). When a task force has its first meeting, or a college faculty gets together after a summer break, the initial uneasiness is natural and usually is broken by some tension-relieving humor. *Secondary tension,* which is the more serious kind, occurs later in the discussion. Power struggles, role demands, and leadership challenges all lead to a variety of rewarding and punishing communication acts until people accept certain roles. Research indicates that both of these types of tension are normal, but learning how to deal with secondary tension is vital. Although some tolerance for the social conflict usually occurs, groups must learn to deal with conflicts. Because the conflict can overshadow the group process, we have chosen, in this text, to deal with conflict management in a separate chapter. Groups will experience both types of tension as they go through the process of dealing with the task at hand.

Membership in some groups feels better than others. Your work group might greet you with a chill, but in your meeting with fellow new managers you are welcomed warmly. We are describing *group climate,* which is "defined as those molar factors, objective and/or perceived, which affect the message sending and receiving process of members within a given organizational group" (Latane, Williams, & Harkins, 1979, p. 104).

## Group Climate

How group members feel toward each other and the group process can be gauged by examining the group climate. Four conclusions regarding group climate in organizations can be drawn (Falcoine, Sussman, & Herden, 1987, pp. 209–210):

1. Member satisfaction increases to the extent that leadership style allows for participation and equal distribution of control across participants.

2. Groups are a form of network. Therefore, the perceptual presence of the network is significant. In fact, objective measures of organizational behavior may miss the point regarding effectiveness.

3. Communication climate plays a central role in the development and productivity of groups.

4. Regardless of the specific nature of the group, the elements of climate are relatively few in number. These include one's role within a network, style of the leader within the network, accuracy of communication within the group, warmth, and task facilitation. Climate is not a stable issue. As we discussed earlier in the text and chapter, climate comes and goes depending on the factors influencing the interaction. One of these is the process of group development.

Clearly, the factors affecting message sending and receiving include interpersonal behavior, listening, networks, and issues we discuss later in this text regarding leadership, conflict management, and motivation. Groups have an additional responsibility to coordinate member activities and to have some consensus regarding group decisions and goals. We return to group climate in this chapter when we explain group cohesiveness.

Consensus is the value most sought for a decision-making group. Although there are no guarantees, extensive research supports the importance of (a) active participation, (b) increased group cohesiveness, (c) managing conflicts by dealing with the issues not the personalities, and (d) communication intended to clarify and share information in achieving consensus (Frank & Brownell, 1989, p. 150). How this communication is achieved is called *group talk.*

## Group Talk

The quality of communication is a major factor in how effective the group will be (Hirokawa & Pace, 1983). In general, group members need to provide information, analyze and evaluate the information, listen effectively, question, participate, and think and act as a unit (Kelly, Lederman, & Phillips, 1989, pp. 122–125).

How do we actually talk in a group? Four approaches, labeled group talk, have been identified. When work groups try to solve problems, they use problem-solving, role, consciousness-raising, and/or encounter approaches (Cragan & Wright, 1991, p. 51). Returning to the frame perspective, a task group's primary purpose is to do work (structural frame), so the task dimension involving problem solving and the social dimension (human resources) involving roles, take precedence. But, as you are already aware, the symbolic and political frames must be dealt with.

Consciousness raising might seem to be outside the realm of organizational behavior, but it is used in numerous ways to enhance team performance. Team development is so important that we cover it in detail later in this chapter. Team pride frequently is built through raising consciousness regarding quality, customer service, or successes (Cragan & Wright, 1991, p. 41). Sometimes, management teams use retreats and outdoor problem-solving activities to foster teamwork skills. Executive Adventure, an Atlanta-based company, has served more than 20,000 participants from more than 300 companies (Hicks, 1990). In 1987, Colorado's governor Roy Romer took 27 staffers on a weekend of roughing it in the Rockies "to promote better cooperation, communication, and teamwork" ("Colorado Governor," 1987, p. 2A). As team pride works to overcome individual orientations, people become better able to orient themselves to the entire group.

The end product of team building is a common symbolic identity. A sense of oneness is formed, which leads to "group fantasies" (Bormann, 1975). The effect of a group fantasy is to put "in each of its members a feeling he has entered a new realm of reality—a world of heroes, villains, saints, and enemies—a drama" (Bales, 1970, p. 152). In other words, the same process that leads to a cultural identity discussed earlier (e.g., chapters 3 & 8) creates a team spirit that helps explain events and guide behavior. Employees may pass on stories of extraordinary efforts that lead to great successes as a team or relate how management (they) prevented the team (us) from succeeding, providing the essence of a bad guy/gal-good guy/gal drama replete with villains, heroes, and morals. Competition between work units, such as sales and delivery, provides fodder for the fantasy canon. This process is useful for many groups and provides enjoyment as the group works toward being a cohesive unit. Humor, as we explained in our analysis of verbal communication, is vital to effective working relationships and it can make a significant contribution to the effectiveness of groups (Westcott, 1988). Competition also can lead to alienation because of the group ideology.

## Group Ideology

Group differentiation occurs when there is polarization and stereotyping of the opposition (Putnam & Poole, 1987, p. 580). This tendency of groups to utilize the "other" groups as a rallying point has been observed for years by sociologists (Coser, 1956). In fact, the fine line between esprit de corps and a hardening of the group's perceptions toward other groups has disturbed many leaders of diverse subunits. Groups develop ideologies, which are "the beliefs the group holds about the 'structure of action' in the social system and about itself and other groups" (Putnam & Poole, 1987, p. 580). Obviously, when the group members all hold the same ideology, they will act as a unit. As a means for developing substantive organizational issues such as quality production, customer service, or efficiency, this likeness of mind is clearly useful. To the degree that the process leads to a fortress mentality, subversion of cooperative intergroup behavior, or a we/they perspective (e.g., employee/manager, union/company, student/teacher), it can be counterproductive.

Many organizations will set up groups to compete with each other for the purpose of achieving a specific goal (e.g., increased sales, new product line, different public relations approach). In these cases, competition is focused on improving performance and not on simply beating the other groups. There are a variety of approaches and expressions used in these organizations. Some examples are: "a free for all among brands with no holds barred" leading to "creative conflict" and "counterpartism" exists in Procter & Gamble; "IBM is the acknowledged master in fostering competition among would-be product ideas" leading, at some point, to performance "shoot-outs" among the competing groups; a product developed at Hewlett-Packard must "sell it to the sales force" (Peters & Waterman, 1982, p. 216–217). Further, according to Peters and Waterman, "Internal competition as a substitute for formal, rule- and committee-driven behavior permeates the excellent companies" (p. 218).

Groups can become so absorbed by their own ideology that they begin to make bad decisions. You were introduced to the concept of groupthink earlier in this text, and we now examine it once again in light of its influence on groups.

## Groupthink Revisited

An excessive amount of peer pressure, combined with a powerful leader, lets groups go along to get along. The potential for disastrous decisions is significant. As we explained in an earlier chapter, sending up the Challenger, invading Cuba, breaking into the Democratic headquarters at Watergate, or the arms-for-hostages deal provide support for the concept of groupthink (Whyte, 1989, pp. 46–48). On a smaller scale, Our Lady of Elms College in Massachusetts decided to raise $1 million for student financial aid by publishing a cookbook ("School Burned," 1988). You can imagine the deliberations leading up to this decision (e.g., everyone loves our recipes, people are seeking ways to give money to our college). The group's enthusiasm led to the ordering of 100,000 cookbooks which cost $400,000 to print. Now, they are left with 94,000 copies of the cookbook and an enormous debt. The inflated expectations of success (e.g., selling 100,000 books for a $1 million profit) and the group's desire to solve a problem led to groupthink. Ironically, they initially had ordered 200,000 but were talked down by the printer. Every year, struggling small businesses find that they also have purchased a dream supported by a band of loyal family members and friends that really believed that their cookie recipe was as good as Mrs. Fields' or Famous Amos'.

Over 50% of all new businesses fail within the first 2 years. Ineffective planning, based on unrealistic expectations, is the chief cause (Bangs, 1988, p. 11). According to various studies of small-business failures, only 2% are due to factors beyond control of the persons involved (Bangs, 1988, pp. 28–29). Put in simple terms, groups can become self-reinforcing, and therefore self-destructive, during the decision-making process.

Fear of the impact of exposing a bad decision often leads to continued fabrication of false information. In 1990, for example, the Air Force decided not to tell Defense Secretary Dick Cheney that the F-117A Stealth jet fighter-bomber used in the Panama invasion had seriously missed its target. So, Cheney repeatedly touted the "pinpoint accuracy" of the jet despite its failure ("Stealth's Miss," 1990). The same problem occurs when an organization makes a poor decision regarding issues such as product development.

***Decision Framing and Risky Shift.*** You also should be aware that the concept of groupthink can be explained further by looking at how people make decisions. Specifically, given the choice between certain loss and a risky alternative, the vast majority of groups will take the chance (Whyte, 1989, pp. 40–56). In a study reported in the *New England Journal of Medicine,* 44% of the people questioned were prepared to accept a risky treatment for lung cancer if told it would give them a 68% chance of surviving. When the same treatment was described as having a 32% chance of dying, only 18% said they would undergo the treatment ("Safety Risk," 1989). The second description paints a very different decision alternative than the first. Groups also can frame discussions and alternatives in a manner that guarantees groupthink. Remember, the framing of the decision can be the deciding variable.

Imagine the group discussions preceding the establishment of a position titled "Manager of Competitive Assessment" (e.g., industrial espionage). Given the immense competition from other firms and the enormous costs of product development, many American corporations now accept, or at least engage in, spying. Yes, we just framed the issue in a manner that makes the spying concept palatable. In fact, The Society of Competitor Intelligence Professionals, a 1,400-member group, is an organization of corporate spies whose sole purpose is helping companies gather information about other company products ("Corporate Snooping," 1990). The Futures Group is a consulting company that helps corporations design, develop, and operate their own intelligence organizations. Futures' vice president added fuel to the fire by concluding, "The Japanese are professionals. They're the ones who started it. They do it almost by second nature" ("Corporate Snooping," 1990, p. 7E). Given "their" sins, what choices do American corporations have but to follow suit? And, while they are at it, they might as well spy on each other (after all, everyone is doing it, so we had better also). Although corporations probably have engaged in spying for a long time, framing the decision by providing a certain loss (e.g., product knowledge, competitive advantage, Japanese threat, plant closing) compared to a viable alternative, practically guarantees many groups will opt for endorsing snooping, sans the midnight break-ins or bugging and the cloaks and daggers. Both of these represent a significant shift from earlier attitudes about organizations regarding corporate espionage.

This propensity to frame decisions in such a manner as to lead to poor decisions can be altered by strong cultural guidelines, as we outlined in our analysis of symbolic behavior. Steelcase, America's premier office manufacturing company, pierces the groupthink fog through a milieu of information sharing (Waterman, 1987, p. 147). Steelcase involves a combination of beliefs that encourages everyone to do it right, fosters an environment that encourages extensive informal communication, and views policy decisions as ones made last week and therefore easily reversed, altered, or reconsidered. Developing a system that overcomes groupthink requires extensive interaction within the organization, or feedback.

## Feedback

Groups operate within the organization's realm. So, how much support or criticism a group receives can influence its effectiveness. As Cusella (1987) put it, "Positive feedback leads to favorable outcomes for the group while negative feedback leads to less favorable outcomes" (p. 663). Outcomes from positive feedback include group pride, task motivation, team accuracy, group attraction and group esteem, and involvement. Upon receiving favorable feedback, groups tend to rate themselves as more cohesive, motivated, and open to change, and have greater attraction, more participation, and a greater readiness to reduce status incongruence (Cusella, 1987, p. 662).

Although unfavorable feedback is needed to unfreeze habits or change problem behaviors, it also leads to defensiveness, less pride and more task-oriented behavior, lower aspiration levels, less attraction to the group, and more distortion in team scores, increased coping, and attribution of cause of behavior to outside factors (Cusella, 1987, p. 663).

Feedback also has an impact on group members. For example, "when the individual thinks his or her own contribution to the group cannot be measured, his or her output tends to slacken. This notion we call '*social loafing*' " (Falcoine et al., 1987, p. 205). As we have discussed at various times in this text, feedback is critical to keep the system functioning. Group norms are one of the most stable forms of feedback.

## GROUP NORMS

The behavioral expectations we must adapt to are called *norms*. Norms are the standards or rules of behavior that provide order, allow understanding of the group's activities, and ensure that we will orient ourselves toward the group's performance (Gutknecht & Miller, 1986, p. 143). The norms of a group are "the set of assumptions or expectations by members of a group or organizations concerning what kind of behavior is right or wrong, good or bad, appropriate or inappropriate, allowed or not allowed" (Schein, 1969, p. 59).

Not all norms apply to every group member with the same intensity. New members might observe, for example, that they are expected to be attentive by being quiet. In other cases, the group expects the newcomer to go through some hazing in order to prove their willingness to accept the group's standards. Although the hazing process is well known in college Greek societies, being assigned grunt work—a phrase derived from military service where the menial jobs require only a grunt during acceptance and performance—or completing an assignment nobody wants, are important rites of passage for the newcomers as they join the group. As Huber (1986) put it, "More than any other aspect of group life, they serve to define the nature of the group" (p. 158) by expressing the collective values of its membership. These collective values reinforce the group's symbolic frame and lay out the norms of behavior expected in order to complete the job (structural frame), work with other people (human resources frame), and not alienate anyone (political frame).

### Types of Norms

Norms are crucial or peripheral. *Crucial norms* help the group survive, and a violation of these will lead to censure. *Peripheral norms* represent more of an indiscretion than a transgression. In prison, a fink (e.g., stoolie, stool pigeon) violates a crucial norm regarding inmate behavior and punishment, when the violation is discovered, is quick and certain. Codes of behavior exist in almost any group and are articulated with pejorative labels (e.g., teacher's pet, company man, double-dealer, Judas, Brutus, snake in the grass, squealer, cop-out, back-stabber). Jealousy over a new colleague's success probably would suggest that a peripheral norm (e.g., don't rock the boat or reduce other group member's credibility) is close to being violated. Fear that a younger, healthier, or more energetic group member might "break the curve" or "create new work standards" can bring strong group sanctions ranging from statements about the behavior to warnings about the implications of continuing to surpass production quotas or shine too bright as an individual performer.

Norms also are expressed explicitly or implicitly understood (Daniels & Spiker, 1991, p. 180). *Explicit norms* are standards such as policies (structural frame), and *implicit norms* are learned by observing the group in action. To repeat an earlier observation, these shared expectations arise from the external culture (e.g., organization) and the group itself, and conformity is expected in most cases.

***Sanctions.*** Group members have a large number of actions they can take to alter norm violations by nonconformists. For example, verbal threats, criticisms and ridicule can be directed at the individual. Gossip and rumors can be spread behind the person's back to discredit him or her. Simple exclusion from social gatherings (e.g., lunch, bowling teams) and unfriendliness at work can be used to intimidate the individual. Work tools, memos, personal items, and important records can be misplaced to make life difficult. Although it might seem bizarre to have such activities occur at work, the determining factor is the importance placed on the norm to the group's sense of survival. On the flip side of this picture, the group can take significant actions to reward individuals who conform and support group norms. How individuals carry out the perceived norms is called *roles*.

## ROLES

The way we act in a group is a role. Whereas norms are expectations regarding similar behaviors for everyone, roles suggest that members may be expected also to act differently from each other. As Johns (1988) said, "Roles are 'packages' of norms that apply to particular group members" (p. 246). There are two ways of examining roles. The first is a deterministic view where roles are assigned to an individual (Offerman & Gowing, 1990, p. 96). Depending on the group, we may be expected to act as a secretary, chairperson, or a passive participant. These assigned roles are based on normative standards.

*Emergent* roles occur through the dynamics of the group process. For example, you can be assigned the role of leader, but in many groups the actual leader emerges as the discussion carries forward. One of the complexities of fulfilling a role is the difference between how we perceive the role, how we are expected to act out the role, and how we actually perform, or enact, the role (Wooford, Gerloff, & Cummins, 1979, p. 39).

For many years, group researchers have utilized a set of group roles based on the group task, the group building and maintenance, and individual roles (Phillips, Pedersen, & Wood, 1979, pp. 78–95). These are outlined in Table 10.1 with an explanation of each role. Because it is unlikely that you will have the luxury of moving from one of these behaviors to the other and then on to another during the group

TABLE 10.1
Group Role Behavior

| *Group Maintenance Behavior* | |
|---|---|
| Encouraging: | Praising, expressing support/warmth; recognizing value of others. |
| Harmonizing: | Helping to relieve tension; mediating differences. |
| Gatekeeping: | Keeping communication channels open; helping "quiet" members to be heard. |
| Process Observing: | Making comments on how the group is working; how the members are coordinating and working together. |
| Following: | Accepting others' suggestions and contributions. |
| Setting Standards: | Helps set goals and standards for the group; assists in setting norms. |
| *Group Task Behavior* | |
| Initiating: | Proposes new ideas; offers suggestions and approaches. |
| Elaborating: | Clarifying ideas, suggestions; expanding on ideas, suggestions. |
| Coordinating: | Integrating; putting together parts of various ideas. |
| Summarizing: | Pulling work and ideas together; orienting group. |
| Recording: | Keeping track of the group's work. |
| Evaluating: | Critiquing ideas or suggestions. |
| Seeking or Giving Information: | Presenting data; asking questions about information provided by others; requesting evaluations; asking if group is prepared to test for consensus. |
| *Self-Oriented Behavior* | |
| Blocking: | Preventing group from reaching consensus; refusing to go along, accept, or support group. |
| Being Aggressive: | Criticizing, threatening other group members, being a "noble fighter" preventing collaboration. |
| Withdrawing: | Remaining indifferent, refusing to contribute. |
| Dominating: | Interrupting, refusing to accept others conclusions as being as valid as one's own, forcing a leadership role. |
| Special Interest Pleader: | Not allowing any group influence over one's perceived self-interests (e.g., department, other group membership). |

process, this delineation of role activities is more useful to remind you that different behaviors create different outcomes. With this knowledge, you can work at using some versatility in how you enact your roles.

*Role assumption* occurs when you take on the expected behaviors outlined by your team, department, or group. Although a particular role may seem quite simple "on paper," the actual acceptance and acting out of the role can be very difficult. Demographic studies indicate, for example, that today's youth are less willing to accept restrictive roles if the only rationale is that they must "pay their dues" (Daniels & Spiker, 1991, p. 182). When the expectations are unclear, there is considerable *role ambiguity*. Being told to be assertive, innovative, patient, and a team player would seem to be a call for a set of actions filled with ambiguities and potential conflicts. *Role conflict* occurs when we are faced with incompatible role expectations. New supervisors who have come up through the ranks often find difficulty in being a team leader and maintaining their friendships with their new subordinates (former colleagues). This does not have to occur, but it often does. As we already observed, effectively managing conflict is a major issue for small groups.

### Group Leadership

A very important role is group leadership. Because of the central nature of leadership, we devote an entire chapter to this issue. Fortunately, you are already privy to the differences between the four perspectives. In addition, we spent a great deal of time in chapter 3 explaining the evolution of managerial theory. One of the central problems for a leader is how to effectively motivate the group members. We also devote an entire chapter to motivation. For now, we offer two suggestions for effective group leadership. These suggestions assume the leader does not want to employ a political or structural approach to the meeting.

First, the leader must be able to adapt to the situation (Fieldler, 1981, pp. 630–631). Every group, as a living system, is unique because of the differing membership, task, and environment (Bolman & Deal, 1991, p. 112). Most groups also have a history that establishes expectations regarding how the leader should act. As such, leaders, and group members, must adapt to the situation (Beene & Sheats, 1948). Leaders should consider the individual strengths, weaknesses, and limitations of each member before and during the meeting. Some attempt should be made to structure the initial stages of the meeting with an agenda or set of issues. Finally, the leader must be willing to adapt his or her personal style to the needs of the group (Phillips et al., 1979, p. 82). Table 10.2 summarizes the difference between traditional leadership and group-centered leadership.

Second, leaders should adopt a functional approach. Instead of managing a meeting, the effective leader works to facilitate the discussion (O'Connoll, 1979, p. 161). We return to adaptive and functional group leadership when we discuss teams, and leadership, as a concept, is developed in greater depth in a later chapter.

### GROUP DEVELOPMENT

As living systems, groups develop as the members interact. Various investigators have studied this process. Early research, which is still popular and widely used, described a specific sequence for group development. According to these studies, groups inevitably will pass through the four basic stages of orientation, conflict, emergence, and reinforcement while arriving at a decision (Fisher, 1970). Another popular format argues that groups go through four phases: forming, storming, norming, and performing (Tuckman, 1965). Later, a fifth phase of adjourning was added (Tuckman, 1977). For both of these models, the process involves four or five stages that occur in sequence. As neat a package as this appears, not all small groups actually follow this pattern (Cragan & Wright, 1991, p. 34). Although the phases are descriptive of what events will occur, they are not prescriptive regarding the pattern

TABLE 10.2
Group Leadership

| *Traditional Leadership* | *Group-Centered Leadership* |
|---|---|
| 1. The leader directs, controls, polices the members, and leads them to the proper decision. Basically it is his group, and the leader's authority and responsibility are acknowledged by members. | 1. The group, or meeting, is owned by the members, including the leader. All members, with the leader's assistance, contribute to its effectiveness. |
| 2. The leader focuses his attention on the task to be accomplished. He brings the group back from any diverse wandering. He performs all the functions needed to arrive at the proper decision. | 2. The group is responsible, with occasional and appropriate help from the leader, for reaching a decision that includes the participation of all and is the product of all. The leader is a servant and helper to the group. |
| 3. The leader sets limits and uses rules of order to keep the discussions within strict limits set by the agenda. He controls each time spent on each item lest the group wander fruitlessly. | 3. Members of the group should be encouraged and helped to take responsibility for its task productivity, its methods of working, its assignment of tasks, its plans for the use of the time available. |
| 4. The leader believes that emotions are disruptive to objective, logical thinking, and should be discouraged or suppressed. He assumes it is his task to make clear to all members the disruptive effect of emotions. | 4. Feelings, emotions, conflict are recognized by the members and the leader as legitimate facts and situations demanding as serious attention as the task agenda. |
| 5. The leader believes that he should handle a member's disruptive behavior by talking to him away from the group; it is his task to do so. | 5. The leader believes that any problem in the group must be faced and solved within the group and by the group. As trust develops among members, it is much easier for an individual to discover ways in which his behavior is bothering the group. |
| 6. Because the need to arrive at a task decision is all important in the eyes of the leader, needs of individual members are considered less important. | 6. With help and encouragement from the leader, the members come to realize that the needs, feelings, and purposes of all members should be met so that an awareness of being a group forms. Then the group can continue to grow. |

followed by many groups. In other words, all groups are likely to cover these steps, but not necessarily in the following order.

## Orientation/Forming

During this phase, group members are uncertain about the other members or the actual group process (Wellins, Byham, & Wilson, 1991, pp. 191–197). So, communication tends to be tentative with a great deal of agreeing. Members attempt to clarify by asking questions. The task functions center around becoming oriented to the group's goals and establishing some operating procedures. Members feel a great deal of dependence, so any conflict is played down, ignored, or shelved.

Studies indicate that groups need to ask a lot of questions to make this an effective stage. In addition, the orientation stage might have to be returned to several times in the course of the group process (Cragan & Wright, 1991, p. 34).

## Conflict/Storming

Once the social niceties are over, members begin to vie for control of the discussion and the outcome. Often, there are emotional responses to demands and resistance by various members. There are interpersonal hostilities with members openly expressing disagreements. Even when the discussion remains on the task, individuals take sides, align themselves with different factions, form coalitions and substantiate their beliefs on a given proposal.

This is the most complex phase of the process. Members are trying out for leadership roles and often find themselves avoiding the inevitable conflicts over ideas or individual roles. Cragan and Wright (1991) asserted, "The more ideational conflict a group can tolerate without taking flight, the better the group decision will be" (p. 35).

## Emergence/Norming

The storm subsides and members sense that a possible decision is developing. Although the interaction remains tentative, there are expressions of opinion and cooperation. Polarization is reduced as the disagreements turn toward a possible solution. Group cohesion begins to occur. Research indicates that groups will be more successful if they proceed through phase two before offering solutions (Cragan & Wright, 1991, p. 35). Of course, in many organizations, individuals bring their own solutions to problems and try to impose them before the conflict phase even occurs.

## Reinforcement/Performing

At this point, group members emphasize consensus regarding the decision and the group is mobilized to follow through. A sense of relief occurs as tension is replaced by group cohesion. Solutions and problem solving predominate during this phase.

These four/five phases are extremely useful to emphasize the importance of accepting conflict and disagreement as a natural part of decision making. For the time-pressured executive, this model forces a realization that all decisions cannot be made within a 30-min time span or without some chaos.

So far, you have been introduced to a vast number of variables regarding the group process. It should be fairly clear that informal groups will occur regardless of the organization's goals, product, or structure. Formal, or sanctioned groups, are used for a vast variety of tasks. In the opening discussion, we pointed out that chief executives spend 17 hr a week in meetings, which translates into 852 hr or 21 40-hr work weeks a year. If aspiring to the top is not of interest to you, nonexecutives often spend 50% to 80% of their time communicating in or leading small groups (Leonard, 1986, p. 32). This is an expensive proposition. A 2-hr executive meeting can cost $1,000 or more. So, one company of 6,000 people holding 1,000 meetings a year has invested over $1 million (Sigband, 1985, p. 48). Are these meetings worth it? The answer is "yes" with 58% of senior managers and 54% of middle managers in one survey finding their meetings to be productive ("Survival Guide," 1988). But these managers recognize many of the drawbacks to meetings. One solution for making meetings more productive is to pick the meeting format carefully. Before turning to some of these tailored small-group techniques, you might find it useful to have a summary of the advantages and disadvantages of small groups.

## ADVANTAGES

There are a large number of advantages to using groups. First, they provide a broader perspective and input regarding issues. As such, groups generate more and better solutions when synergy is in action. Successful organizations thrive on small-group successes. Digital Equipment and Hewlett-Packard openly boast about the value of small-group activity (Fletcher, 1983, p. 25). 3M uses groups to cut production costs (e.g., cut unit costs 10%, reduce manufacturing cycle time by 50%), develop a system for increasing customer satisfaction (e.g., responses to customer complaints were reduced from 49 days to 5), and cut the development time of new products (e.g., from 6 to 3 years for a new digital color proofer) (Kelly, 1991). The diversity of opinion and the possibility of focusing the group's energy on a particular issue can lead to excellent results. For a manager or supervisor, the group can allow insights not available through interpersonal discussions.

A second advantage, for the leader, is the work group learns more about the issues behind the decision-making process, which should enhance understanding. Even when making an excellent decision, managers can leave subordinates feeling confused or resistant simply because the rationale is not clear.

Making good decisions is a third advantage. Groups allow for a testing of a large number of options. Increased creativity can occur, along with some excellent "piggybacking" by group members on ideas already formulated by the organization and the manager.

Fourth, groups can create a scenario for collaboration. The group lends its power to group decisions. If you want a new operating procedure, letting the group examine the needs and come up with a solution adds credence, the likelihood of group enforcement (remember our discussion on sanctions at the beginning of this chapter), and a peer group mechanism for explaining the rules.

Increased morale is a fifth reason for using groups. Meeting your colleagues in a group setting can help lower interpersonal barriers, enhance team spirit, and provide for common goals. Groups also allow you the opportunity to develop networks of people to call on at different times for other purposes.

Finally, groups allow individuals a chance to demonstrate personal value to the organization. Assuming you are making contributions to the meeting, a variety of individuals will be able to form an impression regarding your abilities and talents (Peters & Waterman, 1982, pp. 14, 121–134).

## DISADVANTAGES

Not all groups work well. Without a moment's hesitation, we can generalize that the biggest problem is a lack of training in how to use groups. This leads to significant problems.

First, the corporate culture and style set the tone for the meetings. Of course, when the culture is proactive, decentralized, and team/group oriented, this is excellent. However, a study by the 3M Meeting Management Institute of the meeting experiences of middle- and senior-level managers at nine organizations found "that meetings are intimately connected to other aspects of an organization's mode of operation" (Cole, 1989, p. 14). You were introduced to this conclusion in chapter 3 when we outlined the four perspectives. The structural frame uses meetings as formalized places for decision making. The human resource frame has informal meetings to increase involvement. Meetings become competitive events under the political frame, with winning one's points the most important issue. The symbolic frame uses meetings as opportunities to celebrate and transform the culture.

Corporate culture can create problems in several ways. When the company's first priority is "Never make a mistake," meetings can become a place for placing blame. Who would openly commit organizational suicide by admitting in a meeting that their department was responsible for the recent losses because of poor judgment, cost overruns, or stupidity? Because of the ruthless self-interest displayed by the company, any attempts at developing effective meetings would have to fail.

The relationship between corporate culture and leadership style also can subvert meetings. If a company values authoritarian leadership and structure, group decision making, extended discussion, and teamwork comes across as soft and unbusinesslike. One study of 275 members of high-level teams at 26 major American corporations by Psychological Associates, Inc. of St. Louis "found that one-third of the managers characterized the meetings they attended as authoritarian" (Cole, 1989, p. 14). Another 19% carried on their teamwork bureaucratically because of top management messages such as "Don't rock the boat" and "Don't make waves." We already have examined a variety of poor decisions (e.g., the Challenger Disaster, Sears, Allegis). In these cases groups are a disadvantage because they only serve to use time and resources without enhancing the outcome. Lacking trust, individual members continually will look out for number one.

A second problem with groups is they consume an enormous amount of time.

Taking the time away from other activities is fine as long as the meetings are productive. Quick decisions rarely justify the use of groups unless "signing off" (e.g., covering one's posterior, forcing agreement, requiring public acceptance) are desired. One solution for this problem is to use tailored small-group activities, which we discuss shortly.

You are already familiar with the third problem, the possibility of groupthink, freezethink, or risky shift. Actually, these are three different problems, but they fit within the discussion of group influence on individual members. Overly homogenous groups will avoid healthy conflicts, which diminishes the possibility for a strong solution to many problems (Goddard, 1986, p. 12). Other groups will influence members to take chances that they would not take individually.

Finally, groups require excellent planning, leadership, and facilitating skills, which some managers do not have. Committing an organization to extensive training in effective meeting behavior is an obvious solution. But, many managers do not see the need. Requiring the development of these skills is difficult and can be counterproductive.

These five advantages and four disadvantages to groups provide you with some insights into the group process. Table 10.3 provides you with a comparison of effective and ineffective groups on a variety of characteristics. This summary places much of the preceding analysis in perspective. In the end, picking the group members, providing organizational support, and choosing the correct format will enhance the quality of group decision making. Because groups can operate through a variety of networks and procedures, we now examine some of the most popular small-group techniques.

## TAILORED SMALL-GROUP TECHNIQUES

The systems concept of *equifinality* certainly applies to the structuring of small groups. There are numerous options available on how to use the group. These different approaches alter focus, emphasis, or process. We overview the Delphi, nominal group, brainstorming, and PERT techniques. Each of these techniques has been developed to solve a particular type of problem with groups. As such, they tend to be very prescriptive in nature and work only if they are carried out in a manner close to the formula. In addition, they tend to be most useful when used judiciously, rather than for every group meeting. Later, we examine the broader and more significant use of small groups as employee involvement techniques.

### Delphi Technique

Developed by the Rand corporation, this small-group approach does not require all the members to sit around a table. In fact, people may be spread throughout the corporation, country, or world. It allows a large collection of people to reach group decisions without face-to-face meetings (Tersine & Riggs, 1976). In brief, any number

TABLE 10.3
Comparison of Effective and Ineffective Groups

| *Effective Groups* | *Ineffective Groups* |
| --- | --- |
| Goals are clarified and changed so that the best possible match between individual goals and the group's goals may be achieved; goals are cooperatively structured | Members accept imposed goals; goals are competitively structured |
| Communication is two-way, and the open and accurate expression of both ideas and feelings is emphasized | Communication is one-way and only ideas are expressed; feelings are suppressed or ignored |
| Participation and leadership are distributed among all group members; goal accomplishment, internal maintenance, and developmental change are underscored | Leadership is delegated and based upon authority; membership participation is unequal, with high-authority members dominating; only goal accomplishment is emphasized |
| Ability and information determine influence and power; contracts are built to make sure individual goals and needs are fulfilled; power is equalized and shared | Position determines influence and power; power is concentrated in the authority positions; obedience to authority is the rule |
| Decision-making procedures are matched with the situation; different methods are used at different times; consensus is sought for important decisions; involvement and group discussions are encouraged | Decisions are always made by the highest authority; there is little group discussion; members' involvement is minimal |
| Controversy and conflict are seen as a positive key to member's involvement, the quality and originality of decisions, and the continuance of the group in good working condition | Controversy and conflict are ignored, denied, avoided, or suppressed |
| Interpersonal, group, and intergroup behavior are stressed; cohesion is advanced through high levels of inclusion, affection, acceptance, support, and trust. Individuality is endorsed | The functions performed by members are emphasized; cohesion is ignored and members are controlled by force. Rigid conformity is promoted |
| Problem-solving adequacy is high | Problem-solving adequacy is low |
| Members evaluate the effectiveness of the group and decide how to improve its functioning; goal accomplishment, internal maintenance, and development are all considered important | The highest authority evaluates the group's effectiveness and decides how goal accomplishment may be improved; internal maintenance and development are ignored as much as possible; stability is affirmed |
| Interpersonal effectiveness, self-actualization, and innovation are encouraged | "Organizational persons" who desire order, stability and structure are encouraged |

From Gutnecht and Miller (1986). Copyright © 1986 by University Press of America. Reprinted by permission.

of individuals can be polled, in writing, for their input regarding certain issues. The ideas then are synthesized by a small group of experts who prepare a master list. This list is resubmitted and the process can continue until the responses do not change significantly. The Delphi technique is excellent as a means for reducing personality conflicts, overcoming physical distance (all the work is done through the mail or via a computer bulletin board), and providing an orderly process for reaching group consensus (Dalkey, 1967).

## Nominal Group Discussion

Having people work together seems to produce more and better ideas than if they work separately on the same task (Huseman, Lahiff, & Wells, 1974). However, sometimes talking takes away from the goals of a group and there can be dominance by a few members. The discussion can be sidetracked to a few, secular issues, and the value of the meeting can be lost.

The nominal group technique attempts to overcome these barriers by eliminating verbal interactions. There are a variety of ways to approach the process, but four steps usually occur. First, each group member writes down the major issues the group is to discuss. Second, the leader records all responses as read by each participant so everyone can see. Third, ideas are clarified and duplications are eliminated. Finally, there is a straw vote on the ideas (Delbecq, Van de Ven, & Gustafson, 1975, p. 71). You should note that computerized and face-to-face discussions can produce equally good results, but consensus is more difficult with computers (Hiltz, Johnson, & Turoff, 1986). With face-to-face meetings, you still have individual limitations.

## Brainstorming

Groups can reach a point where new ideas are needed. A very popular technique is brainstorming (Osborn, 1959). Once the problem is identified (e.g., employee motivation, new markets, new uses for old products), members are encouraged to engage in a freewheeling session where all ideas are welcome. During the process, no negative criticism can be used, quantity is desired, and piggybacking on other ideas is encouraged. Once the creative part of the meeting is over, the ideas are broken down into acceptable and unacceptable ones. Brainstorming serves to eliminate the naysayers and encourage an open analysis.

## Program Evaluation and Review Technique

When we discussed symbolic behavior, we provided you with an example of how the Navy used Program Evaluation and Review Technique (PERT) to impress visitors. PERT is an elaborate planning system that begins with the goal of the group or project and then proceeds systematically through all the stages required to implement the plan. For example, when a group has agreed to purchase a new fleet of trucks for their organization. PERT outlines the steps and provides for coordination of all the necessary steps as a group attempts to accomplish an accepted, common goal. This logical, structured approach to policy implementation allows a group to carefully plot the various issues, stages, and obstacles in carrying out the solution (Phillips, 1966, pp. 89–104).

These four techniques are used to facilitate group decision making. Although they cannot resolve the limitations imposed by an organization's culture, they are extremely useful for overcoming some of the problems encountered by groups. Every small-group technique is designed to enhance employee involvement. Even the stiffest, most formalized, leader-controlled meeting, which is masquerading as a small group-activity, is designed to include employees in an organizational activity. The remainder of this chapter is spent examining the concept of employee involvement, the use of parallel structures, and semiautonomous work units.

## EMPLOYEE INVOLVEMENT

You probably have reached the conclusion by this point in your analysis of organizational communication that informing and involving individuals in the organization's ongoing activities is vital. All employee involvement (EI) programs are efforts to include employees in the information-gathering, decision-making, and/or implementation stages (Truell, 1991). In the same vein, one of the primary goals of small-group activity in most organizations is involving employees (Abbott, 1990, pp. 1–3). In fact, small groups represent one of the most successful means for EI. As a leader, manager, or group member, you will have to make some important decisions regarding the techniques you employ when involving subordinates, colleagues, and superiors. Before discussing the relationships between small groups and employee involvement, we should outline the values and scope of EI in American corporations.

### Values of Employee Involvement

Actively involving employees in an organization is a vital component in any developmental effort (Kouzes & Posner, 1990; Peters, 1987). EI programs enlist various degrees of participation in the management process ranging from making suggestions to semiautonomous work units. In the view of many analysts, EI will become the way to manage in the 1990s (*Employee Involvement in America,* 1989, p. 6; Olsavsky, 1990). Because they influence efficiency, quality, and morale, EI programs provide an important method for making America more competitive (Marshall, 1987; Truell, 1991). Innovation is tied directly to the use of effective communication through EI (Kouzes & Posner, 1990, pp. 56–59).

### Scope of Employee Involvement Programs

These programs already exist in the majority of organizations. A study of the Fortune 1,000 companies by the American Productivity and Quality Center revealed that 80% of the responding companies have some type of EI activity (*Employee*

*Involvement in America,* 1989). In a survey of Fortune 500 industrial and service companies and federal organizations, the Government Accounting Office (GAO) found that more than 80% of the responding companies had some form of EI in the past 3 to 5 years, and that 67% of the employees were covered by these programs (GAO, 1989).

The GAO categorized EI programs ranging from suggestion systems, which have the lowest amount of active employee participation, to self-autonomous work units. The types most used, the study concluded, are the least effective. Although there are dramatic examples of successful teamwork in some organizations (e.g., Corning, Motorola, Xerox, GE, A. O. Smith, Boeing, Kodak, Cummings, Polaroid, Procter & Gamble), and the concept is spreading to banks, insurance companies, and other financial service businesses, "fewer than 10% of all U.S. employers have installed what the Commission on the Skills of the American Workforce, a private, nonpartisan group, called 'high-performance work systems' " (Hoerr, 1990, p. 78).

In our earlier chapter on networks and channels, we discussed communication techniques used to keep employees informed. Suggestion systems, long seen as an important upward communication technique, represent the least amount of actual involvement because the message's ultimate fate is passed on to managers who may not respond quickly or appropriately (Rowe & Baker, 1984). In one study of 5,300 employees, less than 30% of the employees believed that management acted on employee suggestions (Wyatt Company, 1987). Although gaining input from the individuals doing the job is a key factor in increasing competitiveness, employee suggestions have little power to produce change unless managers decide to pay attention. Sharing information, grievance resolution procedures, and employee participation programs that involve employees in workplace decisions are primary characteristics needed to make EI effective (Delaney, Lewin, & Ichniowski, 1989, p. 4).

Approaches that have the greatest potential impact, such as semiautonomous work units, cover the smallest number of employees. The GAO survey concludes that the most powerful programs cover only 25% or less of the responding firms' employees. A study of 429 companies with innovative programs for first-level employees, representing a cross section of organizations practicing cooperative labor-management relations, revealed only 33 semiautonomous work unit programs (Olsavsky, 1990). At the same time, numerous EI programs were being used, including the extensive use of labor-management committees, quality circles, quality of work life programs, task forces, incentive plans, and employee communication programs. So, although employee involvement is a valued tool for organizational development, it is not utilized widely in its most effective form. Effective EI requires programs that incorporate two way communication, provide information so employees understand the business, and allow these employees to actively participate in the decision-making process (Haas, 1990). Clearly, the use of teams, already overviewed as a type of network, deserves further attention.

## TEAMS AND TEAMWORK

Teams are ongoing, coordinated groups of individuals working together even when they are not in constant contact (Dyer, 1987). These groups can include special task forces, intact work groups, new work units, or people from various parts of an organization who must work together to achieve a common goal (Johns, 1988, p. 592). Teams differ substantially from many small groups because they involve team rather than leader control over the group process. Figure 10.1 outlines the traditional leader/member relationship. Although group communication textbooks recognize the value of a diminished leadership role in many situations (Brilhart & Galanes, 1989, pp. 193–194), the means for diminishing the inherent power and influence of a manager on a particular employee group is not outlined as clearly. The continuous working relationships required by teams is a widely used mechanism.

### Importance of Teams

The importance of teams and teamwork is obvious to anyone working with organizations (French & Bell, 1984, p. 101; Gutkneckt & Miller, 1986, pp. 214–215; Peters, 1987, p. 297; Truell, 1984, p. 116). Examples of the power of teamwork to assist in transforming organizations are provided in practically any discussion of renewal and change (Dalziel & Schoonover, 1988; Nora, Rogers, & Stramy, 1986; Wellins et al., 1991, pp. 10–15). Team building represents the most widely used form of organizational development because it offers a systematic method for improving the interpersonal and task aspects of regular work groups (DuBrin, Ireland, & Williams, 1989, p. 629). Teams provide a productive means for achieving EI (Waterman, 1987, pp. 81–85). As Naisbitt and Aburdene (1985) put it, "Fast, flexible, loaded with talent, the small-team model is the most popular and widespread alternative to bureaucratic organization" (p. 38).

For our purposes, teams are divided into groups seeking solutions to particular problems (e.g., task forces, specialized work groups, quality circles), and the semi-autonomous, self-directed, or *self-managing work teams* (SMWT). Although both approaches represent important attempts to involve employees in the problem identification and solution processes, the SMWT encompasses participative management. As such, SWMTs are becoming an even more potent means for organizational development, transformation, and renewal.

We cover four issues regarding teams. First, the role of problem-solving groups as parallel organizational structures is examined. We examine quality circles as an example of the successes and limitations of parallel problem-solving groups. Second, three inherent limitations to the use of parallel problem-solving groups are provided. Third, we examine the successes of SMWTs. Fourth, the concepts behind the SMWT are outlined.

PARTICIPATION CHART

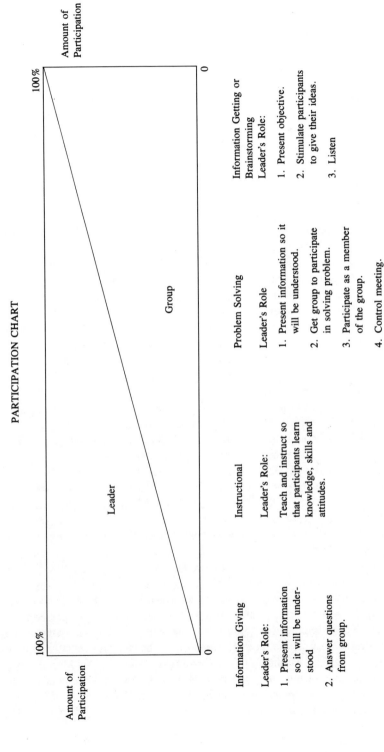

Amount of
Participation

100%

Leader

Group

Amount of
Participation

100%

0

0

Information Giving

Leader's Role:

1. Present information
so it will be under-
stood

2. Answer questions
from group.

Instructional

Leader's Role:

Teach and instruct so
that participants learn
knowledge, skills and
attitudes.

Problem Solving

Leader's Role

1. Present information so it
will be understood.

2. Get group to participate
in solving problem.

3. Participate as a member
of the group.

4. Control meeting.

Information Getting or
Brainstorming
Leader's Role:

1. Present objective.

2. Stimulate participants
to give their ideas.

3. Listen

FIG. 10.1.   The traditional leader/member relationship.

353

## PROBLEM-SOLVING GROUPS

*Parallel organizational structures,* such as quality circles, teams, labor-management cooperation committees, and other issue-specific employee participation groups, are a commonly utilized approach for increasing EI. These groups are different, however, from the ongoing informal groups or your department, office, team, or crew membership. We are examining parallel organizational structures first because they provide an insight into the advantages and limitations of creating problem-solving groups outside of the ongoing work process.

### Quality Circles

*Quality circles* (QCs) are one of the best known parallel approaches. Although there are a variety of definitions for QCs, "in essence, such circles are voluntary groups of employees who work on similar tasks or share some area of responsibility, and who agree to meet on a regular basis to discuss — and perhaps solve — key problems related to their work" (Baron, 1983, p. 558). The groups have 6 to 12 members who focus on specific issues to resolve a quality problem (Bain, 1982, p. 202). QCs meet, usually once a week, to analyze these work-related problems and to propose solutions to them. Typically, a QC has little or no authority to spend organizational resources and has no direct control over the acceptance or implementation of the QC's solution. Most QCs are limited to making an analysis and providing recommendations for improvement to management.

Pushed by the Japanese success in the early 1980s, American businesses rushed to adopt QC approaches, with 80% of the Fortune 500 companies having some type of QC and 44% of all companies with more than 500 employees using QCs (Lawler & Mohrman, 1985). There are numerous documented examples of QC successes (Johns, 1988, pp. 594–595), especially in specific quality areas, and in the general area of morale building (Baron, 1983, p. 558). A sample of the Fortune 1,000 companies indicated that 68% of the companies had some form of QC (Jacobs, 1982; Marks, 1986). These companies report a 69% success in productivity improvement and a 72% success in quality improvement (*Employee Involvement in America,* 1989, p. 6).

This rush also led to a failure rate "in more than 60 percent of the American organizations in which they have been tried" (Marks, 1986, p. 38). Many organizations abandoned their QC program within a year (DuBrin et al., 1989, p. 636).

Some experts argue that the problem is not in the patient, but in the prescription. Too often, QCs have been used as quick fixes for serious problems. Given the natural tendency to resist change, the lack of incentive for managers to actually listen to employees, and inadequate training, QC are bound to fail (Karp, 1983; Marks, 1986). In addition, consulting firms seem to have marketed QC effectively without actually adapting them to specific organizational needs (Wood, Hull, & Azumi, 1983, p. 39).

Even when they are successful, programs using problem-solving groups (QCs included) tend to decline into disuse within 2 to 5 years (Lawler & Mohrman, 1985). This life cycle may be due to inadequate implementation and inflated expectations (Smeltzer & Kedia, 1985), or the actual solving of the type of problems being addressed by the group (Blair & Whitehead, 1984).

## INHERENT LIMITATIONS TO TEAM-BUILDING EFFORTS

There are numerous other reasons for the failure of team-building programs such as QCs. At various times, union objections, time away from the job by employees, unrealistic expectations, threat of change, and inadequate training have led to failures (Gutknecht & Miller, 1986, p. 237).

Three very specific problems confronted in most team-building efforts are the tendency toward individual rewards, inappropriate management style, and segmentalism (Kanter, 1983). Because these barriers can be countered by SMWT, they warrant further analysis.

### Individual Rewards

First, the reliance on individual rewards is counterproductive to team building. One of the vital components in effective organizational change is teamwork (Egan, 1989). The tendency of American organizations to reward individual performance is a major stumbling block in team-building efforts (Crocker, Charney, & Chui, 1984). The outcome is intrateam conflict over perceived scarce resources (Lefton, 1988, p. 20).

The measurements used by organizations to gauge individual success provide one of the major reasons for choosing personal recognition and glory over positive team-building behavior. For American corporations, success often is based on short-term criteria such as the department's or subunit's profit (*Employee Involvement in America,* 1989). Because effective team building requires time, there is a natural inclination to circumvent the group process in order to qualify for the short-term rewards. Organizations reinforce this perspective by focusing on market leadership, strong profits, and high stock prices rather than developing team concepts based on strong cultural affiliation (Schaef & Fassel, 1988, p. 3).

One study, based on interviews, small-group meetings, and reviews of corporate information, concludes that current corporate bureaucracies establish the counterproductive norms of good management behavior (defined as behavior leading to advancement and job security), which include ignoring the long term, avoiding responsibility, concentrating on appearances rather than reality, hypocrisy, and slavish acceptance of current dogma (Jackall, 1983). In a nutshell, looking out for number one is an impediment to many team-building efforts.

## Inappropriate Management Style

Second, many managers and supervisors are ill equipped to encourage team building. This is true for two reasons.

*Loss of Power.*   Often, managers and supervisors view employee involvement in the decision-making process as a threat to their own power and authority (Meyer & Stott, 1985). This perceived loss of power had led first-line supervisors to resist QC and team efforts (Klein, 1984, p. 93).

*Managing Versus Leading.*   Underscoring the difference between managing and leading has become a very popular means for focusing on productive and counterproductive behaviors (Bennis, 1989, pp. 17–24; Kotter, 1990, pp. 3–18). Managing is required to plan, budget, organize, and control. Overuse of these managerial tools tends to sabotage EI programs. Leading involves developing strong subordinates (Kotter, 1988, p. 26). Although the leader does bear the responsibility for implementing effective team-building concepts (Blake, Mouton, & Allan, 1987, p. 11), overreliance on the leader for heroic attempts at motivating and developing individuals is counterproductive (Bradford & Cohen, 1984). Leaders need to empower individuals and teams by strengthening the control individuals and groups have throughout the decision-making process (Conger, 1989).

Autocratic management and heroic leadership can be significant impediments in the team process. If team-building efforts are successful, supervisors and managers will be expected and required to assume entirely different roles from their traditional ones (Klein, 1984). Instead of being the boss, reward dispenser, and coordinator, managers and supervisors become liaisons, linking pins, and facilitators. Power will shift through the empowerment process and leading, not managing, becomes the expected behavior. Without proper training, managers and supervisors will conduct business as usual rather than deal with the uncertainties inherent in employee involvement through teams.

## Segmentalism

Segmentalism, which is the tendency of units to be indifferent—or actually competing—as an organization works toward change, prevents effective team building. According to Egan (1988), "Isolationism and empire building instead of system-enhancing integration of the subunits of a corporation or institution constitute one of the main forms of corporate irrationality" (p. 146). Universities provide an excellent example with their "untouchable departmental system" (Egan, 1989, p. 273). Groups isolate and tend to take on problems that are particular to their own areas of interest. So, they are limited in their abilities to respond to problems that are not "theirs."

So ingrained is this issue that it is labeled the *NIH* factor (Not Invented Here), which we discussed in an earlier chapter. You will recall that in any operation, NIH prevents collaboration in at least two ways. First, NIH suggests that the idea cannot be very good because it was created somewhere else. Apple Computer became so ingrained in the NIH syndrome that during the 1990 corporate reorganization process Chief Operating Officer Spindler decreed that NIH no longer would be tolerated (Buell, Levine, & Gross, 1990). His reasoning was simple—Apple's arrogance was decreasing productivity and marketing effectiveness. Second, the group asked to produce the product, or sell the product, does not understand or identify with it. In the extreme, the process of developing a product in engineering and handing it over to production is called the "over the wall" syndrome.

The cross-disciplinary team allows for the reorganization of communication and power (Egan, 1988, p. 152). According to Naisbitt and Aburdene (1985), "*Fortune* magazine's eight most innovative companies—American Airlines, Apple, Campbell Soup, General Electric, Intel, Merck, 3M, and Philip Morris—are masters of the cross-disciplinary team" (p. 38). As a careful reader, you already have noted that Apple appears on the most innovative list and had to reorganize in 1990. Although Apple successfully built the Macintosh, and became a leader in easy-to-use computers, the refusal by different teams to accept outside information and inventions created excessive costs and diminished Apple's ability to be cost competitive. Building empires, guarding turf, and preventing loss of control are all powerful deterrents to effective team building (Kanter, 1983).

This examination of the limitations of parallel problem-solving groups, and the three inherent limitations to many team-building efforts, underscore the differences between parallel problem-solving groups—as manifested through QCs—and SMWTs.

In almost all cases, QCs do provide a useful initial step in the SMWT process (Gmelch & Miskin, 1984). In addition, teamwork, either through parallel structures or SMWTs, creates opportunities for social-emotional growth and increased productivity (Egan, 1988, p. 153).

What differentiates the parallel structure approach to problem solving and SMWTs are the powers vested in the two types of problem-solving groups. Although QCs maintain the traditional reporting structure and do not provide for control of resources, SMWTs provide for team management of the problems involved in the production process. Parallel structure groups tend to be impeded by the three problems of individual rewards, management style and perception, and segmentalism. Figure 10.5 shows the difference between traditional management, parallel structures, and SMWTs.

## SELF-MANAGING WORK TEAMS

SMWTs are self-regulating. This independence from outside authority represents a significant movement from small problem-solving groups to a more participative management system (Torres & Spiegel, 1990).

TABLE 10.4
Employee Involvement Stages

| | | | |
|---|---|---|---|
| *From*<br>Manager<br>Solves<br>Problems | | Traditional<br>Organization | |
| | *To*<br>Employees Help<br>Identify and Solve<br>Problems | Quality<br>Circles | |
| | | Task Forces | |
| | *To*<br>Problem-Solving<br>Part of Employees'<br>Jobs | | Self-Managing<br>Work Teams |

After sufficient training and experience SMWT members work together as one to complete a total job. As the teams develop, they increase the group's knowledge and understanding and gradually take shared responsibility for planning, organizing, decision making, controlling, scheduling, and goal setting. SMWTs work toward regulated, continuous improvement in the performance of their work unit. When they are introduced carefully into subunits of many organizations, SMWTs have a remarkable record of achievement in a variety of organizational settings.

This record can be measured in the six performance areas of quality, absenteeism, turnover, productivity, cost savings, and grievances (Hampton, 1987; Olsavsky, 1990; Osborn et al., 1990; Peters, 1987; Wellins et al., 1991). For example, in quality, reject rates were down 39% at Harmon International, service quality was improved at Citibank, and there was a 15% reduction in scrap at Eaton Corporation. Absenteeism was 2.5% at Sherman Williams, which is 63% below the plant average. At General Motors the absenteeism rate went from 7.5% to 2.5% where SMWTs were used. At Eaton Corporation, a range of 6% to 12% absenteeism was replaced by a .5% to 3% rate. Turnover dropped from 53% to 14% in 7 years at SAAB. Harmon International had a 7.2% decrease in turnover after the development of SMWTs.

Productivity, the ultimate measuring stick for many improvements, showed a 33% increase in 4 years at Guardian Life. Malden Mills showed a significant increase in productivity and Eaton Corporation had a productivity rate 5% higher than in their plants still operating under the traditional format. Midland-Ross had a cost savings of $300,000 through one SMWT program. Finally, grievances were reduced at General Motors in 7 years to 32 a year from 2,000 a year.

SMWT, as represented by the success of Ford's Team Taurus, demonstrate "the power of empowerment," with decisions being made by the people actually implementing the solutions (Waterman, 1987, p. 84). The Toyota-General Motors joint venture in California, New United Motors Manufacturing, Inc. (NUMMI), set the stage for the use of the team concept being used in "at least 17 GM assembly plants, six Chrysler plants, Ford's Rouge Steel operation and Romeo Engine plant in Michigan, and in all of the wholly or partially Japanese-owned plants in the U.S." (Parker & Slaughter, 1989, p. 53). A comparison between traditional GM production and NUMMI underscores the success of the SMWT. At NUMMI it takes 20 hr of labor to assemble a car, there is a 2% rate of unexcused absences in the work force, and NUMMI's Chevy Nova ranked number two in quality for cars produced in America. At GM it takes 28 hr of labor, there is a 9% rate of unexcused absences, and no car ranked in the top 15 (Parker & Slaughter, 1989, p. 58).

## CONCEPTS UNDERPINNING SELF-MANAGING WORK TEAMS

SMWTs represent a structural and procedural change in traditional organizational operations (Rees, 1991; Torres & Spiegel, 1990). Rather than operate as a parallel structure, the problem-solving group becomes a fundamental work unit. The team employs participative practices so that the supervisor and employees form a single operating unit. They represent a team of individuals, working together as one to complete a total job. With experience and training yielding knowledge and understanding, these individuals gradually take shared responsibility for planning, organizing, decision making, controlling, scheduling, goal setting, and in general, regulating continuous improvement in the performance of their work unit. For example, in the past a typical employee response to a production problem in a traditional organization would be to sit down and wait for a foreman. However, in SMWTs employees take the responsibility to solve the problem. They do so because their knowledge, involvement, power, and responsibilities are expanded. Table 10.5 outlines the changes occurring as organizations move toward SMWTs.

### Traditional Organizational Approaches

The goal is to move from control by management to commitment by the team members. Under the traditional orientation, controls are imposed to increase efficiency. This approach has seven elements. In sum, it:

1. separates planning from implementing;
2. uses standards for minimum acceptance performance,
3. applies a management structure based on specialization and top-down control;
4. has management prerogatives and authority;
5. establishes status symbols for rank and importance,
6. provides compensation based on a fair day's pay for a fair day's work,

TABLE 10.5
Evolution of Employee Involvement

| Traditional | Transition | Semiautonomous |
|---|---|---|
| "Not my job . . . see my supervisor" | Supervisor with some team participation | Each team's job . . . part of daily work—internal control by team |
| Control by management | Employee input sought | |
| Solve problems based on supervisor's guidance and instructions | Investigate problems—suggest solutions | Accurately predict problems and develop workable controls for them |
| Few, well-trained specialists responsible | Some people trained with time off-line to apply | All people trained with time to apply |
| Work to meet predetermined standards | Problem solving | Continuous improvement based on team's own analysis |
| External control | No power to implement Meetings in addition to normal job functions | |
| Narrow-based jobs | Some team activity | Broad-based jobs |
| Task focus | Function focus | Business focus |
| Little information to employees | Limited information to problem-solving groups | Full information |
| Specialized functions | Specific problem orientation | Integrated functions |
| Single-skilled jobs | Focus on production, morale, or quality issue | Multiskilled jobs |
| Performed by supervisor | Controlled and judged by supervisor or management | Performed by team |

7. encourages an adversarial relationship between worker and employer or management and union.

Moving from traditional management to SMWTs often requires a transition through the use of problem-solving groups (e.g., QCs), as was discussed earlier in this chapter. During this phase, management style must shift toward increased EI. Because old habits die hard, limited use of problem-solving groups seems to set the stage for the expanded use of employee involvement through SMWTs.

## Characteristics of the SMWT

Commitment by employees to higher performance is the key ingredient in the success of the SMWT. Eight characteristics make the SMWT different. They are:

1. broader, more flexible job design—broad-based jobs;
2. planning and implementation combined in one unit—increased autonomy and integration;

3. ambitious performance expectations replacing work standards—self-management;

4. compensation given for learning and teamwork—pay for knowledge and performance;

5. strong employee voice—greater involvement;

6. union/management or employee/organization relations tending toward mutuality;

7. employee assurances of secure future;

8. leaner, more flexible management—flat structure.

In sum, a team is not just a group. Although problem-solving groups are important, a team shares common boundaries, interdependent tasks, articulated purpose, and understood, owned goals. In addition, SMWTs seem to overcome the three barriers faced by many problem-solving groups.

## SMWTs and the Inherent Barriers to Team Building

First, SMWTs help overcome the impact of individualized rewards because SMWTs are designed to create member interaction and interdependence. In the examples cited earlier regarding the effectiveness of SMWTs, employees are also better paid, because they are rewarded on a team success basis (Hampton, 1987; Nora et al., 1986). Rather than viewing colleagues as competitors, individuals have powerful incentives for working together to maximize success. In addition, SMWTs provide for group identification and increased job satisfaction (Dalziel & Schoonover, 1988; Nora et al., 1986; Wellins et al., 1991). Task excellence is achieved because employees identify with the issues and the solutions. Because they are part of the solution, individuals feel a greater obligation to guarantee successful implementation.

Second, the role of managers and supervisors is dramatically different in the SMWT. In traditional organizations, leadership is based on the manager having the decision-making power, the information, the rewards, and in many cases, the expertise. The impact of this approach already has been discussed. The manager tells people what to do and becomes an administrator rather than a leader. Shared responsibility and control take the place of the traditional manager carrying the responsibilities and burdens of managing performance alone. The primary role of the manager is that of a coach. This coaching role includes setting high standards, forwarding all knowledge, working with the team members, while delegating increasing responsibility, and inspiring increased collaborative effort. The SMWT leader constantly asks: "How can each problem be solved in a way that further develops my subordinates' commitment and capabilities?" Managers empower others, move decisions to the proper levels, provide a vision and communicate it, and build trust and openness.

Third, SMWTs overcome segmentalism. The perspective of subordinates and managers is broadened beyond a narrow concern for a specialized area. Instead, team members identify with the problems associated with the overriding issues of productivity and quality. In addition, learning to solve problems makes each team member even better qualified to solve future problems.

**The Benefits of SMWTs.**   At this point, it is useful to summarize the outcomes occurring because of SMWTs. After reviewing the various studies (Hampton, 1987; Nora et al., 1986; Olsavsky, 1990; Osborn et al., 1990; Wellins et al., 1991), several conclusions can be drawn. As might be expected, there are benefits and costs.

Although SMWTs are touted as solutions to a vast variety of organizational issues, seven specific benefits consistently occur. They are:

1. improvement in work methods and procedures,
2. gains in attraction and retention of employees,
3. increases in staffing flexibility,
4. increases in service and product quality,
5. improvements in output,
6. enhanced quality of decision making,
7. reductions in supervision and staff support.

These factors lead to better productivity. Teams set the production goals, which tend to be higher. Feedback is employed effectively to improve performance. Cross-training enhances the ability of team members to help out and replace each other. The SMWTs do their own set up, thereby eliminating the need for supervisory assistance. The cost of labor is reduced 20% to 40% in many cases.

If this sounds too good to be true, the various analyses of SMWTs also highlight some significant impediments. If SMWT programs are to be implemented successfully, these factors must be considered carefully.

**Costs and Pitfalls of SMWTs.**   Five costs occurring in many programs are:

1. increased training costs, including the use of staff or outside consultants to facilitate the implementation;
2. unmet expectations for organizational change,
3. conflicts between participants and nonparticipants perhaps occurring if only a few teams are formed;
4. time lost in team meetings and slower decisions, and
5. resistance to the change by some staff support groups.

The seven pitfalls include:

1. insufficient or too late training for the teams,
2. management too impatient for results,
3. failure to acknowledge that people will test the system,
4. trying to implement when the technology for a particular change is insufficiently known,
5. inadequate time allowed for the experience to gel before it is evaluated,
6. inappropriate boundaries chosen for team membership or responsibilities, and
7. the corporate culture radically counter to the self-managing team philosophy.

As should be apparent, SMWTs require a substantial investment in time and forethought in order to be successful. Implementation can be difficult, but the successes of SMWTs make this approach to EI and organizational transformation exciting and important.

Under the very best of circumstances, change is difficult. When attempting to redefine employment relations, identifying and pursuing common interests seems to be a vital component (Cutcher-Gershenfeld, 1988, p. 24). The learning process, which requires management and employees alike to reconsider many underlying, and often incorrect assumptions, might be the most important outcome of any SMWT process.

## PLACING EI AND SMWT IN PERSPECTIVE

Facilitating the communication process in organizations is an important goal. EI programs provide a significant means for involving employees in the various stages of decision making. For most organizations, change is inevitable. Given the current pressure on organizations to increase competitiveness and transform into more productive entities, using the most successful forms of EI would seem to be required.

Faced with increasing costs, uncertainty, complexity, and the pace of change, many organizations have turned to teamwork and team building as a solution. Because teamwork represents one of the best means of EI, efforts in this direction are extremely useful. There is a difference between creating parallel problem-solving structures and empowering a team by making it self-managing. SMWTs represent a significant change in employee involvement.

You will be asked, at many points in your organizational career, to solve problems, enhance teamwork, and use groups effectively. We have risked belaboring the discussion of teams and semiautonomous work units to explain the actual impediments and possible success you should consider as you organize the communication processes in your group.

In this section, we have discussed five issues. First, the role of problem-solving groups as parallel organizational structures was presented by using QCs. The successes and limitations of parallel problem-solving groups, as represented by QCs, offer insights into the use of teams. Second, three inherent limitations to the use of parallel problem-solving groups, QCs included, suggested a need for an alternative.

A summary of the successes of SMWTs points to one viable alternative. Because SMWTs are a significant structural and psychological change, the basic concepts behind the SMWT were outlined.

Too often, organizations have rewarded values such as "If it ain't broke, don't fix it." EI programs tend to be superficial and lack credibility with employees. By passing managerial power to SMWTs, new values can be encouraged, such as "If it ain't broke, fix it anyway" or "Do your job well and find ways to constantly improve it!" The goal is to create work environments where power, knowledge, information, and rewards are shared. By assuming more responsibility for quality and continuous improvement, employees ultimately become self-managing through their work teams. Although implementation is difficult, the rewards can be remarkable for the organization and its members.

## CONCLUSION

Depending on the expertise of a particular organizational researcher, different factors will be seen as the most important part of an organization. So, for one group networks and channels are critical. Others peg theory, leadership, or motivation and the important knowledge areas. Still others look to the one-to-one relationship as the key factor. However, one area where the interest of scholars converge is small groups. As we stated in the introduction, groups are the gears and inner workings of an organization. Regardless of the organization you join, the coordination, complexity, and working of small groups will be important to you. We discussed the scope of small-group activities.

This chapter has provided you with a definition of small groups that explains why the scope is so broad. We further explained small groups by outlining the types and characteristics.

A great deal of time was spent on group cohesiveness, including an analysis of the various climate, ideology, and interacting factors. All groups develop norms of behavior that are enforced by group members. Part of the process of fitting into a group is understanding the roles and group leadership patterns. Groups also have their own patterns of development, and two of the most popular processes were explained.

There are advantages and disadvantages to the use of groups. One means of overcoming these is to use one of the four tailored methods. Another is to examine the critical role of employee involvement and groups.

The last part of this chapter provides you with an extensive analysis of how employee involvement, teams, and semiautonomous work units are used in organizations. A careful reading of these concepts will provide you with an in-depth understanding of how organizations actually employ the group process.

# REFERENCES

Abbott, J. R. (1990). *New approaches to collective bargaining and workplace relations: Do they work?* Washington, DC: Bureau of Labor-Management Relations & Cooperative Programs.

Bain, D. (1982). *The productivity prescription: The manager's guide to improving productivity and profits.* New York: McGraw-Hill.

Bales, R. F. (1950). *Interaction process analysis.* Reading, MA: Addison-Wesley.

Bales, R. F. (1970). *Personality and interpersonal behavior.* New York: Holt, Rinehart & Winston.

Bangs, D. H., Jr. (1988). *Business planning guide.* Portsmouth, NH: Upstart.

Baron, R. A. (1983). *Behavior in organizations: Understanding and managing the human side of work.* Boston; Allyn & Bacon.

Beebe, S. A., & Masterson, J. T. (1990). *Communicating in small groups: Principles and practices* (3rd ed.). Glenview, IL: Scott, Foresman.

Beene, K. D., & Sheats, P. (1948). Functional roles of group members. *Journal of Social Issues, 4,* 41–49.

Bennis, W. (1989). *Why leaders can't lead: The unconscious conspiracy continues.* San Francisco: Jossey-Bass.

Blair, J. D., & Whitehead, J. D. (1984). Can quality circles survive in the United States? *Business Horizons, 27,* 17–23.

Blake, R. R., Mouton, J. S., & Allan, R. L. (1987). *Spectacular teamwork.* New York: Wiley.

Bolman, L. G., & Deal, T. E. (1991). *Reframing organizations: Artistry, choice, and leadership.* San Francisco: Jossey-Bass.

Bormann, E. G. (1975). *Discussion and group methods* (2nd ed.). New York: Harper & Row.

Bostrom, R. (1970). Patterns of communicative interaction in small groups. *Communication Monographs, 37,* 257–258.

Bradford, D. L., & Cohen, A. R. (1984). *Managing for excellence: The guide for developing high performance in contemporary organizations.* New York: Wiley.

Brilhart, J. K., & Galanes, J. K. (1989). *Effective group discussion* (6th ed.). Dubuque, IA: Brown.

Buell, B., Levine, J. B., & Gross, N. (1990, October 15). Apple: New team, new strategy. *Business Week,* p. 88.

Campbell, D. T. (1958). Common fate, similarity, and other indices of the status of aggregates of persons as social entities. *Behavioral Science, 3,* 14–25.

Cartwright, D., & Zander, A. (Eds.). (1968). *Group dynamics: Research and theory* (3rd ed.). New York: Harper & Row.

Cole, D. (1989, May). Meetings that make sense. *Psychology Today,* pp. 12–14.

Colorado governor staff "rough it" in a team effort. (1987, July 13). *USA Today,* p. 2A.

Conger, J. A. (1989). Leadership: The art of empowering others. *The Academy of Management Executive, 3,* 17–24.

Corporate snooping refined to fine art. (1990, April 29). *The Tuscaloosa News,* p. 7E.

Coser, L. A. (1956). *The functions of social conflict.* New York: Free Press.

Cragan, J. F., & Wright, D. W. (1991). *Communication in small group discussions: An integrated approach* (3rd ed.). St. Paul, MN: West.

Crocker, O., Charney, C., & Chui, S. L. (1984). *Quality circles: A guide to participation and productivity.* Toronto: Methuen.

Cusella, L. P. (1987). Feedback, motivation, and performance. In F. M. Jablin, L. L. Putman, K. H. Roberts, & L. W. Porter (Eds.), *Handbook of organizational communication* (pp. 624–678). Newbury Park, CA: Sage.

Cutcher-Gershenfeld, J. (1988). *Tracing a transformation in industrial relations.* Washington, DC: Bureau of Labor-Management Relations & Cooperative Programs.

Dalkey, N. D. (1967). *Delphi.* Chicago: Rand.

Dalziel, M. M, & Schoonover, S. C. (1988). *Changing ways: A practical tool for implementing change within organizations.* New York: AMACOM.

Daniels, T. D., & Spiker, T. D. (1991). *Perspectives on organizational communication* (2nd ed.). Dubuque, IA: Brown.

Delaney, T., Lewin, D., & Ichniowski, C. (1989). *Human resource policies and practices in American firms* (BLMR Report No. 137). Washington, DC: U.S. Department of Labor.

Delbecq, A. L., Van de Ven, A. H., & Gustafson, D. H. (1975). *Group techniques for program planning: A guide to nominal group and Delphi processes.* Glenview, IL: Scott, Foresman.

DuBrin, A. J., Ireland, R. D., & Williams, J. C. (1989). *Management & organization.* Cincinnati: South-Western.

Dyer, W. G. (1987). *Team building: Issues and alternatives* (2nd ed.). Reading, MA: Addison-Wesley.

Egan, G. (1988). *Change agent skills a: Assessing & designing excellence.* San Diego: University Associates.

Egan, G. (1989). Model a: A design, assessment, and facilitation template in the pursuit of excellence. In J. W. Pfeiffer (Ed.), *The 1989 annual: Developing human resources* (pp. 267–275). San Diego: University Associates.

*Employee involvement in America.* (1989). Washington, DC: General Accounting Office.

Falcione, R. L., Sussman, L., & Herden, R. P. (1987). Communication climate in organizations. In F. M. Jablin, L. L. Putman, K. H. Roberts, & L. W. Porter (Eds.), *Handbook of organizational communication* (pp. 195–227). Newbury Park, CA: Sage.

Festinger, L. (1957). *A theory of cognitive dissonance.* Stanford, CA: Stanford University Press.

Fisher, B. A. (1970). Decision emergence: Phases in group decision-making. *Speech Monographs, 37,* 53–66.

Fletcher, W. (1983). *Meetings, meetings.* New York: Morrow.

Frank, A. D., & Brownell, J. L. (1989). *Organizational communication and behavior: Communicating to improve performance* (2 + 2 = 5). New York: Holt, Rinehart & Winston.

French, W. L., & Bell, C. H. (1984). *Organization development: Behavioral science interventions for organization improvement* (3rd ed.). Englewood Cliffs, NJ: Prentice-Hall.

General Accounting Office. (1989, June). Miles to go . . . Or unity at last. *Journal of Quality and Participation,* pp. 60–67.

Gmelch, W. H., & Miskin, V. D. (1984). *Productivity teams: Beyond quality circles.* New York: Wiley.

Goddard, W. (1986). The healthy side of conflict. *Management World, 15,* 10–12.

Goodall, H. L., Jr. (1990). *Small group communication in organizations* (2nd ed.). Dubuque, IA: Brown.

Gutknecht, D. B., & Miller, J. R. (1986). *The organizational and human resources handbook.* Lanham, MD: University Press of America.

Haas, M. S. (1990). Labor-management partnerships in the U.S. *International Productivity Journal, 1,* 11–13.

Hampton, W. J. (1987, June 8). Why image counts. *Business Week,* p. 130.

Harris, T. E. (1990). Organizational cultures: An examination of the role of communication. In S. Thomas & W. A. Evans (Eds.), *Communication and culture: Language, performance, and media* (pp. 143–155). Norwood, NJ: Ablex.

Hicks, R. (1990, April 10). Retreat firm molds executives into team. *Birmingham Post-Herald,* p. B6.

Hiltz, S. R., Johnson, K., & Turoff, M. (1986). Experiments in group decision-making: Communication process and outcome in face-to-face versus computerized conferences. *Human Communication Research, 13,* 225–252.

Hirokawa, R. J., & Pace, R. (1983). A descriptive investigation of the possible communication-based reasons for effective and ineffective group decision making. *Communication Monographs, 50,* 363–379.

Hoerr, J. (1990, December 17). Sharpening minds for a competitive edge. *Business Week,* pp. 72, 74, 78.

Huber, G. P. (1986). *Human behavior in organizations* (3rd ed.). Cincinnati: South-Western.

Huseman, R. C., Lahiff, J., & Wells, R. (1974, February). Communication thermoclines: Toward a process of identification. *Personnel Journal,* 124–135.

Jablin, F. M. (1982). Organizational communication: An assimilation approach. In M. E. Roloff & C. R. Berger (Eds.), *Social cognition and communication* (pp. 255–286). Newbury Park, CA: Sage.

Jablin, F. M. (1985). Task/work relationships: A life-span perspective. In M. L. Knapp & G. R. Miller (Eds.), *Handbook of interpersonal communication* (pp. 615–654). Newbury Park, CA: Sage.

Jablin, F. M. (1987). Organizational entry, assimilation, and exit. In F. M. Jablin, L. L. Putman, K. H. Roberts, & L. W. Porter (Eds.), *Handbook of organizational communication* (pp. 679–740). Newbury Park, CA: Sage.

Jablin, F. M., & Sussman, L. (1983). Organizational group communication: A review of the literature and model of the process. In H. Greenbaum, R. Falcoine, & S. Hellweg (Eds.), *Organizational communication: Abstract, analysis, and overview* (Vol. 8, pp. 1–28). Newbury Park, CA: Sage.

Jackall, R. (1983). Moral mazes: Bureaucracy and managerial work. *Harvard Business Review, 61,* 118–130.

Jacobs, N. A. (1982). Quality circles alone can't hike productivity. *Industry Week, 212*(3), 28–29.

Johns, G. (1988). *Organizational behavior: Understanding life at work* (2nd ed.). Glenview, IL: Scott, Foresman.

Kanter, R. M. (1983). *Change masters: Innovation for productivity in the American corporation.* New York: Simon & Schuster.

Karp, H. B. (1983). A look at quality circles. In L. D. Goodstein & J. W. Pfeiffer (Eds.), *The 1983 annual for facilitators, trainers, and consultants* (pp. 157–163). San Diego: University Associates.

Kelly, K. (1991, September 16). 3M run scared? Forget about it. *Business Week,* pp. 59, 62.

Kelly, L., Lederman, L. C., & Phillips, G. M. (1989). *Communicating in the workplace.* New York: Harper & Row.

Klein, J. A. (1984). Why supervisors resist employee involvement. *Harvard Business Review, 62,* 87–95.

Kotter, J. P. (1988). *The leadership factor.* New York: Free Press.

Kotter, J. P. (1990). *A force for change: How leadership differs from management.* New York: Free Press.

Kouzes, J. M., & Posner, J. M. (1990). *The leadership challenge.* San Francisco: Jossey-Bass.

Latane, B., Williams, K., & Harkins, S. (1979, October). Social loafing. *Psychology Today,* pp. 102–104.

Lawler, E. E., III, & Mohrman, S. S. (1985). Quality circles after the fad. *Harvard Business Review, 63,* 65–71.

Lefton, R. E. (1988). The eight barriers to teamwork. *Personnel Journal, 67,* 18–21.

Leonard, J. W. (1986). Gather "round!": Putting a method in your meetings. *Management World, 15,* 30–32.

Lewin, K. (1951). *Field theory in social science.* New York: Harper & Row.

Management meetings mount. (1988, March 2). *USA Today,* p. B1.

Management Recruiters International. (1986, January 8). Wasting time at work. *USA Today,* p. B1.

Marks, M. L. (1986, March). The question of quality circles. *Psychology Today,* pp. 36–44.

Marshall, R. (1987). *Unheard voices.* New York: Basic.

Meetings unpopular, but still a staple. (1990, February 25). *The Tuscaloosa News,* p. 1E.

Meyer, G. W., & Stott, G. W. (1985). Quality circles: Panacea or Pandora's box? *Organizational Dynamics, 13,* 34–50.

Miller, G. R. (1990). Interpersonal communication. In G. L. Dahnke & G. W. Clatterbuck (Eds.), *Human communication: Theory and research* (pp. 91–122). Belmont, CA: Wadsworth.

Mooreland, R. L., & Levine, J. M. (1982). Socialization in small groups: Temporal changes in individual-group relations. In L. Berkowitz (Ed.), *Advances in experimental social psychology* (Vol. 15, pp. 140–178). New York: Academic.

Naisbitt, J., & Aburdene, P. (1985). *Re-inventing the corporation.* New York: Warner.

Nora, J. J., Rogers, C. R., & Stramy, R. J. (1986). *Transforming the workplace.* Princeton, NJ: Princeton Research Press.

O'Connoll, S. (1979). *The manager as communicator.* New York: Harper & Row.

Offerman, L. R., & Gowing, M. K. (1990). Organizations of the future: Changes and challenges. *American Psychologist, 45,* 95–108.

Olsavsky, M. A. (Ed.). (1990). *The new work systems network: A compendium of selected work innovation cases* (BLMR Report No. 136). Washington, DC: U.S. Government Printing Office.

Osborn, A. F. (1959). *Applied imagination.* New York: Scribner's.

Osborn, J. D., Moran, L., Musselwhite, E., & Zenger, J. H. (1990). *Self-directed work teams: The new American challenge.* Homewood, IL: Business One Irwin.

Pace, R. W., & Faules, D. F. (1989). *Organizational communication* (2nd ed.). Englewood Cliffs, NJ: Prentice-Hall.

Parker, M., & Slaughter, M. (1989). Worked to the limit. *Best of Business, 11,* 52–58.

Pascale, R. (1984, May 28). Fitting new employees into the company culture. *Fortune,* pp. 28–43.

Peters, T. (1987). *Thriving on chaos: Handbook for a management revolution.* New York: Knopf.

Peters, T. J., & Waterman, T. J., Jr. (1982). *In search of excellence.* New York: Harper & Row.

Phillips, G. M. (1966). *Communication and the small group.* Indianapolis: Bobbs-Merrill.

Phillips, G. M., Pedersen, D. J., & Wood, J. T. (1979). *Group discussion: A practical guide to participation and leadership.* Boston: Houghton Mifflin.

Putnam, L. L., & Poole, M. S. (1987). Conflict and negotiation. In F. M. Jablin, L. L. Putman, K. H. Roberts, & L. W. Porter (Eds.), *Handbook of organizational communication* (pp. 549–599). Newbury Park, CA: Sage.

Rees, F. (1991). *How to lead work teams: Facilitation skills.* San Diego: Pfeiffer.

Reich, R. B. (1987). Entrepreneurship reconsidered: The team as hero. *Harvard Business Review, 65,* 77–83.

Rogers, E. M., & Agarwala-Rogers, R. (1976). *Communication in organizations.* New York: Free Press.

Rowe, M. P., & Baker, M. (1984). Are you hearing enough employee concerns? *Harvard Business Review, 62,* 126–130.

Safety risk and cost debated. (1989, May 14). *The Sunday Courier,* p. B1.

Schaef, A. W., & Fassel, D. (1988). *The addictive organization.* San Francisco: Harper & Row.

Schein, E. H. (1969). *Process consultation: Its role in organizational development.* Reading, MA: Addison-Wesley.

School burned over cookbook. (1988, November 9). *The Evansville Courier,* p. 2.

Shaw, M. E. (1976). *Group dynamics: The psychology of small group behavior* (2nd ed.). New York: McGraw-Hill.

Sigband, N. B. (1985). Meetings with success. *Personnel Journal, 64,* 47–50.

Smeltzer, L. R., & Kedia, B. L. (1985). Knowing the ropes: Organizational requirements for quality circles. *Business Horizons, 28,* 30–34.

Stealth's miss kept from Cheney. (1990, April 7). *The Birmingham News/Post-Herald,* p. 3A.

Sundstrom, E., De Meuse, K. P., & Futrell, D. (1990). Work teams: Applications and effectiveness. *American Psychologist, 45,* 120–133.

Survival guide to the office meeting. (1988, June 26). *Wall Street Journal,* p. B1.

Tersine, R. E., & Riggs, W. E. (1976). The Delphi technique: A long-range planning tool. *Business Horizons, 19,* 51–56.

Tompkins, P. K. (1987). Translating organizational theory: Symbolism over substance. In F. M. Jablin, L. L. Putman, K. H. Roberts, & L. W. Porter (Eds.), *Handbook of organizational communication* (pp. 70–96). Newbury Park, CA: Sage.

Torres, C., & Spiegel, J. (1990). *Self-directed work teams: A primer.* San Diego: University Associates.

Truell, G. F. (1984). *Building and managing productive work teams.* Buffalo, NY: PAT.

Truell, G. F. (1991). *Employee involvement: A guidebook for managers.* Buffalo, NY: PAT.

Tuckman, B. W. (1965). Developmental sequences in small groups. *Psychological Bulletin, 63,* 384–399.

Tuckman, B. W. (1977). Stages in small-group development revisited. *Group and Organizational Studies, 2,* 419–427.

Waterman, R. H., Jr. (1987). *The renewal factor: How the best get and keep the competitive edge.* New York: Bantam.

Watson, K. W., & Barker, L. L. (1990). *Interpersonal and relational communication.* Scottsdale, AZ: Gorsuch Scarisbrick.

Wellins, R. S., Byham, W. C., & Wilson, J. M. (1991). *Empowered teams: Creating self-directed work groups that improve quality, productivity, and participation.* San Francisco: Jossey-Bass.

Westcott, J. M. (1988). Humor and the effective work group. In J. W. Pfieffer (Ed.), *The 1988 annual: Developing human resources* (pp. 139–142). San Diego: University Associates.

What business meetings cost. (1988, September 12). *USA Today*, p. B1.

Whyte, G. (1989). Groupthink reconsidered. *Academy of Management Review, 14,* 40–56.

Wilmot, W. W. (1987). *Dyadic communication* (3rd ed.). New York: Random House.

Wood, R., Hull, F., & Azumi, K. (1983). Evaluating quality circles: The American application. *California Management Review, 1,* 37–51.

Wooford, J. C., Gerloff, E. A., & Cummins, R. C. (1979). Group behavior and the communication process. In R. S. Cathcart & L. A. Samovar (Eds.), *Small group communication: A reader* (3rd ed., pp. 28–38). Dubuque, IA: Brown.

Wyatt Company. (1987, September 12). Employee satisfaction: What hurts, what soothes? *Behavioral Sciences Newsletter,* p. 2.

Yang, D. J., & Buderi, R. (1990, August 13). Step by step with Nike. *Business Week,* pp. 115–116.

Ziller, R. C., & Behringer, R. D. (1960). Assimilation of the knowledgeable newcomer under conditions of groups success and failure. *Journal of Abnormal and Social Psychology, 45,* 288–291.

# CHAPTER 11

# Effective Leadership
# in Organizations

Although observers and authorities differ regarding the specific elements needed to create and maintain a successful organization, they all agree that leadership plays a pivotal role (e.g., Bennis, 1990; Kotter, 1988; Kouzes & Posner, 1987; Peters, 1987). The leadership by key individuals makes a difference in the performance of organizations, groups, and individuals (Weiner & Mahoney, 1981; Zaleznik, 1989). Because leadership is something people do, communication plays a vital role in all leadership activities (Clemes & Mayer, 1987). As Cybert (1990) put it, "Communication is perhaps the most important mechanism of leadership" (p. 35). Leaders are judged by their communication behaviors, which provides the focus for this chapter.

Anecdotal material abounds regarding specific leaders (e.g., Deal & Kennedy, 1982, pp. 37–45; Peters & Austin, 1985; Peters & Waterman, 1982). The importance of Lee Iaccoca to Chrysler, Mary Kay to Mary Kay Cosmetics, Walt Disney to Walt Disney Co., and other well-known celebrities to their companies is legend. The less flamboyant founders or leaders of the IBMs, Maytags, and many other organizations are still leading forces in shaping their organizations (Harris, 1990, p. 149). These leaders have gained stature and recognition as their companies' success stories become well known.

Many corporate and business leaders take on a larger-than-life celebrity status thanks to an effective strategy for organizational turnarounds (e.g., Iacocca), best sellers (e.g., Iacocca, Donald Trump), personal promotion (e.g., T. Boone Pickens, Trump, Ted Turner), and/or capital accumulation as touted by the annual listings of the richest people in America (e.g., Sam Walton) (Bennis, 1990). Other individuals appear for their 15 min. of leadership fame and then are dethroned by changing events or error of judgment (e.g., Ivan Boesky).

This chapter places leadership in perspective. You are already privy to a great deal of leadership information. Our goal here is to collect our understanding of leadership in one chapter. This is accomplished by following these steps. First, we define leadership. Second, a differentiation between management and leadership is provided. Because communication is vital to leadership, the third part of this chapter explains this link. Fourth, several major behavioral approaches to understanding leadership are examined. Finally, an analysis is offered for three leadership types: heroic, transformational, and learning.

## DEFINITION OF LEADERSHIP

Being an effective leader is an admired attribute and a sought after skill. But, what is leadership? For a moment, stop reading and make a list of 10 leaders.

What do they have in common?

Do you have some criteria for calling someone a leader?

Is your list similar to the one I overviewed at the beginning of this chapter? That is, composed of famous and infamous – but well-known – individuals.

Did effectiveness in a particular activity make them a good leader?

Were they successful in every leadership activity they tried?

Accepting that a leader must lead someone, what is the difference between being in charge and leading?

Finally, compare your list of leaders with someone else's list.

Do not be surprised if this exercise raises as many questions as it answers. Leadership is a skill best defined by examining its characteristics.

Leaders have a sense of direction. The nature of leadership includes (a) directing others to behave in a desirable manner, (b) providing a vision that operates as a map for the members of the organization, (c) focusing attention toward specific activities by allocating the leader's time carefully, and (d) setting some central goals that allow individuals and groups to work together (Cybert, 1990, pp. 31–33).

A second major factor is *influence* (Bass, 1960, p. 90; Stogdill, 1950, p. 4). As Hollander and Offermann (1990a) put it, "Leadership clearly depends on responsive followers in a process involving the direction and maintenance of collective activity" (p. 179). One operational definition of leadership is "any attempt to influence the behavior of another individual or group" (Hersey, 1984, p. 14).

In some ways, influence is the capacity to set priorities and goals. As Cybert (1990) observed, "Leadership is the ability to get participants in an organization to focus their attention on the problems that the leader considers significant" (Cybert, (p. 29).

Third, leadership is *situational*. The activity called leadership is defined by what an individual does in the context of the situation. A war hero may fail miserably in running a local bakery. As Clark and Clark (1990) put it, "Leaders deserve to be so-called only when they have been the key players in acts of leadership" (p. 20). A remarkable number of books define leadership by pointing to specific successes and failures, followed by a list of particular activities and attributes effective leaders possess. This is not an unreasonable approach. According to Kotter (1988) "Effective leadership, research suggests, is remarkably chameleonlike . . . [it] is a function of the situation in which it is found" (p. 21). Put another way, there is no "single comprehensive list of leadership qualities and . . . no single path to leadership" (Clark & Clark, 1990, p. 70). Although certain individuals might be predisposed toward leadership, leaders are more made than born.

Before we examine leadership theory in depth, we need to respond to an important issue. What is the difference between leadership and management?

## LEADERSHIP AND MANAGEMENT

Management is defined as the process of getting work done through others. As Albanese (1988) put it, "A manager is an organizational member who is formally accountable for the job performance of others in the organization" (p. 28). Most examinations of management outline four broad functions: planning, organizing, leading, and controlling (DuBrin, Ireland, & Williams, 1989, pp. 4–10). Clearly, these are important skills for most of us, or we will fail when we try to lead others. But, there are important distinctions between leadership and management.

### Perspective

There is a difference in perspective. Leaders focus on innovation, change, and dealing with turbulence whereas managers create stability, harmony, and constancy (Kouzes & Posner, 1987, pp. 31–32). A survey of 90 successful corporate and public leaders found that managers are people who do things right and leaders are people who do the right things (Bennis & Nanus, 1985, p. 21). Effective leaders are able to understand the organization's needs and adapt their individual style to facilitate change (Bolman & Deal, 1984, 1991).

Because there is a difference between controlling and changing, there are a large number of actions by organizational leaders that have come under increased attack for diminishing growth, team development, and company loyalty (Egan, 1988; Pascale & Anthos, 1982; Zaleznik, 1989). Traditional managerial behaviors often are seen as roadblocks to effective change (Hickman & Silva, 1984). Too often, managers act in ways counterproductive to facilitating change (Brown, 1987). Although everyone believes that organizations need leadership, most individuals act as managers. Managers "administer, allocate resources, resolve conflicts, and go home at night convinced that they have done a good day's work" (Cybert, 1990, p. 29). Managers tend to maintain the status quo instead of responding to demands for change.

The same can be said for leaders with ascribed status. Extensive anecdotal information indicates that some leaders articulate the importance of change, but do not act in a manner conducive to change (Peters, 1987; Schein, 1985). The argument, presented in various forms, is that many individuals in situations requiring leadership (e.g., internal and external change, competition, quality, customer service, loyalty) are relying on well-tuned, time-honored, and control-centered managerial responses instead. Rather than acting like leaders, many executives revert back to the very managerial behaviors that limited the effectiveness of their response in the first place.

## Power

Leaders work toward empowerment of subordinates whereas managers concentrate on developing power rather than people (Jackall, 1988). Behind-the-scenes lobbying, formation of secret coalitions, and empire building takes the place of developing subordinates and facilitating change (Zaleznik, 1989). Early writings outlining the human relations and human resources approaches (e.g., Likert, 1961; McGregor, 1960), and numerous other scholars calling for increased participatory activities (e.g., Bradford & Cohen, 1984; Egan, 1988; Ouchi, 1981), set the stage for differentiating between management and leadership. Leaders develop strong subordinates (Kotter, 1988, p. 26), and empower individuals and teams (Conger, Kanungo, & Associates, 1988). In many cases, teaching others to lead themselves is required. The goal is to inculcate habits of self-leadership in employees. In the end, employees will be self-directive. One leadership analysis calls this a *Superleader*. This is someone "who leads others to lead themselves" (Manz & Sims, 1989, pp. 3, 10–11). They become teachers and coaches rather than directors. The Superleader gets others to command and instruct themselves.

Stories that surface in organizations demonstrate empowerment and often define leadership. For example, at Procter & Gamble, an hourly employee noticed that the labels on Jif peanut butter in the store were off-center. He bought all the bottles assuming that P & G would pay him back. They did, of course, and he became a hero and a leader in the pursuit of quality (Peters & Austin, 1985, p. 279). A Domino's Pizza driver was passing a home where there had been a bad fire. The owners were sifting through the damage. He took the initiative to return to his store, explain the situation to the manager, and return with two pizzas. One of the owners acted perplexed and pointed out that, with the fire, they certainly were not ordering pizza. The driver replied that he knew that, but figured they must be really hungry. The pizzas were on the house—and the driver offered to take them back if they were the wrong kind! Now that's situational empowerment and leadership! And a confirmed Domino's customer (Hart, Heskett, & Sasser, 1990–1991, p. 16). Marriott Hotels have been leaders in empowering employees. For example, at the Minneapolis Marriott City Center, employees are authorized to spend $10 at their discretion to satisfy guests. In one case, a guest complained about not finding a particular book in the hotel gift shop and the cashier, at the end of her shift, walked to a local bookstore and purchased the book with her $10. The guest was astonished, and a confirmed Marriott customer for life (Hart et al., 1990–1991, p. 16). These examples demonstrate empowerment. They also show how leadership becomes a matter of doing the right thing at the right time. Each of these employees took a leadership position with regard to a particular problem.

Leaders have a different perspective regarding their organizational roles and the use of subordinates and power. Bennis (1989) provided a useful conclusion. The difference, he stated, between managers and leaders is fundamental. The manager administers, the leader innovates. The manager maintains, the leader develops. The manager relies on systems, the leader relies on people. The manager counts on control, the leader counts on trust.

Kotter (1990) outlined four major differences between leadership and management (pp. 6–9). As can be seen in Table. 11.1, Kotter's analysis highlights the difference between management and leadership. Remember, planning, budgeting, organizing, and controlling are the watchwords of effective management (Kotter, 1988, pp. 21–22). Leaders, on the other hand, orient themselves toward active goals rather than dealing with deviations from the prescribed direction, and excite followers toward new options and ideas (Zaleznik, 1989). All of these comments might be unimportant if change was not a fundamental characteristic of all organizations.

## Leadership and Change

Two observations about organizations are almost axiomatic. First, change is a fact of organizational life (Steers, 1988). Every organization will grow, diminish, gain and lose personnel, alter product lines, have new and different customers, and be influenced by a multitude of other environmental factors (Peters, 1987). Even the best-run organizations must cope with international competition, a shifting domestic market, evolving internal characteristics, and major demographic transformations. For example, through the 1990s, the touchstone for success may well be quality. Effective leadership is needed to support the changes in priorities, develop managers, and alter the prevailing culture (Juran, 1989). For banks, hospitals, and numerous other organizations, customer service and developing a sales culture will rank as vital issues (Harris, 1990).

Second, leadership behaviors are pivotal to effective change management (Danziel & Schoonover, 1988). The relationship between leadership behaviors and organizational success is well documented (Allcorn, 1988). Leaders are the driving force behind, and the heart of, the change process (Egan, 1988). Stories about the various actions taken by successful leaders are repeated within the organization and often create a standard of excellence for other organizational members to follow (Peters & Austin, 1985; Peters & Waterman, 1982). Because leaders control the resources, the communication opportunities, and the goal-setting mechanisms, their behaviors have a critical impact on change efforts. In order to deal effectively with the changing job attitudes and concerns of workers, shared leadership through par-

TABLE 11.1
Four Major Differences Between Leadership and Management

|  | Management | Leadership |
|---|---|---|
| Creating an Agenda | Planning and budgeting<br>detailed steps<br>timetables for achieving results<br>allocating resources | Establishing direction<br>vision of the future<br>often distant future<br>producing changes |
| Developing a Human Network for Achieving the Agenda | Organizing and staffing<br>structure to accomplish a plan<br>staffing<br>delegating responsibility and authority for carrying out plan<br>providing policies and procedures<br>create systems to monitor implementation | Aligning people<br>communicating direction<br>words and deeds to all<br>creation of teams and coalitions that understand the vision<br>gaining acceptance of vision |
| Execution | Controlling and problem solving<br>monitoring results vs. plan in some detail, identifying deviations, and then planning and organizing to solve these problems | Motivating and inspiring<br>energizing people to overcome major political, bureaucratic, and resource barriers |
| Outcomes | Produces a degree of predictability<br>potential of consistently producing key results expected by various stakeholders (e.g., customers, always on time; for stockholders, being on budget) | Produces change, often dramatic<br>potential of producing extremely useful change (e.g., new products, more competitive) |

From Kotter (1990). Copyright © 1990 by Free Press. Reprinted by permission.

ticipation and teamwork is required (Offermann & Gowing, 1990, p. 103). Empowerment and power sharing are used to reflect the shift in focus from leader domination to follower involvement through groups and team efforts (Burker, 1986; Gutknecht & Miller, 1986, pp. 214–215; Nora, Rogers, & Stramy, 1986).

## Leadership and Communication

Leading is a process that is tied directly to communication (Pace & Faules, 1989, pp. 166–168). There cannot be leadership without communication. Besides the obvious fact that a leader must "lead" someone and that can be done only through some type of communication, leaders also use symbols to create reality (Hackman & Johnson, 1991, p. 7). Leaders must make a conscious use of symbols to reach their goals and to discuss the past, present, and future.

A quick review of the last section highlights the interdependence between leadership and communication. Consider the following leadership activities, which represent proactive communication behaviors:

1. articulating a vision by communicating a great deal to all the individuals involved (Bennis, 1990, p. 20; Kotter, 1990, p. 52);
2. applying effective interpersonal skills to develop trusting relationships (Kotter, 1988, p. 29);
3. creation of meaning (Bennis, 1990, p. 168);
4. exercising influence through communication (Pace & Faules, 1989, p. 168);
5. using symbols to clarify visions (Zaleznik, 1989);
6. innovating, developing, and trusting (Bennis, 1990); and
7. motivating and inspiring (Kotter, 1990, pp. 61–73).

In summary, effective leaders employ numerous behaviors (e.g., communication activities) to achieve these needed changes based on the requirements of the specific situation (Beck, 1982).

In the end, leaders are the users of symbols and they learn to present themselves effectively. We covered this concept in our chapter on symbolic behavior when we outlined impression management. At this point, we have differentiated between leadership and management and linked leadership and communication. We now review several leadership theories.

## LEADERSHIP THEORIES

There are numerous approaches to defining and explaining leadership. We present an overview of these by concentrating on trait approaches, two-dimensional models, contingency leadership, path-goal theory, situational leadership, transformational, and leadership that creates a learning environment in an organization. This is a prodigious task worthy of an entire textbook. Therefore, we will examine the essence of each approach and conclude with some observations regarding effective leadership.

### Trait Theory

According to the trait approaches, effective leadership is best understood in terms of certain traits, or specific personal characteristics possessed by leaders. During the early part of the 20th century, numerous studies concluded that certain psychological and physical characteristics predisposed individuals toward leadership positions (Hackman & Johnson, 1991, p. 43). Attempts at compiling these characteristics can take two forms. One is the *great person theory*,which focuses on past heroes, leaders, or successful individuals. Although it is interesting to discover characteristics common to various leaders, researchers have had little success in developing a profile of physical or psychological traits held by the majority of leaders. Research concentrated on collecting examples of proven leaders and developing a list of the characteristics they possessed. Whereas age, height, and appearance might be evident as a contributory factor for some leaders, no research has been able to provide a universal list of leadership characteristics. In conclusion, there does not appear to be a comprehensive list of physical leadership traits.

The psychological testing movement, also emerging during the early part of the 20th century, attempted to establish certain traits. Stodgill (1974) reviewed these studies and concluded that leaders have a strong drive for responsibility and task completion; are adventuresome and original; exercise initiative in social situations; have self-confidence; accept consequences of decisions and actions; can influence behavior; tolerate stress, frustration, and delay; and structure social situations to the issues at hand (pp. 72, 81; see also Kirkpatrick & Locke, 1991). This established a *leadership type* concept.

Recent tests of leadership potential provide additional insights into certain behaviors that make someone more likely to succeed as a leader. *Personality type*, as an indicator of leadership potential, has long been of interest to organizational investigators. To date, there is an absence of measures of leadership personality (Clark & Clark, 1990, p. 50). This has not deterred the use of personality measures, such as the California Psychological Inventory (CPI) and the Myers–Briggs Type Indicator (MBTI), to try and determine the factors that make leaders successful. Dominance on the CPI scale appears to have the highest relationship to leadership (Gough, 1990). But, this makes sense. CPI merely identifies persons of prosocial ascendency dispositions that, in organizations, would be individuals who hold positions of authority and decision making. MBTI might be the most widely used psychological test instrument. The MBTI data bank holds over 500,000 records, and this does not account for all the American adults who have discovered their personality type through casual testing. In a very general sense, persons in higher levels of management are more likely to reach closure, prefer impersonal, logical decision making, and are practical (McCaulley, 1990). There is evidence that all 16 MBTI types assume leadership positions, which would support the assumption that everyone, given the proper response to a situation, has the potential to be a leader. In addition, these conclusions do not account for how a person becomes a leader, nor how they respond to a variety of situational variables. These psychological measures were not designed to predict leadership and they do not provide clear evidence of what personality factors will create a successful leader—yet. With longitudinal studies of managerial success, there is every possibility that particular personality flaws, and specific orientations, will surface as the underpinnings of leadership (Clark & Clark, 1990, p. 54).

Sometimes, the leader must evoke loyalty and trust, which has been labeled *charismatic leadership*. Originally, this meant leadership based on emotional appeal. *Charisma*, a Greek word, means divine gift, and early researchers saw such a leader as having considerable power over followers, especially in times of crisis (Hollander & Offermann, 1990b, p. 88). In its revised form, charismatic leadership involves (a) articulation of a strategic vision, (b) inspiration and empowerment of followers, and (c) superior articulation and impression management skills (Conger et al., 1988, chapters 1 & 3).

There is a dark side to charisma in organizations. As Clark and Clark (1990) pointed out, "The attractiveness of the charismatic leader makes it easy to overlook critical weaknesses" (p. 50). Three examples are the *Highly Likeable Floater, Hommes de Ressentiment*, and *Narcissists* (Hogan, Raskin, & Fazzini, 1990). Highly Likeable Floaters are positive, facilitate individuals and meetings, and make no enemies. As such, they float up in the organization without any agenda or performance. But, they do not know how to lead. *Hommes de Ressentiment* are able to be charming with great social skill. But, below this surface is an independent set of resentful tendencies based on a passive-aggressive personality. So, on the surface everyone likes this individual. But no one knows these people and cannot trust or follow them through the change process. Finally, *Narcissists* carry feelings of entitlement, expectation of special privileges, omnipotence, and self-centeredness. Why are these people charismatic? Because they come across with a great deal of self-composure, assertiveness, and self-confidence. Their external picture of leadership is hiding a true willingness to exploit subordinates, curry favor with superiors, and use any measure necessary to self-promote.

Although pointing to physical and psychological attributes is overly simplistic, no examination of leadership theory would be complete without some understanding of how variables such as personal characteristics contribute to effectiveness. How a leader comes across interpersonally and in front of a group has been linked consistently to effectiveness. "Appearance, self-image, friendliness, the projection of a favorable self-image, and motivation to be attractive to others" (Williams & Huber, 1986, p. 473) are all related to the leader's impact on others. An individual's personal integrity, mental ability, emotional maturity, problem-solving skills, motivational patterns in terms of a high activity level, and administrative skills all contribute, as traits, to effective leadership (Barrow, 1977; Harrell & Harrell, 1973; Sank, 1974). The operative variable is the word *contribute*. Intelligence, personality, and task-related characteristics are important to leadership success. Because many leadership tasks are ambiguous until the specific situation is encountered, no list of traits can be made that will predict effective leadership. Clearly, an inability to communicate, or to make cogent decisions, ultimately will restrict any potential leader. On the other hand, being an effective strategist without the commensurate ability to motivate also will create problems. We can conclude that certain salient characteristics of leaders have been identified, but there are few definitive guidelines. Effectiveness, situational adaptation, group influence on the leader, and the lack of uniformity at all levels of leadership remain issues not resolved by the trait approach (Gutknecht & Miller, 1986, p. 155).

Finding a list of reasons leaders most often fail proves to be a little easier than finding traits that lead to success. In a study conducted at the Center for Creative Leadership, ten reasons were identified:

1. insensitive to others. Abrasive, intimidating, bullying style;
2. cool, aloof, arrogant;
3. betrayal of trust;
4. overly ambitious, playing politics, thinking of next position;
5. specific performance problems with the business;
6. over managing, cannot build a team or delegate;
7. unable to staff effectively;
8. unable to think strategically;
9. unable to adapt to a boss with a different style;
10. over dependence on mentor or advocate (McCall & Lombardo, 1983, p. 28).

In conclusion, leaders pursue activities that enhance their effectiveness. Certain traits clearly contribute to their capacity to lead other people, or to their inability to lead. But, there are too many intervening variables to predict that a particular set of traits will lead to being a leader.

## Two-Dimensional Models

Another way to examine traits is to decide if an individual is more oriented toward the job or people. In chapter 3 we discussed the three general types of leaders: authoritarian, participative, and laissez-faire. The authoritarian leader places a strong emphasis on task completion, the participative leader looks to subordinate needs, and the laissez-faire leader almost abdicates the leadership role. According to Hackman and Johnson (1991), "Researchers have concluded that the democratic style of leadership communication is often most effective" (p. 29). Authoritarian leadership can create increased output, but it diminishes satisfaction. Hackman and Johnson continued, "Laissez-faire leadership damages productivity, satisfaction, and commitment in most groups" (p. 29). Before you decide that you will pursue a democratic leadership style, you would be wise to return to chapter 3 and examine the findings regarding contingency theory. The need for structure by the leader and the degree of control required to accomplish the task make a difference in terms of successful leadership. This leads, naturally enough, to the important observation that there is no one best way to lead.

We now review some of the research attempting to establish traits and leading to situational leadership. Two sets of studies demonstrate efforts that have been made to explain how a leader should behave.

***Ohio State Studies.*** After World War II, investigators at Ohio State University used a questionnaire approach, which revealed a set of nine key factors that characterize the nature of leadership behavior (Stodgill & Coons, 1957). With a factor analysis, two dimensions of leadership emerged—consideration of others and initiating structure. Consideration includes an emphasis on good human relations with the leader being friendly, approachable, and a good listener. The initiating involves directing the organization, helping to define its goals, and determining the organization's structure (Cybert, 1990, p. 30). These assist in helping the organization achieve its objectives. Although the findings, over the years, have been somewhat inconsistent, one conclusion can be drawn. Leadership, to be effective, must employ a high level of consideration and initiating (Stodgill, 1965). The Ohio State studies focused on two interacting variables — people and task — that are the basis for almost all leadership tests. The University of Michigan studies supported the focus on these two variables with additional insights regarding work-group satisfaction.

***University of Michigan Studies — Institute for Social Research.*** Rather than just focusing on productivity, several studies conducted at the Institute for Social Research at the University of Michigan tried to identify styles of leadership behavior that would result in increased work-group performance and satisfaction. Although these studies have been criticized as being naive in their attempts to offer simple conclusions for very complex issues, they highlighted the difference between employee-oriented and production-oriented communication (Katz, Macoby, & Morse, 1950). Employee orientation included an emphasis on delegation of responsibility and a concern for employee welfare, needs, advancement, and personal growth. Production orientation included close supervision, legitimate and coercive power, work performance, and meeting schedules and deadlines. These initial studies established the groundwork for follow-up studies showing that leaders should use both concerns to be effective. Production and employee concerns are not dichotomies, but descriptions of how a leader behaves.

***Blake and Mouton's Managerial Grid.*** Using two axes — concern for people and concern for production — Blake and Mouton (1985), and more recently Blake and McCanse (1991), offered five possible leadership postures as shown on Fig. 11.1. They considered the team management leadership style, which is a goal-directed team approach that seeks a high level of productivity through involvement and redirection of potentially disruptive conflict, as the best possible approach for all managers. As indicated on Table 11.1, their scheme assigns a value of 1 (least) to 9 (most) on the two axes of concern for people and concern for productivity. This provides the following categories:

1. *9,9 Team Management.* As already indicated, this involves a high concern for people and production. The leader facilitates followers in a manner that allows excellence in team and personal achievement. As a team, leaders and followers work together to achieve high productivity while guaranteeing personal accomplishment.

2. *9,1 Authority-Compliance.* The leader is concerned with the task (9) while showing little regard for relationships (1). Directing, controlling, and planning are the major focus of this type of leader. Followers are not encouraged to participate in decision making.

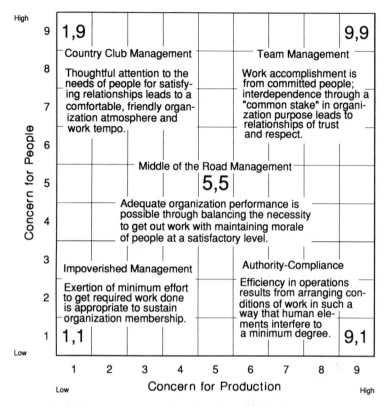

High

9 | **1,9** | | | | | | | **9,9**

Country Club Management — Team Management

8

Thoughtful attention to the
needs of people for satisfying relationships leads to a
7 comfortable, friendly organization atmosphere and
work tempo.

Work accomplishment is
from committed people;
interdependence through a
"common stake" in organi-
zation purpose leads to
relationships of trust
and respect.

6

Concern for People

Middle of the Road Management

5 | | | **5,5**

Adequate organization performance is
possible through balancing the necessity
4 to get out work with maintaining morale
of people at a satisfactory level.

3

Impoverished Management — Authority-Compliance

Exertion of minimum effort
to get required work done
2 is appropriate to sustain
organization membership.

Efficiency in operations
results from arranging conditions of work in such a
way that human ele-
ments interfere to
1 | **1,1** | | | | | a minimum degree. | **9,1**

Low

1  2  3  4  5  6  7  8  9

Low — **Concern for Production** — High

FIG. 11.1. The Leadership Grid. From "Leadership Dilemmas – Grid Solutions," by
Robert R. Blake and Anne Adams McCanse. Houston: Gulf Publishing Company, p.
29. Copyright © 1991, by Scientific Methods, Inc. Reproduced by permission of the
owners.

3. *5,5 Middle of the Road.* Enforcing rules, not rocking the boat, and generating
adequate results are the mainstays of this type of leader. With a 50% effort on task
and a 50% effort on people, this individual will get along with some success but
always will have mediocre results.

4. *1,9 Country Club Management.* By placing interpersonal relationships at the
top (9), this leader fails to set goals or assist accomplishments. An overemphasis
on supportive relationships creates a failure in achieving goals.

5. *1,1 Impoverished Management.* With a low concern for people (1) and a low
concern for task (1), this leader does not try to influence subordinates. Instead, he
or she exerts a minimum of effort to get the required work done.

As we explained in chapter 3, arguing for "one best way" will create controversy.
Blake and Mouton (1985) have been criticized (Yago & Vroom, 1981), but they

argued that there are certain principles that should not be sacrificed. The ultimate goal of the 9,9 style is that employees will grow, become autonomous, and find satisfaction. Although some versatility is needed, they agreed a consistent path toward a team management approach is necessary. Managerial Grid theory allows us to visualize the interactive patterns created by the two dimensions. As important as these two issues are, they still do not account for the specific situation. In other words, attempting to maintain a high concern for people and task may not be useful in certain situations.

## Contingency Approach

Ironically, the search for heroes as models for leadership highlights an important issue. Different individuals succeed in different leadership situations. What it takes to save a company, or to invent a new product may not be the same leadership skills needed to work with a mature organization. Although you may make a great Little League coach, you may not be able to create a 5-year vision for an organization. But, winning the Little League title still is heralded as an example of exemplary leadership. Right! The most important leadership activities are those that are appropriate to the situation. The environment is as important as a particular style.

*Fiedler's Contingency Theory.*     Contingency theory speaks to this concept. In chapter 3, we discussed Fiedler's contingency theory, House's Path-Goal theory, and the Vroom–Yetton Model. Briefly, Fiedler's (1972,1981) theory is that a leader's effectiveness in achieving high group performance is contingent on (a) the need of the leader for a relationship or task orientation, and (b) the degree to which the leader has control and influence over a particular situation. He argued that changing leadership behavior is difficult, so it would be better to change the circumstances. Leaders who are task oriented belong in situations that are very favorable or unfavorable, whereas people oriented leaders perform best in situations that are intermediate in terms of favorableness. His theory has been most useful for determining if a leader is task or people oriented. To be optimally effective, subordinates would have to be selected to fit the leader's predisposition. Although this is unrealistic, the emphasis on the interdependence between a large number of variables (e.g., subordinates, leaders, situation, task) is an important perspective toward understanding the impact of the environment on leadership effectiveness (Ford, 1981).

*Path-Goal Theory.*     Path-Goal theory points to the leader's job in developing more desire by subordinates for achieving organizational goals (House & Mitchell, 1974). At the same time, leaders are expected to help their subordinates find satisfaction in their work. At times, the leader will improve the motivation of employees by making the rewards for productivity more attractive (e.g., recognition, raises, promotions). Sometimes the employees' work is poorly defined and the leader will respond by clarifying the job structure or task requirements (e.g., goal setting, training, supportive supervision). At other times, the work is highly structured. In this case the leader would strive to meet the personal needs of the subordinate (e.g., praise, understanding). The leader develops the path that will help the subordinate reach the appropriate goal. The bond between leaders and followers occurs because of the leader's ability to grip subordinates with a program of action involving a goal, with a path to achieve it.

*Vroom–Yetton Model.* The Vroom–Yetton Model points to the important leadership variable of decision style. It requires the leader to choose a style on a continuum from autocratic to democratic depending on the problem and its contingencies (Yago & Vroom, 1981). You will remember that this is position taken by most contingency theorists and it directly challenges the assumption that democratic approaches are the best.

Putting the leader's behavior into the context of the environment provides a reality that is not as apparent from two-dimension approaches. To the degree possible, leaders should choose their actions based on research concerning the situation. Contingency leadership attempts to specify the relationship between managerial action (e.g., MBWA, delegating) and other relevant variables (e.g., type of work or product, abilities of subordinates). A more specific approach, situational leadership, argues that the organizational environment must be analyzed before taking any action. One of the best known examples is the LEAD approach.

## Situational Leadership-LEAD

Arguing that there is no one best way, Hersey and Blanchard's (1977) Situational Leadership Test (LEAD) is based on the premise that different leadership approaches should be used depending on the requirements of the situation. LEAD uses the traditional divisions of task-oriented and relationship-oriented behaviors, but focuses on the subordinate's ability and willingness to do a particular activity. This "follower's readiness" is recognized by Hersey and Blanchard as a catch-all for several variables the leader must be able personally to take into account given the particular employee or task.

The four styles are telling, selling, participating, and delegating. As Fig. 11.2 indicates, each style employs a variation of task and relationship orientation in order to effectively lead.

Additional information about the leaders is provided by LEAD because each of the four choices on LEAD's 12 situations has a different likelihood for success. By weighing the leadership behavior with the highest probability for success with a +2, the behavior with the least likelihood for success with a −2, the second best alterna-

**LEADERSHIP BEHAVIOR – APPROPRIATENESS**

RELATIONSHIP BEHAVIOR, CONSIDERATE, INTERPERSONAL

HIGH

LOW

| SITUATION 3 | SITUATION 2 |
|---|---|
| *PARTICIPATING* | *SELLING* |
| High relationship & low task | High task & high relationship |
| MODERATELY HIGH ON TASK READINESS, BUT NOT FULLY WILLING (CONFIDENT) Follower needs support, indications of rewards for achievement — low directive behavior by superior, because follower knows how to do job. | LOW TASK READINESS, BUT WILLING AND ABLE TO DO TASK Leader is both task-directive & openly considerate with relationship supportive behavior. Leader provides direction & keeps follower's willingness to do new challenges high. |
| SITUATION 4 | SITUATION 1 |
| *DELEGATING* | *TELLING* |
| Low task & low relationship | High task & low relationship |
| HIGH TASK READINESS Follower needs almost no direction & little support. Leader uses interpersonal relationship behaviors for quality of leader-follower relationship. | LOW TASK READINESS Subordinate needs clear & specific instructions to learn to do job. Leader's willingness to take time & effort acts as evidence of concern — not impersonal but task-oriented. |

LOW                              HIGH

TASK BEHAVIOR, DIRECTIVE

FIG. 11.2.   The Hersey–Blanchard situational leadership model (1988). Copyright © 1988 by Leadership Studies. Adapted by permission.

tive with a +1, and the third with a −1, the leadership style adaptability profile for each leader can be established. This instrument has been tested under a variety of circumstances to determine its usefulness as a leadership training tool.

Criticisms of the LEAD approach include a lack of clear correlation between how task, maintenance, and subordinate maturity can be manipulated (Graeff, 1983); a tendency toward a circular explanation for effectiveness as a guide for future actions (Vecchio, 1987); and an orientation toward groups, not individuals (Johansen, 1990). At the same time, studies by Hersey and Blanchard (1988) establish the validity of the LEAD instrument.

Further experimental examinations have substantiated LEAD's ability to differentiate between leadership styles and quality of decisions (Hambleton & Gumpert, 1982; Hersey, Angelini, & Carakushansky, 1982). Other studies have found partial support for the instrument as it relates to the value of high relationship activities by leaders (Beck, 1982). A valid conclusion is that the LEAD instrument probably cannot function alone as a means for prescribing specific changes a manager should make in a given circumstance.

The most important limitation of this instrument, and probably any single test of leadership, is it cannot take into account all the variables. In fact, it is widely agreed that organizations make a serious mistake when they use a particular test to measure leadership ability or potential.

Finally, in some leadership situations, specifically academic medical centers, a prevailing view of leadership is that "it doesn't matter what kind of management style one uses" because the various interest groups ultimately will view management as SOBs anyway (Pettegrew, 1982, p. 179). This pessimistic view of leadership supports the importance of understanding the impact of organizational environment and culture, as we discussed in chapter 3. If the culture creates a strong political orientation where protecting one's turf is more important than cooperating with other interest groups, the leader is unlikely to be perceived in a positive light regardless of his or her activities. In other words, in a highly divisionalized setting, such as a hospital where various interest groups (e.g., administrators, doctors, nurses) vie for control, leaders will find any type of action criticized by someone. This leads to one of the dangers of leadership—misunderstanding heroic behaviors for leading.

## Heroic Leadership

In their analysis of effective leadership, Bradford and Cohen (1984) identified 10 organizational characteristics that must be taken into consideration by leaders as they choose their managerial approach. Their premise is that good managers must be leaders who pick the correct response to the needs of their subordinates and organization. These 10 characteristics are: (a) subordinates work independently, (b) subordinates do simple tasks, (c) environment is stable, (d) subordinates have low technical knowledge compared to boss, (e) subordinates commitment not needed for success, (f) subordinates do complex tasks, (g) subordinates require considerable coordination, (h) environment is changing, (i) subordinates have high technical knowledge, and (j) subordinate commitment necessary for excellence.

Bradford and Cohen (1984) outlined three styles that are likely to be used. They were not concerned with the actual situational correctness as much as the leader's view of their jobs in relation to their subordinates. There exists, they argued, a basic difference between the types of management traditionally practiced and the type needed for organizational development and change. Basing their views on a careful and extensive review of the current studies of management, they identified three types of leadership behavior.

Many managers have become accustomed to overcontrolling their subordinates through an heroic approach to their jobs, which encompasses the first two styles of management: *manager-as-technician* and *manager-as-conductor*. Whenever problems occur, the manager-as-technician is the one who will provide the answers. The manager-as-technician, as the person promoted from within, or brought in because of some specific expertise, has all the answers and will take over any situation. For example, some expert sales representatives, who get promoted to manager, tend to have all the answers for any difficult sales situation. Each time a problem occurs, the new manager second-guesses the representatives or comes up with a better answer. Faced with continued correction, the representatives become accustomed to waiting for the insights by the experienced boss. As long as employees are not expected to take a great deal of initiative or responsibility, and the boss remains sensitive to the field issues, this style can work well.

The manager-as-conductor assists individuals or units in working together, prevents or resolves conflicts, and establishes a smooth work flow. This individual coordinates the various individuals or units involved. However, this individual can become overly concerned with everyone's activities. Meetings, with everyone in attendance, become more important than successes by individuals. Large organizations, like universities, banks, or hospitals, create these positions.

These heroic management styles work, but they do not encourage employee development, individual excellence, or group cohesion, because the leader is always center stage. In fact, they cause reliance on the manager who is acting out a self-concept of being tough, reliable, and able to handle situations. The manager becomes a cross between John Wayne and the Lone Ranger through the use of behaviors that centralize the manager's importance and thereby diminish the growth of subordinates. Bradford and Cohen (1984) were not suggesting these two types of management—manager-as-technician and manager-as-conductor—cannot succeed. However, both of these styles limit organizational change.

What is needed, Bradford and Cohen (1984) argued, is a postheroic style called manager-as-developer. This is the style used by the excellent leaders they studied at the National Training Laboratories and in organizations. This style views the organization's members as capable of handling change and works to facilitate individual and group responsibility.

For many years, consultants and researchers have pointed to an apparent leadership paradox: Reducing control actually increases control, and sharing power increases power (Hocker & Wilmot, 1985, pp. 87–90). The various processes of participative management, leveling, team building, and so on all require leaders to recognize the impact of their behaviors on the capacity of the organization to change. For example, in chapter 10, we examined the values of increasing group control (e.g., quality circles, teams, self-managing work units) in order to increase the organization's productivity. Throughout our examination of organizations, we have offered examples of the importance of proactive, collaborative approaches. When leaders learn to empower subordinates, the potential for growth can be remarkable. The concept of transformational leadership offers important insights into how leaders should act.

### Transformational Leadership

Postheroic leadership brings into focus one additional leadership concept. Although many of the day-to-day activities between leaders and subordinates consist of a transactional exchange of rewards for services, something more is needed to truly effect organizational change. When the big picture is brought into focus—changing companies or countries—a special type of leadership is required. Transformational leaders try to change the outlook and behavior of their followers (Burns, 1978). This type of leader (a) articulates a realistic vision of the future that can be shared, (b) stimulates subordinates intellectually, and (c) pays attention to the differences between subordinates (Bass, 1985, chapter 2).

This approach contrasts with the *transactional* leader. The majority of leadership approaches, according to the proponents of transformational leadership, concentrate on the transaction between leader and subordinate (Tichy & DeVanna, 1986). Transactional approaches call for an initiation and clarification of what is required of subordinates (e.g., Path-Goal). The two factors of initiating structure (task) and consideration (people) are emphasized as means for determining how to lead various individuals (e.g., contingency, situational). Because they clarify what is expected of subordinates, and assist them in achieving these goals, satisfactory performance is achieved. Although these approaches will work for the ongoing leadership process, they will fall short when major change is required. As Senge (1990) observed, "Ironically, by focusing on performing for someone else's approval, corporations create the very conditions that predestine them to mediocre performance" (p. 7). What is needed, many observers agree, are transformational leaders who can develop learning organizations. These are organizations that provide extensive opportunities for individuals, groups, and systems to accept information from the environment (e.g., new technologies, innovative approaches, customer input) and change.

***Learning Organizations.*** All organizations operate as open systems. However, some merely adapt to changing conditions rather than effectively managing the process in order to grow and develop. Transformational leaders go beyond heroic acts to actually help their organization receive feedback and alter the course of direction. Successful organizations will focus "on generative learning, which is about creating, as well as adaptive learning, which is about coping" (Senge, 1990, p. 8). These two types of learning are the differences between single-loop learning, in which individuals or groups adjust their behavior relative to fixed goals and assumptions, versus double-loop learning, in which goals, assumptions, and behavior are open to change (Argyris & Schon, 1978).

Leading-edge firms are learning to predict what the customer might want rather than what market research states they expect. The total quality movement in Japan demonstrates what learning organizations will be. At first in Japan, there was an orientation toward zero defects while producing a product. Once defects were reduced, these organizations focused on making the customer satisfied by fine-tuning existing parts of the product. The Mazda Miata demonstrates the third stage by looking at the customer's latent needs (Senge, 1990, p. 8). These are things the customer might value but never has experienced. The Miata required a leap of imagination into what the customer might want, rather than a dependence on market research.

According to Senge (1990), "In a learning organization, leader's roles differ dramatically from that of the charismatic decision maker. Leaders are designers, teachers, and stewards" (p. 9). Leaders must build a shared vision, test mental models to help other people cope with the changes, and adopt a systems, interrelationships, process point of view. This is a weighty demand for leaders and promises to be a difficult task.

## UTILIZING LEADERSHIP SKILLS

You will be expected to perform leadership tasks at some time in your organizational career. There is every reason to believe that you also will find being a leader the most gratifying part of your career. Leadership occurs at three levels. Interpersonally, you will help guide and direct colleagues and subordinates, and serve as an advisor, mentor, or a role model to promising newcomers. To make the most of your dyadic experiences, recent evidence suggests that you should work toward the manager-as-developer style. Accepting that a situational approach is most likely to be effective, you will want to examine leadership tests such as LEAD or the Grid to see how you actually approach problem situations. The chapter on interpersonal communication provides specific guidelines.

Small-group leadership offers you the chance to see how difficult it can be to balance task and relationship. For your group to work well, either in meetings, informally, formally, or as teams, you will be expected to facilitate the development. Through the use of delegation, well thought-out meetings, and some excellent climate-enhancing skills, you will find small-group leadership a very rewarding means for accomplishing tasks.

Leading a larger group, division, or organization requires some special skills that need to be developed as you work interpersonally and as a small-group leader. For the transformational leader, "the essential point is that the leader strives to go beyond the bounds of the usual to bring about a change in follower thinking that will redirect follower actions" (Fiedler & House, 1988, p. 75).

Leadership brings us foursquare with the structural, human resources, symbolic, and political frames (Bolman & Deal, 1991, pp. 403–441). Effective leaders must balance structural and human resources frames while providing a strong symbolic presence. They do this through a clear understanding of the positive aspects of the political frame. The political frame encompasses the issue of power. Power is the "capacity to translate intention into reality and sustain it. Leadership is the wise use of this power. . . . Vision is the commodity of leaders, and power is their currency" (Bennis & Nanus, 1985, pp. 17–18). Although we deal with power more fully in the conflict management chapter, leaders understand that political skills are needed to organize others and to win support for visions (Pfeffer, 1981). Recognizing that standing still means losing ground, and that the future is the key to survival, leaders must use power over others to gain the necessary changes (Hollander, 1985; Kanter, 1981).

The techniques used by the leader to exercise power, ranging from establishing a vision to self-managing work units to positive recognition, have been discussed in earlier parts of this text. Learning to develop teams, negotiate results, communicate effectively, build networks, and maintain a vision are all part of transformational leadership (Waterman, 1987, pp. 207–208).

Leadership is a learning process. In some ways, it is like flexing a muscle. The more you try to use effective leadership techniques, the better you will be as a leader. Leaders understand that adaptation and growth are the key factors in being a proactive force in an organization. They recognize that if organizational members do what they always have done, they will get what they always have gotten. As obvious as that observation may seem, managers tend to reinforce the current activities, whereas leaders work toward change.

## CONCLUSION

Leadership is a vital component of organizations. Our definition of leadership includes three overriding characteristics. These are a sense of direction, the ability to influence, and effective situational adaptation. To make the definition even clearer, we examined the differences between leadership and management. Although there are many, they center on differences in perspective, power and empowerment, and orientation toward change. Finally, the critical link between leadership and communication reminds us that leaders are judged by what they do, not how they manage.

We then examined various leadership theories. The first is trait theory, which may seem too easy to dismiss. In fact, some traits do indeed help leaders. As a trait approach, psychological theories offer promise for the future but are incomplete at this time as explanations for effective leadership.

The two-dimensional models explain the importance of exhibiting both concern for people and a concern for production. The Blake–Mouton Grid offers a specific application of this approach.

This led us to contingency theories, which make the correct assumption that the situation requires adaptation. Fielder, House, Vroom–Yetton, and Hersey and Blanchard all offered means for understanding the interrelatedness of elements.

We completed our analysis by offering a discussion of heroic leadership, transformational leadership, and learning organizations. These are an appropriate place to end this chapter. They offer a vision for us as we pursue leadership. The next two chapters, motivation and conflict management, put us back in the trenches.

In some ways, we never leave the topic of leadership. Clearly, it is one of the most exciting facets of organizational communication. Being in charge creates numerous paradoxes that force us to continue reevaluating how we lead. This is called double-loop learning. An age-old vision of leadership, from Lao Tsu, offers appropriate closure:

> The wicked leader is he who the people despise.
> The good leader is he who the people revere.
> The great leader is he who the people say, "We did it ourselves."

## REFERENCES

Albanese, R. (1988). *Management*. Cincinnati: South-Western.

Allcorn, S. (1988). Leadership styles: The psychological picture. *Personnel, 65*, 46–54.

Argyris, C., & Schon, D. (1978). *Organizational learning: A theory-in-action perspective*. Reading, MA: Addison-Wesley.

Barrow, J. C. (1977). The variables of leadership: A review and conceptual framework. *Academy of Management Review, 2*, 231–251.

Bass, B. M. (1960). *Leadership, psychology, and organizational behavior*. New York: Harper & Row.

Bass, B. M. (1985). *Leadership and performance beyond expectations*. New York: Free Press.

Beck, D. E. (1982). Beyond the grid and situationalism: A living systems view. *Training and Development Journal, 36*, 76–83.

Bennis, W. (1990). *Why leaders can't lead: The unconscious conspiracy continues*. San Francisco: Jossey-Bass.

Bennis, W. & Nanus, B. (1985). *Leaders: The strategies for taking charge*. New York: Harper & Row.

Blake, R. R., & McCanse, A. A. (1991). *Leadership dilemmas—Grid solutions*. Houston: Gulf.

Blake, R. R., & Mouton, R. R. (1985). *The managerial grid III: The key to leadership excellence*. Houston: Gulf.

Bolman, L. G., & Deal, T. E. (1984). *Modern approaches to understanding and managing organizations*. San Francisco: Jossey-Bass.

Bolman, L. G., & Deal, T. E. (1991). *Reframing organizations: Artistry, choice, and leadership*. San Francisco: Jossey-Bass.

Bradford, D. L., & Cohen, C. J. (1984). *Managing for excellence: The guide for developing high performance in contemporary organizations*. New York: Wiley.

Brown, D. S. (1987). *Management's hidden enemy*. Mt. Airy, MD: Lomond.

Burker, W. W. (1986). Leadership as empowering others. In S. Srivasts & Associates (Eds.), *Executive power: How executives influence people and organizations* (pp. 51–77). San Francisco: Jossey-Bass.

Burns, J. M. (1978). *Leadership*. New York: Harper & Row.

Clark, K. E., & Clark, M. B. (1990). *Measures of leadership*. West Orange, NJ: Leadership Library of America.

Clemes, J. K., & Mayer, D. F. (1987). *The classic touch: Lessons in leadership from Homer to Hemingway*. Homewood, IL: Dow Jones Irwin.

Conger, J. A., Kanungo, R. N., & Associates (1988). *Charismatic leadership: The elusive factor in organizational effectiveness*. San Francisco: Jossey-Bass.

Cybert, R. M. (1990). Defining leadership and explicating the process. *Nonprofit Management and Leadership, 1*(1), 29–38.

Danziel, M. M., & Schoonover, S. C. (1988). *Changing ways: A practical tool for implementing change within organizations*. New York: American Management Association.

Deal, T. E., & Kennedy, T. E. (1982). *Corporate cultures: The rites and rituals of corporate life*. Reading, MA: Addison-Wesley.

DuBrin, A. J., Ireland, R. D., & Williams, J. C. (1989). *Management & organization*. Cincinnati: South-Western.

Egan, G. (1988). *Change-agent skills a: Assessing and designing excellence*. San Diego: University Associates.

Fiedler, F. E. (1972). How do you make leaders more effective? New answers to an old puzzle. *Organizational Dynamics, 1*, 3–18.

Fiedler, F. E. (1981). Leadership effectiveness. *American Behavioral Scientist, 24*, 630–631.

Fiedler, F. E., & House, R. J. (1988). Leadership theory and research: A report of progress. In C. L. Cooper & I. Robertson (Eds.), *International review of industrial and organizational psychology* (pp. 73–92). London: Wiley.

Ford, J. D. (1981). Departmental context and formal structure as constraints on leader behaviors. *Academy of Management Journal, 24*, 274–288.

Gough, H. G. (1990). Testing for leadership with the California Psychological Inventory. In K. E. Clark & M. B. Clark (Eds.), *Measures of leadership* (pp. 355–380). West Orange, NJ: Leadership Library of America.

Graeff, C. L. (1983). The situational leadership theory: A critical view. *Academy of Management Review, 8*, 285–291.

Gutknecht, D. B., & Miller, J. R. (1986). *The organizational and human resources handbook*. Lanham, MD: University Press of America.

Hackman, M. Z., & Johnson, C. E. (1991). *Leadership: A communication perspective*. Prospect Heights, IL: Waveland.

Hambleton, R. K., & Gumpert, R. (1982). The validity of Hersey and Blanchard's theory of leadership effectiveness. *Group and Organizational Studies, 7*, 225–242.

Harrell, T. W., & Harrell, M. S. (1973). The personality of MBA's who reach general management early. *Personnel Psychology, 26*, 127–134.

Harris, T. E. (1990). Organizational cultures: An examination of the role of communication. In S. Thomas & W. A. Evans (Eds.), *Communication and culture: Language, performance, technology, and media* (pp. 143–155). Norwood, NJ: Ablex.

Hart, W. L., Heskett, J. L., & Sasser, W. E. (1990–1991, Winter). Soothing the savage customer. *Best of Business*, pp. 12–20.

Hersey, P. (1984). *The situational leader*. Escondido, CA: Center for Leadership Studies.

Hersey, P., Angelini, A. L., & Carakushansky, S. (1982). The impact of situational leadership and classroom structure on learning effectiveness. *Group and Organizational Studies, 7*, 216–224.

Hersey, P., & Blanchard, K. H. (1977). *Management of organizational behavior: Utilizing human resources* (3rd ed.). Englewood Cliffs, NJ: Prentice-Hall.

Hersey, P., & Blanchard, K. H. (1988). *Management of organizational behavior: Utilizing human resources* (5th ed.). Englewood Cliffs, NJ: Prentice-Hall.

Hickman, C. R., & Silva, M. A. (1984). *Creating excellence*. New York: New American Library.

Hocker, J. L., & Wilmot, W. W. (1985). *Interpersonal conflict* (2nd ed.). Dubuque, IA: Brown.

Hogan, R., Raskin, R., & Fazzini, D. (1990). The dark side of charisma. In K. E. Clark & M. B. Clark (Eds.), *Measures of leadership* (pp. 343–354). West Orange, NJ: Leadership Library of America.

Hollander, E. P. (1985). Leadership and power. In G. Lindzey & F. Aronsonn (Eds.), *The handbook of social psychology* (3rd ed., pp. 485–537). New York: Random House.

Hollander, E. P., & Offermann, L. R. (1990a). Power and leadership in organizations: Relationships in transition. *American Psychologist, 45*(2), 179–189.

Hollander, E. P., & Offermann, L. R. (1990b). Relational features of organizational leadership and followship. In K. E. Clark & M. B. Clark (Eds.), *Measures of leadership* (pp. 83–97). West Orange, NJ: Leadership Library of America.

House, R. J., & Mitchell, T. R. (1974). Path-goal theory of leadership. *Journal of Contemporary Business, 3*, 81–97.

Jackall, R. (1988). *Moral mazes: The world of corporate managers*. New York: Oxford University Press.

Johansen, B. P. (1990). Situational leadership: A review of the research. *Human Resource Development Quarterly, 1,* 73–85.

Juran, J. M. (1989). *Juran on leadership for quality: An executive handbook.* New York: Free Press.

Kanter, R. M. (1981). Power, leadership, and participatory management. *Theory into Practice, 20,* 219–224.

Katz, D., Macoby, N., & Morse, N. C. (1950). *Productivity, supervision, and morale in an office setting.* Ann Arbor: University of Michigan, Institute for Social Research.

Kirkpatrick, S. A., & Locke, E. A. (1991). Leadership: Do traits matter? *The Executive, 5,* 48–60.

Kotter, J. P. (1988). *The leadership factor.* New York: Free Press.

Kotter, J. P. (1990). *A force for change: How leadership differs from management.* New York: Free Press.

Kouzes, J. M., & Posner, B. Z. (1987). *The leadership challenge: How to get extraordinary things done in organizations.* San Francisco: Jossey-Bass.

Likert, R. (1961). *New patterns of management.* New York: McGraw-Hill.

Manz, C., & Sims, H. (1989). *Superleadership: Leading others to lead themselves.* New York: Simon & Schuster.

McCall, M., Jr., & Lombardo, M. (1983, February). What makes a top executive? *Psychology Today,* pp. 27–29.

McCaulley, M. H. (1990). The Myers–Briggs type indicator and leadership. In K. E. Clark & M. B. Clark (Eds.), *Measures of leadership* (pp. 381–418). West Orange, NJ: Leadership Library of America.

McGregor, D. (1960). *The human side of enterprise.* New York: McGraw-Hill.

Nora, J. J., Rogers, C. R., & Stramy, R. J. (1986). *Transforming the workplace.* Princeton, NJ: Princeton Research Press.

Offermann, L. R., & Gowing, L. R. (1990). Organizations of the future: Changes and challenges. *American Psychologist, 45,* 95–108.

Ouchi, W. G. (1981). *Theory z: How American business can meet the Japanese challenge.* Reading, MA: Addison-Wesley.

Pace, R. W., & Faules, R. W. (1989). *Organizational communication* (2nd ed.). Englewood Cliffs, NJ: Prentice-Hall.

Pascale, R. T., & Anthos, A. G. (1982). *The art of Japanese management.* New York: Warner.

Peters, T. (1987). *Thriving on chaos.* New York: Knopf.

Peters, T. J., & Austin, N. (1985). *Passion for excellence: The leadership difference.* New York: Random House.

Peters, T. J., & Waterman, R. H., Jr. (1982). *In search of excellence: Lessons from America's best-run companies.* New York: Harper & Row.

Pettegrew, L. S. (1982). Organizational communication and the s.o.b. theory of management. *Western Journal of Speech Communication, 46,* 179–191.

Pfeffer, J. (1981). *Power in organizations.* Marshfield, MA: Pitman.

Sank, L. I. (1974). Effective and ineffective managerial traits obtained as naturalistic descriptions from executive members of a super-corporation. *Personnel Psychology, 27,* 423–434.

Schein, E. H. (1985). *Organizational culture and leadership.* San Francisco: Jossey-Bass.

Senge, P. M. (1990). The leader's new work: Building learning organizations. *Sloan Management Review,* pp. 3–14.

Steers, R. M. (1988). *Introduction to organizational behavior* (3rd ed.). Glenview, IL: Scott, Foresman.

Stogdill, R. M. (1950). Leadership, membership and organization. *Psychological Bulletin, 47,* 1–12.

Stogdill, R. M. (1965). *Managers, employees, organizations.* Columbus: Ohio State University, Bureau of Business Research.

Stogdill, R. M. (1974). *Handbook of leadership: A survey of theory and research.* New York: Free Press.

Stogdill, R. M., & Coons, A. E. (1957). *Leader behavior: Its description and measurement.* Columbus: Ohio State University, Bureau of Business Research.

Tichy, N. M., & DeVanna, M. A. (1986). The transformational leader. *Training and Development Journal, 40,* 27–32.

Vecchio, R. P. (1987). Situational leadership theory: An examination of a prescriptive theory. *Journal of Applied Psychology, 72,* 444–451.

Weiner, N., & Mahoney, T. A. (1981). A model of corporate performance as a function of environmental, organizational, and leadership influences. *Academy of Management Journal, 24,* 452–470.

Williams, J. C., & Huber, G. P. (1986). *Human behavior in organizations.* Cincinnati: South-Western.

Yago, A. G., & Vroom, V. H. (1981). An evaluation of two alternatives to the Vroom/Yetton normative model. *Academy of Management Journal, 24,* 714–728.

Zaleznik, A. (1989). *The managerial mystique: Restoring leadership in business.* New York: Harper & Row.

# CHAPTER 12

# Effective Conflict Management in Organizations

Like death and taxes, organizational conflicts always will be with us (Putnam & Poole, 1987). Unlike death and taxes, organizational conflicts can be positive, used to enhance creativity, productivity, and job satisfaction, and managed successfully. Not only is it impossible to eliminate conflicts, but we would create a host of new problems (e.g., groupthink, freezethink, lack of creativity, reduced motivation, strikes, sabotage, stress) if we forced the submission by organizational members to a strict set of cooperative behaviors (Boulding, 1962; McNeil, 1965).

Conflicts have a significant impact in organizations. First, organizations are changing, as we have stated throughout this text, and the 1990s promise to be even more turbulent (Carnevale, 1991; Offerman & Gowing, 1990. ). Uncertainty and change increase conflicts over turf, perceived scarce resources, and power (Lippitt & Lippitt, 1986, pp. 2–3, 6). At the very least, change requires people to alter their current job-related activities. In the case of downsizing, for example, change includes unemployment for some individuals or a new job.

Second, conflicts affect every member of an organization. One study revealed that chief executive officers, vice presidents, and middle managers spend 24% of their time dealing with conflict (Thomas & Schmidt, 1976). The same study found that conflict management was seen as equal or slightly more important as a skill than topics like planning, communication, motivation, and decision making. School and hospital administrators, mayors, and city managers consider this estimate quite low. According to Lippitt (1982), "In these and similar fields, conflict resolution commands nearly 49% of the attention of such officials" (p. 67).

For the college graduate, being proficient at managing conflict is an expected skill (Harris & Thomlison, 1983). In a realistic response to these reports regarding conflict, graduate courses in business administration put aside a significant amount of their time to teaching conflict management skills. One content analysis of course syllabli for graduate students in business administration revealed that conflict resolution is ranked fifth among the 65 topics most frequently taught (Rahim, 1981). In a recent survey of the skills expected of college graduates, conflict management was listed as being very important (Harris & Thomlison, 1983). Seasoned managers, business school graduates, and college graduates must be proficient in managing conflicts. In addition to managers and college graduates, there are those individuals, dubbed flak catchers in many organizations, specifically assigned the job of managing conflicts (e.g., customer service representatives, gatekeepers, administrative assistants, assistants to the president). In fact, conflict management is a needed skill for all members of an organization (Carnevale, 1991, pp. 118–119).

One last observation regarding the need for individual conflict-managing skills: A careful examination of most organizational conflicts will show that focusing on personalities and ideologies unnecessarily limits our understanding of why conflicts occur. In fact, conflicts are just as likely to occur because of the roles, rules, incentives, and constraints of the organizational structure within which the participants interact (Brett, Goldberg, & Ury, 1990, p. 163). Put another way, although you may end up working for or with someone you cannot stand, you are more likely to experience conflicts over goals, procedures, and the distribution of rewards (e.g., resource allocation, wages, perks).

Having the skills necessary to get along with other people are important. For example, if you work for someone and they cannot stand you, then you are likely to be fired. One study concluded that "for every person who is fired for incompetence, two people are fired for personality factors. The major contributor: lack of communication skills" (Walton, 1991, p. 6). Another study examined why managers were fired (Odiorne, 1978). Of the 14 reasons reported, none included technical knowledge, lack of education, or taking too many chances. They were fired for not controlling emotions, being immature, not responding to change, poor employee relations, and not communicating effectively—they could not deal with conflicts. For managers, technical competence is not the deciding issue when they are fired (Steinmetz, 1983, p. 133). Not only do conflicts have a significant impact on interpersonal relationships, they also affect the organization.

Third, organizations are conglomerates of individuals, groups, departments, special interests, and divisions. If you already have had organizational experience, you probably can list the conflicts that occur among these different groups. For example, "the marketing, quality control, and personnel department may all be part of the same company, but their self-interests may pull them in different directions" (Muniz & Chasnoff, 1987, p. 8). The traditional adversarial relationship between management and employees, symbolized in management/union confrontations, has caused mutual distrust regarding methods and motives (Abbott, 1989, pp. 1, 5). Inflexibility and resistance to change, manifested through hostility between internally competing forces, has hastened the demise of various organizations (Hoerr, 1988).

Unfortunately, rather than seeking a proactive, cooperative relationship, energy is expended in defending power bases or seeking additional control.

Conflicts are a part of all organizations at all levels. They consume a great deal of time and effort. Throughout this chapter, we continue to underscore that the issue is effective conflict management (Hocker & Wilmot, 1985, chapter 1).

First, we need to establish the vital link between communication and conflict. With this groundwork in place, we provide several definitions of conflict.

## COMMUNICATION AND CONFLICT

Although communication can occur without conflict, conflict cannot occur without some type of communication. As Hocker and Wilmot (1985) put it, "Communication and conflict are inextricably tied" (p. 19). Interpersonally, the expression of conflict is carried through the message (e.g., your work is substandard) and the relationship (e.g., superior/subordinate). According to Egan (1988) "One of the most important types of communication in organizations, institutions, and community centers around the management of conflict" (p. 167). Conflicts are formed and sustained through social interaction (Folger & Poole, 1984, p. 4).

Examining conflict offers us a chance to see the systems approach to organizational communication in action (Hocker & Wilmot, 1985, pp. 130–133). One cannot communicate, as we already know, and all actions have the potential for creating collaboration or conflict. In addition, our perception of events, our interpretation of verbal and nonverbal messages, and our use of networks and channels, interpersonal skills, small-group activities, and leadership all contribute to how cooperative or competitive we may appear. The systems/communication perspective allows us to isolate the levels (e.g., systems, subsystems, suprasystems) of conflict in an organization (Gutknecht & Miller, 1986, pp. 69–71):

1. Intrapersonal: Conflict within one's self over goals or cognition—created because of inconsistencies in our thoughts. When we feel dissonance between our thoughts and actions, two or more goals, or two or more values, we will experience intrapersonal conflict.
2. Interpersonal: Conflict between two or more people. This can be a personality, task, or combined conflict.
3. Intragroup: Conflict within the group over the task (substantive conflict) and interpersonal relations (affective conflict). Teams, task forces, and small groups must experience some types of conflict or they will "go along to get along." The secret is to channel the energy into collaborative efforts.
4. Intergroup or department: Conflict due to competition between groups over achieving goals or over issues such as power, status, and resources. In many organizations, this is the most difficult type of conflict to manage.

5. Intraorganizational: Conflict between levels such as supervisors/subordinates, line-staff (people who have direct responsibility for some organizational function and the staff that advises them), role conflict and role ambiguity (unclear tasks make the job difficult), horizontal conflict (between departments at the same level in the organization).

6. Interorganizational: Conflict due to competition between two or more organizations. Although this is a positive mechanism for producing creative alternatives and innovation, resources can be diverted to this battle and away from other, critical organizational needs.

The systems perspective also reminds us that all behavior is potentially meaningful and that the cultural rules play a major role in how the conflict is played out. This serves to remind us that there is a thin line between cooperative and conflicting behaviors. For example, tacit communication has been used to describe communication occurring via the common understandings of the two parties in a conflict situation (Schelling, 1960). Even in an all-out "war" over market share, employee rights, promotions, budgets, or company ownership, a great deal of collaborative activity occurs without the use of explicit messages sent through identifiable (e.g., spoken, written) channels (Nicholson, 1971, p. 3). We make tacit assumptions regarding other people's actions based on the corporate culture, the past behaviors of the other party, or the unwritten rules of behavior, and we can coordinate or compete using this information (Harris & Smith, 1974, p. 82). For example, in various studies, parties faced with conflicting demands, but intent on maintaining a relationship, tacitly agree to a 50-50 split of a small amount of cash. The same is true when jockeying for position in a traffic jam, boarding a crowded elevator, getting along with a co-worker you do not speak to but must work with to complete a task, or limited conflicts where some boundaries are set without any overt discussion. This reminds us that organizational conflicts represent complex communication behaviors. Our first step in unraveling this complexity is to define organizational conflict.

## DEFINITION OF CONFLICT

Communication behaviors are the underpinning of any definition of conflict. Conflict is a process, and communication is the mechanism for combat, cooperation, and collaboration. As Hocker and Wilmot (1985) put it, "From a communication perspective, conflict is an expressed struggle between at least two interdependent parties who perceive incompatible goals, scarce rewards and interference from the other party in achieving their goals" (p. 23). Other researchers add opposition by the other party in realizing goals, aims, and values (Putnam & Poole, 1987, p. 552).

Before accepting this as the definitive perspective, keep in mind that the study of conflict has a rich heritage. For Coser (1956), conflict is "a struggle over values and claims to scarce status, power, and resources in which the aims of the opponents are to neutralize, injure, or eliminate the rivals" (p. 8). Other definitions include the existence of incompatible activities (Deutsch, 1973, p. 156), disagreement or controversy (Simons, 1972), and an opportunity for interference with another's goal attainment (Schmidt & Kochan, 1972).

Finally, conflict can be viewed as "the explicit or implicit antagonism between participants in an interpersonal communication transaction arising from incongruency in the transaction" (e.g., misunderstandings because of different interpretations of meaning, differences between verbal and nonverbal message systems, contradictions between message and context) (Smith & Williamson, 1981, p. 249). These types of conflicts occur when organizations attempt to become more participatory and empower employees (Putnam, 1983, pp. 43–44). A supervisor might ask everyone to take part in goal setting and getting the work accomplished, but step in each time there is any delay to the work. Employees are faced with a double-bind (damned if they do and damned if they don't) because their boss is saying they should get involved but is acting in a manner that makes it clear that they should be passive. A vicious conflict cycle can begin because the supervisor will note a lack of action by the employees and perhaps accuse the subordinates of not caring. Of course, the subordinates will withdraw more, creating additional proof that the supervisor is correct, and only his or her heroic efforts will get the work done. The complexity of organizational behavior, fostered by the multiple interacting systems, creates numerous dilemmas for members.

At this point, a summary provides us with a list of criterion that lead to organizational conflicts. Organizational conflicts occur because of

1. incompatible goals,
2. scarce rewards (e.g., power, status, and resources),
3. interference or opposition,
4. disagreement or controversy,
5. incongruency in the transaction,
6. incompatible activities.

The interdependence inherent in all organizational activity creates the potential for conflicts and communication is the vehicle for the expressing the struggle.

## ORGANIZATIONAL CONFLICT

Conflict is essential to the healthy growth of any organization. No examination of developing teams, for example, bypasses conflict management or fails to note the importance of conflicts over content (Phillips & Elledge, 1989, pp. 45, 104–154; Truell, 1984, pp. 55–71). According to Lippitt (1982), "Management of human conflict is an objective of organizational renewal" (p. 70). In order to effectively manage conflicts, we need to distinguish between nonrealistic and realistic conflicts and functional and dysfunctional conflicts.

## Nonrealistic Versus Realistic Conflicts

Although realistic conflict is the struggle of perceived scarce power, status, or resources, *nonrealistic conflict* arises from the need to release tensions or aggressive impulses. This type of conflict is not goal oriented but is designed to express aggression (Coser, 1956, pp. 41–49). Arguments over petty procedures as a means of venting anger are good examples.

The U.S. Postal Service offers a prime example of conflicts arising from the need to release tensions (Monroe, Riley, & Traver, 1989). Although the Postal Service had a $585 million high-tech makeover from 1987 to 1989, performance on first-class mail delivery was at a 5-year low in 1988. In response, supervisors have increased surveillance of employees leading workers to complain of being shadowed by foremen toting stopwatches, being warned "not to take little baby steps" while moving around, and denied permission to go to the bathroom. Between 1987 and 1989, there were 355 attacks by workers on supervisors, and 183 by bosses on workers (Monroe et al,1989, p. 30). By all accounts, this stress is enhanced because of a top-down management style where there is a rule for everything. The outcome is 150,000 grievance proceedings and 69,000 disciplinary actions a year! The Postal Service is trying to change the prevailing management style by increasing employee involvement and quality of work life processes. Postal employees are well paid and have generous benefits and job security (e.g., in none of the 69,000 disciplinary hearings was there a firing). But problems abound because of nonrealistic conflicts.

This distinction requires an understanding that conflict can develop intangibles (e.g., power and status) as well as tangibles (e.g., resources) (Smith & Harris, 1974). It also reminds us that conflict can require some bargaining strategies even when our interests are not totally divergent (Carnevale, 1991, pp. 118–119). We can be in a realistic conflict and still share mutual goals. We can change an unrealistic conflict by adopting an overarching, realistic goal (e.g., company survival, increased employment).

In some ways, conflicts are caused because we perceive the need for them. So much has been written about the values of competition that an absence of conflict can create dissonance. Early in this text we examined the tendency to perceive issues differently, even when there was little difference. When we see power, status, or resources as finite, then there is the potential for conflict. Our analysis of self-managing work units (e.g., chapter 10) explains the difference between the traditional manager–subordinate relationship—which exacerbates the power, status, and resources issues—and empowerment, which is one means for overcoming these types of conflicts (Frost, 1987, p. 539).

One promotion spot for two people or limited funds for new projects serve as examples of how organizations create a "sense" of competition. Couple this with a lack of ability by most people to manage conflicts, and these issues tend to spiral into counterproductive conflicts. Filley (1975) lists nine antecedent conditions leading to organizational conflict: differentiation between parties; communication barriers; conflict over prestige, power, or resources; ambiguous jurisdiction; dependence on one another; association and interrelatedness of the parties; need for consensus; rules regulating behavior; and unresolved prior conflicts (pp. 9–12).

As this last paragraph should make clear, there are realistic reasons for conflicts to occur. So, the next step is to distinguish between dysfunctional and functional conflicts.

## Dysfunctional Conflict

Developing an understanding of the nature of conflict is vital as a preliminary step in learning how to manage it. Conflicts have positive and negative effects on organizations.

A conflict is *dysfunctional,* or generally negative, when it demands too many of the resources of a unit where it occurs compared to the benefits received from the conflict itself. If energy is diverted, or morale is destroyed, the conflict inevitably will lead to decreased productivity.

Conflicts become destructive when the focus is on the personalities involved rather than the department, team, group, or company's objectives. When the conflict is interpersonal, employee turnover, refusing to cooperate, working to the rule, and absenteeism all can increase (Edwards & Scullion, 1984). To prevent alienation or a threat to their self-image, individuals will suppress a conflict. This means that it grinds away without producing a positive response to the situation.

The energy of people or groups can be drained by the conflict, making it dysfunctional (Pareek, 1982). Distrust and suspicion increase and the result will be polarization. Intradepartmental conflicts can decrease motivation and reduce job satisfaction (Schnake & Cochran, 1985). Interdepartmental conflicts lead to frustration, anxiety, and wasted resources (Robey, 1991, pp. 153–156).

Third, positions can become polarized, creating the demand for winners and losers and face-saving activities. The competition in some companies between union and management is seen as a major impediment to the implementation of new technologies. The compliance/adversarial approach, where the supervisor is an enforcer and a we/they attitude develops, works against the effective use of teams, innovation, and organizational adaptation to change (Walton & McKersie, 1989, p. 33). When the original foe or issue disappears, there is a tendency to search for enemies to maintain the power base, togetherness, and focus (Coser, 1956). In some cases, issues are invented that serve to support the polarization, rather than assist in resolving the conflict.

Finally, because there are few rules and acquired skills for conflict management, most conflicts carry the potential for counterproductive outcomes (Truell, 1984, p. 56). Sadly, the original issue can become lost.

For example, when group members feel highly competitive, the following activities are decreased in effectiveness: listening to others, understanding actual statements, high achievement, coordination, assisting others, and liking of work and colleagues. In addition, there is more duplication of effort, less efficiency, and lower quality work (Pace & Faules, 1989, p. 217).

In a recent consulting experience I had with a highly successful national sales organization, the impact of a competitive environment was made very clear. Sales representatives receive individual recognition on a quarterly basis for achieving higher sales than their colleagues. Because the rewards were based on internal competition, there was no incentive to share insightful sales practices because that would diminish that each sales representative's chance for individual success. In addition to preventing team development, the practice was based on a perspective that having the representatives compete with each other would make everyone more productive. Instead, successful representatives were excluded from discussions by other representatives on how to develop a broader customer base. Energy was being expended on the contest rather than the growth and development of the company. And, whatever special approach was developed by an individual representative, it was not shared for the good of the company. This would seem harmless enough, except referrals (one customer to the next), repeat buying (continued use of a particular product), and cross-selling are all part of the company's national strategy. The successful representatives, naturally enough, were concentrating on those items they could sell, which was counterproductive to the company's goals. The culprit was the highly competitive environment. Our solution was to create district teams that could win as a group, thereby allowing some competition but focusing on the success of a large number of people. Teams also were rewarded for increased referrals, repeat buying, and cross-selling.

Conflict has many negative aspects. Time allocation, focus, misspent energy, polarization, search for enemies, and a lack of skills all contribute to conflict being dysfunctional.

## Functional Conflict

There are excellent reasons for an organization to encourage and foster goal-oriented conflicts (Bolman & Deal, 1991, p. 200). First, there is ample research to demonstrate that healthy conflict will improve the quality of the decision-making process (Whyte, 1989, p. 53). We can avoid the traps inherent in groupthink, and openly challenge ideas in an effort to achieve the best possible solutions to problems.

Creating independent subunits who compete for the best final product is a characteristic of most successful companies (Peters & Waterman, 1982, pp. 215–218). Procter & Gamble has competition between brand managers described in a special language such as "counterpartism," "creative conflict," and "the abrasion of ideas" (Peters & Waterman, 1982, p. 216). Hewlett Packard has a competitive routine: "Sell it to the sales force." This represents an excellent attempt to overcome the issue of Not Invented Here (NIH) that we discussed earlier. Internal competition, in the excellent companies, is substituted for rule- and committee-driven behavior that diminishes incentive and development.

Second, conflict allows us to define our own territory and responsibility. In the process, conflict can challenge us to extend ourselves (Truell, 1984, pp. 55–56). As Buell (1990) reported, "John Sculley (chairman of Apple Computer) says that both he and his company thrive on crisis" (p. 92). For example, after many initial successes, Apple needed to overcome its own NIH syndrome—in Apple's case viewing all other computer companies as not being worthy opponents in the fields of research and development (Buell, Levine, & Gross, 1990). So, the other companies were able to push ahead with innovations Apple had not even considered, and people at Apple had a blind spot (NIH) regarding these advances in the constantly evolving computer industry. This complacency has been replaced with a willingness to compete by examining competitors products with the goal of developing even better innovations. As a result, Apple has increased its own product development cycle, hastened the decision-making process, and developed new approaches (Buell, 1991).

In addition, a small conflict can "clear the air" and establish working relationships. Creativity can be fostered and our own thinking can be clarified.

Two examples show how conflict can be functional. First, teams provide an excellent paradigm for differentiating between dysfunctional and functional conflict. Our earlier discussion of semiautonomous work units shows how teams can be structured to be highly successful. General Foods found that the best way to respond to rapid market changes was to set up a nine-person team with the freedom to operate like entrepreneurs starting their own business (King, 1989, p. 16). Although it normally takes 5 to 7 years to get new products onto the shelves, this team had Jell-O Pudding Snacks in grocery stores nationwide in 3 years. This established a $100 million ready-to-eat dessert sales for General Food. Why did it work? Because of the difference between dysfunctional and functional conflict.

In one study of teams, less than 40% of the interaction could be considered teamwork. The rest was formalistic, perfunctory, leader-position ratifying, and collegiality mistaken for true teamwork. In the General Foods case, and in any effective team situation, there is an easy frankness, arguing and disagreement over goals, and a spirited seriousness (King, 1989, p. 17). In other words, the conflict is over accomplishing a goal, not beating someone else.

Rewarding mistakes is a second example. In this case, risk is rewarded even when the employee ends up doing something wrong. Returning to the last chapter, employees are rewarded for doing things right (e.g., innovation and leadership) rather than doing the right thing (e.g., managerial behavior).

Put another way, for many innovative organizations mistake making is one road to progress (Hillkirk, 1990). You can win a "Doobie" (dubious achievement award) at the Public Broadcasting System as a manager who lays the biggest egg. At Pepsi-Co's Pizza Hut subsidiary, John Lauck launched a big promotion featuring futuristic sunglasses for the film *Back to the Future, Part 2*. The promotion was a disappointment, but he was promoted because he tried something innovative. Employees can receive a duck's head mounted on a toilet plunger at Esso Resources Canada for challenging management or for doing something without the boss's approval. The "Order of the Duck" award represents vision (e.g., duck's head) and the neck of the plunger represents sticking your neck out. "Bureaucracy . . . strangles all big business. To us, loyalty means not letting the boss do a stupid thing," said Shaun Murphy, one of the duck's creators (Hillkirk, 1990). Managers can receive $100 if they make the biggest mistake of the month or quarter at Temps & Co. Two recent winners were Temps' president, Steve Ettridge, who took a plane to the wrong city and a secretary who typed a social security number for a check amount, creating a multimillion dollar check. Ettridge observes: "The object is to get people to take risks—and tell us about their mistakes early and fast."

Communication strategy becomes the intervening variable (Borisoff & Victor, 1989, chapter 1). Many organizational conflicts can be viewed as bargaining situations where there is the opportunity for one party to influence the other (Tedeschi, 1970). The difference is the procedure, or communicative behavior, each side takes. The outcomes of conflicts can be functional when both sides use their reward power, which consists of promises and exchanges of information regarding the positive outcomes each side has in store for the other (Raven & Kruglandski, 1970). This contrasts with punishment, where the threats intensify the distrust, which makes the conflict dysfunctional. This brings us to the ways we approach conflicts.

## STYLES AND STRATEGIES OF CONFLICT MANAGEMENT

The most popular approaches to conflict management offer a five-category scheme that is based on the two factors of concern for self and concern for others (Blake & Mouton, 1964; Filley, 1975; Hall, 1986; Harris, 1967; Killman & Thomas, 1977). Various tests have been devised that measure whether you are most likely to:

1. compete—be a "tough battler" and use position power, verbal dominance, perseverance, and assertiveness in striving for a win/lose solution;
2. compromise—be a mediator and split the difference;
3. accommodate—be a "friendly helper" and smooth over or trivialize the conflict where one person loses the conflict to win the relationship;
4. avoid—removing yourself physically or psychologically from the scene that results in a lose/lose outcome; and
5. collaborate—be a "problem solver" and use a win/win approach by confronting the conflict directly and working for an integrative solution.

Each of the measuring instruments has been given extensive scrutiny. For example, an entire issue of the Management Communication Quarterly (Putnam, 1988) was devoted to examining the strengths and weaknesses of the various conflict tests, because of the importance of conflict-training programs for organizations. In almost all cases, they "subscribe to collaborative or problem solving approaches to conflict management" (Monroe, DiSalvo, Lewis, & Borzi, 1990, p. 12). You will recognize this perspective as an argument for "one best way," which has cropped up in our discussions of other organizational behavior (e.g., leadership).

## Contingency Approach

Based on earlier chapters, you probably will have predicted the next sentence. A contingency approach is the best means of managing conflicts. As with organizational design, management, and leadership, contingency approaches suggest that the conflict managing strategy should come after the conflict has been analyzed (Hocker & Wilmot, 1985, pp. 59–66).

Studying the five conflict styles is very useful. Remember, without any training in conflict management, we develop certain responses, or trained incapacities, for dealing with conflicts (Folger & Poole, 1984, pp. 65–68). Many of these are formed early in life, and tend to be self-reinforcing. When they work, we attribute our success to our strategy. When we fail, we tend to fault the other party, or group (Groder, 1989). Our internal reasoning usually follows a pattern such as the following. We received the promotion because we fought for it (or laid back, or befriended the boss), but we lost the promotion because we were outmanned (or the other side was crooked, or the evaluation process was biased).

For whatever reasons, we have patterns we follow during conflicts that make sense to us at the time (Hocker & Wilmot, 1985, pp. 37–38). The boss who explodes (necessary to relieve tension; keep employees on their toes), the subordinate who calls in sick (cannot face another failure; it's a terrible job anyway; everyone's doing it), or the student who cuts class (too much work for 3 hr. credit; the professor is unfair; the material is too hard) are all using a conflict management style that makes sense to them. With training and insights, most people can learn to adapt their styles and increase their conflict-managing abilities. Without some understanding, our conflict-managing techniques become trained incapacities.

A contingency approach becomes particularly useful when dealing with difficult people. As long as we assume the parties to a conflict are reasonable, then picking a strategy is largely a question of management. When we are operating in an irrational situation, rationality might not work. Difficult people are willing to pursue their own perception of reality without a great deal of concern for the other person's needs. In addition, they often take self-defeating actions in the process.

The old fable about the scorpion and the frog may help clarify this issue. The scorpion, unable to swim, asked the frog to carry him across the stream, but the frog resisted on the grounds that the scorpion would sting him to death. "Look," said the scorpion, "use your head. If I sting you while we're in the stream, we both die." A reassured frog finally agreed. Of course, when they reached the deepest part of the stream, the scorpion stung the frog. As the frog was dying, he cried: "Why? Now we both die." To which the scorpion replied, "Once a scorpion, always a scorpion. It's my nature." In a real sense, the scorpion was willing to use counterproductive behavior to achieve his own personal goals.

As with most fables, there are additional lessons. The adversarial relationship between labor and management, supported by a long history of backstabbing and subversive activities, prevents cooperation until the system can be altered (Abbott, 1989). Organizations that request sacrifices on the part of employees and then give enormous bonuses to the top officers demonstrate a lack of trust (e.g., Chrysler, General Motors). Promising to cooperate with a colleague and then taking credit for the work is a more personal example.

Finally, some people are so accustomed to being a scorpion that you may have to avoid them in order to get ahead or survive (Grothe & Whlie, 1987, pp. 218–294). Lawyers use a "scorpion defense," which means making the sting of litigation (e.g., years in court, massive legal fees, uncertain outcome) so severe that most people back down. We will deal with this group more fully under competitive styles of conflict management.

In most organizations, collaboration and cooperation are required to achieve certain goals. However, there are times when conflicts cannot be resolved, when pushing for "one best way" is unrealistic, and individuals are simply unapproachable — unless you want to get stung.

What you will want to do is become aware of all five styles and develop a proficiency in choosing the correct style for the situation. Figure 12.1 places all five styles within the context of the the chapters on organizational and management theories, interpersonal and group communication, and leadership. We now offer a fuller examination of each of the five styles, discussing what the style entails, when it should be used, and when it would be inappropriate to use the style.

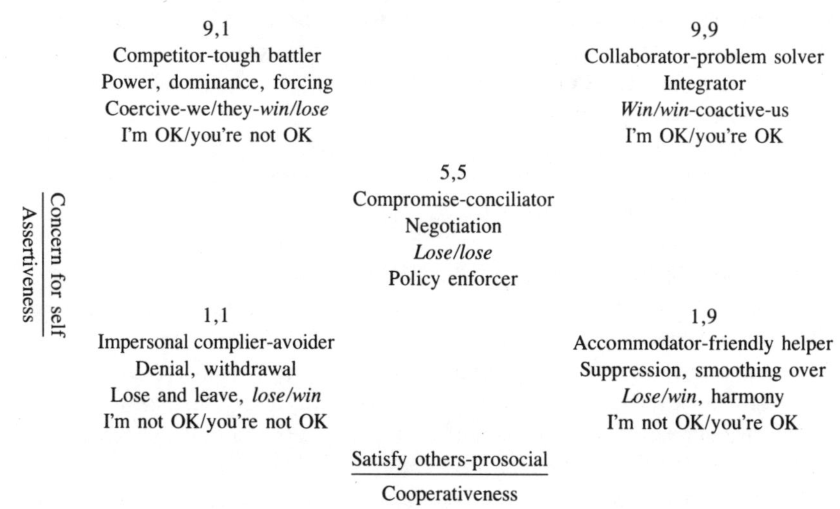

9,1
Competitor-tough battler
Power, dominance, forcing
Coercive-we/they-*win/lose*
I'm OK/you're not OK

9,9
Collaborator-problem solver
Integrator
*Win/win*-coactive-us
I'm OK/you're OK

5,5
Compromise-conciliator
Negotiation
*Lose/lose*
Policy enforcer

Concern for self
Assertiveness

1,1
Impersonal complier-avoider
Denial, withdrawal
Lose and leave, *lose/win*
I'm not OK/you're not OK

1,9
Accommodator-friendly helper
Suppression, smoothing over
*Lose/win*, harmony
I'm not OK/you're OK

Satisfy others-prosocial

Cooperativeness

FIG. 12.1.   Five styles of conflict management.

## Competitive

This is a zero-sum, win/lose strategy whereby you must make the other person lose so you can win. Competition is ingrained into our way of thinking. Law courts are based on adversarial behaviors, politicians win elections, and a clever "put-down" can be seen as wit. As Ruben (1980) said, "There are virtually no areas of human interaction which are free from the urge to 'win' " (p. 3). We "win a promotion," "beat" the competition, and pursue the "competitive edge." According to Keltner (1987), "We have been conditioned from childhood to seek to be 'winners' in almost all of our human relations" (p. 5).

As we described earlier under dysfunctional conflict, competition is used to increase productivity. Merit systems, performance appraisals, and ratings make people competitive (Gabor, 1990–1991, p. 9). This approach involves coercion and control with the assumption that "might makes right." When translated into communication tactics, the goal is to get the other person to change. W. Edwards Deming, America's apostle of quality management and one of the individuals credited with the successes of many of the Japanese manufacturing operations, concluded that the biggest problem facing American management today is "the system of reward, which makes people, teams, divisions, companies competitive. Companies should manage so as to optimize the system, whereby everyone would gain—employees, stockholders, customers, suppliers" (Gabor, 1990–1991, p. 8).

On an interpersonal level, hostile questioning, threats, faulting, and avoiding responsibility are examples. In 1981 and 1984, *Fortune Magazine* ran articles on the toughest bosses in America. They described John Welch, Jr., Chairman of General Electric (GE), in the following manner: "(He) conducts meetings so aggressively that people tremble. He attacks (subordinates) almost physically—criticizing, demeaning, ridiculing, humiliating." He was nicknamed "Neutron Jack," because after he visited a GE facility the building was left standing, but the people were gone (Grothe & Whlie, 1987, pp. 7–8). Robert Malott, Chairman of FMC Corporation, also was chosen. It was observed about him, "Employees say he can grill subordinates mercilessly when there's no good reason." Malott once was quoted as saying, "Leadership is demonstrated when the ability to inflict pain is confirmed" (Grothe & Whlie, 1987, p. 8).

Two general examples of incompetent, competitive bosses are the *petty bureaucrats* in love with paperwork, rules, and by-the-book behavior, and the *commandants* who are bullies using their power to get their way (Grothe & Whlie, 1987, p. 4). Numerous articles about success tout the competitive edge, the sacrifices to overcome odds, and the great coaches, players, and teams that exemplify the values of a winning perspective. Modern management folklore and recent corporate history resembles a battlefield, at times, with takeovers, price wars, poison pill maneuvers (e.g., making the company worthless because of debt), propaganda (e.g., negative advertising), intelligence gathering, and merger skirmishes. Some companies see their survival as being based on an amalgam of offensive and defensive strategies, designed to obtain market share, ward off competitors, or survive (Ramsey, 1987, p. xv; Rogers, 1987). Perhaps because of the perception of it being a "jungle out there," or because we take note of assertive—and therefore dramatic—actions, the reward process in most American companies seems to reinforce a competitive outlook. In a 1985 study of 3,445 managers in 12 countries, advancement in American organizations was associated closely with noncooperative actions (Rosenstein, 1985)! Before you decide that being competitive is the gateway to success, consider a broader viewpoint.

Unbridled "competition generally does not promote excellence because trying to do well and trying to beat others are simply two different things" (Kohn, 1986, p. 28). In cooperative situations, which are ones designed to focus on the job and not personalities, others are depending on you to succeed. In competitive situations, others hope to see you fail. In study after study, psychologists have found "that making one person's success depend on another's failure—which is what competition involved by definition—simply does not make the grade" (Kohn, 1986, p. 22).

When large companies compete for market share, the evolving strategies are designed to deliver a knock-out punch. But, the deciding factor—as with all competing strategies—is the capacity of the opponent to respond in like form. For example, in 1990 Coca-Cola introduced Coke II, which is simply New Coke (the sweeter version of Coke introduced in 1985 to compete head-on with Pepsi), in a new can with a new ad campaign in Spokane, Washington (Konrad, 1990). To Coke's surprise, Pepsi responded with a $1-million counterattack that greatly limited Coke II's success. The point: Pepsi had the resources to compete and the willingness to commit them.

The same is true for individuals or groups. Studies of attempts to enforce work rules or safety procedures provide numerous examples of the failure of punitive measures to get people to wear safety glasses or helmets. Competition can work, but the strategy is open to being countered by someone with more power, influence, finances, or tenacity.

*Behavioral Characteristics of the Competitive Style.* This style is high in assertiveness and low on cooperativeness. Power and dominance are the primary tools for implementing this strategy. The outcomes desired favor the individual or his or her group and the goal is to force the other party into submission. Uses of "you" language (e.g., accusing, blaming, labeling), sarcasm, and invasion of "space" are common tactics of this style.

*Appropriate Uses of the Competitive Style.* There are times when being competitive is a valuable style. You will want to take note of the difference between competition, compromise, and collaboration. Under compromise, we discuss additional dangers of not seeking the right solution. Confrontation, which is not a competitive stance, is discussed as a collaborative strategy.

When a quick, decisive course of action is required (e.g., emergency) or an unpopular, but necessary, course of action must be followed (e.g., enforcing safety rules such as protective gear; limiting gatherings at the Xerox machine; establishing strict lunch hours and break times) a competitive approach can be appropriate (Ross, 1982, p. 136). Finally, conflicts can force individuals and groups to become aware of specific problems and demand a solution.

When you know you are right, this can be a viable approach (e.g., safety issues). Especially with issues that must be dealt with, a competitive stance can be very important. A competitive stance can make other parties to the conflict aware of just how committed you are.

***Inappropriate Uses of the Competitive Style.*** The differences between a bully and a hero bring the problems of a competitive style into focus. When your opponents have no way to express their needs, they will suppress the conflict or find other outlets. In organizations, supervisors might "kick the dog" when a manager tears into them. The subordinates (e.g., the kicked dog) then take it out on the customers or their colleagues. In other words, simply being able to force compliance (e.g., bully your way) does not foster commitment by others. Carrying the bully analogy one step further, competition results in a win/lose, we/they, for me or against me structure that mitigates against many important organizational activities (e.g., teamwork, motivation). A competitive strategy should be used only when the consequences have been considered carefully and other alternatives ruled out.

## Compromise

This approach is expedient. In an effort to maintain the relationship, while achieving some goals, conflicting parties decide to "split the difference." Essentially, we are willing to win a little and lose a little and establish some type of détente. In this lose/lose approach both parties must give up something to reach the compromise. This middle of the road solution often ignores the real diversity in the issue.

This approach involves a heavy reliance on the democratic process and a willingness to abide by majority rule for the "common good." To be effective at this approach, you will need negotiating abilities, persuasive talents, the ability to swap, and some adaptability and flexibility. Bosses who are "company people" or POPOS (Passed Over, Put On the Shelf) tend to work on compromises as the easy way to manage. Employees who work late, take unlimited trips, and accept bad assignments often are compromising their own needs for the demands of the boss or organization.

***Behavioral Characteristics of the Compromise Style.*** When democratic methods are employed, this signals a compromise approach. Negotiation talk (e.g., "Let's make a deal"; or "Can we split the difference?") makes it clear that the parties are looking for a settlement.

In most cases, there is acknowledgment of only the surface needs of both parties.

The underlying needs, feelings, and perceptions rarely are dealt with through compromise.

***Appropriate Uses of the Compromise Style.***          Compromising is quicker than collaborating and less dangerous than competing. If a balance of power has been reached between the parties, compromise perpetuates it. When other styles fail, this is a useful option.

When the competing parties have equal power, this might be the only choice. If nothing else, it provides a temporary settlement. In so doing, it establishes a working relationship, which can be a steppingstone to additional conflict management.

At the end of 1990, MTV Network's "Ha! The Comedy Channel" and Home Box Office's "The Comedy Channel" announced a merger. "After months of duking it out for subscribers (e.g., system operator to carry their programming)" both sides decided to compromise and transfer all assets and control to a 50-50 venture called Comedy TV (Collingwood 1990, p. 61). Both sides realized dividing the market was better than expending unlimited resources in an effort to defeat the other side. Sometimes, compromise is the best solution.

***Inappropriate Uses of the Compromise Style.***          Compromise can lead to the use of formulas to solve problems. When individuals call for a flipping of the coin to solve a problem, this is not true compromise. In this case, the arbiter is chance (Hocker & Wilmot, 1985, p. 46).

Compromise does not work if both parties cannot afford to yield. For example, compromising on major safety or ethical issues can be disastrous. Examinations of the Challenger space mission explosion and the Hubble Space Telescope mirror malfunctioning conclude that quality continually is compromised (Howard, 1990). Manifestations of this compromising approach include cutting funds for the quality assurance team so money can be spent on other parts of a project, no independence or clout for the safety team so it can be overridden easily by the project manager, hundreds of "flight waivers" granted on important components of the space shuttle so some substandard parts might be used, and quality control underfunded in comparison to other parts of the NASA program. Frank Pizzano, head of the maintainability and reliability engineering division at NASA's Marshall Space Flight Center, concluded that when the quality division goes up against the project offices, the projects have the upper hand because they have more money. He observed: "There is a saying about the Golden Rule: 'He who has the gold rules' " (Howard, 1990). The Hubble fiasco, Challenger disaster, cost overruns, and the grounded space shuttle fleet because of hydrogen leaks all point to the potential dangers in compromising specific standards. U.S. Senator Al Gore was so frustrated with the decline in quality that he quoted the comedian Jay Leno to explain the Hubble telescope problem: "You know there's new information about the Hubble. It's actually working perfectly but the universe is all blurry" ("Space Program," 1990). Compromise is not appropriate when the stakes are too high for one side in the conflict.

When one side lacks the resources to make a compromise, it is not an appropriate conflict-managing tool. Asking employees to take a 10% wage cut when they are working for $4.50 per hr, in the name of saving the company, is coercion, not compromise. Shaving corners on health and disability insurance in order to have more take-home pay or greater profits represents a dangerous compromise. Disability is a worker's biggest risk on the job, yet 70% of American companies do not have disability insurance (New York Times News Service, 1990). A recent, and frightening, headline was "Research Finds Workplaces More Deadly Than Cars" (1990). The reason, according to the Chicago-based Safe Workplace Institute, is the "financial starvation of enforcement agencies and inadequate standards" ("Research Finds," 1990). Forcing financial sacrifices, cutting back on insurance, and underfunding safety organizations provide very specific examples of how compromise can lead to disastrous outcomes. Competition and compromise are only two alternatives. We also can choose to make the relationship more important than the issue.

### Accommodating

In organizations, we defer to others when it does not make sense to push for our own needs. The phrase, "kill your enemies with kindness," describes the underlying principle. This is the opposite of competing (e.g., kill your enemies). In this approach, we are willing to forgo our own goals in order to satisfy the relationship. Generosity, self-sacrifice, and yielding to the other person's point of view characterize this approach. We become a friendly helper and find ourselves in a lose/win situation. We modify our needs to maintain the relationship.

*Behavioral Characteristics of the Accommodating Style.* Sometimes, this style involves being easy to get along with. The nonassertive use of language (e.g., "It seems to me," "It probably wouldn't work anyway," "It's really up to you"), or an extensive use of qualifiers can signal an accommodating approach. This style assumes that the relationship is more important than the issue.

*Appropriate Uses of the Accommodating Style.* When harmony, future good will, or the relationship are more important, this is a useful approach. At the risk of being called an "apple polisher," "brown noser," or "company person," this style allows us to keep in contact with the other individual while putting the issue on the back burner. When we are working for someone who has a great deal more experience than we do, it can be a useful approach while we are learning. This ultimately will allow us a better position from which to be recognized and heard.

Second, when you are wrong, this is an important alternative. Accommodating demonstrates that you are willing to keep working with the other person even when you "lose" an argument or issue. At work, this will happen, and it pays to have a strategy to employ.

Third, you could have raised the issue at the wrong time (e.g., when serious discussion cannot occur; opponent is upset about other issues), in the wrong setting (e.g., in a meeting rather than face-to-face), or at the wrong place. You also might perceive that a cooling-off period is needed and the best bet is to take a break, sleep on it, or let it go for a while.

Finally, when continued competition would damage your case, accommodating can be useful. Essentially, you are trying to minimize your losses. Sometimes, even when you are right, you are "outgunned." Given that reality, keeping the working relationship intact can be important.

***Inappropriate Uses of the Accommodating Style.*** Accommodation should be a short-term solution to major problems. Make no mistake, being easy to get along with is an asset, as we demonstrated earlier in this chapter. But giving up on significant issues is not. Too much accommodating simply proves that you really do not have any power.

This style, when it becomes a company-wide approach, can lead to a shallow, unrealistic approach to real problems. There are times when people should demonstrate their concerns and worries and accommodating does not allow for this. Carried to the extreme, people can avoid a conflict altogether, which is the next style we consider.

## Avoiding

When we rely on sidestepping, denying, postponing, or withdrawing, we are adopting the avoiding approach. This appears to be a passive strategy because people using the avoiding approach seem to be stating that there is little that can be done to solve the problem. These individuals might be willing to forgo personal gain in order to avoid a conflict. In organizations, patience, detached objectivity, and disengagement are the primary modes. When we let "fate" decide, call in third parties, procrastinate, or withdraw to fight another day, we are avoiding. This style is labeled "I'm not OK/You're not OK" because you do not stand up for your own needs, you do not concern yourself with the other person's needs either, and you leave the relationship. It is a lose/lose situation.

***Behavioral Characteristics of the Avoiding Style.*** This style involves a denial of the problem. Often people will refuse to disclose their own feelings, change the subject, focus on someone else, or relabel the situation. People use a complex set of responses to avoid dealing with conflicts. For example, they may leave their jobs, move, change friendships, or withdraw.

***Appropriate Uses of the Avoiding Style.*** As with the accommodating approach, this is an important choice if the timing is wrong, you are wrong, or a cooling-off period is needed. In addition, you might need more information, and avoiding would allow you to obtain it. If the issue is unimportant, this can be a very realistic approach.

For most of us, organizations are filled with numerous dilemmas and paradoxes. When we discussed symbolic behavior, it became apparent that people search for meaning. *Ambiguous situations* can drive some individuals to use avoidance tactics. According to Roskin (1982), "Avoidance can help keep routines in place, allow planning, delegation, and the continued best use of technology and resources. It can also lead to perceptual distortion, insensitivity, indecision, and construction of elaborate defense mechanisms" (p. 108).

The list of avoidance tactics is extensive. Some representative examples are denial of the conflict, underresponsiveness, joking, and topic avoidance (Hocker & Wilmot, 1985, p. 112). Sometimes, avoiding can be "a productive, power-shifting ploy for persons in high-power positions who would have to give up some of their autonomy to make decisions if they entered into the negotiation process" (Hocker & Wilmot, 1985, p. 113). Large organizations, with the incredible diffusion of responsibility, offer some executives, vice presidents, or college deans the opportunity to avoid taking responsibility by pointing to an apparent lack of power. Responses such as "It's in the policy manual" or "they make the ultimate decision" allow middle managers to escape responsibility and, depending on the issue, can be positive or negative uses of avoiding.

***Inappropriate Uses of the Avoiding Style.***   We already have discussed the problem with significant issues. Clearly, avoiding a life-threatening, or sanity-threatening, issue can be a serious mistake. If the issue will not go away, then this is not a useful method.

Avoidance can signal that you simply do not care to get involved. For example, managers when dealing with disciplinary issues must be careful about hoping a problem will "work itself out." Instead, managers should employ a collaborative, "*we* have a problem," approach.

## Collaboration

This is called a win/win strategy because both parties are able to achieve mutually desired goals. Collaboration focuses on problem solving and depends on the concept "two heads are better than one." Each party has a maximum concern for his or her own goals, for the goals of the other party, and for their working relationship. Although this might sound naive or counterintuitive and it definitely challenges the importance of unbridled competition, "study after study shows nothing succeeds like cooperation" (Kohn, 1986, p. 22). By getting both parties involved in the solution, many conflicts can be managed to everyone's satisfaction (Ury, Brett, & Goldberg, 1988).

Earlier, we distinguished between dysfunctional and functional conflict. Conflict that is designed to produce some winners over losers rarely surpasses the benefits of functional conflict. Remember, competition generally does not promote excellence because trying to do well and trying to beat others are simply two different things (Waterman, 1987, pp. 195–197). The trick, as they say, is to create proactive conflict behaviors. As Ury et al. (1988) put it, "If successfully managed, conflict can produce high quality, creative solutions that lead to innovation and progress" (p. 163). Some authors describe this approach as *confrontation* (Schein, 1969). Taken in the vein of a win/win strategy, confrontation means confronting the issues, and emotions, head-on, dealing with them, and resolving the issues to everyone's satisfaction.

***Behavioral Characteristics of the Collaborative Style.***    As indicated on Fig. 12.1, the collaborative style is high on concern for self and a willingness to satisfy others. Combining strong assertiveness and a prosocial, cooperative approach produces a problem-solving, integrative style. This is called a non-zero-sum approach because neither side must lose in order for the other side to win. Sharing power is the most apparent example because the more a leader shares power, coupled with clear goals, the greater the leader's power.

Both parties must approach the conflict in a problem-solving mode. In so doing, the goals, opinions, attitudes, and feelings of all parties are recognized as legitimate and everyone takes part a constructive role in solving the problem. The conflict must be depersonalized so that the energy can be channeled into a solution rather than into the combat. Communication skills are at a premium in this approach with excellent listening, supportive climate, and positive verbal and nonverbal behavior being used by everyone.

As Fig. 12.1 indicates, this is a win/win approach because both parties come out ahead. The perspective is "us" and, drawing from transactional analysis, this approach suggests that "I'm OK/You're OK." In chapter 9, Interpersonal Communication, we discussed games and the devastating effect they can have on organizations. Collaborative behavior is game-free, problem oriented, and mutually satisfying. Given this conclusion, it would seem that we always should operate in a collaborative mode. Returning to the contingency perspective, there are appropriate and inappropriate times to use this approach.

***Appropriate Uses of Collaboration.***    When the individuals or groups are willing to commit the time and energy necessary to work through the problem, collaboration can succeed. When we discussed small groups, we indicated that collaborative efforts often fail because we are not willing to allow time for the search for an effective solution. We conclude this chapter with some examples of collaboration.

***Inappropriate Uses of Collaboration.***    There are times when collaboration simply cannot work—for example, two people vying for the same promotion or starting position on the basketball team. Sometimes the issue does not deserve the time and energy required for collaboration. Third, the individual, group, or organization might be a scorpion and "not OK" which would make any effort at collaboration a waste of time and potentially dangerous. Finally, the issue might not be open to collaboration. For example, drinking or drug use on the job is not acceptable, regardless of the reasons. Offering alternatives for dealing with the problem (e.g., counseling, goal setting) can be done in a collaborative manner, but the unacceptable behavior must stop.

At this point, we have outlined the five strategies that can be used to manage conflicts. There are advantages and disadvantages to all five, and effective management brings us back to a basic point. To be skilled in organizational communication, we constantly must attempt to do the right thing at the right time. One of the intervening variables is the amount and types of power being used in the conflict.

## POWER

Regardless of the conflict management approach, we are exercising power and influence in a conflict. Each of the styles defines the relationship and is a power move (Hocker & Wilmot, 1985, p. 69). Because we cannot not communicate, we also cannot not exercise power once interdependence has occurred (Watzlawick, Beavin, & Jackson, 1967). The use of power is a form of communication (King, 1987, pp. 4–8). The choice we do have is how the power will be used.

You are also aware that power is not a finite source. When we discussed empowerment and leadership dilemmas, we established that power increases as more people are brought into the solution phase of a problem. There are seven sources of power in most organizations.

Power can be defined as the capacity to control or influence the other person or persons (DeVito, 1986, p. 234). Others have observed that, "In the broadest sense, power is the capacity to reward or punish as a result of one's position, personality, or proficiency" (Frank & Brownell, 1989, pp. 416–418; Hocker & Wilmot, 1985, p. 73). Although these definitions are helpful, a fuller examination of the sources of power proves useful.

### Sources of Power

There are seven sources of power in organizations (Bolman & Deal, 1991, pp. 196–197; Frank & Brownell, 1989, pp. 416–418; French & Raven, 1959; Hocker & Wilmot, 1985, p. 73). Although different investigations have provided alternative slants to these seven, the important point is that power is a complex, diverse issue.

***Expert Power.***    When someone has special knowledge or expertise, they have power. Knowing how to operate a computer, complete a budget, or solve a problem makes someone powerful. For it to work in an organization, the expertise must be essential to the functioning of the organization, concentrated in the hands of a few individuals, and irreplaceable (Mintzberg, 1983). Because organizations are designed to be able to operate without a high dependency on any one individual, a person must be critical to getting the job done before they are granted expert power (Brass, 1984, p. 522).

**Reward Power.** Inherent in all organizations is the hierarchical arrangement whereby someone has the capacity to give or withhold rewards. Even the CEO is rewarded by the board of directors or the holding company. Reward power is the ability to dispense rewards ranging from time off to pay increases. When resources are available to us based on the discretion of someone else, they have reward power.

**Coercive Power.** Marching along with the capacity to reward is the ability to force people to comply. If someone believes you have the ability to punish them, then you have coercive power over them.

**Legitimate Power.** When the person's position gives the right to exercise power over us, it is called legitimate power. In addition, if you believe a person has the right to control you, with or without a formal position, that person has—for you—legitimate power.

**Referent Power.** When someone wants to be identified with someone else, there is referent power. Power attracts people, and power holders can be important sources for our own future. This personal power reflects our willingness to let someone influence us because of respect, liking, or a feeling that they can provide us with important psychological rewards (e.g., security) or advancement (Sashkin & Morris, 1984, pp. 296–297).

**Connection Power.** The importance of connections was established in our chapter on channels and networks. Interpersonal linkages, places in the networks or channels, or being "in the know" give an individual a resource that others might want. When it is apparent that you are connected to important or influential people, you will have power over other individuals wishing to gain favor or avoid disfavor with those people (Goodstein, 1981, p. 285).

**Information Power.** At various times in our analysis of organizational communication, we have established that information is power. If someone possesses information that you need or want, or has access to that information, he or she has power. According to Fowler (1988), "Legend has it that the priests of ancient Egypt knew much about the flood patterns of the Nile, knowledge that would have been useful to farmers, but they kept it to themselves because they knew that knowledge is power" (p. 79).

Our earlier discussion of information (chapter 9) as being based on the four modes of rational, limited capacity, expert, or cybernetic places the discussion of information power in context. In addition, controlling the access or flow of information (chapter 6, Networks and Channels) can be as powerful as being the source of the information.

Power is an exciting and important topic. These seven sources demonstrate the diversity of power. Clearly, individuals and groups can possess several types of power and can switch from one power base to another during a conflict. Finally, everyone has power in a relationship. When organizational members sense a lack of power, they may turn to alternative means of influence.

## Passive Aggressive Behavior

People without power also can take control through passive aggressive behavior (Hocker & Wilmot, 1985, pp. 81–82). This is a strategy that can work very well when an individual wishes to avoid certain tasks or responsibilities.

Let us assume that you want someone to run off 500 copies of a memo. If they do not want to do this type of work, they can make poor copies (e.g., off-center, dark) or continually call you to help with operating problems with the machine. Pretty soon, you simply will give up, do the job yourself, or assign it to someone else.

Passive aggressive behavior means someone is pursuing their own self-interests, without regard for the other person, by being passive or unconcerned when the other person needs a response. As Hocker and Wilmot (1985) explained, "Especially when people feel they have low power, whether they do or not, passive aggression may be used since it appears to be a safer way of expressing anger, resentment, or hostility than stating such feelings directly" (p. 82). For some people, engaging in conflict is viewed as not being nice, so they use passive aggressive behaviors. Examples of passive aggressive behavior include scheduling two things at once; being late so others must wait; forgetting appointments, promises, and agreements—your own or your superiors; evading so other people in the organization cannot get their work completed; getting sick when you have promised to do something; and acting confused or disoriented when certain topics come up (Hocker & Wilmot, 1985, p. 82).

A partial price tag can be placed on passive aggressive behavior in organizations. Employee pilferage of company property is costing American business between $5 billion and $10 billion a year, according to the U.S. Department of Justice ("Workers Admit," 1983). In the same 3-year study, more than two thirds of the sample engaged in counterproductive behavior such as excessively long lunches and breaks, slow or sloppy workmanship, sick-leave abuse, and using alcohol or drugs on the job. The report concluded that "a feeling of being exploited by the employer figured more as a cause of employee theft than economic pressures on the worker" ("Boss' Pockets," 1983, p.1). Part of the problem is the "Draconian security hardware, such as cameras, one-way glass, mirrors, and the like," which convey a message of distrust ("Boss' Pockets," 1983, p. 1). The solution, according to the report, are social controls including treating employees with respect, trust, and greater responsibility.

## Empowerment

Shifting responsibility, self-determination, and power are vital organizational issues. We already discussed empowerment, and we return to it again in the next chapter on motivation. According to Conger and Kanungo (1988), "The need to empower employees becomes critical when subordinates feel powerless" (p. 474). Empowerment is "a process whereby an individual's belief in his or her self-efficacy is enhanced" (Conger & Kanungo, 1988, p. 474). And, as we discovered with leadership and self-managing work units, empowerment leads to greater productivity, job satisfaction, and success.

Under the sobering title "Can You Compete?" *Business Week* examined the various reasons American companies might not survive the 1990s (Hoerr, 1990). One of the recommendations was greater empowerment of employees through self-managing work units, educational advancement, and internal training. All attempts to open communication channels, create a positive climate, and involve employees lead to empowerment. Although not a cure for powerlessness, making employees part of the solution rather than part of the problem does seem to be a move in the right direction.

## STEPS IN CONFLICT MANAGEMENT

There are a variety of formulas for managing conflicts. Generally, they all include five steps. They are: Clearly identify the conflict or problem, identify mutually acceptable goals, openly communicate, negotiate a possible solution, and implement the solution (Stewart, 1986, p. 142).

At the interpersonal level, communication (e.g., listening, sensitivity, empathy) and patience (e.g., tolerance, separating personal from professional role, control temper, check your perspective) are very important. If you are part of the problem, you will want to remember that "lack of performance isn't usually why people get fired" (Walters, 1985, p. 3D). When we approach a conflict situation, we have three basic options: Try to change the other party, try to alter the conflict conditions, or change our own behavior (Hocker & Wilmot, 1985, pp. 157–158). A strong temptation in any conflict is to try and change the other person. In most instances, this will not be highly successful. In organizations, we can work to change the conflict conditions and this is a fertile area for exploration. In the vast majority of situations, the first step we should consider is changing ourselves. This requires a careful examination of how we respond to situations (e.g., conflict styles) and how well we perceive the problem. If we are in a position where we must change the other person, looking to the conflict conditions should be our second step.

When we are assigned the job of helping other people change, there are guidelines. Table 12.1 outlines the confrontation/collaborative process for conducting a disciplinary interview. Note the focus on issues not personalities, clarity of the messages, and concern for communication style. The same concern for changing the conflict from a potentially dysfunctional one to a functional one can be seen in the guidelines for a coaching interview. Table 12.2 explains the coaching process, which is used by managers and supervisors to assist subordinates in improving specific performance items. Once again, note the concern for communication style and process.

When there are conflicts between employees, managers can be called in to manage them. Managers are counseled to listen to both sides, ask each employee to repeat the other's point of view to check for accuracy, point out areas of similarity (e.g., goals, interests, needs), ask each employee to make suggestions as to what can be done to resolve the situation, come to an agreement on an action plan, and offer a follow-up opportunity (Rosenbaum, 1982, pp. 144–146). This process is intended to empower the combatants so they will have to accept responsibility for managing the conflict.

Interdepartmental conflicts are the most difficult to manage because of the nature of the interactions. Because departments and teams strive for an esprit de corps,

TABLE 12.1
Key Steps in the Disciplinary Interview

State problem and/or rule violated.
Give relevant facts related to the disciplinary infraction.
Obtain employee's view of the problem.
State management's expectation for improvement.
Inform employee of consequences if there is failure to improve.
Set a follow-up meeting, if appropriate.

*Style*

Key the interview to the point.
Listen, be open-minded.
Maintain the employee's self-esteem.
Maintain privacy.
Avoid being hostile.
Avoid putting the employee down.
Do not be defensive or apologetic.
Control temper.

*Other Points*

When there are genuinely extenuating circumstances do not discipline.
When the infraction is minor, and has not arisen previously, make a genuine effort to see if the problem can be dealt with through problem solving rather than discipline.
Do not handle the problem of a single employee by generalizing about the problem in departmental or staff meetings.

TABLE 12.2
Ten Guidelines for a Coaching Interview

Conducting a coaching session successfully depends very much on the skills of the coach. No set of rules or guidelines can substitute for those skills. Still, the coach will find it helpful to keep some basic guidelines in mind and to practice them during the coaching session.

The Framework

Don't try to hold a coaching session during an appraisal. If specific problems are identified during an appraisal session, they should be recorded and dealt with at a later coaching session, perhaps the next day or later in the week.

Plan regular automatic coaching sessions at least once a quarter. These need not take up a lot of time, but it is important to sit down with subordinates on a regular basis to see what concerns or problems they might have and how one might be helpful.

The Skills

Take time to learn and practice basic communication skills and specific coaching communication skills:

basic—effective listening
specific coaching—giving helpful feedback; goal setting

The Coaching Interview

*Preparation*

Begin only after a clear statement of basic job performance elements has been developed and agreed on by boss and subordinate.

Boss prepares by reviewing this statement and trying to identify the specific activities and skills of top performers.

*Conduct*

Take a positive approach; focus on solutions and on the fact that you are there to solve problems, not to lay blame. Focus on rewards available for performance improvements, not on punishments. Treat the interviewee as an equal, if at all possible; take the role of a supportive helper, not that of a judge. Never criticize in a personal way. When it is necessary to discuss specific problems and the subordinate's performance, be as descriptive as possible; be detailed, but do not evaluate. Do not use words like "poor," "inferior," "lousy," "rotten," etc.

Identify specific solution actions that the subordinate can actually carry out to correct specific performance problems.

Set specific measurable performance goals and targets. Try to involve the subordinate in goal setting, but do not accept goals that are too low or that seem unrealistically difficult.

Identify agreed-upon milestones for checking on and reporting progress toward goal attainment.

Try to identify ways that such performance feedback can be designed so as to be more or less automatic and a normal part of the job activity. In other words, try to find ways for the job itself to provide feedback.

*Note.* From Sashkin and Morris (1984). Reprinted by permission.

competition is a useful means for developing cohesion and goal orientation (Gutknecht & Miller, 1986, p. 71). But, unbridled competition creates all the problems inherent in any competitive approach. To move toward a collaborative approach, departments and teams must have the overall goals of the organization as their first priority (e.g., customer service, quality). When this happens, the conflict can present an incentive for each team.

In organizations, we have the opportunity to reorient conflicts toward overarching goals. Communicating goals is central to any effective conflict-managing technique (Hocker & Wilmot, 1985, p. 91). Goal setting begins with the participation of all parties. As Fisher and Ury (1981) put it, "Give them a stake in the outcome by making sure they participate in the process" (p. 27). We leave goal setting at this point because it is a central issue in our next chapter on motivation. What is apparent is the central concept of empowering employees through leadership, effective teams, proactive interpersonal behavior, and collaborate conflict management practices.

Our four-frames approach offers a further explanation of how conflict is managed (Bolman & Deal, 1991, pp. 147–150, 198–200; Harris, 1990). The structural frame tends toward a competitive or compromise stance. When problems occur, they reflect an inappropriate structure and they can be resolved through redesign or reorganization. The human resources frame espouses collaboration, and attempts to teach individuals how to confront issues. Because of the concern for people, however, this frame also uses compromise or accommodation. The political frame is highly competitive, with a belief in scarce resources, need for coalitions, and bargaining. As we pointed out when discussing leadership, a political approach can be an attempt to create change with the eventual goal of collaboration. The symbolic frame, with its emphasis on symbolic behavior, looks for shared values to resolve the conflicts that arise from the complexity, ambiguity, and incongruency in any organization.

When attempting to manage a conflict, you will want to decide if you are the problem. If not, or if you are expected to manage the conflict because of your position, focus on issues, goals, and expectations. Make certain that all parties own the conflict and the proposed solution. No one can provide a perfect solution for managing all conflicts. Your goal is to minimize the dysfunctional aspects and maximize the values of conflict.

## CONCLUSION

Conflict management is a significant issue in all organizations. Conflicts are a source of concern and growth. Individuals are expected to manage conflicts successfully, and organizations must respond to external competition. In all conflicts, communication is a basic component and a systems perspective reminds us of the interdependence and complexity of all organizations. To manage conflicts, we must understand fully the complex communication behaviors involved in conflicts.

Conflicts occur because of:

1. incompatible goals;
2. scarce rewards (e.g., power, status, and resources);
3. interference or opposition;
4. disagreement or controversy;
5. incongruency in the transaction;
6. incompatible activities.

Any definition of organizational conflict must take into account the levels and types of conflicts. Conflicts can be nonrealistic and realistic and dysfunctional and functional.

We have choices in dealing with conflicts. Adopting a contingency approach is important for effective conflict management. The five strategies are: (a) compete—be a "tough battler" and use position power, verbal dominance, perseverance, assertiveness striving for a win/lose solution; (b) compromise—be a mediator and split the difference; (c) accommodate—be a "friendly helper" and smooth over or trivialize the conflict where one person loses the conflict to win the relationship; (d) avoid—remove yourself physically or psychologically from the scene, which results in a lose/lose outcome; and (e) collaborate—be a "problem solver" and use a win/win approach by confronting the conflict directly and working for an integrative solution. Each of these approaches has strengths and weaknesses.

Power is the influence we use in an organization and during our conflicts. Expert, reward, coercive, legitimate, referent, connection, and information power are all used in organizations. Organizational members feeling powerless can exercise their power through passive aggressive behaviors. Effective use of power involves the process of empowering all parties to a conflict, problem, or issue.

Resolving conflicts requires a concern for issues over personalities. In addition, we must identify clearly the conflict or problem, identify mutually acceptable goals, openly communicate, negotiate a possible solution, and implement the solution.

This is a very important chapter for understanding how communication operates to increase or decrease organizational effectiveness. Conflicts are inherent and can be very useful. The issue is effective management and properly applied communication techniques are the mechanisms.

## REFERENCES

Abbott, J. (1989). New approaches to collective bargaining and workplace relations: Do they work? *Readings on Labor-Management Relations*. Washington, DC: U.S. Department of Labor.

Blake, R., & Mouton, J. (1964). *The managerial grid*. Houston: Gulf.

Bolman, L. G., & Deal, T. E. (1991). *Reframing organizations: Artistry, choice, and leadership*. San Francisco: Jossey-Bass.

Borisoff, D., & Victor, D. A. (1989). *Conflict Management: A communication skills approach*. Englewood Cliffs, NJ: Prentice-Hall.

Boss' pockets being picked of huge sums. (1983, June 11). *The Evansville Courier*, p. 1.

Boulding, K. E. (1962). *Conflict and defense: A general theory*. New York: Harper & Row.

Brass, D. J. (1984). Being in the right place: A structural analysis of individual influence in an organization. *Administrative Science Quarterly, 29*, 522–531.

Brett, J. M., Goldberg, S. B., & Ury, W. L. (1990). Designing systems for resolving disputes in organizations. *American Psychologist, 45*, 162–170.

Buell, B. (1990, October 15). Sculley: Up against the lab wall. *Business Week*, p. 92.

Buell, B. (1991, January 28). The second comeback of Apple. *Business Week*, p. 68.

Buell, B., Levine, J. B., & Gross, N. (1990, October 15). Apple: New team, new strategy. *Business Week*, pp. 86–96.

Carnevale, A. P. (1991). *America and the new economy* (U.S. Department of Labor Grant No. 99-6-0705-75-079-02). Alexandria, VA: American Society for Training & Development.

Collingwood, H. (1990, December 21). Is one laugh channel better than two? *Business Week*, p. 61.

Conger, J. A., & Kanungo, R. N. (1988). The empowerment process: Integrating theory and practice. *Academy of Management Review, 12,* 471–482.

Coser, L. A. (1956). *The functions of social conflict.* New York: Free Press.

Deutsch, M. (1973). Conflicts: Productive and destructive. In F. E. Jandt (Ed.), *Conflict resolution through communication* (pp. 148–160). New York: Harper & Row.

DeVito, J. A. (1986). *The communication handbook: A dictionary.* New York: Harper & Row.

Edwards, P., & Scullion, H. (1984). Absenteeism and the control of work. *The Sociological Review, 32,* 547–572.

Egan, G. (1988). *Change-agent skills a: Assessing and designing excellence.* San Diego: University Associates.

Filley, A. C. (1975). *Interpersonal conflict resolution.* Glenview, IL: Scott, Foresman.

Fisher, R. & Ury, W. (1981). *Getting to yes: Negotiating agreement without giving in.* Boston: Houghton Mifflin.

Folger, J. P., & Poole, M. S. (1984). *Working through conflict.* Glenview, IL: Scott, Foresman.

Fowler, R. D. (1988, October). User-friendly psychology. *Psychology Today,* p. 79.

Frank, A., & Brownell, J. (1989). *Organizational communication and behavior: Communicating to improve performance.* New York: Holt, Rinehart & Winston.

French, J. R., & Raven, B. (1959). The bases of social power. In D. Cartwright (Ed.), *Studies in social power* (pp. 150–167). Ann Arbor: University of Michigan Press.

Frost, P. J. (1987). Power, politics, and influence. In F. M. Jablin, L. L. Putnam, K. H. Robert, & L. W. Porter (Eds.), *Handbook of organizational communication* (pp. 503–548). Newbury Park, CA: Sage.

Gabor, A. (1990–1991, Winter). Deming's quality manifesto. *Best of Business Quarterly,* pp. 5–11.

Goodstein, L. D. (1981). Getting your way; A training activity in understanding power and influence. *Group and Organizational Studies, 6,* 285–292.

Groder, M. G. (1989). *Business games: How to recognize the players and deal with them.* Springfield, NJ: Boardroom Classics.

Grothe, M., & Whlie, P. (1987). *Problem bosses: Who they are and how to deal with them.* New York: Facts on File.

Gutknecht, D. B., & Miller, J. R. (1986). *The organizational and human resources sourcebook.* Lanham, MD: University Press of America.

Hall, J. (1986). *Conflict management survey and conflict management appraisal.* The Woodlands, TX: Telometrics International.

Harris, T. (1967). *I'm o.k.–You're o.k.* New York: Harper & Row.

Harris, T. E. (1990). Understanding organizational communication: Applying the four frame approach. *The Bulletin, 13,* 50–54.

Harris, T. E., & Smith, R. M. (1974). An experimental verification of Schelling's tacit communication hypothesis. *Speech Monographs, 41,* 82–84.

Harris, T. E., & Thomlison, T. D. (1983). Career-bound communication education: A needs analysis. *The Central States Speech Journal, 34,* 260–267.

Hillkirk, J. (1990, May 22). Employees blunder into rewards. *USA Today,* p. B1.

Hocker, J. L., & Wilmot, W. W. (1985). *Interpersonal conflict* (2nd ed.). Dubuque, IA: Brown.

Hoerr, J. P. (1988). *And the wolf finally came: The decline of the American steel industry.* Pittsburgh: University of Pittsburgh Press.

Hoerr, J. (1990, December 17). Sharpening minds for a competitive edge. *Business Week,* pp. 72–78.

Howard, J. (1990, January 5). Quality, safety message lost? *The Birmingham News/Birmingham Post-Herald,* p. C1.

Keltner, J. W. (1987). *Mediation: Toward a civilized system of dispute resolution.* Urbana, IL: ERIC Clearinghouse on Reading & Communication Skills.

Killman, R., & Thomas, K. (1977). Developing a forced-choice measure of conflict-handling behavior: The "MODE" instrument. *Educational and Psychological Measurement, 37,* 309–325.

King, A. (1987). *Power & communication*. Prospect Heights, IL: Waveland.

King, P. (1989, October) What makes teamwork work? *Psychology Today*, pp. 12–18.

Kohn, A. (1986, September). How to succeed without even vying. *Psychology*, pp. 22–28.

Konrad, W. (1990, November 26). The real thing is getting real aggressive. *Business Week*, p.100.

Lippitt, G. L. (1982). Managing conflict in today's organizations. *Training and Development Journal*, *36*, 58–67.

Lippitt, G., & Lippitt, G. (1986). *The consulting process in action*. San Diego: University Associates.

McNeil, E. B. (Ed.). (1965). *The nature of human conflict*. Englewood Cliffs, NJ: Prentice-Hall.

Mintzberg, H. (1983). *Power in and around organizations*. Englewood Cliffs, NJ: Prentice-Hall.

Monroe, C., DiSalvo, V. S., Lewis, J. J., & Borzi, M. G. (1990). Conflict behaviors of difficult subordinates: Interactive effects of gender. *The Southern Communication Journal, 56*, 12–23.

Monroe, S., Riley, M., & Traver, N. (1989, December 25). Mailroom mayhem. *Time*, pp. 30–31.

Muniz, P., & Chasnoff, R. (1987). Assessing the causes of conflict—and confronting the real issues. In *Practical negotiation and conflict resolution* (pp. 1–12). New York: American Management Association.

New York Times News Service. (1990, April 29). Disability: Workers' biggest risk. *The Tuscaloosa News*, p. 6E.

Nicholson, M. (1971). *Conflict analysis*. New York: Barnes & Noble.

Odiorne, G. S. (1978, October). Executive effectiveness. *The George Odiorne Newsletter, No. 5*, p. 1.

Offerman, L. R., & Gowing, M. K. (1990). Organizations of the future: Changes and challenges. *American Psychologist, 45*, 95–108.

Pace, R. W., & Faules, D. F. (1989). *Organizational communication* (2nd ed.). Englewood Cliffs, NJ: Prentice-Hall.

Pareek, U. (1982). *Managing conflict and collaboration*. New Delhi: Oxford & IBH.

Peters, T. J., & Waterman, R. H., Jr. (1982). *In search of excellence: Lessons from America's best-run companies*. New York: Harper & Row.

Phillips, S. L., & Elledge, R. L. (1989). *The team-building source book*. San Diego: University Associates.

Putnam, L. L. (1983). Lady you're trapped: Breaking out of conflict cycles. In J. J. Pilotta (Ed.), *Women in organizations: Barriers and breakthroughs* (pp. 42–47). Prospect Heights, IL: Waveland.

Putnam, L. L. (1988). Communication and conflict styles in organizations. *Management Communication Quarterly, 1*(3), 293–301.

Putnam, L. L., & Poole, M. S. (1987). Conflict and negotiation. In F. M. Jablin, L. L. Putnam, K. H. Roberts, & L. W. Porter (Eds.), *Handbook of organizational communication* (pp. 549–599). Newbury Park, CA: Sage.

Rahim, M. A. (1981). Organizational behavior courses for graduate students in business administration: Views from the tower and the battlefield. *Psychological Reports, 49*, 583–592.

Ramsey, D. K. (1987). *The corporate warriors: Six classic cases in American business*. Boston: Houghton Mifflin.

Raven, B. H., & Kruglandski, A. W. (1970). Conflict and power. In P. Swingle (Ed.), *The structure of conflict* (pp. 69–109). New York: Academic.

Research finds workplaces more deadly than cars. (1990, August 31). *Birmingham-Post Herald*, p. A7.

Robey, D. (1991). *Designing organizations* (3rd ed.). Homewood, IL: Irwin.

Rogers, D. J. (1987). *Waging business warfare*. New York: Scribner's.

Rosenbaum, B. L. (1982). *How to motivate today's workers: Motivational models for managers and supervisors*. New York: McGraw-Hill.

Rosenstein, E. (1985). Cooperativeness and advancement of managers: An international perspective. *Human Relations, 38*, 1–21.

Roskin, R. (1982). Coping with ambiguity. In J. W. Pfeiffer & L. D. Goodstein (Eds.), *The 1982 annual for facilitators, trainers and consultants* (pp. 108–116). San Diego: University Associates.

Ross, M. B. (1982). Coping with conflict. In J. W. Pfeiffer & L. D. Goodstein (Eds.), *The 1982 annual for facilitators, trainers, and consultants* (pp. 135–139). San Diego: University Associates.

Ruben, H. L. (1980). *Competing, understanding and winning the strategic games we all play.* New York: Lippincott & Crowell.

Sashkin, M., & Morris, W. C. (1984). *Organizational behavior: Concepts and experiences.* Reston, VA: Reston.

Schein, E. H. (1969). *Process consultation: Its role in organizational development.* Reading, MA: Addison-Wesley.

Schelling, T. C. (1960). *The strategy of conflict.* Cambridge, MA: Harvard University Press.

Schmidt, S. M., & Kochan, T. A. (1972). Conflict: Toward conceptual clarity. *Administrative Science Quarterly, 17,* 359–370.

Schnake, M. E., & Cochran, D. S. (1985). Effect of two goal-setting dimensions on perceived intraorganizational conflict. *Group and Organizational Studies, 10,* 168–183.

Simons, H. (1972). Persuasion in social conflicts: A critique of prevailing conceptualizations and a framework for future research. *Speech Monographs, 39,* 227–247.

Smith, D. R., & Williamson, L. K. (1981). *Interpersonal communication: Roles, rules, strategies, and games* (2nd ed.). Dubuque, IA: Brown.

Smith, R. M., & Harris, T. E. (1974). Methods for introducing conflict theory into the speech communication classroom. *Central States Speech Journal, 25,* 288–295.

Space program troubles shake Congressional support. (1990, July 16). *Birmingham Post-Herald,* p. C3.

Steinmetz, L. L. (1983). *Nice guys finish last: Management myths and realities.* Boulder, CO: Horizon.

Stewart, D. (1986). *The power of people skills.* New York: Wiley.

Tedeschi, J. T. (1970). Threats and promises. In P. Swingle (Ed.), *The structure of conflict* (pp. 155–191). New York: Academic.

Thomas, K. W., & Schmidt, W. H. (1976). A survey of managerial interests with respect to conflict. *Academy of Management Journal, 19,* 315–319.

Truell, G. F. (1984). *Building and managing productive work teams.* Buffalo, NY: PAT.

Ury, W., Brett, J., & Goldberg, S. (1988). *Getting disputes resolved: Designing systems to cut the costs of conflict.* San Francisco: Jossey-Bass.

Walters, J. (1985, January 2). Getting along can help you get ahead. *USA Today,* p. 3D.

Walton, D. (1991, January 15). *Are you communicating?* New York: McGraw-Hill. (Reported in *Bottom Line, 12,* 6).

Walton, R. E., & McKersie, R. B. (1989). Managing new technology and labor relations: An opportunity for mutual influence. In D. C. Mowery & B. E. Henderson (Eds.), *The challenge of new technology to labor-management relations* (BLMR 135, pp. 33–43). Washington, DC: Bureau of Labor-Management Relations & Cooperative Programs.

Waterman, R. H., Jr. (1987). *The renewal factor: How the best get and keep the competitive edge.* New York: Bantam.

Watzlawick, P., Beavin, J. H., & Jackson, D. D. (1967). *Pragmatics of human communication: A study of interaction patterns, pathologies and paradoxes.* New York: Norton.

Whyte, G. (1989). Groupthink reconsidered. *Academy of Management Review, 14,* 40–56.

Workers admit pilferage toll is $5 billion. (1983, June 12). *Chicago Tribune,* p. 3.

# CHAPTER 13

# Motivation

Would you like to be rich? Would you prefer to be famous? If you can devise a foolproof motivational system, you will not have to make a choice between the two. Write a book that provides a viable solution for effectively motivating employees (or children, sports teams, bosses), and people will flock to the bookstores to purchase your insights. As some tongue-in-cheek observers have said, also explain how to lose weight, and you will have a best seller forever! In fact, the question most asked of business consultants is: "How do you motivate employees?" (Cavanagh, 1984, p. 26). Developing effective means for enhancing employee motivation is a primary concern for all organizations. Three additional observations help put motivation in context.

First, motivation is a vital issue in every organization. Few subjects have received as much attention in organizational behavior textbooks and journals in the last few years as motivation (Cooper & Robertson, 1986; Katzell & Thompson, 1990; Landy & Becker, 1987; Locke & Henne, 1986). In facilitating management seminars, I have found that the participants list motivation as one of the most important, and difficult, issues their organizations face.

Second, managers and leaders are expected to effectively motivate others. As Quick (1985) observed, "Effective performance of your employees is your highest priority as a manager [and] . . . ultimately your success as a leader is measured by how well you enable your employees to achieve your and the organization's goals, to work up to their potential, to become even more valuable assets to the organization, and to identify and promote the well-being of the operation of which they are a part" (p. vii). Fewer than 25% of American employees believe they are well managed (Quick, 1991, p. 5). Even if we were to dismiss the importance of helping individuals, in most cases, labor is the largest cost factor in a business enterprise (Delaney, Lewin & Ichniowski, 1989, p. 3).

Some managers respond that people are different now and do not even want to work. Pollsters have attempted to determine the validity of this viewpoint. Although the exact percentages vary with each survey, they find that "an overwhelming 88 percent of all working Americans feel it is important to them to work hard and do their best on the job" (Yankelovich, 1982, p. 5). To demonstrate the ongoing difference between employees and managers, in one study almost two thirds of American and Canadian office workers polled felt they were working as hard as they could (Memmott, 1987). In the same poll, 40% of the senior managers polled said their office workers could do more. These conflicting views make a fuller understanding by managers of the motivational process an organizational imperative.

Finally, motivating ourselves or others is a difficult task. Although people may be the most valuable resource in terms of getting the work done and making the organization viable, they are also the most varied, least predictable, and hardest to manage factor (Delaney et al., 1989, p. 33). People do things for their reasons, not our reasons. Later in this chapter, we develop a complete definition of motivation. For now, it is important to understand that organizations give messages to employees that dehumanize the workplace and lead to demotivation. Whereas motivation is the willingness to accomplish tasks, demotivation is used to describe situations where employees lack any real desire to commit themselves to the organization, the task, or the group.

Some of the reasons for demotivation are easy to spot. Delaney et al. (1989) pointed out that, "Recent work has emphasized that firms should not expect good, let alone outstanding, performance from workers who are treated as interchangeable parts of the production process" (p. 3). Employers need to: "Treat people as adults. Treat them as partners; treat them with dignity; treat them with respect. Treat them—not capital spending and automation—as the primary source of productivity gain" (Peters & Waterman, 1982, p. 238).

The causes of demotivation vary widely. One study concluded that six factors lead to a loss of motivation. They are lack of constructive feedback, inconsistent behavior by those who directly affect success, lack of sensitivity to individual needs, denial of sufficient information, lack of behavioral and psychological support, and intrusion into predefined psychological and actual job space (Meyer, 1978). All of these factors are based on communication behaviors. The demotivation activities do have an impact on employees. The Public Agenda Foundation found that only 22% of American workers felt there is a direct relationship between how hard they work and how much they are paid (Quick, 1991, p. 6).

In this chapter, we discuss the major theories of motivation and introduce you to the insights provided by two broad constructs. The first examines the general need theory model. The need hierarchy, two-factor, and acquired-needs theories provide a focus for this examination. Process-oriented theories, which concentrate on the interactions that occur in organizations, then are presented. These include expectancy, equity, and goal-setting theories. In addition, the factors external to the individual, such as the quality of work like, are examined. To set the stage, we provide a definition of motivation.

## DEFINITION OF MOTIVATION

For the sake of clarity, we confine ourselves to work motivation, which "is the process by which behavior is mobilized and sustained in the interest of achieving organizational objectives" (DuBrin, Ireland, & Williams, 1989, p. 358). This is "a broad construct pertaining to the conditions and processes that account for the arousal, direction, magnitude, and maintenance of effort in a person's job" (Katzell & Thompson, 1990, p. 144). The issues of individual uniqueness and job performance deserve further examination.

All major theories of motivation account for the uniqueness of individuals in one way or another (e.g., different values, attitudes, needs, expectations) (Mitchell, 1984, p. 10). Earlier, we offered the paradoxical statement that "everyone is unique, just like you." Two guiding principles of the major theories help us cope with the danger of generalizing. These theories consider work motivation to be intentional and multifaceted. Put another way, people have reasons for everything they do and whatever behavior they choose. They believe it is good for them (Quick, 1985, pp. 20–21). This premise does not suggest people will not engage in dumb activities. It does suggest that some form of reasoning is behind an individual's behavior.

Second, for organizations the critical issue is the link between motivation and individual job performance (Baron, 1983, p. 123). Operationally, job performance (P) is a person's ability (A) times their motivation (M), $P = A \times M$ (DuBrin et al., 1989, p. 359). For example, being fired up to provide excellent customer service (e.g., motivated), without the commensurate training (e.g., handling complaints), means an employee may or may not be able to complete the task (e.g., providing customer service). Performance is a criterion for judging individual and group motivation. By examining behavior (e.g., complaints by customers, number of letters written, reduction of waste, attendance, team performance), organizations can draw conclusions concerning the motivation of their employees. But, as the performance criterion moves from individually controlled and well-specified behavior to more ambiguous behaviors (e.g., initiative, enthusiasm, team spirit, creativity), it becomes more difficult to know if the behavior is based on motivation or something else (e.g., natural ability, circumstances, support staff) (Mitchell, 1984, p. 13). So, setting a performance standard for the more abstract demands placed on an individual in an organization is difficult.

We need to clarify further the factors affecting a person's ability. In all jobs, at least four additional variables determine if a person can perform up to some standard. These include (a) understanding the job expectations (e.g., quality of customer service); (b) working in a climate and culture that allows employees to translate their intentions into performance (Mitchell, 1982, p. 82); (c) having the opportunity actually to do the task (Stewart, 1986, p. 158); and (d) having the necessary technology or equipment (Mitchell, 1984, p. 9). In other words, effectively motivating organizational members requires a broad view of the various contingent factors that can facilitate or limit job performance. This brings us to an examination of the theories of motivation.

## THEORIES OF WORK MOTIVATION

Without an understanding of how people are motivated, we are likely to respond intuitively and idiosyncratically. You can drawn an analogy between conflict management style (chapter 12) and motivational approaches. When we attempt to motivate other people, we tend to draw on our own past experiences, which may or may not be generalizable to others. So, our efforts at motivating others can depend more on luck and the applicability of our type of experience than on a knowledgeable response.

Motivation theories divide into two broad types, needs and intentional choice. Both theory types focus on internal (e.g., intrinsic or endogenous theories) and/or external (e.g., extrinsic or exogenous theories) factors. The needs theories concern themselves with the content, or what is identifiable, in the motivation "picture," whereas the intentional choice theories concentrate on the process, or what goes on between employees and their environment. In a sense, the need approach is similar to a still picture, whereas the intentional choice approach is similar to a video camera. Table 13.1 provides a broad map of the theories of motivation we discuss. These have been chosen because they are representative, but not necessarily inclusive, of a voluminous amount of research. We examine the need approaches first.

### Need-Drive-Satisfaction Theories

One of the most prevalent themes in motivation theory is that people have certain inner needs (e.g., a craving or imbalance) that lead to drives (e.g., tension or drive to satisfy the need). In response to these needs and drives, we take actions or goal-

TABLE 13.1
Approaches to Motivation

| *Needs* | | *Intentional Choice* | |
|---|---|---|---|
| *Internal* | *External* | *Internal* | *External* |
| Maslow's Hierarchy | McClelland | Expectancy | Rewards |
| ERG | Acquired Needs | Equity | Quality of Life |
| Herzberg's Two-Factor Theory | | Goal setting | Culture, Management, Social Interaction |

TABLE 13.2
The Motivational Process:
A Basic Model of Need/Drive/Satisfaction

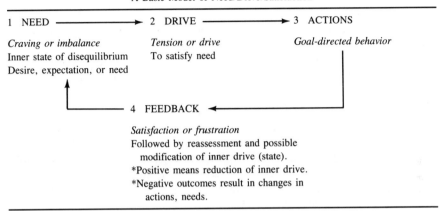

1 NEED ⟶ 2 DRIVE ⟶ 3 ACTIONS

*Craving or imbalance*     *Tension or drive*         *Goal-directed behavior*
Inner state of disequilibrium    To satisfy need
Desire, expectation, or need

4 FEEDBACK ⟵

*Satisfaction or frustration*
Followed by reassessment and possible
   modification of inner drive (state).
*Positive means reduction of inner drive.
*Negative outcomes result in changes in
   actions, needs.

directed behaviors. We then receive feedback indicating the degree to which we have satisfied the need. If we satisfy the need, we repeat the behavior. If we experience frustration, we try another approach. Table 13.2 shows the process indicating that it occurs on a step-by-step basis. Applying these theories answers the question, "What causes behavior to be started, changed, or eliminated?"

This is an accurate, although simplistic, view of need motivation. Missing from this formula are environmental factors (e.g., culture, opportunity, economic conditions). To clarify the need approach, we highlight the major theories, including Maslow, ERG, Herzberg, and McClelland.

### Maslow's Need Hierarchy

Based on his clinical studies, Maslow (1954) offered his hierarchy of needs explanation for motivation. People are goal seeking throughout their lives and have internal motives for taking action. We are motivated (e.g., driven) to satisfy certain needs. These needs occur in a hierarchy of preeminence throughout our development and maturation. The ascending occurrence of the hierarchy suggests that we cannot really address a higher need until the lower one has been satisfied. This leads to the important conclusion that individuals must largely satisfy or fulfill their lower needs before the next level can motivate them.

A second conclusion follows: A relatively satisfied need no longer is a motivator of behavior, and the next higher level comes into play (Maslow, 1943). These are divided into a hierarchy of needs with five categories, which can be subdivided into the two general types of deficiency and growth needs (Maslow, 1968, p. 10). *Deficiency needs* (e.g., physiological, safety, belongingness and love) are those that must be satisfied in order for us to be secure and healthy. *Growth needs* (e.g., esteem, self-actualization) allow us to grow and develop toward our full potential. In an ascending order of importance of satisfaction and complexity, they are defined as follows.

**Physiological.**   These are the biological needs that are related directly to self-preservation. These include food, oxygen, rest, exercise, sex, drink, and sleep. The threat of losing a job might trigger a response from this lowest level, but most people do not believe they will starve if they are temporarily unemployed.

Examples of physiological needs in organizations could include hazardous working conditions (e.g., radiation levels at nuclear power plants, chemical emissions, a debilitating illness), excessive heat or cold (e.g., lack of air conditioning, heating, protection), inadequate nutrition (e.g., no breaks for meals, no food supply), and remarkably low wages. These types of working conditions have diminished or been eliminated for many Americans, but reading about the conditions during the Great Depression, or events leading up to the passage of the child labor laws will provide ample support that these conditions can occur. Certainly, they remain common in many third-world countries even today.

**Safety and Security.**   Our desire for security, stability, protection, and freedom from fear is a major motivator. In addition, we prefer a safe, predictable environment, creating a need for structure and order.

Examples of safety needs and security needs include unexpected or undesirable changes in our work environment, lack of adequate salary or fringe benefits, and dangerous working conditions (e.g., asbestos and insulation workers, timber loggers, fire fighters). Each year, more than 60,000 people died from work-related illnesses or accidents ("Jobs That," 1989). In 1987, 1.8 million workers were disabled on the job (e.g., cumulative trauma disorders such as carpal tunnel syndrome, falls) and occupational diseases (e.g, cancer, pulmonary, neurological, and cardiovascular) killed between 47,377 and 95,479 according to the National Safe Workplace Institute and the National Center for Health Statistics ("Research Finds," 1990). In 1988, there were 105,265 instances where workers were exposed to measurable radiation at U. S. power plants ("Study Shows," 1990). Although this appears to be an almost ghoulish recitation of death and injury, it reminds us that the lower levels of need figure prominently in the minds of many employees.

On a less dramatic level, millions of individuals worry about their job security or company's strength (e.g., possible bankruptcy, downsizing, takeover). According to the General Accounting Office (1989), "Each year about 1 million U.S. workers lose their jobs because of business closures and permanent layoffs" (p. 10). The economic stresses of job loss take a toll on the mental and physical health of dislocated workers, with prolonged unemployment increasing anxiety, depression, physical ailments, alcoholism, and family strife (U.S. Office of Technology Assessment, 1986). Although you probably do not need additional reasons to pursue a college degree, in the 1990 economic downturn, 99% of the net job losses were among production and nonsupervisory workers (e.g., sales, technical and clerical, skilled and unskilled blue collar, bank tellers) (Koretz, 1991).

Office workers face fewer hazards than industrial workers, but accidents still can happen because of falls, dangerous equipment, unsafe conditions (e.g., asbestos, pollution, hermetically sealed—energy efficient offices), or job-related disorders (e.g., chronic fatigue syndrome, carpal tunnel syndrome from operating computers, computer sprains) (Associated Press, 1991; Simmons, 1990; University of Alabama Office of Health and Safety, 1990). For other employees, the threat of electronic monitoring creates insecurity, and charges that electronic sweatshops have been created (Garson, 1988, pp. 205–224). In 1990, over 10 million American workers were being scrutinized electronically (e.g., reading employees' electronic mail; computer tracking of time per task; telephone call accountability including time, tracking of outgoing phone numbers dialed, and duration of conversations; listening in on service personnel including long-distance operators, airline reservation agents, and telemarketers; coming and going of employees based on their use of coded cards to open doors) (Lee, 1990).

Later in this chapter, we deal with motivational techniques managers and organizations can implement to motivate employees. However, it is important to realize that, for many individuals, safety is still a significant concern.

***Belongingness and Love.*** People have a need to love and to be loved. At work this translates into a sense of friendship, approval, and acceptance. Our family and friends can be a primary source of belongingness and love, but working relationships also figure into this need. Professional relationships and the quality of our supervision can have a significant impact on this need. Tightly knit work groups offer a strong sense of belongingness, and excellent organizational cultures create a symbolic bond. At numerous places in this book we have outlined the characteristics of excellent cultures, supervision, self-managing work units, and symbolic behaviors. For Maslow, these all would be examples of a sense of belongingness.

***Esteem.*** These needs include our self-evaluation regarding how useful, competent, and important we feel. There are two facets of the esteem need—a sense of self-esteem as well as respect from others. Maslow (1943) saw achievement and strength as one part of esteem and recognition and attention from others as the other part (p. 382). For Americans, esteem needs are very important. As Ross (1990) put it, "The satisfaction of the esteem needs leads to self-confidence and a feeling of personal worth" (p. 49).

Recognition is an obvious type of esteem need, and we discuss it in greater detail later in this chapter. In addition, merit pay increases, job titles, increased responsibility, the window and the corner office, and the quality of the interactions between colleagues and supervisors can lead to an increase in esteem.

***Self-Actualization.*** When we seek self-fulfillment or self-realization, we are trying to reach the top of our own personal best. We are striving to achieve our full potential, and to become more of what we are capable of being. In most cases, we are bound by the transactional nature of success in that we only realize we have reached a new plateau when someone provides us with the appropriate recognition. Self-actualized people seem to transcend the other four areas of need. They are able to get started on a spontaneous, deeper sense of being (Maslow, 1970, pp. 153–157).

For entry-level employees, this is one of the hardest needs to satisfy. Once on the job, allowing creativity, offering challenges, providing advancement, and supporting achievement all will lead to some self-actualization.

**Applying Maslow's Theory.**    The hierarchy can be viewed conveniently as a ladder, with our hands and feet on different levels (Ross, 1990, p. 47). At any one time, we might have most of our strength pulling toward esteem, but still have our feet on belongingness and love. During our lives, we dynamically move up and down the ladder. For example, a Louis Harris survey of 1,250 United States and Canadian workers asked what they considered to be "very important" work characteristics; 82% said a challenging job. In Maslow's schema, this would be an esteem or self-actualization need. At the same time, 80% said good benefits, and 74% said pay, free exchange of information, and being able to make significant contributions to the organization (Memmott, 1987). The survey respondents may have their hand on the self-actualization rung of the ladder, but their other hand and feet seem to be planted firmly on a variety of other rungs.

The model has been accepted widely without a great deal of solid evidence regarding its validity. To his credit, Maslow (1965) cautioned against a literal transfer of his clinically derived theory to organizational behavior. Because he was studying a limited number of people, Maslow was not comfortable that other motivational theories should be based solely on his analysis.

So, how do we utilize Maslow's theory? First, as we already stated, Maslow highlighted the important point that a satisfied need is no longer a motivator. Techniques that have worked well in the past to motivate individuals may need to be examined to make certain they still motivate. Although pay is a primary need and reward, once a fair compensation program is established, high quality job performance depends on "giving employees opportunities for their personal growth, achievement, responsibility, recognition, and reward" (Hanna, 1987, p. 2).

Second, he reminded us of the difficulty of focusing on higher level needs when the basic ones are not being met. There are two interrelated, but different issues. The *activation/gratification proposition* states that needs become activated and thus become motivators only as lower level needs are gratified and therefore lose their motivational force (Williams & Huber, 1986, p. 94). As a corollary, the *deprivation/domination proposition* states that the greater the deprivation of the need, the greater its motivational force.

Even if Maslow's hierarchy cannot be verified, his categories provide organizations and managers a starting place for understanding the relationship between deficiency and growth needs (Wilson, Goodall, & Waagen, 1986, p. 54). An extended discussion of the responses by organizations to child care illustrates the loss of motivational power of a satisfied need, and the impact of lower level needs on our ability to concern ourselves with higher needs.

Although there is little comprehensive research regarding the relationship between child-care difficulties and personnel issues (e.g., productivity, absenteeism, tardiness, turnover, recruitment, quality of work, competitiveness), there is an excessive amount of anecdotal information provided by parents regarding their child-care concerns (U.S. Department of Labor, 1988). Working parents suffer stress over the quality of child care, and in families where both parents work, 73% said one parent would stay home if money were not an issue (Hellmick, 1988, p. 1A). Organizations have responded to this need. A 1987 survey by the Bureau of Labor Statistics found that 61% of all establishments had one or more work practices that facilitate parents caring for their children (e.g., flexible work schedules, voluntary part-time arrangements, flexible leave policies) (U.S. Department of Labor, 1988, p. 4). Parents' concern for the safety of their children clearly invokes lower level, basic needs involving safety and security.

We can assume that parents were pleased with these policies that facilitated adequate care of their children. However, in line with Maslow's prediction, they soon regarded these practices as foregone conclusions. Therefore, these practices have lost their value as motivators.

In addition, these policies may not alleviate all of the parents' child-care concerns. Remember the second point. It is difficult to focus on higher level needs when the basic ones (e.g., safety and security) are not being met. To extend the child-care example, parents continue to feel the need for quality child care. An AT&T survey in 1986 of 5,000 employees found that 57% of the women and 33% of the men with children under 6 years of age reported spending unproductive time at work due to child-care concerns (U.S. Department of Labor, 1988, p. 5). In 1986, the California Governor's Task Force on Child Care questioned 1,200 parents. One fourth of all homemakers and unemployed parents, including half of all single parents, said they were prevented from working or attending a training session as a result of inadequate child-care arrangements (U.S. Department of Labor, 1988, pp. 126–128).

Many organizations have accepted the importance of trying to meet this basic need in order to assist employees in focusing on higher needs. Limited, but impressive, evidence exists that in the areas of recruitment, retention, public relations, productivity, turnover, absenteeism, and morale, employer-sponsored child care benefits, competitiveness and productivity (U.S. Department of Labor, 1988, pp. 128–130). In response to the issue, companies have chosen to operate child-care centers (e.g., Stride Rite shoe company in Boston, Zale Corporation in Texas, Merck Pharmaceuticals in New Jersey), help pay for child-care costs (e.g., CINGA Corporation in Connecticut, Allendale Insurance Company in Rhode Island, and others contract with Kindercare, a proprietary child-care center, for a 10% discount for their employees), offer voucher/subsidy programs to help with tuition (e.g., Ford Foundation in New York, Zayre Corporation in Natick, Massachusetts, Polaroid Corporation), or offer child-care subsidies as an option within a flexible benefits program (e.g., Procter & Gamble Company, American Can Corporation) (U.S. Department of Labor, 1988, pp. 133–135). The bottom line is quite simple. Organizations accept that the parents' basic needs must be met so that the parents can be free to focus on higher order needs.

*Analysis of Maslow's Theory.* Maslow's theory has been very popular among managers because it is clear and intuitively appealing (Tuzzolino & Armandi, 1981). According to Cummings, Long, and Lewis (1988), "Maslow is probably the most widely quoted motivational theorist, both in universities and in the thousands of management training programs conducted every day in business and industry" (p. 227). The motivation prescription is quite simple. If employees appear to be undermotivated, managers should create conditions that alleviate the lower level needs. In this way, employees will be able to concentrate on higher level needs and work toward individual growth and job satisfaction. Although simplistic, there is a great deal of truth in the assumption that people having a hard time paying their bills (e.g., clerical positions, fast-food servers), worrying about their personal safety (e.g., nuclear power plants, occupational hazards), or concentrating on their family (e.g., child care, health insurance) will experience difficulty worrying about the more elegant corporate themes such as improved quality or customer service. As long as an organization can meet a person's current needs, we can assume that some motivation will occur (Baron, 1983, p. 209). For example, high school students, seeking money to pay for school supplies, dates, other basic needs, or even that first car, might experience little difficulty in accepting jobs with minimal esteem or self-actualization need fulfillment.

There is, however, little research to support the general application of Maslow's theory to organizations (Miner, 1980, pp. 28–37). For one thing, "it has been impossible to demonstrate that everyone has the same need hierarchy" (DuBrin et al., 1989, p. 362). Returning to our child-care example, how can we effectively generalize regarding the needs of individual parents? Some may be satisfied with adequate child supervision programs, whereas others want child development programs.

Even more troubling is a basic question regarding how to satisfy specific employee needs. For upper level managers, good pay, extensive benefits, and numerous challenges mean that their growth needs are more likely to be satisfied. In one study comparing the satisfaction of upper and lower level managers, however, the more routine jobs of the lower level managers made it much more difficult to fulfill their growth needs (Porter, 1964). In addition, in the 1990s "the steady pruning of middle management presents companies with a problem. Fewer layers mean fewer promotions for promising young managers" (Weber, Driscoll, & Brandt, 1990, p. 192). As we progress further down the corporate ladder (e.g., telephone operators, computer operators), we will find it even more difficult to satisfy the higher order needs. How do we satisfy the self-actualization needs of a McDonald's crew member whose job is taking orders or cleaning floors? For any routine job, what aspects can be modified to enhance a sense of belongingness and esteem? There are answers to these questions, but implementing them is difficult.

Maslow provided a starting point for an examination of the relationship between individual needs and motivation. An attempt to simplify Maslow's approach is offered by Alderfer's (1972) ERG theory. He proposed that there are three basic needs: *existence* (physiological and safety), *relatedness* (need for meaningful interpersonal and social relations), and *growth* (need for developing one's potential). Although similar to Maslow, Alderfer also discussed what occurs when an individual attempts to reach a higher level need, but fails. When this happens, the importance of relatedness and existence needs are intensified. His theory also recognizes that there is no hierarchy in how the needs will be met. Any need can be activated regardless of whether the other ones are met. Because Alderfer's model simplifies Maslow's, it holds a great deal of promise for researching motivational approaches.

As murky as Maslow's categories might appear, he has had a major impact on how organizations approach motivation. His contributions are limited by the lack of empirical research verifying the categories or the correlation between specific needs and motivation. Herzberg's motivator-hygiene theory, drawing on many of Maslow's ideas, attempts to establish that link.

### Herzberg's Motivator-Hygiene Theory

In research on the job attitudes or opinions of 200 accountants and engineers, Herzberg, Mausner, and Snyderman (1959) and Herzberg (1966) asked two questions: "Can you describe, in detail, when you felt exceptionally good about your job?" and "Can you describe, in detail, when you felt exceptionally bad about your job?" The interviewees also were asked to connect the time with a specific objective event and to report the intensity and duration of their feeling about the event.

Based on this research, Herzberg (1966) made an important finding. The job experiences, or factors that related to a good feeling on the job, were related most often to the job content. The ones leading to negative feelings most often related to the surrounding or peripheral aspects of the job. He classified the content factors as *satisfiers* and the context factors as *dissatisfiers*. The satisfiers and dissatisfiers function, respectively, as *motivator* and *hygiene* factors. We are motivated, according to Herzberg's research, by achievement, recognition, work itself, responsibility, and growth. We become dissatisfied because of company policy, supervision, salary, interpersonal relations, working conditions, status, job security, and personal life. Table 13.3 provides a detailed description of the satisfiers and dissatisfiers.

Herzberg (1966) hypothesized that if an organization removes all the dissatisfiers, employees no longer will be dissatisfied. However, they will not be motivated. This perspective is useful because it explains why simply getting rid of some problems (e.g., inadequate child care, low wages) does not lead to increased productivity.

TABLE 13.3
Herzberg's Two-Factor Theory of Motivation

| | |
|---|---|
| *Satisfiers — Motivational Factors* | |
| Achievement: | the successful completion of a job. |
| Recognition: | that which is received by an individual from any source with the accomplishment or achievement of a task or job. |
| Work Itself: | the actual content of the job itself. |
| Responsibility: | satisfaction derived from being in charge of one's work or others' work. |
| Growth: | growth and advancement to higher level tasks including potential through training, etc. |
| *Dissatisfiers — Hygiene Factors* | |
| Company Policy & Administration: | feelings about the inadequacy or adequacy of some overall aspect of the company. |
| Supervision: | the competency of supervision. |
| Salary: | all responses involving compensation. |
| Interpersonal Relations: | relationships with superiors, subordinates, and peers. |
| Working Conditions: | the physical environment of the job. |
| Status: | indications of status (e.g., nonverbal, executive washroom, company car). |
| Job Security: | objective signs such as tenure or company stability. |
| Personal Life: | job factors affecting personal life. |

*Applying Herzberg's Theory.*    Dissatisfiers constitute hygiene factors because they are preventable and environmental (e.g., external). The first group we listed, satisfiers, are seen as motivators and they are internal factors. There is clear correlation between Maslow and Herzberg. Maslow's physiological, security/safety, and social needs correspond to Herzberg's job security, pay, and working conditions. Maslow's esteem and self-actualization needs correspond to Herzberg's task identification, feedback, and task variety issues.

Herzberg's theory explains why environmental factors alone do not motivate performance. Having poor interpersonal relations, run-down facilities or equipment, and coercive supervision, according to this theory, means employees will be dissatisfied with their work. Getting rid of these simply will remove dissatisfaction.

Perhaps most important, his research indicates that reaching point zero, where there are no more dissatisfiers, simply means employees are no longer dissatisfied, angry, or unhappy. No additional motivation has occurred. What has happened is the way has been cleared for increasing motivation.

Our child-care discussion shows how Herzberg's hygiene/satisfier approach makes sense. Just because organizations alleviate the worries by parents about the safety of their children, there is no reason to assume that the parents will be more motivated or productive. They will be less distracted because there is one less reason not to concentrate on work. A very practical application of Herzberg's perspective has been to explain to managers why money (a dissatisfier) cannot be depended on to motivate people.

Herzberg also shifted the emphasis from human relations to increasing the amount of responsibility required for each employee (e.g., human resources) as a means for motivating. He believed that opportunities should be designed for each employee through such means as job redesign and open-system career paths (Frank & Brownell, 1989, pp. 262–263). His research has stimulated work on job design and job enrichment (Baron, 1983, p. 211).

***Analysis of Herzberg's Theory.*** Because the methodology for the research makes duplication difficult, the two-factor theory has been criticized extensively (Miner, 1980, pp. 81–99). In addition, in some attempts to replicate Herzberg's findings, it was found that hygiene and motivators exerted powerful effects on both satisfaction and dissatisfaction (House & Wigdon, 1967; Schneider & Locke, 1971). Once again, our child-care example can help explain the point. It a parent has always wanted to work hard anyway, removing the burden of worrying about child care could increase the parent's satisfaction, sense of responsibility, and pride in the organization, which are all satisfiers and motivators. Another parent could respond simply that company policies, safety, and fringe benefits finally have removed the dissatisfier of worrying about child care.

In 1990, for example, more than 102,000 New Yorkers applied for a trash collector's job with the City Sanitation Department ("The Promise," 1990). Working conditions (e.g., dissatisfier/hygiene) would not seem to warrant this outpouring of applications. The average city sanitation worker lifts 5 tons of garbage per day, which is the equivalent of two Toyotas. But, the salary level is high (over $23,000 with a pay increase to $35,000 in 5 years), with a 35-hr work week. In this case, the high salary might function as a recognition factor (e.g., satisfier/motivator) and the promotion possibilities are a definite plus. Although working as a trash collector might not be attractive to everyone, being outside – with job security and relatively short hours – does seem to be appealing to a large number of people. Returning to our discussion of perception (chapter 2), in this case one person's trash is literally another person's treasure.

Despite the difficulty in finding an operational definition for Herzberg's categories, this approach is a healthy reminder of the difference between preventing people from being unhappy and motivating people to be more productive. In addition, the theory reminds us of the importance of psychological growth as a basic condition for lasting job satisfaction (Baron, 1983, p. 211). There are basic similarities between Maslow, ERG, and Herzberg, as Table 13.4 indicates. Whereas Maslow, ERG, and Herzberg concerned themselves with needs that are intrinsic to human beings, McClelland focused on acquired needs.

### Acquired Needs Theory

Taking a different view of needs and motivation, McClelland proposed that certain needs are acquired from our culture (Maehr & Kleiber, 1981; McClelland, 1962). When a need is strong enough, it prompts a person to engage in work activities to

TABLE 13.4
Comparison of Need Theories

| Higher Order Needs | | Intrinsic Motivation |
| --- | --- | --- |
| Maslow's Need Hierarchy | Herzberg's Two-Factor Theory | Alderfer's ERG Theory |
| Self-actualization | | |
| | | Growth |
| Esteem | | |
| | Motivators | |
| Belongingness | | |
| | | Relatedness |
| Safety | | |
| | Hygiene Factors | |
| Physiological | | |
| | | Existence |
| Basic Needs | | Extrinsic Motivation |

satisfy that need. Because the needs are learned, dramatic changes should be possible by encouraging the growth of certain needs in individuals by the organization. The three needs he identified are achievement, power, and affiliation. Each of these needs warrants further discussion.

***Need for Achievement.*** There are specific traits exhibited by individuals with a high achievement motive. For example, they are likely to examine how to do a job better or how to accomplish something unusual. They view monetary rewards as feedback about how well they are doing (DuBrin et al., 1989, p. 364). Entrepreneurs and fast-track managers in organizations tend to be strongly achievement oriented (Stahl, 1976). They seek responsibility and take calculated risks. People who are high achievers prefer to set their own performance goals (McClelland, 1953). These individuals prefer immediate and efficient feedback on their performance and wish to grapple with moderate goals that are achievable. Driven by these moderate goals (as opposed to easy or difficult ones), they enjoy the responsibility of solving problems. High-achievement managers are characterized by candor, openness, sensitivity, receptivity, participative leadership style, and work satisfaction. Low-achievement managers are more secretive, insensitive, and separated from their work (Mitchell, 1984, p. 14).

***Need for Power.*** McClelland originally thought that the need for achievement was the most important source of managerial motivation. His later research indicated that the need for power is the primary motivator of successful managers (McClelland & Boyatziss, 1982; McClelland & Burnham, 1976). Other research substantiated this conclusion (Cornealius & Lane, 1984). The power motive is demonstrated through a desire to control, influence, and be responsible for other people's behavior (McClelland, 1975).

The desire to control is a form of personalized power where managers are informed about "how things are going." This seems to be an important need or motive in managerial behavior (Pareek, 1986, pp. 121–122). Influence, or having an impact, is a straightforward desire for power. Power also has a socialized dimension. When managers take the responsibility for others, they use their power to benefit people or groups within the organization.

In summary, power-oriented individuals like to control resources and spend time determining how to influence and control others. From a managerial perspective, power is seen as a means to influence subordinates to do the right thing. Effective leaders have high power motives (Kotter, 1988, p. 30).

***Need for Affiliation.***   People driven by a desire to establish and maintain friendly and warm relationships with others are high in a need for affiliation. Sometimes, this need can create an unnecessary focus on smoothing feelings, avoiding disruptive situations, and seeking positions that enhance a great deal of companionship (DuBrin et al., 1989, p. 366). Because many leadership positions require a certain amount of assertiveness, someone with a high need for affiliation probably will avoid some managerial work. Several studies have shown that successful leaders do tend to have a low need for affiliation (McClelland & Boyatziss, 1982).

***Application of Acquired Need Theory.***   This approach offers a different mirror for examining needs. Rather than assuming that motivation comes from internal driven needs, McClelland offered the view that some needs are created and reinforced by our culture. Studies indicate that achievement motivation can be developed through training, with favorable consequences for job success (McClelland & Winter, 1969, p. 69). Other applications of this theory would include training individuals to be more assertive and dominant in work relationships (O'Donnell & Colby, 1979). McClelland (1978) developed training programs that teach the participants about the theory, achievement motives, and includes a variety of exercises to help them practice achievement behavior. Increased performance and firm survival rate for a number of entrepreneurs have occurred because of his training programs.

***Analysis of Acquired Need Theory.***   In spite of its important contributions, McClelland's approach is an incomplete theory of work motivation. First, some needs would seem to be inherent (e.g., security). Second, if we accept that some needs occur because of our environment, rather than early adaptation, two additional needs, recognition and autonomy, should be considered.

***Need for Recognition.***   Receiving praise, attention, and approval for our personal efforts works to motivate people (Hunt, 1989, pp. 68–70). We already provided information regarding the importance of feedback earlier in this book (e.g., chapter 7). At this point, we are concentrating on recognition. But, you should remember that there is a fine line between a need for recognition and the use of reinforcement, which we discuss shortly.

There are two explanations for the importance of recognition. First, in the presence of others, we tend to try to perform at a higher standard. Simply put, we want to look good in the eyes of others. Two studies demonstrate the power of recognition. The first confirms something most of us have experienced. Drivers will accelerate at a significantly higher rate of speed from a stoplight when another car is next to them (Bozzi, 1984). This study confirmed that an audience will increase our performance of simple, already-learned tasks, such as driving. Given the number of repetitive tasks in most organizations, wanting recognition can be a potent need. Another study reported that watched joggers run faster when they were being watched by someone who was in the position to judge them (Bridgewater, 1984). The study reported that in the "mere presence" situation, where the watchers had their backs turned to the joggers, no change occurred. This is a subtle, but important, addition to the social sciences theory that joggers will run faster, not just because they are in the presence of others, but because they feel they might be judged. That leads to the second point.

We are confirmed by the wishes and desires of co-workers and supervisors. Shared offices, team development, and pep rallies (e.g., Mary Kay Cosmetics) are all examples of how an organization might utilize this principle. Effective sales representatives are high in achievement motivation, but recognition follows closely.

There is a great deal of research to indicate that organizations that recognize employees for work well done, extraordinary actions, or special efforts succeed in motivating employees (Cerrington & Wixom, 1983, p. 87). Recognition programs range from "zero-defects" awards to certificates and dinner for the completion of a training program. Informally, "atta-ways" highlight successes and provide recognition for a job well done. Because handing out praise and recognition is an underutilized motivational technique, it has great value as a potential motivational technique. As our discussion should make clear, for some individuals recognition functions as achievement and for others it works as a reinforcer of desired behavior.

*Need for Autonomy.*    Regardless of the possible rewards presented by organizational membership and companionship, some individuals would prefer to be autonomous. In the extreme, a high degree of autonomy, independence, and control of their own destiny might lead them to want to be isolated. Excellent salespeople, for example, often are motivated by the desire to be self-managers as much as by achievement (Hopkins, 1982, p. 1). When the entrepreneurs we discussed under a need for achievement decide to be independent, they operate their own enterprise. The "desire to be one's own boss is what drives both male and female entrepreneurs to accept all the social, psychological, and financial risks and work the numerous hours needed to create and nurture a new venture" (Hisrich, 1990, p. 214). This is a strong motivation because 75% of all new businesses fail within 5 years (Hisrich, 1990, p. 214). In order to keep autonomy-seeking high achievers, organizations have created intrapreneurial opportunities where innovations can be pursued without going through bureaucratic red tape (Hisrich, 1990, p. 220). In our discussion of networks and channels, we discussed the role of the isolate in organizations (e.g., chapter 6).

In conclusion, acquired needs can be understood further by adding recognition and autonomy. All five of these needs provide an additional means of examining the types of motivation acquired by individuals.

### Analysis of Need Theory

Organizations have found the needs approach useful in three ways. First, the folly of making broad generalizations regarding why individuals are motivated becomes apparent. For managers, the need approach opens the window to appreciating the major differences and complexities in motivating individuals. Employees do things for their reasons, not the manager's reasons.

Michael Faraday, the inventor of the first electric motor, experienced this principle when he went to the British prime minister, William Gladstone, for financial backing. Faraday took the crude model, a little wire revolving around a magnet, and showed it to the statesman. Gladstone was obviously not interested: "What good is it?" Gladstone asked Faraday. "Someday, you will be able to tax it," answered Faraday. And with that answer, the great scientist won his point, and the endorsement of his research, by applying his efforts at motivation to the other person's needs (Quick, 1985, pp. 158–160).

In chapter 2, we examined the differences in perception between what managers thought employees wanted and what the employees reported they wanted from work. Maslow's need hierarchy encourages a more sophisticated view of human motivation. ERG clears up some of the confusion by simplifying Maslow's categories and changing the importance of meeting one need before turning to another.

Second, the difference between relieving employees from the stress of dissatisfiers and providing motivation clears the way for ongoing efforts at motivating. Herzberg forced managers to understand that treating people well is not the same as motivating them. Maslow introduced this perspective by making clear that a satisfied need no longer motivates people.

As a consultant, I am asked constantly to address the issue of motivation. Numerous managers firmly believe that employees will be motivated only by more money. Although there is extensive documentation that money, by itself, will not sustain motivation, the hygiene/motivator explanation forces managers to come to grips with the complexities inherent in motivating individuals through needs (Conklin, 1979). As with Maslow, Herzberg offered some additional insights on the question of motivation.

Organizations increasingly have attempted to alleviate the basic needs. The vast majority of American corporations have paid vacations (almost 100%), paid holidays (99%), health insurance (97%), life insurance (96%), and pension benefits (87%) (Mitchell, 1984, p. 17). The amount these corporations provide for benefits averages 38.4% of payrolls, which is $12,402 per year, per employee ("Rising Benefits," 1992).

Accepting that employees want and need different things, organizations have developed a broad range of motivational programs. We already discussed flexibility in work hours (e.g., flextime; 4-day, 40-hr work week), location (e.g., home-based operations, telecommunicating), and benefits. One benefits approach features a cafeteria-style plan where employees are allowed to change the makeup of their benefit package to meet their particular needs (e.g., increase amount to day care, vary amounts to medical or dental coverage). More exotic, and increasingly popular, approaches are sabbaticals, extended leaves, early retirement, stock options, and company-obtained group memberships for discounts (e.g., buying household appliances, wholesale discounters).

Finally, McClelland's acquired need theory has practical training applications. In a variety of programs, McClelland succeeded in increasing the achievement need (McClelland, 1961). Assertiveness-training programs provide opportunities to increase the uses of power as do the various theories in our chapter on leadership. The current level of a particular need can be tested (Pareek, 1986). In response, organizations can adopt training and development strategies for helping individuals develop job-related needs (e.g., power for a manager, achievement for intrapreneural projects).

The needs approach has had a substantial impact on how organizations attempt to motivate their employees. Because there are limitations to the need approach (e.g., determining individual worker needs, knowing when needs are fulfilled, establishing a priority for needs), in recent years research has concentrated on alternative means for motivating employees.

## PROCESS THEORIES

Once we shift our concern from an individual's characteristics as a means for understanding and enhancing motivation, to the social and information cues given to the individual, we are examining motivational theories that involve choice and process. These theories are concerned with the situation and how communication processes influence our decisions to act one way or the other (Mitchell, 1984, p. 19). As with the need approach, we can examine process approaches by examining three major internal motivation theories, then turn our attention to external approaches.

### Internal Motivation Approaches

Internal motivation approaches presume that "people are practical, reasoning beings who have anticipations and expectations about their future in the organization" (Sample, 1984, p. 257). Essentially, "people make conscious choices among outcomes according to their estimated probabilities of occurrence and the personal values attached to them" (Casio, 1982, p. 283). Put in behavioral terms, individual behavior is energized through the anticipation of reward. The value we place on various outcomes gives direction to our behavior. We examine three different explanations of the relationship of reward and direction. Expectancy theory sees individuals as decision makers weighing different options. Equity theory points to the perceptions employees hold of what rewards others are receiving based on a comparison of effort put forth. Goal-setting theories predict that employees will be more successful in completing their work if the organization's and manager's expectations are clearly laid out.

### Expectancy Theory

Expectancy theory attempts to explain motivation in terms of the beliefs people have about their organization. People will work if they have the expectancy that the environment will provide them with the things they are looking for. Fundamental to expectancy theory's predictions are the assumptions that people (a) are rational, (b) think about what they must do to be rewarded, and (c) determine how much the reward means to them.

Expectancy theory argues that motivation is a product of three intervening factors (Tosi, Rizzo, & Carroll, 1986, pp. 240–246; Vroom, 1964). First, the *expectancy*, or anticipation of what will occur, influences the individual. Expectancy involves an estimate of the probability that a certain action or effort (e.g., studying) will lead to achieving the desired end or performance (e.g., better grades). Second, the anticipated satisfaction, or how much someone wants something, provides the *valence*. A final term is *instrumentality*, which is the probability assigned by the individual that the performance will lead to certain outcomes. In sum, expectancy is a subjective hunch that increased effort will lead to the desired performance.

So, assume you are trying to get a raise and that you place a high valence on this outcome. If you also can place a high instrumentality (e.g., a certain performance will lead to the reward) that visiting more customers for your organization will lead to being considered for the raise, you probably will pursue this behavior. You make this choice by examining possible alternative activities (e.g., make larger sales to fewer customers, departmental meetings, bring the boss a present) and deciding the best route to pursue. Individuals will make deliberate choices to engage in certain activities in order to obtain predetermined outcomes, according to expectancy theory. There is a clear economic tone because it is assumed that people try to maximize their payoffs by looking at various alternatives. If you believe that cutting class will provide more benefits than going, you are likely to cut class.

**Applying Expectancy Theory.**   There are practical applications for this theory. Organizations can outline the link between performance and rewards in a clear manner. If the expectancy level is low, organizations should consider training and encouragement to increase employees' willingness to pursue the desired actions. When rewards that are forthcoming are not readily apparent, such as long-term advancement, managers should make these very clear (DuBrin, 1988, p. 87). In other words, the expectancy must be realistic and explicit if it is to be expected to motivate employees. If the goal of higher education is for students to achieve excellent grades, we would have to examine the valence of this goal to each student (good chance for some variation here). Then we would have to see if students could be made to believe that certain behaviors (e.g., papers, research groups, test performance) were realistic means to the end. If so, then the students' expectancy could be utilized to motivate them to achieve better grades. In organizations, specific communication activities, including sharing information, providing ongoing feedback, and clarifying expectations, are required (Mitchell, 1984, p. 22).

**Analysis of Expectancy Theory.**   There has been extensive research on expectancy theory. On issues such as predicting occupational choice and job satisfaction the correlations have been excellent, and there are some results supporting the relationship between expectancy and job effort (Mitchell, 1984). Our example with students and grades highlights the problem with expectancy theory. Because individuals do differ, establishing the various components can prove difficult. However, expectancy theory has been used in designing employee participation programs, leadership development approaches, and reward systems (DuBrin et al., 1989, p. 377). The research on expectancy theory continues to be promising (Aldag & Stearns, 1987, p. 450).

Finally, expectancy theory is based on a *normative model*. As we stated in the opening discussion, the assumptions are that people should think about all the alternatives, know all the outcomes, be aware of the action-outcome relationships, and understand how they feel about those outcomes (Mitchell, 1984, p. 20). The drawbacks to applying expectancy theory are clear. The way people actually think, as opposed to a normative model that tells people how they should think, is less systematic. Even when we are rational, we rarely have all the information to follow this process. Sometimes our expectation regarding grades, for example, is based on how fairly we feel we are rewarded in comparison to others. This leads to our analysis of equity theory.

### Equity Theory

The power of social comparison is the basis for equity theory. Although you may not gather all the necessary information in order to maximize your decisions (e.g., expectancy), equity theory argues that you will be motivated to choose a behavior when there seems to be a fair exchange to be made. We have a type of internal balance sheet that helps us figure out what to do. As with expectancy theory, we compare the overall favorableness of different behaviors. Unlike expectancy theory, no attempt is made to decide the probability between actions and outcomes.

When applied to organizations, this theory concludes that if you perceive a discrepancy between what you are receiving and what others are receiving, you will feel an inequity (Adams, 1965, p. 280). These comparisons between ourselves and other individuals are based on what we get out of our jobs (e.g., *outcomes*) and what we contribute to our jobs (e.g., *inputs*). Different outcomes (e.g., pay, promotion, recognition, praise, status) can appear fair or unfair in comparison to other people's inputs (e.g., background, education, training, effort, time).

The theory further proposes that people compare their outcomes with that of specific reference persons whose inputs to the organizations are comparable to their own (Goodman, 1974). These comparisons result in three different conditions. The first, underpayment inequity, means we feel we are getting less out of the job than other people. The second, overpayment inequity, means that in comparing our input/outcome formulation, we are getting more out of the job than other individuals. Finally, if we feel the contributions we make give us the same gain as our comparison group, we experience equity. In one study, employees feeling equity in their pay were more satisfied with their jobs than under- or overpaid employees (Prichard, Dunnette, & Jorgenson, 1972). In the same study, overpaid workers were more productive and underpaid workers less productive than the group perceiving equity.

The most harmful comparison state is underpayment inequity. Employees who feel that they are underrewarded can reduce their efforts (e.g., become demotivated), increase their efforts (e.g., take a proactive means for establishing equity), or change their means of determining equity (e.g., reexamine inputs and/or outputs). Research indicates that perceived underpayment generally leads to decreased efforts (Mitchell, 1984, p. 21). For employees already alienated, recognizing the inequity simply will increase the alienation, or encourage them to leave the organization (Finn & Lee, 1972). Alienation can manifest itself in subtle forms of nonproductive behavior (e.g., increased absenteeism, lowered quality, hounding for raises) (Dittrich & Carrell, 1979). All of these responses (e.g., decreased efforts) indicate that the employee is trying to restore his or her sense of fairness regarding the inequity (Gould, 1979).

Inequities are not difficult to find. As Auster (1989) pointed out, "Women in the U.S. still earn an average of only 50 to 75 percent of the wages of men, depending on the occupation, and this gap persists despite legal and social advances" (p. 173). The subtle nonverbal inequities in status and power (e.g., office size, dress, assigned parking spaces) discussed earlier in this text demonstrate how difficult it can be to resolve perceived inequities.

***Applying Equity Theory.***    This theory takes a broad view of an employee's perception of his or her contribution to the organization. A contribution can be anything that the employee values (e.g., loyalty, dependability, zero defects, education level). In order to prevent feelings of inequity, organizations would have to go to some lengths to keep employees from feeling that they are not being rewarded fairly. Clearly, pay levels provide an ideal example of unfairness, but many other issues also are involved. In a study of Boeing Aircraft Company, for example, feelings of inequity were related to grievances, absenteeism, turnover, and dissatisfaction

(Telly, French, & Scott, 1971). Managers can examine the comparisons employees make with conditions within and outside the organization and attempt to respond to the perceptions (Gutknecht & Miller, 1986, p. 119). Because rewards are relative, not absolute, managers must implement effective communication practices (e.g., frequent and evenhanded feedback, objective recognition, listening) (Quick, 1985, pp. 52–55). Otherwise, employees will use their own internal standards regarding what appears inequitable to them, and managers will attempt to remove the wrong perceived inequity (Huseman, Hatfield, & Miles, 1987).

*Analysis of Equity Theory.* Because examples of unfair treatment are not difficult to find, this approach has a great deal of intuitive appeal. The majority of equity theory studies have focused on pay levels, so it is difficult to measure the other, less tangible, forms of payment. One set of studies does demonstrate that in collaborative, interdependent settings, people perform better when pay is tied to long-term criteria (Mitchell, 1984, p. 22). In other words, trying to pay people by their own individual performances does not work well in a collaborative setting.

But, how can an organization or manager know the employee's equity perceptions? Even if the inequity is identified, should it be mitigated? If mitigated, how can this prevent other employees from seeing an inequity? These, and many other questions, make the application of equity theory difficult. One possible alternative is to make the person's job more goal oriented so individual and group accomplishments are relatively simple to measure, which leads to the third approach.

### Goal-Setting Theory

Implicit in expectancy and equity theories is the concept of goals (Locke, 1968, 1978; Locke & Latham, 1983). Goal setting argues that the critical antecedent to task-relevant behavior is our intention to reach some goal (Wood & Locke, 1991). So, we are influenced by our expectations of rewards (expectancy theory) and comparisons to other people (equity theory) when these factors affect our goals. This is an important distinction because it concludes that the goal causes the motivation, not the reward. Ample evidence exists that goal setting does affect work performance (Tubbs & Ekeberg, 1991).

Goals provide order and structure, measure progress, give a sense of achievement, and provide closure (Quick, 1985, p. 124). Using the analogy of shooting at a target, goals explain what you are aiming for, how close you came to a bull's eye, possibly a feeling of success, and an identifiable end to the sequence of behavior. Virtually every discussion of performance appraisals, coaching, and training includes goal setting as a linchpin concept.

*Applying Goal Setting Theory.* Mitchell (1984) observed, "Goals are a major source of work motivation" (p. 21). Almost every study indicates that when individuals have clear goals, they perform at a higher level than when they do not have goals

(Latham & Yukl, 1975). To be effective, goals must be very specific (e.g., finish seven books by Friday), rather than general (e.g., read as many books as you can). In addition, goals must be realistic, relevant to the organization, and to the person (Quick, 1985, pp. 126–128).

In addition to being specific, realistic, and relevant, research indicates that difficult goals lead to better performance than easy goals (Klein, 1989, p. 163). Indicating to the employee that the manager has a high expectancy for success in the employee's ability to reach the difficult goals works to further enhance the process (Eden, 1988). In addition, when the goals are specific for a group of employees, there is higher performance and less performance variance across individuals. So, a manager, utilizing excellent communication skills, can negotiate difficult, but obtainable, goals with her or his subordinates.

The use of management by objectives (MBO) is a straightforward attempt to utilize goal setting (Latham & Baldes, 1975). When managers operate with an MBO system, they work with subordinates to arrive at a mutually acceptable set of goals for the subordinates (Baron, 1983, p. 271). The goals are stated in concrete, measurable terms. The methods for reaching the goals also are agreed on, and the subordinate's performance evaluation is based on the extent to which he or she reached the goals. However, "the success record of MBO as a practical management technique is spotty at best" because a general program of goal setting must fit into the prevailing culture (Muczyk & Reimann, 1989, p. 137). While acting as a consultant to a military training program, I was intrigued by the unexpected outcome of their goal-setting expectations. They placed a strong emphasis on "support your analysis (S.Y.A.)" as a means of demonstrating that you had examined all data carefully before submitting your suggestions regarding a goal. However, with its strong emphasis on a command structure, this branch of the military had tended to make goal setting a one-way, top-down process. So, S.Y.A. took on a different meaning. Subordinates went out of their way to prove they had fulfilled the leader's demands in order to "Save Your A." All too often, goal setting is leader centered. Unless the goals are discovered, developed, and accepted mutually, managers still retain the power to accept or reject an employee's work based on the manager's perception of quality.

***Analysis of Goal-Setting Theory.*** Effective goal setting requires skills that might not be utilized currently by managers (Mitchell, 1984, p. 23). In most cases, there must be a collaborative goal-setting process between managers and subordinates (Mitchell, 1984, p. 23). This is the principle behind the effective use of MBO.

Goal setting appears to be most effective when combined with feedback (Cusella, 1987). As Klein (1989) explained, "Results from studies in which goals and feedback were systematically varied suggest that both are necessary to improve performance" (p. 155). In fact, when goals are provided without feedback, or feedback is given without goals, employees often will try to fill the gap. Klein continued, "Specific feedback, like specific goals, will lead to higher levels of performance and less performance variation among individuals" (p. 163). Effective listening and feedback, as we indicated earlier in this text, are learned skills. In addition, managers must develop a sense of trust to encourage upward communication.

In summary, intentional choice approaches provide an exciting avenue for increasing work motivation by external stimulation of internal motivators. The motivational process between the individual and the organization's components provides the impetus to act. Expectancy theory proposes a quasi-rational employee making a decision regarding tasks. Equity theory sees the same employee looking at other individuals to decide if his or her efforts are correctly rewarded. Goal-setting theory argues that individuals will perform better with realistic and demanding goals. There is a clear crossover in the actual application of these theories in organizations. There are additional external motivators of intentional choice. We discuss three.

## External Approaches

We highlight several specific means that can be used by organizations to enhance employee motivation. Because almost all approaches to organizing, ranging from the structural to symbolic, are concerned with motivation, we confine our examination to several approaches. These include employee involvement and rewarding performance, Pygmalion and the self-fulfilling prophecy, and quality of work life. Because the opportunities for external approaches are almost unlimited, a summary of the primary external approaches is presented. First, we need to consider employee involvement.

### Employee Involvement and Rewarding Performance

These two approaches have been utilized extensively by organizations. According to a survey of 1,598 organizations by the American Productivity Center and the American Compensation Association, the 1980s witnessed a strong growth in programs designed to increase involvement and rewards (Horn, 1987). One of the major findings is that no one employee involvement or performance-rewarding mechanism guarantees motivation. The study "stresses that incentive programs tied to productivity work best in combination with supportive human resource practices . . . [and] without adequate and timely information sharing, employee involvement, and assurance of some employment stability" reward systems (e.g., compensation) will not increase productivity (Horn, 1987, p. 57). However, correctly applied incentives do work. Yankelovich (1982) reported, "One review of 103 experiments which were designed to test whether an improved incentive system—including money and great control over one's work—would lead to higher individual productivity, found that it did in 85 of the experiments" (p. 8). Avis Inc., the nation's number two car rental company, uses employee ownership (Employee Stock Option Plans—ESOP) to create involvement and reward performance. Between 1987 and 1989, customer complaints fell 35%, the value of workers' shares rose from $5.22 a share to $15.47, and employees offered valuable input on issues ranging from providing multilingual information cards for international customers at John F. Kennedy International Airport to detecting car theft in Baltimore (New York Times News Service, 1989). We discussed ESOP earlier in this text as an example of effectively using employee involvement.

Intrinsic to an understanding of positive reinforcement is an examination of negative messages. These are verbal and nonverbal, and create discouragement. For example, the *red-pencil effect* involves circling the mistakes of others in a literal form (e.g., typos, memo format) or behaviorally (e.g., management by exception, subtle statements regarding specific behaviors). As Eckstein (1983) observed, "A frequent consequence of such 'constructive criticism' is that the receiver of the message becomes preoccupied with his or her mistakes" (p. 142). The red-penciling lets the subordinate know who is in charge, who can exercise arbitrary power, and clearly ignores the predominately positive aspects of the work. Basic to the impact of external influence is the impact of reinforcement on self-image.

### The Self-Fulfilling Prophecy or the Pygmalion Effect.
In chapter 2, we discussed the impact perception has on ourselves and others with self-fulfilling prophecies and self-fulfilling stereotypes (Snyder, 1982). In motivation, what we expect often can be what we get. And, according to Hackman and Johnson (1991), "This makes communication of expectations one of a leader's most powerful tools" (p. 159). In the Greek myth, Prince Pygmalion created a statue of a beautiful woman whom he named Galatea. The Prince was so taken with the statue that he fell in love with it. In the myth, the god Venus took pity on the Prince and brought Galatea to life. In essence, the Prince acted toward the statue as if it were real, and it became real.

There are studies and extensive anecdotal information to support the impact that a manager's beliefs can have on the motivation of subordinates (Eden, 1984). In chapter 2, we presented the conclusions regarding the self-fulfilling prophecy and linked the manager's expectations to the motivation of subordinates (Single, 1980, p. 19). In one study of Israeli army trainees, instructors were told that the trainees had either high, regular, or unknown command potential. In actuality, the groupings were random (e.g., no one group had more or less command potential). The trainees were not told to which level of command potential they were assigned. The high-potential recruits outperformed the other two groups, had higher motivation toward advancement, and were more satisfied with the training (Eden & Shani, 1982). In a study at AT&T, when managers had high, but realistic, expectations, employees performed better than for managers who expected too much or too little (Berlew & Hall, 1966). Even low performers seem to respond to expectations. In a study of the U.S. Navy, performance improved markedly when problem sailors were given special training designed to enhance personal growth and were given mentors (Crawford, Thomas & Fink, 1980).

There is a great deal of overlap between goal setting and the Pygmalion effect. In essence, when we are given a realistic goal to strive toward, and a great deal of support in the process, we are responding to goals. A broader approach is to attempt to improve the overall quality of work life.

### Quality of Work Life

At various times, we have offered examples of mechanisms that can enhance motivation (e.g., semiautonomous work units, feedback, office design, culture, channels, information, and power sharing). Based on the research reported earlier in this text, these approaches hold great promise. Table 13.5 summarizes the approaches that can be taken to enhance quality of work life.

In summary, external sources of intentional choice influence range across all the topics we have covered in this text. Operating in a cultural context, numerous activities can be undertaken to create a motivational environment. We can summarize the means for external motivation under seven categories. Table 13.6 provides an explanation for matching workers' motives and values with the job, making work satisfying, reinforcing effective performance, clear work goals, eliminating restraints, developing social and group factors, and reducing incongruences between the personal, social, and technological elements. The examples we have introduced throughout the text can be used to amplify these concepts. In addition, we can provide some specific suggestions regarding effective motivation.

## KUDOS REGARDING THE PRINCIPLES
## UNDERLYING MOTIVATION

From our discussion of expectancy, equity, and goal-setting theory, and the addition of rewarding performance, self-fulfilling prophecies, and quality of work life

TABLE 13.5
Improvements in Quality of Work Life

| From | To |
|---|---|
| 1) Detailed job descriptions with specific tasks and rigid instruction for how to do work | 1) Flexible, diverse work assignments allowing self-regulation, variety, and challenge |
| 2) Structured chain of command, managers making decisions and supervisors bossing | 2) Worker involvement in planning, decision making, and operating procedure |
| 3) Hierarchical channels of communication | 3) Direct, fast two-way communication |
| 4) Limited on-the-job instruction | 4) Advanced training, educational, and career opportunities |
| 5) Job specialization in one task | 5) Leeway allowed for every employee to complete many tasks by crossing lines of specialization |
| 6) Obscure, irregular job evaluations | 6) Objective job performance standards with measures fairly administered |
| 7) Careless or neglected safety and health conditions | 7) Clean, safe, and healthful working conditions |

TABLE 13.6
Motivation – Summation of External Approaches

---

1. Matching workers' motives and values with the job. Select the right workers for the situation. Develop the motives needed for the situation.
   Examples:   interviewing procedures, personnel selection, job previews, socialization, acculturation, training.
2. Making work satisfying, interesting, and attractive. People want interesting work, good pay, control of their own working life. The person-environment fit is important.
   Examples:   participation, job enrichment, benefit package, job security, promotion, flexible hours, child care, recognition programs, cafeteria-style plans.
3. Programs to positively reinforce effective performance. Eliminate reinforcement of negative performance.
   Examples:   self-management, praise and criticism, coaching, financial incentives pay programs, increased vacation time, feedback.
4. Clear, challenging work goals. Goal-setting techniques must lead to attainable and attractive goals.
   Examples:   quality circles, self-managing work units, management by objectives (MBO), modeling, goal-setting programs.
5. Eliminate restraints on performance due to inadequate resources.
   Examples:   training and development, coaching and counseling, trained supervisors, problem-solving groups, advanced technology.
6. Develop social and group factors. Have interpersonal and group processes support goal attainment.
   Examples:   team development, semiautonomous work units, leadership training, division of labor, change group composition, conflict management training, interpersonal and group process training.
7. Make the personal, social, and technological parameters harmonious.
   Examples:   ESOPs, Scanlon Plan, organizational development, quality of work life programs, sociotechnical systems designs.

---

*Note.* From Katzell and Thompson (1990). Copyright © 1990 by the American Psychological Association. Adapted by permission.

programs, we can draw four major conclusions that are consistent with all these theories and with our earlier discussion of needs (Quick, 1985, pp. 20–23). Accepting that all generalizations about human behavior should be questioned strongly, these four conclusions do offer some useful advice regarding motivating others. First, people have reasons for everything they do. All human behavior is directed at some goal. In the process, people must choose between goals. As with perception, the reasons can be idiosyncratic and may not make sense to outside observers. So, voluntary behavior is not always conscious. Often, we act based on sets and habits learned in other activities. For example, our responses to leadership and conflict management can be gut-level and intuitive, rather than well thought out.

Second, whatever people choose as a goal is something they believe is good for them. If you decide not to come to work, it is because you think this is a good idea. Just because we do not understand someone else's behavior does not make it any less valuable to the person pursuing it. According to Quick (1985), "Thus the key to behavior that is mystifying, self-destructive, and counterproductive is in understanding the reward that the person perceives. If you want to change that person's behavior, or more accurately, if you encourage him or her to act in a different man-

TABLE 13.7
Imperatives for Motivation:
Summary of Recent Motivation Research in Organizations

1. Ensure that workers' motives and values are appropriate for the jobs on which they are placed.
2. Make jobs attractive to and consistent with workers' motives and values.
3. Define work goals that are clear, challenging, attractive, and attainable.
4. Provide workers with the personal and material resources that facilitate their effectiveness.
5. Create supportive social environments.
6. Reinforce performance.
7. Harmonize all these elements into a consistent sociotechnical system.

*Note.* From Katzell and Thompson (1990). Copyright © 1990 by the American Psychological Association. Adapted by permission.

ner, you must substitute a more valuable reward for the one the person is enjoying now" (p. 21).

Third, the goals people choose must be attainable. By and large, people will not continue to pursue a reward that is clearly out of reach. To tell an incoming employee that someday he or she may become president of the organization is tantamount to no goal at all. The exception is with people who would play the odds anyway. Gamblers, for example, bet on the dark horse. The fallacy of large numbers explains why people believe that when a coin flips heads in a repeated fashion (e.g. 20 times), the odds are greater on the next flip that it will be tails. Or, people playing slot machines really believe that the machine gets "hot." Actually, since the late 1970s slot machines have been controlled by microprocessors to give a very precise payoff. So each pull of the handle, like each flip of the coin, is a random event (Crevelt, 1991).

The difficulty of enacting these three principles takes us back to our chapter on perception. Often, managers project their own perceptions of employee needs, rather than asking employees what motivates them. Asking people to explain what motivates them, however, is not an easy solution. Many of us do not have a clear notion of why we act in certain ways.

Fourth, working conditions can effect the work's value to the employee, and his or her perceptions of attainability or success. Motivation does not occur in isolation. So, implementing quality of work life programs, developing a positive climate and culture, and paying attention to individual needs assist in the motivational process.

## PLACING MOTIVATION IN CONTEXT

In a sense, motivation brings us full circle to our earlier examination of management and organizational theories. An historical perspective is useful for our examination of motivation. Most observers have concluded that in the post-World War II expansion era, organizations would have made money regardless of what they did (Peters & Austin, 1985; Peters & Waterman, 1982; Quick, 1985, p. 2). America was the world economic leader, backed by an impressive industrial capacity and a strong domestic setting. Ineffective management practices (e.g., Theory X, management by terror, country-club settings), weak responses to undermotivated employees (e.g., coddling, ignoring, arbitrarily dismissing), and poor quality (e.g., loss of market, consistently poor evaluations) were of little consequence because, in most cases, these organizations were the only game in town. This analogy fits well, because American corporations controlled the gaming table (e.g., viable production facilities, technology), the size and type of the stakes (e.g., resources, accessibility to the market), and the list of participants (e.g., who gets what business, rewards to be distributed). People who stayed with the corporation became "Organization People" and those who used job hopping as a means for advancement became the "Migrant Managers."

More recently, the challenges from international trade, coupled with a decline in quality, demands for increased customer responsiveness, and economic fluctuations, have required American organizations to grapple with demands for increased productivity without the traditional increase in perks. As Marks (1988) observed, "Shaken by mergers and cutbacks, today's managers fend for themselves, placing their trust not in corporations, but in their own capabilities" (p. 34). The Employment Management Association found that 79% of the 259 companies it studied had reduced their staff for economic reasons in the last 5 years (1983–1988). This included more than half a million positions cut in some companies since 1984 (Marks, 1988, p. 34). Although new technologies, the globalization of economic activity, and organizational changes will create new job opportunities for qualified individuals, these new jobs "almost never go to the people who have lost their jobs because of these forces" (Carnevale, 1991, p. 82).

Employment trends provide a backdrop for this analysis. Most of the jobs that will decline are blue-collar (e.g., hands on, direct labor jobs, production workers) (Bureau of Labor-Management Relations, 1987, p. 2). Indirect labor jobs (e.g., white-collar, nonproduction) accounted for 55% of the work force in 1990 (Carnevale, 1991, pp. 81–94). By the turn of the century, these could rise to 90% (Bureau of Labor-Management Relations, 1987, pp. 1–4). The service sector is the other area of rapid labor growth. Between 1970 and 1984, manufacturing jobs grew by only 1.2%, whereas service-sector jobs grew by 46.4% (Bureau of Labor-Management Relations, 1987, pp. 1–4).

Both white-collar and service-sector jobs create difficult motivational issues. For the white-collar worker, advancement traditionally has been a key motivator (Weber et al, 1990). Now, with the career ladder having fewer rungs as a result of cutbacks, downsizing, or automation, how can this group be motivated? The solution is a careful mix of the various approaches we have discussed in this chapter.

The message is clear. Techniques used to motivate employees in the past will have to be altered to meet the new working conditions and employee expectations. For example, measuring productivity for a blue-collar worker is relatively easy (e.g., number of units, time taken, specific tasks accomplished). White-collar workers might have one outstanding idea that saves the organization. Service workers often do the same task over and over again, but would end up slighting a customer if the service process were speeded up.

For the 1990s, creating a climate that enhances motivation, with the commensurate increase in productivity, is a requirement (Carnevale, 1991). Being motivated, as a path toward job security, is also vital. So, understanding motivation has become even more important. For certain, we can conclude that motivation to work varies widely between people, and that different jobs offer substantially different reasons to be motivated (Stanton, 1983). We also can underscore the difference between hard-management issues (e.g., technology, systems, capital investment, structure) and soft-management practices (e.g., employee involvement, communication).

Finally, we can argue realistically that all organizational and management theories are concerned with motivation (Quick, 1991). Our discussion of situational strategies explains why some individuals and tasks require controlled environments whereas others require flexibility. Each of the four frames represents a means for responding to the motivational challenges. And, returning to a broader perspective, the ongoing interest in organizational cultures underscores the importance of the environment in determining motivation.

## COMMUNICATION AND MOTIVATION

Communication is the driving force behind motivational efforts (Cusella, 1987). Various management practices, including goal setting, reinforcement, feedback, and evaluation, require communication. According to Rosenbaum (1982), "Goal setting and regular communication increase the challenge of the job, make it clear to workers precisely what they are expected to do, and deliver a sense of pride and achievement" (p. 103). Based on our previous discussion in this text, a multitude of other elements (e.g., nonverbal messages, symbolic activities, leadership) are communicated, at all times, to all members of the organization. In addition, because behavior, which indicates performance, is the yardstick by which we measure motivation, there is a clear link between examining motivation and communication.

There are two strategies for enhancing organizational effectiveness. One is to deal with the human process and the other is to change the technostructural approach (e.g., equipment, innovation, sales territory, computerization). Clearly, the first issue is based in communication activities. The second "assumes motivation and behavior are powerfully influenced by job design (and its underlying technology), organization structure, and control, and information and reward systems" (Beer & Walton, 1990, p. 155). Goal-setting theories provide specific explanations for why people are motivated. Difficult, specific, and mutually developed goals will assist individuals in being motivated. Although goal setting is extremely useful, many individuals are motivated more by climate, culture, and affiliation.

Finally, the organization's culture functions as a means of motivating individuals.

Effective communication practices are essential to any effective motivational program. An appropriate means for concluding this chapter is to present a story offered by one highly successful motivator.

Jan Carlzon, president of Scandinavian Airlines (SAS), is fond of the story of two stone cutters who were chipping square blocks out of granite. A visitor asked them what they were doing. The first stone cutter grumbled, "I'm cutting this damned stone into a block." The second, who looked pleased with his work, replied, "I'm on a team that's building a cathedral."

A worker who can envision the whole cathedral and who has been given responsibility for constructing his portion of it is far more satisfied and productive than the worker who only sees the granite before him. A true motivator is one who designs the cathedral and then shares the vision that inspires others to build it.

## REFERENCES

Adams, J. S. Inequity in social exchange. In L. Berkowitz (Ed.), *Advances in experimental and social psychology* (pp. 267–299). New York: Academic.

Aldag, J. R., & Stearns, T. M. (1987). *Management*. Cincinatti: South-Western.

Alderfer, C. P. (1972). *Existence, relatedness, and growth*. New York: Free Press.

Associated Press. (1991, January 20). Are we keeping up with brave new world? *The Tuscaloosa News*, p. 7E.

Auster, E. R. (1989). Task characteristics as a bridge between macro- and microlevel research on salary inequality between men and women. *Academy of Management Review, 14*, 173–193.

Baron, R. A. (1983). *Behavior in organizations: Understanding and managing the human side of work.* Boston: Allyn & Bacon.

Beer, M., & Walton, E. (1990). Developing the competitive organization: Interventions and strategies. *American Psychologist, 45*, 154–161.

Berlew, D., & Hall, D. (1966). The socialization of managers: Effects of expectations on performance. *Administrative Science Quarterly, 1*, 208–223.

Bozzi, V. (1984, September). Step on it: Somebody is looking. *Psychology Today*, p. 76.

Bridgewater, C. A. (1984, September). Watched joggers run faster. *Psychology Today*, p. 76.

Bureau of Labor-Management Relations. (1987). *Participative approaches to white-collar productivity* (BLMR Publication No. 116). Washington, DC: U.S. Department of Labor.

Carnevale, A. P. (1991). *America and the new economy*. Washington, DC: U.S. Department of Labor.

Casio, W. F. (1982). *Applied psychology in personnel management*. Reston, VA: Reston.

Cavanagh, M. E. (1984, March). In search of motivation. *Personnel Journal*, pp. 22–26.

Cerrington, D. J., & Wixom, B. J., Jr. (1983). Recognition is still a top motivator. *Personnel Administrator, 28*, 85–87.

Conklin, R. (1979). *How to get people to do things*. Chicago: Contemporary Books.

Cooper, C. L., & Robertson, I. T. (Eds.). (1986). Editorial forward. In C. L. Cooper & I. T. Robertson (Eds.), *International review of industrial and organizational psychology* (pp. ix–xi). Chichester, England: Wiley.

Cornealius, E. T., III, & Lane, F. B. (1984). The power motive and managerial success in a professionally oriented service industry organization. *Journal of Applied Psychology, 69*, 32–39.

Crawford, S. K., Thomas, E. D., & Fink, J. J. (1980). Pygmalion at sea: Improving the work effectiveness of low performers. *Journal of Applied Behavioral Science, 16*, 482–505.

Crevelt, D. (1991, January 30). All about slot machines . . . And how to improve your odds. *Bottom Line*, p. 13.

Cummings, H. W., Long, L. W., & Lewis, M. L. (1988). *Managing communication in organizations: An introduction* (2nd ed.). Scottsdale, AZ: Gorsuch Scarisbrick.

Cusella, L. P. (1987). Feedback, motivation, and performance. In F. M. Jablin, L. L. Putnam, K. H. Roberts, & L. W. Porter (Eds.), *Handbook of organizational communication* (pp. 624–679). Newbury Park, CA: Sage.

Delaney, J. T., Lewin, D., & Ichniowski, C. (1989). *Human resource policies and practices in American firms* (BLMR Publication No. 137). Washington, DC: U.S. Department of Labor.

Dittrich, J. E., & Carrell, M. R. (1979). Organizational equity perceptions, employee job satisfaction, and departmental absence and turnover rates. *Organizational Behavior and Human Performance, 24,* 29–40.

DuBrin, A. J. (1988). *Human relations: A job-oriented approach* (4th ed.). Englewood Cliffs, NJ: Prentice-Hall.

DuBrin, A. J., Ireland, R. D., & Williams, J. C. (1989). *Management & organization.* Cincinnati: South-Western.

Eckstein, D. G. (1983). Encouragement: Giving positive invitations. In L. D. Goostein & J. W. Pfeiffer (Eds.), *The 1983 annual for facilitators, trainers, and consultants* (pp. 140–144). San Diego: University Associates.

Eden, D. (1984). Self-fulfilling prophecy as a management tool: Harnessing Pygmalion. *Academy of Management Review, 9,* 64–73.

Eden, D. (1988). Pygmalion, goal setting, and expectancy: Compatible ways to boost productivity. *Academy of Management Review, 13,* 639–652.

Eden, D., & Shani, A. B. (1982). Pygmalion goes to boot camp: Expectancy, leadership, and trainee performance. *Journal of Applied Psychology, 67,* 194–199.

Finn, R. H., & Lee, S. M. (1972). Salary equity: Its determination, analysis and correlates. *Journal of Applied Psychology, 56,* 283–292.

Frank, A. D., & Brownell, J. L. (1989). *Organizational communication and behavior: Communicating to improve performance.* New York: Holt, Rinehart & Winston.

Garson, B. (1988). *The electronic sweatshop: How computers are transforming the office of the future into the factory of the past.* New York: Penguin.

General Accounting Office. (1989). *Dislocated workers: Labor-management committees enhance reemployment assistance* (GAO/HRD-90-3). Washington, DC: U.S. Department of Labor.

Goodman, P. S. (1974). An examination of referents used in the evaluation of pay. *Organizational Behavior and Human Performance, 12,* 170–195.

Gould, S. (1979). An equity-exchange model of organizational involvement. *Academy of Management Review, 4,* 53–62.

Gutknecht, D. B., & Miller, J. R. (1986). *The organizational and human resources sourcebook.* Lanham, MD: University Press of America.

Hackman, M. Z., & Johnson, C. G. (1991). *Leadership: A communication perspective.* Prospect Heights, IL: Waveland.

Hanna, J. B. (1987). *Techniques for productivity improvement.* Washington, DC: Small Business Administration, U.S. Government Printing Office.

Hellmick, N. (1988, November 28). 73% would stay home, if they could. *USA Today,* pp. 1A–1B.

Herzberg, F. (1966). *Work and the nature of man.* Cleveland: World Publishing.

Herzberg, F., Mausner, B., & Snyderman, B. (1959). *The motivation to work* (2nd ed.). New York: Wiley.

Hisrich, R. D. (1990). Entrepreneurship/intrapreneurship. *American Psychologist, 45,* 209–222.

Hopkins, T. (1982). *How to master the art of selling* (2nd ed.). New York: Warner.

Horn, J. C. (1987, July). Bigger pay for better work. *Psychology Today,* p. 57.

House, R. J., & Wigdon, L. A. (1967). Herzberg's dual-factor theory of job satisfaction and motivation. *Personnel Psychology, 20,* 369–389.

Hunt, G. T. (1989). *Communication skills in the organization* (2nd ed.). Englewood Cliffs, NJ: Prentice-Hall.

Huseman, E. C., Hatfield, J. D., & Miles, E. W. (1987). A new perspective on equity theory: The equity sensitivity construct. *Academy of Management Review, 12*(2), 222–234.

Jobs that are most hazardous. (1989, January 6). *USA Today*, p. 2B.

Katzell, R. A., & Thompson, D. E. (1990). Work motivation: Theory and practice. *American Psychologist*, *45*, 144–153.

Klein, H. J. (1989). An integrated control theory model of work motivation. *Academy of Management Review*, *14*(2), pp. 150–172.

Koretz, G. (1991, February 4). A white-collar recession? Wrong color. *Business Week*, p. 20.

Kotter, J. P. (1988). *The leadership factor*. New York: Free Press.

Landy, F. J., & Becker, W. S. (1987). Motivation theory reconsidered. In L. Cummings & B. M. Staw (Eds.), *Research in organizational behavior* (Vol. 9, pp. 1–38) Greenwich, CT: JAI.

Latham, G. P., & Baldes, J. J. (1975). The practical significance of Locke's theory of goal setting. *Journal of Applied Psychology*, *60*, 122–138.

Latham, G. P., & Yukl, G. A. (1975). A review of research on the applications of goal setting in organizations. *Academy of Management Journal*, *18*, 824–845.

Lee, E. (1990, July 8). High-tech monitoring invades the work place. *The Tuscaloosa News*, pp. 1E–2E.

Locke, E. A. (1968). Toward a theory of task motivation and incentives. *Organizational Behavior and Human Performance*, *3*, 157–189.

Locke, E. A. (1978). The ubiquity of the technique of goal setting in theories and approaches to employee motivation. *Academy of Management Review*, *3*, 594–601.

Locke, E. A., & Henne, D. (1986). Work motivation theories. In C. L. Cooper & I. T. Robertson (Eds.), *International review of industrial and organizational psychology* (pp. 1–35). Chichester, England: Wiley.

Locke, E. A., & Latham, G. P. (1983). *Goal setting: A motivational technique that works*. Englewood Cliffs, NJ: Prentice-Hall.

Maehr, M. L., & Kleiber, D. A. (1981). The graying of achievement motivation. *American Psychologist*, *36*, 787–793.

Marks, H. L. (1988, September). The disappearing company man. *Psychology Today*, p. 34.

Maslow, A. H. (1943). A theory of human motivation. *Psychological Review*, *50*, 370–396.

Maslow, A. H. (1954). *Motivation and personality*. New York: Harper & Row.

Maslow, A. H. (1965). *Eupsychian management*. Homewood, IL: Irwin.

Maslow, A. H. (1968). *Toward a psychology of being* (2nd ed.). New York: Van Nostrand.

Maslow, A. J. (1970). *Motivation and personality* (2nd ed.). New York: Harper & Row.

McClelland, D. C. (1953). *The achievement motive*. New York: Appleton-Century-Crofts.

McClelland, D. C. (1961). *Achieving society*. Princeton, NJ: Van Nostrand.

McClelland, D. C. (1962). Business drive and national achievement. *Harvard Business Review*, *40*, 99–112.

McClelland, D. (1975). *Power: The inner experience*. New York: Irvington.

McClelland, D.C. (1978). Managing motivation to expand human freedom. *American Psychologist*, *33*, 201–210.

McClelland, D. C., & Boyatziss, R. E. (1982). Leadership motive pattern and long-term success in management. *Journal of Applied Psychology*, *67*, 725–739.

McClelland, D. C., & Burnham, D. H. (1976). Power is the great motivator. *Harvard Business Review*, *54*, 159–166.

McClelland, D. C., & Winter, D. G. (1969). *Motivating economic achievement*. New York: Free Press.

Memmott, M. (1987, May 19). We work more and like it less. *USA Today*, p. B1.

Meyer, M. C. (1978, May). Demotivation—its cause and cure. *Personnel Journal*, pp. 8–14.

Miner, J. B. (1980). *Theories of organizational behavior*. Hinsdale, IL: Dryden.

Mitchell, T. R. (1982). Motivation: New directions for theory, research, and practice. *Academy of Management Review*, *7*, 80–88.

Mitchell, T. R. (1984). *Motivation and performance*. Chicago: Science Research Associates.

Muczyk, J. P., & Reimann, B. C. (1989). MBO as a component to effective leadership. *Academy of Management Executive*, *3*, 131–138.

New York Times News Service. (1989, September 24). Workers' input pays off. *The Tuscaloosa News*, p. 10E.

O'Donnell, M., & Colby, L. (1979). Developing managers through assertiveness training. *Training, 16,* 36–37.

Pareek, U. (1986). Motivational analysis of organizations-behavior (MAO-B). In J. W. Pfieffer & L. D. Goodstein (Eds.), *The 1986 annual: Developing human resources* (pp. 121–133). San Diego: University Associates.

Peters, T. J., & Austin, N. (1985). *Passion for excellence: The leadership difference.* New York: Random House.

Peters, T. J., & Waterman, R. H., Jr. (1982). *In search of excellence: Lessons from America's best-run companies.* New York: Harper & Row.

Porter, L. W. (1964). *Organizational patterns of managerial job attitudes.* New York: American Foundation for Management Research.

Prichard, R. D., Dunnette, M. D., & Jorgenson, D. O. (1972). Effects of perceptions of equity and inequity on worker performance and satisfaction. *Journal of Applied Psychology, 56,* 75–94.

Quick, T. L. (1985). *The manager's motivation desk book.* New York: Wiley.

Quick, T. L. (1991). *Training managers so they can really manage.* San Francisco: Jossey-Bass.

Research finds workplaces more deadly than cars. (1990, August 31). *Birmingham Post-Herald,* p. A7.

Rising benefits bills: Medical costs the key. (1992, April). *Behavioral Sciences Newsletter,* p. 4.

Rosenbaum, B. L. (1982). *How to motivate today's workers.* New York: McGraw-Hill.

Ross, R. S. (1990). *Understanding persuasion* (3rd ed.). Englewood Cliffs, NJ: Prentice-Hall.

Sample, J. A. (1984). The expectancy theory of motivation: Implications for training and development. In J. W. Pfieffer & L. D. Goodstein (Eds.), *The 1984 annual: Developing human resources* (pp. 257–261). San Diego: University Associates.

Schneider, J., & Locke, E. A. (1971). A critique of Herzberg's incident classification system and a suggested revision. *Journal of Applied Psychology, 6,* 441–457.

Simmons, L. (1990, March 22). Carpal tunnel work injury incidence spreads. *Birmingham Post-Herald,* p. A7.

Single, J. L. (1980). The power of expectations: Productivity and the self-fulfilling prophecy. *Management World, 9,* 19–21.

Snyder, M. (1982, July). Self-fulfilling stereotypes. *Psychology Today,* pp. 60–68.

Stahl, M. J. (1976). Achievement, power, and managerial motivation: Selecting managerial talent with the job choice exercise. *Harvard Business Review, 54,* 159–166.

Stanton, E. S. (1983, March). A critical reevaluation of motivation, management, and productivity. *Personnel Journal,* pp. 4–7.

Stewart, D. (1986). *The power of people skills.* New York: Wiley.

Study shows most ever radiation exposure. (1990, April 11). *Birmingham Post-Herald,* p. A2.

Telly, C. S., French, W. L., & Scott, W. G. (1971). The relationship of inequity to turnover among hourly workers. *Administrative Science Quarterly, 13,* 164–172.

The promise of cold, hard trash calls New Yorkers. (1990, September 20). *Birmingham Post-Herald,* p. A4.

Tosi, H. L. Rizzo, J. R., & Carroll, S. J. (1986). *Managing organizational behavior.* Marshfield, MA: Pitman.

Tubbs, M. E., & Ekeberg, S. E. (1991). The role of intentions in work motivation: Implications for goal-setting theory and research. *Academy of Management Review, 16,* 180–199.

Tuzzolino, F., & Armandi, B. R. (1981). A need-hierarchy framework for assessing corporate social responsibility. *Academy of Management Review, 6,* 21–28.

University of Alabama Office of Health and Safety. (1990). The office—Hazards of a different kind. *Safety and Environmental Issues, 1,* 2.

U.S. Department of Labor. (1988, April). *Child care—A workforce issue: Report of the secretary's task force.* Washington, DC: U.S. Government Printing Office.

U.S. Office of Technology Assessment. (1986). *Technology and structural unemployment: Reemploying displaced adults* (OTA-ITE-250). Washington, DC: U.S. Department of Labor.

Vroom, V. H. (1964). *Work and motivation.* New York: Wiley.

Weber, J., Driscoll, L., & Brandt, R. (1990, December 10). Farewell, fast track. *Business Week,* pp. 192–193.

Williams, J. C., & Huber, G. P. (1986). *Human behavior in organizations* (3rd ed.). Cincinnati: South-Western.

Wilson, G. L., Goodall, H. L., Jr., & Waagen, C. L. (1986). *Organizational communication*. New York: Harper & Row.

Wood, R. E., & Locke, E. A. (1991). Goal setting and strategy effects on complex tasks. In E. A. Locke & G. P. Latham (Eds.), *A theory of goal setting and task performance* (pp. 293–319). Englewood Cliffs, NJ: Prentice-Hall.

Yankelovich, D. (1982, May). The work ethic is underemployed. *Psychology Today*, pp. 5–8.

# CHAPTER 14

# New Communication Technologies

Marshall McLuhan (1964; McLuhan & Fiore, 1967) observed that we shape our tools and then our tools shape us. For example, the wheel extended the foot's ability to cover distances leading to changes in working, traveling, and living arrangements. The telephone extends the ear's hearing range, develops new patterns of interaction, and significantly alters the ways people approach communication. For organizations, the telephone "made it possible for managers to leave the factory floor, for salespeople to change orders in quick response to client demands, for customers to order products directly, [and] for companies to establish branch offices" (Kiesler, 1986, p. 47). Finally, the telephone allowed for the creation of a single corporate headquarters.

McLuhan (1964) also argued that television extends the visual and audio senses, and creates a simultaneous awareness of events by individuals who otherwise are not connected. Time Warner Inc. is introducing a fiber optic cable system to replace the standard coaxial cable system. The system will make 150 channels available to its subscribers, and it will be interactive "allowing viewers to order a movie, buy something from a home shopping service, or book a travel package by pushing a button" ("TV Viewers," 1991).

Finally, computers extend the mind by offering assistance in completing numerous mental functions (e.g., keeping track of finances, spelling checks, research). For researchers, inventors, and designers, computers allow simulations of complex events heretofore requiring years of investigation. As we see, new communication technologies have a significant impact on every organization. As Dizard (1989) put it, "Of all the changes taking place in our time, none has more profound effect than the new ways in which we communicate with each other" (p. 1).

As we move toward the 21st century, the tools and communication technologies we are shaping definitely will shape our organizations. Technology is a cornerstone of organizational activity, and information is the mechanism for reducing uncertainty, so it is extremely important that we understand the impact of the new communication and information technologies (e.g., electronic mail, teleconferencing, computer conferencing, personal computers and local area networks [LAN], interactive cable television, videotex and teletext, satellite communications, computer networks, computer-aided manufacturing [CAM, e.g., robotics] and computer-assisted design [CAD]).

The remainder of this chapter examines three facets of technology. First, we analyze the relationship between organizations and technology. Second, we provide an overview of the new communication technologies. Finally, we examine six information systems.

## ORGANIZATIONS AND TECHNOLOGY

Two claims place the impact of new technology on organizations in context. First, technology always has a major impact on any organization (Culnan & Markus, 1987; Kleinschrod, 1986; Osterman, 1989). It is "the set of tools, techniques, and actions used to convert an organization's inputs into outputs. In an open systems model, technology is a firm's transformation process" (DuBrin, Ireland, & Williams, 1989, p. 188). For example, elevators were introduced to create a more efficient use of energy and space. While accomplishing this task, elevators also made it possible to build structures capable of housing a large number of people in close proximity who do not know one another (Kiesler, 1986). The advent of the skyscraper to house corporations, although efficient, left many people feeling more alienated and distant from each other because they do not interact. Historically, the industrial revolution was created because of the introduction of machines, assembly lines, and technological advances.

Second, almost every observer of the 1990s speaks of turbulent times. For example: "Rather than abating, the pressures on organizations to alter existing policies, patterns, and practices are likely to increase" (Bolman & Deal, 1991, p. 371). We live in a world of "permanent white water" (Vail, 1989, p. 6). The rapid pace for most organizations provides one clear example of the pressure on organizations. As Dumaine (1989) observed, "General Electric used to take three weeks after an order to deliver a custom-made industrial circuit breaker box. Now it takes three days. AT&T used to need two years to design a new phone. Now it can do the job in one. Motorola used to turn out electric pagers three weeks after the factory got the order. Now it takes two hours" (p. 29). So, technologies not only offer organizations a means for transforming themselves, but the environment requires that organizations be highly adaptable to the demands of new technologies. A further examination of the interface between automation, information technologies, and people is in order.

## Mechanization, Automation, and Technology

As we already mentioned, the early applications of technology included mechanization and automation (Daniels & Spiker, 1991). In chapter 3, we examined the development of modern management and organizational theories. We traced their roots to the introduction of machines and the need for individuals to be able to work together in conjunction with this machinery. When an individual operates a machine that is substituted for the mechanical capabilities of an individual, we are witnessing *mechanization*. The greater the technological complexity, the lower the human input. The development of more sophisticated technology led to *automation*, where machines are capable of self-regulation and act as substitutes for an employee's sensory mechanisms (Laufer, 1984, p. 11). *Robotics* is a melding of mechanization and automation (Whitney, 1986). This technology ranges in sophistication from simple, repetitive assembly-line operation where the steps are stored in the robot's program to machines capable of making decisions regarding the production process. An extended example demonstrates the varied impact of technology on organizations.

At the Golden Flake Snack Foods plants located in Alabama, Tennessee, and Florida, raw unwashed potatoes are processed into potato chips in 4 min (Rupinski, 1991b). Up to 350,000 pounds of potatoes per day are scrubbed, peeled, sliced, graded, fried, sorted, seasoned, and bagged without being touched by humans. Computerized scanners on conveyor belts reject blemished potatoes and slices as well as chips that exceed a precisely defined golden color. These plants are highly mechanized and automated and these *computer-aided manufacturing (CAM)* systems are used to produce the entire line of snack foods. At this point, machines are substituted for humans.

But Golden Flakes has progressed well beyond mechanization and automation to *mediated communication processes* where information is processed through electronic media to and between individuals. To prevent stale products, Golden Flake does not build up inventories. Instead, the 670 delivery routes operating in 12 states feature trucks equipped with on-board computer systems to track sales and orders based on the information relayed from these trucks to headquarters and the production plants. In the next few years, Golden Flake plans to plug its portable computers into retail customers' computers to relay order information. Using this combination of mechanization (e.g., delivery trucks, loaders, production machines), automation (e.g., 4-min production process), and mediated information processes (e.g., customer to delivery person to computer to plant), Golden Flake successfully competes with many larger producers (e.g., Frito-Lay, Keebler, Eagle Snacks).

According to the executive vice president of Golden Flake, F. Wayne Pate, technology is an important addition to the company's basic business philosophy: "We try to run our business on the basis of the 'Golden Rule.' In doing that, we want everyone who has an association with this company to feel that treatment whether they be a consumer, business customer, employee or supplier" (Rupinski, 1991b. p. B1).

The Golden Flake example offers us a quick insight into the impact of technology on organizations. They use mechanization, automation, robotics, and interactive communication technologies to produce a highly competitive product.

At some point, Golden Flake might use *computer-assisted design* (*CAD*) systems to develop new products. The M&M/Mars Company, for example, uses CAD to design candy products (DuBrin et al., 1989, p. 194). For years, CADs have been used for research and development with a wide variety of products (Szakonyi, 1988).

To summarize, there is a synergistic relationship between people and machines. The industrial revolution was created, in part, because of the feasibility of replacing manual operations with machines (DuBrin et al., 1989). With mechanization, employees either facilitate the machine's operation (e.g., operators, maintenance) or coordinate the people/machine process (e.g., managers, supervisors). Second, as the technology advanced to create automated machines, people changed from merely being an extension of the machine to managing the machines (computer-aided manufacturing [CAM]). In some cases, the machines relieved individuals of laborious tasks (e.g., repetitive functions — peeling potatoes; meticulous detail work — bad potatoes). In other cases, machines have taken over because they do a better job (e.g., printers for computers, detail work). Finally, our Golden Flake example shows how the capacity of individuals to use computerized technology to facilitate the actual selling of the product can be combined effectively with a state-of-the-art manufacturing facility. Although the interface between manufacturing and technology is interesting, the new information technologies offer even greater promise for changing the nature of organizations.

## THE NEW INFORMATION TECHNOLOGIES

Information processing is a fundamental element of all organizational activity (Robey, 1991). Information technologies include all types of computing and communications hardware and software (e.g., microcomputers, telephones, integrated management systems, electronic mail). These systems can process, transfer, store, analyze, and communicate information (Davis & Olson, 1985, p. 29). Information technologies are changing the workplace in a variety of ways. Personal computers (PCs) and video display terminals (VDTs) provide two important examples.

In 1991, U.S. companies hooked up 3.8 million PCs into small office networks bringing the total number of PCs that are connected to other electronic sources to over 18 million (Verity, Coy, & Rothfeder, 1990). This represented a 48% increase over 1989. These networks also are tied into minicomputers and mainframes that control thousands of terminals and printers in offices, banks, factories, and supermarkets. Expanding beyond the office, laptop computers will account for 35% of all PCs sold in the United States by 1993 (Depke, Gross, & Buell, 1991). The VDT first appeared in America's workplaces in the 1960s. In 1976 there were less than a million and in 1991 there were more than 40 million. And according to an article in *Labor Relations Today*, "By the year 2000, experts estimate that half of all Americans will be operating VDTs at work" ("VDTs: Fitting," 1991).

The changes produced by these new information technologies are widespread. Already, many secretarial functions have been altered or taken over by automated office systems (Daniels & Spiker, 1991, p. 171). In addition, these technologies assist individuals in sending and receiving information, attending meetings, filing reports, and keeping records (Daniels & Spiker, 1991, p. 171). As individuals utilize the new communication technologies, the richness of the media seems to have an impact of individual satisfaction.

## Media Richness

*Media richness* refers to "the speed of feedback permitted by the medium, the number and types of sensory channels utilized by the medium, the perceived personalness of the source when communicating over the medium, and the richness of language used with the medium" (Komsky, 1991, p. 314). So, face-to-face communication is very rich based on these four criteria, followed by the telephone, interactive media, personal written communication, other written communication, and numeric communication such as computer printouts. The concept of richness is important because predictions are that people enjoy greater communication satisfaction with a richer media. So, richness is one means for organizing our understanding of the new communication technologies.

## TYPES OF SYSTEMS

A second means for organizing the various types of information systems is to consider the primary function each performs. Using this approach, there are five types of information systems: communication, operational, control, decision support, and interorganizational (Markus, 1984). Although there is a great deal of overlap, the categories offer a clearer picture of the various components.

## Communication Systems

Communication systems are designed to augment human communication. *Computer-mediated communication systems* (CMCS) "have become a cornerstone to the activities of knowledge workers in the information age and the office of the future" (Compton, White, & DeWine, 1991, p. 23). CMCS change the type of information people receive, overcome temporal and geographical barriers for the information exchange, and can "break down hierarchical and departmental barriers, standard operating procedures, and organizational norms" (Kiesler, 1986, p. 47). The remainder of this chapter examines the impact, uses, and limitations of information technology.

Voice messaging, electronic mail (E-mail), video conferences, and integrated systems are all examples of how organizations can use electronically mediated messages. Proponents of these technologies point to "the speed of message delivery, the efficiency of asynchronous communication (because all the parties need not participate at the same time), and the number and geographic spread of participants (no longer constrained by physical location and size of meeting facilities)" (Culnan & Markus, 1987, p. 431). Examples include telephones, FAX machines, interactive networks, voice mail, computer conferencing, mail delivery, and teleconferencing. Organizations have used these systems "to create the proper network configuration for a task, increase transmission speed and accuracy, and reduce human travel" (Robey, 1991, p. 462).

The new telecommunications process links telephones, televisions, and computers together in a vast digital network. According to Byrne (1984), "Computers and communications technologies are converging, linking with telephone systems and satellites, and producing an unprecedented network for connecting individuals and organizations" (p. 78). Unique to this process is "the microchip, which makes the synergistic three-way interplay possible, and the technology of digital data transmission" (Hanson, 1982, p. 224). Voice, print, picture, and telegraph can all be reduced to one channel whereby they can be transmitted simultaneously. As Hanson concluded, "The vocal message of the telephone call, the visual signal of the television set, the bits and bytes of the computer system—all these forms of electronic information are becoming the same" (p. 224).

These changes offer some novel opportunities for different types of organizational communication. E-mail "enables a network of uses to communicate more extensively with one another, to tap new sources of information, and to save time consumed in business travel" (Robey, 1991, p. 462). E-mail has important features that change the nature of organizational communication (Robey, 1991). Message transmission is almost immediate. The messages are *asynchronous*, which means they do not have to be received at the same time they are sent because they can be stored until the receiver is prepared to read them. Being *screen-based*, messages may be composed, edited, sent, received, stored, and filed at a terminal with a keyboard. With no intermediaries (e.g., secretaries, receptionists, couriers), mail is scanned by the receiver, protecting confidentiality and eliminating delays. Finally, there is broad audience reach because the message can be routed to any number of receivers in the network.

With an electronic bulletin board, employees can address a message to a communication space rather than to an individual (Culnan & Markus, 1987, p. 432). This anonymity may increase the likelihood that disgruntled employees will post messages reflecting a great deal more honesty than what would be required in a written memo to the manager or CEO. In one case, the network was renamed GRIPENET because so many managers used it to complain about company policy (Kiesler, 1986). Communicating to a space also creates an effect called *flaming* (Kiesler, 1986). When they are ignorant of the social context and feel free to express themselves, some senders and receivers flame.

The capacity of a mainframe to retain entire transcripts also changes the nature of meetings. Individuals not attending the electronic conference can eavesdrop. They might take this as an opportunity to learn and add to the quality of the meeting. On the other hand, this record can inhibit managers from even using the electronic channels because bad judgment, loss of information power, and a change in role are all recorded in the main frame (Byrne, 1984).

*Teleworking* or *telecommuting* is the ability to work at locations away from the traditional office. F-International is a computer-consulting company based in the United Kingdom using more than 1,000 freelancers in three countries (Collins, 1986). Individuals work at home and integrate their activities with a regional manager. Workers have increased control over their schedules, less commuting time, and greater flexibility (Long, 1987). The laptop computer allows individuals to work anywhere. By 1992, AT&T will have 10,000 salespeople who will be operating from portable offices. They will be equipped with a modem to communicate to AT&T's corporate computers and have a portable printer and a cellular phone (Armstrong, 1991). AT&T will save the cost of office rental, and the salespeople will have much greater control over their time.

These changes, involving the linking of communication and computers, are matched by the major changes in operations.

## Operational Systems

*Operational systems* help with the structural aspects of work. As the name implies, routine activities can be examined to see where inefficiencies are occurring. Because procedures are standardized, a great deal of time and effort can be eliminated. An overdependence on these systems, however, leads to a significant amount of depersonalization in the organization (Robey, 1991). At the very least, "computers and information technologies link previously semi-independent aspects of the production system more closely" (Osterman, 1989, p. 7). For some, these operational systems depersonalize the workplace.

A useful example of the speed gained and the personal influence lost, is with the credit-approval process for a Visa charge. When a Visa card is used for a purchase, the elapsed time between the moment the clerk passes the card through a credit-verification terminal and the approval code is 15 sec (Verity et al. 1990, p. 144). The approval path begins with National Data Corp.'s (NDC) computers in Cherry Hill, New Jersey. The request transfers to NDC headquarters in Atlanta for acceptance. If the amount is over $50, the Visa microcomputers send the query to the mainframes in McLean, Virginia or San Mateo, California. The mainframe verifies the card and checks with the individual issuing bank to see if the money is available. The approval, or denial, is back—in 15 sec. The denial of credit, or the inadvertent late payment, is greeted by the "system," which automatically penalizes you. Only a frantic phone call to an 800 number and a conversation with a human can prevent the system from making an electronic notation of nonpayment. Banks have seen the number of transactions through the nation's 80,000 automatic teller machines (ATM) grow from 400,000 in 1975 to 6 billion in 1991 (Woolley, 1991). While you are obtaining funds from your account at many ATM locations nationally, you are communicating, your transactions are recorded immediately and your account is charged. Electronic banking services soon may make checks obsolete by allowing individuals to pay bills through electronic transfers accomplished with a push-button telephone (Rupinski, 1991a).

## Control Systems

*Control systems*, using data collection and entry, monitor and evaluate organizational performance. In their advertisement, Andersen Consulting forwards information processing for its Time Compression Management users ("Are You Making," 1991). For their clients, they analyze every aspect of the organization (e.g., work flow, product delivery, market dynamics) with the goal of using information technologies "to compress each stage to its minimum time. Activities that don't add value are eliminated" ("Are You Making," 1991). Management obtains "up-to-the-second views of inventories, receivables, and market demand at businesses ranging from fast food to industrial chemicals to toy retailing. For many companies, networks have become essential means of production—their very nervous system" (Verity et al. 1990, p. 143).

Supermarkets now stock almost 19,000 different items, up from 14,000 in 1985 (Mandel, 1991), which are monitored through computer checkouts. More than 2,200 new supermarket items were introduced in 1985, and most of them failed because the tracking system reported inadequate sales figures nationally. The new information technologies allow supermarkets to control inventories and respond to the demands from the environment (e.g., customers, producers, distributors).

Earlier in this text, we discussed the *computer monitoring* now occurring in many organizations. Some 10 million U.S. workers already are scrutinized through electronic monitoring (Lee, 1990). There are two types of monitoring. One is to actually read the messages placed in the computer. The second, which includes two thirds of the 7 million workers in the United States who use terminals (Brophy, 1984), is to count the number of keystrokes by the word-processing operator (Markus, 1984, pp. 23–24). Other cases of computer monitoring include a check on phone numbers dialed by employees (Emery, 1989). In both cases, the manager can compare the output (e.g., keystrokes) or nonessential calls with the productivity standards of the office or organization. One response by operators is to type "garbage" into the computer, which creates rapid, but random keystrokes to get the average up. According to Robey (1991), "This version of 'strategic measurementship' arose with manual typewriters during the heyday of scientific management. Equipped to count keystrokes mechanically, the machines were outsmarted by typists who never used the tab key, always the space bar, to increase their count" (p. 464).

Computer games now are being used to test trolley operators for drug use. In an experiment in San Diego, drivers at Old Town Trolley Tours check in each day by playing a 30-sec computer game designed to test their eye/hand coordination and reaction time ("Trolley Games," 1990). Stress, fatigue, or substance abuse will show up in slowed responses, because results are measured against individualized baseline responses. Drivers may wait 10 min and try again. A second failure means reassignment to another job (e.g., ticket taker) for that day, and repeated failures may result in the company asking employees to take a conventional drug test. Don Harrison, Vice President for Public Affairs for the parent company, Historic Tours of America, concluded that: "It saves employees the humiliation of traditional drug testing and it starts the driver's day with a gentle reminder that safety comes first" (Trolley Games, 1990).

Communication, operational, and control are three important types of new technology systems. However, the communication/computer link also assists in decision making.

## Decision Support Systems

*Decision support systems* (DDS) operate as extensions of the planning and decision-making processes. Many management information systems (MIS) provide important information to managers to enhance the decision-making process. These systems range from relatively simple data support systems to complex forms of expert systems. These systems have had limited application because of the complexity of managerial decision making (Luconi, Malone, & Scott-Morton, 1984). Systems that provide information to help the user can be quite successful, but systems that take the place of human decision making can be troublesome and lead to a loss of productivity (Kaye & Sutton, 1985).

A more powerful application is the formalized management of group meetings in an effort to make better use of participant's time (DeSanctis & Gallupe, 1987, p. 638). Each person in the electronically mediated group meeting can use his or her terminal to volunteer information or withhold comments. At any time, the leader can poll the members. Using this group decision support system (GDSS) can speed up data processing, ensure more balanced participation, and deal with routine matters. When face-to-face communication is necessary, the GDSS can be eliminated.

## Interorganizational Systems

*Interorganizational systems* link different organizations. Organizations have been able to increase their competitive advantage by cooperating in the design and use of interorganizational systems (Johnston & Vitale, 1988). For example, by linking airlines and travel agents, direct booking can be accomplished in seconds. This benefits the airlines, travel agents, and the traveler. Inherent in any system is the potential for the use of power. A case in point, airline reservation systems have an architectural bias in the software that confers marketing advantages to the airlines sponsoring the system. The sponsoring airline allows travel agents to "hook-up" with their system (O'Brian, 1989). Delta and American Airlines merged their reservation systems in 1989 so that they now control 46% of the domestic travel agency market. If you go to an agency with this system, you are most likely to "Love to fly" (Delta) or Fly American, rather than some other airline, because the system is set to give Delta or American routes first.

## IMPLICATIONS

There are extensive arguments concerning the impact of new technology (Compton et al., 1991). On the positive side, information flow up, down, and across organizations has been enhanced (Rogers, 1986; Spelt, 1977); access to information has been increased leading to power sharing, better decision making, and more creativity (Gengle, 1984; Kiesler, Siegel, & McGuire, 1984); and there has been an increase in information distribution and consumption (Pool, 1983). Functional groups have seen increased communication activities and superior–subordinate relationships have developed more communication behaviors (Rice, 1980). Communication with external environments has occurred and there have been more open organizational networks (Rice, 1987). Less time in shadow activities such as telephone tag are often the result of the new technology (Francas & Larimer, 1984). From the task perspective, new technology, such as CMCS, "has been associated with improvements in planning, promoting timely and complete feedback, controlling organizational activities, managing time, initiating action plans, responding to the environment, planning flexible work schedules, eliminating manual labor, composing documents, and preparing written documents" (Compton et al., 1991; see also Rice & Bair, 1984).

At the same time, information overload has occurred (Rogers, 1986); a disparity between information-rich and information-poor parties has evolved; there has been a decrease in face-to-face communication (Kay & Byrne, 1986); alterations in the organizational structure have occurred (Allen & Hauptman, 1987); some portions of the work force have become obsolete (Rogers, 1986); a technological elite has evolved (Hiemestra, 1983); and desktop computers, and other technologies, serve as a status symbol (Rice & Case, 1983; Rogers, 1986).

We examine in further detail three specific issues: access to information, power and relationships, and impact on users.

### Access to Information

New technologies have increased the access of information once available only to top-level or middle managers. Information has become more accessible and widely shared across all levels meaning that many decisions once made only at the upper levels of the organization now can be made by those closer to the immediate situation (Bolman & Deal, 1991, pp. 74–75). According to Drucker (1989a), "the information based organization needs far fewer levels of management than the traditional command-and-control model. By now a great many—maybe most—American companies have cut management levels by one-third or more. But the restructuring of corporations—middle-sized ones as well as large ones, and eventually, even smaller ones—has barely begun" (p. 20).

The pressure to eliminate layers of management emanates from a variety of sources. In manufacturing, for example, firms cannot remain competitive without speeding up the process. In traditional firms, only 5% to 10% of the total time needed to get a product to the market is in the manufacturing process (Dumaine, 1989). The remainder of time is administrative, and largely unnecessary.

Benetton, the Italian sportswear company, used computers and redesign to enhance distribution of new products. They created an electronic loop linking sales agent, factory, and warehouse (Dumaine, 1989, p. 31). If salespeople anywhere in the world find that they are running out of a best-selling sweater, they enter an order in their PC, which then sends it to the mainframe in Italy. Because the sweater originally was created on a CAD system, the mainframe has all the measurements on hand in its digital code, which can be transmitted to the knitting machine. The machine makes the sweaters, which factory workers put in boxes with a computer bar code containing the address of the store. The box goes to a central warehouse in Los Angeles, which serves 5,000 Benetton stores in 60 countries. Run by only eight people, the warehouse moves 230,000 pieces of clothing a day. The box in the central warehouse is placed in one of 300,000 slots and it is retrieved by a robot that reads the bar code, picks up the merchandise, and loads them onto a truck. Whereas other garment industry suppliers can take forever to fill an order, Benetton can get the order to Los Angeles in 4 weeks. If the sweaters are in stock, it only takes 1 week (Dumaine, 1989).

On the other side of the coin, people without terminals, or who are unwilling to adapt to the new communication technologies, can find themselves excluded from critical information (Robey, 1991). New channels of communication, such as computers, also can lead to a neglect of the traditional patterns of interaction such as face-to-face meetings and conversations at the Xerox machine (Zuboff, 1988). Therefore, increased reliance on new technology actually increases the importance of the remaining face-to-face meetings.

## Power and Relationships

A major shift of power has occurred because of the impact of technology. A useful analogy is between the mainframe computers of the 1960s and the individualized PC of the 1980s and 1990s. In order to use the mainframe in the 1960s, individuals had to go through a centralized bureaucracy that controlled access and time. Now, individuals can work at home, call up significant amounts of information, and operate independently. With a freer flow of communication, decision making can be decentralized.

But, these technological advances can disrupt severely the organization's social system because of the loss of face-to-face interactions, increased isolation, and maximizing of status distinctions (Cummings, Long, & Lewis, 1988, p. 188). The computer is symbolic, as much as any other factor in the evolution of an organization, of the impact of information access and control. Desktop computers are as fast as mainframes were just a few years ago (Brandt, 1991). The electronic pulses make journeys that take mere billionths of a second, which makes many of the assumptions regarding horizontal and vertical channels seem outdated.

Finally, because information technologies do alter organizations, the complex interactions between the system are always changing (Robey, 1991). Individual managers feel a greater sense of *global venerability* because information technologies link together disparate areas of the organization (Osterman, 1989). Actions in any one part of the organization immediately can have an impact on many other areas. Information technologies act to break down traditional barriers and force changes in how supervisors and managers act.

Although new technology starts with a rational, goal-oriented perspective (e.g., increased efficiency, fewer layers), the dynamic interface between humans and machines means that the outcome is rarely under the control of the designers. According to Robey (1991), "Information systems carry implications for power, control, and growth, as well as efficiency" (p. 473). In her long-term study of a major drug corporation, Zuboff (1988) documented the transformations occurring within the technological system by focusing on the distinctions between *automate* and *informate*. In fact, the new communication technologies can have a significant impact on users.

## Impact on Users

The distinction between automate and informate is important (Zuboff, 1988). Information technology can distance workers from the physical feel of production and require them to deal with computer-generated data. Unless workers are offered means to continue to feel good about their work, they will lose a sense of identity and purpose (Hirschhorn, 1984).

In order for technology to have a positive impact, basic worker functions and needs cannot be ignored. A recent study of 2,000 U.S. companies that had implemented office technologies found that 40% had not achieved the intended results. But, only 10% of the failures were technical in nature (Bikson & Gutek, 1984). Information technology will reshape work in many ways, but the training and development required to make the changes successful must come first (Rogers, 1986).

*Isolation.* Although much of the discussion regarding the information age is upbeat, many workers are left feeling isolated (Cohen, 1984; Ruprecht & Wagoner, 1984). In offices and factories, individuals can feel that their job is reduced to pushing buttons and dealing with other people through impersonal electronic extensions (e.g., telephone, E-mail). In one case, workers cut holes in partitions so they could peek through and see someone else (Zuboff, 1988, p. 145). The computer has had a major impact on office work. As we discussed previously in this text, electronic automation is sweeping corporate offices. Often, the worker is given a smaller and smaller part of the overall problem, thereby decreasing satisfaction and productivity (Greenbaum, 1979, p. 151). Worker isolation leads to decreased satisfaction (Ruprecht & Wagoner, 1984, p. 588). Wineman (1986) observed, "When introducing electronic technology into the office, it is becoming increasingly important for social interaction and a sense of belonging to the company to be built into the environment" (p. 128). For example, automating an office requires a commensurate investment in the training and development of the equipment users. According to Green (1984), "The productivity of any system depends upon the attitudes and abilities of the people who work with it" (p. 84). New technology has a significant impact on the people using the equipment (Blacker & Osborne, 1987; Zuboff, 1988). Technology has been viewed as a tool for increasing both productivity and the quality of the employee's life. From this optimistic view, employees will be liberated from mundane activities (e.g., filing, typing, attending meetings), thereby allowing them to concentrate on other important task objectives (e.g., planning, coaching, customer service). A more pessimistic view sees technology as a contributor to unemployment, deskilling, and a tightly controlled workplace.

*Decreased Motivation.*    There are numerous generalizations regarding the impact of technology on individuals. In manufacturing, for example, U.S. firms now face a failure rate of 50% to 75% when implementing new technologies (Ettlie, 1986). In many cases, the problem is that technological innovation can degrade work and reduce creativity (Shaiken, 1988). For example, as a consultant to one of the paint suppliers for Ford, I observed the impact of standards demanded by the "Quality is Job 1" program. Pigment mixers, a specialized and coveted job, learned their trade and mixed batches by eye. Ford demanded statistical quality control for the process. So, the mixers, although keeping their jobs, were reduced to pushing a few buttons at the appropriate time. For Ford, there was a guarantee of uniform quality. For the mixers, there was no job satisfaction or a sense of accomplishment. The same type of problem has been observed in a study of a biscuit-manufacturing company (Buchanan & Boddy, 1983). Although these problems can be alleviated, an insightful human resources approach is required. A 1989 survey by the American Management Association concluded that "insufficient education and management training in this area [technology] may be halting progress in technological innovation" (Berk, 1989, p. 50). In fact, only 30% of the surveyed companies have in-house programs. The investment in technology is a waste unless the people are incredibly well trained (Abetti, 1989).

## Coping with Uncertainty

One definition of uncertainty is the difference between the information that an organization already has and the information it needs (Galbraith, 1977). An increase in uncertainty, which is endemic in organizations facing rapid change, requires either an increase in the capacity to process information or a reduction in the need for information processing (Galbraith, 1977). Apple Computer, Inc. provides a useful example (Richards, 1991). Founded in a garage shop, and financed by the sale of a red-and-white Volkswagen bus, Apple developed a culture that featured annual meetings with well-paid employees treated to rock concerts, and Friday afternoon beer busts. Underlying all of these activities was a sense of egalitarianism. Now, with the major changes in direction, employees are wondering about the future of the company. One anonymous writer to the electronic bulletin board asked the top four Apple executives if they were even reading the numerous complaints being placed in the system. As Richards (1991) observed, "Employees are not clear anymore what the vision is, and they will therefore be less committed and more resistant" (p. 2D). Apple's reorganization has created an entire set of highly competitive products based on working with outside suppliers, adopting off-the-shelf technology from other companies, accepting Japanese subcontractors, and getting the product out the door as soon as possible (Buell, Levine, & Gross, 1990). This urgency is Apple's own response to the speed demanded by the new electronic age they helped to create (Buell, 1991).

The second goal, reducing the need for information processing, can be accomplished through increased use of lateral relationships (e.g., self-managing work units, liaisons, direct contact). We discussed these concepts at several different points in this text. Increasing the capacity to process information can be accomplished through the use of vertical information systems (e.g., computers, information technologies).

According to Schleh (1989), "Executives who look forward to the day when they can depend on stable conditions are living in a fantasy world" (p. 50). Schleh further observed that, "Flexible management requires authority to be pushed downward as far as possible" (p. 52). The computer is a perfect example of how executives attempt to resist change (Schleh, 1989, p. 50).

At this point, it would be impractical to conclude all the arguments for and against the new technologies. Several observations are valid, however. All technological innovations have an impact on organizations. Second, carefully introducing the innovation will lead to a more successful transition. One additional issue should be mentioned to put the impact of new technologies into perspective.

## GLOBALIZATION

During the 1980s, business shifted from multinational to transnational (Drucker, 1989b). The traditional multinational corporation, invented in the middle years of the 19th century by U.S. and German industrialists, centered the design of products at the parent company and produced them in various foreign markets. But, as Drucker observed, "In the transnational economy, companies design products anyplace within the system" (p. 90). Major pharmaceutical companies have research labs in many countries. IBM produces personal computers for all of Europe in two locations. Japanese companies now operate over 1,000 businesses in the United States including service organizations, trading companies, marketing and distributing firms, and industrial concerns (Bowman, 1986). Because of the interdependence of national economies, the majority of businesses operate in the world economy rather than in just one or two countries (Szakonyi, 1988).

For example, Ford Motor Company "based its turnaround and recovery in the U.S. market based on products and processes developed in Europe and by its Japanese affiliate, Mazda" (Drucker, 1989b, p. 90). Ford used reverse engineering to make the Ford Taurus. Adopted from the Japanese approach to understanding the competition, over 50 imported cars were taken apart piece by piece to understand the factors creating high customer satisfaction (Waterman, 1987, p. 158). By conducting the process Ford called a "layered strip-down," they were able to identify 400 features that should be considered for the Taurus.

The new technologies make transnational organizations a reality. Teleconferences can link various countries, E-mail can overcome the national boundaries, and telephones can be used to confirm information. As our examples have shown throughout this chapter, most organizations combine the various technologies to create the most effective means for producing a product or for transferring information.

## CONCLUSION

The new technologies are having a major impact on organizations. Because of the link between information and organizations, the developments in electronic technology are particularly relevant to our study of organizational communication. These changes are creating important developments at every level. Mechanization, automation, and information technology represent the phases in the introduction of machines into organizations.

All parts of the modern organization are effected by the new technologies. Ranging from secretarial functions to corporate meetings, the use of mediated communication techniques has had a profound impact. Because media richness remains an important element in communication satisfaction, the new technologies will not replace face-to-face communication.

There are five types of information systems: communication, operational, control, decision support, and interorganizational. Each of these provides an organization with important opportunities for growth. With the transnational nature of most corporations, the new technology will continue to be a major force. At the beginning of this chapter, we examined the permanent state of white water for most organizations. In order to be an effective organizational communicator, each of us must become well acquainted with the new technology in order to effectively navigate our way throughout the 1990s.

## REFERENCES

Abetti, P. A. (1989, February). Technology: A key strategic resource. *Management Review*, pp. 37–41.

Allen, J. T., & Hauptman, O. (1987). The influence of communication technology on organizational structure. *Communication Research*, *145*, 575–587.

"Are you making the most of your time?" (1991, March 11). *Business Week*, p. 77.

Armstrong, L. (1991, March 18). Who needs a desk when you've got a lap? *Business Week*, p. 124.

Berk, S. (1989, February). Managing technology for a competitive edge: An AMA survey. *Management Review*, pp. 49–51.

Bikson, T. K., & Gutek, B. (1984). *Implementation of office automation*. Santa Monica, CA: Rand Corporation.

Blacker, F., & Osborne, D. (Eds.). (1987). *Information technology and people: Designing for the future*. Cambridge, MA: MIT Press.

Bolman, L. G., & Deal, T. E. (1991). *Reframing organizations: Artistry, choice, and leadership*. San Francisco: Jossey-Bass.

Bowman, S. J. (1986). The rising sun in America. *Personnel Administrator*, *31*(9), 63–67, 114–117.

Brandt, R. (1991, March 4). The next great leap in computing speed. *Business Week*, p. 76.

Brophy, B. (1984, June 13). Unions object to computer monitoring. *USA Today*, p. 3B.

Buchanan, D. F., & Boddy, D. (1983). Advanced technology and the quality of working life: The effects of computerized controls on biscuit-making operators. *Journal of Occupational Psychology*, *56*, 109–119.

Buell, B. (1991, January 28). The second comeback of Apple. *Business Week*, p. 68.

Buell, B., Levine, J. B., & Gross, N. (1990, October 15). Apple: New team, new strategy. *Business Week*, pp. 86, 88–89, 93, 96.

Byrne, R. B. (1984). Overcoming computerphobia. In S. H. Evans & P. Clarke (Eds.), *The computer culture* (pp. 76–101). Indianapolis: White River Press.

Cohen, B. G. F. (Ed.). (1984). *Office automation: Vol. 1. Human aspects of office automation*. Amsterdam: Elsevier.

Collins, E. G. C. (1986). A company without offices. *Harvard Business Review*, *1*, 127–136.

Compton, D. C., White, K., & DeWine, S. (1991). Techno-sense: Making sense of computer-mediated communication systems. *The Journal of Business Communication*, *28*, pp. 23–43.

Culnan, M. J., & Markus, M. L. (1987). Information technologies. In F. M. Jablin, L. L. Putnam, K. H. Roberts, & L. W. Porter (Eds.), *Handbook of organizational communication* (pp. 420–443). Newbury Park, CA: Sage.

Cummings, H. W., Long, L. W., & Lewis, M. L. (1988). *Managing communication in organizations: An introduction* (2nd ed.). Scottsdale, AZ: Gorsuch Scarisbrick.

Daniels, T. D., & Spiker, B. K. (1991). *Perspectives on organizational communication* (2nd ed.). Dubuque, IA: Brown.

Davis, G. B., & Olson, M. H. (1985). *Management information systems: Conceptual foundations* (2nd ed.). New York: McGraw-Hill.

Depke, D. A., Gross, N., & Buell, B. (1991, March 18). Laptops take off. *Business Week*, pp. 118–124.

DeSanctis, G., & Gallupe, R. B. (1987). A foundation for the study of group decision support systems. *Management Science*, *33*, 589–609.

Dizard, W. P., Jr. (1989). *The coming information age* (3rd ed.). New York: Longman.

Drucker, P. (1989a, October 21–27). Peter Drucker's 1990s. The futures that have already happened. *The Economist*, pp. 19–20, 24.

Drucker, P. (1989b). The world according to Peter Drucker. *Best of Business Quarterly, 11*(2), 86–92.

DuBrin, A. J., Ireland, R. D., & Williams, J. C. (1989). *Management & organization.* Cincinnati: South-Western.

Dumaine, B. (1989). Business speeds up. *Best of Business Quarterly, 11*(2), 26–31.

Emery, C. E., Jr. (1989, January 1). Computer monitoring raises question about on-job privacy. *The Sunday Courier,* p. F4.

Ettlie, J. E. (1986). Implementing manufacturing technology: Lessons from experience. In D. D. Davis (Ed.), *Managing technological innovation* (pp. 72–104). San Francisco: Jossey-Bass.

Francas, M., & Larimer, E. (1984, May). *Impacts of an enhanced electronic message system.* Paper presented at the International Communication Association Convention, San Francisco.

Galbraith, J. (1977). *Organization design.* Reading, MA: Addison-Wesley.

Gengle, D. (1984). *The netweavers sourcebook: A guide to micro networking.* Reading, MA: Addison-Wesley.

Green, J. H. (1984). *Automating your office—How to do it, how to justify it.* New York: McGraw-Hill.

Greenbaum, J. M. (1979). *In the name of efficiency.* Philadelphia: Temple University Press.

Hanson, D. (1982). *The new alchemists: Silicon Valley and the micro-electronics revolution.* New York: Avon.

Heimstra, G. (1983). You say you want a revolution? Information technology in organizations. In R. E. Bostrom & B. H. Westley (Eds.), *Communication Yearbook 7* (pp. 802–828). Beverly Hills: Sage.

Hirschhorn L. (1984). *Beyond mechanization: Work and technology in a postindustrial age.* Cambridge MA: MIT Press.

Johnston, H. R., & Vitale, M. R. (1988). Creating competitive advantage with interorganizational information systems. *MIS Quarterly, 12,* 153–166.

Kaye, A., & Byrne, K. (1986). Insights on the implementation of computer-based messages system. *Information and Management, 10*(5), 275–284.

Kaye, A. R., & Sutton, M. J. D. (1985). Productivity and quality of working life for office principles and implications for office automation. *Office: Technology and People, 2,* 267–286.

Kiesler, S. (1986, January-February). The hidden messages in computer networks. *Harvard Business Review, 64,* 46–48, 52, 54, 58–59.

Kiesler, S., Siegel, J., & McGuire, T. W. (1984). Social psychological aspects of computer-mediated communication. *American Psychologist, 39*(10), 1123–1134.

Kleinschrod, W. A. (1986). *Critical issues in office automation.* New York: McGraw-Hill.

Komsky, S. H. (1991). A profile of users of electronic mail in a university. *Management Communication Quarterly, 4,* 310–340.

Laufer, A. C. (1984). *Production and operations management* (3rd ed.). Cincinnati: South-Western.

Lee, E. (1990, July 8). High-tech monitoring invades the work place. *The Tuscaloosa News,* pp. 1E–2E.

Long, R. J. (1987). *New office information technology: Human and managerial implications.* London: Croom Helm.

Luconi, F. L., & Malone, T. W., & Scott-Morton, M. S. (1984). *Expert systems and expert support systems: The next challenge for management.* Cambridge, MA: MIT Press.

Mandel, M. J. (1991, March 4). There's a silver lining in the service sector. *Business Week,* pp. 60–61.

Markus, M. L. (1984). *Systems in organizations: Bugs and features.* Marshfield, MA: Pitman.

McLuhan, M. (1964). *Understanding media: The extensions of man.* New York: McGraw-Hill.

McLuhan, M., & Fiore, Q. (1967). *The medium is the massage: An inventory of effects.* New York: Bantam.

O'Brian, B. (1989, February 6). Delta, American plan to merge reservations. *The Wall Street Journal,* p. A4.

Osterman, P. (1989). New technology and the organization of work: A review of issues. In D. C. Mowery & B. E. Henderson (Eds.). *The challenge of new technology to labor-management relations* (pp. 5–15) (BLMR Publication No. 135). Washington, DC: U.S. Department of Labor.

Pool, I. (1983). *Technologies of freedom.* Cambridge, MA: Harvard University Press.

Rice, R. E. (1987). Computer-mediated communication and organizational innovation. *Journal of Communication, 37*(4), 65–94.

Rice, R. E. (1980). The impacts of computer-mediated organizational and interpersonal communication. In M. Williams (Ed.), *Annual review of information technology* (pp. 221–249). White Plains, NY: Knowledge Industry Publications.

Rice, R. E. & Bair, J. H. (1984). New organizational media and productivity. In R. E. Rice (Ed.), *The new media: Communication research and technology* (pp. 185–215). Beverly Hills, CA: Sage.

Rice, R. E., & Case, D. (1983). Computer-based messaging in the university: A description of use and utility. *Journal of Communication, 33*(1), 131–152.

Richards, E. (1991, February 25). Apple losing its core—Prized corporate culture. *The Birmingham News*, p. 2D.

Robey, D. (1991). *Designing organizations* (3rd ed.). Homewood, IL: Irwin.

Rogers, E. M. (1986). *Communication technology: The new media society.* New York: Free Press.

Rupinski, P. (1991a, March 19). No more checks? High-tech puts buzz in banking. *Birmingham Post-Herald*, pp. C1, C5.

Rupinski, P. (1991b, March 12). Rule has done well unto Golden Flake. *Birmingham Post-Herald*, pp. B1, B6.

Ruprecht, M. M., & Wagoner, K. (1984). *Managing office automation.* New York: Wiley.

Schleh, E. C. (1989, June). Meeting change with open arms. *Management Review*, pp. 50–52.

Shaiken, H. (1988). *Work transformed: Automation and labor in the computer age.* Lexington, MA: Lexington.

Spelt, P. F. (1977). Evaluation of a continuing computer conference on simulation. *Behavioral Research Methods and Instrumentation, 9*(2), 87–91.

Szakonyi, R. (1988). *Managing new product technology.* New York: American Management Association.

Trolley games. (1990, September/October). *Labor Relations Today.* Washington, DC: U.S. Department of Labor.

TV Viewers could get "limitless" selections. (1991, March 8). *Birmingham Post-Herald*, p. B9.

Vail, P. B. (1989). *Managing as performing art: New ideas for a world of chaotic change.* San Francisco: Jossey-Bass.

VDTs: Fitting the job to the person. (1991, January/February). *Labor Relations Today*, p. 1.

Verity, J. W., Coy, P., & Rothfeder, J. (1990, October 8). Taming the wild network. *Business Week*, pp. 142–146, 148.

Waterman, R. H., Jr. (1987). *The renewal factor: How the best get and keep the competitive edge.* New York: Bantam.

Whitney, D. W. (1986). Real robots do need jigs. *Harvard Business Review, 64*, 112–115.

Wineman, J. D. (Ed.). (1986). *Behavioral issues in office design.* New York: Van Nostrand Reinhold.

Woolley, S. (1991, February 18). Banks make a statement with fatter fees. *Business Week*, pp. 138–139.

Zuboff, S. (1988). *In the age of the smart machine: The future of work and power.* New York: Basic.

# Author Index

# Subject Index

Delphi technique, 347–348
Disciplinary interview, 418
Double-loop learning, 295
Doubling, 215
Downward communication, 202–209
Downsizing, 232
Dramatistic, 273–275

## E

Environmental uncertainty, 57
Employee involvement, 350–364, 448–449
  parallel organizational structures, 354–355
  problem-solving groups, 354–355
  quality circles, 354–355
  scope, 350–351
  self-managing work teams, 357–359
    benefits, 362
    characteristics, 360–361
    costs and pitfalls, 362–363
    definition, 359
    inherent barriers, 361–362
    traditional teams, 359–360
  teams, 352–353, 359–360
    limitations, 355–357
    loss of power, 356, 361–362
    managing versus leading, 356, 361–362
    segmentalism, 356–357, 361–362
  values, 350
Employee stock ownership plans (ESOPs),
    192–193, 448–449
Empowerment, 373–374, 417
Equity theory, 444–446
Ergonomics, 156
Espionage, 337–338
Ethics, 266–267, 269
Excellent companies, 74–76
  characteristics, 75
  fluidity, 74–75
  small groups, 75
Expectancy theory, 443–444

## F

Feedback, 12–13, 249–253
  effective techniques, 252–253
  feedforward, 250
  negative, 250–251
    management by exception, 250

  positive, 250–251
    rewarding mistakes, 250–251
  supportive and defensive climates, 251–252
Frames, 78–86
  applied to the excellent companies, 85
  human resources, 79–83, 85
  organizational processes, 76–86
  political, 80–83, 85
  structural, 78–79, 82–83, 85
  symbolic, 82–84
Freezethink, 174–175
Functional illiteracy, 207

## G

Gain sharing, 211
Globalization, 473–474
Goal setting, 238, 446–447
Grapevines, 167, 217–223
Groups, 263, *see also* Small groups
Groupthink, 174–175, 336–337

## H

Heroic leadership, 385–383
Home office, 157
Human relations management, 47–53
  excesses, 50
  goals in conflict, 49–50
    individual growth, 49
    organizational control, 49–50
    PATCO strike, 51
  Hawthorne studies, 47–49
    attention to human needs, 49
    de facto managers, 48
    lighting, 47
Human resource management, 52–59
  contingency approach, 52, 55–59
  core behaviors, 59
  differentiated subsystems, 56–57
  environmental uncertainty, 57
  mechanistic, 56
  no one best way, 55–59
  organic, 56
  situational appropriateness, 56
  strategy, 57
  structure, 57
  structural diversity, 56
  impact of participation, 54–55